UNMASKING TERROR

Unmasking Terror
A Global Review of Terrorist Activities

Edited by Jonathan D. Hutzley

The Jamestown Foundation
Washington, DC

THE JAMESTOWN FOUNDATION

Published in the United States by
The Jamestown Foundation
1111 16th Street NW
Suite 320
Washington, DC 20036
http://www.jamestown.org

Copyright © 2007 The Jamestown Foundation

For more information on this book of the Jamestown Foundation, e-mail pubs@jamestown.org

ISBN 978-0-9675009-6-6

Jamestown's Mission

The Jamestown Foundation's mission is to inform and educate policy makers and the broader policy community about events and trends in those societies which are strategically or tactically important to the United States and which frequently restrict access to such information. Utilizing indigenous and primary sources, Jamestown's material is delivered without political bias, filter or agenda. It is often the only source of information which should be, but is not always, available through official or intelligence channels, especially in regard to Eurasia and terrorism.

Origins

Launched in 1984 after Jamestown's late president and founder William Geimer's work with Arkady Shevchenko, the highest-ranking Soviet official ever to defect when he left his position as undersecretary general of the United Nations, The Jamestown Foundation rapidly became the leading source of information about the inner workings of closed totalitarian societies.

Over the past two decades, Jamestown has developed an extensive global network of experts - from the Black Sea to Siberia, from the Persian Gulf to the Pacific. This core of intellectual talent includes former high-ranking government officials and military officers, political scientists, journalists, scholars and economists. Their insight contributes significantly to policy makers engaged in addressing today's new and emerging global threats, including that from international terrorists.

Contents

Articles by Chapter

Part I: Jihadi Doctrine and Methods of Terrorism

Part II: Middle East and Africa

Part III: South Asia

Part IV: The Caucasus and Central Asia

Part V: Southeast and East Asia

Part VI: Europe and the Americas

Acknowledgements

The list of those who have contributed to this publication is quite extensive given that the contributors to *Unmasking Terror Volume III* are the analysts themselves who wrote for our two flagship publications, *Terrorism Monitor* and *Terrorism Focus*. This core group represents nearly 50 analysts residing in over 200 countries around the globe who have used their insights and analysis of indigenous source material to provide Jamestown's readers with a diverse array of perspectives not found in the Western media.

A special thanks is due to Jonathan Hutzley who labored endless hours putting this publication together, editing the proof, and who created the marvelous index which makes this publication so valuable to the analysts who use it for their research. The next person I want to thank is Kristi Marks who designed the cover and who made many wonderful contributions to our publications program while at Jamestown. Obviously, one of the most important people to thank would be Erich Marquardt, our Program Manager for Global Terrorism Analysis and managing editor of *Terrorism Monitor* and *Terrorism Focus*. His dedication not only to these publications but to The Jamestown Foundation itself has been of a great service to the policymaking community as he liaised with analysts around the globe to guarantee the high quality that we set for our publications. All of his hard work and dedication is deeply appreciated.

We would also like to thank Alexandra Frasca and Joseph E. Lin for their help in editing and proofreading sections of this publication. Their dedication and attention to detail have helped considerably.

We also wish to extend our gratitude to the Jamestown board, in particular its Chairman, James G. Gidwitz, for his guidance and direction in overseeing our work and support to the terrorism program.

The Jamestown Foundation owes its gratitude to our generous donors who have made the work of the terrorism program and this book possible. Finally, our utmost gratitude is owed to the readers of Jamestown's publications for their continuing support, feedback and encouragement.

Glen E. Howard

Introduction

Every week, I can't wait to read the latest issue of the two online journals published by The Jamestown Foundation. *Terrorism Focus* and *Terrorism Monitor* have become the indispensable tools for any consultant on terrorism. They cover new events in the field and always provide provocative interpretations of new trends. In a world of self proclaimed "expertise," the Jamestown Foundation is an oasis of sanity giving justice to the complexity of terrorism. It is one of the few places, where concerned citizens can turn to for well reasoned analysis. Terrorism is an unfortunate reality of our world. It is doubly unfortunate that this issue is often cynically exploited for political gains, and the popular media plays along by reducing these complex tragedies to sound-bites. These bumper-sticker arguments lead to false policy choices for combating terrorism. Fanned by political commentators, these options are often as popular in the United States as they are disastrous abroad. The end result is not a decrease in terrorism, but an expansion of the pool of terrorists worldwide.

I am deeply honored to have been asked to write the introduction to this book, which collects the most significant articles from the Foundation's two online journals in a convenient and accessible volume. This is a true public service, for it educates the reader about the true nature of terrorism, stripped away from any ideological obfuscation. Our understanding of this present form of terrorism has matured through the efforts of organizations like The Jamestown Foundation. Discussions on terrorism are starting to shed their simplistic Manichean positions and be replaced by more sophisticated arguments based on solid data instead of unrepresentative anecdotes. A more fruitful societal dialogue is slowly emerging in government agencies and think tanks as to the appropriate policy necessary to deal with this social threat to the West. Much of the credit for this positive development must go to The Jamestown Foundation.

The authors of the articles in this volume constitute a virtual who's who of genuine terrorist experts, who are well acquainted with their subject. Many come from the countries they write about, are posted there or have spent a long time there. Their field experience and local knowledge provide a needed context to the terrorist incidents they describe. Most other commentators neglect the circumstances surrounding these incidents. Terrorist operations, especially those perpetrated by homegrown groups, can not be understood out of context for it is the specific situation of these groups, which explains their radicalization and transformation into terrorist groups.

The first two volumes *Unmasking Terror* are simply the best overview of terrorism worldwide, especially as it relates to al-Qaeda and its global affiliates. I have learned a lot from them over the years. I never fail to find something new in each article. Even when I have disagreed with the arguments of some of their authors, I always respect their views. This new volume surpasses the high standards they set. It should be part of the library of every citizen concerned about terrorism.

Marc Sageman
Principal,
Sageman Consulting, LLC

Preface

The Jamestown Foundation is pleased to release Volume III of its *Unmasking Terror* series. With the release of Volume III, Jamestown continues its mission of providing the policymaking community with timely information and analysis based upon indigenous sources of the regions we monitor in Eurasia. The uniqueness of this publication is first and foremost a result of the rich analysis provided by the 200 analysts scattered around the globe who write for The Jamestown Foundation. Located in over 40 countries, these analysts represent the best that Jamestown has to offer the policymaking community. By sifting through all the indigenous sourced information they use for their reports, these analysts have created a unique asset in the realm of open source information. As one foreign journalist described Jamestown, *"where the intelligence of the CIA ends, Jamestown's begins."*

In its more than twenty years of existence, Jamestown is proud to have continually received this sort of recognition and praise for its contributions to open-source analysis, making us one of the top research and analysis institutions in the world. We would not be able to continue our work if it were not for the support of our readers and the donor community which makes it possible for us to maintain our activities.

As our readers over the years have realized, each volume of our series is packed with unique information comprised of the best analytical insight available on al-Qaeda and other global terrorist activities around the globe. Using their access to indigenous sourced information, Jamestown's writers have accumulated some of the best analytical expertise and insight on these topics. With the strategic frontlines of this information war moving to the World Wide Web, we are pleased to provide the readers of *Unmasking Terror* with some of the best in-depth analysis of the electronic battleground being waged on the Internet. Jamestown has been at the forefront in analyzing the content of these forums and making this information available to the policymaking community at large.

As the readers of this volume will learn, Jamestown has made a valiant effort to provide our readers with analysis concerning the use of training and intelligence manuals, electronic counter-measures and other means by which the jihadi community aims to spread open source intelligence. On the frontlines of conflict and instability, our analysts have made this volume of *Unmasking Terror* truly unique as analysts like James Brandon traveled throughout northern Iraq to obtain first-hand insight into the PKK. His insider look at Mount Qandil in northern Iraq, where units of the PKK and other Kurdish insurgent groups have relocated, offers a rare examination of the new generation of leaders and the camps where they are trained. Yemen has been a special area of interest at Jamestown since we began covering terrorism because it is often under-reported in the Western media and the expertise Jamestown provides on the Arabian Peninsula is even rarer. Jamestown has provided extensive coverage of recent developments in Yemen, providing a profile piece of Sheikh Abd al-Majid al-Zindani as well as another one on the Aden-Abyan Islamic Army.

Elsewhere in Eurasia, Jamestown has followed the advice of Winston Churchill, who once said, "that there is no such thing as history, only biography." Indeed, as someone who traveled and reported from the Northwest Frontier, Churchill knew that the events that shaped this important region were dominated by the tribes and their tribal chieftains. For this reason we have followed his insight by focusing much of our analysis by conducting in-depth profiles of the people shaping the Taliban insurgency on both sides of the Durand Line. We have provided our readers with bios of Mullah Dadullah (the military mastermind of the Taliban insurgency), Baitullah Mehsud, Haji Omar and other top Taliban operatives. Once again, Jamestown's information came from indigenous sources and analysts located in Pakistan and Afghanistan.

By no means is Jamestown's analysis concentrated on any one region. We have consciously sought to balance our coverage throughout Eurasia, devoting extensive coverage to the Thai insurgency, including a breakdown of southern Thailand's secretive insurgent groups. We also have given our readers an in-depth look at Jemaah Islamiyah – including a profile piece of Noordin Mohammad Top and an article on the role of kinship in JI's operations, provided by an analyst who interviewed many jailed JI operatives.

About the Book

One of the most critical themes analyzed in this book is an in-depth look at al-Qaeda's doctrine, and the doctrine of jihadi terrorists at large. This is largely anchored by Jamestown Senior Fellow Michael Scheuer. Over the course of several articles, Dr. Scheuer examines the real purpose behind al-Qaeda's existence and how it is imperative that the West learn these lessons so that it will be more capable of combating this force, not only militarily, but also through winning the hearts and minds of those who might be otherwise inclined to heed al-Qaeda's clarion call. This section also explores the general methods of terrorism, ranging from a continuation of last volume's examination of jihadi use of the internet to propagate not only jihadist teachings, but also jihadist training manuals ranging from an examination of manuals distributed that teach jihadis how to avoid being detected by law enforcement agencies to a discussion of liquid explosive training manuals that jihadis can obtain on the web; both of which were contributed by analyst Abdul Hameed Bakier. Furthermore, this section also examines the growing links between terror networks and organized crime, anchored by Hayder Mili's excellent article showing how terrorist organizations have stepped into the role previously played by criminal outfits in the "triangular trade," or the steadily evolving trade that consists of weapons, stolen/contraband goods and narcotics.

Unmasking Terror also contains a unique collection of articles that focus on various important figures and groups in the terrorist world, giving a unique insight into the lives of these men and groups that is not easily obtainable elsewhere. Chief among these is an important interview conducted by Scott Atran of the alleged leader of Southeast Asia's Jemaah Islamiyah, Abu Bakar Ba'asyir, that provides excellent insight into that organization. Other such articles look at Abu Ayyub al-Masri, the successor to Abu Musab al-Zarqawi in al-Qaeda in Iraq. *Unmasking Terror* also features articles on the evolution of trends that are important to consider, such as the history and roots of Somali Islamism, as illustrated by Anouar Boukhars, or the rise of the jamaats in the North Caucasus, and the role they play in furthering the struggle for independence of the various peoples in that region.

Unmasking Terror is also crucial because it examines areas of the world or topics that are not frequently discussed as arenas in the War on Terror. For example, The Jamestown Foundation is proud to feature an article by Olimpio Guido looking at the threats that Japan faces in this struggle. There is an excellent series of articles by Chris Zambelis which examine the potential for terrorism threats emanating from Latin America and the Caribbean. Also, there is an excellent article by Andrew Holt that gives many recommendations that could be useful to policymakers on how to ensure that mass surface transportation is not such a large attraction for terrorists to wreak their havoc.

In short, we feel that *Unmasking Terror* is a unique source because it condenses materials that could be crucial for policymakers, academics, and others interested in understanding the world of terrorism and terrorist threats into one easy-to-use desk reference that provides information on subjects simply not being covered elsewhere, and provides much more depth than can be gleaned from traditional news sources.

Glen E. Howard
President, The Jamestown Foundation
February 2007

Part I

Jihadi Doctrine and
Methods of Terrorism

Al-Qaeda

Al-Qaeda's Insurgency Doctrine: Aiming for a "Long War"

Michael Scheuer

Originally published on February 28, 2006

Conventional national militaries train, think, and fight according to their doctrine. To date, however, America and the West have not sufficiently appreciated that al-Qaeda, too, is fighting the insurgencies in Iraq and Afghanistan according to a doctrine of its own. That doctrine has been developed from the group's experiences during the Afghan war against the Red Army, and has matured through each of the insurgencies in which bin Laden's fighters have since been involved, from Eritrea to Xinjiang to Mindanao. In presenting their doctrine, al-Qaeda's strategists also have tipped their turbans to the significant lessons they have learned from Sun Tzu, Clausewitz, Mao, General Giap, and even Ahmed Shah Masood, as well from the training manuals of U.S. and UK Marines and Special Forces. Ironically, al-Qaeda strategists have discussed all of these matters for years in their internet journals, but this discussion has garnered little interest in Western essays.

The corpus of al-Qaeda's writings on the development and application of its insurgency doctrine is too diverse and voluminous to discuss in a single article. For present purposes, it will suffice to look at some of the insurgency-related work of five of the group's strategists: the late Abu-Hajer Abd-al-Aziz al-Muqrin, Abu Ubyad al-Qurashi, Abu-Ayman al-Hilali, Abd-al-Hadi, and Sayf-al-Din al-Ansari. These writings discuss the need to conduct the political and military facets of an insurgency in tandem. They are especially worth reviewing now because of the success al-Qaeda is having in using its doctrine against U.S.-led forces in Iraq and Afghanistan, a success that has prompted U.S. Defense Secretary Rumsfeld to rename the Global War on Terror as the "Long War" and to publicly lament that al-Qaeda is beating the U.S. in the political war being fought in the media. The essays used herein to analyze al-Qaeda's insurgency doctrine were published between January 2002 and February 2004 in the al-Qaeda internet journals *al-Ansar*, *al-Neda*, and *Mu'askar al-Battar*.

Al-Qaeda Doctrine in Iraq and Afghanistan: The Military

Religious obligation is the central point on which al-Qaeda's insurgency doctrine was and is grounded. Osama bin Laden and—since the U.S.-led invasion of Iraq—hundreds of Islamist leaders and clerics have declared a "defensive jihad" against the United States, a form of jihad that mandates the participation of every Muslim through taking up arms, financial donations, prayer, providing safe haven, or some other form of support. This is what Abu-Hajer Abd-al-Aziz al-Muqrin called the "First Axis of Jihad," the axis that requires complete victory over the infidels, a goal that "is not subject to discussion" and which permits "no half-solutions" and "no bargaining." In this form of jihad, however, bin Laden and al-Qaeda's strategists have firmly declared that universal participation does not mean that each Muslim acts on his or her own, but rather they act in unity with other Muslims. "A feeling of [individual] responsibility," Sayf-al-Din al-Ansari explained, "does not mean embodying jihad in scattered individual actions. The feeling needs to be deepened by striving for well-planned actions emanating from a position of collective activity."

This "collective activity" is what al-Muqrin termed the "Second Axis of Jihad," the one that covers military strategy and operations, and features a doctrine that is "flexible," "depends on conditions and circumstances," and can easily "accept half-solutions." This adaptability among the mujahideen, Abu-Ubayd al-Qurashi wrote, "is done on the basis of practical experience and field results. This means that jihad military doctrine is constantly changing, thus denying America the chance to know it well or train its troops on how to confront it decisively and permanently." As important, Abu-Ayman al-Hilali wrote, the insurgents' doctrine must address all aspects of the country and society in which the war is being fought. "[W]orking in an organization dedicated to jihad," al-Hilali argued, "requires a fundamental working knowledge of planning, administration, security, psychology, sociology, history, geography, politics, strategy, law, education, preaching, and military science, not to mention religious knowledge."

In terms of fighting the U.S.-led coalitions in Iraq and Afghanistan, al-Muqrin spoke for each al-Qaeda strategist when he explained that Islamist forces must be prepared to fight a "long war of attrition," a struggle in which "the enemy of God will feel that it is impossible to finish off the mujahideen's military power." In both the Iraqi and Afghan "arenas of jihad," the overriding goal for mujahideen leaders should be to prepare to fight the mightiest military power on earth; the insurgent leadership, al-Muqrin advised, must "know the enemy it is fighting." The mujahideen chiefs must be "psychologically prepared for the worst" and, on this basis, they must build an organization "so if one link falls, whatever its organizational size is, the organization [as a whole] does not suffer lethal blows." Before widespread attacks began, Abd al-Hadi added, it was essential that leaders conduct extensive "reconnaissance and surveillance operations to find the enemies' weak points," as well as to "build a vital [dynamic?] database on each target, as well as every change in enemy movements in all regions [of the country] before taking any action."

When military operations based on this data are ready to begin, al-Muqrin urged the mujahideen to follow "the 1,000-wound" policy of guerrilla war with the goal of prolonging the war to "exhaust" the enemies' patience and resources, and to avoid set-piece battles and attacks on "hardened targets" that would be too costly in terms of mujahideen casualties. "We can exhaust him [the enemy]," Abd-al-Hadi wrote, "without fighting any real battles with him." Al-Qaeda's strategists believe that they could find no better foe than the Americans against which to implement this doctrine. The Americans love "fixed bases," al-Qurashi argued, and even in the field their combat forces are awkward, with troops who are "highly paid and overloaded with comfort facilities that often restrict their movements." The key to victory lies in a simple reality, al-Muqrin noted, American bases are "known and immovable," while those of the mujahideen are "light and movable."

Al-Qaeda Doctrine in Iraq and Afghanistan: The Media

Among the strategists referenced in this article, the Saudi al-Muqrin most thoroughly discussed the essential interconnectedness of the military and media dimensions of insurgency. Al-Muqrin argued that the military and media campaigns must be accelerated simultaneously. While al-Qaeda's military doctrine required that the mujahideen wage war in all areas of Afghanistan and Iraq, this widespread activity was no less essential from the perspective of influencing the Muslim and Western worlds. "[There must be] no trace of doubt left on anybody's mind that they [the mujahideen] are present all over the land," al-Muqrin explained. "This will prove the mujahideen's power, rub the nose of the enemies in the dirt, and encourage young men to take up arms and face the enemy—Jews, Christians, and their collaborators." Such demonstrations, moreover, will stimulate donors to increase funding for the mujahideen. This is vital, al-Muqrin noted, because "jihad eats up enormous funds" and those funds are "the nerves of the jihad." In addition, broad and continuous mujahideen military activity will send a warning "through the language of blood or fire" to the people of nations allied with America that "their governments are getting them involved in wars and conflicts with which they have nothing to do."

Conclusion

The insurgency doctrine used by al-Qaeda has been evolving for more than a quarter-century, and is designed to defeat conventional Western military forces. It calls for the group's fighters to be able to fight in the mountains, in desert regions, in maritime conditions, and to be able conduct what al-Muqrin refers to as "covert action" in urban areas. These multifaceted military operations must be matched by the mujahideen "excelling in their organized media action." Tellingly, however, al-Qaeda's insurgency doctrine pays virtually no attention to what the West would identify as "terrorist" operations. While such attacks, al-Muqrin wrote, are an essential contribution to the mujahideen's war effort—especially "qualitative operations" like those of 9/11—they are best left to other units of the al-Qaeda organization.

[From Terrorism Focus, Volume III, Issue 8]

Al-Qaeda's Tactical Doctrine for the Long War

Michael Scheuer

Originally published on March 14, 2006

While the February 28 issue of *Terrorism Focus* outlined al-Qaeda's strategic doctrine for insurgency, it is worth examining how al-Qaeda believes its doctrine should be applied at the tactical level. As was the case for strategic doctrine, the best place to find a discussion of al-Qaeda's tactical doctrine is in its own electronic publications. The following analysis is based on essays published by al-Qaeda writers in March 2003 and August 2004 (http://www.alfjr.com, March 5, 2003; *Sawt al-Jihad*, August 17, 2004; *Muaskar al-Battar*, February 2, 2004). Since the essays were published prior to the intensification of the insurgencies in Iraq and Afghanistan, they allow the reader to compare this outline of tactical doctrine to the events on the ground in both countries since summer 2004.

Building on Experience

The building-block on which al-Qaeda and many of its allies define and refine tactical doctrine is the experience of the mujahideen who fought and defeated the Soviet military occupation of Afghanistan (1979-89). Al-Qaeda's fundamental tactical doctrine emerged from that conflict and has been refined in each of the following jihads— Tajikistan, Chechnya, Bosnia and Kashmir. Indeed, al-Qaeda writers constantly stress the importance of learning from every battle—the need to incorporate what they call "event-related experience" into their doctrine. "Hardships make men," the doctrine holds. "All noble qualities come with time and battles."

Small Groups, Small Arms

According to al-Qaeda military chief Sayf al-Adil, turning a large insurgent force "into small groups with good administrative capabilities will spare us big losses." Al-Qaeda, therefore, emphasizes that insurgent units be limited to between six and ten fighters. A team of this size is mobile, can be kept well-supplied, and has enough manpower to take on many different tasks: reconnaissance, ambushes, raids on small bases, surveillance, kidnappings and other urban operations. Beyond this "flexibility of the organization," a six- to ten-man unit presents a relatively small physical signature, which limits the ability of enemy airpower to fix the position of a group and eliminate it.

Al-Qaeda's tactical doctrine stresses the need to use weapons that are easily available, reliable, and relatively cheap. While the doctrine instructs fighters that "you must prepare weapons of all kinds" to fight the enemy, it concludes that the most important is "the Kalashnikov [AK-47] and ammunition, and there must be large quantities of this because it is the substance of war." Also to be acquired are grenades, medium-caliber mortars and recoilless rifles, 107mm rocket launchers, rocket-propelled-grenade launchers (RPGs) for "anti-armor use," and SAM-7's and 12.7 and 14.5mm machine guns, which are "effective against helicopters." (Interestingly, al-Adil clearly admits that al-Qaeda does not have an effective anti-aircraft weapon. The SAM-7's, he says, are "not useful at all" against jets, and recommends that enemy fixed-wing aircraft not be fired at because the planes can locate and destroy the source of the fire.) Overall, al-Qaeda favors weapons made by Russia and its former communist allies because they are dependable and readily available at "low prices" on the black market; in August 2004, for example, insurgents were urged to quickly purchase as many RPGs as possible "due to its falling price."

In the area of Improvised Explosive Devices (IEDs), al-Qaeda's doctrine instructs the mujahideen to depend on the supplies of explosives that are available in the country in which they are fighting. Most of these countries are awash in explosives; time and money should not be wasted trying to bring explosives in from outside. The insurgents also are told to focus on acquiring stocks of "anti-tank mines" not only for their use against armored vehicles, but because they are a "multi-use weapon" containing components that can be used for building bombs of several sorts. In terms of bomb-making expertise, al-Qaeda doctrine acknowledges "that the production of different types of bombs and explosives must be mastered," but adds this is not difficult because "the ways to do this are available and explained in many places." In addition, "people with experience…[are] many in number in Saudi Arabia and elsewhere."

Logistics

"There is no jihad without power," al-Qaeda's doctrine holds, "and there is no war without resources that ensure the flow and continuation of power. Men without weapons will be useless unless God wishes otherwise." Not surprisingly, there is no specific discussion in the group's electronic journals about the international networks that acquire arms for the mujahideen. Yet, inside a country in which insurgents are engaged, al-Qaeda encourages its fighters to acquire as much ordnance as possible from abandoned or captured regime stockpiles, battlefield recovery, and from deserters and captives. Ordnance acquired internally and from abroad is to be hoarded in "scattered" depots that are in or near the mujahideen's areas of operations. In establishing ordnance depots, the insurgents are instructed to make sure they do not use old and well-known military positions. Al-Qaeda's military chief, Sayf al-Adil, stressed that this was a lesson learned in Afghanistan, where the Taliban had used decades-old positions that were identified to the U.S. military by the Pakistani and Russian intelligence services. Depots should be relatively small so that an enemy success against one depot does not paralyze operations in a given area. The combat team in a particular area, in fact, should be supported by "several logistics cells...in order to ensure the continuity of [military] action within the group" they support. In addition, the logistics cells should not be known to each other in order to prevent communication between them from being discovered by the enemy.

Al-Adil also suggests that the insurgents' logisticians use "fast and light Corolla vehicles" to move men and supplies whenever possible, claiming that, against the U.S.-led coalition in Afghanistan, the vehicles could carry four men and all their equipment and "proved their efficiency, maneuverability, and deceptive qualities." Al-Adil claims that the vehicles were so good that the Japanese company should acquire video of their use in the Afghan war for its advertisements. He also adds that logisticians should look for opportunities to use motorcycles, horses, and camels because the mujahideen in Afghanistan found that coalition soldiers would often let these conveyances pass without inspection.

Combat

Al-Qaeda's tactical doctrine teaches that the key to insurgent success in warfare is patience. An insurgency is by definition a long war, and "there is no harm in delaying action if there is a real interest in doing so." For instance, Sayf al-Adil explained in March 2003, "We want to say to those [Muslims] who want a quick victory that this type of war waged by the mujahideen employs a strategy of the long-breathe and the attrition and terrorization of the enemy and not holding on to territory."

Al-Qaeda's doctrine identifies U.S. airpower as the overwhelming problem facing the mujahideen in combat situations. Al-Qaeda writers are universally dismissive of the quality of U.S. and coalition ground forces, believing that those forces cannot win battles unless they are supported by airpower. U.S. tactical operations are described as very predictable: bombing, troop advance, troop retreat if casualties are suffered, more bombing, and repeat until ground troops can advance with minimal casualties. "The enemy lost the ground battle, which was the norm with us in Afghanistan," Sayf al-Adil has written. "The situation has not changed and will not change, God willing, in the Iraq battle." Almost wistfully, al-Adil also noted that any group could defeat U.S. ground forces if it had a "good, long-range air-defense missile system."

In the face of U.S. airpower, al-Qaeda recommends that insurgents focus on ambushes, mining, and stand-off attacks using crew-served weapons on enemy bases, airfields, and convoys. These attacks should be prepared after extensive surveillance of enemy behavior patterns and a thorough reconnaissance to choose attack sites that can be camouflaged and are at least somewhat shielded by topography from enemy aerial observation. In addition, attack sites should be chosen with an acute concern for maintaining several possible escape routes. If an attack goes poorly, mujahideen forces should immediately break off the fight and flee. Finally, attack sites always should be chosen to minimize the negative impact of a fight on the local population. The mujahideen benefit from active and passive support from local non-combatants, and the best way for the insurgents to maintain both is "to pay attention to the affairs of the public and the people" and to avoid operations that significantly disrupt people who "are busy with life and are pursuing their livelihood."

Al-Adil recommends ambushes as the least costly and most lucrative form of attack on U.S. ground forces. Ambushes, he argues, allow the mujahideen to close with the enemy and thereby deprive him of support from fixed-wing aircraft. In this situation, the insurgents will find that "an American soldier is qualified to fulfill movie roles only"; in ambushes "the enemy will suffer its biggest human losses" because his aerial advantage is largely negated. Al-Qaeda's tacticians have little concern about helicopters coming to the rescue of ambushed U.S. forces because the attacking insurgent unit will have veteran gunners experienced in using SAM-7s, RPGs, and 14.5mm machine guns mounted on pick-up trucks.

Outlook

Al-Qaeda's tactical doctrine for insurgency, like its strategic doctrine, is the product of more than a quarter-century of adapting U.S. and British doctrine—mostly from each country's Marines and Special Forces—to Muslim culture, and a dedication to learning-from-fighting in guerrilla wars across the Islamic world. Both doctrines have been reduced to texts written in several languages, and have been distributed in hard-copy manuals and electronic formats across the Islamic world. For now, al-Qaeda's doctrine is not only its own guiding light, but the doctrine of choice among numerous like-minded Islamic insurgent groups.

[From Terrorism Focus, Volume III, Issue 10]

Al-Qaeda Doctrine: Training the Individual Warrior

Michael Scheuer

Originally published on March 28, 2006

While *Terrorism Focus* previously examined al-Qaeda's strategic and tactical doctrine (February 28, March 14), this article looks at the type and purpose of the non-military training that is given to the individual al-Qaeda fighter or mujahid. Based on al-Qaeda sources (see notes for complete listing), this training appears to be common to both the organization's insurgents and their special forces, and is intended to produce fighters who are pious, disciplined and unity-minded, fatalistic, and cognizant of the requirements and attitudes of those they are defending.

Piety

When training each mujahid, al-Qaeda's doctrine declares that the first priority must be "spiritual preparation ... because it is necessary to attain victory." The key to this preparation is two-fold, al-Qaeda's Ma'adh al-Mansur explained. First, each fighter must completely accept the fact that God has promised victory to the Muslims if they obey His word. Second, the fighter must recognize that victory has not yet come because most Muslims love life and hate death, and thus have strayed from God's path, most specifically from the path of jihad. As a result, al-Mansur directs that each trainee be taught that "God has set the infidel nations against them [the Muslims] to inflict on them humiliation and lowly status. This is an inevitable and ordained punishment that befalls those who abandon jihad." For this degraded status, each Muslim man should be deeply ashamed, and should "die of grief if he does not ward off the calamities inflicted on his fellow Muslims and Kinsmen."

In other words, al-Qaeda doctrine does not argue that the current predicament of Muslims is the fault of what al-Faruq al-Amiri calls "the campaign and reality of the crusader enemy." Rather, that predicament flows from the refusal of Muslims to resist the infidels' attack. The commonly held Western view that al-Qaeda and its followers blame the West for all of Islam's woes—an understanding most stridently advocated by Bernard Lewis—thus falls by the wayside.

Al-Qaeda trainees are taught that the humiliation God has inflicted on Muslims for their failure to obey Him can only be lifted by Muslims accepting God's word and "returning to jihad." If they do so, they will win victories like those the Prophet Muhammad and his companions won in the battles of Badr and The Trench in Islam's first years of existence. "Although the Muslims [with Muhammad] were few and had scanty military means, and the infidels were many and well-equipped," al-Mansur reminds today's mujahideen, "victory was in the hands of God."

Discipline and Unity

If an al-Qaeda trainee is not thoroughly inculcated with the discipline of the Sharia, Abu-Hajar Abd-al-Aziz al-Muqrin warned, "[he] will turn into an outlaw." Abu Jandal, bin Laden's former bodyguard, noted that each trainee must learn that his "mission in life is to protect the ummah," and that this is the "cause" all fighters "carried in our hearts wherever we are able to go." Reflecting on his own training, al-Muqrin recalled that he and his colleagues, "the sons of the Arabian Peninsula," came to the Afghan training camps with much to learn. We were "not used to military order and discipline," al-Muqrin wrote, and found "many things full of restrictions and difficult." After receiving what al-Amiri called intense training for "faith, spirit and heart," however, al-Muqrin said that he and his comrades became mentally "tough and arduous" and knew that they "must fear no one but God and must be ready to sacrifice everything for upholding God's word."

While Sharia instruction develops a disciplined, focused mindset, al-Qaeda doctrine acknowledges that unity of belief does not automatically yield a consistently united organization. Of the other factors impacting unity, al-Qaeda doctrine focuses most on eliminating animosities between trainees, or groups of trainees, that are based on national origins. Abu Jandal, for example, said that in the late 1990s he was often called on by al-Qaeda leaders to travel to camps in Afghanistan to settle disagreements between different nationalities, most commonly Saudis and Egyptians. Al-Qaeda is unique for a number of reasons, but most of all because it is the only Islamist insurgent organization that has been able to remain cohesive and effective despite a heterogeneous membership drawn from several dozen Muslim and non-Muslim states. Abu Jandal has written that bin Laden has long contended that to successfully confront the United States and its allies al-Qaeda fighters "needed to entrench amity among ourselves and eliminate regional rivalries." Part of the training regimen is to ensure, according to Abu Jandal, that "the issue of nationalism was put out of our minds, and we acquired a wider view than that, namely the issue of the ummah."

Fatalism

"What does a mujahid seek from jihad?" Sheikh Yusaf al-Alyiri answers his own question: "He seeks one of two happy endings, either victory or martyrdom. He will be victorious when he achieves either of them." Of all the non-weapons training an al-Qaeda trainee receives, this seems the most simple and straightforward. The mujahid, al-Muqrin concludes, "must be eager to enrage God's enemies and he must believe that God's victory is certain, as promised." He must not worry about the future. "Whatever is going to happen to you," al-Muqrin instructed would-be insurgents, "will not miss you, and whatever is going to miss you will not happen to you; if it were your fate to be killed, taken prisoner, or wounded , then this would be your fate, and caution will not save you from fate."

Area Awareness

Al-Qaeda's training in piety, discipline, unity and fatalism is designed to produce a mujahid who is part of an elite vanguard organization that is deployed in multiple areas of the Muslim world. Al-Qaeda doctrine tells each mujahid that he is "fighting for the whole [Islamic] nation to preserve its religion, sanctities, the blood, honor, and property of the [Muslim] people, and to repulse injustice and aggression." That said, the doctrine notes that al-Qaeda fighters may not encounter a fully supportive population when they first arrive in the theater of fighting. This is because the mujahideen themselves are outsiders as far as the locals are concerned, and they have not yet proved they can protect the local population. In many instances, therefore, the most the mujahideen can expect is passive assistance. "The mujahideen," al-Muqrin explained, "must pay attention to the fact that most people are busy with life and pursuing their own livelihood. If the mujahideen keep this in mind they will realize that in many circumstances they will not get great support unless God wishes otherwise."

Since this situation will be common across the Muslim world, the mujahideen must be disciplined and behave according to the tenets of their training. To turn passive support into active support, al-Muqrin claims, each mujahid must "be known for his nobility of character, ethics, and loyalty to the believers." He continues:

"The troops must be marked by their good manners and conduct. A mujahid must serve as a beacon to lighten the road for the people and a model for other colleagues to follow. He must be careful not to be like those whom God referred to as: 'Do ye enjoin right conduct on the people, and forget [to practice it] yourselves?'"

Conclusion

For national militaries and insurgent groups military doctrine is a set of ideals that cannot be perfectly applied during the unpredictable course of a war. Clear, demanding and repetitive doctrinal training probably is the best means of ensuring the fullest possible application of doctrine in war situations. The fact that al-Qaeda has remained a united and disciplined fighting force in a war against the world's greatest military power, and continues to be welcomed in multiple Muslim countries in which insurgencies are underway or being kindled, suggests the inculcation of its training doctrine for individual fighters has been largely successful.

Notes

1. Ma'adh al-Mansur, "The Importance of Military Preparation According to the Sharia," *al-Mu-askar al-Battar*, January 3, 2004.
2. Yusaf al-Alyiri, "The Illumination on the Path of Jihad. The Road to Battle," *Sawt al-Jihad*, November 1, 2004.
3. Al-Faruq al-Amiri, "What is Our Duty toward Our Ummah?" *al-Mu-askar al-Battar*, August 17, 2004. Ibid., "God is Your Refuge, al-Fallujah," *al-Mu-askar al-Battar*, November 10, 2004.
4. "Interview with Abd-al-Aziz al-Muqrin," *Movement for Islamic Reform*, October 13, 2003.
5. Abu Hajar Abd-al-Aziz al-Muqrin, "The Second Stage: The Relative Strategic Balance," *Mu-askar al-Battar*, January 15, 2004.
6. "Interview of Bin Laden's Former Body Guard, Abu Jandal," *al-Quds al-Arabi*, August 3, 2004 and March 15, 22, 24, and 25, 2005.

[From Terrorism Focus, Volume III, Issue 12]

Al-Qaeda Doctrine: The Eventual Need for Semi-Conventional Forces

Michael Scheuer

Originally published on May 23, 2006

Earlier in 2006, *Terrorism Focus* published three articles on al-Qaeda's doctrine for what the United States government has taken to calling the "Long War." In recent weeks, Western media reporting on developments in the Iraq and Afghan insurgencies seems to make a fourth article relevant. Media reports from both Iraq and Afghanistan have suggested the appearance of a slow evolution of the Islamist insurgents' tactics in the direction of the battlefield deployment of larger mujahideen units that attack "harder" facilities. These attacks are not replacing small unit attacks, ambushes, kidnappings, assassinations and suicide bombings in either country, but rather seem to be initial and tentative forays toward another stage of fighting. In the past month, reports have suggested Abu Musab al-Zarqawi and his Iraqi resistance allies are trying to train semi-conventional units, and last week's large-unit action by the Taliban at the town of Musa Qala in southern Afghanistan may be straws in the wind in this regard.

As was explained in the earlier *Terrorism Focus* articles, al-Qaeda believes that it and its allies can only defeat the United States in a "long war," one that allows the Islamists to capitalize on their extraordinary patience, as well as on their enemies' lack thereof. Before his death in a firefight with Saudi security forces, the leader of al-Qaeda in the Arabian Peninsula, Abu Hajar Abd al-Aziz al-Muqrin, wrote extensively about how al-Qaeda believed the military fight against the United States and its allies would unfold. He envisioned a point at which the mujahideen would have to develop semi-conventional forces. He identified this period as the "Decisive Stage" [1].

Al-Muqrin told his insurgent readers that the power of the United States precluded any expectation of a quick victory. He wrote that the war would progress slowly through such phases as initial manpower mobilization, political work among the populace to establish trust and support, the accumulation of weaponry and other supplies, the establishment of bases around the country and especially in the mountains, the initiation of attacks on individuals and then a gradual intensification of the latter until a countrywide insurgency was underway. Each of these steps was essential and none could be skipped, al-Muqrin maintained; the steps would prolong the war, thereby allowing the mujahideen to grow in numbers, experience and combat power. "We should warn against rushing from one stage to the next," he wrote. "Rather, we should be patient and take all factors into consideration. The fraternal brothers in Algeria, for instance, hastily moved from one stage to the other...The outcome was the movement's retreat...from 1995-1997."

As these steps were traversed by the mujahideen, al-Muqrin argued that the resources, political will, morale and manpower of the insurgents' enemies would be eroded, and that their forces would assume more static positions in order to limit the attrition they suffered. In this stage of the insurgency, al-Muqrin predicted that the United States and its allies would conduct far fewer large-scale combat operations in the countryside and would turn toward conducting smaller raids on specific targets, while simultaneously hardening their bases and protecting their supply routes and lines of communication. At this point, al-Muqrin wrote, the mujahideen could begin the final stage of preparation for victory, "which is building a military force across the country that becomes the nucleus of a military army."

With the end of the constant pressure and danger generated by major enemy sweep operations, al-Muqrin wrote that the mujahideen should begin "taking advantage of the areas where the regime has little or reduced presence" to train semi-conventional military units. In these areas, "the mujahideen will set up administrative centers and bases...They will build camps, hospitals, Sharia courts and radio transmission stations at these areas, which will serve as a staging area for their military and political operations." Currently, al-Anbar province in Iraq; Nuristan, the Kunar Valley, Kandahar and Paktika provinces in Afghanistan; and swathes of Pakistan's border provinces would seem to meet the requirements laid down by al-Muqrin.

It should be clearly noted that al-Muqrin neither envisioned nor called for mujahideen units that could evenly square-off with the units of their foes. Although the formation of such insurgent units would mark "the era of victory and conquests for the mujahideen," al-Muqrin wrote, the development of "semi-regular forces that gradually become regular forces with modern formations" will not yield forces equivalent to those of the enemy. "By modern," al-Muqrin wrote, "I mean the need for these troops to be knowledgeable about regular warfare, the army formations [and] their function in urban areas. I do not mean following the suit of the regimes..." The purpose of these forces? "Through these regular forces," al-Muqrin explained, "the mujahideen will begin to attack small cities and publicize the conquest and victories in the media to lift the morale of the mujahideen and the people in general and break the morale of the enemy." Al-Muqrin continued, stating, "The reason the mujahideen should target the small cities is that when the enemies' soldiers see these [small] cities falling into the hands of the mujahideen it will destroy their morale and they will realize that they are no match for the mujahideen."

Interestingly, al-Muqrin uses for his example the activities of the Afghan mujahideen from 1988-1992. In Afghanistan, this period encompassed the era after the Soviet military terminated its large-scale, hammer-and-anvil sweep operations—leaving most of the country's non-urban areas to the mujahideen—and after the Soviet withdrawal when the Afghan communists were hunkered down in a few urban bastions. In these years, Ahmed Shah Masood and Jalaluddin Haqqani began to train small, semi-conventional units to use in attempts to take small cities of the kind to which al-Muqrin refers. Both Afghan commanders successfully used these units; Masood took several small cities in northern Afghanistan—including Takhar—and Haqqani took Khost, then the capital of Paktia province. These relatively small victories produced a substantial morale boost among the Afghan mujahideen and their supporters and produced equal dismay among their enemies. In a similar but more recent example of this phenomenon, the Iraqi insurgency's morale received a boost—and the U.S.-led coalition was embarrassed—when al-Zarqawi's forces took and temporarily held the small city of al-Qaim near the Syrian border in September 2005 [2].

In closing, it is again important to note that al-Qaeda's doctrine as explained by al-Muqrin does not call for semi-conventional units to replace guerrilla forces; the latter will remain a main force of the insurgency, as well as its safety net. At this stage, al-Muqrin wrote, "we should keep the guerrillas because the mujahideen may need them in some cases." Al-Muqrin argued that it was always possible that the enemy would revert to large-scale aggressive offensive operations and force the insurgents back into an earlier stage of the war. He also noted that the enemy's airpower would always afford it great mobility. "It should be noted here that the main bases on the mountains must maintain a strong garrison and that the conquests [taking small cities] should not tempt the mujahideen to abandon their fortified bases," al-Muqrin warned. "This is [done] so not to give the enemy an opportunity to conduct a rear-landing operation, taking advantage of the absence of the mujahideen in these bases. This is why we mentioned earlier that the mujahideen must keep the guerrillas constantly prepared."

The larger-size insurgent units that have been sporadically operating in Iraq and Afghanistan during the last year may signal the initial, limited success of al-Muqrin's call for the building of semi-conventional mujahideen units. The data to make a definitive judgment, however, is currently not available. It will suffice to say that what is known about al-Qaeda doctrine for the "Long War" calls for the eventual creation of such units, and that Ayman al-Zawahiri's instructions to al-Zarqawi—in al-Zawahiri's letter of July 9, 2005—clearly infers that the mujahideen will need semi-conventional forces to control Iraq after the withdrawal of the U.S.-led coalition [3].

Notes
1. Abu-Hajar Abd-al-Aziz al-Muqrin, "The Second Stage: The Relative Strategic Balance," *Mu'askar al-Battar*, February 2, 2004.
2. Ellen Knickmeyer, "Zarqawi Militants Seize Key Town in Western Iraq," *Washington Post*, September 6, 2005.
3. Zawahiri to Zarqawi, July 9, 2005, Director of National Intelligence, http://www.dni.gov.

[From Terrorism Focus, Volume III, Issue 20]

Al-Qaeda's WMD Strategy after the U.S. Intervention in Afghanistan

Robert Wesley

Originally published on October 21, 2005

With the loss of its Afghan sanctuary following the U.S. intervention in 2001, there was a question as to what role weapons of mass destruction (WMD) would play in al-Qaeda's newly evolving strategy. Al-Qaeda has taken advantage of its recently assumed role as the ideological and strategic brain for the global jihad to create an environment from which a variety of jihadi elements can participate in acquiring and employing chemical, biological, radiological, and nuclear (CBRN) weapons.

Al-Qaeda has opened the door for its supporters to use CBRN weapons to further the goals of the global jihad. To this end, al-Qaeda has provided the religious, practical, and strategic justifications to engage in CBRN activities. These steps have served to strengthen the acceptance of such weapons within sympathetic audiences, dispelled objections to unconventional attacks and prepared the ground for jihadi leaders to operationalize CBRN weapons into their repertoire of tactics. Departing from its previous reliance on in-house production and management of CBRN weapons, al-Qaeda is now encouraging other groups to acquire and use CBRN weapons with or without its direct assistance.

Over the years, al-Qaeda has stepped up its efforts to seek justifications to conduct increasingly brutal attacks. Correspondingly, the group has attempted to frame the acquisition and use of CBRN weapons as the religious duty of Muslims. Al-Qaeda began the process of incorporating this dynamic before the U.S. intervention in Afghanistan. In response to the testing of Pakistan's nuclear arsenal in 1998, Osama bin Laden praised the efforts of the first Muslim state to defend itself through WMD and encouraged other Muslims to follow Pakistan's example [1]. Shortly after these developments, bin Laden was interviewed by Jamal Isma'il in December of 1998 over U.S. charges that al-Qaeda was aggressively pursuing CBRN. Bin Laden asserted that using the word "charge" was misleading in that it implies a wrong doing. Rather, according to bin Laden, "it is the duty of Muslims to possess them [WMD]," and that "the United States knows that with the help of Almighty Allah the Muslims today possess these weapons" [2].

These events illustrate al-Qaeda's early gravitation toward promoting CBRN weapons that the network was attempting to produce before the U.S. intervention in Afghanistan. Al-Qaeda's pre-9/11 activities also display a sense of confidence in its preparation to use CBRN weapons. However, in response to the 9/11 attacks, the terror network came under increasing criticism from its Muslim audiences to more correctly follow Islamic traditions of warning, offers of conversion, and significant religious authorization before committing such highly destructive attacks in the future.

Through a series of subsequent statements, al-Qaeda is believed to have sufficiently fulfilled these prerequisite obligations for high-impact attacks. The lesson of 9/11 has also been applied to its WMD strategy, in that further preparations have been taken to justify CBRN attacks prior to the actual events. Al-Qaeda seems to frame its argument around references from the Qur'an that they interpret as instructing Muslims to respond to aggression with equal aggression (Qur'an 16:126; 2:194; 42:40); similar to the expression of "an eye for an eye."

In this regard, Osama bin Laden stated in 2001 that, "if America used chemical and nuclear weapons against us, then we may retort with chemical and nuclear weapons. We have the weapons as a deterrent" [3]. Al-Qaeda also received much needed outside theological assistance from the radical Saudi Sheikh Nassir bin Hamad al-Fahd. In 2003, al-Fahd issued an important and detailed fatwa on the permissibility of WMD in jihad. He stated that since America had destroyed countless lands and killed about 10 million Muslims, it would obviously be permitted to respond in kind [4]. Al-Fahd's ruling provided support to the previous assertion of al-Qaeda spokesman Suleiman Abu Gheith in 2002, stating that, "we have the right to kill four million Americans, two million of them children… and cripple them in the hundreds of thousands. Furthermore, it is our obligation to fight them with chemical and biological weapons, to afflict them with the fatal woes that have afflicted Muslims because of their chemical and biological weapons" [5].

However, these do not constitute the most direct threats of WMD deployment by the terror network. In fact, purported al-Qaeda trainer Abu Muhammad al-Ablaj continued the preparation for eventual

WMD use when he forebodingly said in 2003 that, "as to the use of Sarin gas and nuclear [weapons], we will talk about them then, and the infidels will know what harms them. They spared no effort in their war on us in Afghanistan and left no weapon unused. They should not therefore rule out the possibility that we will present them with our capabilities" [6]. Al-Ablaj again emphasized the thematic justification of reciprocity concerning WMD. Later in 2003 al-Ablaj provided further explanation that a chemical, biological, or nuclear weapon is a strategic weapon that has "reactions commiserate with its size." He added, "It must therefore be used at a time that makes the crusader enemy beg on his knee that he does not want more strikes" [7]. Apparently al-Ablaj is convinced that al-Qaeda has fulfilled its preparatory duty for using CBRN and it is now only a matter of appropriate circumstances presenting themselves.

Although the core of al-Qaeda has been primarily concerned with justifying WMD attacks based on reciprocity, Mustafa Setmariam Nasar (a.k.a. Abu Mus'ab al-Suri), a highly experienced jihadi, veteran of the Afghan conflicts and associate of al-Qaeda and the Taliban, has taken another line of justification. Al-Suri's position is similar to the legal judgment of al-Fahd when he wrote that "if those engaged in jihad establish that the evil of the infidels can be repelled only by attacking them with weapons of mass destruction, they may be used even if they annihilate all the infidels" [8].

Mustafa Setmariam Nasar was forced out of Afghanistan after the U.S. intervention at the end of 2001. He then devoted the next several years to, as he explains, "plug one of the Muslims' major gaps: reflection on past experience... and comparing it with the confrontation and battles which the future holds for us, as I am one of the few mujahideen remaining who specialized in this matter" [9]. The fruit of al-Suri's contemplative hiatus is an unprecedented 1600 page treatise of strategic and military guidance which should be taken very seriously in terms of its impact on the future strategy of the global jihad. He has concluded that CBRN weapons are the "difficult yet vital" means to ensure final victory, partially due to ineffectiveness of current tactics. He also stated that "the mujahideen must obtain them [WMD] with the help of those who posses them either buying them," or by "producing primitive atomic bombs, which are called dirty bombs [RDD]" [10]. His prescription of WMD will serve to strengthen the direction of the global jihad towards using CBRN in the future as he has essentially bound the aforementioned broad strategic parameters created by al-Qaeda's traditional leadership into a more actionable logic. Al-Suri, in a sense, has departed from the current strategy of al-Qaeda's traditional leadership. Al-Qaeda's leadership has been primarily concerned with providing the justification for jihadis to use WMD, while al-Suri advances this to actively advocating CBRN weapons as essential to the "end-game" strategy.

It must be recognized that although what has constituted "al-Qaeda" as an organization or network is now undergoing considerable realignment into more of a guidance and support base, it still retains operational capabilities which will be demonstrated in the future. Figures such as Abu Khabab, a director of al-Qaeda's chemical and biological weapons programs believed to be at large, or other members of the former weapons programs, may play a significant role in any future attack. Abdullah al-Muhajir, previously Jose Padilla, is an example of al-Qaeda's traditional cadres' continued intention to plan and execute such attacks. Padilla is accused of meeting with "senior al-Qaeda operatives" while in Pakistan and Afghanistan in 2001 and 2002, who instructed him to return to the United Sates to explore advanced plans for attacking America, including an attack with a radiological weapon (RDD) [11]. Lastly, it is also worth noting that the rising class of "e-mujahideen," who are increasingly integrated into the internet yet have little connection to established jihadi groups, have displayed enthusiasm for WMD.

There are several "encyclopedias" online claiming to contain formulas for chemical agents or construction plans for dirty bombs [12]. Although much of the information provided in these manuals is usually flawed from a technical perspective, the fact that e-mujahideen are promoting WMD procurement and use while disseminating CBRN manuals is quite alarming. It is only a matter of time before more accurate manuals will begin to surface, an eventuality that will make countering CBRN terrorism increasingly more difficult.

Conclusion

Al-Qaeda's leadership has made a concerted effort to prepare its audiences for a WMD attack. However, it has been argued that since the historical volume of direct references to WMD by al-Qaeda has been relatively low, this somehow displays a disinterest in or unlikelihood of WMD playing a role in the terror network's future. Al-Qaeda operative Muhammad al-Ablaj has already responded to this argument when he asked: "Is there a sane person who discloses his [WMD] secrets?" [13] A second explanation is that what has already been presented has adequately justified WMD use, and thus there is little more to be said until a need for further guidance presents itself, such as it did for al-Suri. Whether by al-Qaeda core cadres, those answering al-Suri's calls, or e-mujahideen inspired by their own arguments and supported by al-Qaeda's justifications, CBRN weapons are likely to be employed by jihadi forces in the not-so-distant future.

Notes:
1. *Al-Quds al-Arabi*, June 1, 1998.
2. Interview rebroadcast on al-Jazeera, September 20, 2001.
3. *Dawn* (Pakistani Daily), November 10, 2001.
4. Nassir bin Hamad al-Fahd, Risalah fi hokum istikhdam aslihat al-damar al-shamel didh al-kuffar, May 2003.
5. Suleiman Abu Gheith, www.alneda.com.
6. *Al-Majallah*, May 25, 2003.
7. *Al-Majallah*, September 21, 2003.
8. Al-Fahd, Risalah fi hokum istikhdam aslihat al-damar al-shamel didh al-kuffar.
9. *El Pais*, June 6, 2005.
10. Ibid.
11. United States court of Appeals for the Second Circuit, Docket No. 03-2235.
12. Examples of sites have included: http://elaqsa.2islam.com/; www.alm2sda.net; www.tawhed.ws; www.geocities.com/i3dad_jihad/.
13. *Al-Majallah*, September 21, 2003.

[From Terrorism Monitor, Volume III, Issue 20]

Toronto, London and the Jihadi Spring: Bin Laden as Successful Instigator

Michael Scheuer

Originally published on June 6, 2006

Over the past two years, U.S. and Western commentators have concluded that Osama bin Laden is largely irrelevant as the leader of the worldwide Sunni insurgency. *Newsweek's* Fareed Zakaria, for example, has said that "by now it is surely clear that al-Qaeda can produce videotapes but not terrorism...And the bad guys are losing" (*Newsweek,* March 15, 2004). James S. Dobbins at the *National Review* added that bin Laden "made many threats of course, but was never able to back them up, creating an unbridgeable credibility gap" (*National Review Online,* September 28, 2005). The new CIA chief, General Michael Hayden, has described bin Laden's recent audiotapes as a public relations campaign to prove he is still alive. "These attempts," Hayden said, "may be an attempt on their part [bin Laden and Ayman al-Zawahiri] to kind of re-establish authenticity with their followers" (AP, February 5). Finally, from Sarah Lawrence College, Fawaz Gerges all but dismisses bin Laden's relevance, arguing that "we are in the throes of the beginning of a new wave [in the Muslim world]—the freedom generation—in which civil society is asserting itself" (*Christian Science Monitor,* February 4, 2004). In short, these arguments assert that the situation has improved.

Well, maybe. The issue of bin Laden's continued relevance as a major leader of Sunni militancy—and as an enemy of the United States and the West—can surely be assessed through the lens these authors used. Put most simply, this lens is built on the assumptions that bin Laden leads a gang of criminals who have hijacked Islam and is nihilistically attacking the United States because they hate democracy, freedom, elections and gender equality. Based on this analysis, the above-noted quotations suggest that a U.S.-led victory over al-Qaeda is in the offing because bin Laden's popularity is withering and because there has been no post-9/11 al-Qaeda attack inside the United States.

The purpose of this article is not to attack either the distinguished individuals quoted or the views and analyses they put forth. The tent under which attempts are made to understand bin Laden, al-Qaeda and the threat they pose must be a large one that accommodates a broad range of heated but civil debate. The point of this piece is to examine where bin Laden might believe he and al-Qaeda stand vis-à-vis his primary goals today, nearly 10 years after his late-August 1996 declaration of war on the United States. This is an opportune moment to try to view the war from bin Laden's perspective, as the West is sorting out the broader meaning of last week's major police actions against al-Qaeda-inspired Islamists in the United Kingdom and Canada.

It often comes as a surprise to people to discover that bin Laden has never claimed that al-Qaeda can or would defeat the United States, much less that al-Qaeda's goal was to destroy the "American way of life" or "Western civilization." He is not a man given to grandiose pronouncements and has limited his goal to incrementally increasing the pain inflicted on the United States and its allies in order to force them to disengage from the Middle East to the greatest extent possible. If achieved, bin Laden believes, this would then allow al-Qaeda and its allies to focus on its main targets: the tyrannies that rule most Arab states, and the state of Israel.

In examining where bin Laden thinks he stands in attaining this goal, it is also vital to understand that he has never claimed that al-Qaeda could achieve this goal by itself. Quite the contrary, he has consistently maintained that al-Qaeda is only the vanguard of the large-scale movement that is needed to achieve this goal. The working title of my first book on al-Qaeda was "Allah's Humble Incendiary." That title was not used, but I believe that it remains a useful short-hand summary of the role bin Laden seeks for himself and al-Qaeda in the present war. He intends to be the instigator and inspirer of Muslims to follow the path of jihad and aims to agitate their souls until they do so. Even in this, he claims no original role for himself, explaining that he is honored to "provide our ummah with the inspiration it requires" [1] because "Allah asked it from the best of humans, the Prophet" [2]. It is in this context that bin Laden assesses the current status of the effort he publicly launched in 1996. "I must say," bin Laden reemphasized just after the 9/11 attacks, "that my duty is just to awaken Muslims, to tell them what is good for them and what is not...Al-Qaeda was set up to wage jihad against infidelity, particularly to encounter the onslaught of infidel countries against the Islamic states. Jihad is the sixth undeclared element of Islam. Every anti-Islamic element is afraid of it. Al-Qaeda wants to keep this element alive and active and make it part of the daily lives of Muslims. It wants to give it the status of worship" [3].

If bin Laden is taken at his word—that his goal is to incite Muslims to jihad and that he and al-Qaeda will not and cannot be the sole agent forcing substantial U.S. disengagement from the Middle East—some of the judgments of the individuals quoted above become problematic. It also makes irrelevant the argument by some commentators and government officials that bin Laden is losing control of international Sunni militancy. The reality is that he has never sought universal command-and-control and has always tried to foment widespread, anti-Western Islamist violence that would need nothing from al-Qaeda except for inspiration. Indeed, the data surfacing since last week's disruption of what appears to have been preparations for major terrorist attacks in Britain and Canada—perhaps a chemical attack in the United Kingdom—strongly suggest that bin Laden's unrelenting focus on instigation and agitation is having an impact among Muslims worldwide (AP, June 3; *International Herald Tribune*, June 4).

Some will correctly argue that last week's events are not enough to validate the contention that bin Laden is succeeding in his main goal of instigation. The aborted operations in London and Toronto, however, are both said to have been inspired by bin Laden and al-Qaeda. Moreover, they are two more in a series of events that now stretch back over three-plus years. Kuwaiti Islamists, for example, said that the attack that killed one U.S. Marine and wounded another before the 2003 invasion of Iraq was a gift to bin Laden. In the same period, a Yemeni cleric killed a senior member of Yemen's socialist party and announced the same motivation as the Kuwaitis. More recently, the bombers who hit Madrid's Atocha Train Station in March 2003 and London's transit system in July 2005, as well as the Islamist militant cell taken down by Australian authorities in late 2005, are said to have been inspired by al-Qaeda's example (AFP, November 10, 2005). Even in such places as Nigeria's oil-rich Niger Delta and the teeming cities of Bangladesh, Islamist leaders claim to have been inspired by bin Laden. In each of these events and places, national authorities have yet to document direct training, financial or command-and-control links to al-Qaeda; indeed, in the case of the actual and thwarted attacks, the required training appears to have been done in the country where the attack occurred. In addition, Islamist leaders in Syria, Lebanon, Palestine, Egypt, Jordan and Jerusalem in 2005-2006 declared the formation of insurgent organizations that have pledged their allegiance to al-Qaeda and the goals enunciated by bin Laden.

Other incidents also suggest the viability of bin Laden's clear intention to incite Muslims by keeping them focused on what the United States and Europe do in the Muslim world, and not on how they conduct their domestic political and social affairs. Islamist networks established to recruit Muslims to fight U.S.-led forces in Iraq, for example, have been found in France, Belgium, Australia, Germany, Switzerland and elsewhere. European intelligence officers have said that up to 1,000 European Muslims have been sent to fight in Iraq; British officials claim that up to 150 Muslims from the United Kingdom alone have gone to Iraq. In these cases, both Europe-born Muslims—some third generation—and local converts have been attracted and motivated by the Iraqis' jihad, a cause that for Islamists pivots on the U.S.-led invasion and occupation of Iraq, and not on opposition to elections, democracy and liberty. They will return home, moreover, with significant military skills and imbued with the jihadi spirit [4].

Taken at his own word, then, it seems likely that bin Laden is quite pleased with where he and al-Qaeda stand a decade after declaring war. This is not to say that U.S. military and intelligence forces have not hurt al-Qaeda; they have, although not to the catastrophic extent some claim. It is to say, however, that bin Laden's main goal of using his words, al-Qaeda's actions and a tight focus on what the United States does in the Islamic world to instigate Muslims to join the anti-U.S. jihad has not only found traction, but is increasingly successful worldwide. Today, the United States and Europe are not only confronted by a still undefeated al-Qaeda, but by an increasing number of Muslims in their own populations who—inspired and religiously agitated by bin Laden—are prepared to pick up arms and spend their lives to act on that inspiration.

Notes
1. "Exclusive Transcript of Previously Unaired Interview with Osama bin Laden," *Qoqaz* (internet), May 23, 2002.
2. "Exposing the New Crusader War—Osama bin Laden—February 2003," *Waaqiah* (internet), February 14, 2003.
3. "Interview with Osama bin Laden," *Ummat*, September 28, 2001.
4. *Sydney Morning Herald*, January 7; BBC News, January 12; *Washington Post*, February 18; *The Sunday Times*, June 4.

[From Terrorism Focus, Volume III, Issue 22]

Can al-Qaeda Endure Beyond bin Laden?

Michael Scheuer

Originally published on October 31, 2005

The question of al-Qaeda's longevity after the demise of its figurehead is ultimately unanswerable until bin Laden is actually gone. There are those who believe bin Laden is dead—which would surely be one of history's best kept secrets—and argue that al-Qaeda has proven its survivability. While never saying never, it seems exceedingly likely that bin Laden is alive, and on that presumption the following analysis is based.

Man or Organization

Too often, al-Qaeda's post-bin Laden future is discussed solely on the basis of who will replace him. It is asked whether the successor will have bin Laden's intelligence, charisma, and jihadi credentials. Or, can Zawahiri, Sayf al-Adil, Zarqawi, one of bin Laden's sons, or a now-unknown mujahid fill the top position? Thus, much of the analysis about a new al-Qaeda leader's impact focuses on personalities and their respective strengths and weaknesses, and frequently fails to examine the nature of the organization bin Laden's successor will inherit.

The al-Qaeda organization, as all know, was formed in the last months of Moscow's occupation of Afghanistan, around mid-1988. Bin Laden played the lead role in its formation, but his colleagues— Wali Khan Amin Shah, Abu Hajir al-Iraqi, Wael Julaidan, Muhammed Jamal Khalifah, etc.—also played a part. What was the group's goal in establishing al-Qaeda? It was meant to maintain the Islamist momentum attendant to the Red Army's defeat. It was also intended to be an organization governed by Islamist principles. Furthermore, it was meant to be patterned on the Afghan Islamist insurgent groups—those of Khalis, Hekmtayar, Sayyaf, and Masood—which had defeated the Soviets. (It always is worth noting that al-Qaeda is not modeled on a terrorist group.) Finally, from its inception, al-Qaeda has targeted the United States.

Yet, the foregoing are intentions to be accomplished, they are not the basic reason for al-Qaeda's creation. The best phrase to describe why al-Qaeda was created is "long-term durability." At the most fundamental level, al-Qaeda's founders wanted to build an organization that would preserve and—here bin Laden's CEO talents came into play—institutionalize the mechanisms built during the 1980s to support the Afghan mujahideen and, once institutionalized, use them to support militant Islam worldwide. How to enumerate these mechanisms is an open question, but it fair to list five mechanisms that al-Qaeda's founders thought essential to the long-term durability of their organization, regardless of who was serving as its chief.

Funding

The Afghan jihad was expensive, and bin Laden saw this reality first hand. Bin Laden, moreover, was directly involved in the funding process, serving early in the war as a channel through which private and official Saudi monies went to the mujahideen. (Bin Laden's counterpart in funding was Sheikh Abdullah Azzam, who brought money from the non-Gulf Middle East and the Muslim Brotherhood.)

By the Afghan war's mid-point, moreover, bin Laden and other Arab mujahideen began forming all-Arab insurgent units. While it is likely that Pakistani intelligence diverted some official U.S. and Saudi funds to the groups, bin Laden has explained that the Arabs did not want to be tainted by U.S. support and so developed funding sources and channels independent of those supporting the Afghans.

Since the end of the Afghan war, al-Qaeda's funding capability has been solidified and expanded on the basis that established it in the 1980s. Al-Qaeda's worldwide growth and multifaceted activities— attacking America, supporting Islamic insurgencies, training fighters, etc.—demanded reliable funding. The group's well-documented record of success suggests funding is ample and that the channels carrying the funds are hidden and not susceptible to interdiction.

Procurement

Many wealthy Muslims were willing to buy weapons for the Afghans but were unwilling to work with Riyadh or the U.S. government. Faced with this reality, bin Laden and other Arabs crafted a weapons-procurement system for the Afghan mujahideen that, like the funding mechanism, ran parallel to the U.S.-Saudi system. Bin Laden and his colleagues ran this parallel mechanism and used it to arm the Afghans and themselves. Before al-Qaeda was formed, therefore, its leaders were well-versed in clandestine procurement and transportation of arms, communications gear, and military accoutrements.

Since 1988, bin Laden and his lieutenants have improved their procurement system to accommodate al-Qaeda's needs, as well as to arm its allies. There is no evidence that al-Qaeda and its allies have ever suffered more than a temporary shortage of conventional weapons. Al-Qaeda also has created a second, separate procurement channel for acquiring weapons of mass destruction (WMD), particularly nuclear weapons. This system benefits from al-Qaeda's successful recruitment of scientists, engineers, technicians, and hands-on practitioners of building such weapons from, at least, Pakistan's WMD programs. The extent of this second system's success is not known, but if the targeted application of money, time, expertise, and leadership pressure can yield success, it would be a mistake to assume that WMD-acquisition is too difficult for a non-state actor like al-Qaeda.

Manpower and Logistics

Bin Laden, Abdullah Azzam, and their colleagues began their jihad careers building and managing a network that supplied men for the Afghan war. Bin Laden et al brought non-Afghan Muslims from across the Islamic world to Pakistan to serve as fighters and as workers in hospitals, arms dumps, refugee camps, clinics, and NGOs. Their effort was successful and created a network of travel routes, trusted facilitators, and way stations where jihad-bound travelers could be succored. By war's end, this system had matured to the extent that very few volunteers could not reach the jihad.

At its founding, al-Qaeda faced the task of turning this single-direction system—all roads led to Afghanistan—into one that could continue bringing men to South Asia for training, transport trainees to camps in Yemen and Sudan, and move trained fighters to combat theaters in Tajikistan, Bosnia, and Chechnya. Al-Qaeda obviously succeeded in a systemic expansion which has accommodated ever larger numbers. Indeed, manpower never has been a problem for al-Qaeda; it is now present in 75-plus countries, has sizeable contingents in Afghanistan and Iraq, and has combat trainers, logisticians, and veteran fighters involved in most of the world's Islamist insurgencies. Al-Qaeda's manpower and logistical capabilities—like those for funding and procurement—can be described as effective and relatively immune from disruption.

Training and Personnel Services

Bin Laden's 1988 operational priority was for al-Qaeda to train Muslim militants from around the world at the groups' camps, and provide far-flung Islamist insurgencies with a cadre to train fighters locally and be a "stiffening agent" for local forces. The al-Qaeda cadre added to Taliban forces in 1996, for example, added skill and professionalism to Mullah Omar's campaign against the Northern Alliance around Kabul. The al-Qaeda cadre had the same impact on Kashmiri insurgent forces in the late 1990s. Today, al-Qaeda's training capability in Afghanistan is constrained, but the steady pace of combat in the insurgencies in the Philippines, Chechnya, Afghanistan, Iraq, and elsewhere suggests training remains an al-Qaeda priority and is being executed outside Afghanistan.

As for any military organization, al-Qaeda's personnel services for combatants and their families are vital both to maintain morale and prevent disgruntled fighters or their families from publicly denigrating the group or, worse, providing information about it to the enemy. After a decade of war with the United States, we know little about how al-Qaeda's personnel services work. We do know, however, that no individual has come forward in the media to attack al-Qaeda for the treatment he or she received from the group, nor have there been intelligence leaks about an ill-treated al-Qaeda fighter or family member providing information that damaged group—data Western governments surely would have leaked if it existed. On the other hand, anecdotal accounts abound of al-Qaeda providing health care and financial aid to the families of fighters killed in battle or absent on operations; doing everything possible to provide special care such as prosthetic devices for wounded fighters; and delivering monthly stipends to families of imprisoned fighters. In sum, al-Qaeda's personnel services seem to help maintain high morale and stubborn loyalty toward the organization.

Propaganda

From al-Qaeda's first day to the present, bin Laden's priority has been to incite and instigate Muslims to support and participate in a defensive jihad against the United States and its allies. He and his lieutenants have spent large amounts of money, time and imagination to build a world-class media and propaganda apparatus. Today, that apparatus is in full operation. Bin Laden and Zawahiri appear on and dominate the international media at times of their choosing. As important, al-Qaeda's multifaceted internet presence keeps its religious views, political and ideological commentary, and news reports constantly before its most important constituency, the Muslim world's computer-literate middle- and upper-middle classes.

Al-Qaeda also has used the internet to drastically reduce the need for would-be mujahideen to travel to places like Afghanistan, Yemen, or Sudan for training. By mounting military and intelligence manuals on the internet, al-Qaeda has created a situation where training can be conducted in virtually any country on earth, thereby increasing the chance of evading the eye of Western governments.

Conclusion

Al-Qaeda's post-bin Laden effectiveness will, in significant measure, depend on leadership qualities of his successor. Realistically, there is little reason to think a potential successor will have the same credentials and talents that have powered bin Laden's leadership. Yet, his successor may not need equivalent credentials and talents. Al-Qaeda is now a well-established, 17-year-old firm; indeed, the parts of it that developed from mechanisms that supported the Afghans against the Soviets have been operating for 25 years. In short, al-Qaeda is now what its founders intended: a reliable, professional organization that has demonstrated long-term durability. Thus, bin Laden's successor will inherit a proven, well-functioning organization, one that will give him time to grow on the job without the need to spend most of his time keeping the organization running.

[From Terrorism Focus, Volume II, Issue 20]

Al-Qaeda's Next Generation: Less Visible and More Lethal

Michael Scheuer

Originally published on October 4, 2005

Experts speculate widely about the composition and tactics of the next generation of mujahideen. This speculation stems from the fact that transnational groups are harder collection targets than nation-states. Such ambiguity and imprecision is likely to endure indefinitely, and is particularly worrisome concerning "next-generation" terrorism studies.

Osama bin Laden has been planning for the next generation of mujahideen since he began speaking publicly in the mid-1990s. Bin Laden has always described the "defensive jihad" against the United States as potentially a multi-generational struggle. After the 9/11 attacks, bin Laden explained that, even as the anti-U.S. war intensified, the torch was being passed from his generation to the next. "We have been struggling right from our youth," bin Laden wrote in late 2001:

"We sacrificed our homes, families, and all the luxuries of this worldly life in the path of Allah (we ask Allah to accept our efforts). In our youth, we fought with and defeated the (former) Soviet Union (with the help of Allah), a world superpower, and now we are fighting the USA. We have never let the Muslim Ummah down.

"Muslims are being humiliated, tortured and ruthlessly killed all over the world, and its time to fight these satanic forces with the utmost strength and power. Today the whole of the Muslim Ummah is depending (after Allah) upon the Muslim youth, hoping that they would never let them down." [1]

The question arising is, of course, what threat will the next generation of al-Qaeda-inspired mujahideen pose? Based on the admittedly imprecise information available, the answer seems to lie in three discernible trends: a) the next generation will be at least as devout but more professional and less operationally visible; b) it will be larger, with more adherents and potential recruits; and c) it will be better educated and more adept at using the tools of modernity, particularly communications and weapons.

Religiosity and Quiet Professionalism

The next mujahideen generation's piety will equal or exceed that of bin Laden's generation. The new mujahideen, having grown up in a world dominated by the internet and satellite television, will be more aware of Muslim struggles around the world, more comfortable with a common Muslim identity, more certain that the U.S.-led West is "oppressing" Muslims, and more inspired by the example bin Laden has set—bin Laden's generation had no bin Laden.

While leaders more pious than bin Laden and Ayman al-Zawahiri are hard to imagine, Western analysts tend to forget that many of bin Laden's first-generation lieutenants did not mirror his intense religiosity. Wali Khan, Abu Zubaidah, Abu Hajir al-Iraqi, Khalid Sheikh Mohammed, Ibn Sheikh al-Libi, and Ramzi Yousef were first generation fighters who were both swashbuckling and Islamist. Unlike bin Laden and Zawahiri, they were flamboyant, multilingual, well-traveled, and eager for personal notoriety. Their operating styles were tinged with arrogance—as if no bullet or jail cell had been made for them—and each was captured, at least in part, because they paid insufficient attention to personal security. Now al-Qaeda is teaching young mujahideen to learn from the security failures that led to the capture of first-generation fighters.

> "The security issue was and still is one of the aspects that most influence the practical course of the conflict [with the West] and one of the fronts that most affect the war's outcome. As long as the Islamic movement does not take this aspect seriously, the promised victory will continue to lack the most important means for its realization.

> "What is required is that the security consciousness be present with a strength that causes it to mix with the natural course of daily action.... However, a consideration of history and a study of events lead us to conclude that the enemy's gain in the

security conflict [with al-Qaeda] basically cannot be due to the extraordinary strength of those organizations or to the superior skill of those in charge of them. They are derived from the state of defenselessness caused by the sickness of [security] laxity in Islamic circles!" [2]

The maturing mujahideen are less likely to follow the example of some notorious first-generation fighters, and more likely to model themselves on the smiling, pious, and proficient Mohammed Atef, al-Qaeda's military commander, killed in late 2001 and, to this day, al-Qaeda's most severe individual loss. A former Egyptian security officer, Atef was efficient, intelligent, patient, ruthless—and nearly invisible. He was a combination of warrior, thinker, and bureaucrat, pursuing his leaders' plans with no hint of ego. Atef's successor as military commander, the Egyptian Sayf al-Adil, is cut from the same cloth. Four years after succeeding Atef, for example, Western analysts cannot determine his identity—whether he is in fact a former Egyptian Special Forces colonel named Makkawi—or his location—whether he in South Asia, Iraq, or under arrest in Iran. Similarly, the Saudis' frequent publication of lengthening lists of "most wanted" al-Qaeda fighters—many unknown in the West—suggests the semi-invisible Atef-model is also used by Gulf state Islamists. Finally, the U.K.-born and -raised suicide bombers of July 7, 2005 foreshadow the next mujahideen generation who will operate below the radar of local security services.

Numbers

At the basic level, the steady pace of Islamist insurgencies around the world—Iraq, Chechnya and the northern Caucasus, southern Thailand, Mindanao, Kashmir and Afghanistan—and the incremental "Talibanization" of places like Bangladesh, Pakistan, and northern Nigeria, ensure a bountiful new mujahideen generation. Less-tangible factors will also contribute to this bounty.

- Osama bin Laden remains the unrivaled hero and leader of Muslim youths aspiring to join the mujahideen. His efforts to inspire young Muslims to jihad against the U.S.-led West seem to be proving fruitful.

- Easily accessible satellite television and streaming video on the internet will broaden Muslim youths' perception that the West is anti-Islamic. U.S. public diplomacy cannot negate the impressions formed by real-time video from Palestine, Iraq, and Afghanistan that shows Muslims battling "aggressive" Western forces and validating bin Laden's claim that the West intends to destroy Islam.

- The adoption of harsher anti-terror laws in America and Europe, along with lurid stories about Guantanamo Bay, Abu Ghraib prison, and the handling of the Qur'an will give credence to bin Laden's claim that the West is persecuting Muslims.

- The ongoing "fundamentalization" of the two great, evangelizing monotheist religions will enhance an environment already conducive to Islamism. The growth of Protestant evangelicalism in Latin America, and the aggressive, "church militant" form of Roman Catholicism in Africa, has and will revitalize the millennium-old Islam-vs.-Christianity confrontation, creating a sense of threat and defensiveness on each side.

Compounding the threat posed by the next, larger generation is the possibility that analysts underestimated the first generation's size. Western leaders have consistently claimed large al-Qaeda-related casualties; currently, totals range from 5,000-7,000 fighters and two-thirds of al-Qaeda's leadership. If the claims are accurate, we should ponder whether the West has ever fought a "terrorist group" that can lose 5,000-7,000 fighters, dozens of leaders, and still be assessed militarily potent and perhaps WMD-capable? The multiple captures of al-Qaeda's "third-in-command"—most recently Abu Ashraf al-Libi—and the remarkable totals of "second- and third-in-commands" from Abu Musab al-Zarqawi's organization suggests the West's accounting of Islamist manpower—at the foot soldier and leadership levels—is, at best, tenuous.

Modernity

Recent scholarship suggests al-Qaeda and its allies draw support primarily from Muslim middle- and upper-middle classes [3]. This helps explain why bin Laden places supreme importance on exploiting the internet for security, intelligence, paramilitary training, communications, propaganda, religious instruction, and news programs. It also points to the West's frequent failure to distinguish between the Islamists' hatred for Westernization—women's rights and secularism, for example—and their openness to modernity's tools, especially communications and weaponry.

Several features of Abu Musab al-Zarqawi's forces demonstrate that the mujahideen embrace modern tools. Two-plus years after the U.S. invasion, for example, Zarqawi's technicians continue building Improvised Explosive Devices (IEDs) and car bombs that defeat the detection/jamming technology fielded by U.S. forces. Indeed, each new iteration of defensive technology has been trumped by improved insurgent weaponry.

Zarqawi's media apparatus is likewise the most sophisticated, flexible, and omnipresent U.S.-led forces have encountered since 9/11. Al-Qaeda-in-Iraq's media produce daily combat reports, near real-time video of attacks on coalition targets, interviews with Zarqawi and other leaders, and a steady flow of "news bulletins" to feed 24/7 satellite television networks. In doing so, Zarqawi's media are telling the Muslim world al-Qaeda's version of the war professionally, reliably, and in real-time. So good has Zarqawi's media become since joining al-Qaeda that it is fair to assume the most important help he has received is from bin Laden's world-class media organization.

Conclusion

Despite satellites, electronic intercept equipment, and expanding human intelligence, the West does not understand al-Qaeda the way it knew the Soviet Union. Transnational targets are substantially more difficult collection targets than nation-states. We are, for example, unlikely to build an accurate al-Qaeda order-of-battle or recruit assets to penetrate the al-Qaeda equivalent of Moscow's politburo. As a result, Western analysts must closely track broad trends within al-Qaeda and its allies, and the trends toward greater piety, professionalism, numbers and modernity merit particular attention.

Notes

1. Osama bin Laden, "Message to Muslim Youth," *Markaz al-Dawa* (internet), December 13, 2001.

2. Sayf-al-Din al-Ansari, "But Take Your Precautions," *Al-Ansar* (internet), March 15, 2002.

3. See especially, Marc Sageman, *Understanding Terror Networks*, (University of Pennsylvania Press, 2004), and Robert Pape, *Dying to Win: The Logic of Suicide Terrorism*, (Random House, 2005).

[From Terrorism Focus, Volume II, Issue 18]

Setmariam Nasar: Background on al-Qaeda's Arrested Strategist

Stephen Ulph

Originally published on March 28, 2006

Since November, reports from Pakistan of the possible arrest of a leading al-Qaeda ideologue have been engaging the interest of media analysts on the war on terrorism. In mid-March, Pakistan security authorities again hinted that they were seeking confirmation that the man arrested last October 31 during a police raid in the southern city of Quetta was a leading Syrian linked to al-Qaeda, Mustafa Setmariam Nasar, also known as Abu Mus'ab al-Suri or Umar Abd al-Hakim. Jihadi forums now regularly append the term "fakka Allahu asrahu" ("may God set him free") after his name. The arrest is significant since Nasar is linked both to the 2004 train bombings in Madrid, Spain, that killed 191 people, and to the July 7 attacks in London that left 56 dead. He has had a $5 million bounty placed on his head by the U.S. State Department for training terrorists, including in the use of poisons and chemicals, in which he worked closely with Abu Khabab al-Masri, the poisons and chemical explosives expert killed during a Pakistani air strike in mid-January (see *Terrorism Focus*, January 25, 2006).

Nasar is one of al-Qaeda's top ideologues, ceding place only to Abdullah Azzam and Abd al-Qadir bin Abd al-Aziz. In terms of his practical analyses on political and military policy, he has proved to be the movement's most significant strategic brain. Nasar had consciously set out to take on this role. In a response written to the statement issued on November 18, 2004 by the U.S. State Department, he denied having collaborated with Abu Mus'ab al-Zarqawi, regretting it as "an honor I was not granted to share in since I had difficulties in getting to Iraq, and because of my isolating myself to devote my time to filling one of the Muslims' most important gaps—the analysis of our past experiences, drawing lessons from them, and examining the nature of the confrontations and battles that await us, since I am one of the few that are left among the mujahideen specializing in this" (www.fsboa. com/vw).

His jihad experience prepared him well for this task, since it covers all the main arenas of conflict. According to the Minbar al-

Tawhid wal-Jihad website, after studying mechanical engineering in Aleppo, Nasar joined the Syrian jihadist movement al-Tali'a al-Muqatila ("The Fighting Vanguard") and deepened his military expertise at the hands of refugee Syrian military officers in Jordan and Egyptian and Iraqi instructors in Baghdad and Cairo. Specializing in explosives engineering and urban guerrilla warfare, Nasar trained recruits in the military camps of the Muslim Brotherhood in Jordan and Baghdad. Following the Syrian Brotherhood's dramatic reverse in the Hama massacre of 1982, Nasar left the movement and moved to Afghanistan with the intention of reconstructing the dismantled jihadist movement in Syria. There he fought against the Russians and joined the fledgling al-Qaeda movement, deepening his doctrinal and historical training. Subsequently Nasar traveled to Spain and from there in 1995 to Britain, where he collaborated in the founding of the Algerian Groupe islamique armé (GIA). The success of the Taliban movement then brought him back to Afghanistan, where he worked both in propaganda and military training. After the U.S. destruction of his al-Ghurabaa training camp at Kabul and following the fall of the Emirate following the September 11, 2001 attacks, Nasar ostensibly devoted his energies to writing, re-emerging active in the field following a November 2004 warrant by the U.S. State Department and the posting of $5 million reward for his arrest (www.tawhed.ws).

The range of his works in the form of treatises, books and audio lectures indicate the caliber of the man and his prodigious energy. Since well before September 2001, Nasar has been authoring works on the organization of the jihadi movements, detailing its ideal doctrinal and political methodology and leadership structures. Reflecting his pedagogical role in Afghanistan, Nasar has written wide-ranging works covering treatises on the present world order and the illegitimacy of modern democratic systems. There are a number of tactical works from his pen, focusing on guerrilla warfare and the use of terrorist cell structures, but a large portion of his oeuvre are "jihad culture" works that focus on the history and development of Islamic political systems. As a result of his deep analysis of history, Nasar's most original contributions are the works concentrating on reasons for failure in the jihadist movement. These include works on "Aspects of the Jihadi Crisis" such as the experience of the jihad movements in Central Asia, North Africa, the Arabian Peninsula and his influential 18-

chapter Mulahazat hawl al-Tajriba al-Jihadiyya fi Suria ("Observations on the Jihadi Experience in Syria"), published in 1987 and circulated in the form of an e-book by the Minbar al-Tawhid wal-Jihad site (www. tawhed.ws).

His most ambitious work is the 1,600 page treatise written in December 2004, entitled Da'wat al-Muqawama al-Islamiyya al-'Alamiyya ("The Call of the International Islamic Resistance"), which outlines future strategies for the global jihad movement, prioritizing terrorist attacks and decentralized urban warfare as the only method to guarantee success. Excerpts from the work are continually circulated on the jihadi forums, and the recent attacks on the Abqaiq oil facilities in Saudi Arabia increased the distribution of sections urging attacks on oil installations.

Strategists of the caliber of Mustafa Setmariam Nasar are few and far between, and the loss of such a figure is highly significant, particularly since he saw his role as one of educating the "third generation" of mujahideen. By these are understood later, dispersed jihadi formations, not subject to the systematic training in Afghanistan and who are in danger of losing the lessons learned from the experiences of earlier jihadi arenas. While Nasar's works continue to populate the web, his own website "al-Muqawama al-Islamiyya al-'Alamiyya," ("The International Islamic Resistance") hosting his works and statements (www.fsboa.com/vw) no longer functions properly. Nasar's last dated statement was a general salvo made on August 20, 2005, following the London bombings, in which he encouraged sleeper cells the world over to launch a general front against western nations, as "a battle against a single entity that is comprised of all the allies" in what is "a global conflict" (from the Tajdeed jihadi forum www.tajdeed.org.uk).

[From Terrorism Focus, Volume III, Issue 12]

Jihadi Use of Internet

Technology and Security Discussions on the Jihadist Forums: Producing a More Savvy Next Generation

Jeffrey Pool

Originally published on October 11, 2005

Jihadist groups operating online appear to be raising awareness about information and communications security, and stressing the importance of technical know-how in conducting successful operations. Two training manuals recently found on internet discussion forums promoting militant Islam illustrate the importance of technical savvy to the jihadist movement. Formerly used chiefly as a platform for al-Qaeda statements and claims of responsibility for attacks by numerous groups, these forums have become a grassroots medium through which individuals without any particular group affiliation can post a document or manual of their own creation, which is then subsequently usable as standard procedure for terrorist cells.

Although the technology discussed is simple in nature, the dissemination of basic security guidelines for hacking and for mobile phone use could greatly enhance the effectiveness of aspiring mujahideen, as they would make fewer security mistakes and create fewer leads for Western intelligence services. A former CIA official commented that several notable arrests and intelligence coups have come about through simple security errors on the part of the terrorists. For example, Ahmed Ibrahim al-Nagar, a member of the Egyptian Islamic Jihad group operating in Albania, was arrested and ultimately convicted due to his lax personal security habits. Information recovered from his laptop yielded many new insights into the EIJ organization and its future plans, never before available to human intelligence personnel.

We have seen numerous examples of this phenomenon in recent months. Italian Islamic militants employed a simple strategy involving the use of multiple SIM cards when making mobile phone calls. Each call, very brief, would consist of a short series of code words, after which the caller would dispose of the old SIM card and install a new one, repeating the process until the message was complete. In this way, tracking the caller's location and monitoring the transmitted message was nearly impossible. Similarly, Yasser Arafat and his cadre were forced to improvise to continue their communications when Israeli security forces had them confined. Their headquarters compound was under constant human and electronic surveillance, and yet the Palestinians were able to maintain their privacy and efficacy through a series of simple security precautions.

The first of the recently posted documents was found on the forum "Minbar ahl al-Sunna wal-Jama'a" ("The Pulpit of the People of the Sunna;" www.minbar-islam.com/forum), a user calling himself "albattar" posted an article instructing readers on how to become hackers. The article is written in a pedagogical style, giving aspiring hackers a brief overview on the subject followed by an analysis of the motives and incentives for computer-based attacks. These factors are separated into several categories: political, strategic, economic and individual.

The article outlines three different activities that constitute categories of hacking. The first consists of direct intrusions into protected corporate or government networks. Such an attack may begin by defeating the firewalls set up to protect the network, which the author claims can "contribute to the demise of a protected system." Once inside, an attacker would immediately seek to obscure and ultimately misrepresent their location and identity, through a technique called "spoofing." This technique is used in conjunction with "source routing" to maneuver throughout the network. Source routing is a method in which the path a particular set of data packets takes is outlined by the hacker in such a way that computers normally isolated from the internet (using only internal IP addresses) can be accessed. Intruders take advantage of the fact that source routing is a routine element of network maintenance, used when troubleshooting internal communication problems.

The second type of hacking is the infiltration of privately-owned computers, to steal personal information. This type of attack is possible due to both "the naïveté of personal computer owners," and the widespread availability and effectiveness of exploitative software.

The final category involves the interception of sensitive information in transit, such as credit card numbers and Personal Identification Numbers. The author lists examples where such information is at risk, including online merchants lacking the most recent or most advanced protections. In addition, the article includes links to numerous applications and instruction manuals outlining their use.

While the author exhibits considerable knowledge of computing throughout the article—making extensive references to important personalities and events in computing history, as well as key terms in English—numerous other examples given of software and tactics are well out of date. This is likely due in part to the level of computer technology and internet service available to the author.

Another manual, posted to the "Muntadiyat al-Farouq" forums (www.al-farouq/vb), informed readers about the fundamentals of cell phone security. Reprinted from the "Tawheed wal-Jihad" forum, the manual explains the basics of mobile phone communications, outlining the security risks inherent in the use of such a device to coordinate operations. This manual is an example where a rather basic document circulates across different internet forums, becoming more valuable with each exposure to new readers. In the past, such a text might have been prepared for a specific audience and then destroyed after reading. With the rise in popularity among aspiring mujahideen of such sites as the al-Farouq forums, documents like this become rapidly disseminated to new individuals and groups.

The article discusses the route a call takes when communicating between two mobile users, and how much information about the caller is available to companies and law enforcement authorities. When a call is placed on the mobile network, the identity and general location of the caller are automatically recorded. Other relevant data includes the model number and production date of the mobile phone, as well as the duration and recipient of the call. The author stresses however that the precise location of the caller is impossible to determine through routine records, and no information is transmitted while the device is powered off.

In their training and in the execution of their operations, these aspiring mujahideen prefer to employ the simplest or most direct method possible, to avoid complications and to facilitate self-instruction. This often means they will choose less sophisticated methods, opting for simplicity over advanced technology. They know they cannot prevail in an even contest against national intelligence services without the finest (and most costly) technology available, so they seek instead to outsmart the strategy behind the gadgetry.

As the online community supporting terrorist groups evolves and attracts new members with increasing levels of technical and tactical prowess, analysts and security services will need to monitor such communications closely. Without the information and insight gained through such evaluation, no meaningful understanding of overall methods and ideology will be possible.

[From Spotlight on Terror, Volume III, Issue 11]

Liquid Explosive Training Manuals Easily Attainable on Jihadi Forums

Abdul Hameed Bakier

Originally published on August 15, 2006

In light of the information emerging from the foiled London attack, the terrorists involved in the operation planned on destroying commercial aircraft by mixing together explosive chemical substances while aboard the planes. The chemicals necessary to create such explosions are easily attainable. More concerning, however, is the fact that the technical information on how to create such explosives is accessible on many jihadi forums and websites. The most significant and frequently discussed subjects in the jihadi forums are topics pertinent to military tactics and how to create deadly explosives.

The website of the al-Aqsa Martyrs Brigade (http://www.kataebaqsa.org), for example, carries links to a colossal amount of data on creating explosives, part of a more extensive training document called "The Preparation Encyclopedia—All the Mujahid Needs." The training manual contains whole sections on topics such as:

- Types of explosives, mines, detonators, explosive engineering and electronics;
- Chemical and biological weapons;
- Nuclear weapons;
- How to make rockets;
- How to make silencers;
- Poisons.

The encyclopedia also includes informative topics on U.S. and British weapon systems, radar jamming and regular military operations. Furthermore, some training materials are very well prepared with illustrative drawings and photos, especially in the explosives section.

Concerning the latest terrorist threat in London, a closer look at the chemicals section and what the terrorists are capable of and willing to do to elicit explosive substances could explain how and why this threat is very serious. In these training manuals, the jihadis are learning how to extract a wide range of explosive components from readily available materials. Most of these chemicals are very hazardous, and include such things as: hydrochloric acid, potassium permanganate, potassium cyanide, information on how to extract potassium from goat excrement, red mercury, sodium nitrite, hydrogen peroxide, ammonium nitrite, nitroglycerin and hexamine (which is a very combustible white crystalline sand-like solid), in addition to other acids. In addition, the manual lists the ingredients for many types of explosives and how to mix them, in addition to diagrams that display different ways of packaging and transporting them.

To what extent do jihadis benefit from and try to utilize this knowledge? It is clear how useful these documents are to jihadis since many of them post inquiries in other forums requesting further explanation or information on the manufacturing of specific types of explosives. For example, one forum, called "al-Bramj" (http://www.bramjnet.com), explains in plain and thorough language how to make the highly explosive acetone peroxide as a main explosive charge and how to make a detonator from the same substance. The jihadi who posted the instructions was also aware of the precautionary details necessary when handling or mixing the components.

In the same context, Matiur Rehman, who apparently worked as an explosives instructor in al-Qaeda's camps, is allegedly one of the mentors of two of the suspects who plotted to blow up the jetliners, explaining to them, in detail, how to produce and use the explosive device (ABC News, August 9, 2006). If Rehman proves to be the mastermind and mentor of the suspected plotters, it appears that al-Qaeda operatives could be implementing the training found in the jihadi forums. Further corroboration of this hypothesis is the fact that the intended explosives appear to be analogous to those mentioned in the training manuals, and the confiscation, by British authorities, of materials related to the investigation from internet cafes in the United Kingdom.

[From Terrorism Focus, Volume III, Issue 32]

Jihadis Adapt to Counter-Terror Measures and Create New Intelligence Manuals

Abdul Hameed Bakier

Originally published on July 13, 2006

Islamist websites are filled with security manuals and training information for jihadi militants. These manuals are often posted on forums sympathetic to violent Islamists, and the visitors to the forums are able to ask questions to different jihadi security experts regarding fighting tactics and intelligence strategies. In intelligence training and sharing practices, the jihadi sites have posted three significant documents: *The Great Jihad Encyclopedia*, a letter from al-Qaeda operative Abu Yahia al-Libi and a document titled "How to Confront and Cope with Intelligence Agency Interrogators."

The Great Jihad Encyclopedia

It is not clear when *The Great Jihad Encyclopedia* was prepared, but it was originally released in 2002. The encyclopedia is a manual on security and intelligence techniques collected from different sources and from experienced jihadi militants. The encyclopedia is broken up into different sections spanning 70 pages, and the sections suggest that the document was prepared from the archives of the renowned services office Maktab al-Khidamat in Pakistan (the Afghan Services Bureau). Maktab al-Khidamat was, essentially, a guesthouse rented by Osama bin Laden in 1984 in Peshawar to receive and organize Arab mujahideen volunteering in the war against the Soviets in Afghanistan [1]. *The Great Jihad Encyclopedia* was written by "Abu al-Qaidan." The true identity of Abu al-Qaidan is unclear since covert al-Qaeda operatives use pseudonyms. The fact that there was an Algerian intellectual called Abu al-Qaidan suggests that the author could be an Algerian [2].

The jihad manual consists of 11 separate postings. The first posting by Abu al-Qaidan occurred on February 22, 2002, and he continued posting intermittently. His last one is dated September 27, 2002. Some sections of the encyclopedia articulate the fundamentals of security and intelligence trades, while others explain serious intelligence work such as the use of cover stories, surveillance and safe houses.

Similar to any training curriculum, the manual commences the training with definitions of security and intelligence terminologies, interjecting pertinent Islamic perspectives of the practices. Furthermore, it explains the process of acquiring, analyzing and presenting information as a finished intelligence product followed with a section on how to preserve the confidentiality of the gathered intelligence and the means of utilizing it.

The encyclopedia elaborates on many intelligence skills such as espionage, counter-terrorism, sabotage, the importance of human intelligence (HUMINT) and agent handling. Moreover, it includes training on quality intelligence work such as the use of safe-houses, defensive and offensive intelligence, operating behind enemy lines, preventive security and a detailed explanation of reconnaissance. In command and control situations, the manual recommends security inspections of current operatives every six months to uncover any possible moles, although it does not explain how to conduct such inspections. In addition, the manual teaches the mujahideen how to resist arrest and interrogation. Finally, the course talks about the two most important prerequisites for any successful intelligence operation: good cover stories and casing a target.

Advanced intelligence agencies focus on the creation of good cover stories that allow for the efficient performance of their agents. The section on cover stories was very explicit and elaborate. Remarkably, the example used for cover training to distract suspicious enemy agents is the Soviet-style method called "secret exhibition," which was used by ex-KGB agents. The "secret exhibition" method is when the covert operative himself plants false evidence for the probing enemy to find. The evidence, then, corroborates the cover story. For instance, if the operative is posing as an Italian using a fake Italian passport, it is useful to also have in his possession fake personal letters supposedly sent to him from a friend in Milan to his address in Rome; another example would be for this particular agent to keep a bus ticket used in Italy.

Casing is another important tool in the intelligence world necessary to eliminate enemy targets successfully. The manual's section on casing is presented in a clear and standard form akin to that of any intelligence service. It provides practical examples of casing a target. In the manual, the example used was a house in the al-Ansar wa al-Mohajireen district, which is most likely in Peshawar.

Al-Libi's Letter Outlining U.S. Interrogation Techniques

The same forum posted a letter, at a different date, regarding U.S. interrogation techniques sent by one of four terror suspects who escaped from the U.S. prison in Bagram in Afghanistan in July 2005. The suspect, Mohammed Hassan (known as Sheikh Abu Yahia al-Libi), is a Libyan national in his mid-30s who studied Sharia doctrine in Mauritanian universities and wrote a book entitled *al-Ijmah Wa Mafhoumeh fi al-Sharia al-Islamia (The Concept of Consensus and its Meaning in Islamic Law)*. In his letter, al-Libi describes, in four major parts, U.S. arrest and prisoner transfer procedures, the locations of five different U.S. prison facilities in Afghanistan, torture methods, interrogation issues and the information that U.S. operatives are seeking to extract from the mujahideen. Al-Libi states that U.S. interrogators are seeking information on the following:

- Information on preparations for future terrorist attacks;
- The whereabouts of Osama bin Laden, Ayman al-Zawahiri and other prominent al-Qaeda leaders;
- The whereabouts of Mullah Omar and other Taliban leaders;
- The sources of mujahideen funds;
- Training facilities, launch pads and routes used by the mujahideen.

Al-Libi reiterates that there is a variety of other information constantly sought by U.S. interrogators throughout the incarceration period [3]. Al-Libi is a prominent member of al-Qaeda who recently posted a videotape on the internet inciting Muslims to attack France, Norway and Denmark for mocking the Prophet Muhammad in political cartoons (*Middle East Online*, May 12, 2006). In November 2005, he sent a message to al-Zarqawi in Iraq calling upon him to review, reform, revise and evaluate his jihad activities. It was not clear from the short message whether al-Libi was reprimanding al-Zarqawi for faulty techniques or simply advising him to avoid failed terrorist operations (al-Arabiya, December 19, 2005).

How to Confront and Cope with Intelligence Agency Interrogators

Contextually, another mujahideen site also released an extensive training manual on interrogation called "How to Confront and Cope with Intelligence Agency Interrogators" [4]. Although it is not as exhaustive as the encyclopedia, it thoroughly covers the different aspects of interrogation. The subject was prepared from three different jihadi sites by an individual named al-Kandahari, a very common alias name that refers to the city of Kandahar in Afghanistan. The subject defines the objectives, methods of interrogation and interrogation resistance techniques. The training is a step-by-step guide to almost every procedure the mujahideen might face during interrogation. Interestingly, it even tells the mujahideen how to manipulate the interrogator into drawing preferable conclusions. To manipulate the interrogator and even to intimidate him, al-Kandahari suggests that the mujahid:

- Restrain from answering the same question twice;
- Smile at the interrogator and remind him of God's punishment for persecuting innocent mujahideen;
- Make eye contact and tell the interrogator that he will one day leave his job and will no longer enjoy the protection of the agency he works for, insinuating that the mujahideen know his name and where he lives;
- Try to figure out the information that the interrogator is after and give seemingly accurate but false information.

The use of interrogation is a very essential technique used by the security apparatus to extract information. It is, basically, a struggle between two individuals. The more that one party understands the technique, the better chance he or she has of prevailing in the struggle. Therefore, al-Kandahari's document is very useful knowledge for the mujahideen because it teaches them what to expect and how to resist releasing important information.

Conclusion

The encyclopedia and the other different training materials that jihadis are preparing and sharing remain within the normal practice of the intelligence cycle. It is clear that parts of *The Great Jihad Encyclopedia* were prepared from non-Arabic and government sources. In addition, the training style used in the documents appears to originate from military intelligence, and the encyclopedia is organized in a logical, sequential training order. The only unique aspect of the mujahideen training manuals is the interjection of Quranic verses and stories of intelligence practices in the Islamic epoch, apparently introduced to different parts of the text to justify certain intelligence work—a necessary addition since much of the manual appears to have originated from governmental sources. For instance, in one stark contradiction, under the "general guidelines for intelligence operatives" section, the manual advises the operative not to drink too much alcohol or to trust women; a stark contradiction to Islamic code that the writer failed to omit from the final document.

From the documents, it is clear that many of the intelligence lessons were drawn from the Eastern intelligence school style of training. This makes sense in light of the information that some ex-Iraqi intelligence officers have joined al-Qaeda in Iraq. In the future, it is possible that these jihadi planners will find a Quranic verse to justify non-conventional intelligence operations involving non-Islamic behaviors such as deep cover operations in the West that could expand rapidly via the advanced technology in communications that has previously helped radical Islamists perpetrate terrorist acts and evade capture.

Advancement in communication technology is the key to the success of any counter-terrorism operation by security and intelligence agencies; unfortunately, the same applies to terrorist operations that use the same technological systems to utilize and disseminate their ideology and methods. Consequently, the internet is the most preferable means of terrorist communication and regardless of how hard the security agencies attempt to control the terrorists' propaganda and communications by shutting down their websites, the terrorists are always able to find an outlet on the internet to communicate and share their experiences to better confront the security forces.

[From Terrorism Monitor, Volume IV, Issue 14]

The Evolution of Jihadi Electronic Counter-Measures

Abdul Hameed Bakier

Originally published on September 8, 2006

After each attempted terrorist attack, whether botched or successful, government security forces worldwide are typically tasked with reviewing and analyzing the incident to draw lessons from the mistakes made in order to better prepare for possible future attacks. The same process, however, takes place in the opposite camp. Jihadis analyze their failed attacks and try to train their members to penetrate the defenses of international security forces. Since communication is essential for any operation and the internet is a favorite tool of Islamist militants, jihadi forums and websites contain information on the secure use of computers and mobile phones.

Electronic training explains to jihadis the vulnerability of the internet. It warns against electronic methods that security services use to penetrate jihadi networks, such as computer viruses as well as actual infiltration of jihadi computers by using trojan viruses. In addition, the training lessons discuss security gaps in mobile communications by explaining the basics of mobile technology and giving real examples of cases where security forces tracked jihadi militants using the mobile phone system. As part of this discussion on electronics, jihadis also provide information on how to beat polygraph tests.

Internet Communication Security

In a forum relating to internet security, located at http://www.gsm4arab.net, jihadi users begin by highlighting the importance of internet forums for reciprocation among members and for propaganda against the enemy, acknowledging the fact that intelligence services are constantly attempting to penetrate these forums [1]. The training underlines a few steps that forum participants should take in order to avoid being identified by security forces. Some of the paraphrased steps are below:

- Be aware that some participants are pretending to be sincere, asking many questions on ways to travel to mujahideen war zones to take part in the holy war—these "participants" are often intelligence officers logged on from their offices. The officers will defend the mujahideen and write long articles praising jihad. They will ask you to cooperate with them in furthering the cause. If you fall for their bait, you will end up in jail.

- By signing up in a forum, forum owners can obtain a participant's IP address and pinpoint the location of the computer to a very precise proximity. We recommend that honest owners of forums cancel the IP address option. Nevertheless, be aware that IP addresses can also be obtained by tracking e-mails. If you are tasked with publishing mujahideen news or if you are wanted by the intelligence services, it is better to use internet café computers. Do not forget, however, that most internet cafés spy on their clients.
- Do not provide accurate personal data when signing up in any forum.
- Always use different internet cafés to post in the forums, delete internet temporary files and do not stay long in the café.
- Be careful of spyware when downloading files from the forums.
- Do not install any software on your computer if requested by the forum.
- Do not give your e-mail address to anyone in the forum.
- Use different passwords and nicknames for different forums.
- Do not mention critical information in the forum and apply the need-to-know principle.
- Remember that jihadi forums are not for making friends.

The training provides solutions to some of the points mentioned in the lessons such as how to hide the computer's IP address. Furthermore, the training covers other aspects of internet security such as safe web surfing, avoiding sites and forums already penetrated by some authorities and the secure use of e-mail and messenger programs. Finally, the training advises jihadis to frequently update their anti-virus, anti-spy, IP hiding and network identity card software.

The training also discusses electronic dead letter boxes. An example of an electronic dead letter box is sharing the same e-mail address and password with all the individuals/parties communicating. Rather than send an e-mail from that e-mail address, the user instead saves the message that they want to convey as a "draft" so that the other parties can log in and read the draft—if an e-mail is not sent over the internet, it is very difficult to intercept. Acknowledging the fact that al-Qaeda's global jihad depends on the internet to instigate and train Salafi-Jihadi adherents to commit terrorist acts makes secure internet usage a critical component of Islamist militant strategy.

Mobile Communications

The training documents at http://www.almaqdese.net explain the basics of mobile communication such as handover or communication towers and repeaters that convey the conversation of the caller to the tower closest to the receiver of the call [2]. In the process, each mediating tower will register all technical details of the caller such as the phone number, SIM card serial number and the location of the caller. The mobile phone lessons also explain the ability of phone company operators to locate mobile phones by using the paging and signaling technique to an accuracy of a few centimeters; if intelligence services are able to identify a phone as belonging to a potential suspect, they are able to track the movement of the suspect through this technology. Citing examples from Palestine, the training refutes the misconception that powered-off mobile phones can still be remotely activated as a listening device. One example explains how secret Israeli agents managed to plant eavesdropping equipment in mobile phones that were then sent to Palestinian suspects as gifts. In general, the writer advises methods for jihadis to avoid capture by authorities. These methods include.

- All jihadis in contact with a captured member must eliminate the mobile phone numbers they used to contact the arrested and destroy the SIM cards.
- Refrain from calling officials who know your identity from your unofficial/secret number because that will reveal the fact that you are using a phone under a fake name. This will make your behavior suspicious if the official ever spoke with security agents. The "unofficial number" refers to the phone numbers that the jihadis purchase under false names and use for operational communication.

- Do not give your unofficial number to anyone except your jihadi contacts. If the number becomes known by relatives and uninvolved friends, discard the mobile phone and the SIM card.
- Do not use the unofficial phone from the same location (such as your home) repeatedly.
- Do not keep phone numbers under surveillance turned on in the same location for long periods of time because security forces will uncover your address.

In a related topic, the training touches on the subject of voiceprint, warning jihadis of intelligence services' capabilities to establish voiceprint through eavesdropping on the jihadis and later uncovering any attempted terrorist acts even if the jihadis use fake names and unknown phone numbers. To further explain the voiceprint notion, the lesson draws an example from Israeli intelligence and air force operations against four members of the al-Qassam Brigade. The four members of the al-Qassam Brigade were meeting in an open area at the Gaza beach. Israeli intelligence, which had established the voiceprints of the four in an earlier encounter, was able to intercept their calls and pinpoint their location even though they were using different numbers and fake names. Finally, the writer suggests preventive measures such as:

- Change the tone of voice from hoarse to soft or vice-versa.
- Shield the phone speaker with a piece of cloth.
- Change breathing rhythm.
- Change the accent.
- Speak in a noisy environment.
- Avoid commonly used phrases.
- Use computers to change the tone of voice in recorded messages or communiqués.

Needless to say, like other jihadi training documents, the mobile communication lessons are thorough and scientific. Also, keeping up with the latest technology that the intelligence services are using, the writer added to the lesson at a later date a warning about the capability of some advanced intelligence services to send out magnetic signals to locate mobile phones that are turned off.

The Polygraph

In a section on polygraph testing, located at http://www. tawhed.ws, jihadi training describes the test as a psychological hoax to pressure the mujahideen during interrogation, reiterating the mythology that Western security services propose about the machine's ability to detect lies [3]. Furthermore, the training identifies the functions of the polygraph machine such as how it registers the physiological reflexes of the subject and how the interrogator uses control questions to convince the mujahid of the capability of the machine. The control questions, the training explains, are a group of question with known answers for both the interrogator and the mujahid designed to register the mujahid's normal reflexes to be compared later with reflexes from the serious questions. Therefore, the training outlines steps to counter the polygraph, especially during control questions, such as:

- Controlled breathing. The mujahid must train on controlling the rate of his breathing all through the test.
- Controlled blood pressure. Blood pressure must be raised above the normal rate by solving complicated mathematical problems in his mind while the interrogator asks polygraph control questions or by imagining mind stimulating situations like falling from a high cliff.
- Biting the tongue to induce pain.
- Give short answers and deny any knowledge of polygraph machine technology.

The polygraph training concludes with a few reminders of interrogators' behaviors in pretending that the mujahid has failed the test even if he or she did pass because the overall objective is to extract information from the subject by any possible means. To further convince mujahideen that the test is a hoax and to protect them from collapsing during interrogation, the postings quote former presidents of the United States and ex-FBI and CIA officials criticizing the effectiveness of the polygraph system.

Conclusion

Terrorists and suicide bombers communicate on jihadi sites and forums to learn different terrorist tactics. The internet remains jihadis' favorite means of tactical support since it is easy to access and easy to remain relatively anonymous, consequently directing and guiding the global jihad movement. The small cells and temporary groups of this global movement, inspired by jihadi ideology, are acting increasingly independently from al-Qaeda. Jihadis are also using the technological evolution for propaganda and for the recruitment of new terrorists. For instance, there are many successful cases of recruitment through the internet in Iraq and in other countries, such as the case of the German citizen of Moroccan origin Redouane EH, who German prosecutors say was recruiting suicide bombers through internet chat rooms [4]. Jihadi leaders, like Abu Musab al-Zarqawi before his last appearance in a televised message, regularly sent promotional and justification messages through the internet such as the ones sent after the Amman hotel bombings in November 2005. The promotional campaign through two electronic jihadi magazines—*Sawt al-Jihad* and *al-Battar Training Camp*—in Saudi Arabia is another example of internet employment by Salafi-Jihadis [5]. Therefore, the jihadi groups are capable of adapting to security constraints and pressures by using contemporary means and shifting tactics.

Notes
1. http://www.gsm4arab.net/vb/archive/index.php/t-42312.html.
2. http://www.almaqdese.net/r?i=963&a=p&PHPSESSID=50a931aff 534b807a0a5348f4a5635bd
3. http://www.tawhed.ws/r?i=3165&PHPSESSID=7633aa0416e42bef d58f43b63d8164c3
4. CNN, August 24, 2006.
5. *Middle East Report*, September 21, 2004.

[From Terrorism Monitor, Volume IV, Issue 17]

Secret Camps Offer Operational Courses in Jihad Tactics

Stephen Ulph

Originally published on March 28, 2006

An interesting recent posting on the "Abu al-Bokhary" jihadi forum (http://www.abualbokhary.net/) provides some useful insight about the current conditions and the priorities in the training of mujahideen. The anonymous author of a "Basic Course for Beginners in Secret Mujahideen Camps," describes a "five day course for beginners in jihadist activity." He states that it is derived from practical experience in a fast-tightening environment, in which "time is against the brothers, and in which there is the necessity to train by any means available." This means camps "in secluded places whose existence is limited to one week." After first detailing the type of equipment, communications and weaponry to be brought, the posting gives an hour-by-hour program of events.

Day one of the course is taken up with constructing the camp and establishing the group dynamics of the 14-member team, apportioning roles and appointing the amir (commander). The 30-by-10 meter site of the camp is to contain a mosque, sleeping rooms, latrine and kitchen, for each of which the details on measurements, location and camouflage are provided. Time is to be set aside for instilling the importance of discipline, "the fear of God and obedience to the amir" and of banishing levity, while each day is to contain time slots both for physical training and spiritual exercises in the form of readings from the Quran.

On day two the military training begins in earnest and includes the following sections:

- Hand weapons: assembly and disassembly of revolvers and Kalashnikovs;
- Training in Islamic law and appropriate Islamic conduct;
- Lessons in night patrols and the use of security measures, such as passwords.

Day three is made up of lessons that may last from 30 minutes up to one hour and include the following subjects:

- The concealment of light weapons in clothing: how to conceal a Kalashnikov in the clothing of two persons and maneuver with these Kalashnikov parts; practice in throwing the parts from one to another while moving;
- Assassination techniques: throttling, knife assault, obtaining the enemy's knife, how and where to deal fatal blows to the body;
- Setting up cells, maneuvering and communications between them;
- Bodyguard duties and the defense of the commander;
- Maneuvering while armed or firing the weapon;
- Map reading, route analysis and distance calculation, and determining the enemy's armor;
- Rapid trench digging, dugouts behind enemy lines, camouflage;
- Intelligence gathering, the planning and study of targets, and access and escape.

Day four is devoted to live-fire exercises. The course lays emphasis on the use of silencers for training exercises, the importance of collecting and burying spent cartridges and the restoration of the area to its pristine state after use. Courses then follow on discreet food preparation, cooking and storage of food supplies for up to two weeks.

Day five consists of a performance assessment by the commander and elaborate measures to disguise the camp's brief existence. An unexpected feature of this last day is the time given to lessons on the life and military campaigns of the Prophet Muhammad, on the nature of God and the afterlife and the punishments of hell. A feature of this section, with no further details offered, is the "instilling of fear in others of Hell and of God's punishments."

The author finally concludes with the promise to provide more information subsequently on details of the course. Immediately noticeable from the posting is the sense of concern that training should to be carried out under greater levels of secrecy and in ever-shorter timeframes than before. Some of these camps, the author explains, "have lasted less than two days, made up of 48- or 72-hour courses." It is also interesting to note that even under such perilous conditions, elements relating to doctrine are still retained.

[From Terrorism Focus, Volume III, Issue 12]

Internet Mujahideen Intensify Research on U.S. Economic Targets

Stephen Ulph

Originally published on January 18, 2006

A series of documents recently (re)circulating on the internet continue to underline a pressing jihadist interest in targeting U.S. economic assets. Some of these documents are quite explicit and detailed, giving indications of specific pipelines and facilities to attack—not only in the Gulf, but wherever in the world such assets can be targeted. *Terrorism Focus* highlighted last month (December 13, 2005) how Ayman al-Zawahiri has been urging the targeting of oil installations in the Gulf States as part of the "bleed-until-bankruptcy" strategy against the United States. More broadly, this strategy was underlined in posting last October on the forum "Minbar Suriya al-Islami" of Abu Musab al-Najdi's "Al-Qaeda's Battle is an Economic Battle, Not a Military One," in which the targeting was extended to Kuwait, Saudi Arabia and Venezuela (www.nnuu.org.vb).

Yet a more detailed treatment on this strategy re-appeared last month on the Al-Safinat forum (http://202.71.102.108/~alsafnat/vb). The document authored by "Abu Yusuf 911" and entitled "Targets for Jihad: A Response to the Words of Sheikh Ayman al-Zawahiri," is an extended exposition of the potential vulnerabilities of Western economies in the Middle East and around the world. The author details how best the mujahideen can strike America's "economic joints," understood in the sense of strategic centers of gravity. He divides the targeting for the mujahideen into sectors. The first is "Islamic lands seized by the Crusaders." Iraq heads the list, and here the treatise advises that the effort should not be on destroying what remains of the oil infrastructures but rather on depriving the enemy of financial gain from this "booty of war"—either by limiting exports or preventing the Americans from using the oil as fuel for their tanks, armored vehicles, aircraft, or ships. The author therefore advises the striking of bases used for these purposes. This is accompanied by URLs providing information, maps, and images on distribution networks, transportation hubs and military fuel supply depots.

Following Iraq are the Afghanistan and Central Asian arenas. The treatise cites (with accompanying URLs) U.S. and Western strategic theories on the region, mentioning by name the book *The Grand Chessboard* by former National Security Advisor Zbigniew Brzezinski, and featuring analyses by Vice President Dick Cheney and U.S. Congress Reports. This section, which also cites revenue from heroin production as a U.S. strategic target, gives details on pipeline, refineries, and pumping stations, focusing in particular on the Caspian Sea sector, and providing names and addresses of companies associated with the industry.

The second sector for activity are territories through which oil wealth passes, focusing on the United States and the state of Alaska in particular. The Alaska section is furnished with URLs that provide information on its oil distribution infrastructure, capacities, routes, facts and figures, and notably the *Wall Street Journal* article by Jim Carlton (October 8, 2001) detailing the attack on the pipeline and its "vulnerability to sabotage." The author suggests attacking it during the months of June and July, and at the pipeline's most isolated point, ideally in a heavily-wooded area so that an accompanying forest fire will maximize the delays to repairing the pipeline. States crucial in oil production and storage such as Texas, California, Louisiana and Oklahoma are also featured. As to the mujahideen most suitable for such operations, Abu Yusuf suggests "our Muslim brothers living in the land of the American rabble," (non-American) Muslims temporarily residing in the U.S., or mujahideen groups of four to five members that can enter the U.S. either directly or via Canada or Mexico. Each group should define itself according to the principal pipeline networks, so that their operations should cover the area covered by each major pipeline, and include production facilities, oil fields and pumping stations.

"The Targets for Jihad" treatise earlier appeared in March 2005 on the Risalat al-Umma forum (www.alommh.net). Again, at that time the posting followed a recent warning by Ayman al-Zawahiri's, on a videotape message aired by al-Jazeera, that the Western powers faced defeat through the collapse of their economies. The smaller original of the present 12-page treatise was first posted with reference to the sermon by bin Laden on 'strategic directives on jihadist targets' posted on May 3 2003, and concluded with a note that these were "initial thoughts" to which readers could make "major additions."

Since then, interest in the potential of catastrophic reverse for the U.S. and western powers has been re-kindled on the jihad forums by the recent spate of natural disasters (Hurricane Katrina and Hurricane Rita) or accidents (the UK oil depot fire at Hemel Hempstead). While in Iraq attacks and threats of attacks on pipelines, refineries and oil-related transportation are frequent, the planned jihadi application of this strategy has not yet been observed outside Iraq.

The strategy is certainly being taken seriously on the web and is generating research traffic. The same day as the "December Targets for Jihad" posting, one identifying himself as Abu Saqr called for the updating of the document's links that had lapsed, and the collation of "all the available illustrations for the project into one file." Convinced that the attacks on U.S. oil interests "will inflame the final war between them and us, and lead to their downfall," Abu Saqr further took up the baton, promising to collaborate with "friends who have completed advanced studies in aerial photography and surveying" on a "complete and professional study of the subject, so as to offer it to the mujahideen and those who are at the forefront of jihad initiatives." He also once broadened the call for "participation from forum readers who are experts in petrochemical engineering, distribution networks and pumps," specifying the need for ".pdf documents of books relevant to the subject." Abu Saqr then concludes by promising that the completed .pdf document "will be distributed over the largest possible number of forums."

This treatise is notable for two reasons, which more broadly underlines the significant of the internet for the jihad. One is the element of collective endeavor that the author encourages, highlighting the speed of communication and the potential power that dispersed jihadi sympathizers across the globe can focus on a single project. The second is the facility for data mining that the web provides, allowing instant access not only to academic research data but also sensitive infrastructure details of utilities, distribution and transport networks, as well as threat and vulnerability perceptions of these facilities—which governments are now offering at ever greater levels of transparency. With official discussion papers circulating on strategically useful areas such as the functioning of intelligence and security agencies (often highlighting their deficiencies) or counter-terrorism methodology, the internet eloquently illustrates the dictum made by an al-Qaeda training manual recovered in Afghanistan: "Using public sources openly and without resorting to illegal means, it is possible to gather at least 80 percent of all information required about the enemy."

[From Terrorism Focus, Volume III, Issue 2]

Methods of Terrorism

Al-Qaeda's Clandestine Courier Service

Sohail Abdul Nasir

Originally published on February 21, 2006

The recent release of audio and videotapes from Osama bin Laden and Ayman al-Zawahiri call attention to al-Qaeda's couriers and how they transport tapes to major media outlets (al-Jazeera, January 21, 2006). Audiotapes, videotapes and the internet are the major mass media tools of al-Qaeda and are used to tilt and blur the realities of the locations of al-Qaeda leaders. They are an effective means to threaten the U.S. and the West. Al-Qaeda's videos are produced by the organization's in-house production team, al-Sahab, identified by the al-Sahab logo that appears in the videos. It appears that al-Sahab consists of multiple individuals and is not centrally located. While the videos have improved in quality, at its most basic level the videographers require computer images, e-mail transmission, and a production expert who uses a computer to compile it together in broadcast quality.

After the tapes are produced, they make their way to a major media outlet. The previous route of the videotapes was from southern and eastern Afghanistan to South Waziristan, and then to Peshawar. The final destination used to be the al-Jazeera office in Islamabad. It became easy, however, for various intelligence agencies to track this route. In at least two instances—in 2003 and in 2004—the tape messenger was intercepted. In 2003, the carrier was of Central Asian origin and was captured by security agents while traveling through South Waziristan. The second incident occurred in late 2004 and the carrier was arrested near Dera Ismail Khan in southern Pakistan. Nevertheless, little information was gleaned from the messenger because the tape had already passed through more than a dozen different carriers. Through this method, the tapes are handed over in a manner so that the next carrier does not know the other carriers.

The amount of time that each carrier handles the tapes depends on the prevailing security conditions in that particular area. Carriers attempt to pass on the tapes as quickly as possible, which is usually in one or two days. If security is tight then it is passed on in quick succession in order to keep the tapes secure, otherwise each carrier may travel more than 100 kilometers. On a few occasions, the content of the tapes were electronically transmitted to their final destination through e-mail.

The carriers of the tapes are diehard local and Central Asian operatives. The carriers are always young, tough and experienced; the task of a carrier is a specialized job. Simple sympathizers are not usually carriers because if the carrier is arrested, he is tried under anti-terrorism laws, deterring those who are not completely committed to al-Qaeda's cause.

For the last year, the tape route has been modified due to repeated successful interventions by Pakistani authorities and continuous surveillance of known transfer locations. Currently, tapes are dispatched to Herat, in the western province of Afghanistan, to coastal areas of Iran and then to the final destination. The tapes are generally made inside Afghanistan. Additionally, the Taliban is now also involved in producing tapes in a new campaign of media warfare. Taliban guerrillas are often accompanied by a videographer who films their attacks against Afghan or international security forces. These tapes are later used within the Taliban ranks to boost the morale of Taliban fighters and the participating mujahideen.

[From Terrorism Focus, Volume III, Issue 7]

Reinforcing the Mujahideen: Origins of Jihadi Manpower

Michael Scheuer

Originally published on May 9, 2006

Much is written about how non-indigenous, would-be Islamist fighters enter the battlefields of Iraq and Afghanistan to join the mujahideen fighting U.S.-led coalitions in both countries. Do they enter Afghanistan from Pakistan? Or Iran? Perhaps Central Asia? What about Iraq? Which border is the most porous? Does that dubious honor belong to Syria, Saudi Arabia, Jordan or Iran?

These are, of course, important questions. To know and close the entry points of these aspiring mujahideen would slow the pace at which foreign fighters could join the fray. It also would make local insurgent field commanders unsure about the dependability of the flow of replacement fighters for their units, and thereby probably limit their willingness to undertake operations that are likely to result in sizeable manpower losses.

A more basic question, however, is seldom asked or debated. While it is clear that closing points of entry would give the U.S.-led coalitions a better chance to reduce the level of each insurgency, the more important path to victory probably lies in determining exactly from where these prospective insurgents emanate. There has been an intense concentration in both the media and academic literature on the role that madrassas play in producing young men eager to join the war against the West. Indeed, has this been discussed and analyzed so thoroughly that we are nearing the point where it will become common wisdom that if Washington, London and their allies can close down the madrassas, we could halt the flow of reinforcements to the Iraqi and Afghan mujahideen.

On the basis of at least two factors, it would be wise to hold off on enshrining as common wisdom the belief that madrassas are the main producers of nascent mujahideen. The first lies in some recent academic work. Marc Sageman, in his excellent book *Understanding Terrorist Networks* (Philadelphia, 2004), and Robert Pape, in his equally outstanding study *Dying to Win* (New York, 2005), demonstrate that few of the non-indigenous Islamist fighters the West is encountering in the Iraq and Afghan insurgencies are the products of madrassas.

Both Sageman and Pape show that these fighters are, more often than not, young men educated in areas beyond the strictly religious studies that dominate the madrassas' curriculum. Many have studied sciences and engineering and hail from stable, middle-class families. In short, Sageman, Pape and a few other analysts have concluded after extensive research and statistical study that the largest number of foreign fighters who travel to participate in the insurgencies in Iraq and Afghanistan are not madrassa graduates. (NB: The exception to this conclusion is Pakistan, where it seems likely that madrassas produce the majority of Pakistanis who join the Afghan insurgency.)

The second factor that argues against accepting that madrassas are the main source of the insurgencies' reinforcements requires a bit of historical background. During the Afghan jihad against the Soviet Union (1979-89), the Afghans played the overwhelming role in defeating the Red Army. Non-indigenous Muslims did, of course, travel to Afghanistan to assist the Afghans. Their numbers grew as the war wore on, and among the foreign fighters were Osama bin Laden, Ayman al-Zawahiri, Ibn Khattab, Mustafa Hamza and many others who later helped to form al-Qaeda and other like-minded organizations. Others simply returned to their homes in Egypt, Jordan and Saudi Arabia and began to attack their national governments.

Where did the non-indigenous Muslim fighters come from during the Afghan jihad? Their travel to the battlefield was certainly facilitated by the Muslim Brotherhood and other Islamist organizations—and some members of those groups, like Sheikh Abdullah Azzam and the Saudi Wael Julaidan, joined the fight—as well as by some wealthy Muslim individuals and Arab governments. It is well-known, for example, that the bin Laden family business helped aspiring mujahideen travel to Afghanistan, and that Riyadh ordered Saudia, its international airline, to offer reduced-fair "jihad" tickets to young men on their way to Afghanistan.

Many of these non-Afghan Muslim mujahideen came out of the prisons of Arab states. The West often forgets that Arab prisons are built not only to house criminals, but to confine ideological opponents of the regime. Thus, the prisons are generally full-to-overflowing with Islamic militants who, for example, oppose the brutality of Egyptian President Hosni Mubarak's regime or the al-Sauds' greed, corruption and opulence in Saudi Arabia. Incarcerating these militants helps the regimes maintain societal control. Their detention, however, also has proved to increase their Islamic militancy because the extremist inmates tend to congregate and to be easy targets for instruction by jailed radical Islamic scholars and clerics, both of which breed a sense of fraternity. Al-Qaeda's deputy leader Ayman al-Zawahiri emerged much more militant after his incarceration and torture in post-Sadat Egypt, as did Abu Musab al-Zarqawi after his imprisonment in Jordan and his instruction by the renowned Salafi scholar Abu Muhammad al-Maqdisi.

Faced with a large population of young, Islamic-extremist prisoners during the Afghan jihad, governments across the Arab world found a release valve for radical religious pressures in their societies by freeing ideological prisoners on the condition that they would go to fight the atheist Soviets in Afghanistan. Many such prisoners agreed and were released by regimes that hoped they would go to Afghanistan, kill some infidels, and be killed in the process. Many of these fighters were killed, but many were not and returned to bedevil their respective governments to this day. Still, for more than a decade, the Afghan jihad allowed Arab governments to redirect domestic Islamist activism outward toward the hapless Red Army. Although the policy proved shortsighted, it reduced domestic instability for most of the 1980s and the first half of the 1990s.

Today, it is hard to know for sure whether this trend is repeating itself. Yet, we do know three things for certain: (a) every Arab government faces a domestic Islamist movement that is broader and more militant—though not always more violent—than in the 1980s; (b) the insurgency in Iraq, because the country is the former seat of the caliphate and is located in the Arab heartland, is an attraction for Islamists far more powerful than was Afghanistan; and (c) the flow of foreign fighters into Iraq and, to a lesser extent, Afghanistan seems to be more than sufficient to allow a steady increase in the combat tempo of each insurgency. Thus, the situation seems ideal for Arab governments to try a reprise of the process that lessened domestic instability during the Afghan jihad.

This circumstantial argument that the current situation in Iraq is an almost ideal opportunity for Arab regimes to export their Islamic firebrands to kill members of the U.S.-led coalitions and be killed in turn is augmented—if not validated—by the large numbers of Islamic militants that have been released by Arab governments since the invasion of Iraq. The following are several pertinent examples drawn from the period November 2003-March 2006:

November 2003: The government of Yemen freed more than 1,500 inmates—including 92 suspected al-Qaeda members—in an amnesty to mark the holy month of Ramadan [1].

January 2005: The Algerian government pardoned 5,065 prisoners to commemorate the feast of Eid al-Adha [2].

September 2005: The new Mauritanian military government ordered "a sweeping amnesty for political crimes, freeing scores of prisoners... including a band of coup plotters and alleged Islamic extremists" [3].

November 2005: Morocco released 164 Islamist prisoners to mark the end of the holy month of Ramadan [4].

November 2005: Morocco released 5,000 prisoners in honor of the 50th anniversary of the country's independence. The sentences of 5,000 other prisoners were reduced [5].

November-December 2005: Saudi Arabia released 400 reformed Islamist prisoners [6].

February-March 2006: In February, Algeria pardoned or reduced sentences for "3,000 convicted or suspected terrorists" as part of a national reconciliation plan [7]. In March, 2,000 additional prisoners were released [8].

February 2006: Tunisian President Zine el-Abidine Ben Ali released 1,600 prisoners, including Islamist radicals [9].

March 2006: Yemen released more than 600 Islamist fighters who were imprisoned after a rebellion led by a radical cleric named Hussein Badr Eddin al-Huthi [10].

The justifications offered by Arab governments for these releases vary. Some claim they are to commemorate religious holidays or political anniversaries; others claim they are part of national-reconciliation plans. In some of the official statements announcing prisoner releases, Islamists are said to be excluded from the prisoners freed; in others, they are specifically included. In all cases, the releasing governments are police states worried about internal stability in the face of rising Islamist militancy across the Islamic world, the animosities of populations angered at Arab regimes for assisting the U.S.-led invasions of Iraq and Afghanistan, and the powerful showings Islamist parties have made in elections across the region. While the motivation of Arab governments in releasing large numbers of prisoners is impossible to definitively document, it seems fair to conclude that those governments are not ignorant to the attraction that the U.S. occupation of Iraq and Afghanistan will exert on newly freed Islamists, nor of the chance that it might take no more than a slight incentive to dispatch some of the former prisoners to the war zones. It may well be that the West is seeing but not recognizing a reprise of the process that supplied manpower to the Afghan mujahideen two decades ago.

Notes
1. "92 al-Qaeda Suspects Freed in Amnesty," *Los Angeles Times*, November 17, 2003.
2. "Algeria Pardons 5,065 Prisoners to Mark Muslim Feast," http://www.deepikaglobal.com, January 18, 2005.
3. "Mauritania: Junta Declares General Amnesty for Political Prisoners," Reuters, September 5, 2005.
4. Said Moumni, "One-hundred and Sixty-four Detainees Belonging to the Salfia Jiahdia Group are Pardoned," *Annahar al-Maghribiyah*, November 5, 2005.
5. "Morocco Pardons 10,000 to Mark Independence," Reuters, November 17, 2005.
6. "Saudi Arabia: Almost 400 Prisoners Released," http://www.adnki.com, December 19, 2005.
7. "Algeria to Pardon or Reduce Sentences for 3,000 Terrorists," http://www.eveningecho.ie/news, February 2006.
8. "Over 2,000 Algerians to be Released Under Reconciliation Charter," Radio Algiers/Channel 3, March 1, 2006.
9. "Ben Ali Frees 1,600 Tunisian Prisoners," http://www.middle-east-online.com, February 27, 2006.
10. "Yemen Frees 627 Zaidi Rebels," http://www.middle-east-online.com, March 3, 2003.

[From Terrorism Focus, Volume III, Issue 18]

The Salafi-Jihadist Movement in Iraq: Recruitment Methods and Arab Volunteers

Murad al-Shishani

Originally published on December 2, 2005

The experience of Arab fighters in Iraq is the latest and most important development of the global Salafi-jihadi movement, as they constitute the third generation of Salafi-jihadists. An examination of the social structure of these fighters provides important insights into this generation and the similarities and differences with the previous two generations.

While the secrecy surrounding foreign fighters in Iraq and the lack of impartial sources on their activities make the collection of quality information very difficult, "Islamic Forums" have become a key outlet for information. These forums specialize in providing information on slain fighters, and in recent times have divulged the names and details of 429 such fighters in Iraq [1]. The analysis in this article is largely based on these figures.

Two recent articles have extensively studied the phenomenon of "Arab Volunteers" in Iraq. The first is by Israeli researcher Reuven Paz, who has analyzed 154 names and found that 94 (61%) were Saudis and came from the following regions: 61 from Najd, 12 from Qassim Burida, 7 from Mecca and Hijaz, 5 from the South and 2 from the North [2]. Paz also found that these Saudis perpetrated 23 suicide attacks, and that roughly 45% of the suicide bombers were from Najd.

The remaining fighters found in Paz's study were: 16 Syrians (10.4%); 13 Iraqis (8.4%); 11 Kuwaitis (7.1%); 4 Jordanians, and 2 from Algeria, Morocco and Yemen each; and one each from Palestine, United Arab Emirates and Sudan. Paz also noted that their ages ranged from 25-30 years. Some of them were married, some had earned higher education degrees, most of them went to Iraq through a friend or relative, and the majority came from neighboring countries.

The second article is a study by Anthony Cordesman and Nawaf Obaid, who question the credibility of the lists published by al-Qaeda supporters, and contend that they were published for mobilization and recruitment purposes [3]. They also argue that many of the persons mentioned in the list have been found to be living in Saudi Arabia and were never involved in jihadi activities in the first place. But the Saudi magazine *al-Osbu'iah* and al-Arabiya.net had previously published a report based on the same list and no response was forthcoming from the people whose names were mentioned [4].

Using methodology and information generated by the aforementioned articles, this article further studies the social structure of Salafi-jihadists in Iraq by analyzing the following factors: country of origin (geography), age, marital status and participation in other conflicts.

Geography

Based on a list of mujahideen posted on the al-Saha web forum (http://alsaha.fares.net), the ranks of the Salafi-jihadists fighting in Iraq—most of whom are part of Zarqawi's al-Qaeda in Iraq organization—come from all over the Arab World, with Saudis being the majority (200 fighters – 53%), 13% from Syria, 8% from Iraq, 5.8% from Jordan, 4% from Kuwait, 3.8% from Libya, with the rest distributed among other countries (see Figure 1) while the geographical origin of 52 names remains unknown.

While these numbers are not comprehensive, they do give an idea as to the complexion of the mujahideen in Iraq, and indicate that the largest percentage belongs to countries surrounding Iraq, presumably because accessing Iraq is easiest for these fighters. Moreover, jihadi leaders in neighboring countries (particularly in Saudi Arabia) regularly call on mujahideen to join the jihad in American-occupied Iraq. In addition, the ongoing conflict between the Saudi regime and the Saudi al-Qaeda network is forcing many young Saudi Salafi-jihadists to migrate to Iraq. Many of these jihadis are prominent fighters and ideological trainers; a good example being the Salafi-jihadist ideologue Abdullah Rashid al-Rashoud, whom Zarqawi eulogized after he was slain by American forces near al-Qaim.

In addition, there are many North Africans—principally Moroccans, Algerians and Libyans, among the Arab fighters. This is because local Salafi-jihadist movements in these countries are in conflict with their governments. Therefore, as in Saudi Arabia, overwhelming security pressures are forcing fighters to search for new havens.

Interestingly, in the list posted on the al-Saha forum, the number of local Iraqis among the ranks of the Salafi-jihadists is very low (around 8%), which indicates that insurgent Iraqis prefer to join indigenous "nationalist" resistance networks, rather then foreign-led extremist ideological movements. Another interesting fact is that Egyptians no longer represent a significant constituency among Arab fighters as was the case in Afghanistan and Bosnia. This is primarily because the role of jihadist movements has receded in Egypt and many former leaders of jihadist organizations have now publicly renounced violent methods.

Finally, it is worth re-iterating the seriousness of the threat posed by those returning from the Iraq conflict, especially in light of recent reports that the United States intends to substantially reduce its forces in Iraq over the next two years. The Arab volunteers in Iraq are acquiring cutting-edge fighting skills, and are exposed to an extremely powerful ideological influence in an environment of total war, characterized by concepts such as wala' and bara' (loyalty and disavowal) and mufasala (dissociation). It is imperative on the authorities of neighboring countries to devise effective rehabilitation programs and avoid resorting to typical security solutions.

Age, Education, Recruitment and Previous Combat Experience

Out of the 429 fighters listed in the al-Saha study, only the ages of 85 of them are known. Based on these statistics the average age of foreign fighters in Iraq is 27. Moreover, out of 429 fighters only 22 (5.1%) have had fighting experience in other regions, demonstrating that the foreign fighters in Iraq do indeed constitute the third generation of Salafi-jihadists. Furthermore, the average age is similar to that of the Saudi fighters whose names were released in the new list of the 36 most wanted [5].

It is worth noting that 17 out of 31 fighters (58.6% - only 31 of the 429 had data available on education) quit their education to join the fight against the American occupation. This is also evident in the high percentage of BA degree holders (19.4%), which is different from what typically occurs in Salafi-jihadist movements, whose ideologues are normally the ones with high levels of education while the fighters are mostly young men who have not completed their education (see Figure 2).

Another interesting fact is that 22 of those fighters are married, and among those whose career status is known, 8 out of 18 (44%) work in the private sector, with some even being investors. This lends further credence to the notion that the occupation of Iraq, and all the excesses that surrounds it, is generating new developments in erstwhile socioeconomically stable Salafi-jihadi networks.

Finally, in regards to recruitment, the majority of those coming from the same area, for instance Burida in Qassim or Hael in Saudi Arabia, have entered Iraq together or were recruited through relatives. This is evident in the recurrent names of major tribes such as Shammari, Otaibi, Shahri and Motairi, which indicates that kinship and friendship are major modes of recruitment.

Conclusion

American-occupied Iraq is both the catalyst and incubator for the birth and evolution of the third generation of Salafi-jihadists. Without the Iraqi theater, the entire al-Qaeda-inspired global jihad movement would be faced with critical ideological and recruitment problems.

It is compellingly clear that the American occupation of Iraq, with its associated human rights abuses such as the Abu Ghraib scandal, has played a major role in driving young men to join al-Qaeda and affiliated organizations. At the same time, it is equally clear that Salafi-jihadist discourse does not appeal to Muslims in general and Iraqis in particular. Indeed, despite the changes to their socioeconomic make-up, recruitment into Salafi-jihadist networks is still primarily based on kinship and friendship and not only on their religious-political ideology.

Two important conclusions can be drawn from assessing the make-up al-Zarqawi's fighters in Iraq. First, as long as the United States remains in Iraq as an increasingly unpopular occupation force, more young people will be drawn to radical Islamist movements. Second, Arab countries—especially those neighboring Iraq—need to begin planning in earnest for the arrival of Iraq returnees. It is imperative for these countries to design effective cultural and political programs to deal with these young men and reintegrate them into society, and not simply resort to the already tried-and-failed security solutions.

Figure 1

Percentage of Salafi-Jihadists Foreign Volunteers in Iraq Compared to Native Iraqi Salafi Jihadists

Country/Region	Percentage
Saudi Arabia	53%
Syria	13%
Iraq	8%
North Africa	8%
Jordan	6%
Kuwait	4%
Yemen	2%
Egypt	1%
Palestine	1%
Other	4%

Source: the figures have been compiled by the author from the source mentioned in note 1 of the endnotes

Figure 2

Educational Status of Arab Fighters in Iraq

Education	Number	Percentage
Quit Education	17	54.8%
High School	3	9.7%
Diploma	3	9.7%
BA	6	19.4%
Higher Education	2	6.4%
TOTAL	31	100%

Source: the figures have been compiled by the author from the source mentioned in note 1 of the endnotes

Notes

1. This list has been published in 3 parts in a variety of online Islamist forums. The author downloaded the list from the al-Saha Forum http://alsaha.fares.net/sahat/.ee6b2ff.
2. Reuven Paz, "Arab Volunteers Killed in Iraq: An Analysis, Project for the Research of Islamist Movements," *PRISM, Series of Global Jihad*, No. 1/3 – March 2005.
3. See: Anthony H. Cordesman and Nawaf Obaid, "Saudi Militants in Iraq: Assessment and Kingdom's Response" (revised September 19, 2005), Center for Strategic and International Studies (CSIS).
4. Mustfa al-Ansari, "Asma'a al-Muqatleen al-Saudieen fi al-Iraq", (the Names of Saudi Fighters in Iraq), *Al-Osbu'iah*, Issue 40, 13 June, 2005, also see this link: http://www.alsahfe.com/modules.php?name=News &file=print&sid=248.
5. See two articles by the author in the Jordanian newspaper, *al-Ghad*: "Al-Qaeda in Saudi Arabia: the Determinants of Age and Participation in Fighting", Jan. 6, 2005; and "The Future of the Salafi-Jihadist Way in Saudi Arabia", July 7, 2005.

[From Terrorism Monitor, Volume III, Issue 23]

Muslim Female Fighters: An Emerging Trend

Farhana Ali

Originally published on November 3, 2005

Muslim women are increasingly joining the global jihad, some motivated by religious conviction to change the plight of Muslims under occupation, and recruited by al-Qaeda and local terrorist groups strained by increased arrests and deaths of male operatives. Attacks by female fighters, also known as the mujahidaat, are arguably more deadly than those conducted by male jihadists, attributed in part to the perception that women are unlikely to commit such acts of horror, and when they do, the shock or "CNN factor" of their attacks draws far greater media attention than male bombers. Increasing awareness with instant media attention can motivate other women to commit similar attacks.

The use of Muslim women for suicide attacks by male-dominated terrorist groups could have implications on the jihadi mindset, challenging more conservative groups such as al-Qaeda to reconsider the utility of the Muslim woman on the front lines of jihad. These groups will likely exploit women to conduct operations on their behalf to advance their goals and achieve short-term tactical gain. Convinced of the operational advantages of using female fighters, and the media attention she garners—including some sympathy from the Muslim world—men began to rely on women to carry out attacks.

While women enlisted and played a pivotal role in operations, including the veteran Palestinian female Leila Khalid for a myriad of successful hijackings in the late 1960s and early 1970s, counterterrorism experts and analysts have rarely focused on female terrorists. According to Dr. Marc Sageman, a forensic psychiatrist, the notion of a woman perpetrating acts of violence "runs counter to Western stereotypes and misconceptions of male terrorists; we assume that women are second-class citizens and rely on the men to run the organization," rather than challenging our prejudices of women in these terror networks [1].

Why Now?

Since at least 2000, there has been a gradual progression of suicide attacks conducted by Muslim women in new theaters of operation, including Uzbekistan, Egypt, and more recently, Iraq [2]. The attack in Talafar, northern Iraq, by a female suicide bomber came as a surprise, but was predictable. Al-Qaeda claimed responsibility for the latest coup de main at an army recruitment center on September 28, 2005 by a "blessed sister." The Iraqi woman stood among job applicants before detonating; a similar tactic was used by women in the Irish Republican Army, who carried bombs beneath their clothing feigning pregnancy or wheeling weapons in baby carriages. The attack in late September was not the first by an Iraqi woman; in April 2003, two women, one pretending to be pregnant, blew up a car at a coalition checkpoint, killing three soldiers [3]. Although attacks by women in Iraq are still a relatively new trend, women will likely play a wider role in operations where jihad mobilizes an entire population against a clear aggressor. That leaves Iraq vulnerable to attacks by female suicide bombers in the near future.

The attacks in Egypt earlier this year by two women remain an anomaly. For years, Egyptian men, not women, fostered the growth of the jihadi movement, which led to the formation of different groups, varying in their membership and orientation. Yet, the April 30, 2005 shooting on a tourist bus in Cairo by two veiled Egyptian women is evidence that women in the Arab Muslim world can play an increasing role in operations. The women, both in their 20's, were related to the male perpetrator, Ehab Yousri Yassin. Negat Yassin was the bomber's sister and Iman Ibrahim Khamis his fiancée; they reportedly shot at the bus in revenge for Yassin's death by Egyptian authorities and then shot themselves [4], probably to avoid capture. It remains unclear if the two women intended to commit suicide or chose the tactic to evade arrest by Egyptian police.

While little is known about the two Egyptian women and their intentions for suicide, the story of a young Uzbek girl illustrates her determination to participate in a suicide attack in March 2003. Nineteen-year old Dilnoza Holmuradova detonated explosives at Tashkent's Chorsu Market, killing at least 47 people, including ten policemen [5]. Dilnoza came from a solid middle-class background, was well educated, spoke five languages, and, unlike the vast majority of Uzbek women, she had a driver's license [6]. After dropping out of the police academy she was attending in 2002, Dilnoza began praying regularly, and in January 2004 she and her sister left home without a word to their parents, taking the Islamic literature in the house with them [7]. Her recruitment by the Islamic Jihad Group, a radical offshoot of the Islamic Movement of Uzbekistan (IMU), likely resulted in her decision to carry out the operation.

The attacks by women in Iraq, Egypt, and Uzbekistan—three women unrelated in culture, religion, and national identities—are reflective of a crisis in Muslim societies. In both instances, women who had never before conducted terrorist operations, are beginning to challenge their perceived enemies and male-only terrorist groups. Their actions could provide an example for other Muslim women to either enlist in extremist organizations or volunteer for future attacks.

Historical Precedence for Female Fighters

For centuries, Muslim women in different struggles and communities have joined men on the front lines of war, and have died alongside them. The most prominent example of an early Muslim woman in jihad is Nusayba bint K'ab, who fought in the Battle of Uhud with her husband and two sons and during the Caliphate of Abu Bakr. She joined the Muslim troops, suffered eleven wounds, and lost one arm [8]. The Prophet's own female relatives took part in jihad; his wife Ayesha led the Battle of the Camel, and his granddaughter Zaynab bint Ali fought in the Battle of Karbala. Other women were recognized for tending to the wounded, donating their jewelry for the jihad, and encouraging their male family members to fight to ensure the survival of Islam [9].

The involvement of the early Arab women in jihad is celebrated today throughout the Muslim world and they serve as icons and a precedent for contemporary Muslim women who choose suicide operations. In modern day resistance movements, a Christian Lebanese woman, Loula Abboud, "may have been the model for the first Palestinian women who became suicide bombers in 2002" [10]. The dark-eyed petite girl of 19 conducted a suicide operation in the Bekaa valley in southern Lebanon in April 1985, "exceeding all expectations" for men and women in war [11]. Described by her brother as a woman "fighting for the liberation of her own homeland," Aboud's struggle for "self-defense" is echoed by other women around the world, including women of the first Palestinian intifada, who led a campaign to re-open schools, teach underground classes for children, and participate in "street activism that directly confronted the occupation forces" [12].

However heroic the modern day female fighter may be regarded by her community, contemporary women warriors do not resemble their predecessors. The involvement of early women in jihad is recognized in the Qur'an and hadith. Women were also rewarded for performing the same duties as men. A Qur'anic verse was revealed to reflect the equal status of both men and women: "Lo! Muslim men and Muslim women, and believer men and believer women, and men who obey and women who obey...Allah has prepared for them forgiveness and a vast reward" (Surat al-Ahzab 33:35).

Diverse Motivations

Local conflicts are critical motivators, but each conflict is unique and must take into account the historical framework from which conflict emerges. For instance, aside from being linked by gender, the mujahidaat in Chechnya have little in common with women in Palestine, and women in Saudi Arabia share absolutely nothing with their "sisters" in Uzbekistan.

While conflicts and motivations vary, a woman's decision to pursue violent action is impacted by personal experiences and outcomes. Coupled with the absence of change to her own local conflict, of which she is a part, a woman is more apt to volunteer or be recruited for an operation to end her own suffering or that of her people. Suicide becomes the preferred tactic when Muslim women perceive they have no other alternative to affect change to their local environment; coupled with a heightened sense of anger, disillusionment, and despair, some women choose suicide as a way to communicate and channel their frustration. This is particularly true for those who believe there are no other social, economic, or political opportunities available to them.

The perceived threat against Islam is another powerful motivator that sanctions the use of violence as an effective means of communication. Convinced that the local Muslim community can no longer afford inaction, some Muslim women enlist in operations to ensure the survival of the Muslim community. For the believer of martyrdom, subjugation to the faith is rewarding. The individual, knowing that death is likely, "inspires other Muslims to continue the struggle and the martyr's death is kindling wood for jihad and Islam" [13].

Assured of the rewards of martyrdom, women perceive they have nothing to lose. Printed in a HAMAS monthly publication *al-Muslimah*, Palestinian operative Reem Rayishi said, "I am proud to be the first female HAMAS martyr. I have two children and love them very much. But my love to see God was stronger than my love for my children, and I'm sure that God will take care of them if I become a martyr" [14].

A Short-Lived Panorama

The liberal door that now permits women to participate in operations will likely close once male jihadists gain new recruits and score a few successes in the war on terrorism. At the same time that a Muslim woman is indispensable to male-dominated terrorist groups and the war effort, she also is expendable. The sudden increase in female bombers over the past year may represent nothing more than a riding wave of al-Qaeda's success rather than a lasting effort in the global jihad. In the short term, male fighters could encourage Muslim women to join their organizations, but there is no indication that these men would allow the mujahidaat to prevail authority and replace images of the male folk-hero. There is also no evidence that Muslim female operatives will have contact with senior male leaders, except to execute attacks.

Notes
1. Interview with Dr. Marc Sageman in October 2005.
2. Two female suicide bombers killed themselves and three U.S. Army Rangers at a checkpoint in western Iraq. One of the women appeared to be pregnant, and as she exited the vehicle, she screamed for assistance. "Women Kill 3 Rangers in Suicide Bombing," April 5, 2003. www.chicagotribune.com/news/nationsworld/.
3. "Woman Suicide Bomber Strikes Iraq," http://news.bbc.co.uk/1/hi/world/middle_east/4289168.stm.
4. "Attacks Injure Nine in Egypt," *Columbia Daily Tribune*, published May 1, 2005. http://www.showmenews.com/2005/May/20050501News020.asp.
5. IWPR Staff in Central Asia, "Uzbekistan: Affluent Suicide Bombers,"

RCA No. 278, April 20, 2004.
6. Ibid.
7. Ibid.
8. Busool, Assad Nimer, *Muslim Women Warriors*, Chicago, Illinois: Al Huda, 1995. p.35-37.
9. Ibid, p. 34-35.
10. Davis, Joyce. *Martyrs: Innocence, Vengeance and Despair in the Middle East*, New York: Palgrave MacMillian, 2003, p. 68.
11. Davis, p.68-72.
12. Jennifer Plyler interview with Hanadi Loubani, founding member of Women for Palestine. "Palestinian Women's Political Participation," WHRnet, November 23, 2003. www.whrnet.org/docs/interview-loubani-0311.html.
13. Lustwick, Ian S., "Terrorism in the Arab-Israeli Conflict: Targets and Audiences," in Martha Crenshaw, ed., *Terrorism in Context*. University Park, Pennsylvania: The Pennsylvania State University, 1995, p. 536.
14. *Al-Muslimah*, February 2004.

[From Terrorism Monitor, Volume III, Issue 21]

Jihad Without Rules: The Evolution of al-Takfir wa al-Hijra

Hayder Mili

Originally published on June 29, 2006

The September 11 attacks precipitated the uncovering of extensive al-Takfir wa al-Hijra (Excommunication and Exile) networks across Europe specialized in logistical support to terrorist groups. While the obscure group had been previously encountered by law enforcement, many were surprised at the extent and reach of its networks. Once thought of as nothing more than a fringe group in Egypt, in the last 15 years the ideology has undergone a surprising internationalization and evolution with Takfir groups involved in terrorist attacks, criminal activities and cooperating with the al-Qaeda network in its jihad against the West.

The Doctrine

Most contemporary Takfir doctrine was forged inside Egyptian jails following the great wave of arrests targeting Muslim Brotherhood in the mid-1960s where many of its members were tortured and/or executed. One of those arrested, the sheikh of Egypt's al-Azhar mosque, Ali Ismael, postulated that not only were Egyptian President Nasser and his entourage apostates, but so was Egyptian society as a whole because it was not fighting the Egyptian government and had thus accepted rule by non-Muslims. This was another radical turn in the concept of takfir (to excommunicate), first enunciated by Sheikh Ibn Taymiyyah and further developed by Sayyid Qutb, both intellectual pillars of the contemporary jihadist ideology. While the sheikh later rejected this doctrine, his remaining followers quickly gravitated around a young charismatic agronomist by the name of Shukri Mustafa, who became the spiritual leader of Jama'at al-Muslimin (as they called themselves) but whom Egyptian police came to call al-Takfir wa al-Hijra (ATWAH).

Takfir members exiled themselves (al-Hijra) in the desert practicing complete isolation (al-Uzla) from excommunicated (al-Takfir) Muslim societies. While jihad certainly remained an imperative, Shukri Mustafa initially believed that an imminent world war between the superpowers would leave free reign to the jihadists—then too weak—to take power. Arguing that Egyptian man-made laws were illegitimate, ATWAH was able to justify theft, kidnapping, forced marriages and even the assassination of anyone who was not part of the group (such as apostates). Most of these core precepts are still loosely followed by contemporary Takfir groups.

Globalization

After Shukri Mustafa's execution in 1977, what remained of the original group, along with its ideology, dispersed across the Muslim world. Throughout the last decade especially, numerous Takfir groups, unconnected to one another, sprang up and took violent actions in a number of Muslim countries. In Sudan, ATWAH has been responsible for at least five attacks on worshippers since 1994, resulting in scores of fatalities and hundreds of injuries. On December 31, 2000, in an uncommon display of power for the secretive group, hundreds of Takfiris organized a sudden attack in Northern Lebanon, killing civilians and clashing with the Lebanese army in its biggest operation since the civil war. Across the border in Syria, more than 24 Takfiris are imprisoned in Syria's Saidnaya prison alone, and there have recently been deadly battles between security forces and Takfiris suspected of preparing terrorist strikes (*Agence France Presse*, July 12, 2005) [1]. Similar clashes erupted in November 2002 in Jordan, where Takfiris may also have been involved in the murder of U.S. diplomat Laurence Foley. In Turkey, at least 12 Takfiris were arrested in 2004 [2]. In Africa, Kenyan security services warned of an al-Zarqawi-linked ATWAH group in the country and there are reports of ATWAH cells in Somalia where the group is also said to have a training camp (AFP, June 16, 2005; *Les Nouvelles d'Addis*, February 2006).

Many Takfiris also "immigrated" to jihad lands like Afghanistan or Bosnia where they participated in logistical support for the foreign mujahideen. In Egypt itself, the group, or rather the ideology, periodically resurfaces; there have been hundreds of arrests since 1990 and a "botched" plot (killing four people) to blow up al-Azhar University (*Hebdo al-Ahram*, April 20, 2005). While there have been arrests (and executions) of Takfiris in Saudi Arabia, there is some confusion on whether these were "real" Takfiris since the media uses this term interchangeably for those who only consider the house of Saud, and not other Muslims, apostates. In Morocco, a number of Takfir cells have sprung up since 2000, culminating with the attacks on Casablanca in 2003. In Iraq, there are reports that ATWAH is involved in some of the violence, particularly targeting police and government officials. There are also a number of groups with very similar ideologies who do not adopt the name of the original group; for example, Morroco's Salafiya Jihadiya and Assirat al-Mustakim are almost indistinguishable from ATWAH in doctrine (*Maroc Hebdo*, May 23, 2003).

Excommunicate and Purge

A threshold was crossed in early-1990s Algeria under where Takfir was the main inspiration behind the decade-long, wholesale massacres of "excommunicated" Muslim civilians following the annulment of elections that the Islamic Salvation Front (FIS) looked poised to win. The Algerian civil war provided the ideal life-size laboratory for the Takfir ideology, which gradually permeated the GIA (Groupe Islamique Arme) groups spread out across Algeria until the GIA's ideology became effectively indistinguishable from the Takfir's. It is this "merger," the first of its kind for ATWAH, which would further shape the ideology of many contemporary Takfir groups toward a less exclusionary vision of jihad. While initially Takfir members turned on fellow Muslims and were primarily concerned with Muslim societies, starting in the mid-1990s several things changed for ATWAH: some of its branches—starting with the North African branch that had fused with the GIA—became involved in jihadi support networks in Europe, and a "true" Islamic state had finally been founded in Afghanistan where many Takfiris would migrate. Beginning in 1999, for example, ATWAH offered support to al-Qaeda's strategy, turning its sights on the West (*Le Nouvel Observateur*, October 18, 2001).

The Western Exile

The rise of the Taliban, the Algerian civil war and the Western exile produced changes in the Takfir modus operandi. Far from breaking with infidel society, the neo-Takfiris were now infiltrating it and have since become the logistical backbone of jihad in the West, maintaining their own networks in countries like Belgium, the Netherlands, France and Germany. Beginning in 1994, members of the group were arrested in Europe, where law enforcement found Takfiris involved in all aspects of logistical support for terrorism: smuggling weapons, trafficking drugs and sheltering and moving operatives from conflict to conflict. Further arrests were made in Switzerland and France in 1998 when Takfir members Tesnim Aiman and Ressous Houari were arrested. In Paris, a 10-men Takfir cell specialized in raising funds through counterfeit clothing was uncovered in 2003 (Proche-Orient.info, November 25, 2003). In North America, the head of the Lebanese Takfir, Bassam Ahmad Kanj, and one of his lieutenants, Kassem Daher, would go on to head a cross-border logistical support network in Canada and the United States, funded from drug trafficking and charity fronts (http://medintelligence.free.fr/arliban.htm, November 27, 2001). Kassem Daher also had links to a number of jihadi groups and individuals, including Jose Padilla (*Sun Media*, November 25, 2005).

Beyond fundraising and logistics, Takfir has been part of a number of foiled plots, including significant operations such as the targeting of Algerian interests in Marseille, the U.S. Embassy in Paris, NATO headquarters in Brussels and a foiled 2002 attack on the St. Denis football stadium in France (*Le Nouvel Observateur*, October 3, 2002). The European ATWAH appears more structured than its Middle Eastern manifestations; a 2002 confidential report titled *La Menace Islamiste Sunnite*, produced by France's intelligence service, cites the Takfir group (along with the GSPC) as one of two groups most likely to attempt terrorist strikes in Europe (*Fides Journal*, November 13, 2002). In Spain, home to a large and structured Takfir network, the group's role in the Madrid attacks has been confirmed by law enforcement, while in Barcelona Takfiris have been cited in a plot to buy materials for a dirty bomb (*El Pais*, December 19, 2005; *Maghreb Arabe Presse*, October 28, 2005). The doctrine itself, now "globalized," seems to have influenced a number of attacks, including the murder of Theo Van Gogh in the Netherlands.

The neo-Takfiris follow a loose or rather dynamic interpretation of Shukri Mustafa's doctrine. Mustafa was anti-modernity and anti-intellectual, whereas the neo-Takfiris use technology and modernity to their advantage. Where Shukri Mustafa preached a physical withdrawal from infidel society, neo-Takfiris are fully immersed in it, using secrecy and dissimulation as a core tactic. Whereas the original Takfir (and some remaining branches) excommunicates even other jihadi groups, the emphasis on excommunicating fellow Muslims is no longer central; instead, cooperation is now favored. Al-Qaeda's growing legitimacy as the harbingers of worldwide jihad may have had an influence on the movement's new direction. For al-Qaeda, an alliance with Takfir would be in keeping with al-Qaeda's drive to put doctrinal differences aside, federating and uniting all jihadist tendencies to fight the West. While some commentators have claimed that al-Qaeda is a Takfiri organization, there is no evidence that al-Qaeda or its leadership have excommunicated Muslim societies other than their governments and its supporters, even if, for al-Qaeda, Muslims who fail to support them are on the wrong path.

Unlike al-Qaeda in Iraq or the GSPC, Takfiris—in part because they are not an organized, structured entity—have not officially joined al-Qaeda or sworn an oath of allegiance to bin Laden. Takfiris can now, therefore, be viewed as semi-aligned "free agents" who may collaborate with other jihadi groups on an ad hoc basis, working toward the same overreaching goal. Most cells consist of 10-15 people and are usually formed from individual initiatives.

Paradise Now

Additionally, unlike Salafi-Jihadists, the Takfiris lack any legitimate scholar and the ideology is not very elaborate since Mustafa himself did not have any religious diploma. As a result of its theological weakness, the doctrine has been interpreted to allow the worst imaginable deviancies. Without any central leadership, the group's ideology, already extreme, now evolves through self-appointed ideologues who double as cell leaders. As stated above, Takfir is able to legitimize criminal activities, justifying these activities through the theory of the fay'e (the licit) by appropriating the goods and property of infidels and apostates. Criminal activities like theft and drug trafficking are thus encouraged if one-fifth of the proceeds are used to fund the jihad. In many Muslim countries, Takfiris have been involved in theft from both private homes and mosques; indeed, before it was uncovered by security services, the Jordanian cell led by Mohammed Chalabi was heavily engaged in robbery and drug trafficking from its headquarters in Maan (AFP, March 27,

2000). In Europe, a Takfir logistical support network based in France and Italy was involved in theft, trafficking and forging documents (AFP, October 26, 2001).

The quintessential sleeper, Takfiris have "theologically" authorized themselves to break any and every Islamic rule to blend into Western society; they do not frequent mosques and often consume drugs and alcohol. The Takfir in Algeria were known to be using artane, hashish and other drugs while many of the Takfiris involved in the Madrid attacks were themselves drug users. Thus, where one expects an austere bearded militant, one may find a boozing womanizer. The Takfiris effectively stand outside the boundaries of Islam itself to better defend it, with the jihad imperative as the only "rule" to keep. Because of this idea of "sinless sin," the disenfranchised, delinquents or criminals are often found within its ranks and are a known target for recruitment because of their ability to raise funds. In truth, nothing is illicit or off-limits for the Takfiris; it is essentially a jihad without rules that allows for any and all transgressions—including bizarre and macabre rituals involving the victim's dismemberment. The aforementioned incursion into Lebanon in 2000 involved a series of mutilations; in Morocco, mutilated corpses became a regular occurrence in cities like Casablanca where the number of civilians ritually murdered by Takfiris reached 166 in 2002 alone (*Maroc Hebdo International*, December 3-9, 2004). In Madrid, Takfiris are reported to have exhumed and dismembered the body of the GEO sub-inspector who died in the anti-terrorist operation in Leganes following the March 11, 2004 rail bombings.

Conclusion

Takfir is first an ideology and then a group or groups who adhere more or less loosely to its founding principles, with the result that ATWAH has now become a brand name. It has, over time, acquired an aura of mysticism and is now transnational, its members having been found in most Muslim countries as well as in Europe and North America. Apart from al-Qaeda and to a lesser extent Hezbollah, no other Islamist group has achieved the same internationalization across cultures and continents. The secrecy and dissimulation of Takfiris makes them particularly difficult to infiltrate, but also highly unpredictable as attacks may be sporadic and improvised, forcing law enforcement to cast an ever-wider net. The spread of the Takfir doctrine through the internet, its reliance on criminal activities and the atomization of small, secretive autonomous cells present a further challenge for counter-terrorism efforts. These efforts need to place a greater focus on recruitment, especially in prisons and high-crime areas, while increasing understanding of the emerging links between criminality and terror.

[From Terrorism Monitor, Volume IV, Issue 13]

Links between Terror and Crime

Tangled Webs: Terrorist and Organized Crime Groups

Hayder Mili

Originally published on January 12, 2006

Since the early 1990s, Western law enforcement agencies have noted an increasing reliance on criminal activity by terrorist networks around the world. Funding sources from Persian Gulf charities and other non-governmental fronts have been placed under pressure. This development, compounded by the arrests of several high-ranking coordinators and financiers of operations in Europe and North America—such as Abu Doha and Fateh Kamel—have compelled jihadi networks to adapt and further diversify their funding sources. Consequently "traditional" criminal activities like drug trafficking, robbery and smuggling are rapidly becoming the main source of terrorism funds. In fact, many recent terrorist attacks have been partly financed through crime revenue.

Funding Shifts

Throughout the 1990s, European law enforcement officers tasked with combating the Algerian Armed Islamic Group (GIA) networks noticed that operatives had penetrated local criminal structures in Europe and North Africa by using ethnic and cultural links. With the jihad in Algeria at its height, the under-funded GIA became actively involved in drugs and weapons trafficking through logistics and financial support cells in Europe. GIA members such as Djamel Lounici and Mourad Dhina also trafficked stolen vehicles and forged documents. Similarly, for years the Fateh Kamel network in Montreal and an affiliated cell in Istanbul benefited from trafficking in stolen vehicles, theft and credit card fraud. One of its Montreal members, the Millennium bomber Ahmed Ressam, had also planned a series of armed robberies to secure funding for his aborted attack on the Los Angeles airport in 1999.

While a number of violent crimes involving jihadists have taken place in North Africa and Europe over the last decade, the full synthesis between criminality and terrorism took place in 1996 with a series of deadly armed robberies in the French town of Roubaix, which police initially assumed were perpetrated by criminals motivated solely by monetary gain. Following the attempted bombing of a G-7 meeting in Lille, French authorities discovered that the Roubaix gang was in fact a small Islamic militant organization that had also committed robberies in Bosnia to fund the jihad. An added benefit of these actions—from the Roubaix gang's point of view—may have been that these unconventional "fundraising operations" were, in fact, terrorizing in themselves.

In December 2005, co-leader of the Roubaix gang and French convert Lionel Dumont was sentenced to 30 years in prison. Moreover, similar groups have been dismantled in France in the past months, including in a December 13th joint operation involving five French law enforcement agencies that netted over 25 suspects as well as high-grade explosives and weaponry. The group included known jihadists, radicalized delinquents and common criminals. Some of the members of this Zarqawi-linked cell—including presumed leader and ex-convict Ouassini Cherifi—were also involved in a number of armored car robberies that were undertaken to raise funds for the movement of recruits to Iraq.

Triangular Trafficking and Specialization

A "triangular trade" is steadily evolving that consists of weapons, stolen/contraband goods and narcotics. New al-Qaeda affiliates, notably the Groupe Salafiste pour la Prédication et le Combat (GSPC), the Moroccan Islamic Combatant Group (GICM) and North African branches of Takfir wa al-Hijra (Excommunication and Exile) have inherited old GIA networks spread across Europe and are actively involved in various types of trafficking to fund operations, trade in weaponry and explosives and move/shelter militants. In Europe, this nexus is mostly active in France and especially Spain, which because of its geography is a major transit (and destination) point for Moroccan cannabis as well as a hub for forged documents and credit cards (*Le Nouvel Observateur*, October 7, 2004).

While networks were initially involved in drugs-for-weapons exchanges, many eventually shifted to direct drug trafficking. Moroccan sources suspect drug money to be the main source of funding for the May 16, 2003 attacks in Casablanca. Moreover, according to Spanish police, the funding for the March 11, 2004 Madrid train attacks came from drug trafficking, and many of those who took part in the preparation and execution of the attack had been involved in criminal activities such as stolen vehicle trading, jewel thefts and various types of counterfeiting (*La Vanguardia*, May 24, 2005). Furthermore, over half of the members of the group planning suicide strikes against the Spanish High Court later that year were already in jail on drug-trafficking-related charges.

Additionally, in June and November of this year, Spanish police uncovered operational and logistics cells of the GSPC and the Zarqawi networks, and discovered that the suspects had engaged in credit card fraud, robberies, drug trafficking and vehicle theft. At times an operational cell may partially fund itself, as when police found seven kilograms of hashish in the hideout of the suspects planning to bomb the Strasbourg cathedral in 2000. Although financed by Abu Doha, the group had been raising funds through drug trafficking in Frankfurt and London. Many other Islamist cells dismantled in Europe following September 11, 2001, had engaged in drug trafficking, including an al-Qaeda linked group operating in Antwerp and Brussels and a cell in the Netherlands involved in the assassination of Ahmad Shah Massoud.

Diversification

Aside from narcotics, militants and sympathizers also traffic in precious stones and metals, mainly because they are easy to transport and difficult to trace. This was the case with a Tunisian man charged in Germany with planning attacks against Western targets, who had used a travel agency as a front for gold and silver trafficking (*Agence France-Presse*, November 30, 2004). Front companies are ideal vehicles to transfer illicit funds and since the mid-1990s, dozens of terrorist front companies have been dismantled in Europe. Recent arrests in France uncovered a GICM support cell (linked to the Madrid bombings) operating various business ventures, just as Ould Slahi—involved in major al-Qaeda plots and closely linked to al-Qaeda financier Khaled

Al Shanquiti—was first arrested in 1999 for laundering drug money through his import-export firm.

Blurring the Lines

Following the arrests of several key players in the GIA's European operations in the mid-1990s, networks reorganized themselves around contraband and arms-smuggling rings influenced by elements of the Russian and Sicilian mafia (the latter has also laundered money for the GIA) [1]. These types of relationships arise from mutual benefit, with the terrorists seeking entry into established trafficking/money laundering channels and traditional criminal groups taking advantage of profit opportunities. Ethnic or religious links are not necessarily essential for collaboration to take place; for example, the Madrid bombings were facilitated by members of local criminal groups and petty thieves. When in 2001 the Spanish police conducted a counter-narcotics operation, which netted, among other items, hashish, explosives and detonators, they initially arrested the procurer of explosives for 3/11, José Suárez. Furthermore, the arrests of Marc Muller and Stephen Wendler in the mid-1990s were two of many examples where arms traffickers knowingly supplied terrorist groups with weapons from ex-soviet bloc states. In a case of direct barter, two Pakistanis and a U.S. citizen were detained in Hong Kong in 2002 in an attempt to exchange 600 kilograms of heroin and five tons of hashish for four Stinger missiles, which they intended to sell to al-Qaeda.

Since traffickers and terrorist organizations have similar logistical needs, there is ample room for collaboration in money laundering and even facilitating illegal immigration. Recent evidence from Morocco strongly suggests that jihadists are increasingly reliant on outsourcing to specialized migrant smuggling networks to infiltrate or exfiltrate targeted countries (*La Gazette du Maroc*, February 9, 2004).

There are additional concerns that trafficking channels can be used to move heavy weaponry and even weapons of mass destruction (WMD) and WMD components. In December 2004 members of Takfir were arrested in Barcelona for allegedly trying to purchase over 400 kilograms of industrial explosives and material from a Czech source to build a "dirty bomb" (*MAP Maghreb Arebe Presse*, October 28, 2005). Moreover, in a recent case of arms smuggling from Russia, traffickers attempted to sell high-powered arms—and reportedly uranium—to an FBI informant posing as a middleman for al-Qaeda.

Justification

To retain legitimacy, contemporary terrorist groups are particularly concerned about providing religious justification for their acts, criminal or otherwise. The writings of a 13th century Islamic jurist, Ibn Taymiyya, are an important source of authorization in regard to seizing the enemy's property during jihad. During the Algerian jihad, Ali Benhadj (a leader of the Islamic Salvation Front—FIS) quoted Ibn Taymiyya in declaring a fatwa authorizing GIA groups to assassinate and seize the property of all Muslims who opposed them. Terrorist mastermind Sheikh Abdel Rahman had also authorized robbery against "the miscreants and the apostate state," while in 1998 Osama bin Laden echoed this in his call to kill Americans and "plunder their money wherever and whenever they find it." In January 2004 a member of the Moroccan group, Salafiya Jihadiya admitted being shown videos that legitimized and promoted robbing "infidels and hypocrite Muslims," suggesting that encouraging criminal behavior is emerging as an integral feature of al-Qaeda's internal propaganda.

While Islamists are widely viewed as uncompromising literalists, pragmatism in the search for funds is evident in the religious decree by Salafist ideologue Nasreddine El Eulmi, which authorized the use and sale of drugs during the Algerian jihad. The most radical of contemporary terrorist groups, the Takfir, explicitly encourages robbery and drug trafficking as long as a fifth of the proceeds are used to fund the Islamist cause (*Le Parisien*, September 8, 2002). Arrests in Morocco in 2002 confirmed that its members were encouraged by their emir to steal "jewels, credit cards and money" from their victims (*Maroc-Hebdo*, August 3, 2002).

Conclusion

For terrorist organizations, the source of funding is irrelevant and only matters because it procures weapons, facilitates movement and produces propaganda. Even major operations cost relatively small sums when compared with the vast revenues of organized crime groups. For example, major operations like the Madrid bombings cost anywhere between $15,000 to $35,000, while the annual profits from cannabis trafficking in Europe alone are estimated at $12 billion.

The incorporation of organized criminality into terrorist ideology and operations shows the flexibility of terrorist organizations in adapting to dynamic fundraising environments. The border between the two worlds is ever more porous, with terror suspects now often imprisoned on multiple charges, both criminal and terrorist. This poses significant challenges to law enforcement agencies, which have traditionally targeted terrorism and criminality separately.

Notes

1. Salima Tlemçani, "Trafic d'armes en Europe," *Les filières du GIA*, January 11, 2000.

[From Terrorism Monitor, Volume IV, Issue 1]

Radical Networks in Middle East Prisons

Chris Zambelis

Originally published on May 4, 2006

Prisons have traditionally been breeding grounds for some of the world's most violent street gangs and organized criminal organizations. The hostile and dangerous environment of prison life inspired the creation of a diverse array of well-organized gangs and networks that thrived behind prison walls in everything from extortion, drug and weapons trafficking, smuggling, gambling and other illicit activities. In a testament to their organizational capacity and reach, many gangs spread to prisons outside of their place of origin and continue to flourish among seasoned members released into the general public.

Originally, U.S. prison gangs such as the Mexican Mafia (MM), also known as La Eme, the Aryan Brotherhood, and its prison offshoot the Nazi Low Riders, and the Black Guerilla Family (BGF), to name a few, were formed in an effort to bolster ethnic and racial solidarity among jailed Hispanic, White, and African-American inmates who competed for power and influence inside the penal system. In varying degrees, penal systems in Latin America, Europe, Africa and Asia are struggling with their own breed of dangerous prison networks.

In many cases, these networks are comprised of effective leadership councils, chains of command, and strict codes of conduct for members that often include sworn oaths of allegiance and a complex system of communication based on secret codes and signs designed to circumvent prison authorities.

Members of prison gangs often include psychologically vulnerable inmates seeking the physical protection that gang membership appears to provide. Many are also forced to join a particular gang on the threat of violence by gangs determined to swell their ranks. For others facing long-term sentences, gang affiliations based on ethnic, racial, or regional allegiances provide aspiring members with what they perceive as a worthy cause or a sense of belonging, in addition to the protection of membership in a larger social network that claims to speak and act on their behalf.

Prisons in the Middle East

Given this background, it is worth considering the recent prison riots in Jordan and Afghanistan reportedly instigated by jailed radical Islamists, including alleged members of al-Qaeda and the Taliban, respectively (al-Jazeera, March 2, 2006; Azadi Radio, March 6). The daring escape of 23 high-profile al-Qaeda inmates from a Yemeni penitentiary also raises interesting questions (*Yemen Times*, February 4, 2006).

Regional sources are convinced that organized radical networks operating within the confines of the prisons in question planned each of these incidents in concert with assistance from the outside and the support of new followers recruited from within. These cases may shed light on the nature and scope of radical networks and organizational structures in foreign prisons in countries of critical importance in the war on terrorism.

These incidents also have serious implications when we consider that the periodic release of incarcerated Islamists that run the gamut from moderate democratic reformers to others tied to violent extremist activities is a favorite political tactic employed by incumbent authoritarian regimes in the region. This strategy is generally aimed at easing internal tensions centered in the Islamist opposition over the lack of progress toward political reforms, increased repression and other grievances.

For example, Egypt recently released over 900 members of the radical Gama'a al-Islamiyya, some having spent over 20 years in prison (al-Jazeera, April 12, 2006). Tunisia recently freed over 1,600 members of its own Islamist opposition. Algeria also released over 2,000 imprisoned Islamist activists in a sign of good faith as part of its plan to promote its Charter for Peace and National Reconciliation initiative (al-Jazeera, March 4, 2006).

It is not in the interest of the governments in question to release inmates considered to pose a credible and immediate terrorist threat, given that the incumbent regimes would likely be targeted in due course as they were in the past. Moreover, the release of jailed extremists is generally accompanied by a negotiated pact with former radical leaders who in turn often praise the incumbent government's action as a sign of goodwill while renouncing the use of violence and terrorism.

In fact, it is precisely this process that contributes to the creation of extremist splinter groups headed by emerging radical leaders determined to carry on their war against the hated incumbent regimes or their benefactors in the West.

A number of prominent Islamist radicals, including Ayman al-Zawahiri and Abu Musab al-Zarqawi, spent years in prison in Egypt and Jordan, respectively. By all accounts, both were subjected to harsh conditions that included systematic torture and often humiliating abuses against them and their fellow inmates. Many observers believe that these experiences contributed to their radicalization and that of many of their followers (see Montasser al-Zayat, *The Road to al-Qaeda: The Story of Bin Laden's Right-Hand Man*).

In March, Jordan's penal system was struck with a series of what appeared to be simultaneous and coordinated uprisings in three separate prisons. Rioting inmates in Jwaideh prison took hostage Colonel Saad al-Ajrami, director of the kingdom's prison system, along with a host of security guards. The Jwaideh inmates reportedly took up arms in a demonstration of solidarity with two prisoners incarcerated in Swaqa prison that Jordanian officials link to al-Qaeda, including one convicted for the 2002 assassination of a U.S. diplomat in Amman. They also demanded the immediate release of the would-be Iraqi female suicide bomber who participated in the November 2005 attacks in Amman and protested conditions inside the jail (al-Jazeera, March 2, 2006).

Jordanian officials claim that over 180 radical Islamists, including extremists linked to al-Qaeda, are currently being held at Jwaideh prison (*as-Sharq al-Awsat*, March 3, 2006). After a period of tense negotiations, the 14-hour siege ended peacefully with all of the hostages released unharmed.

According to Judge Ali al-Dhmour, Jordan's Secretary General of the Justice Ministry, rioting inmates at the Jwaideh facility coordinated their planned takeover of the facility with their fellow inmates in other prisons through an elaborate system that included cell phone and internet communications and messages passed along to visiting relatives. Al-Dhmour also raised questions regarding the wisdom of having violent Islamist extremists serve their sentences alongside their known colleagues, essentially ensuring that already tight-knit networks remain cohesive and operational behind bars. He also questioned the logic of placing ordinary criminals together with hardened extremists in the same facilities due to fears that the latter may influence disaffected prisoners (al-Jazeera, March 2, 2006).

Ibrahim Zeid al-Kailani, Jordan's former religious affairs minister, echoes these sentiments. He believes that radical extremists, especially individuals tied to al-Qaeda, should be insulated from other inmates and separated from their known associates in an attempt to weaken networks. He also claims that because many prisoners suffer from depression and frustration, they are more likely to be attracted to radical and violent strains of Islamism (al-Jazeera, March 2, 2006).

In another incident in April, inmates in the Qafqafa prison rose up violently, taking two guards hostage before Jordanian security forces stormed the facility to end the crisis (*al-Sharq al-Awsat*, April 14, 2006).

Rioting inmates took security guards hostage in Afghanistan's notorious Pol-e-Charkhi prison in Kabul in February, the second uprising of its kind in a little over a year in Afghanistan. Apparently, grievances stemming from systematic abuses and poor living conditions boiled over when prison authorities tried to implement a new policy requiring all inmates to wear bright orange uniforms. According to Afghanistan's Deputy Justice Minister Muhammad Qasim Hashemzai, rioting inmates received instructions from outside of the prison via cell phones. It is still unclear how the inmates managed to acquire the cell phones. Afghan security officials claim that 350 out of the approximately 1,000 inmates estimated to have participated in the uprising are linked to al-Qaeda and the Taliban (Azadi Radio, March 6, 2006).

In February 2006, 23 members of al-Qaeda managed to escape from the maximum security Political Security Central Prison in Sanaa, Yemen. Among the escapees included 13 radicals tied to al-Qaeda cells believed to be responsible for the attack against the USS Cole in October 2000 and the strike against the French oil supertanker Limburg in October 2002. A similar escape orchestrated by ranking al-Qaeda members, this time from the Political Security Central Prison in Aden, occurred in 2003 (*Yemen Times*, February 4, 2006).

Initial reports from the scene claimed that the fugitives managed a daring escape by digging a 300-meter long tunnel from their cells to the women's prayer yard at the al-Awkaf Mosque located just outside the prison. Other reports, however, say that the prisoners left from the main entrance of the facility. Considering the high-profile stature of the inmates and the heightened level of security at the facility, it is inconceivable that the escapees could have succeeded without close coordination and assistance from prison staff and others from the outside (*as-Sharq al-Awsat*, March 10, 2006).

Conclusion

As the incidents in Jordan, Afghanistan, and Yemen demonstrate, the activities of convicted terrorists and other radical extremists inside prisons in countries of strategic importance in the war on terrorism should remain of vital concern. It is also worth considering the effect that systematic and indiscriminate torture in penal systems across the region has on creating potential recruits for al-Qaeda and other extremist organizations.

[From Terrorism Monitor, Volume IV, Issue 9]

Al-Qaeda and the Threat to Mass Surface Transportation

Andrew Holt

Originally published on May 4, 2006

The March 2004 attack on commuter trains in Madrid and the three simultaneous bombings on the London underground in July 2005, which collectively killed 243 people, dramatically underscored the acute terrorist threat to mass surface transportation (MST) in the contemporary era. According to the Mineta Transportation Institute (MTI) in San Jose, California, MST was the target of more than 195 terrorist attacks from 1997 through 2000. Of the 84 incidents resulting in fatalities, nearly a quarter involved ten or more deaths. Similarly revealing are statistics provided by the Brookings Institution in Washington, DC, which show that between 1991 and 2001 a full 42 percent of terrorist strikes worldwide were directed against mass transit. The high incidence of attacks against MST reflect both its inherent attractiveness as a "soft" target of opportunity and the problematic nature of safeguarding this particular mode of transportation—both of which are likely to have particular salience to the organizational and operational dynamics of jihadis.

MST and Terrorism

The attractiveness of MST as a terrorist target essentially stems from four factors. First, mass transit systems, by definition, cater to high volumes of passengers who are typically crammed into narrow, confined spaces. Such venues provide a civilian-centric setting of the sort that might yield a substantial body count if decisively struck. Second, MST is designed to move large numbers of people quickly and efficiently, which necessarily means that protective measures must minimize the disruptive impact of security on people who use this mode of transport. This openness, while allowing for passenger convenience, also means that mass transit remains exceptionally susceptible to covert penetration as security officials are largely unable to enact a definitive regimen of entry/exit surveillance (author interviews, security officials, Canberra, Australia, February 2006). Third, because train and subway cars are enclosed, they necessarily serve to amplify resulting shock waves emanating from explosions. Stated differently, bombing these targets does not require the enormous payload—and associated logistical deployment problems—that is typically used to destroy buildings or more open spaces (author interview, Explosive Ordinance Response Team (EORT), Brisbane, Australia, February 2006). Finally, attacks against MST have the potential to affect wider components of a country's critical infrastructure system as in many cases underground urban transit links are also employed to house major power and communication cables. While this is convenient and cost-effective—in the sense that there is no need to dig a lattice of multiple tunnels—such co-location necessarily exacerbates the probability that a single strike will impact across several networks that are vital to a city's overall functioning (Clive Williams, presentation made before the Australian Urban Transit Security Conference, Melbourne, November 14, 2005).

Exacerbating the vulnerability of MST is the problematic nature of instituting concerted safety measures for this particular mode of transport. Three in particular stand out:

- The culture of mass transportation, which frequently works against effective crisis management to mitigate casualties. This is particularly true in terms of issuing an order to shut down the operations of a system, which even in instances when a terrorist attack is not confirmed may be the safest thing to do (comments made by Brian Jenkins during the National Transportation Security Summit, Washington, DC, October 30, 2001).

- Direct and indirect financial considerations:

  a) On a direct level, installing security improvements for mass transit is likely to prove quite expensive. One agency in the U.S., for instance, estimated that introducing intrusion alarms and passive infrared night-imaging sensors would cost a quarter billion dollars. A General Accounting Office (GAO) survey of transit agencies in 2002 similarly found that identified security improvements would exceed $711 million (General Accounting Office Report GAO-02-1075T, September 18, 2002). Unlike aviation transportation, these costs cannot be offset through add-ons to standing fares (which could amount to between two and four dollars per ticket) without putting it beyond the range of the paying public.

b) Indirectly, problems arise out of the competitive nature of MST, which as noted above, resides in its accessibility and convenience. To retain this comparative advantage and minimize the associated risk of people choosing to travel by alternative means (such as cars), transit authorities must therefore offer an efficient and quality service. Security measures that limit accessibility and create delays obviously do not satisfy this requirement (author interviews, transit and security officials, Canberra, Australia, February 2006).

- Streamlining collaboration between the numerous agencies and departments tasked with safeguarding MST from terrorism and other crimes. Depending on the state concerned, these parties could include police and intelligence authorities, transportation and government officials, owner-operators and contract security companies. Frequently, these various actors transcend national/federal, state and local jurisdictions creating a mosaic of stakeholders with their own interests, priorities and concerns. Effective coordination is, thus, often a major problem, particularly in terms of information dissemination, early response and overall consequence management.

MST and the Evolving Nature of the al-Qaeda Network

In the years since 9/11, al-Qaeda's functional latitude to emphasize assaults against hard targets has progressively atrophied due to setbacks it has suffered in the context of the global war on terrorism. More specifically, because the group is no longer able to exert clear command and control over international attacks, it has necessarily been required to switch prioritization away from centrally-controlled strategic assaults executed by an inner core of jihadist activists toward more tactically-oriented strikes undertaken by affiliated cells (and sometimes individuals) as and when opportunities arise. This forced organizational devolution has been mirrored in an operational pattern that gives overwhelming precedence to attacks that are cheap, easy to execute, offer a high probability of success and whose consequences can be accurately predicted. The focus has, therefore, tended to be on soft, civilian-centric venues that can be hit recurrently with minimal outside support and logistical assistance but that still retain a realistic potential to result in a large number of casualties and accompanying social disruption.

Surface transportation represents an ideal venue for these types of attacks. As noted, trains, buses and metro systems, simply by virtue of their openness and large user-base, are soft targets in the full sense of the term, offering terrorists a high degree of anonymity, few obstacles to movement and a highly visible victim set that can be decisively struck with minimal resources. In short, MST makes for a good "killing field," inflicting the type of collective punishment that can be readily levered to build morale, mobilize additional recruits and supporters and positively sway "fence sitters." Moreover, because of their greater ease of management, strikes against surface transportation fit well with the operational capabilities of local affiliates—as was demonstrated so graphically in Madrid and London.

Mitigation Measures

How can MST be safeguarded from terrorist attacks? In the short term, there are several pragmatic, cost-effective measures that could be taken, including:

- Removing all luggage lockers and trash cans from stations;
- Augmenting and randomizing police and security patrols;
- Regulating vehicular access to potentially sensitive areas (such as loading docks that may be co-located within station perimeters);
- Conducting regular table top exercises and "real-life" simulations to develop, test and refine emergency drill procedures;
- Paying greater attention to security at suburban stations, which often represent highly vulnerable "jump-off" points for covert entry into MST systems and perpetrating attacks further "down the line";

- Retrofitting trains to help dissipate bomb blasts;
- Ensuring that an effective inter-agency crisis communication structure is not only in place but is also well understood and institutionalized by all parties concerned;
- Emphasizing the need for passengers to be aware of their surroundings and attuned to the critical importance of quickly reporting anything out of the ordinary.

Over the longer term, new generation inspection devices might be considered such as fused, multi-threat people screening portals, integrated baggage checks and "smart" video surveillance systems that are capable of facial recognition. Investments in these types of technologies, however, must always be considered in light of what can be reasonably achieved in terms of safeguarding MST and at what expense. Attempting to institute 100 percent security is neither possible nor feasible given the nature and purpose of mass surface transport and the highly open environment in which it operates. Rather, the objective should be the development of a set of counter-terrorist tools to manage risks within acceptable boundaries—measured in relation to both passenger convenience and overall running costs.

[From Terrorism Monitor, Volume IV, Issue 9]

Part II

The Middle East and Africa

Iraq

The Presence of Saudi Nationals in the Iraqi Insurgency

Christopher Boucek

Originally published on April 20, 2006

This article is based upon extensive research with knowledgeable sources that dealt with the author only on the strict condition of anonymity and non-attribution.

It is widely recognized that Saudi nationals are currently participating in the Iraqi insurgency and have been involved in operations that have targeted the U.S.-led coalition force, aspects of the nascent Iraqi security forces, and segments of Iraq's majority Shiite population. The presence of Saudis in Iraq is deeply troubling not just for the future viability of Iraq, but also for the future security of Saudi Arabia and the smaller Persian Gulf monarchies.

Iraq today is the primary jihadi venue. For the first time in recent history, the jihadi movement is centered in the Arab heartland, engaged in what many in the movement interpret as a struggle for a pivotal Arab country. Moreover, Iraq is a target-rich country for those inclined to stage attacks against the U.S.-led coalition military presence. Attackers in Iraq stand a better chance of escaping to fight again due to the severely poor security situation; they also need not fear the ubiquitous security services that exist elsewhere in the Arab and Muslim world. Iraq is also emblematic of a larger jihadi project, the successes of which many in the movement seek to export back to their home countries. Iraq, therefore, is unlike Afghanistan, which as a non-Arab country never quite carried the urgency and fervor of those presently active in Iraq.

The Saudi government is extremely concerned by the presence of jihadi Saudi nationals in Iraq. It is feared that the return of Saudi jihadis to Saudi Arabia will revitalize what has become a waning domestic insurgency. These fighters not only have learned new techniques, but may also alter the insurgent landscape in Saudi Arabia by introducing techniques, methods, and operations that heretofore have not existed in the Kingdom.

To their credit, Saudi authorities have taken significant measures to combat this trend. The Saudi government has launched a multi-pronged strategy comprised of improvement of border security along the Saudi-Iraqi frontier, an uncompromising and thorough investigative monitoring program of people who have spent time in Iraq, a concerted assault on Saudi Arabia's homegrown indigenous terrorists and significant cooperation with foreign intelligence organizations (including a major joint program with their U.S. counterparts).

A major issue for Iraqi security forces and their Saudi counterparts is that nomadic Bedouin tribes (that have previously been suspected of supporting the insurgency) exist on both sides of the Iraq-Saudi border. These tribes frequently move throughout the vast and unpopulated southern Iraqi desert and maintain clan ties in both Iraq and Saudi Arabia. Moreover, these elements intimately know the area and are well versed in avoiding contact with security forces. As such, it is possible that they are assisting in the movement of fighters into Iraq.

Saudi al-Qaeda leader Saleh al-Oufi wrote in support of Saudi jihadis in Iraq in the July 8, 2004 issue of the *Voice of Jihad* online magazine, strengthening suspicions that al-Oufi himself had fought in the strife-torn country. Saudi Islamic militants have also claimed operations such as the assassination of U.S. contractor Paul Johnson and the assault on the U.S. Consulate in Jeddah in the name of the "Fallujah Brigades," demonstrating—at the very least—a symbolic linkage between Saudi and Iraqi insurgents. In April 2005, Saudi national Hadi bin Mubarak Qahtani killed himself in a suicide operation near al-Qaim, Iraq. According to *The Washington Post*, "Five other Qahtanis have been reported killed in Iraq, including Muhammed bin Aedh Ghadif Qahtani, a captain in the Saudi National Guard who allegedly used his guard identification badge to help gain entry into Iraq when he was stopped for questioning."

On March 2, 2006, an al-Qaeda operative identified as Abdullah Salih al-Harbi was captured by Iraqi border guards attempting to cross the Saudi border near Samawah. Reports at the time indicated that he confessed during his interrogation to participating in the al-Qaeda terrorist assault on the massive Abqaiq Saudi oil facility (Sadoun Jabery, spokesman for the southwestern command of the Iraqi border police, March 3, 2006).

Saudi security agencies have taken major steps to monitor possible travel to Iraq and other jihadi locales. It has emerged that some Saudis have sought to hide their travel to Iraq by reporting their passports stolen, thus erasing any consular evidence of either travel to Iraq or Syria, widely seen as the most important way station for those en route to Iraq. In an effort to end this practice, the Saudi government no longer issues replacement travel documents with "no questions asked." Saudis that have presented themselves at embassies abroad claiming either theft or loss of their passports are now subjected to a rigorous investigation upon their return to the Kingdom (Nawaf Obaid and Anthony Cordesman, "Saudi Militants in Iraq: Assessment and Kingdom's Response," September 19, 2005).

A Saudi intelligence agency interrogation revealed that a number of Yemenis served as facilitators for Saudis going to Iraq. The same report summary noted that Syria was the main point of entry into Iraq, largely due to successful Saudi efforts to increase security on the Iraqi frontier (Nawaf Obaid and Anthony Cordesman, "Saudi Militants in Iraq: Assessment and Kingdom's Response," September 19, 2005). There exists a well-worn route into Iraq, from recruitment and indoctrination in Saudi Arabia to hand-off to facilitators in Syria prior to crossing the Iraqi border. Saudi support for the Iraqi insurgency has also included the issuance of a fatwa in 2004 by over two dozen senior Saudi Ulama, including the influential former dissident Salman al-Awda, endorsing Saudi and Muslim support of the insurgency (http://www.islamtoday.net, November 5, 2004; al-Jazeera, November 6, 2004).

The Saudi National Security Assessment Project (an independent consultancy that works closely with the Saudi government on security and oil issues) has produced some original analysis on the subject of Saudi nationals fighting in Iraq (Nawaf Obaid and Anthony Cordesman, "Saudi Militants in Iraq: Assessment and Kingdom's Response," September 19, 2005). Among the findings, the Project has noted that Saudis—and other Persian Gulf nationals—often travel with large sums of cash. This fact makes them especially sought after and recruiting affluent Saudis has been perceived by Iraqi insurgent leaders as a quick method to finance terrorist operations. Furthermore, private intelligence reports have intimated that the Saudis are so valued by insurgents that they have been sold and traded by insurgent "brokers" in Iraq.

While the true number of Saudis fighting in Iraq may never be known, there have been unsubstantiated reports that the number of Saudis that have perished in the insurgency have been exaggerated in a bid to boost recruitment. A March 2005 Israeli report, "Arab Volunteers Killed in Iraq: An Analysis," that has been subjected to wide criticism, claims that 94 (or 61 percent of) insurgents killed in a six month period were identified as Saudis, while 70 percent of suicide bombers in Iraq were Saudi (http://www.e-prism.org/images/PRISM_no_1_vol_3_-_Arabs_killed_in_Iraq.pdf).

A separate confidential U.S. report has identified a Saudi participation rate in excess of 50 percent, while a jihadi internet forum (http://www.qal3ah.net) has stated that Saudis comprise 44 percent of insurgents. According to Nawaf Obaid, however, the Saudi government-controlled press has only acknowledged 47 Saudis that have been identified as participating in the insurgency. These figures, however, have not been independently verified or confirmed (Nawaf Obaid and Anthony Cordesman, "Saudi Militants in Iraq: Assessment and Kingdom's Response," November 6, 2004).

It is extremely worrying that, according to a Saudi national security source, of those Saudis that have been detained and questioned upon their return from Iraq, approximately 80 percent were unknown to the security services (Nawaf Obaid and Anthony Cordesman, "Saudi Militants in Iraq: Assessment and Kingdom's Response," November 6, 2004). This fact—if true—is concerning as it indicates that the Saudi intelligence and security services may not have as good a handle on the issue as they may otherwise attempt to portray.

In the end, this may well be a significant contributor to greater violence and domestic insurgency in Saudi Arabia. Of course, returning jihadis will not simply abandon their worldview and objectives. Moreover, the Iraq war and the U.S. presence in Iraq and Afghanistan have polarized a large segment of the Saudi population. Some senior Saudi sources have even sought to blame the domestic terrorist struggle against al-Qaeda on the situation in Iraq. It is unknown what, if any effect, disaffection with the ruling family and anger over the rampant corruption has had on the motivations of Saudi nationals to travel to Iraq, to engage in terrorism, and learn skills and gain experiences that they can eventually bring back to the Kingdom.

In large part, the problem is greater for the Saudi government than the U.S. military and its Iraqi partners. The overarching question is what the Saudi government will do to neutralize Saudi fighters in Iraq once they have returned as technically-adept jihadis and battle-hardened fighters. At that point, with the fate of the Kingdom potentially in the balance, many analysts fear that the problem of returning Saudi jihadis may have moved well past any comfortable or easily-achievable solutions.

[From Terrorism Monitor, Volume IV, Issue 8]

A Profile of al-Qaeda's New Leader in Iraq: Abu Ayyub al-Masri

Abdul Hameed Bakier

Originally published on June 20, 2006

It did not take al-Qaeda in Iraq long to name the successor to Abu Musab al-Zarqawi, contrary to speculation that the killing of al-Zarqawi would disrupt al-Qaeda's operations. In a defiant spirit, al-Qaeda announced the name of the man it appointed to the helm of its operations in Iraq less than a week after the death of al-Zarqawi: Abu Hamza al-Muhajir, who the U.S. government says is Sheikh Abu Ayyub al-Masri (al-Jazeera, June 15, 2006).

Al-Masri, an Egyptian in his 40's, has been one of al-Zawahiri's disciples since 1982 and lived in Sudan until 1995. From there, he moved to Pakistan and stayed with the Osama bin Zaid Mosque group in Peshawar; the mosque, apparently, is frequented by extremists. In 1999, al-Masri went to Afghanistan and trained at the al-Farouq camp where he met al-Zarqawi. Al-Masri became an expert in making roadside bombs and explosives. In 2001, al-Masri traveled to Iraq and worked with Ansar al-Islam in the north. Later, he joined al-Qaeda and became very close to al-Zarqawi, directing suicide bombers from Fallujah (al-Arabiya, June 12, 2006).

Although al-Masri is unknown to many observers, what little is known suggests that in the last three years he was in charge of the intelligence operations for al-Qaeda in Iraq and was mainly responsible for soliciting new recruits and insurgent groups to al-Qaeda's corral. To fulfill this task, he traveled, using fake names, to countries all over the Middle East and North Africa. Also, being well educated in Sharia law, al-Masri was tasked with receiving and teaching the Salafi-Jihadist ideology to new recruits. At one stage, he was based in al-Qaim, 380 kilometers northwest of Baghdad (al-Arabiya, June 12, 2006).

In his first communiqué on June 13, al-Masri vowed to revenge the killing of al-Zarqawi and threatened to punish the United States and its allies, saying the fortresses in the green area would not protect them. Furthermore, al-Masri pledged to wage formidable battles in the coming days against the U.S. "crusaders" and the Iraqi "apostates" and proselytes collaborating with them. He also sent a strong warning to Shiites, calling them the blasphemous grandchildren of Ibn al-Alqami—the Shiite minister in the last Islamic regime that ruled Iraq who betrayed the Caliph—promising to carry through what al-Zarqawi started. The historic reference to Shiites indicates deep-seated animosity toward them and the continuity of al-Qaeda's endeavors to fuel sectarian violence and, consequently, to induce civil war in Iraq. In the same statement, al-Masri pledged allegiance to Osama bin Laden, testifying that al-Qaeda soldiers in Iraq were awaiting bin Laden's orders (al-Arabiya, June 13, 2006).

Although not much information is known about al-Masri, he sounds just as violent, if not more violent, than his predecessor. The one letter he released on the internet in 2004, titled "The Samiri of our Age," reaffirms his adherence to the Salafi-Jihadist extremist ideology. In this 2004 letter, al-Masri exhibits a strong grasp of the Quran and Quranic teachings. He cites a verse from the Quran that tells the story of the Jew (Samiri) who went against the will and teachings of the Prophet Moses and carved a calf from gold to worship instead of God. God bestowed on the renegade Jew wisdom and grace, but Samiri showed ingratitude and antagonism toward God and the Prophet Moses. Accordingly, al-Masri talked about today's Islamic scholars and clergymen who have learned the true word of God that was revealed to Prophet Muhammad, yet flatter political leaders for a few dinars and dirhams. In al-Masri's opinion, today's leaders are materialists and not true adherents of Islam. He compares these "bad Muslims" with Samiri, in the verse he cites, and calls them the Samiris of our age.

Additionally, in his letter he accuses moderate Muslims, or the non-Salafis, of being more like Samiri and far more astray than Jews. His accusations against moderate Muslims demonstrate his likely fanaticism and potential for violence. He cites additional verses to consolidate his points, calling upon Muslims to declare an Islamic state according to the Prophet Muhammad's teachings; only then, according to al-Masri, will Muslims be victorious (the entire document can be found at: http://www.alokab.com/quran/details.php?id=P455_0_2_0_C).

The connotation of al-Masri's letter is superficial in Islamic ideology and does not necessarily illustrate deep understanding of Islamic doctrine. Regardless of al-Masri's background as an ideologue tasked with non-violent activities during al-Zarqawi's tenure, his communiqué and letter reveal a very extreme, fanatical mindset. Significantly, being an Egyptian and one of al-Zawahiri's disciples—or the so-called Egyptian Mafia composed of Egyptian nationals aligned with al-Zawahiri—al-Masri could be prone to target Iraqis, Shiite and Sunni government forces, as opposed to bin Laden's Saudi mafia—Saudi nationals—whose priority is U.S. and Western targets.

[From Terrorism Focus, Volume III, Issue 24]

The Lord of the Marshes Takes a Mediating Role in Iraq

Lydia Khalil

Originally published on August 22, 2006

The "Lord of the Marshes" is a name that evokes a mythic image of one of Iraq's most illustrious resistance fighters. Abd Karim al-Mahmud Muhamedawi, also known as Abu Hatem, is a legendary figure inside Iraq but is little known to the outside world. A famed guerrilla leader from the southern marshlands, he is the only indigenous resistance fighter, aside from the Kurds, who successfully fought against Saddam's forces. He formed and led Hezbollah (unrelated to Lebanon's Hezbollah), a militia comprised of Shiite tribal members from the Iraqi marshlands. A key figure during the political transition after the fall of Saddam, he lent credibility to the oft-criticized government of mostly exile leaders. Recently, Abu Hatem is focusing on local politics in southern Iraq, playing a mediating role between various Shiite factions.

Abu Hatem was born in 1958 in Amarrah into the Albu Mohamed tribe prominent in the marshlands. He served in the Iraqi army as a non-commissioned officer, and although he was a well respected leader in the military, was later jailed in 1980 by the regime probably for that very reason. He spent seven years in the Abu Ghraib prison; after his release, he initiated resistance activities, forming Hezbollah, a guerrilla group mostly composed of his fellow tribal members in the marshlands. With anywhere from 1,000 to 8,000 mobilized fighters at any given time, Hezbollah fought a "War of the Fleas" against Saddam's forces, using the marsh reeds as cover and shelter. Hezbollah forces were armed with mortars, rocket propelled grenades and machine guns. They participated in arms smuggling, but they were usually low on ammunition, had almost no money and lived off of the marshlands. Hezbollah forces were continually on the move, irritating and foiling the Iraqi army anytime they entered into the marshlands (*Middle East Times*, June 30, 2003). In 1997, Abu Hatem was nearly killed by Iraqi forces when he was ambushed while traveling by car to Maimuna in southern Iraq. Frustrated by their inability to capture Abu Hatem and neutralize Hezbollah, Saddam ordered the marshes be drained, destroying a culture and a way of life in the process. Although Hezbollah no longer had the marshes as natural cover, they continued their campaign. Instead of hiding out in the marsh reeds, they dug bunkers in the dried up water courses.

Abu Hatem's "Party of God" militia is often mistakenly referred to as a branch of the better known Lebanese organization sponsored by Iran. The two organizations, however, are wholly unrelated and Iraqi Hezbollah was never sponsored by Iran or any other country. It is very likely, however, that it received funding from U.S. and British intelligence agencies. Given Abu Hatem's distaste for foreign interference and special distrust of Iran and its other Iraqi sponsors, Iraqi Hezbollah and Abu Hatem are against Iran's interference in Iraqi affairs. His people had always protected Shalamja, a border area under his control, against infiltration by Iran (author interview with an advisor to Abu Hatem, August 2006).

During the 2003 Gulf War, Amarrah, Abu Hatem's hometown, was the only city to liberate itself before coalition forces entered the area. Abu Hatem, his tribal followers and Hezbollah continue to exercise considerable influence in Amarrah. Abu Hatem is largely responsible for keeping the peace in this southern corner of Iraq. His followers are mainly from the marsh areas, although he has considerable following in Nasiriyah and Basra. He commands respect among many Iraqi groups. He once temporarily resigned his post in the interim government to protest against the Fallujah siege and he was courted by Ahmed Chalabi to lend credibility to his political coalition. Abu Hatem has also played a leading role in quelling recent intra-Shiite fighting in Basra.

Abu Hatem's Hezbollah militia is unlike other Shiite militias in Iraq in that Abu Hatem no longer projects himself as a militia leader. When asked if he had an army of 8,000 men, he answered, "I have just this book and pen," pointing to the table in front of him. His militia is no longer a standing force, but they, and members of the Albu Mohamed tribe, can be mobilized by him at a moment's notice. He has tried to integrate his forces into the security services and cooperated with British forces in the area, despite occasional incidents. His followers are largely responsible for securing the Maysan Province (Terrence Kelly, August 2005). Hezbollah is not as strong in number as SCIRI's Badr Corps or Moqtada al-Sadr's Mahdi Army, nor are they as active. Abu Hatem, however, has served as a conduit to al-Sadr before he was active in politics and has influence over many of Moqtada al-Sadr's followers and militia members in Sadr City. Many of the Albu Mohamed tribal members who left the marshes after they were drained relocated to Sadr City and came to also support al-Sadr.

Although Abu Hatem inspires respect among most, he is not free from controversy. His standing as the region's strongman has brought accusations of gangsterism by some in the area. There was a warrant issued for his arrest in 2004 for allegedly ordering the shooting of Majar al-Kabir's police chief after he criticized Abu Hatem. No action was taken on the arrest warrant, and many believe this was because police officers and civil authorities in the area are either Hezbollah members or receive money and favors from Abu Hatem (*Middle East Times*, June 30, 2003). Abu Hatem also has considerable influence over Iraq's new minister of interior, Jawad Bolani. Bolani once served as Abu Hatem's deputy and holds Abu Hatem in high esteem. He often consults Abu Hatem regarding political and security matters and credits Abu Hatem with securing him the position. Abu Hatem's relationship with Bolani, however, only gives him sway over the minister, not the ministry. Bolani has had trouble reining in the unwieldy Interior Ministry which is compromised of mostly SCIRI followers (author interview with an advisor to Abu Hatem, August 2006). SCIRI, along with the Da'wa party, are Abu Hatem's and Hezbollah's main political rivals. He criticizes their uncontrolled militias that are fomenting civil strife and believes that they are doing Iran's bidding in Iraq. He is also critical of SCIRI's plans for a nine province southern region, knowing that his influence would be overtaken by the more powerful Shiite forces if that was to occur (*al-Hayat*, June 2, 2005).

While he has a good working relationship with British troops in his area and cooperated with the coalition's political plan, he has advocated an early end to the occupation and wants more security responsibilities placed into the hands of Iraqis. He has also resisted disarmament by coalition forces. In late 2003, there were clashes between residents of Majar al-Kabir and British troops, and six soldiers were killed. The incident occurred because the British soldiers insisted on trying to disarm the population; the tribesmen saw this as a dishonor to render them defenseless even after they had initially cooperated with British troops. Afterwards, Abu Hatem played a key role in dispersing tensions following the clash (*Middle East Times*, June 30, 2003).

Abu Hatem is no longer a member of parliament since Chalabi's coalition, of which he was a member, did not receive enough votes for a parliamentary representation. He is focusing on local politics, heading up the Council of Notables, a senate-like civic council made up of representatives from Maysan, Nasiriyah and Basra. Now that Abu Hatem is not working on the national level, he is concentrating more on local issues. As intra-Shiite and sectarian violence continues inside Iraq, Abu Hatem will be able to play more of a mediating role in the southern region and serve as a foil against certain Shiite political militias, such as the Badr Corps and the Mahdi Army, that have been responsible for the recent violence.

[From Terrorism Focus, Volume III, Issue 33]

Kurds

Kurdish Officials Provide Information on al-Qaeda Operatives in Custody

Lydia Khalil

Originally published on June 6, 2006

It is widely acknowledged that northern Iraq has escaped the chaos and violence wrought by the Iraqi insurgency, but this does not mean that al-Qaeda and affiliated groups have not attempted to operate in the Kurdish Regional Government's (KRG) territory. Many al-Qaeda members have been arrested before carrying through their operations and are still held in Kurdish jails. Their presence in Kurdish custody, however, is not widely known or acknowledged. Just this past month, three al-Qaeda members, who were arrested in northern Iraq, were publicly acknowledged as being held by the KRG. The high profile arrests (two of the members were on the most wanted list) attest to the capability of Kurdish security forces, made up largely of former peshmerga, under KRG command. The last attack in KRG territory was over a year ago in May 2005 when terrorists targeted a police training center.

The Arabic newspaper *Asharq al-Awsat* recently managed to secure an interview with Abdullah al-Ramiyan and Mohammed al-Rashudi, two al-Qaeda members in Kurdish custody who are on Saudi Arabia's list of 36 most wanted terrorists. They spoke of their arrest and life in Kurdish prison in the presence of Kurdish security officials. According to Lieutenant Artush, a senior Kurdish security official responsible for their custody, the two men confessed that they had traveled to Iraq to conduct terrorist operations. The two men were without identification and although they had given fake names at the border, their cover was blown by their undisguised foreign accents.

On one occasion, al-Ramiyan stated he had traveled to Kurdistan by first leaving Saudi Arabia, traveling to Syria, then Turkey and entering through the Ibrahim al-Khalil pass to visit Iraqi Kurdistan as a tourist. On another occasion, he changed his story and said he had traveled to Iraq only to visit relatives (*Asharq al-Awsat*, May 30, 2006).

It is unclear how the suspects have been treated in Kurdish jails. The prisoners were first interrogated while in solitary confinement, but were then transferred to general quarters. Al-Ramiyan denied being abused or tortured by Kurdish security officials, but also said that his family visited him four times since he had been in jail, a claim denied by Artush who said inmates received no visitors (*Asharq al-Awsat*, May 30, 2006).

The interview with al-Rashudi did not reveal much information about his arrest or experience under Kurdish custody, but he indicated that one of the benefits was that he learned to speak Kurdish and eat Kurdish food. It is unclear why Kurdish officials did not extradite the two men to Saudi Arabia or central Baghdad. Most likely, Kurdish officials wanted to extract more information from the suspects and determine their fate themselves.

Not all al-Qaeda suspects have remained in Kurdish custody. One other al-Qaeda terrorist arrested by Kurdish officials was recently transferred to U.S. custody. Said Saad Said al-Qarni (also known as Abu Qatiba), was a former student of Imam Mohammed bin Saud in Riyadh. He was detained by Kurdish police in Mosul last year after a failed attempt to blow up the Kurdistan Democratic Party headquarters. Abu Qatiba also traveled through Syria to enter Iraq. According to the investigation, Abu Qatiba met an Iraqi named Abu Mohammed and stayed with him and four others. He was chosen to carry out the attack in Mosul and entered northern Iraq on forged documents (*Asharq al-Awsat*, June 1, 2006).

Thus far, none of the al-Qaeda members in custody have yet to stand trial. The Kurdish minister of state for the interior, Abdul Karim Sinjari, explained that they have not stood trial because anti-terrorism laws have yet to be approved by the regional assembly (*Asharq al-Awsat*, May 30, 2006). Yet for Kurdistan, the focus has been more on arrests and anti-terrorism measures through intelligence and interrogation rather than on legislating anti-terrorism laws.

Kurdish security officials rely on the vigilance of the security forces at the border and the cooperation of ordinary Kurdish citizens. Minister Sinjari has said that many people maintain direct contacts with Kurdish police and inform them of any foreigners or unknown individuals in the area. He even related that one woman informed the police that her husband participated in a terrorist attack saying, "It is best I hand over my husband to the police than for 50 women to become widows" (*Asharq al-Awsat*, May 30, 2006).

In a recent interview, Nechirvan Barzani, prime minister of the Kurdish region, extolled the cooperation and cohesion between Kurdish citizens and the security forces. He cited a similar story, but this time it was a mother who turned in her son. Clearly, Kurdish officials are building upon the myth of close citizen-to-security cooperation as a means to deter would-be terrorists (*Asharq al-Awsat*, June 3, 2006).

Why is there such close cooperation with the security services, and could this offer a lesson for other regions in Iraq? According to Barzani, Kurdish citizens have a direct stake in maintaining stability in the region. Establishing the KRG and building Kurdistan's reputation over the past 10 years has been a unified effort. Although they may have grievances with their government as in other regions of Iraq, Kurdish citizens would rather have security and stability through the security services than establish alternative structures.

[From Terrorism Focus, Volume III, Issue 22]

Mount Qandil: A Safe Haven for Kurdish Militants – Part 1

James Brandon

Originally published on September 8, 2006

The following information and assessments are based upon the author's first-hand observations from his March 2006 visit to Kurdish camps on Mount Qandil.

In recent months, Turkey has renewed its threats to enter Iraqi Kurdistan to attack the Kurdistan Workers Party (PKK). Any Turkish attack would focus on the PKK's main base, or series of camps, in the foothills of Mount Qandil (or Kandeel), a 3,500 meter mountain that straddles the Iranian border some 100 kilometers from the Turkish frontier. In August, Mount Qandil was the subject of Iranian artillery attacks as Tehran targeted camps belonging to both the PKK and its Iranian counterpart, the Party for Freedom and Life in Kurdistan (PJAK) (for an in-depth portrait of PJAK, see *Terrorism Monitor*, June 15, 2006). Any attempt by Turkey and Iran to attack the Kurds in northern Iraq will likely involve operations on this strategic mountain.

Geography

Mount Qandil is located on the Iranian border. The area controlled by the PKK is on the mountain's western and southern side where a series of winding valleys fan out toward Lake Dukan. The PKK controls an approximately 50 square kilometer area that also contains around a dozen Kurdish villages. The mountain's sprawling 3,500 meter high summit, a jumble of interlocking peaks and plateaus, is snow-covered for much of the year. The bulk of Mount Qandil itself is in Iranian territory. The southern slopes of Mount Qandil, within PKK-held territory, are largely occupied by PJAK. A four mile-wide sparsely wooded valley separates the PJAK camps from several small Iranian military bases sited on mountain tops facing Qandil.

The main PKK camp is approached up a winding, well-maintained asphalt road that passes over steep valleys. There are at least two simple PKK checkpoints on this road before the road crosses two passes and reaches the PKK base camp. A mud track then leads up

to the main PKK bases. PJAK's camps are reached by a separate mud
track. Cows and sheep grazing along the roads leading to both camps
indicate that the area is not mined and the few barbed wire fences on
the mountain are to stop livestock rather than troops. Where the road
switchbacks up steep inclines, however, there are indications that the
cliffside is rigged with explosives so that rockfalls can be remotely
triggered. Where the hillsides are steep the terrain is rocky, but in the
valley there are fields and fruit trees. Further up the mountain there are
deciduous forests.

Facilities, Weapons and Communications

    Most PKK buildings on Qandil are traditional Kurdish mud
and stone houses. Some larger buildings are built of pre-fabricated steel
or concrete blocks. There is also a PKK cemetery with approximately
30 graves. The PKK has several petrol-powered generators; electricity
consumption, however, is very low. Buildings and tents are often lit by
oil lamps and heated in winter by oil stoves. There is one simple hospital
at the PKK base camp, partially staffed by Kurds educated in Western
Europe. The hospital, which is composed of two long, low huts made
of concrete breeze blocks, offers only the most basic medical facilities.
    Communication within the camp is by a mix of shortwave
radio and Thuraya satellite phone, neither of which appears entirely
reliable. As PJAK and the PKK are separated by the high mountain
ridges, radio communication between the two is patchy. On parts of
the mountain it is possible to receive a weak signal on Korek, the main
Kurdish cell phone operator. The PKK also have internet access on
several computers through satellite uplinks. Travel within the camp is
mainly by foot. Donkeys and mules are also used to transport food
and provisions up and down the mountain. The PKK also have some
4x4 jeeps that are mainly used for traveling outside the base. Food is
brought in from the nearby town of Raniya.
    The PKK's weapons are mainly basic and are often of
considerable vintage. The standard weapon is the AK-47 assault rifle. In
the Qandil camps, there is little visible evidence of any more high-tech or
modern equipment. PKK publicity photographs, however, show Soviet-
era anti-aircraft guns, RPGs and heavy machine guns. PKK members are
often unarmed in camp and it is unclear if there are enough AK-47s to

go around. There was no obvious sign of high-end guerrilla equipment such as sniper rifles or night-vision goggles. There are some guard dogs kept at outlying PKK encampments on Mount Qandil.

History of the Camp

The precise history of Kurdish militant activity on Mount Qandil is unclear but the presence of old, traditional Kurdish villages within PKK territory suggests that Mount Qandil mostly escaped Saddam Hussein's campaigns against the Kurds. In 1988, Jalal Talabani's Patriotic Union of Kurdistan (PUK) had their main guerrilla headquarters nearby which may have encompassed Qandil [1]. Turkish Kurdish militants were active in Iraq from the mid-1980s, but the PKK first came to the region in substantial numbers in 1991. During the 1980s, the PKK were mainly funded by Syria and based in Lebanon's Bekaa valley. The PKK first moved to Qandil after PKK leader Abdullah Ocalan declared a cease-fire after his arrest in 1999 and then in a second wave when Syrian sponsorship of the PKK formally ended in 2000. Mount Qandil was from its inception a PKK retreat rather than part of an offensive strategy.

The PKK's decision to settle in Qandil may have been inspired by the actions of the Kurdish Islamic groups Komala and Jund al-Islam, which by the mid-1990s were starting to coalesce around Halabja where—with Iranian help—they gradually established a shifting zone of control in a dozen villages. Like Mount Qandil, these areas were also mountainous, inaccessible and nestled tightly against the porous Iranian border. The presence of these Kurdish Islamist camps (eventually ruled by Ansar al-Islam) meant that a rigid ideological separation developed among non-Iraqi Kurds; the religious went to Halabja and the secular moved to Qandil [2].

In summer 2003, the U.S. Army surrounded Mount Qandil and established checkpoints on the roads leading to the mountain [3]. The Coalition Provisional Authority refurbished small Saddam-era forts on some of the mountain's approach roads that are now manned by small PUK peshmerga detachments. These men do not interfere with the operations of the PKK or PJAK and their main aim appears to be to prevent non-Kurds from reaching the camps.

Numbers of Fighters and the Role of the Camp

According to their own estimates, the number of PKK fighters in Qandil is around 3,000 [4]. The Turkish government estimates that there are up to 5,000 PKK members in the whole of northern Iraq [5]. The constant migration of people from Qandil makes an exact figure impossible and there is some overlap between PJAK and PKK fighters. Many of the camp's long-term residents are Syrian Kurds who are unable to return to their homeland [6]. The quality of PKK recruits on Qandil compares unfavorably to those of PJAK, the PKK's more urbanized Iranian equivalent. While PJAK's members are young, motivated and highly educated, PKK members on Mount Qandil are largely older, less educated and often from very rural backgrounds.

The PKK operates Mount Qandil more as a mini-state rather than a simple "training camp." While weapons training does take place and forms an important part of training for new recruits, the PKK puts great emphasis on ideological training [7]. Education in Kurdish history, culture and politics aims to create dedication to the Kurdish cause alongside loyalty to Abdullah Ocalan. Yet at the same time, many PKK members are middle-aged and have been in the camp since 1999, or even earlier. The camp is purposely situated far from the frontlines and its primary role today is to act as a safe haven for Kurds from Turkey and further afield. The sense of lethargy that pervades the camp partly comes from the fact that the PKK's leader is still Abdullah Ocalan who, despite being in prison, aims to micro-manage the movement. "The PKK are lost; they are on their mountain and they don't have a clue about where their movement is going," said Peshwaz Faizulla, editor of *Hawlati*, the largest independent newspaper in Iraqi Kurdistan.

Notes
1. Human Rights Watch, "The Anfal Campaign against the Kurds," (New York, 1993), http://hrw.org/reports/1993/iraqanfal/ANFAL3.htm.
2. Author interviews with members of Komala and the Islamic Union of Kurdistan, March 2006.
3. Author interview with Akif Zagros, member of PJAK leadership council, PJAK Camp, Mount Qandil, Iraqi Kurdistan, March 21.
4. Interviews with PKK members, March 20-22, 2006, Mount Qandil.

5. See for example:
http://www.mfa.gov.tr/MFA/ForeignPolicy/MainIssues/Terrorism/
PKK_KONGRA_GEL.htm.
6. Interviews with PKK members, March 20-22, 2006, Mount Qandil.
7. Author interview with Assad Abdul Rahman Chaderchi, member
of PKK leadership council, PKK base camp, Mount Qandil, Iraqi
Kurdistan, March 22.
8. Author interviews, March 2006, Sulaimaniya.

[From Terrorism Monitor, Volume IV, Issue 17]

Mount Qandil: A Safe Haven for Kurdish Militants – Part 2

James Brandon

Originally published on September 21, 2006

The following information and assessments are based upon the author's first-hand observations from his March 2006 visit to Kurdish camps on Mount Qandil.

Since coming to Mount Qandil, the PKK has undergone a series of ideological evolutions. As a result, camp politics have become highly factionalized leading to often apparently contradictory statements being issued by rival leaders at various times. In April 2002, the PKK changed its name to the Kurdistan Freedom and Democracy Congress (KADEK). KADEK announced a commitment to peaceful methods but said that the group's armed wing would retain its weapons for self-defense. In autumn 2003, KADEK/PKK was renamed Kongra-Gel, which claimed to be a grouping of non-violent Turkish Kurdish organizations. During this process, PKK veterans Cemil Bayik and Murat Karayilan emerged as the most powerful leaders in Qandil. These changes had outward effects. The U.S. State Department, however, updated its list of terrorist organizations to include first KADEK and then Kongra-Gel in January 2004. Kongra-Gel's armed wing, the People's Defense Force (HPG), renounced the PKK cease-fire on June 1, 2004.

During every re-branding, new factions emerged and splinter groups broke off of the PKK rump organization. This summer, PKK, KADEK and Kongra-Gel all existed, overlappingly, on Mount Qandil [1]. Following one re-branding, Osman Ocalan, Abdullah's younger brother, left Mount Qandil with several hundred armed supporters to establish his own organization, The Patriotic Democratic Front (*Zaman*, October 25, 2005).

Qandil and Younger Turkish Kurds

The constant, ineffectual re-branding and resultant proliferation of groups on Mount Qandil, together with the confusing evolution of ideologies from Marxist-Leninist to the latest "Democratic Confederalism," have disheartened PKK members on Qandil. Yet as the re-brandings have been poorly publicized, the PKK remains a powerful icon among Turkish Kurds.

As a result, a pattern is visible. Eager to join the PKK's armed struggle, young Turkish Kurds cross into Iraqi Kurdistan and travel to Qandil. Once there, the bucolic, self-sufficient atmosphere of the camps create a vision of how the ideal Kurdish state should be, meshing neatly with Kurdish nationalists' longtime emphasis on traditional Kurdish dress and rural lifestyles. Yet while this vision of Kurdish identity inspires young recruits, it also explains why the Mount Qandil camps are not, as the Turkish government claims, a one-stop factory of Kurdish militancy; rather, the camps are an important waypoint for young Turkish Kurds drifting toward violence.

As even a brief visit to Qandil demonstrates, the long-term residents of the camps are those who want an easy, rural life. They are the uncommitted, the unmotivated or those on the run from Turkish authorities. They are people who pose no immediate threat to Turkey. When young Turkish PKK recruits realize that most of these older PKK members in Qandil would rather stay on the mountain than fight in Turkey, they have to make an important choice. Do they stay on Qandil and become dependent on the PKK's weak and divided leadership, or do they independently return to Turkey to take part in the Kurdish struggle—whether violently or peacefully? Or, do they decide not to play any further role in activism and go quietly home or settle in Iraqi Kurdistan?

The response of many Kurds, simultaneously inspired and disheartened by the atmosphere in the camps, to this question gives Qandil an importance far beyond its obvious role as a "training camp." For while the PKK's weapons training and education in Kurdish culture and history incubates a powerful transnational and militant Kurdish identity, the camps are also where young Kurdish radicals can become disenchanted with the PKK's strategy and leadership. It is this combination of disenchantment, radicalization and militancy among young Kurdish graduates of Qandil that makes the camps most dangerous to Turkey. Qandil has become a place where young Kurds can meet, receive weapons training and then plan to form their own independent cells either back in Turkey or elsewhere in Kurdistan—often against the wishes of the PKK leadership. Turkish Kurds who make this decision to independently split from the PKK are fast emerging as the most potent and unpredictable factor in Turkey's southeast.

One emerging sign of these trends might be the appearance of the Kurdistan Freedom Falcons (Teyrbazen Azadiya Kurdistan, TAK) who carried out a series of bombings in Turkish cities in spring and summer 2006. TAK's operations, often against foreigners, are directly at odds with the repeated calls from Qandil-based PKK leaders like Murat Karayilan for an immediate cease-fire followed by negotiations and an amnesty (Assyrian International News Agency, August 24, 2006).

In addition, the camps provide a way for Syrian Kurds to join an armed Kurdish movement. Syria's tight control over the steppes of Syrian Kurdistan makes militancy much harder there than in Turkey. The death of several Syrian PKK members in clashes just beyond the Iraqi-Turkish border shows the potency of Qandil. It is unclear, however, if such infiltrations are ordered by the Qandil leadership(s) or whether these volunteers headed to Turkey in defiance of PKK commanders.

PKK Actions in Turkey

Although Qandil is far from the frontlines of the Iraq insurgency, there is evidence that PKK-associated Kurds might be learning from Iraq's Sunni Arab jihadists—particularly if some Turkish Kurds have joined Kurdistan's peshmerga and have been deployed in Kirkuk, Mosul and further south. In particular, Turkish Kurds observing the Iraqi insurgency may be abandoning the PKK's Maoist emphasis on rural revolutions in favor of the Arab jihadists' increasing focus on urban guerrilla warfare. There have been signs of this in recent clashes in the Turkish towns of Hakkiri and Van and in the growing cult of martyrdom in the PKK camps—evidenced by numerous pictures of Vian Jaff [4]. The Kurdistan Freedom Falcon's recent attacks on foreign civilians also echo the tactics of Iraqi insurgents.

Inadvertently, Turkey has already made a Kurdish shift toward urban warfare more likely, thanks to its massive anti-PKK campaigns in the 1980s and 1990s that destroyed thousands of Kurdish villages in southeastern Turkey. Many of these displaced villagers settled in towns like Sanliurfa, Batman and Diyarbekir. These impoverished but rapidly expanding cities are the ideal place for Kurds to re-apply the Arab jihadists' military theories rather than trying to challenge the advanced and highly-mobile Turkish army's dominance of rural areas.

Beyond Qandil

Although Qandil is the largest PKK base in Iraqi Kurdistan, it is not the only one. More PKK fighters are believed to be based around Suleimaniya and at a camp at Hakurk near the Turkey-Iran-Iraq border intersection. Additionally, the PKK has periodically maintained a bureau in Baghdad (*Terrorism Focus*, July 25, 2006). Osman Ocalan also has his own quasi-militant political group called The Patriotic Democratic Front with bases somewhere north of Mosul in the territory of Massoud Barzani's Kurdistan Democratic Party. Other armed exile groups in Kurdistan include the KDP-I (Kurdistan Democratic Party-Iran), based not far from Qandil around Dukan, and Iranian Komola, an Islamist Iranian Kurdish movement. Similarly, the Kurdish satellite channel Roj TV, which the Turkish government accuses of working closely with the PKK, is based in Denmark and is funded and operated by Europe-based Kurds rather than being directed from a James Bond-style lair on Mount Qandil (*The New Anatolian*, April 24, 2006).

Iraqi Kurdish Attitudes toward the PKK

Senior Iraqi Kurdish politicians aim to retain their popular support while remaining on good terms with the United States, Arab Iraqis, Turkey and Iran. The PKK are an increasingly important and challenging factor in this equation. Publicly, Kurdish leaders distance themselves from the PKK and periodically take symbolic action against them. In August 2006, for example, the PUK closed the Suleimaniyah offices of the PKK-linked Iraqi Kurdistan Democratic Solution Party (*Zaman*, August 27, 2006). The PKK, however, are popular among ordinary Iraqi Kurds who cooperate with them extensively around Qandil [5]. The enduring presence of Qandil in Patriotic Union of Kurdistan territory strengthens Iraqi President Jalal Talabani's pan-Kurdish credentials—something that Massoud Barzani perhaps aimed to copy by aiding Osman Ocalan.

Iraqi Kurds, however, are largely unwilling to sacrifice their own independence or prosperity for the sake of Turkey's Kurds. Likewise, Iraqi Kurds do not bear a particular grudge toward Turkey, whose policies have deliberately helped Iraqi Kurdistan to flourish economically and politically. At the same time, however, in the event of a large scale Turkish offensive, Iraqi Kurds would likely be happy to help PKK members come down from Mount Qandil and blend into the local population—thus nullifying any Turkish military action.

Turkish Military Build-up

In recent months, Ankara has renewed its threats to invade Kurdistan to tackle the PKK. It has been making such threats since at least 2003 and briefly sent a mechanized brigade into Kurdistan in 2001. Turkish troops have also previously crossed the un-fenced Iraqi-Turkish border to fight PKK infiltrators up to several miles inside Iraqi territory [6]. In the last six months, Turkey has also persuaded Iran to shell Mount Qandil, and on several occasions in August Turkish jets reportedly bombed Mount Qandil (*The Journal of Turkish Weekly*, August 22, 2006; al-Jazeera, August 26, 2006). Turkey has also deployed an extra 60,000 troops to the Iraqi border region and repeatedly leaked information suggesting that an all-out assault is imminent.

Ankara, however, knows that a massive ground offensive reaching 60 miles into Kurdistan will force the United States to choose between the Kurds and Turkey. Ankara is increasingly aware that the historic causes of the close U.S.-Turkey axis—a shared fear of the USSR and then Saddam Hussein—no longer exist and that Turkey's cooperation with Iran against the Kurds runs entirely against U.S. interests. In contrast to Turkey's lessening usefulness, Iraqi Kurdish support is vital to the United States in Iraq. In addition, PJAK, the PKK's Iranian Kurdish allies, are potentially one of Washington's strongest hands against Iran if used in conjunction with nascent Azeri and Arab separatist movements. For these reasons, Ankara is unlikely to force the United States to choose between an increasing Islamic and Iran-allied Turkey and the secular Kurds.

Turkish Prime Minister Recep Tayyip Erdogan's sabre-rattling comes in the context of Turkey's 2007 elections when he needs votes from nationalists as well as from his religious constituency. Blaming the resurgent Kurdish troubles on foreign meddling and threatening military action is an easy way to both deflect blame and win the support of secular nationalists.

Conclusion

If the Turkish army launches a large-scale assault on Qandil, it forces the PKK to move on, to alter its ideology and to find new modes of operation. When the United States destroyed al-Qaeda's training camps in Afghanistan, it temporarily threw Osama bin Laden's movement into flux. This caused a ripple of unplanned and largely ineffective al-Qaeda attacks, but also fragmented the movement, broke chains of command and caused trained al-Qaeda members to disperse and disappear underground. Once underground, the movement was forced to evolve, and its least effective members were caught or killed. It learned from its mistakes and then re-constituted itself into a more disciplined and effective form. There is every reason to believe that a Turkish move against Qandil would have a similar effect. A strike—whether by ground, or air—would not destroy the movement. Instead, it would damage and shake up the PKK's aging, ineffectual and factionalized leadership, enflame the Kurdish sense of victimhood and pave the way for younger, more intellectually mobile people to take over. The present situation is a stalemate that favors Turkey; military action would shatter this situation with consequences that cannot be easily predicted. Turkish economic and diplomatic pressure on Iraqi Kurdistan to control the PKK is likely to prove more effective—if less dramatic.

Notes
1. Author interview with Assad Abdul Rahman Chaderchi, member of the PKK leadership council, PKK base camp, Mount Qandil, Iraqi Kurdistan, March 22, 2006.
2. Author interview with Seb Walker, Reuters correspondent in Iraqi Kurdistan from 2003-2005, August 2006.
3. Author interview with Peshwaz Faizulla, Suleimaniya, Iraq, March 2006.
4. Vian Jaff was an Iraqi-Turkish Kurd who set herself on fire in Ankara to protest against Turkey's policies toward the Kurds.
5. Author interview with Azad Jundiani, PUK spokesman, Suleimaniya, Iraq, March 2006.
6. Author interview with Assad Abdul Rahman Chaderchi, member of PKK leadership council, PKK base camp, Mount Qandil, Iraqi Kurdistan, March 22, 2006.

[From Terrorism Monitor, Volume IV, Issue 18]

Iran

Iran's Kurdish Threat: PJAK

James Brandon

Originally published on June 15, 2006

As Iran faces international pressure over its nuclear program, Tehran is growing increasingly concerned by the internal threat posed by a resurgent Kurdish national movement led by the Party for Freedom and Life in Kurdistan (PJAK). In 2005, according to the Iranian government, PJAK killed at least 120 Iranian soldiers in Iran. In 2006, PJAK may exceed this total. Already, it has launched dozens of attacks both from its camps in Iraqi Kurdistan and from its underground cells in Iran itself. In one of its latest attacks, PJAK troops killed four Iranian soldiers on May 27 in a clash near the town of Mako in Iranian Kurdistan, the PKK's Roj TV reported. PJAK, however, regards its military operations as merely complementing its wider effort to build a new Kurdish national identity among the four million Kurds who make up seven percent of Iran's population. PJAK has around 3,000 troops based in northern Iraq, but claims tens of thousands of activists working inside Iran to promote a Kurdish identity, democracy and women's rights [1].

As the confrontation between Iran and the West escalates, international attention has increasingly focused on Tehran's internal vulnerability. In particular, analysts point out that Iran's "imperial" past has resulted in ethnic Persians—who make up scarcely half of Iran's 80 million people—holding disproportionate power, wealth and influence. If the crisis with Iran escalates further, Iran's neglected and often resentful Kurdish, Azeri and Arab minorities may increasingly play a key role in global events. At the forefront will likely be Iran's Kurds, and chief among them PJAK, which for nearly a decade has worked to replace Iran's theocratic government with a federal and democratic system, respectful of human rights, sexual equality and freedom of expression.

History of PJAK

The exact history of PJAK is widely disputed. Turkey and Iran claim that PJAK is no more than an off-shoot of the Kurdistan Workers' Party (PKK). According to founding members of PJAK, however, the group began in Iran around 1997 as an entirely peaceful student-based human rights movement [2]. The group was inspired by the success of Iraq's Kurdish autonomous region and by the PKK's struggle in Turkey. Discouraged by the failure of previous Kurdish revolts, however, PJAK's leaders initially worked only to maintain and build a Kurdish national identity and to thwart the Iranian government's attempts to re-brand Iranian Kurds as ethnic Persians or Aryans.

After a series of government crackdowns against Kurdish activists and intellectuals, the group's leadership moved to the safety of Iraqi Kurdistan in 1999. Here they settled in the area controlled by the PKK on the slopes of Mount Qandil—less than 10 miles from the Iranian border [3]. Once established at Qandil and operating under the PKK's security umbrella, PJAK adopted many of the political ideas and military strategies of jailed PKK leader Abdullah Ocalan, whose theories had initially inspired PJAK's founders while still in Iran. The PKK's ideological influence also transformed PJAK from a civil rights movement to a more ambitious and multi-directional independence movement, aided by the transfer of many seasoned PKK fighters of Iranian origin into PJAK [4].

Ideology

Since then, PJAK has adopted many aspects of Abdullah Ocalan's ideology, particularly his renunciation of his earlier communist ideologies in favor of democratic liberalism and his belief that civil activists need to be defended by military "cadres." Yet, PJAK retains many traces of its origins as a non-violent student movement. For instance, while the PKK considers Turkish civilians legitimate targets, PJAK operates "according to the rules of war," according to Akif Zagros, a member of PJAK's seven member leadership council [5]. This claim has been reluctantly endorsed by the Iranian government; although it describes PJAK as a "terrorist group," it has never accused them of attacking civilians. While PJAK's leaders have twice kidnapped groups of Iranian soldiers in 2003 and 2004, in both instances they were released unharmed after being tried and acquitted for crimes against the Kurdish people by ad hoc PJAK courts in Iranian Kurdistan.

Equally, PJAK's vision is less radical than the PKK's. PJAK does not openly promote the creation of a single independent Kurdish state. Instead, they favor replacing Iran's velayat-e-faqih (rule by the jurisprudent) system of clerical government with a democratic and highly federalized system which would effectively grant self-rule not only to Kurds, but also to Azeri, Baloch and Arab regions. Privately, however, since PJAK itself is not exclusively composed of Iranian Kurds and contains Kurds from as far away as Russia, many PJAK members hope for the amalgamation of all Kurdish areas into a single fully independent Kurdish republic.

Yet, perhaps the most striking aspect of PJAK's agenda is their call for the emancipation of women from Islamic law and Middle Eastern cultural norms. Ms. Gulistan Dugan, 36, head of Yerjerika, PJAK's women's branch founded two years ago, says that "45 percent of PJAK are women" and adds that "the daughters of our movement play a part in all our operations. There are many military operations that women have taken part in" [6]. PJAK sees women's freedom as a core part of a Kurdish identity and point to the relative equality historically enjoyed by Kurdish women. At the same time, the issue also usefully affirms their commitment to a modern, liberal and democratic government, while also underscoring their ideological, political and cultural opposition to Tehran.

Strategy

PJAK activists are inspired by Cold War socialist revolutions, Iran's own 1979 revolution and the experiences of Iraqi and Turkish Kurds. Akif Zagros describes the group's tactics as follows: "The first stage is to spread our ideas amongst the people, especially among women, students and businessmen." He continues, saying that the "second stage is to organize people underground in schools, universities and in civil society" [7].

As the movement developed, however, the Iranian government reacted with increasingly heavy-handed crackdowns. In response, according to Zagros, "we formed a military force to protect ourselves and protect our movement. The rule of our party is to avenge the blood of our martyrs" [8]. The group's first armed attack took place in 2004 in the Meriwan region of Iranian Kurdistan after Iranian security forces fired on a Kurdish demonstration killing 10 people. This, however, did not mark an overall change of strategy toward military confrontation.

Military Operations

Although PJAK regularly engages Iranian troops, the group's attacks are not intended to defeat Iran militarily, but instead to complement and protect PJAK's political activists. In addition, the attacks aim to reinforce Kurdish national pride and to explicitly avenge the death of Kurdish activists and civilians. Ideally, PJAK would like to be strong enough to deter any crackdown against Kurdish civil activists by the Iranian authorities.

PJAK has adopted hit-and-run assault tactics against Iranian forces, carrying them out with "small arms and grenades," according to Zagros. Afterward, PJAK fighters may either melt back into Iranian society or re-cross the border into Iraqi Kurdistan. PJAK is believed to have some heavier weaponry in its Mount Qandil camp such as RPGs and heavy machine-guns [9]. PJAK's military operations are believed to be funded by Kurdish immigrant communities in Europe and Kurdish businessmen in Iran. Despite Iranian accusations, there is no evidence of any foreign funding.

Escalation

During early 2006, a cycle of Kurdish demonstrations, Iranian repression and Kurdish counterattacks developed in Iranian Kurdistan. This peaked in February when 10 Kurdish demonstrators were killed by police in the city of Maku. PJAK responded with "three attacks against two [Iranian] bases," says Zagros [10]. Shortly afterward, on April 21, and again a week later, Iranian troops fired nearly 100 artillery shells at PJAK positions near Mount Qandil and briefly crossed the Iraqi border, according to the Iraqi Ministry of Defense. "In the second violation, there was bombing against the positions of the PKK," Major-General Abd al-Aziz Muhammad, director of the joint operation center in the Iraqi Ministry of Defense told al-Jazeera, incorrectly assuming that PKK and not PJAK bases had been attacked. "The Iranian troops reached five kilometers into Iraqi territory before they withdrew" (al-Jazeera, May 3, 2006).

The Iranian attack is believed to have killed no more than 10 PJAK fighters, but it sent out a clear message that PJAK's camp was not invulnerable. The U.S. and Kurdish governments barely responded. "If those reports are true, I would expect that the Iraqi government would have something to say to the Iranian government," U.S. State Department spokesman Sean McCormack told a May 1 press conference when asked about the raid.

PJAK and the PKK

One reason for the failure of the U.S., Iraqi or even the Kurdish governments to take action against Iran's April border incursion is the close relationship between PJAK and the PKK. The European Union and the United States officially classify the PKK as a "terrorist organization." Both Iraqis and Kurds believe the PKK presence in northern Iraq damages ties with Turkey, Iraq's best armed and most economically advanced neighbor.

Although PJAK is administratively, militarily and politically separate from the PKK, strong links remain. PJAK uses some PKK facilities—such as hospitals—and remain based inside the PKK's defensive perimeter on Mount Qandil. Additionally, the two groups evidently share common goals [11]. Of course, if PJAK's links with the PKK damages its standing in the West, the close relationship has other advantages. As well as benefiting from the PKK's military expertise, a close relationship also wins PJAK instant respect among the region's Kurds. Nevertheless, PJAK's complete failure to engage with Western governments or media means that Iran has successfully sown confusion by referring to PJAK attacks as being carried out by the PKK.

Conclusion

PJAK has taken a long-term approach. Its core strategy is to promote Kurdish identity and to fight only in order to defend and avenge its civil activists. PJAK's leaders believe that if they can prevent Kurds from losing their ethnic and historic identity, then there will someday be a chance for Kurds to break free from Tehran's rule. Today, however, PJAK's followers believe that a historic opportunity is fast approaching. They point out that civil and insurgent Kurdish groups in Turkey are again vibrant and that Turkey's response is constrained by its ambitions to join the European Union. At the same time, Iraqi Kurds have consolidated their position while anti-Kurdish governments in Iran and Syria are under increasing international scrutiny and pressure. In addition, Kurds, including PJAK, after re-branding themselves as opponents of political Islam and partisans of human rights, women's rights and democracy, are well-positioned to ride out coming geopolitical shifts in the Middle East and any fragmentation of Middle Eastern states.

PJAK's independent and non-state sources of funding and well-established underground network means that Iran will struggle to defeat either PJAK or the Kurdish nationalism it fosters. Yet, given Iran's proven ability to absorb massive casualties, PJAK's ambitions to create a military balance of power and deter future Iranian crackdowns on PJAK activists seem optimistic. In addition, Iran recently adopted the successful Turkish system of employing rural Kurds as "village guards" in an attempt to force PJAK into fighting its own people. Since most PJAK attacks occur in cities, however, this tactic may fail, especially if Iran does not address wider Kurdish grievances through either investment or political reforms.

While PJAK lacks Western support, this has made the group self-reliant, flexible and open to compromise. For instance, PJAK currently talks mainly of reforming Iran's political system and aims to "create a coalition of all democratic and Kurdish parties," according to Zagros. If PJAK can succeed in creating a broader movement, then they might reach a position to challenge Tehran. In particular, PJAK regards Iran's 20 million Azeris as natural allies against Tehran, despite the fact that many Azeris hold key posts in the Islamic regime. In recent weeks, this strategy has become more plausible after the Azeris of Eastern Iran held widespread demonstrations after a Persian cartoonist compared them to cockroaches—perhaps hinting at deeper underlying tensions within Iran. In the meantime, however, as long as Iranian Kurds continue to consider themselves Kurds, rather than Persians or Iranians, then PJAK will consider itself successful.

Notes

1. Akif Zagros, member of PJAK leadership council, interview with author, PJAK Camp, Mount Qandil, Iraqi Kurdistan, March 21, 2006.
2. Akif Zagros and Gulistan Dugan, members of PJAK leadership council, interview with author, PJAK Camp, Mount Qandil, Iraqi Kurdistan, March 21, 2006.
3. Zagros, March 21, 2006.
4. Ibid.
5. Ibid.
6. Dugan, March 21, 2006.
7. Zagros, March 21, 2006.
8. Ibid.
9. Ibid. Allegations of heavier weaponry come from photographs on PJAK's website PJAK.com and Max Chamka's article "PJAK, the unknown entity of the Kurdish resistance in Iran," http://www.caucaz.com/home_eng/breve_contenu.php?id=183, August 31, 2005.
10. Zagros, March 21, 2006.
11. Assad Abdul Rahman Chaderchi, member of PKK leadership council, interview with author, PKK base camp, Mount Qandil, Iraqi Kurdistan, March 22, 2006.

[From Terrorism Monitor, Volume IV, Issue 12]

Violence and Rebellion in Iranian Balochistan

Chris Zambelis

Originally published on June 29, 2006

The escalating insurgency in Pakistan's southwestern province of Balochistan and neighboring regions receives extensive media coverage. Aside from the need to root out radical Islamist opposition movements tied to al-Qaeda and the Taliban, Pakistan faces a series of domestic threats based on ethnic, sectarian and regional rivalries and grievances. Internal tensions also stem from Pakistan's failure to integrate disparate ethnic, religious and tribal communities in its outlying regions into the fabric of a unified state structure that transcends other allegiances (*Terrorism Focus*, March 21, 2006).

In contrast, evidence of a simmering rebellion and escalating violence between Tehran's own ethnic Baloch minority and Iranian security forces in Iran's vast but sparsely populated southeastern province of Sistan-Balochistan is receiving far less attention. Iranian officials and other observers implicate an obscure Baloch militant organization known as Jundallah (Soldiers of God) for spearheading the uprising. The Baloch campaign in Iranian Balochistan, sometimes referred to as West Balochistan by Baloch nationalists, is also being waged online through a sophisticated network of independent news, activist and nationalist websites and chat forums hosted in the region and abroad in multiple languages. Many of these websites openly support the activities of Jundallah and violence in general against Tehran and others perceived to be oppressing Baloch in the region [1].

Ideology and Identity

Iranian Balochs see themselves as the heirs of an ancient and proud tradition distinct from Iran's ethnic Persian population—that make up a slim majority in Iran—and other groups that comprise the Islamic Republic. Iranian Balochs often identify with the larger Baloch community that resides in Pakistan and Afghanistan in what is referred to as "Greater Balochistan" because tribal and family lines traverse all three countries. The Baloch historical narrative is shaped by a collective sense of oppression and victimization by the imperial machinations of regional and colonial powers that have led to the division of the Baloch nation. One Baloch nationalist website directed toward Western audiences compares the historic plight of the Baloch to that of the Kurds and their longing for a Kurdish state (http://www.baloch2000. org).

Unlike most Iranians who are Shiites, the overwhelming majority of Iran's Baloch population adheres to the Sunni branch of Islam. Despite a lack of concrete evidence, Iranian authorities and some analysts believe that Jundallah may have ties to Sunni Islamist extremists associated with al-Qaeda and the Taliban operating across the border in neighboring Pakistan and Afghanistan. These allegations are likely based on Jundallah's reliance on religious symbols and discourse in expressing its nationalist aspirations and deep-seated resentment toward the Shiite-dominated Iranian state. Baloch nationalist organizations also emphasize the Sunni-Shiite element—real or perceived—in the nascent conflict, further proof in Tehran's view of the group's Sunni extremist pedigree. Jundallah is also reported to operate under different names that reflect its purported Islamist bent, including Fedayeen-e-Islam (those who sacrifice for Islam) (*Asia Times*, June 8, 2006).

At the same time, tribal allegiances and centers of authority built on family lineage traditionally supersede strict religious adherence among the semi-nomadic Baloch. Instead, Iranian Baloch practice a form of tribal Islam. Many observers argue that Tehran is exaggerating the alleged role of al-Qaeda in the Baloch insurgency in an effort to divert attention from the problems affecting Sistan-Balochistan and to tarnish the Baloch cause. It could also be a way for Tehran to curry favor with the United States amidst pressure to concede on its nuclear ambitions and its meddling in Iraq. Hardliners in Tehran downplay ethnic and sectarian tensions in Iran. They instead blame foreign intelligence services with an interest in destabilizing the country through the support of restive minorities (*Asia Times*, June 8, 2006; al-Jazeera, October 17, 2005).

Although Pakistani Balochistan remains a stronghold of Taliban elements and their local sympathizers, Baloch nationalists there rely far less on Sunni Islamist discourse in framing their cause and instead emphasize ethnic and tribal identity and economic grievances (*Deccan Herald*, August 12, 2004). Given its large Sunni majority, a Baloch nationalist campaign framed in religious rhetoric would have less resonance in Pakistan. In this sense, Baloch nationalists in Iran may be using Sunni discourse to highlight their distinct place in Shiite-dominated Iran as an oppressed and disadvantaged ethnic and religious minority (*The Nation*, December 23, 2005).

Jundallah Militancy

Little is known about Jundallah's origins. The group is led by Abdulmalak Rigi, a 23 year-old Iranian Baloch (http://www.roozonline. com). It is believed to have emerged on the scene in 2003 and is known for bold attacks against high-profile targets, especially government and security officials. In a May telephone interview with Rooz, an Iranian online newspaper, Rigi defended Jundallah's use of violence as a just means to defend Baloch and Sunni Muslim interests in Iran and to draw attention to the plight of his people whom he describes as Iran's poorest and the victims of genocide. Significantly, Rigi declares himself an Iranian and Iran as his home. He also claims not to harbor separatist aspirations. Instead, according to Rigi, Jundallah's goal is to improve the life of Iranian Baloch (http://www.roozonline.com).

In June 2005, Jundallah claimed responsibility for the abduction of a team of Iranian security and intelligence officers traveling in a convoy in Iranian Balochistan along the Pakistani border. In a videotaped ultimatum released to al-Arabiya television, the group justified its attack as revenge against Iranian security forces for committing alleged atrocities in the region. The tape included a demand for the release of Jundallah members and other Baloch activists detained in state prisons in exchange for the safe release of the hostages. Jundallah released a second video statement three weeks later showing the execution of Shehab Mansuri, whom the group claimed was an Iranian intelligence officer (*Iran Daily*, January 21, 2006; al-Arabiya, June 2005).

Another operation in mid-March included the abduction and assassination of several Iranian security officials, including members of the Islamic Revolutionary Guards Corps (IRGC), and aid officials affiliated with the Islamic Red Crescent. A similar operation in May claimed another 12 victims. The group has also been implicated in several strikes against infrastructure in Iranian Balochistan and outside of the province (al-Jazeera, March 22, 2006).

Baloch nationalist websites frequently post graphic photographs and video footage of alleged Iranian security operations and atrocities committed against Iranian Baloch civilians (http://www.balochwarna. org). The official website of the Balochistan People's Party (BPP), a movement advocating the federalization of Iran and what it describes as Baloch sovereignty within a democratic Iran, describes a recent Iranian military operation that allegedly commenced on May 15 as the "Islamic clerical regime's atrocities towards Sunni Baloch" and included helicopter gunships and airstrikes against civilian centers in Sistan-Balochistan. The website also includes visual evidence of what it claims are innocent victims of Tehran's crackdown and the recent killing of Sunni Baloch clerics by Iranian security forces (http://www. balochpeople.org).

It is unclear whether a group operating under the name Jundallah in Pakistani Balochistan is affiliated with its Iranian counterpart, although Tehran and Islamabad claim that Baloch militants on both sides of the border cooperate in the area of arms and narcotics trafficking and financing (*The News International*, January 8, 2006; *Asia Times*, June 8, 2006). Given the lawless and porous border region dividing Iranian and Pakistani Balochistan, it is difficult to determine whether this cross-border activity is linked to Jundallah's campaign or everyday crime typical in the region.

Historically, Tehran and Islamabad have collaborated in suppressing Baloch nationalism, often through brutal military crackdowns. Both countries see Baloch nationalism as a serious threat to regional stability and the territorial integrity of both states. Ongoing negotiations over the construction of a proposed pipeline that would deliver Iranian natural gas to Pakistan and India, much of which would traverse large swaths of Iranian and Pakistani Balochistan, is another point of concern that brings both sides together on the threat posed by Baloch nationalism and the emergence of groups such as Jundallah (*Dawn*, June 10, 2006).

An Underserved Community

Accurate demographic data on Iran's ethnic Baloch minority does not exist, largely for political reasons. In fact, the same holds for Iran's other ethnic and religious minorities, especially the sizeable Azerbaijani, Kurdish and Arab communities. Unofficial estimates of Iran's Baloch population range between one million and upwards of four million. The overwhelming majority of Baloch reside in Pakistan, while the rest inhabit parts of Afghanistan, totaling between 10 and 15 million.

Iranian Balochistan represents one of Iran's most impoverished and underserved regions. This is partially due to the region's inhospitable and arid climate. Sistan-Balochistan is also considered a lawless territory where the central government holds little sway. Years of systematic neglect and mismanagement by Tehran are also to blame for the social and economic despair and backwardness that characterize the region. Baloch in Iran suffer from high illiteracy and an overall lack of public services compared to the rest of the country. They are also marginalized politically by Tehran. A Baloch website reportedly run by the BLA claims that Tehran and its neighbors maintain a longstanding policy of suppressing Baloch culture and identity. This includes schemes designed to deliberately impoverish the region in order to ensure the inferior status of ethnic Baloch in Iran and elsewhere in the geographic area (http://www.balochvoice.com).

Conclusion

Tehran's resort to force in quelling the uprising in Sistan-Balochistan through deployments of special and regular army units is not likely to contribute to lasting peace and stability in the region. Since Iranian Baloch grievances run deep, movements such as Jundallah will maintain a sizeable following among the population. Although there is no credible evidence implicating the group of al-Qaeda's brand of radicalism or the strain of Taliban-style Sunni extremism violently opposed to Shiite Islam found in parts of Pakistan, Jundallah's cause does have the potential to be hijacked by militants with a different agenda. This has serious implications for stability, not only in Iran's Sistan-Balochistan province, but Pakistani Balochistan as well. At the same time, despite its Sunni Islamist rhetoric, Jundallah's agenda to date remains fixated on Iranian Baloch causes.

Notes

1. For a list of links to a diverse array of Baloch news, activist and nationalist websites that purport to feature detailed accounts of fighting in Iranian Balochistan and Pakistani Balochistan, including graphic photographs and video of alleged victims and military operations, visit the homepage of the Stockholm-based Radio Balochistan, http://www.radiobalochi.org. The Baloch nationalist website hosted by the self-proclaimed "Government of Balochistan in Exile" also contains useful information from a Baloch nationalist perspective, http://governmentofbalochistan.blogspot.com.

[From Terrorism Monitor, Volume IV, Issue 13]

Israel, Lebanon and Hezbollah

Al-Qaeda's Presence in the Territories

Murad al-Shishani and Abdul Hameed Bakier

Originally published on June 2, 2006

Other than launching Katyusha rockets at Israel in December 2005 and attempting to launch rockets at Eilat from Aqaba in Jordan in August 2005, al-Qaeda has not launched significant attacks against Israeli targets in the Middle East. Al-Qaeda has not been active in the Palestinian territories, although fighting Israel is a top priority of Salafi-Jihadist ideology. There were many indications, however, of al-Qaeda's desire to penetrate the Arab-Israeli conflict as a consequence of Israel's pullout from Gaza; this explains why al-Qaeda's second-in-command, Ayman al-Zawahiri, criticized HAMAS' participation in the peace process (al-Jazeera, April 3, 2006). The potential for al-Qaeda to penetrate the Arab-Israeli conflict exists, and it is important to understand the ideological perspective of Salafi-Jihadists toward HAMAS, indications of al-Qaeda's role in the territories and al-Qaeda's chance for success.

Ideological Perspective Toward HAMAS

On March 4, al-Jazeera aired a videotape of al-Zawahiri, who criticized HAMAS for participating in the political process, calling on HAMAS not to recognize Israel and the agreements signed by the "Secular Palestinian Authorities with Israel." It further warned HAMAS not to participate in the "American game called political participation" (al-Jazeera, March 4, 2006). Al-Zawahiri's perspective in criticizing the participation of HAMAS in the political process is not a new one. He previously criticized Egypt's Muslim Brotherhood for participating in the political process in a long book he wrote, titled *Bitter Harvest*, focusing on their "wrong" belief in political participation. Likewise, the Salafi-Jihadist perspective on HAMAS revolves around the same connotation, even though this perspective is not publicized.

The Salafi-Jihadist ideologue Abu Muhammad al-Maqdisi once wrote an article entitled "HAMAS Mojard HAMAS" ("HAMAS is Just Enthusiasm"), resenting its alliance with the secular Palestinian forces and HAMAS' criticism of the suicide attacks by al-Qaeda in Saudi Arabia. He wrote, "we remark that there is no prohibition on the existence of HAMAS or whomever on the right path that seek to elevate Allah's word. There is good in Palestine and elsewhere, but our criticism of the so-called HAMAS is because it has delayed the big holy war in Palestine and distorted the fundamentals of the religion which can never be argued or renounced for political gains" (http://www.tawhed.ws, 2004).

In the same context, an al-Qaeda ideologue currently imprisoned in Saudi Arabia, Abu Jandal al-Azdi (also known as Faris al-Zahrani), criticized HAMAS for its support of late Palestinian National Authority (PNA) President Yasser Arafat and for believing in democracy, deeming the PNA apostates that should be fought on par with Israel (http://www.tawhed.ws, 2003). Also, the Salafi-Jihadist ideologue in Iraq, Abu Anas al-Shami (also known as Omar Yossif Joma'a), called HAMAS an incomplete Islamic movement due to its cooperation with ideas of "citizenship" and "political participation."

Al-Zawahiri's pep talk presents al-Qaeda as an alternative to HAMAS. Al-Zawahiri stated clearly that "Jihad and Sharia" are the only alternatives (al-Jazeera, April 3, 2006). This explains al-Maqdisi's continuing aspiration to move the Salafi-Jihadist ideology "west of the river Jordan" (http://www.alasr.ws, December 25, 2004). Therefore, it is noteworthy that the Salafi-Jihadists are trying to penetrate the Arab-Israeli conflict zone. It is also what Osama bin Laden expressed in two of his speeches—in October 2001 and in October 2004—when he linked the September 11 attacks to the Israeli invasion of Lebanon in 1982 and vowed that the security of the United States is connected with that of the Palestinians. If this is an ideological aspiration of al-Qaeda, what is the potential of implementing that reality?

Al-Qaeda and the Territories

In an interview with *al-Hayat*, PNA President Mahmoud Abbas stated that there are strong indications of al-Qaeda's presence in Gaza and the West Bank (*al-Hayat*, March 2, 2006). Also, Jordanian authorities indicated the presence of an al-Qaeda cell in Gaza (*al-Hayat*, April 4, 2006). In May 2005, the Palestinian Azzam Abu al-Adas from the Balata refugee camp in Nablus, studying in Jordan, was recruited in the Jordanian city of Irbid by Abdullah (also known as Abu Qudama) and Mo'taz Omar Seelawi, both members of al-Qaeda. They instructed Azzam to set up a terrorist cell in Gaza to perpetrate terrorist attacks against Israeli industrial facilities to undermine the Israeli economy; Azzam recruited Bilal Hafanawi from Gaza to assist in the operation. Bilal is a former HAMAS activist who was heading a cell for al-Aqsa Martyrs Brigades/Fatah in Gaza. On January 10, 2006 Israeli authorities arrested Azzam and Bilal as they were crossing from Jordan into PNA territories. On February 2, 2006 both men were tried and charged in an Israeli military court for attempting terror attacks in Israel. This case indicated real mobilization of the Salafi-Jihadist movement westward, particularly to Gaza. This is logical due to the lack of Israeli control over the dense population of potential recruits in the Gaza Strip after the Israeli withdrawal. Furthermore, the pro-HAMAS *al-Risalah* newspaper indicated the increasing support for al-Qaeda ideology in southern Gaza, particularly in Rafah and Khan Yunis districts (*al-Risalah*, March 9, 2006).

The dissidence of HAMAS' right wing that opposes peaceful solution of the conflict and the May 8, 2006 announcement of a group claiming affiliation with al-Qaeda called Jaish al-Quds al-Islami (Islamic Army of Jerusalem) were the expected outcomes of HAMAS' participation in the political process (*al-Ghad*, May 9, 2006). HAMAS' success in the elections increased the chances of al-Qaeda's penetration for the following reasons. By shifting away from the right-wing, HAMAS left Islamic Jihad alone and created a vacuum exploited by al-Qaeda through the rumor that the commander of Izz al-Din al-Qassam brigades (the military wing of HAMAS), Muhammad Daif (also known as Muhammad Diab al-Missri), had switched to al-Qaeda. HAMAS denied the rumor. Regardless of the validity of the rumor, it strongly indicates that the discord between the military and political wings of HAMAS is expected to intensify in the future. On the other hand, pressure on HAMAS will weaken it and prove true what Nehemia Strasler, an Israeli analyst in Haaretz, said: "And so Israel will continue imposing sanctions and a political boycott, and the radicals, such as Islamic Jihad, will become stronger. And when the Palestinian nation comes to the conclusion that neither HAMAS nor Islamic Jihad have managed to improve the conditions, it will turn to the most radical of all, to al-Qaeda" (*Haaretz*, February 21, 2006).

Externally, HAMAS is facing a real challenge to proceed from political participation to the peace process. Internally, HAMAS has to improve the economic conditions of the Palestinians, a top priority according to recent polls conducted in the territories. It seems that as a consequence of the external and internal factors, al-Qaeda is counting on the failure of HAMAS. The last factor is connected to Al-Qaeda in Iraq which is more Shami (a geographical term used in Arabic to describe Syria, Jordan, Palestine, Lebanon and Iraq) in its outlook. This explains why it may become active in Lebanon, Jordan, Syria and on the Gaza border in the Sinai desert, a weak area lacking development, education and suffering from poor socioeconomic conditions (*al-Hayat*, May 7, 2006). Sinai was targeted more than five times last year. Tacking westward seems a substantive decision of al-Qaeda considering its constant efforts to create a safe haven for its operations, and the ideological priority of the Palestinian issue.

Conclusion

The factors mentioned above play a major role in the possible penetration by Salafi-Jihadists into the West Bank and Gaza Strip. These factors are divided into local, regional and international levels. Al-Aqsa press noted the increasing popularity of al-Zarqawi among Palestinian youths as a consequence of his latest videotape aired on al-Jazeera (al-Jazeera, May 6, 2006). Al-Aqsa said that even the head cover that al-Zarqawi wore in the tape became a vogue among Palestinian youths. Most significant is that those youths express the duty to fight traitors in the PNA in conformity with al-Qaeda's pep talk instigating the killing of apostates and Israelis. It seems that the proclamation of responsibility for the attempted assassination of the head of the Palestinian intelligence services on May 21, 2006 by a new group calling itself al-Qaeda Organization of the State of Palestine is contextual. Therefore, all parties, including the international ones, should not push the Arab-Israeli conflict into a dangerous slide and escalation that is bound to occur if al-Qaeda enters the conflict. Despite the obstacles that al-Qaeda faces in penetrating the Arab-Israeli conflict area as a result of the highly politicized nature of the Palestinian people, HAMAS' possible failure in the political process and the regression of other Palestinian parties will make it that much easier for al-Qaeda to penetrate.

Palestinian political parties need restructuring to be able to understand the political variants of the region; more importantly, they need to keep their cadres from switching to al-Qaeda. HAMAS has to create a balance between internal support and recognition by the international community. Israel, on its part, has to realize the threat of Salafi-Jihadist success in penetrating the area. Fewer Palestinian political options mean a greater chance of violence prevailing over politics.

[From Terrorism Monitor, Volume IV, Issue 11]

Al-Qaeda's Presence in Lebanon

Murad al-Shishani

Originally published on January 31, 2006

After a missile attack on Israel from south Lebanon on December 27, 2005, the Organization of al-Qaeda in Iraq, or the Land of the Two Rivers, issued an audio-recording for its leader, Abu Musab al-Zarqawi, in which he claimed responsibility for the attack and said it was ordered by al-Qaeda's leader, Osama bin Laden. The attack, combined with the statement of responsibility, raised questions about al-Qaeda's presence in Lebanon. Following the attack, Lebanese authorities arrested a group of al-Qaeda members or followers of the Salafi-Jihadist movement. While the Lebanese authorities did not disclose details about the arrested suspects, the news leaks raised several questions about the presence and nature of the Salafi-Jihadist movement in Lebanon.

Al-Qaeda's Presence in Lebanon

Among Arab societies, Lebanese are least affected by Salafi ideas (al-Jazeera, January 13, 2006). Since independence, Lebanon has been a multi-cultural state with a fairly open society, making Salafi-Jihadist ideology less attractive. This explains why most of the arrested men were not Lebanese. Nevertheless, questions remain about the reasons behind the increase in the number of the movement's followers in Lebanon: some sources indicate that there are more than 100 Salafi-Jihadist followers in the country (*al-Watan*, January 15, 2006). The attack on Israel also raises questions about the movement's true motives in Lebanon.

Among the names announced by Lebanese authorities, four of the suspects were Lebanese nationals. The rest of the accused include seven Syrians, one Palestinian and one Jordanian. They were all accused of the attack on Israel. Among the Lebanese were Khader and Malek Nab'a, who are relatives of the suspects in the Dinnieh incidents of 2000 (see the indictment in Lebanon-based *al-Nahar* newspaper, July 11, 2000).

In addition, Khader Nab'a is associated with the appearance of the Salafi-Jihadist movement in Lebanon, when the leader of the al-Ahbash religious sect, Nizar Halabi, was assassinated in 1995. Since Salafi-Jihadist ideology is less popular in Lebanon than in other Arab countries, recruitment takes place among relatives and friends. The exceptions to this were the suspects in the Dinnieh incidents, since most of them were Lebanese veterans of the Afghan war. Yet, most of the individuals arrested in Lebanon after the Dinnieh incidents were not Lebanese nationals. Indeed, recent arrests of Salafi-Jihadists have uncovered plans to target U.S. interests, restaurants and diplomats (see feature on the record of al-Qaeda in Lebanon, *al-Sharq al-Awsat*, September 23, 2004).

Attacking Israel to Increase Popularity of Salafi-Jihadist Movement

The attack on Israel appears to be an attempt by Salafi-Jihadists to gain popularity among the Arab public after it began losing support in the Arab world due to its violent operations and targeting of civilians. The Arab-Israeli conflict remains one of the major issues that affect Arabs. This does not mean, however, that the conflict with Israel is not important for Salafi-Jihadists; on the contrary, it is considered an "ideological priority."

Nevertheless, it seems that Israel is not the main reason for al-Qaeda to increase its operations in Lebanon. For instance, as mentioned earlier, the ideology of Salafi-Jihadists is generally not popular among Lebanese. Additionally, south Lebanon will not become a base for Salafi-Jihadists because the region is controlled by the Shiite party Hezbollah. Salafi-Jihadists hold intense animosity toward the Shiite sect, which makes unlikely any coalition between the two parties.

The primary reason behind al-Qaeda's increasing presence in Lebanon is that since the assassination of former Prime Minister Rafiq Hariri and the Syrian withdrawal that ensued as a result of that assassination, Lebanon has entered a state of security upheaval. According to Moroccan researcher al-Mahjoub Habibi, the Salafi-Jihadist movement is facing difficulties operating in many regions of the world, and the lack of security in Lebanon is drawing the movement's members to the country (http://www.rezgar.com, March 31, 2005). Habibi, a secularist, also argued that Jordan will serve as new ground for al-Qaeda; like Lebanon, it is close to Israel and fits into al-Qaeda's strategy of establishing a Caliphate after dominating Saudi Arabia and Iraq.

Al-Qaeda and the Salafi-Jihadist movement are always trying to establish a presence in regions suffering from a lack of government security. In light of this analysis, the recent attack on Israel was likely an attempt by Salafi-Jihadists to recover the popularity lost with the Arab public over its recent choices of targets, and to move closer to establishing its presence in all of the Middle East.

[From Terrorism Focus, Volume III, Issue 4]

Salafi-Jihadist Movement Becoming a New Force in Lebanon

Murad al-Shishani

Originally published on April 4, 2006

In July 2005, French scholar Olivier Roy argued that Iraq and Palestine are not factors in the prevalence of the Salafi-Jihadist movement. He based his argument on the fact that there are no Iraqi or Palestinian members in the Salafi-Jihadist organizations. Now, however, this argument must be reconsidered. Afghan authorities have expressed their concern over the "hordes of Iraqi suicide bombers" following the arrest of Noman Eddin Majid, aged 35 years, from Diyala governorate as he was trying to sneak into Afghanistan (*al-Hayat*, February 3, 2006). In addition, the perpetrators of the Amman bombing on November 9, 2005, and most 'of those in the recent disbanded terrorist cell in Amman as well, were Iraqis (*Terrorism Focus*, March 7, 2006). As for the Palestinians, the attention is becoming increasingly focused on Lebanon with its Palestinian refugee camps, particularly Ain El-Hilweh, instead of the West Bank. (Approximately 400,000 Palestinian refugees live in Lebanon.)

While the recruitment of Salafi-Jihadists in Lebanon is not restricted to Palestinians and includes some Lebanese nationals, young men from refugee camps are more fertile material for recruitment. Following the news of the arrest of Salafi-Jihadists in Lebanon and the announcement made by the movement of its responsibility for blowing up a target for the Lebanese army on February 1, 2006 (the movement delivered the threat through a phone call to the Sada al-Balad newspaper the day before the attack, according to the paper), Lebanese authorities arrested 31 suspected jihadists. In light of this claim of responsibility and the arrests, it is important to examine the forms of recruitment that the Salafi-Jihadists use in Lebanon (*al-Watan*, February 8, 2006).

It seems that the activities of the Salafi-Jihadist movement focus on the poor Lebanese and Palestinian communities. The increasing connection with the Iraq factor is due to two reasons: the unattractiveness of the secular Palestinian organizations in the refugee camps compared to the increasing attraction of the Islamist groups, and the waning control of the Future/Hariri Party over the Sunni community.

Palestinian Refugee Camps

Ain El-Hilweh refugee camp was the base for Palestinian President Yasser Arafat in the 1980s. The camp was a stronghold for the "Palestinian revolution" organizations, and it remains to this day under the power of Palestinians to the extent that the Lebanese army does not venture inside the camp (*al-Hayat*, February 26, 2006). The power of the secular organizations, however, is moving to the Islamist organizations, especially since the secular organizations have been implicated in cases of corruption and have not met the demands of the Palestinians. The commander of Fatah's militias in Lebanon, Colonel Mounir Maqdah, proposed "forming a Lebanese-Palestinian military force to eradicate this fundamentalist group [from Ain El-Hilweh]." This clearly indicates the increase in the power of Islamist groups and the Palestinian organizations' fear of losing their control, especially when newspaper sources talk of "returnees from Iraq" who aim at declaring "Lebanon's loyalty" to the "Foundation of Jihad in Iraq" (*al-Sharq al-Awsat*, February 4, 2006).

An indication of the spread of the influence of the Salafi-Jihadist movements amidst Palestinians in Lebanon, promoted by the "returnees from Iraq," is what Hazem Amin in *al-Hayat* calls "al-Qaeda terminology." The volunteers in Iraq are in touch with their parents in a way that connects the parents with information about jihad activities. This terminology is so widespread that Shiites are now described as "heretics" (*al-Hayat*, January 25, 2006), which is a new feature in the Lebanese sectarian system. In addition, death threats were made by the al-Qaeda Organization in Bilad al-Sham to Shiite Lebanese figures (*al-Sharq al-Awsat*, July 27, 2005).

While this is the Palestinians' situation in Lebanon, the influence of the Salafi-Jihadist movement is not restricted to them. There are Sunni Lebanese nationals who have headed to Iraq to volunteer in fighting the Americans (*al-Hayat*, January 26, 2006). Likewise, there was a transformation in the village of Majdal Anjar, which used to be the stronghold of "traditional Salafism," since the arrival of Abu

Muhammad al-Lubnani, who later became a close companion of Abu
Musab al-Zarqawi after he reached Iraq with his 16-year-old son, and
where they both later died. Abu Muhammad al-Lubnani was Mustafa
Ramadan. He began to spread his jihadist ideas since his return from
Denmark around 2003 (*al-Hayat*, January 27, 2006), and was able to
form a nucleus for the jihadist movement. The influence of those ideas
applies to the Sunnis in Lebanon—not just to the Palestinians.

Sunni Lebanese

The Lebanon-based newspaper *Addiyar* indicated on February
7, 2006, following the burning of the Danish Embassy and the riots
in Beirut, that Saad Hariri is losing control over the Sunni scene by
eliminating the subsidies for the poor among the Sunnis and making the
al-Mustaqbal movement exclusive to the rich and powerful. As a result,
Salafi-Jihadist movements (al-Qaeda, Usbat al-Ansar, Jund al-Sham) and
the Islamic Liberation Party are, according to *Addiyar*, now controlling
90 percent of the Sunni scene (*Addiyar*, February 7, 2006).

Despite the unreliability of the 90 percent figure, the Salafi-
Jihadist movement is attracting a host of poor Sunnis who were badly
affected after the death of Rafiq Hariri. The media always spoke of
the role Hariri played in restoring the balance between the Sunnis and
the other sects in Lebanon. This becomes evident if we review the
backgrounds of the people who volunteered in or returned from Iraq;
they were mostly poor who did odd jobs like selling coffee and steamed
beans in the street, or were unemployed in the first place.

Hezbollah's Role

The developments related to the Salafi-Jihadist presence in
Lebanon show that those influenced by the ideology will begin to move
out of the Palestinian refugee camps and into southern Lebanon. This
development means that Hezbollah will be threatened in the region it
has historically controlled. For Hezbollah, this development comes at
a time when the party is under pressure to disarm and to end ties with
Syria. This means that Hezbollah will not allow the Salafi-Jihadists to
extend into their region of influence. While Salafi-Jihadists consider
Shiites as infidels, on February 23, 2006 Hezbollah Secretary General

Sayyed Hassan Nasrallah listed, for the first time, the "Jama'at al-Takfeer" (Excommunication Groups, which is how officials in Arab governments describe Salafi-Jihadists), as one of the three beneficiaries of the bombings of Shiite shrines in Iraq, along with the United States and Israel (for full audio of his speech, see http://www.moqawama. org/sound/details.php?linkid=351).

Conclusion

The factors described above show that the Salafi-Jihadist presence and movement into Lebanon is facing many obstacles, but is also becoming a new force in the country. At the same time, however, the sociopolitical developments in Lebanon are creating the conditions for that presence.

While Sunnis in Lebanon were historically led by old families like al-Huss, Karami and al-Sulh, from the 1990s until his assassination in 2005, Rafiq Hariri became the most prominent leader of Sunnis and enjoyed their support. That is why he was described as the "most Sunni personality" (al-Jazeera, February 13, 2006). One of the most important factors in the popularity of Hariri among Sunnis was his concentration on the grassroots level by helping poor Lebanese.

Among the implications of the assassination was that Sunnis have become prone to polarization by different ideologies, among which is the Salafi-Jihadist ideology. Due to the positions of the above-mentioned political forces—such as the Palestinian organizations and Hezbollah—there will be conflict between them and Salafi-Jihadists. The result will be that the spread of the Salafi-Jihadist ideology in Lebanon will become a destabilizing factor in the country.

[From Terrorism Focus, Volume III, Issue 13]

The Man in Nasrallah's Shadow: A Profile of Sheikh Naim Qasim

Sami Moubayed

Originally published on August 22, 2006

Sheikh Naim Qasim, the deputy secretary-general of Hezbollah, is one of the most interesting politicians in Lebanon. He is also one of the most under-reported by the Western media because he remains overshadowed by the towering influence of his boss, the charismatic 46-year-old Sheikh Hassan Nasrallah. Yet the life and career of the number two man in Hezbollah is important since he is the leader who would likely lead the controversial party if Nasrallah were to step down or get killed by Israel.

Sheikh Naim Qasim was born in the Basta district of Beirut, a predominantly Sunni neighborhood, in 1953. His family was originally from the village of Kafar Vila in South Lebanon. His father had come to Beirut as a young boy, searching for a better life like so many Shiites of his generation, and worked at his uncle's bakery in the Lebanese capital. The Shiites at the time were overwhelmingly poor, underrepresented in the Lebanese parliament and their areas were greatly underdeveloped. When Qasim was born, his father was working as a taxi driver in Beirut. Qasim recalled that his father would start his work day at 6 AM and remain behind the wheel until 8 PM, struggling to earn a living for the young Qasim, his three brothers and one sister. Honest and reliable, the father transported money and goods to customers around Lebanon, earning enough money to buy a house in the Msaytbeh neighborhood, which the family moved to when Qasim was 14. Qasim's father was illiterate but insisted that his son receive a proper education to compensate for the lack of schooling in his own childhood. At school he excelled in French and chemistry. The young Qasim then studied in the Department of Education at the state-run Lebanese University (*al-Rajul*, March 1, 2005).

While still in school, Qasim became interested in religion and Islamic studies. No member of his immediate family was a cleric. At a young age, Qasim went to the local mosque during Ramadan where he was influenced by the clerics of the Shiite community. He began doing his own research into scholarly Islam and journeyed to different parts of Lebanon to attend lectures and read about Shiite history. By 1983, Qasim had decided to wear the turban of Shiite Islam. He was 30 years old. This decision, he recalled many years later, was a "revolution" in his life. He added, "many things changed [after I became a cleric], such as the way of life, the nature of relationships and the degree of social interaction. There are many restraints that come with the turban" (*al-Rajul*, March 1, 2005). When asked what he would do if all the restrictions that came with his political and religious office were suddenly lifted, he immediately replied: "I would walk in the streets," claiming that since 1992 this is something he has been deprived of due to the security restrictions of his job in Hezbollah (*al-Rajul*, March 1, 2005).

When the Lebanese Civil War broke out in 1975, Qasim joined the Amal movement of the Iranian-born cleric Imam Musa al-Sadr. He became active in student politics while studying at Lebanese University and rose among party ranks, becoming "deputy officer" of ideology and culture in Amal (http://www.naimkassem.org). He parted from Amal after the "disappearance" of the party founder Musa al-Sadr in 1978 and devoted his time to research and deeper understanding of Islam. When former members of Amal founded Hezbollah in the early 1980s, Qasim joined their ranks but did not become an active member until 1989. Under the first secretary-general of Hezbollah, Sheikh Subhi al-Tufayli, Qasim became deputy president of the Executive Council. When Abbas al-Musawi became secretary-general, Qasim was chosen as his number two man. Six months later, however, al-Musawi was assassinated by the Israelis and Hassan Nasrallah (only 32 years old at the time) replaced him as secretary-general. The decision to bypass Qasim and choose Nasrallah, who was seven-years his junior and less experienced in political affairs, remains a topic of controversy. It is believed that this was the doing of the Grand Ayatollah Ali Akbar Khamenei due to Nasrallah's connections to Tehran. Qasim, on the other hand, is not as well connected to Iran, although he is allied to the Islamic regime there.

Currently, in addition to his political office, Qasim is the media man for Hezbollah. He is also dubbed the "Hezbollah intellectual" for the numerous books and articles that he has authored, in addition to the interviews and seminars that he gives (al-Arabiya, August 4, 2004). Qasim says that he did not start writing until 2001. Before that he had lectured extensively but never had the time to devote himself to composition (al-Arabiya, August 4, 2004). His first book was a collection of 10 lectures he had given on Imam Ali, the fourth grand caliph of Islam. Recently, he wrote a book about Hezbollah in Arabic, which was translated into English in 2004 and published by Saki Books in London. He then wrote a book about the holy Shiite ceremony of Ashura, following it with a book on good manners, and is currently writing a book on "how to strengthen one's will power" (*al-Rajul*, March 1, 2005). He confesses that he reads a lot of books on education and psychology, but prefers to read politics from newspapers and other media outlets, unlike Nasrallah, who repeatedly said that he spends his free time reading political books authored by the Israelis, mainly the biographies and autobiographies of the political and military leaders of Israel (*Ya Lesarat Ol-Hoseyn*, August 10, 2006).

With regard to his personal life, Qasim says that all of his children are religious but none are considering a religious career, except his youngest son, who is 15 years old. He adds that he will not influence his son's choice of lifestyle or career, saying that his son must navigate his life on his own (*al-Rajul*, March 1, 2005). At a book signing, Qasim thanked his wife for her support, something that raised eyebrows within religious establishments as uncommon for a turbaned cleric. Qasim commented on the matter saying that "I support the rights of women" claiming that women's rights are a must in proper Islam. He adds, "She [in reference to women] is not a slave. She is not only there for delivering children. She is a human being in every sense of the word. She has full rights" (*al-Rajul*, March 1, 2005). In his own words, his wife is "educated and intellectual," proudly saying that she used to lecture on various matters and was very active in public life but had to limit her public activities in order to raise their children. When asked about friends he commented: "Nobody lives without friends" (*al-Rajul*, March 1, 2005). He lamented not having time to see his friends regularly or to spend quality time with them, due to the amount of time his work consumes, pointing out that even when he wants to see his mother, he has to fix an appointment with her in advance.

Looking back at his career, Qasim says: "I feel that I can no longer differentiate between myself and the party. The crossovers are very strong. I cannot imagine myself without Hezbollah" (*al-Rajul*, March 1, 2005).

[From Terrorism Focus, Volume III, Issue 33]

Syria

Syria's Abu al-Qaqa: Authentic Jihadist or Imposter?

Sami Moubayed

Originally published on June 27, 2006

Much has been written about the Aleppo-based Syrian preacher Abu al-Qaqa since Syrian security apprehended an armed group on June 2, 2006 that was attempting to carry out a terrorist attack at early dawn on the Ummayad Square in the heart of Damascus (*Terrorism Focus*, June 13, 2006). It is unclear as to what site the group was targeting since Ummayad Square is surrounded by several important sites, including Syrian TV, the General Customs Department, the Damascus Opera House, the al-Assad National Library, the Ministry of Defense and Army Headquarters. What is known for sure is that one security official was killed along with a guard at Syrian Television, while two others were wounded. The police managed to gun down four militants, wound two and arrest four. Pictures of the dead assailants were displayed in Syria's state-run dailies the next morning to end all speculation that the ordeal was fabricated by the Syrian government. Those who were killed and those who were arrested were carrying CDs with inflammatory speeches by Abu al-Qaqa.

The sermons were being preached under the banner of an unknown group called Ghuraba al-Sham (Strangers of Greater Syria). On the CDs, Abu al-Qaqa is seen screaming: "We will teach our enemies a lesson they will never forget. Are you ready?" When the crowds respond affirmatively with thundering voices, he says: "Speak louder so George Bush can hear you!" Abu al-Qaqa addresses a crowd of hundreds, who are so moved by his speech that they begin to cry. He then begins to weep as he speaks, telling his audience: "Guests have come to our land...slaughter them like cattle. Burn them! Yes, they are the Americans" (al-Arabiya, June 4, 2006).

Abu al-Qaqa—sometimes referred to by his original name Dr. Mahmud al-Aghasi—is a rising phenomenon in Syrian politics. Abu al-Qaqa was born to a Kurdish family in the village of al-Foz, north of Aleppo, in 1973. His father was not a religious scholar, but rather lived the life of a simple farmer. Al-Qaqa studied Islam at Damascus University and obtained his MA and PhD from the Islamic University in Karachi. He began to preach to the pious at the Alaa bin Hadrami Mosque in Aleppo in the 1990s. Loudly anti-American, he attracted a wide audience during the Iraq War in 2003 and his reputation has been spreading ever since. His speeches, which by now were recorded on cassettes and DVDs, began to reach thousands and were distributed in towns and villages all over Syria. One person who has seen his sermons described him, saying, "He is an inflammatory speaker and possesses great oratory skills, in addition to being a master of dialogue" (author interview in Syria, June 22, 2006).

It is said that he has mastered the Arabic language, and uses it with eloquence to appeal to the masses that attend his sermons. In an interview with al-Arabiya TV on June 23, Abu al-Qaqa denied that he was calling on Syrians to go to war in Iraq. He cited an example when he spoke at a youth festival shortly after the fall of Baghdad, attended by 15,000 Syrian young men, advising them not to go to Iraq. He admitted that he received thousands of Arab recruits who visited him in Aleppo and wanted to go to Iraq for jihad; due to Aleppo's proximity with Iraq, and the reputation of its clerics and their history of opposing the U.S. occupation, it was a stop for many jihadists en route to Iraq. He convinced them, however, to return to their countries, saying that warfare at such a stage "harms the nation" (al-Arabiya, June 22, 2006). This seemed to contradict what Abu al-Qaqa had been saying on the recorded CDs, but he qualified his new stance, arguing that he was calling on the youth to "burn" and "slaughter" the Americans only if they came to Syria (al-Arabiya, June 22, 2006).

He insists that anger of religious youth should never be unleashed on their fellow Syrians or their government. This explains why the Syrian government has tolerated him since 2003. Many speculated that he was an agent of the Syrian regime, being used by the government to appease the rising Islamic street that was boiling with anti-Americanism. As long as he was not preaching against the state, it was believed, Abu al-Qaqa could be free to say what he wished in Aleppo. In conversations with friends and supporters, Abu al-Qaqa stresses that he is not against the state, emphasizing: "The state and I are against what is wrong" (author interview with Syrian source, June 22). He always calls for "unification of the security and religious apparatus in Syria." He explains this bizarre argument: "Every believer must see that security is a positive action. The objective of a believer's religion is to prevent harm to human beings. This is done by the security services" (*al-Rai al-Aam*, June 14, 2006).

Abu al-Qaqa has authored a 10-page booklet, which is popular among religious Syrian youth, entitled *The Rights of the Ruler*. The book is dedicated to: "The sons of my country: the rulers and the ruled, the officials and the citizenry, those with ranks and those with beards, preachers of religion and political actors, security officials and soldiers of belief." Jihadists usually see regimes in the Arab World as heretical—but Abu al-Qaqa sees them in a good light, explaining why many people write him off as an imposter and a creation of Syrian intelligence. In page two of his booklet, Abu al-Qaqa adds that he will not wrestle with the government for leadership of the state, saying that he hopes to unite the people of Syria, "governors and those who are governed, on the basis of coherent cooperation" to obstruct all Western and Israeli ploys in Syria. He adds that he is unrelated in any manner to al-Qaeda, seeing it as a U.S. creation to bring havoc to Iraq. He is also unrelated to the Jund al-Sham organization that has emerged in Syria since 2003. He says: "We will be agents of construction not destruction for our country, even if we are oppressed or harmed." He says that the status of the ulema and the rulers (in reference to the Baathists) is untouchable, since if both are tarnished, "lost is belief and lost is Sharia."

It is no secret that Abu al-Qaqa is not on the offensive against the Syrian regime. This mindset is new to men of religion, especially those who preach jihad in the post September 11 world, who are usually at the opposite end of the political spectrums with established governments in the Middle East. He continues to live in Aleppo—unlike previous reports that said he currently has Pakistani citizenship and lives in Chechnya—and walks around the city freely with bodyguards. He drives a luxurious Mercedes Benz 600, has a rented apartment in a residential district of Aleppo and is never short of funds (author interview with an Aleppo-based admirer of Abu al-Qaqa, June 20, 2006). He is connected to the Aleppine mercantile class and is widely supported in his campaign to preach tolerant political Islam. Many people donate funds to him to avoid being harassed for saying no, to appease the government that supports al-Qaqa and because some believe he is truly an honest man of religion who needs to be funded, seeking his blessing as a spiritual cleric.

Since he was supported—although not necessarily created—by the security services to appease rising discontent in the Syrian street, it is likely that certain followers deviated from his path, seeing that he was too closely tied to the government, and created cells on their own that are influenced by his teachings, but carry separate agendas for jihad and political conduct. On April 12, 2006 for example, fighting broke out between al-Qaqa's former supporters and members of Syrian security from a newly created branch called the "Combating Terrorism Unit." The fighting led to the killing of two assailants, two security officials and one bystander in the Naqqarin neighborhood of Aleppo. At the time, the sermons of Abu al-Qaqa were briefly seized in Aleppo—a sign that his rhetoric was what inspired the terrorist attack.

Lately, some have accused Abu al-Qaqa of the would-be terrorist attack on the Ummayad Square. In an exclusive interview with *al-Muharrir al-Arabi*, published on June 16, 2006 Abu al-Qaqa denied all involvement in the incident. He added that these accusations were not directed against him personally, "but rather targets the wise and civilized Islamic project in Bilad al-Sham." The would-be attack on the Ummayad Square was a "bitter event," he added. "My stance on it is similar to my stance on criminal acts: total rejection." As for the CDs found on the terrorists, Abu al-Qaqa pointed out that this recording was among 2,000 others widely distributed and sold in the Islamic world, saying that it is no proof that he planned the attack.

For now, it is not clear who to believe in the entire ordeal of Abu al-Qaqa. What kind of a jihadist dabbles with a secular regime like the Baathists? What kind of a jihadist drives around in broad daylight in a Mercedes Benz? Abu al-Qaqa is one of two things. He might be a regime creation, whose supporters strayed from his loyalty to become terrorists working against the Syrian regime and against Abu al-Qaqa himself. These men might have carried out the failed Ummayad Square operation. Or it might have been executed by his opponents, who purposely planted his CDs, to place him in bad standing with the government. Or he might be a double-agent, working for the Syrians and international terrorist groups like al-Qaeda, wanting to play both sides against each other. History will prove how serious of a man Abu al-Qaqa is and what effects he will have on Syria.

[From Terrorism Focus, Volume III, Issue 25]

Saudi Arabia

Saudi Arabia's Shiites and their Effect on the Kingdom's Stability

John Solomon

Originally published on July 27, 2006

A decade has passed since Saudi Hezbollah, known locally as Ansar Khat al-Imam (Followers of the Line of the Imam), bombed the Khobar Towers, a U.S. military housing compound, killing 19 soldiers and injuring 350 [1]. This attack brought dramatic attention to Saudi Arabia's Shiite community and its potential for political violence and terrorism. Today, in light of an emerging power in Iran, a Shiite-dominated Iraq and an intensifying Shiite-Sunni divide, attention has returned to the Shiites of Saudi Arabia. Although there is little evidence of Shiite militancy inside the Saudi kingdom at present, the violence between Shiites and Sunnis in neighboring Iraq remains intense and could spill over into Saudi Arabia. Indeed, the specter of confessional violence looms as homegrown Saudi Salafi-Jihadists and the fighters returning from the jihad in Iraq could clash with the quiescent Shiites living inside the oil-rich kingdom.

As many as two million Shiites live in Saudi Arabia, where they comprise 10-15% of the population [2]. Most Saudi Shiites reside in the oases of Qatif and al-Hasa in the Eastern Province, which is also home to the world's greatest concentration of oil assets and about 90 percent of Saudi Arabia's oil production [3]. Given the extraordinarily tight world oil supply and demand balance, the kingdom's critical role as a swing producer, which enables it to quickly increase output above normal production levels to reduce the risk of an energy shock in the event of a supply disruption, makes conflict between Salafi-Jihadists and Shiites in the oil-rich province a disturbing scenario not only for Saudi Arabia's oil industry, but also for the world economy [4].

Analysts have highlighted the potential for an "Iraq effect" in which the sectarian violence between Sunnis and Shiites in Iraq spreads to Saudi Arabia [5]. Many observers in Saudi Arabia, including the Saudi leadership, have expressed concern regarding increased Shiite and Sunni tensions. Sheikh Hassan al-Saffar, a former Saudi Shiite dissident and now head of the Shiite Reform Movement, warned recently in *al-Quds al-Arabi* "that confessional conflict in Iraq would move to Saudi Arabia if the Saudi Sunnis were emboldened by the Sunni insurgency in Iraq and the Saudi Shiites by the backing of the Shiites of Iraq" [6]. For this reason, it is useful to examine the relationship of Saudi Sunnis and Shiites to their co-religionists and neighbors in Iraq.

The Iraq Effect

With regard to the Saudi Sunnis, propaganda intended to embolden and encourage support for jihadis returning to the kingdom from Iraq continues to proliferate. On June 30, al-Basha'ir (the Glad Tidings), a Salafi-Jihadist media organization, posted a statement on the Lahdud forum entitled "Who We are, What We Want and What Our Relation is to al-Qaeda in the Arabian Peninsula" (*Terrorism Focus*, July 5, 2006). The group identified itself as supporters of the mujahideen returning to Saudi Arabia from Iraq. Its stated objective is to establish an Islamic caliphate in the land of Muhammad and to remove the murtadayeen (apostates) and "crusaders." Murtadayeen refers to the Shiite population, in addition to other deviant sects. Since Salafis interpret Shiite devotion to their religious leaders as apostasy or polytheism, Shiites are sometimes referred to by these terms in Salafi diatribes. Although al-Basha'ir claimed no direct link between itself and al-Qaeda in the Arabian Peninsula, al-Qaeda welcomed the group and echoed its call to remove "polytheists" and "cross-worshippers" from Saudi Arabia. Through implicit but clear references, these statements indicate that Salafi-Jihadists have taken aim at the kingdom's Shiites.

The perception by Saudi Sunnis that an alliance exists between the Shiite powerbrokers in Iraq and the United States against their Sunni brethren fuels anti-Shiite rhetoric and exacerbates sectarian tensions within Saudi Arabia. Saudi Sunnis generally sympathize with the Sunni insurgency in Iraq and the jihad waged by al-Qaeda in Iraq, which explicitly calls for and carries out attacks against Shiites. Subsequently, by supporting the Sunni insurgency, Saudi sympathizers at a minimum tacitly support anti-Shiite violence. Additionally, Saudi Salafi-Jihadists have an ideological basis for targeting Shiites. Saudi Salafis find Shiite practices and beliefs blasphemous and have a long history of persecuting them both institutionally and culturally. The Salafis consider the Shiites apostates because they display adulation for their religious leaders in a way that the Salafis see as antithetical to the concept of tawhid (unity of God). Therefore, events in Iraq combined with preexisting hatreds could trigger confessional violence in Saudi Arabia.

Alerted to the shared danger of returning fighters and a new balance of power in Iraq, in 2004 King Abdullah extended concessions to the Shiites, including the right to observe Ashura, one of the most important Shiite religious days, in exchange for cooperation with the regime. Since the Iranian Revolution, the Saudi regime has questioned the Shiites' loyalty. In the face of Shiite Iraq and Iran, the regime saw it wise to temper the Shiite community's disaffection due to their second class status by addressing some of their grievances. In addition, Iranian-backed Saudi Hezbollah seems to have tactically decided that political violence is not in their current interests and members of the organization are currently participating in King Abdullah's National Dialogue process. Due to the Saudi government's crackdown following the Khobar attack, Saudi Hezbollah may have decided to participate in the National Dialogue process as a way to bide its time and rebuild organizational strength.

Regarding the perspective of Saudi Shiites in the Eastern Province, although Iran may exert some influence on the kingdom's Shiites, mainstream Saudi Shiites are much more attuned to Iraq than Iran. For example, due to their religious school of thought, ordinary Shiites generally follow their marja (source of emulation) or Grand Ayatollah for direction. For Saudi Shiites, the most prominent maraja happen to be from Najaf. Despite Sistani, Najafi and other major clerics having their own personal Hawzas (Shiite Islamic academy) in Qom in Iran, a Saudi Shiite who travels for religious study to Qom is not necessarily entering the Iranian Shiite cultural orbit. On the contrary, this reflects loyalty to a particular marja and not necessarily to the Iranian regime.

The Saudi Shiite political leadership, however, has a complex set of political loyalties because several former Saudi Shiite dissidents went into exile in various stages starting shortly after the Iranian revolution and through the 1980s. Many spent time in Iran but many also left complaining that the Iranians were seeking to co-opt them as instruments against the Saudi regime. Many in this group then moved to

Syria or Europe. In 1993-94, King Fahd made a deal with this group and they started returning to the kingdom. This group of people, of which Hassan al-Saffar is generally considered the head, is known locally as the "Shirazis" because they used to follow the late Sheikh Shirazi as their marja. Sheikh Shirazi was a prominent Najafi cleric who, after being exiled from Baathist Iraq, eventually landed in Qom at the time of the Islamic revolution but notably took part only as an observer. The Shirazis seem to be the dominant political force in the Eastern Province Shiite community as they control all elected seats in the Qatif municipal council. Adding further complexity, all the elected Shiite members seem to have advanced degrees from the United States.

Apart from the Saudi Shiite leadership, the pendulum on Shiite thinking and jurisprudence seems to be swinging away from Iran and back toward Najaf. With respect to which marja ordinary Shiites follow, anecdotal evidence suggests that 70-85% follow Sistani with the remainder split between Najafi, the two Shirazi camps, Khamenei, Tabrizi and Fadlallah. According to a government source in Saudi Arabia who wished to remain anonymous, many Shiites claim that the issue of "Who is your marja?" is of less interest and importance to Saudi Shiites than in Iraq or Iran and many point out that they are not interested enough in the finer points of theology to feel a need to "emulate" anyone. There is, however, a definite consensus that Sistani's popularity has skyrocketed in the past five years and in 2000 perhaps 30-40% of Saudi Shiites might have had him as their marja. The assassination of prominent alternatives (al-Khoei and al-Sadr) and Sistani's perceived statesman-like role in defending the rights of the Shiites in Iraq have won him great popularity.

Many observers hypothesized that there would be expanding links between the Shiites in the Eastern Province and Najaf. Yet there is little evidence in support of this theory. Unquestionably, the prestige of Sistani has grown in the province during the last several years. Clearly, a certain percentage of khums (taxes) collected in the province ends up in Najaf, probably in institutions mostly associated with Sistani. Again, according to anecdotal evidence, there is little intermarriage, no corpse traffic and little travel to Najaf (the latter mostly for understandable security reasons and the Saudi government's efforts to discourage travel to Iraq).

Shiite-Sunni Tensions

It is unlikely that Sunni and Shiite resistance would ever unite against the regime. Sunni Islamist opposition groups in the kingdom derive their ideology from the Salafi concept of tawhid and takfir (declaring one as an infidel). By this principle, the Salafis generally consider Shiites apostates and rejectionists, so cooperating with the Shiites from a Salafi point of view is anywhere from awkward to unacceptable. From the Shiite perspective, there is not much to be gained by an alliance with the Salafi-Jihadist opposition. In their view, the Salafi-Jihadists will gain strength against the regime while the Shiites will lose the gains they have made through King Abdullah's National Dialogue process.

Despite the concerns of sectarian violence erupting in Saudi Arabia, current evidence of this is limited. There are reports indicating that unknown assailants torched three Shiite places of worship in Tarut Island in the Eastern Province as a Shiite delegation was meeting Crown Prince Abdullah in 2004 [7]. Even though Saudi Salafi-Jihadists have disseminated diatribes against the Shiites, labeled them apostates and rejectionists worse than Jews and "crusaders," and have even gone so far as to circulate rumors of assassinating the leading Saudi Shiite cleric, Hassan al-Saffar, nothing critical has taken place in the three years since the war in Iraq began [8].

Although there is still little evidence of returning Saudi fighters, there is cause for concern with respect to the oil industry. The oil target is a way to attack the Saudi regime, the West and, in the Eastern Province, also the Shiites since they comprise a considerable number of Saudi Aramco's manual labor force. If Saudi Salafi-Jihadists do in fact return home and inject new blood, energy and more sophisticated techniques into homegrown Saudi terrorist movements, it is very likely that there will be increased attacks on oil infrastructure, including the enormous and exposed water-pumping installations which Saudi Aramco depends on to pump crude oil from its aging supergiant fields in the Eastern Province.

Therefore, it will be important to monitor whether returning Saudi fighters breathe new life into the kingdom's Sunni insurgency. If the violent Salafi-Jihadists returning from Iraq decide to fight the Shiites in the Eastern Province, the effect on oil prices would be dramatic and devastating for the Western economies, thus giving the Saudi jihadis one more enticing incentive to bring confessional violence to Saudi Arabia.

Notes

1. See 2001 FBI indictments and Anthony Cordesman's *Saudi Arabia Enters the 21st Century* for the best publicly available evidence of Saudi Hezbollah's complicity.

2. According to the latest figures of the CIA World Factbook, there are approximately 23 million Saudi Arabians living in the kingdom. There are no reliable statistics regarding the number of Shiites in the Saudi Arabia. Community leaders usually put the number around 1.5 million.

3. Matthew Simmons, *Twilight in the Desert*, p. 117.

4. "Saudi Arabian Oil Facilities: The Achilles Heel of the Western Economy," The Jamestown Foundation, May 15, 2006.

5. See Toby Jones, "The Iraq Effect in Saudi Arabia."

6. For more information on Sheikh al-Saffar visit www.saffar.org

7. John Bradley, *Saudi Arabia Exposed*, p. 85.

8. See http://www.d-sunnah.net and http://www.ekhlaas.info/forum/index.php.

[From Terrorism Monitor, Volume IV, Issue 15]

Saudi Security and the Islamist Insurgency

Christopher Boucek

Originally published on January 26, 2006

For over a decade, the Kingdom of Saudi Arabia has fought an ongoing battle against homegrown Islamist insurgents. These forces have sought to overthrow the ruling monarchy and replace it with what they have described as an "authentic" Islamic regime. Throughout the Saudi government's battle with these extremists, observers of the Kingdom have charged that security forces have been compromised and penetrated by al-Qaeda connected Islamists. The natural progression of this argument is that Saudi counter-terrorism forces are ineffective and untrustworthy. This article seeks to address this point, and challenge some of the allegations that have been taken at face value [1].

Perhaps the most disturbing development to come out of the 1979 takeover of the Grand Mosque was the eventual revelation of prime organizer al-Utaibi's connection to the Saudi Arabian National Guard (SANG). The SANG has historically been charged with some of the most sensitive security duties in the Kingdom, and has widely been described as the ruling family's "praetorian guard."

During the past decade, Saudi Arabia has suffered from a terrorist insurgency that intensified in May 2003. Many sources within the Saudi security and intelligence establishment attribute this development to the American-led intervention in Iraq and the associated rise in militancy, the participation of Saudi nationals in the insurgency in Iraq, and their subsequent return home to Saudi Arabia [2].

The pace of violence within the Kingdom is greater than reported in the Western media. According to knowledgeable sources in Saudi Arabia, many gun battles between terrorists and security forces go unreported. The same under-reporting is true for the discovery of foiled terrorist plots and materiel seizures. One of the greatest such plots was an operation reported to have targeted the massive Saudi oil facility at Ras Tanura, the existence of which was only revealed by CBS' "60 Minutes" television newsmagazine. Likewise, the existence of a number of plots against the royal family continue to circulate among Saudi watchers, but these attempted strikes against the regime have never been confirmed by either official Saudi or American sources.

One of these stories involved a disrupted plot to smuggle Soviet-designed Sagger anti-tank missiles into Saudi Arabia to allegedly be used in an ambush on vehicles carrying senior members of the royal family. The fact that these reports continue to be repeated both within the Kingdom and among Western counter-terrorism officials demonstrates the plausibility of these rumors, and on some level is measure of the belief within Saudi Arabia that the ruling order is both a primary target of domestic terrorists and one which has until now narrowly escaped catastrophe.

Terrorist violence in Saudi Arabia saw a large upswing beginning with the devastating coordinated suicide attacks on May 12, 2003, in which three Riyadh housing compounds were assaulted. Since then, terrorists have targeted critical infrastructure, international businesses, foreign residents, Saudi authorities, and the U.S. government. A similar attack to the May Riyadh bombings—also directed against a Riyadh housing compound—occurred several months later in November 2003. More than 50 people were killed in the May and November bombings.

Following the May 2003 compound assault, rumors circulated alleging SANG's complicity in the attack. These charges have not been substantiated and appear to be connected to possible legal action by Westerners claiming the Saudi government is not doing enough to fight terrorism [3]. Other allegations include claims that SANG weapons have been diverted to terrorists. This seems unlikely since SANG uses only American weapons, and those in question have been of Soviet design.

Knowledgeable sources have confirmed, however, that the war and chaos in neighboring Iraq has had a direct impact on the types and quantities of weapons seized by Saudi authorities. The corresponding advancements in IED and car bomb technologies first witnessed in Iraq—and now seen in Saudi Arabia—further demonstrate the flow of skills and experience from strife-torn Iraq.

After the deadly spate of attacks on expatriate housing designed to drive Westerners out of the Kingdom, terrorists again turned their attention on the security forces defending the royal court. On April 21, 2004, the former headquarters of General Security was car-bombed in Riyadh. Some sources indicated that this facility had previously housed security elements responsible in part for the protection of the royal family. Throughout the last several years, numerous shoot-outs and gun battles have occurred between militants and the security forces.

According to Ministry of Interior spokesman Lt. Gen. Mansour al-Turki, more than 40 security officers have died in the line of duty and over 350 have been wounded (including more than 150 serious injuries) [4].

The trend of targeting the support and income of the royal family continued in May 2004 with two devastating attacks. The first occurred at the beginning of the month when gunmen attacked a petrochemical complex in Yanbu on the Red Sea coast. The second attack involved a 25-hour siege, during which terrorists rampaged through the Oasis residential community in al-Khobar, leaving over 22 people—mostly foreigners—dead. Several firms involved in the oil sector, including Royal Dutch Shell, Total SA, Saudi Aramco, Lukoil, and Sinopec had offices in the Oasis at the time of the attack.

In December 2004, the U.S. consulate in Jeddah was attacked, and toward the end of the month two car bombs exploded in Riyadh. One exploded outside the Ministry of Interior, and another was detonated outside a training facility for the Special Emergency Forces, the Kingdom's counter-terrorist SWAT force. The Emergency Forces operate under the Ministry of Interior.

By early 2005, the pace and intensity of terrorist attacks began to recede. Had the level of attacks continued, it is a near certainty that Western expatriate residents and businesses would have begun to evacuate. It is unknown why exactly the pace of terrorist incidents did not continue. The inability to properly answer this question is in part due to the opaque nature of such information in the Kingdom, and it has further added to feelings by some analysts that such attacks will again occur in the future.

Some critics have charged that the security forces are either unwilling to act or are simply incompetent. Most often these allegations are made when suspects escape security dragnets. Yet, in Saudi Arabia, the security forces must act in recognition of conservative societal norms. In the Saudi case, security officers will allow women and children to leave once they have been cleared [5]. The Western media, however, reports only that suspects were able to evade capture. Oftentimes, the security forces have been criticized for waiting days before ending a standoff. Again, in Saudi Arabia it proves more effective to wait out suspects, limit exchanges of gunfire, and to try to negotiate surrender [6].

Perhaps some of the most important questions regarding Saudi Arabia's fight against terrorism arise from what is unknown about the security situation in the Kingdom. For instance, how reliable are the security forces in responding to attacks not on the royal family or the vast hydrocarbon infrastructure, but on Western interests in the Kingdom? Similar unknowns exist regarding the veracity with which certain elements of the security forces would act to defend a Western as opposed to a Saudi target. Will Saudi security forces always act to defend Western businesses, expatriates and diplomatic facilities with the same determination with which they defend the ruling order? Until greater data is available to properly address these questions, a central aspect of the security situation will remain unknown.

Saudi society is beginning to show the changes ushered by recent security measures. Huge banners and signs hang in Riyadh with pictures of destroyed buildings and blown apart vehicles asking questions such as how these incidents could happen in Saudi Arabia. The counter-terrorism message is delivered to people several times a day on television with the message "together against terrorism." The same message is displayed at automated teller machines each time a withdrawal is made. Even satellite television programs like "Circle of Darkness" are raising awareness of the terrorism problem.

It is also important to note that support for jihadi terrorism among the clergy and business and community leaders is declining. This is in no small part due to recent regime efforts to end societal acceptance of jihad [7]. Yet to interpret the recent failure of terrorists to mount a large-scale operation as the demise of terrorism in the Kingdom would be foolhardy. Terrorists in Saudi Arabia may be on the run today, but they are far from defeated.

Notes

1. Much of the material in this article is based upon first hand research and detailed interviews with both high-level Saudi and Western sources in Saudi Arabia in 2005.
2. Based upon interviews and discussions with officials from the Ministry of Interior, General Intelligence Presidency, and private analysts in Riyadh, Saudi Arabia, May 2005, as well as discussions held abroad.
3. Based on interviews with security personnel, Riyadh, May 2005.

4. Interview with Lt. Gen. Mansour al-Turki, Riyadh, Saudi Arabia, May 8, 2005.

5. Based on interviews with security personnel in Riyadh and abroad.

6. Ibid.

7. Beginning in November 2005 Saudi newspapers such as *al-Watan* and *Okaz* ran stories detailing these societal changes.

[From Terrorism Monitor, Volume IV, Issue 2]

Yemen

Yemen's Passive Role in the War on Terrorism

Gregory Johnsen

Originally published on February 23, 2006

For the past five years, Yemen has been what is best described as a passive partner in the U.S.-led war on terrorism. It has taken a number of steps to limit the activities of al-Qaeda and other like-minded groups within the country, but most of these have been at the behest of the U.S., and it is often schizophrenic in its pursuit of Islamic militants. In April 2004, Prime Minister Abd al-Qadir Bajammal claimed that Yemen had eradicated 90 percent of the al-Qaeda organization in the country. Yet rumors that factions within the country's political and security establishment assisted in the recent jailbreak of 23 militants, including prominent figures in the attacks on the USS Cole and the Limburg, have once again raised questions about Yemen's reliability as an ally in the war on terrorism (*Terrorism Focus*, February 7, 2006).

In the immediate aftermath of the September 11 attacks, Yemen was often mentioned in the same breath as Afghanistan as a possible hideout for al-Qaeda. Many Yemenis, including prominent government officials, felt their country was next on a "hit list" after the U.S. finished in Afghanistan. That fear has been expressed more recently by President Ali Abdullah Saleh, during a speech in Aden in December 2005, when he claimed that he dissuaded the U.S. from occupying the country following the attack on the USS Cole in October 2000 (al-Arabiya, December 1, 2005).

The country's fears stemmed from a long and close history with Islamic militants. Following the withdrawal of Soviet troops from Afghanistan in 1989, many of these fighters—known as Afghan Arabs—made their way back to their countries of origin, full of religious zeal and the thrill of victory, and eager to replicate their successes at home. The governments of the Arab world, however, were not as excited with the prospect of a local jihad within their borders. Massive crackdowns by many of these governments forced a number of the Afghan Arabs to flee their countries yet again. Many of them seized on an apocryphal hadith of the Prophet Muhammad: "When disorder threatens, seek refuge in Yemen." Even Osama bin Laden has alluded to the ideas expressed in the hadith and the situation in Yemen during the mid-1990s when he told Abd al-Bari Atwan of *al-Quds al-Arabi* in an interview in November 1996 that he would like to live in Yemen because it was one of the few places in the Arab world where one could still breathe the air of freedom.

The Yemeni government largely welcomed these fighters, and in 1994 it managed to turn them into an effective paramilitary force that helped the government put down a secession attempt by socialists in the south. The Afghan Arabs were led by Sheikh Abd al-Majid al-Zindani, who has since been listed as a "specially designated global terrorist" by both the U.S. and the UN, and Ali Muhsin al-Ahmar, a close relative of the president and one of the most powerful military leaders in the country. Both men had extensive contacts among the fighters. Al-Zindani made frequent trips to Afghanistan in the 1980s and early 1990s, and, according to the U.S. Treasury Department, has been a "spiritual leader" of bin Laden. Al-Ahmar is married to the sister of Tariq al-Fadhli, one of the most prominent Yemeni veterans of the war in Afghanistan, and the former head of the Aden-Abyan Islamic Army. Yet, much like U.S. support for the Afghan Arabs in the 1980s, Yemen's use of these fighters has since come back to haunt the government.

In addition to the attack on the USS Cole, which killed 17 sailors, the French oil tanker Limburg was also attacked in 2002, resulting in the death of a Bulgarian sailor who drowned after jumping overboard. Not everyone, however, attributes the attack on the Limburg directly to al-Qaeda operatives in Yemen. Nasser al-Bahri, bin Laden's former chief bodyguard, who is also known as Abu Jandal, claimed in an interview with *al-Quds al-Arabi* in 2004 that the bombing was a rash reaction to the killing of Yahya Saleh al-Mujalli, a local al-Qaeda operative, by government forces in Sana'a in late September 2002.

Earlier that year, Yemen had invited U.S. special forces into the country as advisers and trainers, and following the attack on the Limburg, it cooperated with the unmanned Predator drone strike on Ali Qaid Sinan al-Harithi, the suspected head of al-Qaeda in Yemen, and five of his companions in November 2002. The Yemeni government paid a high price domestically for allowing the U.S. to strike inside Yemen's borders, following a leak from the Pentagon that broke the agreement of secrecy between the two countries. President Saleh felt personally betrayed by the leak, and when Yemen captured al-Harithi's replacement, Mohammad Hamdi al-Ahdal, one year later in November 2003, it refused to allow U.S. officials to interrogate him directly.

The recent escape of 23 prisoners occurred only a day before al-Ahdal was due to stand trial. In the aftermath of the prison break, there has been a great deal of confusion as to whether al-Ahdal escaped or not. Hussein al-Jarbani of *al-Sharq al-Awsat*, reported on February 5 that al-Ahdal was among the escapees. On February 4, the *Yemen Times* also published what it called the "official list" of the escapees, noting that the list contained only 22 names, "excluding [Mohammad] Hamdi al-Ahdal." Other agencies, however, have stated that the judiciary has merely delayed his trial by a week, and that he is still in custody. On February 13, 2006 the Yemeni government finally announced that al-Ahdal was still in custody, as it officially began his trial under extremely tight security.

Al-Ahdal was originally captured in 2003, reportedly on a tip from a former militant who had recently been granted his freedom under a government program, The Religious Dialogue Council (RDC), headed by Hamoud al-Hitar. The program, which was initiated at the request of President Saleh in September 2002, is designed to convince suspected militants that carrying out violent actions in the name of Islam is not sanctioned by the Quran or the Sunna. It has since released 364 suspected militants in six separate pardons, following their pledges to abstain from violence. Bin Laden's former bodyguard, al-Bahri, is one such graduate. The RDC, which was initially started as part of a multi-pronged approach to remove Yemen from a "hit list" in Washington, appears to have been caught up in its perceived success through a combination of Western media reports and fewer terrorist attacks in Yemen from late 2002 to early 2005. This early euphoria led to the release of more and more detainees in greater frequency, and eventually to Bajammal's claim that Yemen was 90 percent al-Qaeda free.

Yet by the summer of 2005, as the war in Iraq continued to drag on, the RDC ran into problems. On June 1, 2005, al-Hitar told the *Khaleej Times*: "Resistance in Iraq is legitimate, but we cannot differentiate between terrorism and resistance in Iraq's situation because things are not clear in this case." Within a few months, however, his views had shifted slightly and he would only say: "Iraq is not a subject of the dialogue" (AP, October 11, 2005). This shift in thinking, or at least public descriptions of the dialogue sessions, seems to have been brought about by an incident in July 2005 when two former detainees, which al-Hitar had recommended for release, carried out a suicide bombing on U.S. forces in Baghdad. Al-Hitar initially denied this claim, which was originally reported by "anonymous Yemeni security sources" in the armed forces weekly paper *26th of September* (October 13, 2005). Yet Jamal al-Amir, the editor of the weekly independent newspaper *al-Wasat*, has argued that the story is true, and that at least eight men from al-Hitar's program have found their way to Iraq to fight U.S. forces there.

These revelations have essentially spelled the end of al-Hitar's program. In December 2005, while al-Hitar was in Washington participating in a State Department-sponsored conference on religious dialogue, Khalid al-Hammadi of *al-Quds al-Arabi* reported that sources within Yemen's security forces were convinced that al-Hitar's program had failed, and that it should be stopped (*al-Quds al-Arabi*, December 10, 2005). The sources pointed to the fact that al-Hitar had not been able to persuade the released militants to renounce violence, as a number of the former detainees were still in Iraq fighting. Yemen, of course, has worked extremely hard to keep its young men from traveling to Iraq, turning away suspicious passengers at the airport. Yet the borders are simply too porous to keep everyone in the country and out of Iraq.

The threat of violence is no longer one-way. In January 2006, Yemen announced that it had arrested 19 men, who had recently returned from Iraq and were planning to carry out terrorist attacks in the country. The men were reportedly acting on the orders of Abu Musab al-Zarqawi and his al-Qaeda in Iraq organization. One of the targets was a hotel in Aden frequented by Westerners; the men also had instructions to kill U.S. citizens. *The Yemen Observer*, which has recently been closed by order of the prime minister as a result of a story on the "cartoon riots," reported that one of the men, Ali Abdullah Asyan, called himself "Abu Ali al-Harithi, Jr." in honor of the slain al-Qaeda commander (*The Yemen Observer*, January 28, 2006).

The return route of fighters from Iraq to Yemen with the intention of striking Western targets in the country suggests that Yemen's period of relative calm could be nearing an end. It is too soon to tell if this is a new generation of fighters, as the "junior" in Asyan's assumed name would suggest, but what is clear is that Yemen has not destroyed

90 percent of al-Qaeda in the country. Furthermore, following the recent prison break, it is not even clear if the Yemeni government is 90 percent al-Qaeda free. For Yemen to truly reach Bajammal's estimate, it will have to cease being passive and become a more active ally.

[From Terrorism Monitor, Volume IV, Issue 4]

Prosecuting Terrorism: Yemen's War on Islamist Militancy

Andrew McGregor

Originally published on May 4, 2006

Any observer of Yemen's political scene cannot help but notice that Yemen appears to be awash with al-Qaeda suspects. Mass trials follow mass arrests as hundreds of suspects flow through Yemen's legal system. Some are selected for execution and others for lengthy prison sentences, but many avail themselves of early release or periodic amnesties. The system seems designed to weed out those who present a direct threat to Yemen or its regime, while relieving U.S. pressure in the war on terrorism by offering a constant demonstration of activity. In the wings of this performance is the constant threat of an insurgency led by Yemen's powerful Islamist movement.

The Legal Frontline

A continuing irritant in Yemen-U.S. relations is the status of Sheikh Abd al-Majid al-Zindani, the country's most prominent Islamist and leader of the Iman University in Sanaa. In February 2004, the U.S. Treasury Department identified al-Zindani as a "specially designated global terrorist" (*Terrorism Monitor*, April 6, 2006). The U.S. would like to see the sheikh extradited for his al-Qaeda connections and possible involvement in the USS Cole bombing, but al-Zindani enjoys the personal protection of Yemen's president, Ali Abdullah Saleh, who describes him as "a moderate." The president called such extradition attempts "unconstitutional" and noted that "we are not the police of any other country" (*Yemen Observer*, March 1, 2006)

The sheikh met in early April with Khaled Meshaal, the Syrian-based leader of HAMAS. At a fundraising event for the new Palestinian government (which has lost nearly all foreign aid from the West), al-Zindani referred to HAMAS as "the jihad-fighting, steadfast, resolute government of Palestine" (UPI, April 14, 2006). Al-Zindani is a leading member of Yemen's Islah Party, an Islamist opposition party that often works closely with the government. The leader of Islah is Sheikh Abdullah al-Ahmar, chief of the powerful Hashed tribe. President Saleh and many other government figures are members of the Hashed. Al-Ahmar is close to the Saudis, and it is partly through his mediation that many long-standing territorial and security disputes have been resolved in the last few years.

Al-Zindani is one of many Yemeni "Afghans," the term used for veterans of the anti-Soviet jihad in Afghanistan. Rather than alienate the so-called Afghans, Saleh's regime has used them to eliminate opponents of the government, most notably in the assassination campaign against members of the Yemen Socialist Party in the period from 1990 to 94. Others are reported to have been deployed against Zaidi Shiite militants in Northern Yemen.

Meanwhile, Saudi-born Mohammad Hamdi al-Ahdal is facing the death penalty in another U.S.-related prosecution. A veteran of conflicts in Afghanistan and Chechnya, al-Ahdal is charged with being a leading member of Yemen's al-Qaeda network, raising funds and organizing bomb attacks on U.S. interests in the country. He has admitted to collecting over one million Saudi riyals to buy the allegiance of Yemeni tribesmen in the Marib region. Nineteen security men were killed in a three-year pursuit of al-Ahdal that ended in 2003. Al-Ahdal used his chance to speak in court to charge Saudi and U.S. authorities with pressing Sanaa for a conviction. Al-Ahdal's onetime superior in al-Qaeda, Ali Qaid Senyan al-Harthi, was killed in Marib in 2002 by a U.S. unmanned Predator aircraft.

Nineteen men currently on trial in Sanaa are accused of planning attacks against U.S. interests as revenge for the killing of al-Harthi. The suspects, including five Saudis, are accused of operating under the instructions of Abu Musab al-Zarqawi, leader of the al-Qaeda faction in Iraq (*Yemen Times*, April 16, 2006). Two of the accused have admitted to possessing arms and explosives for use in training fighters for Iraq and Afghanistan, but proclaimed that their war was with the United States, not Yemen (*Yemen Observer*, March 4, 2006).

In an interesting case that attracted little attention, a group of former Iraqi army officers were acquitted on appeal in March on charges of plotting to attack the U.S. and UK embassies in Sanaa. Other former Iraqi officers are reported to have found employment in Yemen's military. The two armies cooperated extensively in the Saddam Hussein era, and a large part of Yemen's military received training in Iraq. The Iraqis have spent three years in prison, but appealed to be allowed to stay in Yemen over fears for their safety in Iraq.

Furthermore, on April 19, 2006, a group of 13 Islamists led by Ali Sufyan al-Amari were handed prison terms of up to seven years for plotting attacks against political and security officials in Yemen. Prosecutors announced in late April that 60 more suspected members of al-Qaeda are being brought to trial (26September.com, April 25, 2006).

Though the mass prosecutions suggest Yemen is mounting a successful campaign against Islamist militants, hundreds of convicted extremists have found a quick route to freedom through cooperation with Yemen's Dialogue Committee, which engages the prisoners in a Quran-based rehabilitation program. Other convicted Islamists are released in periodic amnesties, while suspects with political connections are often never brought to trial. Over 800 Zaidi Shiite rebels were freed in March in order to resolve the 2004-2005 conflict that erupted in the mountains of Northern Yemen. While the "revolving door" system of Yemeni justice frustrates U.S. security agencies, dispute resolution, mediation and reconciliation are all traditional art forms in Yemen's fractious social framework. They are what prevent the state from disintegrating, and Saleh's proficiency in these skills keeps the regime afloat.

Hunting Fugitives

Yemeni security forces continue the hunt for the 23 Islamists who escaped prison in Sanaa in February 2006. The facility was run by Yemen's leading intelligence service, the Political Security Organization (PSO). Particularly distressing to the U.S. was that many of the fugitives had been involved in terrorist attacks against U.S. interests, while some were making their second escape from PSO prisons. Eight of the escapees have surrendered or been captured, but the two most prominent fugitives, Jamal al-Badawi and Jaber Elbaneh, remain at large. Al-Badawi was sentenced to death in 2004 for planning the attack on the USS Cole, while Elbaneh was one of the so-called "Lackawanna Six," a terrorist cell based in upper New York state. Of the six, five are serving sentences in U.S. prisons, but Elbaneh escaped to Yemen where Yemeni police eventually detained him.

Security forces are reportedly using tribal and religious leaders in negotiations with the other fugitives for their surrender (*Yemen Observer*, April 3, 2006). Several PSO prison governors were put before a military tribunal on April 27, 2006 on charges of "inadequate conduct" in relation to the escape. The PSO is widely believed to include Islamists in its ranks, and there were serious questions raised at the time of the escape regarding PSO assistance to the escapees.

The escape has created barriers to the release of over 100 Yemeni detainees in Guantanamo Bay. The Yemen government maintains that 95 percent of the prisoners have no involvement in terrorism. According to a government study, most of the captive Yemenis worked in Afghanistan as teachers of the Quran or the Arabic language (26September.com, March 21, 2006). Nevertheless, some prisoners already released from Guantanamo Bay have been charged in Yemen with membership in al-Qaeda. One Yemeni prisoner who is unlikely to be released anytime soon is Sheikh Muhammad Ali Hassan al-Muayad, who is serving 75 years in a Colorado prison for financing terrorism. The sheikh was a member of the Shura Council of the Islah Party and imam of the main mosque in Sanaa before he was arrested in Germany in 2003 and extradited to the U.S. Al-Muayad complains of mistreatment in the U.S. and his family is appealing to President Saleh to intervene.

Yemen and the War in Iraq

U.S. intelligence has identified Yemen as a leading source of foreign fighters in the war in Iraq. The leader of the Islamic Army of Aden-Abyan (one of Yemen's largest Islamist militant groups), Khalid Abd al-Nabi, has complained that members of his group were arrested by PSO officers and then taken before U.S. operatives for interrogation regarding plans to fight coalition forces in Iraq (*Yemen Times*, April 4, 2006). The Islamic Army was formed in 1994 from "Afghans" who had helped Saleh's regime defeat Southern Yemen's socialists. They are accused of maintaining ties with al-Qaeda while sending fighters to join al-Zarqawi's network in Iraq.

In 2002, the government mounted a largely ineffective assault with heavy artillery and helicopter gunships on the group's training camp in the mountains near Hatat in Abyan district. Abd al-Nabi surrendered to the government, but was only briefly detained before being released without charges. Convicted Islamist militants released through the Dialogue Committee program agree to avoid further militancy within Yemen, but there is no mention made of Iraq.

Conclusion

A report released in April by Yemen's Ministry of Planning and International Cooperation revealed that 41 percent of Yemenis are below the poverty line and lack access to basic health and educational services (*Yemen Times*, April 25, 2006). Rising food prices, a 17 percent unemployment rate and a general lack of opportunity for Yemen's youth provide a pool of dissatisfied recruits for Islamist organizations.

The number of Yemenis currently fighting in Iraq is probably not large, but the presence of the conflict provides an external outlet for Yemen's most militant Islamists, much like Afghanistan once did. With the Islamist opposition forming the largest political force in Yemen outside of the current government, the United States will continue to find it difficult to leverage the Saleh regime. Any U.S. intervention at this point would present serious consequences for the stability of the region. For now, Yemen will remain a troubling ally in the war on terrorism.

[From Terrorism Monitor, Volume IV, Issue 9]

The Resiliency of Yemen's Aden-Abyan Islamic Army

Gregory Johnsen

Originally published on July 13, 2006

Yemen has had a long reputation of producing fighters for foreign wars. This tradition, as the current trial of a number of Yemenis for traveling to Iraq to fight illustrates, is still intact (*al-Hayat*, June 4, 2006). The 1980s were no exception, as Yemen contributed a number of young men to the war against the Soviet occupation of Afghanistan. Like most of the other "Afghan Arabs," the Yemenis returned home in the late 1980s and early 1990s eager to replicate their successes from abroad. Yemen, unlike most Arab countries, proved to be a hospitable environment for the returned fighters. Training camps were established, some with quasi-official support from government officials, and the men were kept well-supplied and content.

Many of these men gravitated toward leaders who they had fought under in Afghanistan. In the early 1990s, Abu Hasan Zayn al-Abadin al-Mihdhar, a Yemeni commander from Shabwah, organized a group of such men into what would eventually become known as the Aden-Abyan Islamic Army (AAIA) (*al-Hayat*, October 10, 2005). The group took its name from an apocryphal hadith that claims that in the last days an army will arise from Aden-Abyan to fight for victory in God's name, and that God will grant them success.

The unification of the communist south with the tribal north in 1990 created a unique environment that allowed the AAIA to flourish. Despite the official agreement, the Yemeni Socialist Party (YSP) and the General People's Congress, the ruling party in the north, remained wary of each other. Northern officials welcomed the influx of Afghan Arabs into the south, many of whom were returning to family lands, and used them as a proxy to fight a low-level and unofficial war against the communists.

For its part, the AAIA was eager to combat the YSP, which it considered a party of "godless communists." There was also an element of revenge in the conflict. Many of the members of the AAIA, such as Tariq al-Fadhli, had witnessed the nationalization of their family lands and estates by the communists. Al-Fadhli's father had been sultan of the Abyan governorate under the British, but was forced to flee to Saudi

Arabia along with his three-month old son when the communists came
to power in 1967. It was not until after unification that al-Fadhli was
finally able to return to his birthplace.

Northern officials kept some semblance of control over the
Afghan Arabs through Ali Muhsin al-Ahmar, the shadowy commander
of the 1st Armored Division and a close relative of President Ali
Abdullah Saleh, who is also married to al-Fadhli's sister. Al-Ahmar made
sure the AAIA was well-equipped in its struggle. Other prominent men
such as Sheikh Abd al-Majid al-Zindani, who had himself helped to
recruit a number of Yemenis to fight in Afghanistan, helped to provide
the religious cover for combating the communists. Outside figures, such
as Osama bin Laden, whom al-Fadhli had met in Afghanistan, helped to
provide financial support.

It has since emerged that many of the members of the AAIA
drew military and government salaries. Al-Fadhli, for instance, is an
adviser to the Yemeni Ministry of the Interior and a colonel in the
Yemeni army (*al-Quds al-Arabi*, November 8, 2001). All of this support
eventually paid dividends for the government in the north when in
1994 the south attempted to secede under the leadership of its former
president and then vice president, Ali Salim al-Bidh. Al-Fadhli, the
AAIA as well as a number of other Afghan Arabs played a key role in
defeating the south's secession bid. Yet, much like U.S. support for the
Afghan Arabs in the 1980s, Yemen's use of them to destroy its own
communist threat produced unanticipated blowback.

In 1998, the group kidnapped a number of Western tourists,
some of whom were killed in a botched rescue attempt. Officially at
least, this event marked the end of the AAIA. The Yemeni government
executed al-Mihdhar for his role in the kidnappings. Yemeni Prime
Minister Abd al-Qadir Bajammal told *al-Hayat* in 2005 that this was
the battle that destroyed the AAIA (*al-Hayat*, October 11, 2005). His
views were similar to those expressed by al-Fadhli in an interview with
Khaled al-Hammadi of *al-Quds al-Arabi* in 2001. "I believe," al-Fadhli
said, "that the idea of the army was linked to the person himself, that
is Abu Hasan al-Mihdhar, and when he died that army ended as well"
(*al-Quds al-Arabi*, November 8, 2001).

Since the clash of 1998, al-Fadhli has consistently denied that he
was ever a member of the AAIA. He instead insists that he led a group
focused on the destruction of the communists in Yemen. Once that

task was completed with the end of the civil war in 1994, he claims to have dismantled his organization (*al-Quds al-Arabi*, November 8, 2001). Al-Fadhli has also gone to great lengths since 1998 to distance himself from his former colleague.

Despite both the government and al-Fadhli's insistence that the AAIA was destroyed in 1998, it has since been linked to a number of major terrorist attacks in Yemen, such as the bombing of the USS Cole in 2000 and the attack on the French oil tanker Limburg in 2002. Al-Fadhli has even tacitly acknowledged the link, despite his earlier comments that the AAIA had not survived the death of al-Mihdhar (*al-Quds al-Arabi*, November 8, 2001).

One journalist, Arafat Mudabish of *al-Sharq al-Awsat*, even hinted on March 31, 2006 that the group may have been behind the 1992 attacks aimed at U.S. Marines in Aden. Indeed, al-Fadhli was arrested in the aftermath of that attack, although he was released from prison to participate in the 1994 civil war (*al-Quds al-Arabi*, November 8, 2001).

The links between the AAIA, al-Fadhli and bin Laden in the early 1990s have raised questions as to whether or not the group is in any way affiliated with al-Qaeda. Al-Fadhli, of course, maintains that there is no link between the two groups. "Osama bin Laden provided me with funding as a person and not as a leader," he said. "I have only heard about al-Qaeda recently because there was no such thing when I was in Afghanistan" (*al-Quds al-Arabi*, November 8, 2001).

Other, more neutral sources seem to agree with him. Nabi al-Sufi, the editor of the *News Yemen* website, told *al-Hayat* in 2005 that the AAIA was a local organization that had no roots outside of Yemen (*al-Hayat*, October 11, 2005). Yet, local or not, most independent sources appear convinced that the group was not destroyed in 1998.

Following the execution of al-Mihdhar in 1998, the leadership of AAIA was taken over by one of his former soldiers, Khalid Abd al-Nabi (*al-Hayat*, October 11, 2005). Like al-Fadhli, al-Nabi was born in Yemen but moved to Saudi Arabia in the mid-1980s due to poor living conditions before traveling to Afghanistan to fight. He returned to Yemen in time to take part in the 1994 civil war as part of the AAIA (*al-Hayat*, October 11, 2005).

Despite numerous promises and sporadic crackdowns during the past few years, the government has been unable to completely eradicate the group, largely due to a lack of concentrated effort. The running battles and jail sentences seem to have had little impact on the group's fortunes. This failure, however, has not stopped the government from claiming that the AAIA no longer exists.

Most recently, a government official reiterated this claim to *al-Sharq al-Awsat* following reports of a failed assassination attempt against al-Nabi in May (*al-Sharq al-Awsat*, May 16, 2006). The security official, who refused to be named, would only say: "The Aden-Abyan Army does not exist. Khalid Abd al-Nabi turned himself in [to authorities] in the past, and was then pardoned by President Ali Abdullah Saleh. He now lives as an average citizen and owns a farm."

Following his pardon last year, al-Nabi has been officially known in Yemen as the former leader of the AAIA, but his actions seem closer to those of the current leader. In late June, he warned the government that its security sources were overbearing while at the same time pleading with President Saleh to commute the prison sentences of AAIA members still being held (*al-Wasat*, June 28, 2006). This is something that Salih has done numerous times before, such as in 2003 when he released Salih Mansur Haydarah (*al-Sharq al-Awsat*, October 24, 2003). Saleh's catch-and-release method of dealing with the AAIA has certainly contributed to the group's longevity. Yet in a country where the line between allies and enemies is constantly being blurred, Saleh prefers to play off the many competing actors against each other in an effort to maintain a delicate balance of power. This attitude—despite official government claims—helps to explain why the AAIA has been one of the more resilient groups in the region.

[From Terrorism Monitor, Volume IV, Issue 14]

Profile of Sheikh Abd al-Majid al-Zindani

Gregory Johnsen

Originally published on April 6, 2006

February 2006 was not a good month for Sheikh Abd al-Majid al-Zindani, a man the U.S. has labeled a "specially designated global terrorist." First, a Yemeni government weekly, *26th of September*, published a report claiming President George W. Bush had sent a letter to President Ali Abdullah Saleh demanding that Yemen arrest al-Zindani and freeze his assets (*26th of September*, February 23, 2006; *Terrorism Focus*, March 7, 2006). Then, over the course of the next two weeks, al-Zindani was involved in two vehicle accidents, which were later determined to have been assassination attempts against the aging sheikh (al-Jazeera, March 4, 2006).

Like most incidents involving al-Zindani, the details of the stories were in constant flux, and in the end few really knew exactly what happened. Despite the fact that the newspaper's website eventually published the purported text of the letter from Bush to Saleh on March 4, it was eventually discovered that no such letter existed. The story of the assassination attempts had a similar feel of fluidity.

Al-Zindani's son, Abdullah, told *al-Sharq al-Awsat* on March 5, 2006 that it was not true that his father had been the target of an assassination attempt. Just a week later, however, his father corrected this version of the story in an interview with Khaled al-Hammadi of *al-Quds al-Arabi*. He said that the first accident, in which a tire on his car had "exploded," was worrisome, but he became convinced that he had been targeted a week later when an entire wheel fell off the car. "It is well known that assassination operations designed for cars are carried out in this manner," he said (*al-Quds al-Arabi*, March 12, 2006).

Al-Zindani refused to implicate the U.S. in the affair, saying, in a rare moment of discretion, that "we do not know who the person responsible is, nor do we know who is behind him" (*al-Quds al-Arabi*, March 12, 2006). Nevertheless, despite all of al-Zindani's tact, the issue has strained U.S.-Yemeni relations, and has initiated a meeting between President Saleh and U.S. Ambassador Thomas Krajeski. A video of this meeting was later aired on Yemeni Television, with a voice-over by President Saleh: "Sheikh al-Zindani is a rational, balanced and moderate man and we know him well, and the Yemeni government guarantees [his actions], and I guarantee his character" (*al-Quds al-Arabi*, March 12).

The battle between Yemen and the U.S. over the fate of al-Zindani began on February 24, 2004, when the U.S. Department of the Treasury named al-Zindani a "specially designated global terrorist" for his financial support of al-Qaeda (the UN added him to its list of "individuals belonging to or associated with al-Qaeda," in accordance with Security Council Resolution 1267, three days later).

Al-Zindani is inevitably taken at face-value, as a fire-breathing radical intent on the destruction of the U.S. This image of him as a wild-eyed militant is further aided by his striking appearance, which is highlighted by a bright red, henna-dyed beard, as well as by his oratorical presence, which often borders on bombastic despite his occasional difficulties with Arabic grammar.

All of this, however, tends to disguise the fact that al-Zindani defies labels. His thought is a much more nuanced response to the modern world than the simple tags of Wahhabi or Salafi indicate. In the political arena he is a frightening man, who has advocated violence and destruction for those who disagree with him. On the other hand, intellectually he has tackled some of the most difficult issues facing religion in today's world, namely the tension that exists between religion and science. Additionally, he also specializes in the study of tawhid, or the oneness of God. One of his books on the subject is used as a textbook in Yemeni public schools.

In a country with an unacknowledged HIV/AIDS crisis, he is one of the few public figures working to combat it, opening a treatment center in Sanaa. His methods are rather unorthodox—he believes he can heal patients through Quranic intercession—but he refuses to ignore the problem, unlike many that argue that Muslims do not contract the disease (*al-Quds al-Arabi*, March 12, 2006).

In 2003, he issued a controversial fatwa that was designed to make marriage easier for Muslims living in the West. He was attacked for legitimizing sin, but he maintained his position, saying it was a way for Muslims to interact successfully in modern societies (*al-Sharq al-Awsat*, September 12, 2003).

He heads al-Iman University in Sanaa, where John Walker Lindh studied before heading to Afghanistan to join the Taliban, although al-Zindani has denied that Lindh ever attended the school in numerous interviews (al-Arabiya, August 4, 2004). He is also the head of the consultative council for Islah, the country's largest opposition party, and in the opaque world of Yemeni politics he remains very close to President Saleh, who has often delivered the commencement address at al-Iman.

His following in Yemen is mostly derived from cassette tapes of his sermons that are sold in stores throughout the country. Large signs in stores around the new campus of Sanaa University promise that cassettes of his Friday sermons are available by 7 PM on the day they are delivered. He is also a writer, despite the criticisms of some Western-educated Yemenis that he "doesn't really know Arabic grammar," and has authored at least 14 books on subjects from the rights of women to his latest on fasting (author's interview, Sanaa, 2004). He often contributes the front page editorial to the monthly newspaper of al-Iman University, *Saut al-Iman*, or *The Voice of Faith*.

Two years ago, very little was known about al-Zindani in Western circles, and much of what was known was wrong. This is not necessarily surprising; even Western academics specializing in contemporary Yemeni history seemed unsure of his origins. While this is no longer the case, thanks largely to the internet and the large number of interviews that al-Zindani has given in recent years, the U.S. seems to have done little to update its files. Even the birth date that the U.S. government has for him, "circa 1950," is wildly off the mark (U.S. Treasury Department, February 24, 2004).

Al-Zindani was actually born closer to 1940—most likely in 1938—on Mount Ba'dan, near a village of the same name, which overlooks the southern city of Ibb, a date that becomes clear from reading through al-Zindani's numerous interviews and writings. He spent his primary years in school in Ibb, before moving to Aden, which was under British rule at the time, to continue his studies. In his late teens, he moved to Cairo to attend Ain Shams University.

It was in Cairo, where al-Zindani went to study pharmacology, that he first became interested in the relationship between science and the Quran, which is often termed al-i'jaz al-'almi, or the scientific wonders of the Quran. In an interview with the Yemeni magazine *al-Shaqa'iq* in February/March 2004, al-Zindani said that in 1958 a group of Egyptian communists published what he called "a gray pamphlet" attacking the Quran and claiming that it contradicted modern science.

"This started me on my path," he told the magazine, "of answering those challenging communists." The fact that al-Zindani studied in Cairo during the late 1950s and early 1960s has also been confirmed by his fellow Yemeni students who were in Cairo at the time (author's interview, Sanaa, 2004).

This would eventually become al-Zindani's life, although he spent time fighting with Yemen's "third-way force," Hezbollah, during the civil war in the 1960s. (There is no relationship between the Yemeni Hezbollah and the Lebanese grouping of the same name.) He spent most of the 1970s shuttling back and forth between Saudi Arabia and Yemen, as he slowly imported a more conservative version of Islam into Yemen through the education system.

Finally in the 1980s, following a splintering of the Yemeni Muslim Brotherhood, he convinced Sheikh Abd al-Aziz bin Baz, the Grand Mufti of Saudi Arabia, to support him in establishing the Institute for the Scientific Inimitability of the Quran and Sunnah, which was based at King Abd al-Aziz University in Jeddah (*al-Shaqa'iq*, February/March, 2004). It was here where he first met Osama bin Laden, and where he found a base to recruit and transport thousands of young Yemeni and Saudi Arabian men to Afghanistan to fight against the Soviet Union.

The Department of the Treasury calls him one of "bin Laden's spiritual mentors," and while al-Zindani did guide and teach the younger man during the 1980s, he started downplaying the relationship even before 9/11. He told *al-Sharq al-Awsat* that bin Laden did not finance any part of al-Iman University (*al-Sharq al-Awsat*, June 3, 2001). He went even further after the attacks on New York and Washington, although he was careful to remain ambiguous. In 2004, he avoided a question by Hassan M'awdh of al-Arabiya regarding his relationship with bin Laden, saying only that during the 1980s everyone, even the U.S., had been against the Soviet occupation of Afghanistan (al-Arabiya, August 4, 2004).

Still, the fact remains that he was able to utilize his contacts with the Afghan Arabs to help the Yemeni government put down a secession attempt by the Socialist south in 1994. He returned to Yemen following unification, lured back to his country of birth with promises of positions of power. In 1993, he was named to the five-man appointed presidential council, where he remained until 1997.

More recently in 2000, he was involved in a case labeling the late writer Muhammad Abd al-Wali an infidel for a line in his book, *Sanaa: The Open City*, that allegedly blasphemies God. The fact that al-Wali had been killed in a plane crash in 1973 seemed to matter little to al-Zindani. He has also led the charge, collecting donations, to pursue the prosecution of Muhammad al-Asadi, the editor of the English-language *Yemen Observer*, for re-publishing the now infamous "Muhammad cartoons," despite the fact that *The Observer* published them with a line through the cartoons. The case is still pending.

His fatwas have also been linked to the killing of a Socialist Party politician, Jarallah Omar, on December 28, 2002, as well as the murder of three Baptist missionaries two days later. There have also been rumors that he gave the fatwa that led to the bombing of the USS Cole in 2000, which killed 17 U.S. sailors. He has refused to appear in court to answer questions regarding any of these accusations.

Al-Zindani's future remains unclear, but for the moment he remains what he has always been: an intriguing and complex figure in both the political and intellectual arenas, loathed by the U.S. and championed by Yemen.

[From Terrorism Monitor, Volume IV, Issue 7]

Oman

Islamists Stay Clear of Terrorism in Oman

N. Janardhan

Originally published on March 9, 2006

A sudden crackdown and arrest of "Islamists" in 2004-05 raised fears about Oman becoming entangled in the vicious cycle of terrorism, much like several other countries in the Persian Gulf region. The trial of the "saboteurs"—who attempted to challenge the status quo like in 1994—and the continuing calm thereafter indicates that the scourge of violence in the name of religion has still not reached the shores of the Sultanate.

The reason for terrorism not occurring in Oman is mainly attributed to the peculiar religion of the Omanis, who are followers of Abdallah ibn Ibadah al-Maqdisi's branch of Islam, a breakaway from the Khariji ("quietist") movement in Basra in 650 AD. Some experts suggest that the movement is an offshoot of a dissident Shiite sect hailing originally from Ibadh in Saudi Arabia, which was introduced to Oman in the eighth century.

Oman is the only Ibadhi country in the world, with its tenets closely linked to the Maliki Sunni school. Ibadhism rejects primogeniture succession and asserts that the leadership of Islam should be designated by an imam who is capable and elected by the people. In fact, both political and religious Ibadhi leadership is vested in an imam.

The Ibadhi orientation, which many Muslims consider unorthodox, has conditioned the society in such a fashion that in a region extremely conscious of sectarian affiliations, the 2004 census did not even seek to ascertain the composition of the Omani population along divisive lines, though it is understood that roughly 25 percent of the population is estimated to be Sunni. Further proof of Oman's uniqueness lies in it becoming the first Gulf Cooperation Council country in December 1994 to host an Israeli prime minister—Yitzhak Rabin—though there were murmurs of discontent among the Islamists.

Against this backdrop, it is no surprise that there is no record of Omanis having fought in Afghanistan or being held in

Guantanamo Bay. In fact, the only two available references linking al-Qaeda and Oman are: first, without details, the 9/11 commission report simply mentions that Osama bin Laden's Islamic Army Council (the initial ruling body of the International Islamic Front prior to the 1998 reorganization) included Omani Islamists; second, Kuwaiti-Canadian al-Qaeda member Mohammed Mansour Jabarah— who traveled to Oman, possibly on his way to Saudi Arabia—was arrested in the Sultanate in March 2002. Several months later, Muscat confirmed that it had arrested members of an al-Qaeda cell, but gave no details. While Muscat denied reports that they were extradited, Washington said "they were transferred to the United States" [1].

2005 Arrests

The incident that sounded the alarm bells in Oman and reverberated around the world was the late December 2004 and early January 2005 arrests of "100-300" suspects (as reported initially)— including civil servants, military personnel, preachers, Islamic scholars and university professors from the Ibadhi sect—for allegedly planning attacks in the Sultanate. The arrests—carried out in the interior of the country—were facilitated by a road accident that exposed a truck carrying a consignment of weapons allegedly meant to disrupt the month-long Muscat cultural and trade festival, which was boycotted by Islamists because it was seen as being against the precepts of Islam (*Khaleej Times* (UAE), January 26, 2005).

Police seized and displayed computers, cameras, a GPS system, about 40 Kalashnikov rifles, revolvers, maps of Oman, about 35 books dealing with military training, explosives and how to face interrogations, as well as a large quantity of ammunition.

Relatives of some of the accused denied any link between the detainees and arms shipments or with al-Qaeda. "We were astonished by father's arrest in his Muscat home at dawn on January 9," said Taleb al-Abri, son of Islamic studies professor Ali bin Hilal al-Abri [2]. Taleb acknowledged that, like many Muslims, his father opposed the U.S.-led invasions of Afghanistan and Iraq, but insisted that he had no connection to terrorist activities or to al-Qaeda.

The government initially admitted to a "religious extremist" plot, but insisted "they are not violent extremists." It revealed little information beyond stating that "the reason behind these detentions was an attempt to form an organization to tamper with national security, which is a red line that requires to be dealt with sternly" (*Times of Oman*, January 31, 2005). It was only in March that the government revealed that only 31 were arrested and clarified that "the arrests have nothing to do with terrorism or foreign parties" of the sort that were being undertaken in neighboring countries [3].

Unique Trial

The trial by the State Security Court, which finally began on April 19, 2005 and continued for three consecutive days, was unique because it was the first of its kind to be open to a select public, relatives of the accused, journalists and members of Majlis al-Shura (the elected consultative council) and Majlis al-Dawlah (the appointed state council). The accused appeared in national attire with no handcuffs and there were no barriers separating the trial panel and the audience. Despite their "dangerous" depositions, some of the accused declined the services of defense lawyers, placing their faith in the integrity and fairness of the judicial system [4]. The ruler, Sultan Qaboos bin Said, ordered the authorities to continue paying salaries to the families of the suspects until a verdict was reached.

The charges filed against the accused included joining a secret organization first set up in 1982, forming the al-Bashaer military group, raising funds to finance it and conducting military training, convening secret meetings in wilayats ("districts"), arms smuggling and possession and sales of illegal arms, forming a committee to take control of the oil and gas fields, and organizing seminars and summer camps to spread the group's agenda (*Gulf News* (UAE), April 20, 2005). The prosecution screened videos to support their charges.

During the court deliberations, some of the accused confessed to joining the banned secret organization to spread the ideology of imama ("rule of the imam") and its values, but most argued that their intention was not to overthrow the regime, but to spread the Madhab ("Islamic jurisprudence") of Ibadhi. Some others confessed to taking part in the organization's activities, but denied being its members. A few others claimed they had quit the organization some years after joining it because they viewed the return of the imama as unrealistic. The proceedings revealed that the group regularly met in remote desert areas. Many of the defendants, however, regretted joining the organization and pleaded for forgiveness.

One of the accused confessed to taking part in a meeting of the secret organization in 1997 through a person who had convinced him that the aim was to check the tide of strict interpretation of Islam in the wilayats. Another accused, a cleric, was in charge of securing areas of meetings, which were described as "dinner parties" to avoid attracting attention. A third admitted developing a special way of hiding weapons in hollow cement pillars in his farms. One of them said: "We did not call it an organization; it was a group, and our aim was dawa ("preaching") and correction of deviations in the religious branch." Another said: "I continued contacts until I went to Britain for higher studies during 1990-95 and abstained from the activities afterwards. My mistake is I did not inform the authorities concerned" [5].

A fourth session was convened on April 25, 2005 to hear final defense pleas. Seven lawyers pleaded their clients' innocence, saying they had merely sought to promote Ibadhi teachings in the face of "external currents." They said possession of weapons was in keeping with Omani norms and that the worst their clients can be accused of is holding firearms without a license (*Arab News*, April 26, 2005).

Jailed and Pardoned

On May 2, 2005 the court handed jail terms of between one and 20 years—six defendants, accused of being leaders of the group, were sentenced to 20 years in jail, 12 received 10-year terms, another 12 received seven years, while the 31st, who was acquitted of seeking to overthrow the regime, received a one-year jail sentence for holding weapons without a license. The judge said the defendants could not appeal the verdict but could ask for a pardon from Sultan Qaboos within 30 days (*Arab News*, April 26, 2005).

The same day, the government released the names of those convicted for "treason." Those who received 20 years in jail (age in brackets) were: Saleh bin Saleem al-Rubkhi (45), Yousef bin Ebrahim al-Sarhani (44), Mohammad bin Sulaiman bin Mohammad al-Shaili (50), Humaid bin Mohammad bin Sulaiman al-Yahmadi (45), Saleh bin Rashid bin Ali al-Maamari (48) and Khamis bin Rashid bin Said al-Dawi (39).

Those who received 10-year sentences were: Mohammad bin Salim bin Mohammad al-Harthy (40), Mohammad bin Saif bin Hamad al-Rawahi (49), Nasir bin Sulaiman bin Said al-Sabei (37), Khalifa bin Ahmad bin Humaid al-Qassabi (42), Abdullah bin Said bin Khalfan al-Maamari (33), Ali bin Hilal bin Mohammad al-Abri (45), Hilal bin Yahya bin Zaid al-Ismaeili (43), Khalifa bin Said bin Nasir al-Busaidi (35), Abdul Hamid bin Mohammad bin Harib al-Habsi (33), Mohammad bin Khamis bin Ali al-Shamsi (30), Mahmoud bin Mohammad bin Sulaiman al-Azri (31) and Abdul-Aziz bin Yahya bin Ahmad al-Kindi (44).

Seven-year sentences were given to Kahlan bin Nabhan bin Abdul Rahman al-Kharousi (33), Jabir bin Ali bin Hamoud al-Sadi (40), Mohammad bin Rashid bin Saleh al-Gharbi (37), Khalid bin Salim bin Nasir al-Khawaldi (31), Mohammad bin Zahir bin Said al-Abri (38), Said bin Sultan bin Mohammad al-Khanjri (50), Salim bin Ali bin Ashain al-Namani (39), Said bin Saif bin Salim al-Mawali (45), Yaqoob bin Yousuf bin Nasir al-Azri (35) Abdullah bin Yahya bin Ahmad al-Kindi (35), Said bin Abdullah bin Sallam al-Saqri (35) and Saif bin Salim bin Ali al-Busaidi (31). Nasir bin Sulaiman bin Mohammad al-Shaili, 47, received a one-year sentence (*Times of Oman*, May 3, 2005).

Though Sultan Qaboos ratified the sentences, he pardoned all 31 on June 9, 2005 (*Arab News*, June 10, 2005).

1994 Arrests

Though unconnected, Oman witnessed a similar incident in 1994. After the 1963-76 Dhofar civil war, dissidence was under control until a wave of arrests in May 1994 exposed the existence of opposition factions. About 430 people were interrogated on charges of forming an illegal political party to undermine state security and subversion [6]. A state security court was convened in November 1994, which sentenced about 135 to prison terms and a few death sentences were commuted by the Sultan to life imprisonment. Finally, all prisoners, who the Sultan had accused of being Islamist extremists, were freed as part of an amnesty in November 1995. Thereafter, Omani officials opted for a political, social and educational model that was relatively open and that discouraged large-scale opposition. Islamists, nevertheless, worked in secrecy to keep their agenda alive, but were decisively undermined for a second time in 2005.

In the final analysis, while the 1994 and 2005 episodes may have assumed religious connotations, they were more about changing the status quo than acts of terrorism with broader objectives. The fact that there has been no indication of Omani Islamists colluding with foreign Islamist militants provides optimism for the future.

Notes

1. *Arab News* (Saudi Arabia), August 26, 2002. A German tourist was injured in a shooting incident in November 2003 and an American and a German were killed in Muscat in December, but investigation revealed that these were not acts of "terrorism."

2. See http://www.gulfinthemedia.com (UAE), January 28, 2005.

3. *Arab News*, April 19, 2005. Most of the accused were from the Nizwa region, which was historically a major center of learning and the seat of the Imamate rebellion in the 1950s.

4. *Oman Daily Observer*, April 25, 2005. In its editorial, the paper said: "Preaching religion is achieved by prudence and good advice, not by force...Likewise, the call for reform and guidance to the path of piety does not require underground measures or secret meetings."

5. For more accounts of the trial, see *Times of Oman*, April 20-22, 2005, *Khaleej Times*, April 22, 2005.

6. The Islamists accused the Sultan of being influenced by Western powers and criticized the visit of Israelis to Oman, as well as Muscat's steps to cooperate with Tel Aviv at a time when the Palestinian issue was not resolved. Muscat also swapped economic representation offices with Tel Aviv, which were closed in 2000 for lack of progress in the Middle East peace process and Israel's reaction to the Palestinian intifada.

[From Terrorism Monitor, Volume IV, Issue 5]

Algeria

The Algerian 2005 Amnesty: The Path to Peace?

Audra Grant

Originally published on November 17, 2005

On September 29, Algerians voted in an unprecedented referendum to approve a charter for "peace and national reconciliation," offering amnesty to Algerian insurgents in exchange for laying down their arms. The charter also extends the same offer of clemency to police and security agents involved in crimes during Algeria's turbulent civil war. The charter marks a turning point in resolving Algeria's conflict, as it recognizes for the first time the numerous claims of Algeria's "disappeared" and considers reparations for relatives of those who suffered from the violence.

At least 150,000 Algerians are believed to have died during the country's more than decade-long conflict, ignited in 1992 following nullification of the country's first multiparty elections in which the populist Islamist party, the Islamic Salvation Front (FIS) would likely have been victorious after a second round. Islamist oppositionists responded with brutal violence that was met with similar ferocity by the Algerian authorities. While those killed were mostly civilians, as many as 10,000 are among "the disappeared," kidnapped by the security services or Islamic insurgents.

The peace plan, called the Charter for Peace and National Reconciliation, was overwhelmingly approved (97 percent) in a referendum marked by high turnout (80 percent). The plan is a cornerstone of Algerian President Abdelaziz Bouteflika's political agenda, which seeks to end Algeria's insurgency. Bouteflika assumed power in 1999, and pledged in October 2004 to submit an amnesty plan that would facilitate a reconciliation process first initiated by the 1999 Civil Harmony Law. Yet the amnesty is as much an effort to close the wounds of the insurgency, as it is a test of Bouteflika's legitimacy. He was re-elected for a second term in 2004 in a landslide victory, and hopes to win a third election. Bouteflika's political fortunes are firmly tied to the amnesty.

The charter ends judicial proceedings against Islamist insurgents, including those who disarm, who live abroad and are complicit in terrorism within Algeria, and who were convicted of crimes in absentia. The plan also offers reparations for families of the disappeared. Excluded from the amnesty are individuals involved in massacres, rapes, or bombings.

Yet the accord is not without controversial features. State assistance to insurgents' families, rejection of claims that security forces participated in disappearances of Algerians, prohibition on disparaging Algerian institutions, and restrictions on political activity by perpetrators of terrorism have been lightening rods for commentary. Critics question whether the charter's compensations will translate into justice for Algerian victims, asserting the amnesty lacks adequate mechanisms for debate, punishment and justice [1].

The Impact of the Amnesty on Violent Islamist Activity

Islamist violence has continued to subside since Bouteflika's inauguration, even in areas such as Sidi Rais, known as the Triangle of Death at the height of the insurgency. Approximately 4,000 insurgents surrendered from 1995 to 1998 under the clemency of former president Liamine Zeroual, with an additional 6,000 surrendering after Bouteflika's 1999 amnesty [2]. Tallies on active insurgents vary, but Algerian officials estimate that as many as 800 to 1,000 recalcitrant insurgents have managed to sustain operations throughout the country. This represents a notable decrease since the 1990s when insurgents possibly totaled 28,000. The improved ability of Algerian intelligence and security forces to eliminate insurgents, previous amnesty initiatives, and international assistance has contributed to the depletion in the ranks of violent Islamists.

Despite the decline in violence, Algeria is still plagued by bouts of attacks that continue to pose a challenge to national security. Significantly, the weeks preceding and following the charter referendum have been punctuated by a surge in insurgent violence that is attributed to the Salafi Group for Preaching and Combat (GSPC), an organization that remains in a bitter struggle with the state. The GSPC, now perhaps Algeria's most fortified Islamist group, has vehemently rejected the peace plan and vows to continue hostilities against the Algerian state.

Algerian security officials say remnant insurgents predominantly belong to the GSPC and they expect most members to accept the new amnesty. One prolific affiliate may include former GSPC leader Hassan Hattab, who has been negotiating with the Algerian government over his surrender. Hattab's compliance with the charter reportedly depends on a fatwa from a Saudi imam who would authorize Hattab to bargain with a government he considers impious. Rather than judge the legitimacy of surrender, the fatwa would only address whether Hattab can negotiate with a former enemy in a way that protects his credibility vis-à-vis his cadre of current supporters. If successful, Hattab could both come away with his position intact and with supporters willing to surrender under the amnesty [3].

Ultimately, however, Algerian officials offer tempered assessments of whether all violent Islamists will surrender under the charter. "The most important thing is to bring down their numbers," Prime Minister Ahmed Ouhiya told Algerian daily, *L'Expression*. "We don't have any illusions. ...There will always be the hard core who will never take up the offer of peace" [4].

If current GSPC statements are any indication of its reactions to the amnesty, some violence from the group can be expected. Firm in its opposition to the charter and in its intention to wage violence against the Algerian establishment, the new leader of the GSPC, Abu Musab Abdelouadoud, allegedly posted an internet communiqué reaffirming the organization's position. The statement issued just after the referendum said that Algeria "does not need a Charter for Peace and National Reconciliation, but instead a Charter for Islam. ...The jihad is going to continue" [5].

Indeed, such words appear to be backed by actions, which suggest the GSPC intends to follow through with its goals. In the weeks leading up to the referendum, the mayor of Ammal was allegedly killed by GSPC insurgents [6]. These attacks were accompanied by assaults on Algerian soldiers in the countryside. The aftermath of the vote has been even deadlier, as some 60 Algerians died during October in an escalation of hostilities that coincided with the holy month of Ramadan—20 people were killed in two days alone. On October 17th, security operations east of Algiers resulted in the deaths of eight GSPC militants and four soldiers [7]. The next day, GSPC insurgents killed four militia members west of Algiers, according to *El Watan*, and three civilians were killed by a bomb left at a GSPC hideout [8].

GSPC activities abroad also speak to the group's viability and capabilities. Evaluating GSPC activities in the West African Sahel, Nigerian authorities in October discovered an underground terrorist gang reportedly 10,000 strong in the Niger Delta that they say is linked to the GSPC. Nigerian intelligence officials assert that the GSPC, also an al-Qaeda affiliate, is involved in the ongoing recruiting and training of Nigerians in an effort to attack Nigerian interests [9]. The GSPC has also maintained ties in Europe, the U.S. and the Middle East.

However, the strength of the GSPC has eroded considerably over recent years, due to internal divisions and government efforts that have successfully localized and contained insurgents. Once boasting 4,000 members, the organization has been reduced to 300.

Other violent groups on the Algerian landscape are less active. The Armed Islamic Group (GIA), once the major terrorist entity in Algeria, has been substantially weakened by internal fracturing and surrenders under the earlier 1999 amnesty. The Arme Islamiques du Salut (AIS), the armed wing of the FIS, declared a cease-fire in 1997. The Free Salafist Group (GSL), which also opposed the amnesty, is active, but has been predominantly involved in crime and trafficking, rather than terrorism.

The Future of Islamist Politics in Algeria

Against the backdrop of changing developments in Algeria, it is difficult to precisely predict the future of legitimate Islamist politics. The civil war has produced rejectionists unwilling to cooperate with the establishment and advocate the use of violence against the state. Yet the conflict has, likewise, created a government deeply wary of Islamists. Algerian officials vowed that insurgents will never again be able to bring instability to the country and groups involved in the violence, chiefly the FIS, have been banned from participating in politics.

The isolation of the FIS also has important implications for the fate of moderate Islamist parties. Moderate groups have suffered a noticeable decline in popular support, a phenomenon that may be a consequence of FIS' call to boycott elections and Algerian disaffection with Islamists after years of conflict. For example, the Movement of Society for Peace (MSP) and Movement for National Reform (MRN), each with former FIS members, did not fare well in the recent 2002 election. MSP support dropped by half from 14 to 7 percent between the 1997 and 2002 votes, while the newer MRN earned 10 percent. The Islamic Renaissance Movement received four percent—half its previous share [10].

Critics of the state's staunch approach fear the restrictive policy toward political Islam does little to engender confidence in the government or in the future of democracy in Algeria. Some argue that the government's stance may only exacerbate discontent fanned by the war. With the existence of growing unemployment and poverty, the ground may once again become fertile for extremism.

Therefore, the extent to which political Islam will be kept at the periphery of Algerian politics and in what form are now unresolved issues. Algeria's mainstream party, the National Liberation Front (FLN) could adopt some moderate Islamic principles and bring select Islamist moderates into their fold. Since the banner of the amnesty is to encourage harmony, such a strategy may present some opportunities. However, it is a path that needs to be considered carefully as Algeria braces for the long-term impact of the amnesty.

Notes

1. Al-Bawaba Reporters, "Algerian Charter Risks Reinforcing Impunity and Undermining Reconciliation," September 27, 2005, http://www. Albawaba.com.
2. *L'Expression*, September 7, 2005, and Salim Tamani "On Responsibility," Algiers Liberte, October 3, 2005.
3. Ghania Khelfi, "Algerian Terrorist GSPC Leader Hattab Demanding Saudi Fatwa Prior to Surrender" *Algiers Liberte*, October 27, 2005.
4. Ahmed Fattani, "Ouyahia Face Aux Patrons De Press: Espirit De La Reconciliation, Est-tu la?" *Algiers L'Expression*, September 7, 2005.
5. Nadjia Bouarich, "Algerian Terrorist GSPC Rejects Government Peace Plan," *Algiers La Nouvelle*, October 1, 2005.
6. "Algiers: Algerian Paper Says Mayor Killed by Terrorists in Boumerdes Province," Algiers Al-Khabar Website, September 3, 2005.
7. R.H. "Algerian Terrorist Killed in Bouira Area Search Operation," *Algiers La Tribune*, October 20, 2005.
8. "New Reports: 20 Killed in Two Days in Algeria," *Algiers El Watan*, October 19, 2005.
9. Nigerian Government Uncovers 10,000-Man Gang in Niger Delta," *Lagos Weekend Vanguard*, October 18, 2005, http://www.vanguardngr. com/vag.htm
10. Ministry of the Interior, Algiers, May 31, 2002.

[From Terrorism Monitor, Volume III, Issue 22]

Somalia

Somalia: Africa's Horn of Anarchy

Anouar Boukhars

Originally published on January 12, 2006

Fourteen years after the ouster of authoritarian President Siad Barre in 1991 and the subsequent descent of the country into chaos, Somalia remains a lawless patchwork of warring fiefdoms. Terrorist networks have flourished in Somalia and neighboring countries, contributing to the deadly synchronized bomb attacks on the U.S. Embassies in Kenya and Tanzania, and the 2002 tourist hotel bombing in Mombasa that was planned to coincide with the (failed) shooting down of an Israeli passenger jet with a surface-to-air missile. In the absence of a functioning government, Somalia risks becoming a hub of al-Qaeda's East African network.

Somalia's descent into terror came with the emergence in 2003 of an elusive independent jihadi network with loose links to al-Qaeda's East African franchise headed by Tariq Abdullah (a.k.a. Abu-Talha al-Sudani). These local jihadists are engaged in low-intensity warfare characterized by massacres, intimidation and assassinations. The most visible aspect of their reign of terror came with the murder of the Italian nun Annalena Tonelli in Boroma in the Somaliland region and the desecration of an Italian cemetery in the capital, Mogadishu. Despite their small numbers, these local jihadists unleashed a new wave of terror in Mogadishu and other frontier towns like Mandera.

The New Jihadist Network

The apparent commander of this terrorist network is Aden Hashi 'Ayro, a protégé of Sheikh Hassan Aweys, the once notorious leader of al-Itihaad military wing [1]. Ayro is a graduate of Afghan terrorist camps. It is believed that is where he acquired mastery of low-tech and low-cost weapons. His followers are growing adept at the use of explosives, shoulder-launched missiles and anti-tank systems.

The involvement of former al-Itihaad combat veterans in the new jihadi network, however, has led to the mistaken belief that this network represents a resurrection of the revolutionary movement of al-Itihaad al-Islami, which was most active in Somalia during the first half of the 1990s. It is this false assumption that led to the group being labeled "al-Itihaad."

The new jihadi network headed by Ayro differs significantly from al-Itihaad in a number of ways. Whereas al-Itihaad had a clear hierarchy and direction and was motivated by political ideology, the new jihadists are organized in decentralized and compartmentalized networks that each contribute in a small way to urban terrorism operations. The vague hierarchy and direction of the movement coupled with the multi-layered cellular nature of its operations make it difficult to infiltrate this network or identify its sympathizers. Another major characteristic that sets this movement apart from al-Itihaad is its undeclared political and ideological goals. The network's known leaders also lack the religious authority that distinguished al-Itihaad's leadership [2].

Al-Itihaad first rose to prominence in the early 1990s when it successfully capitalized on the demise of the Siad Barre regime and the subsequent descent of Somalia into deepening chaos and misery. Islamic charities, especially those sponsored by Saudi Arabia and other Persian Gulf states, were of key importance to the group. Al-Itihaad used money raised by charitable networks to establish military training camps, cement its ties with other Islamic terrorist organizations and fund terrorist operations against Ethiopia to force the secession of the Ogaden region, which al-Itihaad claimed as Somali land. The group was intent on reclaiming what they perceive as Somali territory from Ethiopia and establishing a Wahhabi emirate in Somalia.

Ethiopian retaliatory military operations and pinpoint raids against al-Itihaad's Somali bases in early 1997 destroyed the movement's political and military infrastructure and damaged its operational capabilities. This eventually led to the group's disbandment [3]. The heavy losses that it suffered in its confrontation with Ethiopian forces in the mid-1990s set the stage for a gradual change in jihadi discourse. Since al-Itihaad's disbandment, many former jihadists and sheikhs renounced the use of violence and jihad, instead promoting a nativist Islamic ideology that, on the one hand shuns terrorism while on the other emphasizes even greater adherence to Sharia law. A small faction of al-Itihaad veterans, however, still provides logistical support and serves as a communications linchpin for al-Qaeda operatives in Somalia and neighboring countries. Yet disruptions in the flow of cash from Islamic charities in Saudi Arabia and the Persian Gulf have severely curtailed their activities.

Al-Qaeda in Somalia

Fazul Abdullah Mohammed, an expert document forger and bomb builder, tops the list of the most dangerous and most wanted terrorists in Somalia. Counter-terrorism officials have been stymied for years by this deadly and elusive Comoros islander, a conspirator in the 1998 al-Qaeda bombings of U.S. Embassies in Kenya and Tanzania that killed 231 people. He is also believed to have played a role in the Mombasa attacks (*Crisis Group Africa Briefing N° 95*).

Saleh Ali Saleh Nabhan and Abu-Talha al-Sudani are another two of the most-wanted al-Qaeda suspects. Nabhan is believed to have owned the vehicle used in the attack that destroyed an Israeli-owned hotel near the Kenyan resort of Mombasa. He has been able to remain at large in part because he has support from some well-armed friends in Mogadishu. He is also related by marriage to a warlord in Baidoa. Al-Sudani is also believed to be in Mogadishu where he married a Somali woman. Other al-Qaeda suspects include Ali Swedhan, Issa Osman Issa, Samir Said Salim Ba'amir and Mohamed Mwakuuuza Kuza. The foreign jihadi contingent is suspected to benefit from the support and protection of the Ayro network (Ibid.).

The detection and capture of these well-protected foreign members of al-Qaeda and their local collaborators constitute the prime challenge for Western, Ethiopian and Kenyan intelligence and counter-terrorism agencies. The United States has stepped up its counter-terrorism efforts in the region by establishing a new command center in the neighboring country of Djibouti to oversee regional counter-terrorist operations. The Combined Joint Task Force-Horn of Africa (CJTF-HOA) conducts surveillance flights and works with regional and local counter-terrorism officials to deny safe havens and material support to al-Qaeda and its local affiliates.

The complex effects of the U.S. war on terrorism in Somalia and its unintended results are not all positive. The United States and its allies have scored major victories by detaining key jihadists, but widespread allegations of arbitrary arrests, prolonged detentions and abductions of terrorist suspects (who later turned out to be innocent) continue to undermine counter-terrorism operations. The kidnapping and prolonged detention of innocent people has alienated many Somalis who are already mistrustful of the U.S. war on terrorism. The U.S. alliance with a number of Somali warlords adds to these feelings of mistrust and anger (Ibid.). Confronted by a vicious cycle of chaos and anarchy, the U.S. needs warlords' cooperation and manpower to maximize its chances of hunting down fugitive jihadists (*VOA News*, February 23, 2004). Yet there is a real danger that by empowering warlords like Mohammed Qanyare Affra, Osman Ali Atto, Muse Sudi Yalahow, and others, the U.S. might end up empowering the true source of Somalia's problems [5].

Some warlords are motivated by criminality and lucrative deals promised by association with U.S.-led counter-terrorism initiatives in the region. Faction leaders arbitrarily round-up innocent Somalis and Arab foreigners in the hope of linking them to terrorist groups.

The Transitional Federal Government (TFG) for Somalia, established in October 2004, has been actively seeking to exploit the international "war on terrorism" to discredit its opponents and critics [6]. At numerous occasions, the TFG blamed terrorist attacks on its Islamist adversaries when the evidence pointed to the contrary. Disturbing evidence has emerged that incriminates TFG supporters in the murders of BBC producer Kate Peyton, a Somali woman working for an international NGO and two Somali footballers (*Crisis Group Africa Briefing N° 95*). The evidence of seeming cooperation between the assassins and members of the TFG reveals new details on the "dirty war" raging in Somalia between jihadists and counter-jihadist organizations. Death squads, disappearances and torture raise the risk of exacerbating chaos and empowering Islamic militancy in Somalia.

Notes

1. Yet there is growing speculation that Ayro, who is believed to be between 28 and 30 years old, may be not the leader of this new jihadi movement. There are multiple reports that identify Ahmed Abdi Godane, alias Ibrahim al-Afghani, a former al-Itihaad leader, Afghan veteran and al-Qaeda associate as the actual leader of the group. See *Crisis Group Africa Briefing N° 100*, "Somalia's Islamists," December 12, 2005.

2. According to International Crisis Group, this new jihadi network, believed to be headed by Ayro, has no known name, its membership is largely clandestine and its aims are undeclared. *Crisis Group Africa Briefing N° 95*, "Counter-Terrorism in Somalia: Losing Hearts and Minds?" July 11, 2005.

3. See Medhane Tadesse, *Al-Itihaad: Political Islam and Black Economy in Somalia* (Addis Ababa, 2002) pp. 90-93.

4. Alisha Ryu, "Rebuilding Somalia Could Aid War on Terror, say Residents," *VOA News*, February 23, 2004.

5. Crisis Group interview, Sheikh Ahmed Nur Jimaale, Mogadishu, April 13, 2004.

6. Matt Bryden, "No Quick Fixes: Coming to Terms with Terrorism, Islam and Statelessness in Somalia", *The Journal of Conflict Studies* (vol. XXIII, no.2), Fall 2003.

[From Terrorism Monitor, Volume IV, Issue 1]

Somalia's ICU and its Roots in al-Itihaad al-Islami

Sunguta West

Originally published on July 27, 2006

As the Islamic Courts Union (ICU) continues to spread its influence throughout southern Somalia, the international community has reacted with concern since there are accusations that the ICU has ties to international terrorists. These accusations stem from the fact that many of the key leaders of the ICU are former members of al-Itihaad al-Islami (AIAI), a radical Islamist organization that once sought to establish an Islamic state in East Africa and was accused of having ties to al-Qaeda.

Originally, after the initial ICU victories in Mogadishu, the international community reacted with some optimism since the chairman of the ICU was a moderate named Sheikh Sharif Sheikh Ahmad. Ahmad had spoken in favor of dialogue with the Transitional Federal Government (TFG), based in Baidoa, and with the international community. Analysts said that Ahmad exhibited Qutbism, an Islamic ideology that supports political or free interpretation of the Holy Quran. The ideology originated from Sayyid Qutb, an Egyptian Islamic thinker executed in 1966. It attempts to reconcile Islam and modernity. Apart from agreeing to engage his adversaries diplomatically, Ahmad was quick to dispel fears of a Taliban-like government forming in Somalia. Unfortunately, a popular wave seems to have sidelined Ahmad, despite the Somali people's respect for his leadership. Instead, former members of AIAI and other hard-line elements have taken the reins of leadership in Somalia's ICU.

History of AIAI

The Somali organization AIAI came into prominence in 1991 with the objective of overthrowing Somali President Siad Barre. According to wardheernews.com, AIAI was formed in a meeting in 1984 in Burao in northern Somalia following the merger of two other organizations: al-Jamma al-Islamiya (Islamic Association) led by Sheikh Mohammed Eissa and based in the south, and Wahdat al-Shabab al-Islam (Unity of Islamic Youth) led by Sheikh Ali Warsame. Al-Jamma al-Islamiya was formed around 1967 as a reaction to unwanted Western cultural influences; it was then led by Islamic religious leaders in northern Somalia and comprised of several Islamic organizations in the region. The Wahdat al-Shabab al-Islam was formed in the late 1960s by Islamic religious leaders. It was similarly a reaction against Western values, and the organization mainly attracted Muslim youth.

The main goal of AIAI was to form a strong Islamic state in the African Horn countries (Ethiopia, Djibouti, Eritrea and Somalia). Sheikh Ali Warsame assumed the leadership of the organization. Warsame is said to be the person who recruited Sheikh Hassan Dahir Aweys into AIAI near the time of Siad Barre's fall from power. Warsame was charismatic and spearheaded the growth of AIAI in Somalia. According to SomaliaWatch.org, he appeared to be opposed to war even as a leader of AIAI. He is described as a reclusive, ideologue of Islamic fundamentalism, and the brainchild behind AIAI. AIAI had its own army, as well as social and political services. After Barre was ousted from power in 1991, AIAI enlarged its scope to launching cross-border attacks into Ethiopia. At the time of these cross-border attacks, Aweys was the leader of AIAI's military wing.

In the mid-1990s, AIAI initiated attacks on Ethiopian forces (*Terrorism Monitor*, February 10, 2005). The main goal behind the attacks was to gain control of the Ogaden Region of Ethiopia, which borders Somalia. This is a region predominantly occupied by Somali speaking people, but is part of Ethiopia. In 1977, Somalia attacked Ethiopia across the Ogaden Desert taking temporary control of the territory, only to be pushed back out of the region the following year (*Terrorism Monitor*, February 10, 2005). While the attacks by AIAI against Ethiopia were generally small in scale, the terrorist organization did manage to execute operations as far as the Ethiopian capital.

ICU Blends in AIAI Ideology

The ICU and the AIAI are different entities, yet the former appears to have grown out of the latter, bequeathing some of its characteristics in the new body. Ideologically, the ICU and AIAI share many similarities. While the ICU wants an Islamic state in Somalia in the short term governed by Sharia law, media reports allege that the Islamic courts are eyeing a bigger Islamic state in the long term carved out of East Africa, similar to the old goals of AIAI, which wanted to create an Islamic state out of Somalia and Ethiopia. The ICU is also radical in its approach, sustains a charity wing and has militias just as AIAI once did.

The most prominent figure in the ICU is Sheikh Hassan Dahir Aweys, who was a former leader in AIAI. The BBC Monitoring Unit reports that Aweys is the genius behind the brilliant military campaigns of the courts in Mogadishu. For instance, he organized the ICU fighters to attack the warlords at the most unexpected times such as early in the morning and at night. According to Adan Mohammed, a conflict analyst in the Horn of Africa based in Nairobi, Aweys also has been able to ensure that all the ICU fighters are inspired and ready to fight for the ICU cause.

Yet, with the defeat of AIAI by Ethiopian forces, Aweys retreated to his home region in Galguduud Province and later to Mogadishu and embarked on self education and spiritual reflection, which is thought to have finally led him to puritanical Salafi ideology since much of his learning came from Saudi Arabia's Wahhabi school of thought. Sustaining this ideology within the courts with Aweys is Sheikh Hassan al-Turki and a young fighter known as Sheikh Adan Hashi Ayro, who heads the youth league (*Terrorism Focus*, July 11, 2006). Since Aweys heads the Supreme Council of Islamic Courts, which is the courts' parliament, this ideology appears to emerge as he openly declares that the agenda of the ICU is to turn Somalia into an Islamic state and to introduce Sharia law.

The consequence of the Salafi hard-line stance has been the banning of songs during weddings and a clampdown on entertainment facilities, including cinemas. This policy led to the ban on viewing the World Cup soccer games that the cinemas were showing live from Germany. The AIAI pursued similar policies, according to SomaliaWatch. org. Soon after coming to the fore after the fall of Barre, it banned the chewing of qat in some areas like the Gedo Region, reduced the stature of the traditional Islamic leaders and built special mosques that served as communal centers.

At the moment, analysts agree the demarcation between the two is thin. According to Ato Medhane Tadesse who works for Center for Policy Research and Dialogue, a local Ethiopian think tank, the first courts were established by AIAI and multiplied as the organization loosened control. Tadesse told the *Addis Ababa Reporter* on July 15, 2006 that the Somali people supported the courts because they brought peace and stability. "They were better than warlords," he said. According to the analyst, former AIAI leaders oriented the courts in an Islamic way, controlled them and gave them ideological direction and brought in military mobilization. The courts, like AIAI, have a social wing known as al-Islah, and is largely viewed as reformist. It provides clinics, schools, roads and support for children.

In light of these similarities, many East African countries consider the ICU takeover of Somalia a threat. *The East African*, a regional weekly based in Nairobi, reported that the ICU, having seized control of southern Somalia, plans to use local elements to destabilize Kenya. The weekly quoted Somaliland Representative Saad Noor, who was in Washington on July 11, 2006 and warned the U.S. Congress that the ICU wanted to first conquer all of Somalia and then declare it an Islamic state. The next step would be to topple and control Somaliland, a territory in northwestern Somalia that declared its independence from larger Somalia when the country descended into chaos following the collapse of Barre's dictatorship. The next step, according to this representative, would be to topple Kenya and Ethiopia, two other secular states who are Somalia's neighbors.

The same publication quoted David Shinn, former U.S. ambassador to Ethiopia, now a specialist in East African affairs, on July 11, 2006 telling a U.S. subcommittee that some leaders of the ICU militias wanted to re-energize the greater Somalia concept by incorporating into Somalia Somali-inhabited areas in Kenya, Ethiopia and Djibouti. As Shinn explained, this would happen if the Islamists come to be dominated by extremist elements and succeeded in consolidating power throughout Somalia. "It will be only a matter of time before Kenya becomes subject to Somali irredentism," Shinn said. Evidence of this consolidation came on July 20, when ICU fighters advanced toward Baidoa, the seat of the TFG. The TFG, an authority created for Somalia two years ago through the efforts of Kenya and the United Nations, failed to be accepted at the grassroots level in Somalia. By the ICU's advance toward Baidoa, it is clear that the ICU wants to consolidate their rule throughout Somalia.

East African countries cannot throw caution into the wind if recent events associated with Islamic fundamentalism are something to go by. Although radical AIAI activities have generally been recorded in Ethiopia, the group is blamed for the 1993 deaths of 18 U.S. soldiers killed in Mogadishu. Furthermore, it is alleged that the al-Qaeda terrorists who destroyed the U.S. embassies in Nairobi and Dar es Salaam used Somalia as a staging area.

A showdown now looms between TFG President Abdullahi Yusuf and Sheikh Aweys, two former colonels of the defunct Somali army. TFG President Yusuf is banking on international support since Aweys has a history of being connected to AIAI and al-Qaeda. Yet, Aweys claims that Yusuf is unpopular in Mogadishu and is seen as an Ethiopian puppet; Ethiopia remains Somalia's traditional rival. The situation remains very unstable. Before the ICU is able to pursue some of the AIAI's former goals, such as attempting to take the Ogaden region from Ethiopia, it must successfully consolidate control in Somalia, which will be difficult in light of Ethiopia's threats to move across the border and to unseat the ICU.

[From Terrorism Monitor, Volume IV, Issue 15]

Understanding Somali Islamism

Anouar Boukhars

Originally published on May 18, 2006

The security situation in Somalia flared up dramatically in the past few weeks, following a number of acts of provocation between Mogadishu's newly-formed coalition of warlords, dubbed the Alliance for the Restoration of Peace and Counter-Terrorism, and gunmen allied to the Islamic Courts Union. As these provocations escalated into fierce clashes, hundreds of people have been wounded and some 120 people killed. There is widespread concern that Somalia is rapidly becoming a new proxy battleground between Washington—the warlords' alleged supporter and benefactor—and what the UN Security Council describes as "Islamic extremists." The United Nations has warned of the rising influence of Islamic radicals as a "third force" in the country, competing with the transitional government and an alliance of warlord groups that constantly violate the current arms embargo and enrich themselves from selling fishing licenses and exporting charcoal. Rumors abound that the fear of a rising and formidable Islamist threat has pushed Washington to side with the warlords, who have portrayed themselves as capable of defeating the Islamists and their alleged foreign al-Qaeda members.

The challenges ahead are formidable and the threat of jihadi Islamism is real (*Terrorism Monitor*, January 12, 2006). Jihadi Islamism in Somalia has a history and a character of its own. Attempts to lump all Islamic movements in Somalia together as an inherently violent monolith are reductive and fail to take account of the diversity of Islamist movements. There are major differences between Islamists like Jama'at al-Tabligh and the Salafiyya Jadiida, whose motives are non-political, but rather missionary in character, and those that have religious political motives like Harakaat al-Islah and Majma' 'Ulimadda Islaamka ee Soomaaliya, whose goal is either the adoption of a Sharia-based system of government or the application of a certain interpretation of Islam within a modern, democratic framework of government. The third group of Islamists in Somalia are Salafi-Jihadists like al-Itihaad al-Islaami and the new al-Qaeda-linked jihadi network of terror led by Aden Hashi 'Ayro, a protégé of Sheikh Hassan Aweys, the once notorious leader of al-Itihaad's military wing. Somali Islamism is thus composed of three distinct types of activism: political, missionary and jihadi.

Rise of Somali Islamism

Somali Islamism can be traced to a common source, the Waxda al-Shabaab al-Islaami and the Jama'at al-Ahl al-Islaami (also known as the al-Ahli group). These Muslim Brotherhood-inspired groups developed in the 1960s and strove to be key players in liaising with the state and the setting of its mixed ideological agenda [1]. The rise to power of Mohamed Siad Barre in 1969, however, deprived the Islamists of their status. Al-Ahli was forced to disband and al-Wahdat and other Islamist groups went underground or fled to the oil-rich states of the Gulf to join the Somali diaspora.

By the 1980s, the Somali Islamist movement had grown considerably. Nevertheless, it was the ouster of the Barre dictatorship that gave a major boost to Islamic associations and organizations. This growth has been less linear and more of a hybrid product of multiple intellectual traditions. Artificial constructs of Somali Islamism as a linear descendant of one particular intellectual tradition ignore the internal and historical variations of the Islamic movement in Somalia. Even when looking at political Islam and not the religion, the differences between Islamists in religious views, political conceptions and social orientations should not be overshadowed by lumping all Islamic movements together as an organizing principle in the war on terrorism.

I. Political Islamism

A. Harakat al-Islah

Harakat al-Islah originated in the late 1970s as a loose network of affiliated underground groups [2]. Today, al-Islah publicly professes its commitment to the basic tenets of democracy and cultural pluralism. Its stated commitment to this philosophy of inclusion is enshrined in the organization's social make-up and mode of action. The organization's forward-looking views on religion and politics and attempts to reconcile the tenets of Islam with the modern notions of democracy are apparent in its internal structure, where members of its "High Council" are elected by the Majlis al-Shura for a maximum of two terms. Al-Islah's leading members include the organization's chairman, Dr. Ali Sheikh, president of Mogadishu University [3]. Prior to the demise of the Barre regime, the organization operated as a clandestine integrated structure of clusters under the leadership of Sheikh Mohamed Garyare, Dr. Ali Sheikh and Dr. Ibrahim Dusuqi.

With the overthrow of the Barre dictatorship and hence the elimination of the organization's main enemy, al-Islah came out of the shadows and was operated exclusively for the promotion of social and humanitarian activities. Al-Islah members play prominent roles in the state's educational apparatuses. Their domination of Mogadishu University and other educational institutions like the Formal Private Education Network in Somalia (FPENS) has prompted fears that the organization is laying the groundwork for the gradual Islamization of society by using education as a tool to propagate its worldview and recruit cadres [4].

Al-Islah has always been suspected by Somali and foreign security services of involvement in radicalism and association with al-Itihaad. There is much evidence, however, of a power struggle between and within al-Islah and al-Itihaad's competing ideological authorities about the relationship between religion and politics. There are also ideological differences and strong divergences on strategies, tactics and religious interpretations. Al-Islah's leaders, for example, condemn violence and takfir (declaring as an infidel) as un-Islamic and counterproductive. They have long called for building a shared future that transcends the extremism and bigotry embodied in al-Itihaad's and Takfir wal-Hijra's Salafi-Jihadist ideology [5].

B. Ahlu Sunna wal Jama'a

Ahlu Sunna wal Jama'a (ASWJ) is another modern Islamist group created in 1991 as an offshoot from Majma' to counter the influence of the most radical Islamist trends. The movement brings together politically motivated sheikhs whose primary goal is to unify the Sufi community under one unified leadership capable of consolidating the powers of the three primary Sufi Tariqas—the Qadiriyya, Salihiyya and Ahmadiyya—into one front whose sole mission is the rejuvenation of the "traditionalist" interpretation of Islam and the de-legitimization of the beliefs and political views of al-Itihaad and other radical Islamic movements.

C. Majma' 'Ulimadda Islaamka ee Soomaaliya

Majma' 'Ulimadda Islaamka ee Soomaaliya represents, as its name denotes, an assembly of Islamic scholars who follow the Shafi'i madhhab and whose main goal is the establishment of a Sharia-based government. The organization has been led by Sheikh Ahmed Abdi Dhi'isow since the death of its founding chairman, Sheikh Mohamed Ma'alim Hassan, in 2001 [6].

There are differences of views among Majma' 'Ulimadda Islaamka ee Soomaaliya, Ahlu Sunna wal Jama'a and Harakat al-Islah about the nature of the state, but a general consensus seems to have developed among the different factions about the need to apply a certain interpretation of Islam within a modern framework of government.

II. Missionary Islamism

Missionary Islamists largely eschew political activism—even if their brand of activism has some political objectives and implications. The movement is represented by Salafiyya Jadiida (the new Salafis) and the most structured movement in Somalia, Jama'at al-Tabligh.

A. Salafiyya Jadiida

The Salafiyya Jadiida current is best exemplified by Sheikh Ali Wajis, an example of a prominent Salafi ideologue who has gone from supporting and briefly leading al-Itihaad to opposing its violent dogmatic theology. Wajis' qualified repudiation of the irrational jihadi ideology of Salafi-Jihadists and his re-examination of its theoretical position in light of a rational reassessment of Islamic rules of warfare and the prevailing realities on the ground exemplify the fractures rocking the jihadi and Islamist movements. It is also an encouraging sign of the debate occurring within the new Salafis and Salafi-Jihadist circles about the need for contextualized understanding of the issues of jihad and political violence.

B. Jama'at al-Tabligh

The Tabligh movement, launched in India in 1926 by the Jama'at al-Da'wa wal-Tabligh (Group for Preaching and Propagation), as an apolitical, quietist movement constitutes the largest group of religious proselytizers in Somalia. Tablighi missionaries' aggressive and dedicated peaceful and apolitical preaching tactics are part of the reason for the explosive growth of Tablighi sympathizers and supporters. This notable success in recruitment and significant increase in membership left the movement wide open to infiltration and manipulation by radical groups. Out of the 500 to 700 foreign sheikhs present in Somalia, many are from the Arab world but they also come from Afghanistan, Pakistan, Chechnya and other countries [7]. Given the size and heterogeneity of the movement, its infiltration by jihadi elements should come as no surprise. What is troubling, however, is the denial of the movement's leadership of any such infiltration despite mounting evidence of the group's involvement in murdering foreign aid workers in Somaliland. The movement, as the International Crisis Group reported, "lacks any system of screening its members for prior involvement in jihadism and so is poorly equipped to respond to allegations that some may be involved in fomenting extremism and violence" [8].

Jihadi Islamism

The jihadi tendency is the third type of Islamic activism. Unlike the political and missionary current, jihadi activists are committed to violence and armed resistance against what they perceive as the continuing onslaught of the enemies of Islam. This form of Islamic activism has very few sympathizers, although it is actively involved in trying to recruit or infiltrate missionary organizations like Salafiyya Jadiida and the Tabligh movement. The Jihadi movement has had its fortunes ebb and flow during the last decade [9].

Conclusion

Since the collapse of the government in 1991, the Islamic activist movement has expanded throughout Somalia. Islamic organizations like Harakat al-Islah are entrenched at both Somali universities and major educational centers; popular sympathy for the movements appears strong. It would be a grave oversimplification, however, to paint Islamism as a fixed ideological monolith and a dangerous and destabilizing force. There is still a disposition among some observers of Somali Islamism to identify Islamic activism with extremism or terrorism. This mistaken belief derives, in large part, from a failure to recognize the clear distinctions between different forms of Islamisms and appreciate not only the opposition of the majority of Somalis toward terrorism as a form of political action, but the fragmentation that plagues the jihadi and Islamist movements.

By far, the most dangerous militant groups are those composed of jihadi Islamists, such as the now-defunct al-Itihaad al-Islaami and the new, elusive independent jihadi network headed by Aden Hashi 'Ayro. Other Islamist entities like the Islamic Courts Union, whose gunmen are involved in the current fighting with the alliance of warlords, "have more complex agendas," and "appear to exist for chiefly pragmatic purposes." The danger remains, however, that as the courts grow in influence and strength, they may begin "to advocate an increasingly ideological agenda—one that jihadi Islamist elements in the court system will no doubt attempt to define" [10].

The best way for the United States to fight jihadi Islamism in the Horn of Africa and sway the hearts and minds of Somalis is to recalibrate its approach. Without public support, the United States would fail to make more than a modest dent in jihadi forces. The threat of terrorism from Somalia remains a major concern for the United States and its East African allies. This danger, however, can only be effectively tackled through the establishment of a legitimate and functional government in Somalia. The temptation to empower one faction over another or deploy foreign troops in the country might only exacerbate the true source of the problem.

Notes

1. Roland Marchal, "Islamic Political Dynamics in the Somali Civil War," in Alex de Waal (ed.), *Islamism and Its Enemies in the Horn of Africa* (Indiana University Press, 2004), p. 119.
2. Andre Le Sage, "Al-Islah in Somalia: An Analysis of Modern Political Islam," unpublished manuscript, pp. 7-8.
3. Alain Charret, "Mouvements islamiques somaliens soupçonnés

d'être liés au terrorisme international," *Les nouvelles d'Addis 8ème année—*
bimestriel—n°51—January 15-March 15, 2006.
4. Mogadishu University "instructs several thousand students in
seven faculties—four taught mainly in English and three in Arabic.
A significant proportion of the student body is female." ICG Report
"Somalia's Islamists," Africa Report N. 100—December 12, 2005, p.
16.
5. Abdurahman M. Abdullahi, "Recovering Somali State: The Islamist
Factor," unpublished draft.
6. Marc-Antoine Pérouse de Montclos, "Des ONG sans gouvernement:
mouvements islamiques et velléités de substitution à l'État dans la
Somalie en guerre," *Colloque organisé dans le cadre du programme MOST
(UNESCO), en partenariat avec l'IRD, le CEDEJ, le CEPS d'Al Ahram.*
March 29-31, 2000 au Caire.
7. ICG Report "Somalia's Islamists," p. 19.
8. Ibid.
9. Anouar Boukhars, "Somalia: Africa's Horn of Anarchy," *Terrorism
Monitor*, Volume 4, Issue 1 (January 12, 2006).
10. ICG Report "Somalia's Islamists," p. 22.

[From Terrorism Monitor, Volume IV, Issue 10]

Leadership Profile: Somalia's Islamic Courts Union

Sunguta West

Originally published on June 13, 2006

The crisis in Somalia may be entering a new phase. A union of Islamic courts has taken control of the lawless capital, Mogadishu. On June 4, 2006, after months of intense fighting, militiamen loyal to the Supreme Council of the Islamic Courts Union (ICU), headed by Sheikh Sharif Sheikh Ahmed, expelled the Alliance for the Restoration of Peace and Counter-Terrorism (ARPCT) from Mogadishu. Last week, after pushing the ARPCT warlords out of the capital, the ICU asserted its authority by establishing three new Islamic courts in Mogadishu in areas previously controlled by warlords (*Somaliland Times*, June 6, 2006). They also advanced toward the warlord stronghold of Jowhar, a town 90 kilometers north of Mogadishu, sending fears that Somalia was headed for extremist Muslim leadership.

A fluent Arabic speaker, Sheikh Sharif Sheikh Ahmed is viewed as a moderate belonging to an anti-fundamentalist Sufist group known as Ahl Sunnah wal jama'ah. Ahmed taught Geography, Arabic and Religious Studies at Juba Secondary School before being nominated as the leader of the ICU in 2004. He was born in January 1964 in Chabila, a town in Central Somalia, and educated in universities in Libya and Sudan (*Asharq al-Awsat*, May 17, 2006).

His deputies Sheikh Hassan Dahir Aweys and Adan Hashi Ayro, however, are militants who initiated al-Itihaad al-Islami (AIAI), a charity organization—with a militant wing—accused of having links with al-Qaeda. AIAI was responsible for small-scale attacks against Ethiopia in 1996 until Addis Ababa launched cross-border raids and successfully weakened AIAI's operations (*Terrorism Monitor*, February 19, 2005). Since gaining control of Mogadishu, Ahmed's assurance to the international community that the ICU is against terrorism has reinforced his moderate position. Nevertheless, the West has remained reserved about trusting Ahmed due to the presence of Aweys and Ayro inside Ahmed's faction. According to Ahmed, the courts seek to enable the Somali people to choose their country's destiny, terming the ICU takeover as a popular revolution and a response to years of anarchy and plunder by the warlords. He also clarified that the ICU would not start a Taliban-style system of government.

Traditionally, Somalia has had non-violent Islamic courts. With the overthrow of President Siad Barre in 1991, however, warlords, clan elders and religious leaders established new forms of authority that aimed at restoring law and order. In 1996, members of AIAI, mainly from south Mogadishu, established a new type of ruling system that refused to acknowledge the warlords' supremacy; additionally, they provided protection to businessmen who had been overtaxed and harassed by various militants. From the outset, the Islamic courts were more popular than the warlords' militias, since the warlords carried out countless kidnappings—while demanding huge ransoms—and partook in numerous killings. In 2004, the separate Islamic courts joined to form the ICU. The members built a joint militia with 400 men and 15 "technicals" (trucks fitted with guns). Presently, Mogadishu has 11 independent Islamic courts, which try and punish crimes under Sharia law. Criminals' limbs are amputated for lesser crimes, while those thought to have committed more serious crimes, such as murder, are executed (each court has a militia that acts as its police force).

Since 2004, Sheikh Hassan Dahir Aweys, 61, has appeared as the most powerful and outspoken religious figure in the ICU. According to Somali Transitional Federal Government (TFG) MP Awad Ashara, Aweys is a former prisons colonel who started preaching in the late 1970s. At the formation of the Joint Islamic Courts Council in 2000—the merging of Mogadishu's independent courts in south Mogadishu—Aweys automatically became the council's secretary general. The merger of the courts' militias raised the largest force in Mogadishu (Center for Humanitarian Dialogue Report, July 2005). After his name appeared on the U.S. list of the most wanted terrorists, however, Aweys disappeared only to resurface in 2004 to run Ifka Halanka, a powerful court in Malka, south Mogadishu.

Aweys' group, AIAI, has been opposed to the TFG since its creation (SomaliNet, September 5, 2005). Around June 2005, Aweys accused the TFG of selling the country to enemies such as Ethiopia, and indicated that he was preparing for war. He had called for jihad, warning that his faction would not be mere spectators in the Somali crisis. Ashara told The Jamestown Foundation that Aweys, who is opposed to "man-made laws" in favor of Sharia, is using the courts for selfish gains. Although Ashara says that Aweys enjoys some support in Mogadishu, he said Aweys could soon face resistance for those opposed to his interpretation of the Sharia courts.

Working with Aweys is Adan Hashi Ayro, a militia commander of one of the courts. He is considered an extremist Muslim and was trained in Afghanistan. He came to the fore following the recent attacks that involved the desecration of Italian cemeteries in Mogadishu and was blamed for killing five Western aid workers and BBC journalist Kate Peyton last year. He is largely viewed as a newcomer on the Somali scene, being mentored by Aweys. Reports in 2005 said that Ayro and Aweys were running camps where religious extremists received military training. The training also included indoctrination into fundamentalist ideology aimed at advocating jihad in Islamic states.

The true nature of the ICU is emerging. They have already closed down makeshift cinemas to prevent people from watching the Soccer World Cup. They have also broken-up groups watching the soccer matches (*Daily Nation*, June 12, 2006). This may be just the beginning. If they continue to clamp down on Somali society, and refuse to be more democratic, they will likely meet increased resistance from the population, making them just as unpopular as the warlords.

[From Terrorism Focus, Volume III, Issue 23]

Somalia's Regional Proxy War and its Internal Dynamics

Anouar Boukhars

Originally published on June 29, 2006

The scramble for power in Somalia's violent and contorted clan-based politics is occurring at every new stage of development, opening up fresh possibilities and opportunities as well as new risks and dangers. The stunning victory of the Islamic Courts Union (ICU) over CIA-backed warlords left more than 300 people dead and more than 1,700 injured in what was by far the deadliest fighting Somalia has seen since the ousting of Mohamed Siad Barre in 1991. It also took the United States, Ethiopia and all the other players in Somalia's convoluted affairs by surprise and opened a new chapter in the country's troubled political history. Basking in their stunning victory, the ICU has the possibility of becoming a more effective force that transcends clan politics. This will not happen, however, until the movement confronts many of the difficult questions and muddled issues it now faces. Clearly, the ICU is not a homogenous organization and does not possess well-defined political and social principles on the issues of primary concern to its diverse constituency.

There are palpable differences within the different Islamic courts—made up of many interests—about the movement's internal identity and its possible future challenges. The struggle to clarify some of the driving issues within the organization regarding its relation to politics and the social and political alternatives it advances threaten to sharpen the divide between moderate sheikhs led by Sheikh Sharif Sheikh Ahmed and hard-line radical Islamists headed by former army colonel Sheikh Hassan Dahir Aweys, 71, and Afghanistan-trained militia commander Adan Hashi Ayro, who would like to take Somalia down the Taliban road. The recent promotion of Aweys to lead the ICU governing council has raised fears of the growing dominance of the radicals and their determination to impose Taliban-style rule in Somalia. As head of the legislative council, Aweys has been entrusted with making the main decisions, leaving to Sheikh Sharif Sheikh Ahmad the task of implementing them in his capacity as head of the executive committee. The courts' critics saw this promotion as a harbinger of incoming Taliban-style legislation. As proof, they cited the recent incident in which the ICU planned to stone to death five rapists, which was recently postponed.

The similarities between the ICU's rapid ascent to power and the Taliban's rise to leadership in Afghanistan are troubling. Both movements came to power under the banner of religion and gained public support across the religious spectrum as a result of their promises of order and security. Both groups claim that their victory proves that Islam is the solution to their societies' problems and is the only way out of the anarchy and bloodshed that the defeated regimes had brought upon their peoples. Mohamed Ali Aden, 19, an associate of Adan Hashi Ayro, insists that the courts would accept nothing less than the establishment of a true Islamic state. "We've neglected God's verses for so long," said Aden to reporters. "We want our women veiled and we want them at home. We men have to grow our beards." Sheikh Sharif is also said to have pledged that the ICU struggle will end only with the construction of an Islamic state. Aden's conception of an Islamic state, however, differs significantly from the moderates' conception.

The transformation of Somalia into a new version of Afghanistan under the Taliban is highly unlikely even under the nightmarish scenario in which the ICU radical wing manages to tighten its grip on the courts at the expense of the moderates. Many Somalis are secular in outlook. Equally important, moderate Islamists make up the majority of the Union's supporters. With the exception of a few renegade courts, the ICU practices a moderate Sufi form of Islam that can act as a counterweight to the radical militancy of Ifka Halane and Shirkoola courts. Much, however, will depend on whether the moderates can capitalize on their numerical superiority by cementing the Union's internal cohesiveness and initiating negotiations with other competing political tendencies on the formation of a national unity government.

Regional powers are watching restlessly as unwelcome events unfold on their doorsteps. Most support a fast deployment of peacekeepers. Ethiopia, troubled by the promotion of Aweys and what it claims is the preponderant dominance of al-Itihaad al-Islamiya members within the ICU, is pressing hard for some sort of AU intervention to prevent the emergence of an Islamist state in nearby Somalia. Such a move, which would most likely be a cover for Ethiopian intervention, would surely alienate the courts, kill all hope for peaceful negotiation between the government and the courts and further contribute to the emergence of Somali nationalism. It is the revelations of Washington's support for the warlords and Ethiopia's complicity that have angered many Somalis to the benefit of the ICU, which judiciously exploited this nationalist fervor. Somalis are naturally suspicious of any outside intervention. Most regional players had backed various Somali factions and can hardly claim that they have Somalis' best interests in mind. Somalia had been a theater for a proxy war between Eritrea and Ethiopia for well over a decade. Asmara supports the Islamic courts while Addis Ababa backs Washington and its policy of siding with any party that promises to cooperate in the war on terrorism. The Intergovernmental Authority on Development (IGAD), a seven-country regional development organization in Eastern Africa, which includes Djibouti, Eritrea, Ethiopia, Kenya, Somalia, Sudan and Uganda, had its reputation tainted due to its members' competing geopolitical interests. As such, IGAD is ill equipped to play an honest power broker between the Transitional Federal Government and the Islamic Courts Union.

Even a Sudanese and Ugandan peacekeeping force would not escape Ethiopian influence, whose prime minister, Meles Zenawi, has signaled at numerous occasions his determination not to see an Islamic state established on his borders. The prime minister is reportedly anxious of the potential creeping influence of Somali Islamists on Ethiopia's 40 percent Muslim population. The ICU and many Somalis are suspicious that interim Somali President Abdullahi Yusuf and his Ethiopian allies, in complicity with the United States, have designs on their land and would use the peacekeeping mission to take control of the country (*The New Vision*, June 21, 2006). The transitional government—the 14th attempt at central rule since the collapse of the central government in 1991—is supported by the African Union, the United Nations and IGAD. Yemen is also known to back Somalia's transitional government; a number of reports have emerged recently detailing how Yemeni planes have been arriving in Baidoa, bringing arms and ammunition. The Islamic courts, however, are funded by influential local business communities. Nevertheless, it is still unclear how and where the Islamic courts received their weaponry and substantial financing in spite of the embargo on Somalia. The courts' detractors claim that they have the financial backing of rich individuals in Saudi Arabia and the Gulf states.

Eritrea is also known to support the courts through the provision of arms and ammunition, although this is strongly denied by the Eritrean authorities. A United Nations report directly accused Asmara of arming the Islamic courts. The same report pointed fingers at Djibouti, Ethiopia, Saudi Arabia and Yemen for their competing efforts to supply military equipment to the Somali warring groups during the later part of 2005 and the first quarter of 2006. "Arms, military materiel and financial support continue to flow like a river to these various actors," the report said. "On 28 March 2006, 10 metric tons of arms, including mortars, PKM machine guns, AK-47 assault rifles and RPGs (anti-tank weapons), arrived in Jowhar from Ethiopia..." Sources in the region reported that Ethiopia had supplied the Somalia Anti-Terror Alliance when they were in Jowhar with trucks loaded with military supplies brought from Feerfeer on the Ethiopia-Somalia frontier (Shabelle Media Network, May 24, 2006). Djibouti, where the United States has built a military base at the abandoned French Foreign Legion camp, is said to have supplied the TFG with military uniforms and vehicles (*Puntland Post*, May 12, 2006).

The United States and other Western powers, however, are still leery of placing all their bets on the Transitional Federal Government. They are also still reluctant to acknowledge the obvious fact that the success or failure of any initiative to stabilize Somalia is dependent upon the cooperation and inclusion of Somalia's Islamists (*Eritrea Daily*, June 22, 2006). After all, the ICU is the only political force that has proven its capacity to provide security, justice and social services. Its dramatic rise as a national military and political force offers the best chance for the construction of a credible and legitimate representative government in Somalia (*Daily Trust-Abuja*, June 22, 2006). Washington and its regional allies have tried hard to prevent the emergence of such a scenario on the grounds that the Islamists are associated with local jihadists, who are linked to a string of assassinations, and foreign al-Qaeda militants, implicated in attacks on the U.S. embassies in Nairobi and Dar es Salaam simultaneously in 1998 and an Israeli-owned hotel near Mombasa in 2002.

Washington's narrow focus on the capture of these foreign al-Qaeda operatives, who are accused of launching a number of deadly attacks throughout East Africa, backfired and ended up empowering the very same group it sought to undermine (Shabelle Media Network,

June 2, 2006). Without any strategic framework, the Bush administration followed a counter-productive strategy that turned Somalia into a proxy war in its campaign against Islamists. According to Africa expert John Prendergast of the International Crisis Group, the United States had channeled about $100,000 per month to the warlords (Reuters South Africa, June 14, 2006). This operation, conducted from the CIA's station in Nairobi, failed miserably because of the Bush administration's underestimation of Somali nationalism and its lack of understanding about the complex politics of the country and its shifting allegiances. State Department counter-terrorism coordinator Henry Crampton acknowledged that the Bush administration failed to correctly assess the heterogeneity of the ICU, their power and the popular support they enjoy.

Rather than promote stability and reconciliation, any foreign intervention could trigger an action-reaction cycle that could only spiral out of control. Anti-Ethiopian feelings resonate very deeply in Somalia and it would be very difficult to assemble a coalition of peacekeepers that would be acceptable to Somalis. The deployment of foreign troops would certainly anger the newly dominant Islamic courts movement and their supporters, who have everything to lose by foreign intervention (*Hiiraan Online*, June 19, 2006). If the United States and other regional powers continue to discount this resurgence of Somali nationalism, witnessed strongly in the last few months, it could once again backfire. The best move that the United States and the international community can take to ensure that Somalia does not slide once again into anarchy is to increase its aid to the Somali people and facilitate a diplomatic solution between the ICU and the transitional government. The U.S. initiative to form a group of stakeholders and potential donors is an encouraging start. Also, the fact that the State Department seems to be taking the lead on dealing with Somalia is another promising sign that Washington is finally recognizing the importance of pushing the political process forward.

[From Terrorism Monitor, Volume IV, Issue 13]

Africa

Islamic Extremism on the Rise in Nigeria

Stephen Schwartz

Originally published on October 21, 2005

Nigeria, a major oil producer, is the most populous African country with around 130 million people, of whom half are Muslim, 40 percent are Christian and 10 percent follow indigenous faiths. Nigeria has a civilian government, but is troubled by widespread corruption and uneven institutional development.

At the end of September 2005, Nigerian oil production was temporarily stopped by threats of violent protest from the Niger Delta People's Volunteer Force, headed by an adventurer known as Mujahid Dokubo-Asari. Asari, as he is commonly called, is 40; he was born to a Christian family and named Dokubo Melford Goodhead, Jr. Asari is a member of the Ijaw ethnic group, which counts several million people, mainly Catholics and other Christians, although their beliefs also include local spiritual traditions. They represent a majority in the main Nigerian petroleum zone. Asari became Muslim in the 1990s and, after failing in an attempt to enter the legal profession, embarked on an equally unsuccessful political career. But notwithstanding his Islamic rhetoric and reported devotion to the faith and his militant stance, his goals are separatist, rather than theological or ideological [1].

Furthermore, as a southerner and Ijaw, he is out of touch with the majority of Nigerian Muslims. It is increasingly clear that Nigeria has been a target for aggressive, radical Sunni Muslim agents supported by religious charities and other outreach (da'wa) groups headquartered in Saudi Arabia. In recent times, the main aim of Islamists in Nigeria has been the establishment of extreme Sharia, along the lines of the Wahhabi sect, as the exclusive law in the Muslim states of the north.

In addition to penetration across the border with Chad, the activities of Saudi, Sudanese, Syrian, and Palestinian representatives in Nigeria is cause for concern. More important, "scores of Pakistanis" have been arrested in the West African country and charged with inciting violence since September 11, 2001, and early in 2004 a rebellion by a group calling itself "Taliban" broke out in Yobe state, on the northern frontier of Nigeria [2].

A "Taliban" cleric, Alhaji Sharu, told police he had received funds for the Nigerian network from al-Muntada al-Islami [3], an agency headed by Dr. Adil ibn Muhammad al-Saleem and based in Britain, but associated with the official Saudi state charitable and da'wa institutions, the Muslim World League (MWL), World Assembly of Muslim Youth (WAMY), International Islamic Relief Organization (IIRO), and al-Haramain Islamic Foundation. All these groups are alleged by American and international investigators to be terror-financing bodies. Including al-Muntada al-Islami, they are together represented in the U.S. by the "Friends of Charity Association," with a website at www.foca.net, and by the Washington attorney Wendell Belew.

In a recent statement, Belew disclosed, with no-doubt-unintended humor, "FOCA's representatives have met with senior Bush administration officials to offer cooperation in the form of exchange of financial, human resource, organizational and other information about our members. Though these offers have been declined by the administration so far, we are actively cooperating in similar efforts with various members and committees of Congress" [4]. Belew also represents Dallah al-Baraka Holding Co., a Saudi business giant.

In turn, Dallah al-Baraka is headed by Saleh Abdullah Kamel, whose name appears in the "Golden Chain," a roster seized by Bosnian authorities in Sarajevo in March 2002, which records Saudi donors to bin Laden and his associates. Kamel is listed in the "Golden Chain" as a supplier of funds to Adil Abdeljalil Batterjee, founder of the Benevolence International Foundation, also designated a terror-financing entity by the U.S. Treasury Department. Kamel and Batterjee continue to walk the streets of the kingdom unmolested. In the aftermath of the al-Muntada al-Islami scandal in Nigeria—in which Nigerian police charged that "millions of dollars" had been sent from Saudi Arabia to finance local religious conflict—the influential Nigerian branch of the Qadiri Sufi brotherhood held demonstrations calling for the expulsion of Wahhabis [5]. Qadiris are known for their Islamic activism and participation in combat in locations as diverse as Kosovo, Chechnya, and, recently, in Iraq.

Given the status of Nigeria as an ideological arena for radicals, it should perhaps come as no surprise that a prominent cleric from the ranks of the Shi'a Muslim minority in the turbulent northern state of Kaduna, Sheikh Ibraheem el-Zakzaky, recently told the *Daily Independent*, a major national paper: "Al-Qaeda does not exist, please. It is non-existent. It exists only in the records of the CIA. Otherwise, al-Qaeda does not exist anywhere in the world. Similarly, bin Laden does not exist. Those sites in the internet have been traced to Texas in the United States of America." Asked if he believed bin Laden is alive, sheikh Zakzaky commented, "I don't know whether he is alive or not… The United States government, which claims to be the strongest in the world, is fighting someone who does not have a base, no government, no anything, no palace, why can't they go and fight China?" On the topic of the July bombings in London, he declared, "Nobody planted those bombs in London except Tony Blair. The British government is behind it" [6].

Zakzaky summarized the 45-year legacy of Nigerian independence as one of bad leadership because people are bad. But other Islamists in Nigeria have embarked on a campaign against the country's Shi'a minority. Sunni-Shi'a conflict had already broken out in the northern state of Sokoto in May 2005, when Sunni fanatics attempted to prevent Shias from entering a local mosque. A considerable Nigerian immigrant community resides in the U.S. cities of New York and Washington, and Shias among them are perturbed by a recent report from the large northern city of Kano, posted on a popular Nigerian Islamic website, www.gamji.com.

The report's author, Mahmoud Mustapha, warns, "Since Malam Ibrahim Shekarau assumed office as the third civilian governor of Kano state on May 29, 2003, Shi'a followers in this Sunni-dominated city have been under threat of attack from bloodthirsty Wahhabis that have taken control of the machinery of government… [T]he government sponsored a systematic and sustained media campaign against Shi'a followers on its radio station, which refers to suicide attacks by Iraqi Wahhabi dissidents against Shias and their places of worship as Jihad. With this campaign they intend to instill in the minds of the people of Kano the desire and the zeal to attack and kill Shias in the name of Jihad, knowing very well the strong support and respect the Iraqi dissidents enjoy from the majority of the Sunnis in Kano" [7].

The Kano state government allegedly seeks to use 9,000 sharia militiamen or hisbah to harass Shias. The hisbah draw a monthly budget from Kano state of 54 million naira ($385,714) and now work as traffic officers. But Abdullahi Tanko, head of the state Sharia Commission administering the hisbah, has initiated an effort to label Shias a threat to public order by equating them with the "Maitatsine," a millenialist and militant reform sect with a few thousand adherents, derived from Islam but extremely heterodox. The sect was founded by Alhajji Muhammadu Marwa, a Cameroon-born figure, and was blamed for bloody clashes in northern Nigeria in 1980 and 1982.

Tanko complained on official Kano state radio in mid-September 2005, "The Shi'a are fast gaining ground in Kano, like wild fire… in every nook and corner of this state, and if we don't act fast and decisively we will be faced with a disaster worse than Maitatsine." Mahmoud Mustapha, writing on these developments, argued, "It is no coincidence that Tanko made this statement a day after Al-Zarqawi, the leader of the terrorists in Iraq from whom the Wahhabis take [their] lead in fighting Shias all over the world, declared a war against the Shi'a in Iraq." Mustapha further predicted, "Once the attacks start in Kano, they will be extended to other 'sharia implementing states' with similar hisbah outfits. Al-Qaeda in Nigeria is born!" [8]

Although such a portrait of the Nigerian situation may seem sensationalized, it is clear that as the dominant power in the entire West African region, the country will remain a major focus of extreme Islamist attention. In addition, Muslim activists in the West African diaspora living in the U.S. insist, in dismay, that Nigeria, which lacks the widespread influence of Sufis and other mystics found in the coastal Francophone states such as Senegal, is especially susceptible to radical agitation. Finally, Nigeria is also characterized by polarization of Muslims against Christians. In these conditions, Nigeria must be considered a country at serious risk of becoming a major new front for Islamist terrorism.

Notes
1. See www.unitedijawstates.com/articles_abidde.htm.
2. Marshall, Paul, "Nigeria: Shari'a in a Fragmented Country," in *Radical Islam's Rules: The Worldwide Spread of Extreme Shari'a Law*, Lanham, Md., Rowman and Littlefield, 2005.
3. See www.almuntada.org.uk.
4. See www.foca.net/Pr_20050923-Nam.stm.
5. Marshall, op. cit.
6. Bakoji, Sukuji, "We've Bad Leaders because We're Bad –Zakzaky," *Daily Independent* [Lagos], Sept. 30, 2005, at www.independentng.com/life/lssep300506.htm.
7. Mustapha, Mahmoud, "Kano Shias Under Wahabi Threat," www.gamji.com/article5000/NEWS5105.htm.
8. Ibid.

[From Terrorism Monitor, Volume III, Issue 20]

The Niger Delta Insurgency and its Threat to Energy Security

Erich Marquardt

Originally published on August 10, 2006

During the first half of 2006, Nigeria's energy industry was crippled by guerrilla attacks from militants demanding a larger share of the country's oil revenue. The guerrillas, primarily from Nigeria's Ijaw ethnic community, live in the country's Niger Delta region where the majority of its energy resources are extracted. The ethnic roots of the crisis and the terrain of the delta make government attempts to end the insurgency difficult since a military response could lead to the complete shutdown of the country's oil exports. Given the significance of energy exports to the Nigerian economy, the roots of the current crisis and the reasons behind the government's failure to stabilize the delta, it becomes clear that attacks on energy facilities in the delta will continue to be an irritant to Africa's largest oil producer.

Background to a Crisis

Nigeria is Africa's most populated country and is the fifth largest supplier of crude oil to the United States. When pumping at full capacity, it produces an output of approximately 2.5 million barrels per day, making it the world's eighth-largest oil exporter. Its gas resources are just as extensive, with proven natural gas reserves at 184 trillion cubic feet, giving Nigeria the seventh-largest gas reserves worldwide. Ninety-five percent of the country's export earnings, accounting for 40 percent of its GDP, come from the oil and gas trade. This dependence on the energy trade makes any disruption of exports especially threatening to the Nigerian economy (*Angola Press*, July 19). Nigeria's oil and gas reserves are located in the south, in the Niger Delta region. As a result of this uneven resource distribution, there are regular disputes over the distribution of oil wealth; the Nigerian government controls the revenue from energy exports, and distributes this revenue throughout the country. The ethnic groups that live in the delta states believe that the majority of energy revenues derived from their territory and homelands should be controlled locally, rather than by the federal government.

The first significant recent militant stirrings among the residents of the delta began in the 1990s among the ethnic Ogoni community. As a result of the small size of the Ogoni population and the fact that Nigeria was ruled by the Abacha military junta at the time, government forces were able to suppress the Ogoni and they executed nine of their activists. The government's aggressive response permanently weakened the Ogoni resistance. Since this initial outbreak of conflict, much more serious ethnic resistance in the delta has arisen, stemming from a far more threatening community. The latest guerrilla attacks against the government and international oil interests are being led by the Ijaw, the largest ethnic group in the Niger Delta region.

Out of Nigeria's 137 million people, the Ijaw number approximately 14 million, making them the country's fourth-largest ethnic group. They live primarily in the Niger Delta region. The Ijaw are generally Catholic Christians, although they incorporate traditional tribal religious practices into their beliefs. The major grievances of the Ijaw are the wealth distribution policies of the government. For instance, while most of the energy wealth emanates from the Niger Delta region, the Ijaw live in poverty and suffer from extensive environmental degradation as a result of frequent oil spills and gas flaring operations (the burning of unwanted natural gas that rises when drilling for oil; the fumes are a contributor to air pollution and acid rain). The Ijaw demand that a larger proportion of Nigeria's energy wealth be spent on their communities, rather than distributed throughout the country. For example, under the 1960 and 1963 Nigerian constitution, 50 percent of oil revenue was returned to the states in which the resources were derived. Currently, under the 1999 constitution, this "derivation formula" stands at 13 percent. While the federal government has offered to slightly increase the revenue allocation to the states, the Ijaw community is calling for the derivation formula to reach 20-25 percent. They are also demanding ownership and management of the resources located on their land, including offshore oil fields.

As a result of these disagreements, the Ijaw formed militant groups to launch operations against energy infrastructure and energy workers in the delta, as well as against government authorities. They receive support from the local populations, making it difficult for the government to isolate and eliminate them. Their success in damaging oil infrastructure and terrorizing international oil workers resulted in

Nigeria's oil exports being cut by approximately 500,000 barrels per day through much of 2006.

Profile of the Ijaw Militant Groups

One of the major initial Ijaw militant groups in the Niger Delta was the Niger Delta People's Volunteer Force (NDPVF). The group was headed by Alhaji Mujahid Dokubo-Asari, who was apprehended by authorities on September 20, 2005. Asari claims to be fighting on behalf of the Ijaw community, demanding that more energy wealth be distributed to Niger Delta residents. Additionally, he has called for greater political autonomy for Ijaw-majority areas. While the head of the NDPVF, Asari and his men siphoned oil from pipelines—a regular occurrence in the Niger Delta, called "bunkering"—in order to fund the group's operations. His guerrilla operations consisted of laying siege to international oil facilities and kidnapping oil workers in order to extract concessions from oil companies and from the government.

In September 2005, the government successfully apprehended Asari and charged him with treason. After his arrest, Asari called on his supporters to halt attacks against the Nigerian government, and this resulted in the general cessation of NDPVF operations. Shortly after Asari's arrest and his call for a cessation of hostilities, a new Ijaw militant group appeared on the scene, in what would mark the most aggressive campaign by Ijaw militants yet.

After Asari's arrest, the Movement for the Emancipation of the People of the Niger Delta (MEND) stormed into the public spotlight. On January 11, 2006, in one of its first operations, the group raided Shell's offshore EA oil rig and kidnapped oil workers. As part of their demands, they ordered Shell to pay $1.5 billion to local communities in compensation for Shell's environmental damages, and they ordered the government to release Asari from jail. On January 30, 2006, MEND released the oil workers unharmed. Since then, the militant organization has been involved in regular operations against international oil interests and government authorities. They regularly raid both onshore and off-shore oil facilities, kidnap international oil workers and executives and then make excessive demands in exchange for the release of the hostages; once the oil companies, or the government, pays a small ransom (or a promise of community financial projects), the hostages have been released unharmed. The certainty of this equation is fueling these guerrilla attacks since the militants are guaranteed ransom and other payoffs for each operation.

Thus far, in 2006, more than 30 oil workers have been kidnapped, mostly by MEND militants, and all of them have been released unharmed. MEND plans to continue its debilitating campaign. In a recent e-mail sent to Reuters, MEND announced that "We are resuming an all-out war on the eastern sector [of the delta] with an aim to wiping out fields there and the export terminals. This we hope to achieve before the end of August" (Reuters, July 26, 2006). MEND has also executed more aggressive operations. On April 19, for example, MEND militants detonated a car bomb at the Bori Camp military base in Port Harcourt, killing two people.

Additional Ijaw militant organizations are undertaking terrorist operations against government forces and international oil interests in coordination with MEND, such as the Martyrs Brigade. Other groups, however, appear less sophisticated and more militant than MEND, such as the Coalition for Militant Action (COMA). According to a recent statement by the group published on July 23, COMA announced that they would resume hostage-taking operations and would target politicians and high-profile Nigerian citizens (*Vanguard*, July 23, 2006). In the statement, COMA said they disagreed with Asari's call for a cessation of hostilities, advising that "in battle, you do not make peace with an unrepentant enemy" (*Vanguard*, July 23, 2006).

Shortly after COMA's announcement, but not necessarily in response to it, Asari released his own statement from jail, arguing that his followers and the Ijaw community should continue their armed struggle against the government and against international oil firms since that was the only way to achieve political and economic rights. According to his statement, which was released on July 24, "How can we [the Ijaw] negotiate when we are in chains and dispossessed? The only noble and honorable path open to us is the glorious and time-tested path of armed struggle" (*Daily Champion*, July 24, 2006).

Government Failure to Stabilize the Niger Delta

There are a multitude of reasons why the Nigerian government has been unable to stabilize the Niger Delta. One of the most obvious explanations is the terrain of the delta. According to the Niger Delta Development Commission, the delta is the world's third largest wetland and is composed of dense mangrove swamps and waterways, making it an ideal location for guerrilla operations. The various oil facilities and pipelines saturate the area and are easy targets for militants who are able to navigate the dense web of waterways in speedboats, lay siege to a facility, capture international oil workers and then disappear back into the swamps and mangroves. The speed and size of the guerrilla attacks often catch the security forces protecting the energy installations by surprise; these same security forces usually suffer from poor equipment, training and morale, placing their dedication in doubt. The weapons used by the militants are abundant in the country since small-arms filter into Nigeria from conflict zones like Liberia, Sudan, Somalia, the Democratic Republic of Congo and Sierra Leone.

Three recent examples of guerrilla operations demonstrate this security context. On June 7, MEND militants approached a Shell gas plant near Port Harcourt in a speedboat. The guerrillas were equipped with small-arms, including rocket launchers, and they killed at least three of the Nigerian soldiers and police protecting the installation. They then kidnapped five South Koreans who were working for Daewoo and Korea Gas Corp. The attack forced Shell to shut down the plant. On June 8, however, all of the South Korean hostages were released (AFP, June 8, 2006). Another recent attack, on July 12, demonstrates the size of some guerrilla contingents. In this incident, a convoy of boats carrying construction material for Chevron-Texaco was traveling through the delta under the armed guard of Nigerian naval troops. After passing near Chanomi Creek on the way to Chevron's Escravos River installation, the convoy was overwhelmed by 20 speedboats loaded with heavily armed militants. A shootout occurred, resulting in the deaths of four naval soldiers. Several Chevron workers were taken captive, but were quickly released (AFP, July 14, 2006). Other incidents follow this pattern, and militants have even attacked off-shore oil rigs, such as on June 2 when Ijaw guerrillas captured eight foreign oil workers (six Britons, an American and a Canadian) on a rig 60 kilometers off the Nigerian coast of Bayelsa state; all hostages were, once again, released, allegedly after ransoms were paid (AFP, June 4, 2006).

According to the chief of Nigeria's Naval Staff, Vice Admiral Ganiyu Adekeye, the guerrillas operating in the delta have studied Nigerian naval operations and discovered the security forces' weaknesses; additionally, according to Adekeye, the navy lacks proper equipment to combat these militants as many of its ships are in poor condition (*This Day*, July 27, 2006). This is one reason why in 2004 the United States provided special boats to Nigerian authorities to help fight piracy, arms and oil smuggling. The United States also conducted joint military exercises with Nigerian troops in Calabar in 2004 with a focus on water combat (IRIN, June 26, 2006). Stability in the delta is an important concern for the United States as a result of the current tight supplies of oil.

The sheer number of oil installations and pipelines also make protection of the infrastructure difficult. Shell, which is the largest foreign oil company in Nigeria, has more than 1,000 oil wells in the delta region, and these wells are linked to a 6,000-kilometer pipeline network (IRIN, July 26, 2006). Protection against attacks, in addition to preventing sabotage to the pipelines, which causes pipeline leaks and results in the loss of millions of dollars in oil revenue and the destruction of the local environment, is too much of a burden for the Nigerian authorities to handle. The government has already sent thousands of additional troops to the delta, but they have not been able to reestablish stability. Furthermore, the army and security forces are restrained from using overwhelming force against the militants because this would likely result in a larger conflagration with the Ijaw, resulting in a complete shutdown of oil and gas exports, crippling the economy.

In addition to the tactical difficulties in suppressing delta militants, there is also the problem of corruption. In a country where 37 percent of the population lives on less than $1 per day, corruption and crime are major concerns. With the price of oil peaking over $70 a barrel, oil theft (bunkering) is tempting and provides an important source of revenue for guerrillas, civilians and criminal elements. Yet, the process of siphoning oil from pipelines causes leaks, which not only causes supply disruptions, but also destroys the environment—guerrillas and other criminal elements then demand that the oil companies pay certain contractors to repair or clean up the leaks, creating a never-ending cycle of contracting work. Additionally, oil companies are known to funnel money to guerrilla groups covertly so that the group "protects" their installations. Companies consider these pay-offs more efficient than spending millions of dollars repairing the pipelines after they are damaged. Also, the money allocated to the delta states from the federal government often falls victim to cronyism since community leaders and elected officials filter the funds to contracts and firms that pad their own pockets. Much of the revenue never makes it back to the delta communities.

Conclusion

Nigeria's future as a stable energy supplier remains in doubt. Already in the first half of 2006, the effects of guerrilla attacks and sabotage to the country's oil infrastructure has reduced production levels by 20 percent. Attacks on oil infrastructure have completely shut down oil facilities in some parts of the delta. The attacks on oil infrastructure will continue in the future, as the government has not drafted an effective policy to end the guerrilla campaigns. President Olusegun Obasanjo, recognizing the problem, released a report on the Niger Delta on July 18, confirming that the region is "suffering from administrative neglect, crumbling social infrastructure and service, high unemployment, abject poverty, filth and squalor and endemic neglect" (*Daily Champion*, July 27, 2006). Additionally, because the guerrillas are not solely criminal in nature and are part of an ethnic movement, heavy-handed tactics by the government against the Ijaw communities where the militants are sheltered could further enflame the crisis.

In the medium-term, one should expect the government to take measures to respond to the latest uptick in violence. President Obasanjo has tried to negotiate a change in the derivation formula to appease the communities in the delta, and the Bayelsa state government has set up a committee to examine strategies to deal with hostage-taking and other terrorist acts in the region (Abuja Rhythm FM Radio, July 13, 2006). Record high oil prices have also offset the losses that the government has sustained as a result of its oil exports being down 20 percent for the year. Moreover, as a result of high energy prices, international oil firms continue to invest in Nigeria despite its chaotic environment. Nevertheless, in a country where 95 percent of export earnings come from the oil and gas trade, the stabilization of the delta will remain a top government priority.

[From Terrorism Monitor, Volume IV, Issue 16]

The Challenge of Radical Islam in Mauritania

Anouar Boukhars

Originally published on October 7, 2005

Mauritania is grappling with a range of fundamental issues, including religion, development, political and social progress and institution building. After the August 3, 2005 bloodless military coup that toppled Mauritania's autocratic president Maaouiya Ould Taya, the country reached a critical juncture in both its efforts to deal with Sunni Islamic activism and its on-again, off-again flirtation with political reform. Whether the country can come together and reconcile the principles of tradition with modernity is still hard to tell, but the success or failure to develop stable religious and political institutions capable of dealing with the challenges of development, economic changes and radicalism will, as much as anything, determine the fate of radical Islamic activists.

The current structural predicament of the Mauritanian state stems from the unresolved contentious debate over the nature of political and religious authority. Since its independence in 1960, the Mauritanian state has managed to produce neither a coherent political order nor ground its rule in either modern, rational-legal, or traditional legitimacy. Seeking to shore up its Islamic credentials, the state under successive presidencies encouraged the spread of Salafi ideals without seeming to appreciate that such a stance risked diluting its monopoly on Islamic interpretation. The state supported the ideological and motivational sources of Islamic radicalism by providing apolitical radicals like Bouddah Ould Bousseyri and Mohamed Salem Ould Addoud with overall political and strategic guidance, gratifying their wishes and supporting their proselytizing missions inside the country [1].

It was the state's own policies of Islamization and Arabization which served as a strong impetus for the growth of religious and political activism [2]. The Arabization of education, for example, necessitated importing teachers from Egypt and the Middle East. These scholars exercised considerable influence on the introduction, reform and interpretation of Islamic laws. They also provided the needed ideological depth for the upsurge in the Arabist/Islamist trend in Mauritania. Islamism also thrived thanks to the financial donations and incentives coming out from the Persian Gulf, particularly from Saudi Arabia. The latter funded mosques, Islamic study centers, and madrassas to propagate its own rigid and intolerant version of Islam. Some of the institutions sustained by Saudi oil money became conduits for material and ideological support to radical Islamists.

The number of radical Islamist sympathizers in the country is very small though growing in number, especially in urban areas, [3] and this is due in part to the corrupt policies of the ruling elites, the abortion of the democratic experiment launched in 1991, and the state's racist and discriminatory policies towards Haratines (the former slave stratum) [4]. But contrary to the regime's depiction of Islamists as uniform zealous ideologues and its obstinate refusal to recognize the variability and non-violent essence of their doctrinal outlook, it is the political tendency of Sunni activism that has gone furthest, thus acknowledging the need for the establishment of a democratic government. Despite their different readings of religion, different understanding of the dialectic of tradition and modernity and disparate political visions, Mauritanian Islamic political activists have come the closest to recognizing that the best way to rationalize the political culture is by first rationalizing the religious culture of the Islamic movements.

Far from being a fixed ideological monolith existing outside history and in opposition to modernity and democracy, Islamism does not and cannot constitute a single coherent entity because different historical, cultural and social contexts and realities make for different Islamisms. Understanding the dynamics of the competing and sometimes contradictory discourses on any given issue requires an appreciation of the diversity of the contemporary Mauritanian Islamic experience.

Mauritanian Islamism is driven largely by three distinct types of activism: political, missionary, and jihadi. The political movement is less cohesive in membership, consisting of small groups that formed through the construction of alliances between a few eminent personalities like Mohamed Jemil Ould Mansour and Mokhtar Ould Mohamed Moussa, former ambassador to Syria [5]. Each group tries to expand its popular base and political clout through identification or affiliation with well-known ideological movements like the Muslim Brothers or personalities like the Tunisian Rachid Ghannouchi and Sudanese Hassan al-Turabi [6]. Most political Islamists envision acquiring political power through peaceful means and prioritize objectives directed at the coordination of strategic and operational issues between the three main variants of

Sunni activism (i.e. political, missionary and jihadi). Attempts to unify the Islamist movement have all ended in failure because of the highly diffuse nature of the movement and the hostility of the apolitical branches of Sunni activism to political Islamists [7].

Another major reason accounting for the failed attempts to strengthen and unify the Islamist movement are the stringent rules governing the establishment of associations, organizations and political parties. Since opening up the political system in 1991, the regime exhibited a marked suspicion of the Islamists and a reluctance to take serious steps in easing restrictions on political parties for fear that genuine democracy would displace the political prerogatives of the ruling regime. The result has been the shutting out of the Islamists from the constitutional process.

The second type of Islamic activism is the da'wa (missionary) current. It is represented by Salafiyya 'ilmiyya (scholarly or scientific Salafism) and the most structured movement in Mauritania, Tabligh [8]. The Salafiyya 'ilmiyya current is best exemplified by such prominent radical figures like Taki Ould Mohamed Abdellahi and Mohamed el Hacen Ould Dedew. The latter has gained prominence by his daring challenge and criticism of the regime and his fatwas denouncing relations with Israel and consumption of American goods. Both Ould Dedew and Mohamed Abdellahi call for the restoration of the Sharia and encourage jihad against the West to free all Muslim land under foreign occupation [9]. They preach a culture of intolerance that suppresses all discourses of dissent. Other Wahhabis include the Tadjakant, the first importers of Wahhabism to Mauritania [10].

The Tabligh movement, launched in India in 1926 by the Jama'at al-Da'wa wal-Tabligh (Group for Preaching and Propagation), took root in Mauritania in the early 1990s. Like Salafiyya 'ilmiyya, it is fundamentalist in its doctrinal outlook, eschews politics, and is primarily concerned with the preservation of the Islamic faith and moral order in Mauritanian society.

The jihadi tendency is the third type of Islamic activism. Unlike the political and missionary current, jihadi activists advocate the use of violence and armed resistance against what they perceive as the continuing onslaught of the enemies of Islam. The latter can be "impious" rulers (the near enemy) or non-Muslim "infidels" (the far enemy), especially Israel and the United States. This form of Islamic activism has very few mujahideen or sympathizers though it is actively involved in trying to recruit more followers from members of Salafiyya 'ilmiyya who have grown more disenchanted by the rapprochement of the regime with Israel. Salafiyya 'ilmiyya is the most likely group of Islamic activism to forsake the non-violent activism of the da'wa and engage in "defensive jihad" against domestic rulers and the West.

All these three different types of Islamist activism are a response to internal authoritarianism and external (i.e. foreign) manipulation. Islam provides two channels of response to these challenges: islah (reform) and tajdid (renewal). The former represented by the political current of the Mauritanian Islamist movement is a proactive approach that responds warmly to the prospect of spreading technological, scientific and democratic norms into Mauritanian society, believing that some aspects of modernity do not conflict with the established values and principles of Islamic law. The latter is a reactive approach, exemplified by the da'wa and jihadi tendencies, which in their search of indigenization, authenticity, and freedom, turn toward nativism and in the case of the jihadi current into jihadism.

Political Islamists are mainly preoccupied with government corruption and social injustice. They see the contesting of elections as the best means to achieve power and redress the inefficiencies of the state. They disapprove of the missionary activists' obsession with individual behavior at the expense of more important issues. Da'wa activists strive to restore the Islamic identity and moral fabric of Mauritanian society and challenge the state's monopoly on religion and the official religious establishment's interpretive authority. Their discourse of cultural authenticity tries to tap into the collective anger and frustration of so many Mauritanians with the failure of the state. Missionary Islamists are highly critical of political Islam which they see as a perversion of religion. Like the da'wa activists, jihadists condemn political Islamists as defeatists for seeking to exploit religion for political purposes and accommodate modernity within Islam. The jihadists' entire political philosophy is based on the belief that contemporary Mauritanian society has returned to jahiliya (a state of ignorance and unbelief that preceded the revelation of Islam).

These competing factions of Islamic activists are engaged in a struggle among themselves and against state authoritarianism over the essence and direction of the Mauritanian state. There is no doubt that the consequences of this momentous battle between conflicting ideologies over the meaning of Islam and the essence of a legitimate political order are of historical significance for the Mauritanian state and its relations with the West.

Notes

1. Rahal Bobrik, "Pouvoir et homes de religion en Mauritania" *Politique Africaine*, number 70, June 1998, pp. 135-143. Ould Bousseyri is a close associate of the regime. He is a supporter of Wahhabi Islam and a very influential figure in the apolitical Islamist camp. For several decades, he had been imam of the grand mosque of Nouakchott built by Saudi money. Ould Addoud advocates an ultra-conservative form of Islam. He was Minister of Culture and director of the High Islamic Council. He is critical of political Islamists and very supportive of the regime.
2. A. W. Ould Cheikh: "Cherche élite désespérément. Évolution du système éducatif et (dé) formation des élites dans la société mauritanienne," in Pierre Bonte & Hélène Claudot-Hawad (dir.), Élites du monde touareg et maure, Les cahiers de l'IREMAM, (Aix en Provence:Edisud, 2000), number 13-14.
3. Adriana Piga, *Islam et villes en Afrique au sud du Sahara: entre soufisme et fondamentalisme* (Paris: Karthala, 2003).
4. "L'Islamisme en Afrique du Nord IV: Contestation Islamiste en Mauritanie: Menace ou Bouc Émissaire?" *Rapport Moyen-Orient/Afrique du Nord* Number 41, May 11, 2005, p. 19.
5. "L'Islamisme en Afrique du Nord IV: Contestation Islamiste en Mauritanie: Menace ou Bouc Émissaire?" pp. 20-21.
6. Ibid. p. 16.
7. The first setback came in 1991 when efforts to create the movement of Umma ended in failure. The second attempt came in 2003-2004.
8. On Salafiyya, see Ahmed Ould Cheikh: "Le mouvement islamiste en Mauritanie: gros plan" in *Le Calame* number 394, May 28 2003.
9. "L'Islamisme en Afrique du Nord IV: Contestation Islamiste en Mauritanie : Menace ou Bouc Émissaire?" p. 16.
10. Ibid. p. 15.

[From Terrorism Monitor, Volume III, Issue 19]

Sierra Leone: An Obscure Battlefield in the War on Terrorism

Donald Temple

Originally published on December 20, 2005

On the dusty trash strewn streets of the Sierra Leonean capital, Freetown, men, women, and children with missing arms and legs wander aimlessly through half-completed concrete buildings. The surrounding hills are covered with hastily constructed shanties made of corrugated iron, plastic, or any other material that can be turned into shelter. Further afield in the countryside, villages lay barren and evoke only the horrific memories of an almost decade-old civil war. This war-torn West African society, which every passing day teeters on the verge of collapse, is the last place in which one would expect the "cat and mouse" game between the West and Islamic extremists to unfold. As the al-Qaeda network morphs from a defined terrorist group into an amorphous ideology of "al-Qaedism," Sierra Leone--because of its historical ties to terrorism, internal dynamics, and external influences-- could soon be pushed to the forefront of the war against terrorism.

Sierra Leone has a history of harboring Islamic militants. The first group to find sanctuary in the country was Hezbollah. From the 1980s onwards, Hezbollah agents, aided by the local Lebanese population, have operated out of Sierra Leone. In 1986, Yasser Arafat entered into negotiations with former President Joseph Momoh to build a PLO training camp on an island off of the coast of Freetown [1]. Further evidence of the ties arose when The United Nations Mission in Sierra Leone (UNAMSIL) released a report on the relationship between al-Qaeda, Charles Taylor, and the infamous Revolutionary United Front of Sierra Leone (RUF). The report showed that in the months prior to 9/11, al-Qaeda and the RUF, with Charles Taylor serving as conduit, traded money and weapons for diamonds. Sierra Leone's historical ties to Muslim extremists appear to still be intact. According to a December 2004 article in Freetown's *African Champion*, two al-Qaeda operatives returning from Pakistan were arrested while trying to enter Sierra Leone [2]. Moreover, in July 2005 three Middle Eastern "businessmen" with suspected ties to terrorist groups were arrested near the Liberia-Sierra Leone border [3].

These are unlikely to be isolated incidents. Indeed, as the United States and its allies deny terrorists safe havens in the Middle East, Asia, and the Sahel countries, the Muslim states of West Africa will likely become destinations for Islamic terrorist groups. Due to its internal features, Sierra Leone is a likely destination for terrorists. Together, the country's demographics, corruption, and unregulated territories and industries create an environment where terrorists can operate with almost total impunity.

Sierra Leone is a multi-racial society. Although the vast majority of people are of African descent, there are also Lebanese, Pakistani, and Indian communities. 60 percent of the population is Sunni Muslim, 30 percent follow indigenous religions, and the remaining ten percent is a mixture of Christians and Shi'ite Muslims of Lebanese descent [4]. These demographic factors combined with a substantial Lebanese presence enable terrorists to operate in Sierra Leone.

The Lebanese merchant class has historically served as the link between this small West African state and the broader radical Islamist movement. Hezbollah and now al-Qaeda have used their contacts within this community to acquire documentation, travel certificates, and financing for terrorist operations. These activities are aided by the corrupt government of Sierra Leone.

Similar to most states in Africa, Sierra Leone struggles with endemic corruption at all levels of society, especially at the governmental level. The most recent case of the government's collusion with individuals linked to terrorist groups involves a British national named Paddy McKay, who is wanted in the UK for alleged involvement with al-Qaeda. According to a report in the *Freetown Peep*, Paddy McKay with the help of Khalil Lakish, a Sierra Leonean of Lebanese descent who is also under investigation for bribery of government officials and ties to Hezbollah, obtained Sierra Leonean registrations for four planes with fraudulent information. The planes have since been tied to terrorist activity. According to two separate reports in *The Independent* and the *Freetown Peep*, McKay, who they allege also has ties to the Muslim Brotherhood in Egypt and Algeria's Jamaat al-Islamia, has been using the Sierra Leonean registered planes to traffic illicit diamonds and distribute weapons to the Middle East and the Horn of Africa.

Francis Bockari, the Permanent Secretary in the Ministry for Transportation and Communication stated that "McKay enjoys a normal and professional business relationship with the department of Civil

Aviation and the Government of Sierra Leone... all airline operators are properly registered and do not have any terrorist connections" [5]. This incident highlights the relationship between the global terrorist infrastructure, the local Lebanese merchant class and corrupt Sierra Leonean government officials. According to another report in the *Freetown Peep*, al-Qaeda has sought to use their local connections to acquire Sierra Leonean passports on several occasions [6]. Sierra Leone's internal environment offers one final advantage to terrorists: lack of government oversight over the diamond industry that is predominately monopolized by unscrupulous Lebanese merchants.

The diamond industry has long been a source of revenue for the Lebanese militant group Hezbollah and more recently al-Qaeda. Douglas Farah of *The Washington Post* and the UNAMSIL mission in Sierra Leone have conducted extensive research on the links between al-Qaeda, Charles Taylor, and the RUF. Since the end of Sierra Leone's civil war, the country has experienced a "diamond boom," according to Mohammed Deen, the Minister of Mines [7]. In 2004, the country "officially" exported $130 million worth of diamonds; however, according to UN special envoy Daudi Mwakawago, the diamond industry in Sierra Leone actually exported somewhere between $300 million and $500 million in 2004 [8]. These figures indicate that between one-half to two-thirds of the diamond industry is not regulated. In an industry where some of the traders are already known to have ties to terrorist groups, and where the elements of the former RUF still control the diamond mining regions, it is likely that al-Qaeda will again return to Sierra Leone's diamond mines if they have not already.

Despite the presence of over 17,000 UN troops, much of the interior of the country remains ungoverned [9]. Decades of civil war have left the country's transportation network in tatters. This lack of control can create an opportunity for al-Qaeda. Furthermore, with the UN scheduled to completely withdraw in December 2005, a major barrier to terrorist infiltration will have been removed.

External forces have historically played a significant role in shaping Sierra Leone, for better or worse. Sierra Leone's last insurgency was sparked by Muammar Qadhafi's destabilizing external influence. Qadhafi trained rebel leaders like Foday Sankoh and Charles Taylor to be foot soldiers for his pan-African revolution. Sankoh initially justified his insurgency by proclaiming himself the liberator of the Sierra Leonean people from a corrupt government. People followed until they realized he was as corrupt as the government in Freetown. By then, he controlled the diamonds and could, in effect, wage war on Freetown indefinitely. This situation would have persisted without the intervention of British forces.

In 2000, rebel forces began an offensive on UN forces before moving on Freetown. British Prime Minister Tony Blair deployed 800 British soldiers to secure the airport and provide logistical support for the UN troops. British forces remained in Sierra Leone until 2003 to train the Sierra Leone Army. The British intervention and the subsequent UN mission (UNAMSIL) were successful insofar as they resuscitated a failed state and gave its people a chance for a better life. On December 20, 2005 the UN will withdraw completely, leaving behind a modicum of a state where the underlying conditions of corruption and destitution, which led people to initially join the RUF in 1991, still exist today. The country suffers from endemic poverty, where the Sunni Muslim masses are disproportionately poorer than the Lebanese Shi'ites and black Christians; the government is unashamedly corrupt; West Africa as a region is awash in weapons; unemployed child soldiers with no education roam the streets and religious fervor is on the rise. Given this terrible state of affairs, it is not surprising that Daudi Mwakawago, Sierra Leone's UN envoy, described the situation as "very explosive" [10].

Sierra Leone is a Muslim country on the precipice where external pressures, like in the past, will decisively influence the country. The U.S. and UK are the two largest contributors of development aid [11]. The British, in particular, have worked with the Sierra Leone government at all levels to improve government transparency and effectiveness. The Islamic Republic of Iran and Saudi Arabia have also aided Sierra Leone's recovery by funding the construction of mosques, Islamic education and cultural exchanges [12]. While there is nothing to suggest that these activities have had anything but a beneficial effect, the West needs to ensure that the influence of Iran and Saudi Arabia does not promote extremism.

In the final analysis, Sierra Leone remains on the periphery of global terrorism, but it is important that policymakers begin to examine the factors and possibilities discussed here--even as the U.S.-led war on terrorism is focused on the Middle East and Southeast Asia.

Notes

1. Farah, Douglas, *Blood from Stones*. New York: Broadway Books, 2004, p. 23.

2. "Sierra Leone: Police Reportedly Arrest Al-Qa'ida Suspects along Guinean Border," *The African Champion*, December 24, 2004

3. "Terrorists Enter Liberia, National Security Source Confirms," *The News* (Monrovia), July 19, 2005.

4. CIA: The Word Factbook 2005 ed. http://www.cia.gov/cia/publications/factbook/geos/sl.html

5. "International: Profiles of Airline Companies Connected to Arms Dealer Paddy McKay" *AFP Report*, December 22, 2004. The AFP report summarizes reports in Freetown local papers during a month long investigation. The papers cited are *The Independent* (Freetown), September 1, 2004; the *Freetown Peep*, September 2, 2004; the *Concord Times* (Freetown), September 2, 2004.

6. "Al-Qaida Terrorists Seek our Passports… Presidential Affairs Minister Confirms to Symposium," *Freetown Peep*, August 22, 2003.

7. "Sierra Leone: Mines Minister Says Country in Midst of 'Diamond Boom'," *Agence France Presse*, July 12, 2005.

8. "Call For Transparency on Mineral Exports," *The Independent* (Freetown), April 8, 2005.

9. http://www.un.org/Depts/dpko/missions/unamsil/facts.html.

10. "Peacekeepers Prepare to Leave Sierra Leone," AP, October 4, 2005.

11. http://www.oecd.org/dataoecd/63/27/1878706.gif

12. Freetown Sierra Leone Broadcasting Service, transcript of the September 26, 2005 and January 15, 2004 broadcasts.

[From Terrorism Monitor, Volume III, Issue 24]

PAGAD: A Case Study of Radical Islam in South Africa

Anneli Botha

Originally published on September 8, 2005

The threat of Islamic terrorism to the Republic of South Africa (RSA) is surprisingly real. Aside from the possibility of an al-Qaeda strike against U.S. and other Western interests in the country, there are a number of indigenous Islamic networks that have the potential to either engage in serious acts of terrorism on their own or in conjunction with international terrorists. Of these indigenous networks the most important is an organization formerly called People Against Gangsterism and Drugs (PAGAD). This article highlights the emergence, evolution and threats posed by PAGAD and similar organizations, which use legitimate causes as a subterfuge for furthering their radical Islamic agenda.

Background

The Muslim community makes up an estimated 2.3% of the South African population. Although well-established Muslim communities can be found throughout the country, the Muslim community in Cape Town represents 7% of the Western Cape's population. Conditions within that region are substantially different from other parts of the country, which have contributed to PAGAD's initial success. Primarily, poverty and related social problems affect the Muslim community in the Western Cape to a much greater extent than other Muslim communities in the Republic. Secondly, the Muslim community in Cape Town is predominately of Malay origin and came to Cape Town as part of the slave trade during the 18th century, as opposed to Muslims in other parts of the country who are predominately of Indian origin.

An Islamic revival in South Africa began in the 1950s, as teachers and professionals in the Western Cape tried to mobilize themselves into coherent movements. The Islamic revival essentially derived its religious inspiration from modern Islamic movements in Pakistan and Egypt. In December 1970 the Muslim Youth Movement of South Africa (MYM) was established. The Iranian revolution in 1979 had a massive impact on the consciousness of South African Muslims and led to the formation of the Qibla Mass Movement, an anti-apartheid movement inspired by the universal egalitarian message of the Islamic revolution in Iran.

The Qibla Movement

Qibla was created in the early 1980s to promote the aims and ideals of the Iranian revolution in South Africa and in due course transform South Africa into an Islamic state, under the slogan "One Solution, Islamic Revolution." [1]

During the anti-apartheid struggle Qibla also supported the black consciousness movement in South Africa, in particular Pan Africanism. Although Qibla is a purely South African organization, it is manipulated from a safe distance by the Iranian intelligence services, which use the organization not only to propagate the world view of the Islamic Republic, but also as a cover to conduct espionage in RSA. In order to broaden its support base inside the South African Muslim community, Qibla initiated three projects:

1. It played a key role in the formation of the Western Cape-based Islamic Unity Convention (IUC), which was formed in 1994 to serve as an umbrella organization for more than 250 Muslim groups. The objective of the IUC is to promote Islamic unity in South Africa, as a precursor for an Iranian-style Islamic revolution in the country.

2. It positioned itself as the driving force behind the militant/ extreme components in PAGAD, in particular the G-Force.

3. It assumed control over the IUC's Radio 786. This medium proved to be useful in mobilizing individuals within the Muslim community for its cause.

Although clearly not a terrorist organization, Qibla nonetheless has whole-heartedly embraced Iran's Islamic Republic. In his book, *Quest for Unity* Achmad Cassiem (a leader of Qibla and the current head of IUC) provides an insight into the revolutionary ideology of groups like Qibla and PAGAD: "Any social order which does not rotate on the axis of justice is not fit for survival. The minimum demand of the oppressed under the guidance of Islamic ideology is for a just social order. Anything less than a just social order is betrayal, is treason to the oppressed people and their glorious martyrs. The essence of jihad is sacrifice and it is necessary because a revolutionary is not merely an exponent of revolutionary rhetoric but one who attacks what is oppressive and exploitative in order to destroy and eradicate it. No revolutionary worthy of the name is therefore threatened and blackmailed – not even with death." [2]

PAGAD

It was the ideological and spiritual environment created by Qibla that led to the emergence of PAGAD on December 9, 1995. Another major factor in the emergence of this organization was the extraordinarily high crime rate in the Western Cape. Indeed PAGAD's initial primary objective was to serve as a broad anti-crime front. Under its banner a variety of organizations and concerned citizens with diverse ideological, political and religious persuasions sought to combat the criminal gangs and drug dealers in their communities.

From its inception until the eventual split in September 1996, there were three distinct strands within PAGAD:

1. Populist moderates and concerned citizens.

2. Islamic extremists and Qibla infiltrators that became the primary driving force of PAGAD after the split in 1996.

3. Drug dealers that used PAGAD to protect their "turf" against competitors.

Modus Operandi and Target Selection

Initially PAGAD employed a dual strategy, acting as a community pressure group while at the same time forming and activating covert cell structures known as the G-Force. The patterns of militancy evident in PAGAD activities indicated the prevalence of both paramilitary-style attacks on alleged drug dealers perpetrated primarily by G-Force members, and mass marches by PAGAD supporters intended to portray the organization as a grass-roots movement. PAGAD's modus operandi developed in the following stages:

1996-1997: The Fight Against Drug Dealers. Between July 1996 and December 1997, PAGAD's covert structures were implicated in 222 acts of violence against alleged drug dealers and their property. Explosives were used in 124 incidents in comparison to the use of firearms in 98 incidents. [3]

1998: Reaction to Opposition. From July 1998 onwards PAGAD began to target academics and clerics critical of the tactics employed by its G-Force. At the same time, the personnel and facilities of the state's security and intelligence community were attacked by PAGAD. The explosion outside the offices of the police special investigation task team on August 6, 1998 elevated PAGAD into the world of Islamic terrorism. Moreover, the increasing selectivity of targets by PAGAD's covert teams reflected a noteworthy qualitative shift in strategic objectives. Furthermore, PAGAD attacked business linked to the U.S., after the latter launched missile strikes against targets related to al-Qaeda in Afghanistan and Sudan in August 1998.

1999-2000: Restaurants and Public Places. There was a significant change in suspected PAGAD-related acts of violence after 1998. Although the number of bombing and shooting incidents declined, PAGAD became more deadly and indiscriminate. Attacks were no longer focused on drug dealers and gangsters but tended to target public places and places of entertainment. Between January and August 1999, six bomb explosions injured 81 people, while 17 armed attacks killed 17. In 2000, at least 14 prominent acts of terrorism that included attacks against eyewitnesses in PAGAD-related court cases, restaurants and international interests were recorded. For example, on August 29, 2000 a car bomb was detonated near the United States consulate injuring seven people.

PAGAD's covert activities came to a standstill with the arrest and prosecution of its prominent leaders. However, since the underlying reasons for its existence were never addressed, the possible re-emergence of PAGAD or similar organizations cannot be discounted.

Conclusion

Ostensibly created to fight drugs and the socioeconomic problems that are associated with it, PAGAD was essentially a political organization with distinct Islamist objectives. Should the RSA government be able to effectively combat gang violence and drugs it is likely that Muslim extremists—particularly in the Western Cape— would find other issues to bolster public support. Indeed after the establishment of PAGAD, similar structures with seemingly identical aims were formed: People Against Prostitutes and Sodomites (PAPAS), Muslims Against Global Oppression (MAGO), and Muslims Against Illegitimate Leaders (MAIL). Each of these organizations represented a different challenge and therefore a different support-base. In other words, each organization has a specific target from which small numbers of extremists could be recruited.

It is also clear that community-based organizations modeled on PAGAD are heavily penetrated by the highly secretive Qibla organization. Qibla uses this penetration to marshal support for its Islamic revolutionary aims. Although in many respects Qibla is worlds apart from al-Qaeda and the broader Sunni Islamic militancy which it inspires, nonetheless its radical ideology can prepare vulnerable individuals for terrorist recruitment further down the line.

The key question, of course, revolves around the likelihood of an al-Qaeda attack against Western interests in South Africa. For its part, the government of RSA hopes that its neutrality in the so-called war against terrorism and its pro-Palestinian stance will spare it from the wrath of international jihadists.

The real threat is to U.S. and other Western interests in the country; in this respect there are major causes for concern. As a nascent democracy, South Africa is obsessed with protecting basic rights, rights that could be exploited by international terrorists working in tandem with local militants. This "rights-based" environment is compounded by widespread official corruption in South Africa that makes it very easy for skilled and experienced terrorists to operate and further their aims (for instance by acquiring fake documentation) without fear of detection. Moreover, South Africa has porous borders and large immigrant communities that can shelter terrorists. Furthermore, high-value targets, including large embassies and the headquarters of multi-national corporations, proliferate in the country.

Notes
1. N Jeenah, PAGAD: Fighting fire with fire, *Impact International*, Vol. 26, No. 9, 1996, p. 9.
2. A Cassiem, *Quest for Unity*, Cape Town: Silk Road International Publishers, 1992, p. 68
3. R Friedman, "Government Blamed for Lack of Action as War Escalates", January 24, 1997, *Cape Times*, Cape Town.

[From Terrorism Monitor, Volume III, Issue 17]

Part III
South Asia

Afghanistan

Mullah Dadullah: The Military Mastermind of the Taliban Insurgency

Omid Marzban

Originally published on March 21, 2006

On March 12, 2006, Sibghatullah Mujaddedi, the former president of Afghanistan and the current chairman of the upper house of parliament, was wounded in a suicide car bomb attack in Kabul (*Dawn*, March 12). Taliban military commander Mullah Dadullah took responsibility for the suicide attack, warning that "attacks against American puppets will continue" (*Dawn*, March 12, 2006). In December 2005, Dadullah warned that "we have prepared 200 young men who are ready to sacrifice themselves and carry out suicide bombings against the U.S. and its allies in Afghanistan" (*Pajhwak Afghan News*, January 11, 2006).

Mullah Dadullah is a primary spokesman for the current insurgency in Afghanistan. Dadullah is one of the most combative commanders of the Taliban and has survived serious injuries on at least three occasions. For instance, in early February, Yusuf Stanezai—the spokesman for the Afghan Interior Ministry—stated in an interview with Kabul-based Tulu TV that Dadullah had been killed during fighting in Helmand province (Tulu TV, February 3, 2006). Once again, Dadullah somehow survived. Just 10 days after the rumor of his death surfaced, Dadullah appeared on al-Jazeera television announcing his link with and support of al-Qaeda's leader Osama bin Laden (al-Jazeera, February 13, 2006).

Dadullah re-emerged on the Afghan scene two years after the Taliban regime was removed from power. The first time that Dadullah spoke on behalf of this ousted radical regime, his name was not unfamiliar to those who lived in Afghanistan during the five years in which the Taliban ruled the country. Most Afghanis knew Dadullah since he was the commander of the toughest battles fought against the Northern Alliance.

Both Dadullah and Taliban leader Mullah Omar are Pashtun, and Dadullah is one of Omar's most trusted followers. According to Mullah Abdul Salaam Raketi, a former Taliban commander and a current Afghan parliament member, who spoke with *Terrorism Focus* on March 4, 2006, Dadullah joined the Taliban in the very beginning of the regime's formation in 1994. He lost his left leg shortly after the formation of the Taliban. According to Waheed Mujda, a former high-ranking member of staff in the Taliban's Foreign Ministry, "When fighting against Ismail Khan [the current Minister of Water and Energy Supply] in the first months following the Taliban's inception, Dadullah stepped on a land mine near Herat, which caused the loss of his leg." The loss of his leg, however, did not discourage Dadullah from promulgating war, but made him even more combative.

Nevertheless, he was not, however, considered an important character during the first years after the regime's creation. After he was accused of a bloody genocide in the central Bamyan province, Dadullah was disarmed by order of Mullah Omar in 2000. He was later re-armed since the Taliban needed his aggressive command against Northern Alliance troops.

When the U.S.-led war to oust the Taliban began in 2001, Dadullah was under siege by the U.S.-backed Northern Alliance soldiers in Balkh, a northern Afghan province. He disappeared during the siege, however, and it was unclear how Dadullah managed to escape. It is believed that certain Northern Alliance commanders who fought against Dadullah gave him an opportunity to escape. Waheed Mujda says that Dadullah, who comes form Arghandab district—some 15 km northwest of Kandahar—was taken from Balkh to his native province by some senior commanders linked to the Jonbesh Melli Islami Afghanistan (National Islamic Movement of Afghanistan) party, led by General Abdul Rashid Dostum, a former communist officer who formed the party in support of the mujahideen. While Dostum and Dadullah are bitter enemies, Dadullah was apparently given the chance to escape by some of Dostum's followers, possibly without their commander's knowledge.

Indeed, in an exclusive interview on March 3, 2006, Waheed Mujda told *Terrorism Focus*, "When he [Dadullah] was in charge of the Taliban's frontlines in the north, he released several captives based on the friendship he had formed with some opposition commanders."

In the 1990s, Dadullah and the Northern Alliance commanders were allies and their common enemy was the Soviet Union. It was later that Dadullah and the Northern Alliance parted ways.

From Kandahar, Dadullah escaped to South Waziristan province of Pakistan, where he was given shelter by his Kakar tribesmen (*Newsline*, October 2003). The Karachi-based *Newsline* internet publication reports that the tribesmen not only provided shelter to Dadullah, but also collected a sizeable sum of donations for him. In addition to that, they bought him a Land Cruiser. They did this because of his "bravery" and "fighting spirit," and also because he is their fellow tribesman (*Newsline*, October 2003). Later, Dadullah moved to Karachi where he reportedly visited madrassas to foment religious fervor among the students and encourage them to join a holy war against foreign troops in Afghanistan, labeling these troops infidels.

Since the fall of the Taliban, Dadullah has been blamed for many terrorist acts in Afghanistan and Pakistan. In December of 2005, a special anti-terrorism court in the Pakistani city of Quetta sentenced Dadullah in absentia to life in prison on charges of attempting to assassinate Maulana Shirani, a Pakistani parliament member (*Pajhwak Afghan News*, December 29, 2005). Currently, Mullah Dadullah is one of the most wanted men by the United States and, as announced by Mullah Omar, he is a member of the 10-man Taliban insurgency leadership council. He is able to evade capture because of his friendship with mujahideen commanders and due to the support he receives from his Kakar tribe in the southern provinces of Afghanistan and Pakistan.

[From Terrorism Focus, Volume III, Issue 11]

Helmand Province and the Afghan Insurgency

Waliullah Rahmani

Originally published on March 23, 2006

A desolate and largely lawless region with a population of just over one million and a surface area of 23,058 square miles, the strategically-located southwestern Afghan province of Helmand is emerging as the center of the neo-Taliban and the broader Pashtun insurgency.

A string of deadly insurgent attacks this year have claimed the lives of several Helmand officials. The latest attack claimed the life of the Sangin district governor, Amir Jan, on March 3. Amir Jan was killed while vacationing in the Musa Qala district (*Pajhwok Afghan News*, March 4, 2006). Prior to this incident, at least 28 people, including the Musa Qala district chief, Abdul Quddus, were killed on February 2 in intense fighting with over 200 Taliban insurgents. The battle—which lasted more than 10 hours—took place in the Sangin, Nawzad and Musa Qala districts, which are located in the extreme south of Helmand.

According to Amir Mohammad Akhund, deputy governor of Helmand, "fighting erupted when militants attacked a government office in Musa Qala district, killing the local government district chief" (Azadi Radio, February 4, 2006). Meanwhile, a spokesman for the Afghan Interior Ministry, Yousef Istanizai, claimed that the battle in early February had been "the most serious incident in the last year" (Tolo TV, February 3, 2006). Istanizai also claimed that two Taliban leaders—Mullah Dadullah and Mullah Turjan—were killed in the fighting. It is not clear if Istanizai was referring to the notorious Mullah Dadullah, who is believed to be the leader of the resurgent Taliban movement in the south and who is still alive.

Causes of Violence

Following the recent Helmand clashes, some of the representatives in parliament criticized the central government's strategies in counter-narcotics, anti-corruption campaigns and disarmament programs. A Helmand representative in the lower house of parliament, Nasima Niazi, told *Sadi Bamdad* daily on February 4, 2006 that the formation of 200 Taliban militants is a result of the dissatisfaction felt by many distressed Afghan farmers. "Now when the farmers want to harvest their plants, the government has started destroying them," said Niazi. "Though I don't agree with planting opium, I still want the government to have a definite strategy" (*Sadi Bamdad*, February 4, 2006).

Aside from agriculture and the opium trade, widespread unemployment is believed to be a major cause of unrest in Helmand. According to Mukhtar Pidram, an Afghan political analyst, "During the last four years, the government has not established even a small company to employ unskilled youths...unemployment is one of the main factors driving dissatisfaction with the [Hamid] Karzai government and the main factor leading youths to embrace 'Mafias' in Afghanistan" (*Danishjo Weekly*, February 6, 2006).

Moreover, heavy-handedness and perceived oppression by the police and the security forces is undermining efforts to bring stability to Helmand. A group of Helmand elders voiced their concerns about this issue in a February 8 meeting with President Karzai in Kabul. Apparently, Karzai promised the Helmand elders that he would investigate their claims (Radio Afghanistan, February 8, 2006). According to Pidram, heavy-handedness by the security forces goes hand in hand with "warlordism, which is a big challenge facing the government and the people. These elements are still strong and control most of the military and civilian institutions, especially in provinces such as Helmand, which is a center of the narcotics trade" (*Danishjo Weekly*, February 6, 2006).

Furthermore, Helmand, aside from being a largely Pashtun province, is where many senior officials of the former Taliban regime originated. For instance, the culture and information minister of the former Taliban regime, Mullah Amir Khan Muttaqi, was from Helmand. Additionally, Helmand youths formed some of the most effective and fearless units of the Taliban's military. When Kandahar fell in late 2001, it is believed that many Taliban leaders sought sanctuary in Helmand. Given this long and deep-rooted association with the Taliban, it is not altogether surprising that former Taliban elements and sympathetic constituencies in broader Pashtun society are at the forefront of the insurgency in this desolate and wretched province. If the Afghan government and its Western allies are serious about tackling the problems in Helmand, they have to reach some sort of accommodation with aggrieved Pashtuns. Otherwise, the Taliban will be able to count on their support indefinitely.

Foreign Influence

Following every clash and suicide attack, Afghan officials customarily point an accusing finger at Pakistan and its notorious Inter-Services Intelligence Directorate (ISI). For instance, following the 10-hour long clashes in early February, Afghan Interior Minister Zarar Ahmad Muqbil, while speaking at the lower house of parliament, claimed that the "eastern" neighbor of Afghanistan (Pakistan) has equipped and sent the Taliban to fight against the central government. According to Muqbil, "Helmand, Kandahar, Paktia, Paktika, Kunar and Nuristan are those provinces which are insecure and restive. I must say clearly that these are the provinces which have joint borders with Pakistan" (Azadi Radio, February 13, 2006).

Moreover, Afghan Defense Minister Abdul Rahim Wardak, while speaking at the lower house of parliament, implicitly accused Pakistan of causing unrest and chaos in Helmand. "The terrorists who attack our young democracy have been trained, equipped and sent from abroad," Wardak stated (Azadi Radio, February 13, 2006). Furthermore, the national security chief, Amrullah Saleh, recently argued that the Afghan government "must put pressure on a specific country which trains and cooperates [with the terrorists] and from where they have been sent to instigate terrorist attacks" (*Pajhwok Afghan News*, February 12, 2006).

An Afghan journalist, Omid Ahmadi, believes that more than 60 countries with different strategies and policies are united in their stand against terrorism in Afghanistan. The only exception, according to Ahmadi, is Pakistan. "Among these countries, Pakistan is sparking chaos, and it has to review its policies," said Ahmadi (*Murdum Weekly*, February 16, 2006).

A Holy War?

Most of the gunmen and suicide attackers in Helmand are believed to be ideologically-motivated and fully committed to the cause of jihad. Waheed Mujda, a senior former foreign ministry diplomat during the Taliban regime, said in an exclusive interview that the "insurgents, mostly Taliban, are not fighting for power in Helmand or the rest of the provinces; they are fighting against foreigners...those

who are coming from abroad or are already present in Helmand attack
the government institutions because of Sharia" (Azadi Radio, March
13, 2006).

At the same time Hezb-e-Islami's Afghanistan leader,
Gulbuddin Hekmatyar, claimed he will "never negotiate with the
foreign established government in Afghanistan" (Tolo TV, February
16, 2006). This is a very important statement by the once all-powerful
Hekmatyar (a former Afghan prime minister), whose current influence
is perhaps underestimated. While Hekmatyar's influence in Helmand
does not exceed that of the Taliban, his statement is a clear sign to his
followers in this region to engage in jihad against government forces
in Helmand and other southwestern provinces. Moreover, despite
having been militarily defeated by the Taliban in 1994, Hekmatyar is
now cooperating with the neo-Taliban and al-Qaeda. This development,
coupled with Hekmatyar's recent statement, is very bad news for the
Kabul government.

The British in Helmand

According to a Kabul daily, "the bloodshed on Saturday
[February 2] underscored the challenge facing thousands of British and
Canadian troops in coming months as they gradually relieve American
forces in southern Afghanistan, a hotbed of insurgency and the drug
trade" (*Outlook Afghanistan Daily*, February 4).

The consensus in Afghanistan is that the surge in violence is
directly linked to the new mission of the British-led NATO International
Security Assistance Force in Helmand. This force will be dominated by
the British 16th Air Assault Brigade. It seems likely that the insurgents,
alongside al-Qaeda, will seek to test the resolve of the British troops
early, hoping to inflict serious losses on their forces.

The treacherous nature of this desolate and lawless region,
coupled with the complex factors driving the insurgency, make it
unlikely that the British-led NATO force will be able to restore stability
to Helmand in the foreseeable future. It is hoped, however, that the
British military's reputation for skillful handling of insurgencies and
the local populations that sustain it will reduce the grievances of the
Pashtun Helmandis.

[From Terrorism Monitor, Volume IV, Issue 6]

Afghan-Pakistan Border Region

Al-Qaeda's Operational Corridor on the NWFP

Sohail Abdul Nasir

Originally published on March 23, 2006

It is believed that the leadership of al-Qaeda is hiding in the area that encompasses Pakistan's Federally Administered Tribal Areas (FATA) and the North-West Frontier Province (NWFP). For instance, in January 2005, a number of locals, speaking privately, claimed to have witnessed the movement of bin Laden's entourage in the Afghan provinces of Paktia, Paktika, Zabol and Kandahar. These provinces constitute a geographical corridor parallel to the border of Pakistan. At one point, security agencies believed that al-Qaeda leaders Osama bin Laden and Ayman al-Zawahiri were roaming around Kunar province in Afghanistan (*Ghazi*, July 2, 2005).

Bin Laden and al-Zawahiri do not lack hideouts in the areas bordering Afghanistan and they do not need to come down to areas where security forces are searching for them. Some al-Qaeda operatives have been detained after being trapped in NWFP towns. For instance, Abu Faraj al-Libbi was arrested in Mardan, a town in NWFP that leads to Swat, Malakand and Dir (*Dawn*, May 4, 2005). Socially and culturally, Swat, Malakand and Dir, which are administratively settled areas of the NWFP, are not as secure for al-Qaeda when compared to the tribal belt of FATA. In the tribal belt, hospitality, giving asylum and exacting revenge on enemies are the norm. This system prevails in the Pashtun areas of Pakistan's tribal belt and in Afghanistan.

North Waziristan, located in FATA, is one province that is considered to be a bastion of Islamic militants and sympathizers of al-Qaeda. It is generally believed that the leadership of al-Qaeda (bin Laden and al-Zawahiri) is hiding in the area that encompasses FATA and the NWFP. Yet, due to the nature of the tribes and the geography in most of FATA and the NWFP, U.S. and Pakistani intelligence agencies have been unable to discover their whereabouts.

Both al-Qaeda leaders live with their families which consist of wives, sons, daughters, grandsons and protection details. Wherever they live, they must enjoy the support of the local population since tribes do not report their presence to the authorities. No one has been able to predict the movement of bin Laden and al-Zawahiri; speculation, however, remains.

Bin Laden's Regional Allies in the NWFP

Outside of FATA, however, Swat, Malakand and Dir in the NWFP are politically-motivated areas and as such are greatly influenced by the country's three main political parties. Dir and particularly Upper Dir is a stronghold of Jamaat-e-Islami (JI). Malakand and Swat are jointly influenced by the Pakistan People's Party (PPP), Awami National Party (ANP) and JI. Among these, PPP and ANP are liberal democratic parties with a tilt toward the left, while JI is the oldest and most influential Islamic party in the subcontinent. Ideologically, the masses in these towns are not committed to the cause of the Taliban and al-Qaeda; support to the extent of providing them shelter and hideouts does not seem plausible here. Some sections of society, however, are linked with the defunct Tehrik-e Nifaz-e Shariat-e Mohammadi (TNSM) but they do not have the potential to extend permanent help to al-Qaeda.

Indeed, in Swat, Dir and Malakand, security agencies have a deep rooted set-up that has effectively detected and captured Taliban and al-Qaeda operatives. The arrest of al-Libbi in Mardan is an example of this. Also, in March 2005, six al-Qaeda suspects were apprehended in the NWFP (Pakistan Television, March 31, 2005).

Tribes and Geography of the Tribal Belt

On the other hand, unlike the areas of NWFP, Pakistani and U.S. intelligence agencies have been unable to penetrate FATA areas. This is mainly due to the area's unique socioeconomic landscape. FATA consists of seven geographic units called agencies. From north to south, these agencies are Bajaur, Mohmand, Orakzai, Khyber, Kurram, and North and South Waziristan. The whole belt is a part of the great range of the Hindu Kush Mountains. Geographically, FATA is a part of the NWFP but the federal government directly governs through a governor of the NWFP and subordinate political agents. The predominant population is Pashtun with the exception of some nomadic tribes. The Bangash tribe of Kurram Agency is Shiite while the rest of the population belongs to the Sunni deobandi school. The main towns of FATA include Miran Shah, Razmak, Bajaur, and Wana.

Bajaur Agency is inhabited by Yousafzai and some local Pashtun tribes; Mohmand tribe lives in Mohmand Agency; Orakzai are the native dwellers of Orakzai Agency; the famous Afridi lives in Khyber Agency; North and South Waziristan are inhabited by the Wazir and Mehsud tribes, respectively.

Prior to the creation of Pakistan in 1947, this tribal belt acted as a buffer zone between the British-ruled subcontinent and Afghanistan. The Durand Line, the international border, separates the tribal areas from Afghanistan. As part of the war on terrorism, Pakistan has deployed more than 70,000 troops in the tribal areas and on the Durand Line. Among the seven agencies, two of which—North Waziristan and South Waziristan—are suffering the worst from the insurgency. In order to cleanse the areas of al-Qaeda and its local associates, the Pakistani government has employed a two-prong strategy of military operations and dialogue. The governor of the NWFP, Commander Khalil-ur-Rehman, recently announced the end of military operations in North Waziristan Agency and asked the tribal notables to curb the militancy in accordance with local tribal norms (*Daily Times*, February 24, 2006). That being said, however, it was just on March 1, 2006, shortly before Bush's visit to Pakistan, that Pakistani security agencies launched a new strike in North Waziristan.

The tribal areas have been a source of trouble in terms of assistance to al-Qaeda, the Taliban and Central Asian militants. The porous border between Pakistan and Afghanistan provides corridors to militants for free movement across the border. Although tribal maliks in FATA tried to support the government, it is very easy for Islamic militants to identify them as a result. Maliks are not appointed by the government, but they are essentially a product of the traditional tribal jirga system. Leadership qualities, sound financial position and good relations with the broader political administration are hallmarks of this distinct status. Such a person becomes a malik and presents the administrative and economic problems of tribes to the political administration. The government responds to the maliks' requests in return for their services such as maintaining peace, keeping the roads open and the collection of taxes. Known pro-government maliks have been killed at the hands of militants and now no one dares to openly cooperate with government agencies in North and South Waziristan. For instance, gunmen recently killed a pro-government tribal chief, Khair Badshah, in Makeen area in South Waziristan (*Geo News*, February 16, 2006).

Conclusion

After a March 1 operation by Pakistani security agencies, 1000 students of local seminaries paraded the streets of Miran Shah and chanted the slogans of jihad. According to locals, a large number of Taliban gathered in a mosque to devise a future strategy (*Dawn*, March 2, 2006). The situation indicates the increasing influence of the Taliban and the weakening writ of the government. Alluding to the gravity of the situation, Musharraf told the national Defense College: "Pakistan will continue to fight extremism and terrorism in a holistic manner as curbing these menaces is crucial to long term national security and economic development" (*The Nation*, March 3, 2006).

Rhetoric aside, there is little the Pakistani government can do to deny the militants safe refuge in FATA. While mid-ranking al-Qaeda and other Islamic militants will continue to fall into the traps of Pakistani security, it is less likely that the same fate awaits the senior ranks of al-Qaeda in the foreseeable future. Osama bin Laden and a resurgent Taliban movement recognize this all too well and are increasing their activities in this enigmatic region.

[From Terrorism Monitor, Volume IV, Issue 6]

Afghanistan and Pakistan Face Threat of Talibanization

Tarique Niazi

Originally published on May 18, 2006

The bilateral relationship between Afghanistan and Pakistan remains frozen and is governed by the two countries' geopolitical rivalries, which have unwittingly helped Taliban militancy in the region. As a result, both states are in danger of "Talibanization" (*Dawn*, April 27, 2006). The immediate challenges that face Afghanistan and Pakistan have to do with four factors: (a) cross-border infiltration; (b) a territorial dispute centering on the Durand Line; (c) India's growing influence with Kabul; and (d) Pakistan's Afghan policy, which is opposed by all factions in Afghanistan including Tajiks, Uzbeks, Hazaras, Pashtun nationalists and even the Taliban (*Dawn*, November 13, 2005).

Infiltration into Afghanistan

Frustrated by Islamabad's tepid response to his repeated calls for disabling the Taliban's operational bases in Pakistan, Afghan President Hamid Karzai turned to personal diplomacy. On February 15-17, he made a three-day visit to Islamabad to seek its cooperation in ending terrorist violence. He conveyed to Pakistani President Pervez Musharraf his deep concern over the recent spike in lethal violence in southern Afghanistan (*Dawn*, February 16, 2006). In 2005, Afghanistan watched 1,700 people die in insurgent violence. In the three months since December 2005, 70 people, predominantly members of the security forces, were killed in suicide bombings. In March, Taliban leader Mullah Omar vowed that "with the beginning of summer, Afghan soil will turn red for the crusaders and their puppets, and the occupiers will face an unpredictable wave of Afghan resistance" (*The News*, March 17, 2006).

President Karzai believes that the Taliban are based in Pakistan, where even their leader Mullah Omar and Osama bin Laden have found safe haven (*Dawn*, February 26, 2006). In his one-on-one meeting with Musharraf on February 15, Karzai shared with him "verifiable" intelligence about 150 key Taliban suspects who are based in Karachi, Peshawar and Quetta (*Dawn*, February 26). Pakistan's security agencies, however, found Afghan intelligence "unreliable."

Infiltration into the North-West Frontier Province (NWFP)

Like Afghanistan, Pakistan is battling a violent insurgency in its northwestern and southwestern provinces. The situation in Waziristan, northwestern Pakistan and the Federally Administered Tribal Areas, has spiraled out of Islamabad's control. On February 17, 2006, Tolo, an independent Afghan television news channel, aired grisly scenes of men in South Waziristan holding up three severed heads to a crowd chanting, "Long Live Osama bin Laden. Long Live Mullah Omar" (*Dawn*, April 18, 2006). It also showed a half dozen corpses chained to a vehicle and being dragged, while a uniformed Pakistan military officer drives past.

The Taliban have so far executed 150 pro-government tribal chiefs without punishment (*Daily Times*, April 18). Similarly, the losses in life of government troops have grown five times more than those of U.S. troops in Afghanistan (*Dawn*, April 21). Between January 2003 and April 2006, 600 Pakistani soldiers were killed, while 200 U.S. troops have died in Afghanistan since 2001 (*The Nation*, April 29, 2006).

Yet, critics say, the military operation in Waziristan has not yielded a single terrorist either dead or alive since 2003 (*Nawa-i-Waqt*, March 11, 2006). Most terrorists have rather been arrested in Karachi, Hyderabad, Lahore, Faisalabad and Gujrat. Islamabad, however, has claimed for the past three years that these operations have been a success. Pakistan's most pro-Afghan and pro-Karzai Pashtun leader, Asfandyar Wali Khan, blames the ISI (Pakistan's intelligence agency) for orchestrating military operations in Waziristan to deflect attention from its "guests" elsewhere. Mehmood Khan Achackzai, another prominent pro-Afghan and pro-Karzai Pashtun leader from Balochistan, calls the military operation in Waziristan a "genocide of Pashtuns," which he wants ceased immediately. Despite the military operation, Waziristan, which the Taliban has declared as its "Islamic Emirate," has steadily slid into anarchy. Stunned by their sweeping reach, Musharraf publicly announced on April 26 his plan to pull out troops from North and South Waziristan (*Dawn*, April 27, 2006). Despite this lackluster performance, the United States continues to offer Pakistan $840 million a year in military aid for its operations in Waziristan (*Dawn*, April 21, 2006).

Infiltration into Southwestern Pakistan: Balochistan

Similarly, Pakistan is battling an even fiercer insurgency in Balochistan, which it blames on Afghanistan. During his recent visit to Islamabad, Pakistan shared intelligence with President Karzai on "weapons smuggling into Balochistan" (*China Brief*, March 2, 2006). Pakistan also raised the matter at the Tripartite Commission's meeting in Kabul on February 25, 2006.

In addition, Pakistani intelligence officials claim to have proof of India's involvement in Balochistan, which is accused of funding and arming the Balochistan Liberation Army (BLA) and the Balochistan Liberation Front (BLF) (*Khabrain*, February 25, 2006). In April, Pakistan banned the BLA as a "terrorist" organization. The United States has not yet agreed to Pakistan's assessment of the BLA. Most recently, Pakistan claimed to have seized weapons worth 500 million rupees (around $8.3 million), which were shipped from Kabul for subversive activities in Balochistan (*The Nation*, February 12, 2006).

Pakistan wants Afghanistan to have India close its consulates in Jalalabad and Kandahar, each of which borders the NWFP (also known as Pakhtunkhaw) and Balochistan. President Karzai, however, disagrees that his country's scaled-back relations with New Delhi will make Pakistan safe. Responding to charges that Afghanistan is behind the Baloch insurgency, he said: "We will never support an insurgency in Balochistan or allow the use of our soil for terrorist activities" (*Dawn*, February 18, 2006). Pakistan is not convinced, however. As a precaution and at great financial cost, it has already deployed 90,000 troops along the Durand Line since the fall of the Taliban (*Nawa-i-Waqt*, September 13, 2005). In addition, 70,000 members of Pakistan's Frontier Corps are deployed in the border areas.

Fencing the Durand Line

To bolster cross-border security, Pakistan has proposed that a fence be built across the 2,300-kilometer Durand Line. Karzai off-handedly rejected the proposal, saying that "barbed wire is a symbol of hatred, not friendship and hence it cannot stop terrorism" (*Dawn*, February 18, 2006). Earlier, speaking at the National Defense College on February 16, he said: "fencing is separation" of the "inseparable" people living on each side of Durand Line (*The Nation*, February 17, 2006). Pakistan has long been toying with the idea of fencing. In September 2005, Musharraf shared the idea with President Bush, who publicly endorsed it. Karzai's rejection of fencing further confounds the issue of the undefined border between the two countries.

Since it was drawn in 1893, the Durand Line has been a tentative marker between Afghanistan and British Raj, which divided Baloch and Pashtun tribal areas on both sides. Afghanistan gave the British Raj its southern territories in Balochistan and the NWFP on a 100-year lease, which expired in 1993. Pakistan has since been pressing Kabul to accept the Durand Line as an international border. Kabul, however, is unwilling to cede its historical claim to the territories it calls "South Pashtunistan" (*Dawn*, November 13, 2005). Even the Pakistan-backed Taliban government (1996-2001) refused to accept the Durand Line as an "international border." It was this unsolved border dispute that led Afghanistan to oppose Pakistan's entry into the United Nations in 1948, which sowed the first seed of a long-festering disagreement that continues to haunt both countries to this day.

The India Factor

To Pakistan's dismay, however, Afghanistan, with the help of India, crossed the Durand Line into South Asia as the eighth member of the South Asian Association for Regional Cooperation (SAARC). Pakistan fears that Afghanistan will use SAARC to raise "the bogey of South Pashtunistan" (*Dawn*, November 13, 2005). More importantly, Pakistan is concerned about India's increasing influence with Kabul, especially its ruling Northern Alliance. A recent Indian move to deploy 300 members of its special operations forces at its consulate in Kandahar has further unnerved Islamabad (WebIndia123.com). Musharraf, during his meeting with Karzai on February 15, 2006, reportedly broached this matter with serious concern.

With or without Afghanistan's help, India is, nevertheless, well on its way to flanking Pakistan's western border and penetrating Central Asia with its economic allure and military muscle. It has already completed the construction of its first-ever foreign military base in Tajikistan to the west of Pakistan (*Nawa-i-Waqt*, March 6, 2006). It is also building a port at Chahbahar in Iran, Pakistan's southwestern neighbor, that will be connected through a road link to Afghanistan and then to Central Asia. Pakistan, which has problematic relations with all three states—Afghanistan, Iran and Tajikistan—views their triangular axis as an Indian attempt to encircle it at its western border.

Pakistan's Afghan Policy

Pakistan's Afghan policy is not helping matters either. It continues to be based on the ethnic subordination of Afghanistan (*Nawa-i-Waqt*, April 17, 2006). Although Pakistan likes to see Pashtuns get their due share in Afghanistan's governance, it rejects their "ethnic nationalism," compared to the Taliban's "Islamic nationalism" (*The International Journal of Contemporary Sociology*, vol. 42(2), pp. 267-293). Pakistan is apprehensive that Pashtun ethnic nationalism will infect Pakistani Pashtuns, whom Islamabad continues to keep de-politicized and thus theologized (*The International Journal of Contemporary Sociology*, vol. 42(2), pp. 267-293). It bars Pashtun nationalist parties, such as the NWFP-based Awami National Party (ANP) led by Asfandyar Wali Khan, and the Balochistan-based Pashtunkhawa Milli Awami Party (PMAP) led by Mehmood Khan Achakzai, from entering tribal areas of Balochistan and the NWFP, while the Taliban and their militant allies are free to establish an "Islamic Emirate" there.

Conclusions

Not until the "Talibanization" of Afghanistan and Pakistan has been addressed can geopolitical and geoeconomic considerations take center stage. It is, therefore, imperative for Afghanistan and Pakistan to concentrate on stemming cross-border infiltration, which will require the redeployment of Pakistani troops from the tribal areas of the NWFP and Balochistan to jointly patrol the Durand Line. Pakistan should replace its military operations in the NWFP and Balochistan with a political process, allowing Pakistan's mainstream political parties as well as Pashtun nationalists to defuse the ticking bomb of religious fanaticism there. More importantly, Pakistan's Afghan policy needs a makeover from the current ethnic subordination of Afghanistan and the demeaning of Pashtun nationalism to the affirmation of Afghan nationalism and Pashtun ethnic pride in order to counter the Taliban's "religious nationalism."

[From Terrorism Monitor, Volume IV, Issue 10]

The Talibanization of the North-West Frontier

Sohail Abdul Nasir

Originally published on June 15, 2006

In a bid to cope with the worsening security situation in North and South Waziristan agencies and to contain the expanding wave of Talibanization from the tribal areas to the settled areas, Pakistani President Pervez Musharraf has appointed a new governor to the North-West Frontier Province (NWFP). Lieutenant General (Retired) Ali Mohammad Jan Orakzai was sworn in as the new governor on May 24, 2006. In the past two years of the insurgency in the tribal areas, he is the third governor to take the helm. Prior to Orakzai, Lieutenant General (Retired) Iftakhar Hessian Shah and more recently Commander Khalil-ur-Rehman held the post. The quick succession of governors shows the importance that the federal government has placed on controlling the situation in the tribal areas, particularly in North and South Waziristan.

Prior to the start of the military operations in the tribal areas, the NWFP governor ran the administration of the Federally Administered Tribal Areas (FATA) through a carefully woven network of political agents, assistant political agents and subordinate staff (each tribal agency is headed by a political agent). During the last two years of military operations, however, the corps commander of Peshawar has assumed a more important role by managing the security situation on the western border up to Balochistan (the army consists of twelve corps).

New Governor Faces Daunting Task

Ali Mohammad Jan Orakzai is facing a daunting task and great expectations are being attached with his appointment to the position because Orakzai is a tribal man, hails from FATA's Orakzai Agency and understands tribal psyche and norms. Additionally, he was the corps commander of Peshawar from October 2001 to 2004 before retiring that year. Orakzai was born in 1947 and was commissioned in the army in 1968. He is a graduate of the command and staff college in Quetta and has also attended military courses in the United States. Before becoming the governor, he served as the secretary of defense of the production division, putting him in charge of the departments that manufacture weapons (*The Nation*, May 23, 2006).

Some analysts are skeptical about the success of the new governor, arguing that while he was the corps commander of Peshawar in 2002, Orakzai was the first person to deploy government troops to the tribal areas (BBC, May 24, 2006). During this time, he never admitted to the presence of al-Qaeda or the local Taliban in the area. Since Orakzai is considered a hardliner, as compared to former governor Khalil-ur-Rehman, the new appointment gives the impression that the federal government, instead of pursuing dialogue with the militants, is sticking with the military option.

The restoration of peace in North and South Waziristan will be a great challenge for Orakzai. The dilemma is not only that the local Taliban in North Waziristan are not ready to speak with the government, but they also disallow anyone else in the region from speaking with the authorities. In these troubled areas, political agents are seen only in their official functions and troops are limited merely to forts and bunkers. In this context, it is uncertain whether the civil administration—responsible for development work, law-and-order and political and administrative tasks—can be activated again in FATA.

Attempts to Revitalize the Political Administration in FATA

Prior to the appointment of the new governor, the federal government was examining ways to revitalize the political administration in FATA. On May 23, *The Nation* published a detailed report, which said that the federal government was considering the replacement of political agents presently posted in the troubled agencies with more competent ones to improve the administration of FATA. Sahibzada Imtiaz, a retired bureaucrat, has been assigned by Musharraf to make proposals in this regard and to suggest the names of competent officers who can carry out the assignment; Sahibzada has already prepared a reform package to improve the situation in the FATA area.

The president has also endorsed another proposal by Imtiaz to bring the Frontier Constabulary—primarily a border security and paramilitary force, but also one that maintains law and order elsewhere in the country—back under the administrative control of the political agents. Until 1996, the Frontier Constabulary was working under political agents; after 1996, however, the inspector general of the Frontier Constabulary had been given the administration of the paramilitary forces guarding the 1600-kilometer border with Afghanistan and Iran. The government also has decided to strengthen the "levies" (tribal militia forces) in FATA to minimize the deployment of the armed forces in the area. Presently, the levies are only active in Kurrum Agency, Khyber Agency and Orakzai Agency; the government is considering the establishment of levies in North and South Waziristan in order to reduce the deployment of regular army forces.

An additional change involves the manner in which political agents are selected. Political agents are normally selected from the District Management Group, a group of civil service members who run different district-level governments; it was previously considered an elite group due to its extensive powers, but has been weakened recently as a result of the decentralization program undertaken by Musharraf. Under the new arrangement, competent officers from other federal services could potentially be appointed as political agents.

The political administration in the tribal areas certainly needs positive changes if the government sincerely wants to normalize the situation. For a long time, the tribal masses have protested against the way the political administration has treated them. Mistreatment by the political administration and political and economic backwardness drives tribesmen to the local Taliban. A former officer of the Pakistani Army and elder of the Mehsood tribe, retired Brigadier Malik Qayyum Sher, said that the local Taliban have their own agenda and are faithfully acting upon it, and that announcements of development programs by Musharraf will not have any effect on their actions. While speaking to the BBC, he revealed that the Pakistani Army itself maintains contacts with the local Taliban and that local people have sympathies for them. He admitted that he himself was in contact with the local Taliban and did not find any harm in maintaining this contact. He believed that military operations were not the solution and that the government would have to reach a settlement with the local Taliban (*Islam*, April 27, 2006).

Local Taliban Continue to Establish Control

The local Taliban in North Waziristan does not seem to be in a mood to reconcile with the government. Rather, they are busy undertaking actions that include the investigation of the 18 tribal chiefs who met Musharraf and violated the ban prohibiting contacts with the government (*Daily Times*, May 23, 2006). For the past two months, these meetings between tribal chiefs and government officials have been occurring in Rawalpindi and in Peshawar. Musharraf is now frequently consulting every relevant quarter about the situation in the Waziristan agencies. Abdullah Farhad, a spokesman for the local Taliban, told reporters that a shura council would decide the fate of two tribal chiefs, Mir Sharof Ederkhel and Nawab Khan Borakhel, who had met the president. "Sharof and Khan have admitted meeting the president was a mistake and pleaded for mercy," said Farhad. Sharof confirmed contacting the government, saying he had attended the meeting to plead for the military's withdrawal from the tribal regions.

The local Taliban is concerned with not only the enforcement of Sharia law, but also the waging of jihad against intruders (i.e., U.S.-led coalition forces) in Afghanistan. Haji Omar, one of the leaders of the local Taliban in South Waziristan Agency, told the BBC that jihad against foreign troops will continue until U.S. and other foreign soldiers completely withdrawal from Afghanistan. He threatened to increase the attacks on U.S. troops in Afghanistan and said that there would be no negotiation with intruders. He explained that the Taliban have no enmity with the Pakistani Army, but if the military carried out operations against them, they would have to defend themselves. He accused the Karzai government of sending spies into Pakistan's tribal areas to detect the presence of al-Qaeda elements. Haji Omar said that a number of such spies have been captured and killed (*Mashraq*, April 22, 2006).

Some members of the media are doubtful that the government will once again apply the obsolete method of using the political agent system to control the worsening situation in Waziristan where military operations have already aggravated the conflict and hollowed the foundations of the political administration system. After controlling North and South Waziristan, the Talibanization movement is stretching to the southern parts of NWFP, which include Dera Ismail Khan, Bannu and Tank. The Taliban have destroyed the authority and traditional tribal system by killing tribal elders (*Khabrain*, May 12, 2006).

Conclusion

Musharraf stated that military operations in the tribal areas will continue until foreign terrorists are completely eliminated. While addressing a special meeting to review the situation in FATA, he proposed that if tribes were to expel or hand over terrorists to the government, the operations in the region would be stopped. He said that he would expedite the developmental work in the tribal areas and finalize the schemes of industrialization with the cooperation of the United States. Musharraf said that these industries would provide immense employment opportunities for local youth (*Nawa-i-Waqt*, May 10, 2006). Musharraf seems sincere in implementing his designs, although the success of the entire process needs to involve all sections of tribal society (*Nawa-i-Waqt*, May 13, 2006).

Indeed, after being sworn into office, the new governor unexpectedly spoke about the peaceful resolution of the conflict in North Waziristan. Orakzai said that he would prefer using peaceful means instead of force to restore law and order in the tribal regions. In his first remarks after taking the oath of office, he said, "Eventually all problems are resolved through talks." The governor said it would be his endeavor to tackle issues through peaceful means: "I am confident that we will succeed in resolving all issues through mutual consultations and talks." He said that law and order was the most important issue before him and he would strive to restore normalcy in the tribal region. Orakzai said that as a native of the tribal region and as the corps commander of Peshawar for two and a half years, he had observed that tribesmen were peace-loving people. "But some of them who are misguided would be put on the right path," he remarked (*Dawn*, May 25, 2006).

It is believed that the tribesmen can be dealt with only by those who have a true perception about tribal norms and values. The British, when they ruled the region, successfully followed this principle and consequently introduced the system of local political administration, which mainly banks upon the tribal jirga system comprised of elders. Governor Orakzai himself hails from a pure tribal family and is also a retired general. He is the most qualified person available at the moment to tackle the worsening situation in the tribal areas by applying military tactics and extending the political process.

[From Terrorism Monitor, Volume IV, Issue 12]

Baitullah Mehsud: South Waziristan's Unofficial Amir

Sohail Abdul Nasir

Originally published on July 5, 2006

Militancy in Pakistan's tribal areas gave birth to a new generation of leadership. Most of the traditional tribal elders who constitute the jirga system have been killed at the hands of the local Taliban; those who survived this assassination strategy fled to safer locations in other areas in the North-West Frontier Province. In the last two years, this new generation of leaders has established control over certain local Taliban groups. Yet, there are some leaders that have established control all throughout the tribal agencies. Baitullah Mehsud is one of the most prominent leaders among the local Taliban, virtually governing all of South Waziristan Agency (*Daily Times*, March 31, 2006).

Mehsud came into prominence when tribal leader Nek Mohammad was killed by security forces during a missile attack. Thirty-two years-old, Baitullah Mehsud was born in Landidog, a small tribal village situated on the fringes of South Waziristan. He has four brothers—Mohammad Yaqoob, Mohammad Ishaq, Yayha Khan and Zahir Shah—and is the son of the late Mohamad Haroon. Unlike local Taliban leaders in North Waziristan—who are recognized religious scholars who run their own seminaries—Mehsud and other local Taliban leaders in South Waziristan are not as well educated. Baitullah Mehsud did not finish regular schooling or religious schooling. He belongs to Broomikhel, an offshoot of sub-tribe Shabikhel, which is a part of the larger Mehsud tribe. Baitullah is married and is very tough physically and mentally. Although he is not well educated, he is famous for his political acumen and military skills. His colleagues describe him as a natural leader who has great ability to infuse vitality among his followers.

Twelve years ago, as a young madrassa student, he was greatly inspired by Taliban ideology and frequently went to Afghanistan as a volunteer to join in the Taliban's enforcement of Sharia and to offer his services. As a traditional tribal man, he is an expert at using small arms. When speaking to this author in June, a person from Mehsud's native village said that he has not, however, been credited with victory in any significant gun battle or skirmish, unlike Taliban leaders in Afghanistan.

There are a number of analogies between Mullah Omar, chief of the Taliban in Afghanistan, and Baitullah Mehsud. Both leaders shun the media and as a result they have not been photographed. This makes it difficult for security forces and the outside world to recognize them. Omar and Mehsud vow jihad, and they are constantly on the move from one hideout to the next in order to avoid arrest. Baitullah has pledged himself to Mullah Omar, even though he signed a deal with the Pakistani army in February 2005. Baitullah was appointed as Mullah Omar's governor of the Mehsud tribe in a special ceremony attended by five leading Taliban commanders (Rediff.com, March 10, 2006). One of them was Mullah Dadullah (*Terrorism Focus*, March 21, 2006). It is said that Pakistani security forces do not take military action against Baitullah because he has assured them that he will not attack the security forces (Rediff.com, March 10, 2006). The local Taliban are considered to be his own private army—although the exact numbers are not known, it is believed that his armed followers number in the thousands. These men are instrumental in establishing his writ in South Waziristan. Tribal society is already conservative and religious, so Baitullah does not need to do much in order to enforce Sharia.

On February 7, 2005, he signed a deal with the federal government that the government calls his surrender. His associates deny these claims and say that it was a peace agreement. Baitullah Mehsud and scores of his supporters laid down arms in a tribal jirga meeting. He was wanted by the government for allegedly sheltering and assisting al-Qaeda fugitives in areas dominated by the Mehsud tribe (*The Nation*, February 8, 2005).

As part of the peace agreement, Baitullah pledged that he and his associates would not provide assistance to al-Qaeda and other militants and would not launch operations against government forces. Baitullah explained that the peace agreement was in the interests of the tribal regions in addition to the government since many enemies—including Indian- and Russian-backed former Northern Alliance fighters—were benefiting from the lack of unity between the government and the tribesmen (*The Nation*, February 8, 2005).

As a result of the peace agreement, South Waziristan is relatively calm, especially when compared to North Waziristan. Baitullah Mehsud himself is not in the limelight because he consistently avoids connections with the media and displays his powerful presence through other means. His men roam South Waziristan in pickup trucks. They monitor many matters, including day-to-day problems among the people, grievances with the political administration and maintaining law and order.

[From Terrorism Focus, Volume III, Issue 26]

South Waziristan's Veteran Jihadi Leader: A Profile of Haji Omar

Sohail Abdul Nasir

Originally published on August 8, 2006

The recent insurgency in some portions of Pakistan's tribal belt has produced a chain of new leaders who govern their respective areas. A common trait of these new leaders is that they receive inspiration from the Afghan Taliban and openly call themselves the "local Taliban." The local Taliban has been associated with the Afghan Taliban and have also vowed to expel foreign troops from Afghanistan through waging jihad. Some of the new local Taliban leaders, such as Faqir Mohammad, are still actively carrying out their activities, but most of them, such as local Taliban leader Haji Omar, are keeping a low profile as a result of government reconciliation efforts (*Terrorism Monitor*, February 9, 2006).

Haji Omar is a veteran jihadi fighter who fought against the Red Army on the Kabul and Bagram fronts during the Soviet occupation of Afghanistan. He sustained serious injuries on numerous occasions, but despite these injuries he continued to fight against the Soviets until they withdrew from Afghanistan. His jihadi career is spread over three periods: against Soviet forces, on behalf of the Afghan Taliban against U.S. troops before the fall of Kabul and his current jihadi activities in the tribal areas of Pakistan. Omar is tall, well-built, with a long, thick, black beard. He wears a turban in traditional tribal style. He is approximately 55 years old, and was born in the village of Kalushah, which is situated some 10 kilometers from Wana, the headquarters of South Waziristan Agency (BBC, April 20, 2006).

After the withdrawal of Soviet troops from Afghanistan, he moved back to his hometown because war among the different jihadi groups disheartened him. At the end of the 1980s, he moved to the Gulf city of Dubai. When the Taliban established control over most of Afghanistan, he returned and became one of the close associates of Taliban chief Mullah Omar and assisted him in day-to-day routine governing matters. He remained there until the fall of the Taliban in 2001. In Waziristan, he began to organize the local Taliban groups. He has excellent communication skills; while Pashto is his native tongue, he is proficient in Arabic due to frequent socialization with Arabs in Afghanistan and also speaks broken Urdu (BBC, April 20, 2006).

Haji Omar's two brothers, Haji Sharif and Noor Islam, have been on the government's most wanted list (*The News*, February 11, 2005). As a result of the Shakai Agreement on April 24, they were given amnesty along with the late Nek Mohammad, but later this amnesty was revoked. Omar was appointed acting leader of the local Taliban group in South Waziristan when Nek Mohammad was killed in a missile attack (*The News*, June 21, 2004). Haji Omar belongs to the Yargulkhel sub-tribe of the Wazir tribe. This background helped him become the acting chief of the local Taliban in South Waziristan since Nek Mohammad was also a Wazir.

Omar is a staunch opponent of the United States, India and other countries that, according to him, occupy Muslim lands. He appears to have a soft spot for the Pakistani army, and in an interview said that his forces will continue to wage jihad against foreign troops in Afghanistan, but would prefer not to fight the Pakistani army (*The News*, June 21, 2004). Government agencies accuse him of harboring al-Qaeda fighters, yet, while speaking to the BBC, he called this allegation baseless. Omar explained that his forces do not shelter al-Qaeda fighters, but if an individual comes to them to seek asylum, then they allow him to live with them under their conditions.

Haji Omar has said that jihad is the only way to expel U.S. troops from Afghanistan. According to Omar, Afghan spies come to Pakistan to collect information for the Afghan government and the United States. Omar claimed that his forces have captured a number of such spies, and they have been "slaughtered" (BBC, April 21, 2006). Haji Omar was among Pakistan's most wanted militants who were paid approximately 32 million rupees ($530,000) in order to pay off their debts to al-Qaeda, so that they would end hostilities with the government. This deal was the result of an agreement between the late Nek Mohammad and the government. Out of that money, Haji Omar received one million rupees ($16,500) (*Press Trust of India*, June 12, 2005).

Nevertheless, despite Haji Omar's influence, he has been overshadowed by Baitullah Mehsud, another prominent leader in South Waziristan (*Terrorism Focus*, July 5, 2006). This development occurred because of the ethnic fault line that affects South Waziristan. The two main tribes that populate the agency are the Wazir and the Mehsud.

While the late Nek Mohammed and Haji Omar are Wazir, Baitullah is Mehsud. After the death of Nek Mohammed, the Wazirs were unable to maintain leadership and Baitullah took control of the Talibanization movement there. Currently, militants like Abdullah Mehsud are working under Baitullah's command. Therefore, under the present circumstances, Haji Omar has to work under the guidance of Baitullah. According to his close associates, in order to avoid this subordinate role, Omar has maintained a low profile and for the time being is not playing an active role in the insurgency.

[From Terrorism Focus, Volume III, Issue 31]

Balochistan in the Shadow of al-Qaeda

Tarique Niazi

Originally published on February 23, 2006

The sudden surge in violence in southern Afghanistan, which Kabul blames on Pakistan-based al-Qaeda and Taliban fighters, has thrust Balochistan into the international spotlight (*Dawn*, January 21, 2006). Afghanistan's southeastern province of Kandahar and southwestern province of Helmand, which border Balochistan, have recently convulsed with violence. On January 16, Kandahar's border town of Spin Boldak, which adjoins northwestern Balochistan, suffered a deadly suicide attack in which 26 people were killed. Since November 2005, there have been 13 suicide attacks in Afghanistan. Similarly, Helmand, which borders southwestern Balochistan, has witnessed the Taliban's lethal engagements with Afghan and coalition forces; on February 3, for instance, 25 people were killed in a skirmish (BBC, February 4, 2006).

Afghan leaders blamed the violence on the growing presence of al-Qaeda and Taliban fighters in Balochistan, who are reportedly using the area as their logistical base, while keeping their military base in Pakistan's Federally Administered Tribal Areas (FATA), especially its North and South Waziristan agencies. It is worth noting that FATA, including North and South Waziristan, is a geographical extension of northwestern Balochistan. Successive governments in Kabul have described this area as "South Pashtunistan," to which they have laid territorial claims. Whenever al-Qaeda and Taliban fighters have come under military pressure in North and South Waziristan, they have retreated into Balochistan where they then instantly drop off the radar. Balochistan's vast deserts, high-rolling mountains and sparsely populated plains provides many places to hide.

In late 2005, however, al-Qaeda and the Taliban transformed Balochistan from a logistics center to an operational base. Two factors explain this shift. The first factor is that al-Qaeda and the Taliban have brought FATA and North and South Waziristan under their virtual writ. They have successfully immobilized 70,000 Pakistani troops in the area, forcing them into their fortified barracks and checkpoints. In February 2005, the Pakistani military indirectly paid them 32 million rupees (about half a million dollars) in extortion money (*South Asia Tribune*, February

10, 2006). Having tamed the government, they brought in line the local population by executing more than 100 government loyalists in North and South Waziristan alone (*Dawn*, January 19, 2006). None of these executions have been punished by Islamabad. These militants are now regulating moral life, administering justice, and enforcing their version of Sharia in the region. Their control is so complete that one of their clerical allies has set up an FM radio station in the neighboring town of Bara near Peshawar to air his religious broadcasts against non-Salafi Muslims (*Dawn*, January 18, 2006). The government has yet to take the station off the air and dismantle the illegal radio transmissions. These intrepid measures suggest that al-Qaeda and the Taliban feel far safer in FATA and no longer need Balochistan as a safe haven.

The second factor is that the impending redeployment of U.S. troops in Kandahar has further emboldened the insurgents to open another front in Balochistan. They think that NATO forces, which will replace U.S. troops, cannot match their determined assaults. Al-Qaeda and the Taliban think that they can bring Kandahar and Helmand under heavy military pressure by mounting attacks from northwestern and southwestern Balochistan.

Alarmed by the gathering strength of the Taliban and other Pashtun insurgents, Afghan leaders believe that the Afghan provinces along the Durand Line with Pakistan—such as Kandahar, Helmand, Kunar and Paktika—are increasingly vulnerable to insurgent attacks. The Afghan Minister for Foreign Affairs publicly accused Islamabad of allowing al-Qaeda and the Taliban to regroup in Balochistan (*Khabrain*, January 21, 2006). It is pertinent to note that Pashtuns live in the northwest of Balochistan and Balochs in the southwest. Pashtuns in northwestern Balochistan are ethnically linked to those in Kandahar. Spin Boldak, Kandahar's border town, adjoins northwest Balochistan's border city of Chaman, whose residents routinely cross over into Spin Boldak and stay there at will. Many top leaders of Lashkar-i-Jhangvi, a Sunni supremacist terrorist group (and the armed wing of the formerly Sipah-e-Sahaba organization) that has killed hundreds of Shiites in Balochistan and elsewhere in Pakistan, took up residence in Chaman after the fall of the Taliban.

On the other hand, the Afghan province of Helmand has a substantial Baloch population. Although there is no evidence that Afghan Balochs are helping al-Qaeda or the Taliban, Baloch residents of Helmand have long supported the nationalist Baloch armed struggle against Islamabad. Al-Qaeda and the Taliban, however, draw on the religious affiliation of Balochs, who happen to be predominantly Sunni. What fires up this mutuality, however, is the alleged persecution of Sunni Balochs by the Iranian government. Iranian Balochs are spread across southern Khorasan and Sistan-Balochistan provinces in southeastern Iran and have long nursed grievances against Iran's Shiite majority. Such grievances find ready resonance with their nationalist co-ethnics in Afghanistan's provinces of Helmand, Farah, Nimroz and Herat, as well as in Pakistani Balochistan. To avenge the "persecution" of Iranian Sunni Balochs, al-Qaeda and its allied group Jandallah are reported to have established a presence in southeastern Iran. Recently, Jandallah's fighters kidnapped nine Iranian soldiers from Saravan along the Iran-Pakistan border. Iranians asked Islamabad to intervene, but nothing happened. On January 29, 2006, Jandallah, on its own terms, released the soldiers after two months of captivity (*Dawn*, January 29, 2006). Lawlessness in southeastern Iran, on the border of southwestern Balochistan, is so widespread that on December 15, 2005, the motorcade of Iranian President Mahmoud Ahmadinejad came under heavy fire on Zabul-Saravan Highway, and one of his bodyguards was killed (*Jomhouri Islami*, December 17, 2005).

Although southwestern (Pakistani) Balochistan is predominantly Baloch, it also represents a demographic twist. In the 1970s-1980s, the Pakistani government settled hundreds of thousands of Afghan refugees of Pashtun descent as a buffer between Iranian and Pakistani Balochs. The major brunt of this resettlement was borne by the all-Baloch border town of Chaghi, which made its name as Pakistan's nuclear-test site in May 1998, turning its native Baloch population into a minority. Afghan Pashtuns in this restive border area provide much-needed cover to the fleeing operatives of al-Qaeda and the Taliban, as well as to the gangs of gunrunners and drug traffickers, who saturate the place.

In addition, Pakistani Balochistan has been gripped by an active Baloch insurgency before and after the fall of the Taliban, which Pakistan blames on Afghanistan and India. This insurgency is so fierce that on December 14, 2005, Baloch rebels fired scores of rockets at Musharraf while he was present in the heavily guarded Quetta Garrison. Earlier reports indicated that rockets were fired at Musharraf when he was addressing a public meeting in the troubled district of Kohlu in southwestern Balochistan. Although Pakistani intelligence agencies set off rumors of al-Qaeda's presence in Kohlu, there is no evidence that Baloch nationalists have any link with al-Qaeda. The Baloch insurgency and Pakistan's restive western borders with Afghanistan are, however, absorbing almost one-third of Pakistan's military resources, which relieve some pressure from al-Qaeda and the Taliban.

More importantly, al-Qaeda and the Taliban are benefiting from the rising tide of crime in Pakistan, especially in its most populous province of Punjab, where, according to Dr. Mubashar Hassan, Pakistan's former finance minister, 52,000 outlaws are on the run. Many of them have joined jihadi organizations to escape detection. Tens of thousands of them have since moved into Balochistan, where they have set up "ferari (fugitives) camps." Many of them have secured the protection of Balochistan's cabinet ministers, who are largely drawn from the pro-Taliban Jamiat-I-Ulema-I-Islam (JUI). Pakistani intelligence agencies overlook JUI leaders' patronage of feraris to curb Baloch nationalists. Recently, a senior ranking JUI minister unleashed his operatives into the private residence of a prominent Baloch nationalist leader, Attaullah Mengal, in Wadh. Intelligence agencies, as such, are combating "ethnic nationalism" with pro-Pakistan "Islamic nationalism."

While Afghan leaders charge that al-Qaeda and the Taliban are present in Balochistan, the governor of Balochistan, Owais Ghani, emphatically rejects this assertion. "We have swept Balochistan clean of even the shadow of Taliban and al-Qaeda," says Ghani. Instead, he has slapped Kabul with a charge sheet of his own: "We have seen 500 million rupees worth (approximately $8.2 million) of Afghan weapons being smuggled into Balochistan every year" (*Khabrain*, February 4, 2006). Musharraf further berates Kabul and coalition forces for their lax control of the Afghan border that he regards as enabling terrorists to sneak into Pakistani territory.

Contrary to Pakistan's denials, diplomatic sources claim that al-Qaeda's leaders have found refuge in Balochistan. A Western diplomat claims that the Pakistani government squandered a CIA lead that bin Laden was hiding in Balochistan because Islamabad "delayed giving permission for the attack on its soil" (*Dawn*, January 30, 2006). The source said that by the time U.S. officials received the go-ahead, bin Laden had left the suspected hideout in Zhob in Balochistan, where he and "his bodyguards had sought temporary shelter." The source speculated that "elements within Pakistan's ISI [Inter-Services Intelligence] may have sought to protect bin Laden."

Similarly, Afghan President Hamid Karzai recently alleged that Mullah Omar is hiding in Balochistan. Asfandyar Wali Khan, Pakistan's most prominent pro-Karzai Pashtun leader, publicly castigated Pakistani intelligence agencies for holding Afghanistan hostage to their misguided Afghan policy. Wali goes so far as to claim that intelligence agencies are treating al-Qaeda and Taliban leaders as their "guests" (*Dawn*, January 18, 2006).

[From Terrorism Monitor, Volume IV, Issue 4]

The Baloch Insurgency and its Threat to Pakistan's Energy Sector

John C. K. Daly

Originally published on March 21, 2006

While most of the world's media remains focused on insurgent attacks on oil facilities in Iraq and Saudi Arabia, Pakistan is experiencing a rising tide of violence against its Sui natural gas installations located in the country's volatile Balochistan province, where the majority of the energy-starved country's natural gas facilities are located. Pakistan, currently engaged in a drawn-out conflict against al-Qaeda and Taliban remnants in its North-West Frontier Province (NWFP), is slowly descending into conflict with anti-government forces in Balochistan province, raising the unsettling prospect of a rising second internal front against militants. A second internal front would drain resources from Pakistan's ability to maintain control over the country and its campaign against al-Qaeda and Taliban remnants in the NWFP and the Federally Administrated Tribal Areas (FATA).

Balochistan contains 42 percent of Pakistan's total land mass and is the largest of the country's four provinces. The province is strategically vital as it borders Iran, Pakistan, FATA and the Arabian Sea. The capital Quetta lies near the border with Afghanistan and has road connections to Kandahar to the northwest.

Islamabad also sees the province as essential to its future prosperity, building a $1.1 billion deepwater commercial and naval port at Gwadar on the Arabian Sea. China contributed about $200 million toward the construction cost of Gwadar's first phase, which was completed in April 2004. Chinese interest extends far beyond Gwadar; during a recent interview, Pakistani Minister of State for Investment Umar Ahmad Ghumman said that the two countries had discussed $12 billion in investment projects of interest to China including a 60,000 barrels per day oil refinery at Gwadar (Aaj TV interview, March 6, 2006).

India is also interested in Balochistan province as a transit point for a projected $4.5 billion Iran-India natural gas pipeline expected to be operational by 2010. India also discussed with Pakistan plans by both countries to import gas from Turkmenistan via Afghanistan and from Qatar (balochistan.org, March 4, 2006).

Balochistan's natural gas production is critical to Pakistan's economy. The Sui natural gas field in Balochistan's Bugti tribal area produces approximately 45 percent of the country's total gas production, with Pakistan Petroleum Ltd. producing 720-750 million cubic feet of gas daily from more than 80 wells in the field (*Business Recorder*, July 30, 2004). Other natural gas fields in the province include Uch, Pirkoh, Loti, Gundran and Zarghoon near Quetta. A provincial spokesman said that Balochistan has 19 trillion cubic feet of natural gas reserves and six trillion barrels of oil reserves on- and off-shore (*Business Recorder*, May 14, 2004).

Despite the province's wealth of natural resources, Balochistan is Pakistan's poorest province, with 45 percent of the population living below the poverty line. There is rising resentment in the province that despite the fact that its natural gas generates $1.4 billion annually in revenue, the government remits only $116 million in royalties back to the province (*Dawn*, February 6, 2006).

After the U.S. campaign against the Taliban began in November 2001, Balochistan became a critical escape route for al-Qaeda and International Islamic Front refugees attempting to flee via Karachi to Yemen. After U.S. operations against Iraq began in March 2003, Balochistan became an increasingly important theater of operations for al-Qaeda and International Islamic Front guerrillas in their efforts to attack U.S. economic interests in Pakistan in retaliation for the U.S. campaigns in both Afghanistan and Iraq (South Asia Analysis Group, January 24, 2003).

Attacks on Pipelines

In 2003, resentment among Baloch chiefs boiled over into intermittent armed conflict with the Pakistani Army. By July 2004 the rising violence in Balochistan forced a U.S. company involved in offshore drilling to abandon its two test wells between Gwadar and Pasni because of security concerns for a loss of nearly 26 million dollars (*Business Recorder*, July 30, 2004).

On January 18, 2005, a major attack disrupted Sui's output. In the aftermath of the attack, the government rushed hundreds of troops to the area. At least eight people died in the violence, which caused a production loss of more than 43,000 tons of urea and caused a daily electricity shortfall of about 470 megawatts (BBC, January 18, 2005).

Balochistan's turbulent year of 2005 ended with an attack on the head of state. On December 14, Balochistan Liberation Army militants launched six rockets, three of them landing near a paramilitary camp in Kohlu that Pakistani President Pervez Musharraf was visiting 135 miles east of Quetta. Islamabad described the attack as an assassination attempt and three days later launched a full-fledged army operation in Kohlu district's Marri-Bugti areas against local "miscreants" and "saboteurs."

Since the beginning of the year, militants have launched at least a dozen attacks on oil pipelines in the region. The militant tribal Balochistan Liberation Army has claimed responsibility for the attacks. Some analysts believe that Taliban and al-Qaeda guerrillas have also been using Balochistan to move back and forth between Pakistan and southern Afghanistan (Voice of America, March 2, 2006). The year opened with heavy fighting on January 1, 2006 between security forces and tribesmen on the Dera Bugti-Sui Road, while four people were killed and three others injured when a bomb exploded in a house in the Kharan district. Jamhoori Watan Party's secretary-general Agha Shahid Hasan Bugti accused the security forces of opening fire on tribesmen without any provocation (*Dawn*, January 1, 2006). Policeman Sher Ahmed was injured when he attempted to deactivate a rocket that was found in Killi Shiekhan as six bombs blew up between Sibi and Harnai, one near a natural gas pipeline in Kalat. Fighting continued into the next day.

District Coordination Officer Dera Bugti Abdul Samad Lasi accused the tribesmen of launching rockets at the Loti gas field and accused Nawab Akbar Bugti's men of attempting to capture the Sui gas installations. Sui Northern Gas Pipelines Ltd. subsequently halted natural gas supplies to 118 power plants in Lahore-Sheikhupura, Bhai Phero and Gujranwala regions, forcing textile mills to halt their operations for an indefinite period. A Sui Northern Gas Pipelines Ltd. official claimed that the shutoff was because of adverse weather conditions.

On January 15, 2006, Jamhoori Watan Party chief Nawab Akbar Khan Bugti told an audience at the Karachi Press Club's Meet the Press program by telephone that the Pakistani government is committing "genocide" in Balochistan, adding, "As a war has been imposed on

Baloch people, they have every right to defend themselves against the onslaught by the government forces" (*Dawn*, January 15, 2006).

The ongoing military operations in Balochistan were now beginning to worry Pakistan's business community. On January 16, the corporate brokerage house Taurus Securities issued its "Key Risks and Challenges 2006" report, which observed that the ongoing violence in Balochistan will have "a detrimental impact on the reserves of natural resources and disrupt gas supplies," adding that the military operations were worsening the situation (http://www.taurus.com.pk, January 16, 2006). On a political level, the report noted that the military campaign was providing common ground for opposition parties to unite and increasing unrest in other provinces.

Attacks also spread beyond Sui. Even as tribesmen clashed with the military on January 29, two separate attacks on natural gas pipelines supplying the power station at Uch in Nasirabad and a gas purification plant at Loti disrupted production at both facilities (*Dawn*, January 29, 2006). Militants also attacked the Pirkoh gas field. The saboteurs managed to destroy a significant portion of the Uch facility's 24-inch pipeline, setting it ablaze. A spokesman said, "The 586 mw-capacity power plant owned by British and U.S. companies was closed at about 11 p.m." Repairs took several days. The Uch attack certainly caught U.S. investors' intention as a threat to U.S. economic interests.

Even as Bugti remained in hiding, Baloch political leaders demanded increased revenue from the province's natural gas facilities. On March 4, 2006, National Party parliamentary leader and Balochistan Assembly opposition head Kachkol Ali demanded royalties from the proposed Iran-Pakistan-India gas pipeline project, which would transit Balochistan, citing international law (balochistan.org, March 4, 2006).

Certainly, Musharraf shows no sign of avoiding a showdown. Speaking to reporters on March 12, he said that his government will not give in to the "blackmail" of "a handful of miscreants" in Balochistan and will use force to defeat them, adding that he was confident that the situation would improve in a month while force would be used against Baloch militants who have attacked security forces and the province's natural gas infrastructure (*Daily Times*, March 12, 2006).

On March 13, U.S. Energy Secretary Samuel Bodman visited Pakistan to inaugurate a bilateral Enhanced Energy Cooperation program. Bodman made a profound statement completely overlooked in the U.S. media, saying, "The security situation in Pakistan needs to be improved as it is an impediment to investment. Until there is an improvement, substantial foreign investment is not possible" (*Daily Times*, March 16, 2006).

Conclusion

While it seems that al-Qaeda and the Taliban remain focused on their campaign against ISAF and U.S. forces in Afghanistan's eastern provinces and Pakistani Army units in the NWFP, the possibility exists that they could move southeastwards to take advantage of Balochistan's growing unrest, linking up with militants operating out of Karachi. The fact that Musharraf has deployed 40,000 troops to Balochistan, about half the 70,000 currently engaged in the NWFP, indicates that he still believes the problems there to be "containable." If the pressure on Islamist militants in the NWFP becomes too severe, then the distinct possibility exists that rather than face the hammer of ISAF troops in Afghanistan, they could migrate to Balochistan and pressure the Musharraf government by threatening the infrastructure there.

An escalating conflict in Balochistan can only drain resources from Pakistan's war on terrorism on its border with Afghanistan and frighten the foreign investment community away from the province, which will be a key player in Pakistan's future prosperity and stability. Should Baloch militants apply the lessons learned in Iraq and more recently in Saudi Arabia about attacking the national energy infrastructure and target the Sui gas fields in a concerted manner, then not only would Musharraf's government lose foreign investment, but it would also face the nasty possibility of industrial production plummeting and nearly half of the country's natural gas consumers placing the blame squarely on Islamabad's iron-fisted tactics.

[From Terrorism Focus, Volume III, Issue 11]

Baloch Insurgents Escalate Attacks on Infrastructure

Tarique Niazi

Originally published on May 23, 2006

Since 2002, Pakistan's southwestern province of Balochistan has remained gripped by insurgent violence. In the last few months, this violence has increased in frequency and intensity. The favorite targets of insurgents are energy production sites—such as Sui in Dera Bugti—and energy infrastructure that supplies natural gas to Pakistan's industrial hub in Punjab and Karachi (*Terrorism Focus*, March 21, 2006). On May 19, 2006, two main gas pipelines to Punjab were blown up, cutting off gas supplies to the province (*Dawn*, May 20, 2006).

Although it is easy to damage Pakistan's extended but unguarded network of gas pipelines, insurgents are now hitting harder targets such as gas production sites. On May 19, the gas supply line to one of the gas plants in Sui was blown up (*Dawn*, May 20, 2006). Sui sits on the country's largest reserves of natural gas, which has been in production since the 1950s. Pakistan's commercial, industrial and residential consumers are heavily dependent upon gas from Sui, the disruption of which can shut the country down. Besides Sui, there are three other gas fields in Pir Koh, Loti and Uch, each of which make a tempting target for insurgent attacks. On April 17, "the regulator of the Pir Koh gas plant was blown off" (*Daily Times*, April 18, 2006). In a similar incident on May 19, the gas pipeline that supplies gas from the Loti gas field to one of the Sui gas plants was also bombed (*Dawn*, May 20, 2006).

Like gas pipelines, railway tracks are another easy target of insurgent violence to disrupt human as well as freight traffic between Balochistan and Punjab provinces. On April 22, a railway bridge near Kari-Dor in Balochistan was blown up, stopping all major passenger trains—Chiltan Express, Balochistan Express, Jaffar Express and Bolan Mail—that run between Balochistan and Punjab and Balochistan and Sind (*Daily Times*, April 23, 2006). In the past two months alone, insurgents mounted 12 attacks on railroad infrastructure on the Sibi-Harnai section (*Daily Times*, April 23, 2006). On May 19, the railway track between Quetta and Chaman (the latter a border town on the Durand Line between Afghanistan and Pakistan), which largely remains under heavy use by security forces, was blown up (*Dawn*, May 20, 2006).

Islamabad has bolstered security in and around the gas production sites as well as the railroad tracks. The major focus, however, has been on the protection of the Sui area where Pakistan has heavily-deployed military and paramilitary forces that also come under frequent attacks. For instance, "on April 17, 'suspected tribal militants' fired 19 rockets at security forces in Dera Bugti" (*Daily Times*, April 18, 2006). No casualties were reported, however. The day before, on April 16, seven rockets were fired on security forces' check posts in Sibi, which is a land route to Dera Bugti and the Sui area (*Daily Times*, April 17). Bridges on the Sibi-Harnai section, which are major means of transportation for security forces in Dera Bugti, have been routinely hit by insurgents. On April 16, a section of one bridge was damaged in rocket attacks (*Daily Times*, April 17). On April 22, two bridges on Sibi-Harnai section were blown up. On May 13, a civilian official was abducted together with his driver and two bodyguards on his way to Uch (*Dawn*, May 15, 2006). The next day, his beheaded body was found and his driver and bodyguards were missing.

Additionally, insurgents are now using "unmanned" weapons such as landmines to attack security forces. The area around the Sui production site is heavily mined, which has caused significant loss of life. On March 11, 28 civilians were killed in a landmine blast (*Arab News*, March 11, 2006). As recently as April 17, three security officials were wounded in a landmine explosion in Sangsila in Dera Bugti (*Daily Times*, April 18, 2006). Besides security forces, agencies engaged in the exploration of oil and gas in the remote areas of Balochistan are also targets of insurgent violence. One such agency is Geological Survey of Pakistan (GSP). On May 19, a hand grenade was lobbed at the house of an important official in the GSP's residential colony in Quetta (*Dawn*, May 20, 2006). The grenade exploded in the front yard of the house and shattered its windows, but caused no casualties. Such incidents should be seen as warnings for lethal violence to come.

The government blames violence in Balochistan on Afghanistan, Baloch tribal chiefs and the Balochistan Liberation Army (BLA) (APP, April 26, 2006; *Dawn*, May 6, 2006). On April 26, Balochistan's minister for home and tribal affairs said that "foreign hands" are sending "arms and terrorists" into the province. Similarly, the federal minister for the interior claimed on May 19 that a tribal chief, Nawab Akbar Bugti, has links to "trouble-makers" in Balochistan. He has banned Nawab Bugti, many members of his family and his nephew Shahid Bugti, who is a member of the Senate of Pakistan, from traveling abroad. Similarly, the government has recently outlawed the BLA, which it blames for attacks on human and property assets. Yet, the government is far from stemming the raging wave of violence in Balochistan.

Although violence in Balochistan has its own roots, its ebb and flow is amenable to the intensity of violence in neighboring Afghanistan and neighboring northwestern Pakistan, especially the latter's Waziristan agencies. Islamabad's strategy to divide Baloch tribes and arm those who do its bidding is further enflaming the existing perilous situation. It is important to understand that the violence in Balochistan is a reaction to President Pervez Musharraf's illusory "strategic objectives"—such as the building of the Gwadar naval port, air bases around the Arabian Sea coast and military installations in the energy-rich section of the province—which are exacerbating an already difficult "situation that could lead to the break-up of Pakistan" (*Khabrain*, May 21, 2006). The reason the government has thus far failed to end violence in Balochistan is the depth and breadth of mass discontent in the province against the government that knows no political and class divides.

[From Terrorism Focus, Volume III, Issue 20]

Pakistan

Al-Zawahiri's Pakistani Ally: Profile of Maulana Faqir Mohammed

Sohail Abdul Nasir

Originally published on February 9, 2006

Maulana Faqir Mohammed was catapulted into prominence last year when his house was raided by Pakistani security agencies hunting a "high value" al-Qaeda target. In the span of seven months, a combination of public sympathy, treacherous local terrain and the intensifying insurgency in Afghanistan has raised Faqir Mohammed into a position of leadership in the Bajaur Agency. Mohammed's house was raided again on January 22, 2006 by Pakistani security forces who detained three of his relatives.

Since May 2005, Faqir Mohammed has been a wanted man on account of his links to al-Qaeda and Taliban operatives. In order to deter him from cooperating with Taliban and al-Qaeda elements, the authorities have pursued a dual-track approach. On the one hand, they are putting increasing pressure on the tribes of the region to alienate Mohammed; on the other hand, they have deployed Pakistani security forces against his followers. Mohammed's house was burnt last year on the authority of elders enacting tribal norms. On January 24, a tribal jirga that convened at Khar, the headquarters of Bajaur Agency, decided that Faqir Mohammed should be asked—through his relatives—to surrender to law enforcement agencies and sever his association with al-Qaeda and the Taliban. If Mohammed does not abide by the decision, then in keeping with tribal norms, his house will be burnt again.

The central question revolves around Mohammed's ability to evade capture. The primary reason behind this is the region's highly distinctive administrative system, a direct legacy of British colonial rule. There is a dual administrative system in the tribal areas consisting of political agents and tribal jirga. A political agent is directly appointed by the federal government and is tasked with overseeing all administrative matters of the tribal agency. The political agent is assisted by subordinate staff and paramilitary troops. The tribal jirga is comprised of tribal elders and notables who perform the role of a jury in any dispute or controversy and base their judgment on tribal norms. The recent upsurge in militancy in North Waziristan, South Waziristan and now in Bajaur is indicative of the gradual erosion of the legitimacy and effectiveness of this unique administrative system. It is unlikely, however, that this system will be fundamentally altered in the foreseeable future. Customary procedures are deeply-rooted and alternative systems are neither appealing nor practical.

Background of Maulana Faqir Mohammed

Faqir Mohammed hails from Bajaur Agency, a tribal administrative unit of Pakistan, bordering the Kunar province in Afghanistan. He was born in Chopatra, a village that is 20 kilometers away from the Afghan border. He is 37 years old, tall and well-built. He has a long black beard and sports a Taliban-style haircut and turban. Despite the fact that polygamy is a common feature of tribal society, Mohammed has only one wife.

Mohammed belongs to the powerful local Mommand tribe (not to be confused with the Mehmands of the Mehmand Agency). Mohammed has a large extended family and almost everyone who is associated with him (by blood or otherwise) is in some way connected to his activities. His two sons and two first cousins, Mulvi Mohammed Karim and Mulvi John Mohammed, were staunch activists of Tehreek-e-Nafaz-e-Shariat-e-Mohammadi (TNSM), or Movement for the Enforcement of Islamic Laws. They went to fight jihad in Afghanistan with Maulana Sufi Mohammad. They tried to make their way home after the fall of the Taliban in late 2001, but were captured and are now languishing in Dera Ismail Khan jail in southern Pakistan.

Although Faqir Mohammed is not a chief or tribal elder, he has managed to secure a powerful support base in the region and moves relatively freely, accompanied by his personal security team. Normally he is guarded by five to eight diehard followers. When undertaking journeys on foot, Mohammed is usually accompanied by 15-20 followers and guards; when traveling by jeep their number is confined to the capacity of the vehicle. The local tribal administration does not dare arrest him and in recent years, Mohammed has rarely ventured beyond Bajaur and the adjoining tribal belt.

Maulana Abdus Salam and Maulana Sufi Mohammad

Until the age of 20, Faqir Mohammed was known to be an excellent student and was not involved in politics or militant actions. In keeping with local tradition, Faqir Mohammed started his early education in a local madrassa and was taught by the prominent Maulana Abdus Salam. Abdus Salam is widely respected in North-West Frontier Province (NWFP) and is not considered to be involved in politics or militant activities. Maulana Abdus Salam belonged to the Deobandi school of Islam, but recently adopted Salafism and has shifted his madrassa to Peshawar. Faqir Mohammed was greatly inspired by Maulana Abdus Salam and under his guidance, obtained the Dars-e-Nizami, which is equal to graduation.

Faqir Mohammed also studied the Quran at Darul-Uloom Pamjpeer, which is considered to be one of the most influential religious schools in the central Peshawar valley. It has no political or militant affiliations and is well known for its monotheist-oriented religious curriculum. It was the Salafi strands of Maulana Abdus Salam and the teachings at Pamjpeer that impressed Faqir Mohammed the most and eventually led to his embrace of the "Arab" Afghans.

Maulana Sufi Mohammad was Faqir Mohammed's first jihadi mentor, and the one who introduced him to militancy in Afghanistan in 1993. Sufi Mohammad was one of the active leaders of Jamaat-e-Islami (JI) in the 1980s. He was the principal of the JI madrassa in Tamaergra, a town in the northwestern part of NWFP. He was an instinctive hardliner and in due course, developed differences with JI and left them in 1992 to form TNSM. Faqir Mohammed was introduced to Maulana Sufi Mohammad in 1993 when he was 22.

One of the main objectives of TNSM was to enforce Islamic laws through the use of force if necessary. The Afghan Taliban subsequently used TNSM methods to enforce Sharia in their own country. It was this ideological and methodological affinity that led many TNSM activists (including Faqir Mohammed) to wholeheartedly embrace the Taliban.

Faqir Mohammed continued to fight in Afghanistan until the fall of the Taliban in late 2001. According to reliable sources, Faqir Mohammed mainly fought on the Bagram front (north of Kabul) and areas bordering the Panjshir valley. He mostly stayed in the Afghan province of Kunar and, by virtue of his Arabic language skills, quickly developed a rapport with Arab mujahideen. Faqir Mohammed never enjoyed a special position among the Taliban and merely fought as a volunteer. It was this modesty, coupled with Mohammed's status as a trained religious scholar, that significantly boosted his prestige and credibility (this information was derived from an interview with Molvi Hakim Khan, a former TNSM activist in NWFP). Faqir Mohammed was considered a brave fighter and an expert at guerrilla warfare. He is proficient in using all small arms, rocket launchers and anti-aircraft weapons.

After the downfall of the Taliban, Mohammed's native knowledge of the tribal Pakistani regions adjacent to Afghanistan, his status and influence in the region and his ideological commitment to international Islamic militancy proved invaluable to al-Qaeda operatives and other radical elements. Security agencies believe that his house in Chopatra village has been used as a winter headquarters by al-Qaeda, which prompted the security forces to raid it in May 2005. Faqir Mohammed is a key facilitator for al-Qaeda and Taliban activities in this mountainous region, and security sources maintain that Mohammed was financially rewarded by the militants for providing logistical facilities and shelter.

For his part, Faqir Mohammed strongly denies any presence of al-Qaeda or Taliban leadership in the area and says, "According to Pashtun tradition we will definitely exact revenge on America. Ayman al-Zawahiri never came here but if he wanted to come, we will welcome him, and it will be a great pleasure for us to be his host" (*Daily Jang*, January 23, 2006). President Pervez Musharraf, however, is insistent that "al-Qaeda fighters were probably killed in a suspected CIA air strike that killed 18 civilians in Bajaur Agency earlier this month…now that we have started investigating the reality on the ground, yes we have found that there are foreigners there, that is for sure" (*The Nation*, January 25, 2006).

It is noteworthy that JI is politically influential in the area; its only deputy member in the National Assembly (Sabzada Haroon-u-Rashid) from the Federally Administered Tribal Areas is from Bajaur Agency. Notwithstanding the influence of JI, the masses are staunch followers of the Taliban, not least because of strong feelings of Pashtun ethnic kinship and the proximity of the region to Afghanistan (*Mashriq*, July 26, 2004).

[From Terrorism Monitor, Volume IV, Issue 3]

Religious Organization TNSM Re-Emerges in Pakistan

Sohail Abdul Nasir

Originally published on May 17, 2006

Western parts of the North-West Frontier Province (NWFP) are gradually coming under the grip of religious radicalism. People in Malakand and Swat districts, which are populated mainly by the Yousafzai Pashtun tribe, have been gathering in public places to burn electronic equipment such as television sets, tape recorders, VCRs, computers, CDs and so forth. These actions have been motivated by the religious sect Tehrik-e-Nafaz-e-Shariat-e-Mohammadi (TNSM), the Movement for the Enforcement of Islamic Laws.

The leader of TNSM is Sufi Mohammad, who was heavily involved in the battle against the Northern Alliance in Afghanistan at the time of the downfall of the Taliban in 2001. Most of his mujahideen were killed or arrested by the Northern Alliance and only a few were able to return to Pakistan, including Sufi Mohammad. The Pakistani government immediately arrested him and for the past five years he has languished in jail. Locals argue that thousands of mujahideen were killed as a result of Sufi Mohammad's incompetence and lack of combat skills. As a result, Sufi Mohammad lost much of his support. Additionally, TNSM members have been killed and regularly arrested by Pakistani authorities, reducing the organization's effectiveness. TNSM has been almost completely dormant in its stronghold of Swat and the adjoining areas. Recently, however, this situation has changed.

After the devastating earthquake that hit the region on October 8, 2005, Sufi Mohammad's followers capitalized on the incident and are using it to revive TNSM. There is a strong and growing belief among the people of Swat and Malakand districts that the earthquake was punishment for their misdeeds. Remnants of the TNSM have been encouraging them to burn their valuable electronic equipment in order to avoid a sinful life and prevent further retribution.

The magnitude of this movement can be gauged from a news item reported by *Mashraq* on April 15, 2006 that after a short period, once again people have begun to burn their electronic music appliances. According to the report, on April 14 hundreds of people gathered after Friday prayers at two different villages. Maulana Abdullah led the procession in the village Bilogram in Malakand when he and his followers set fire to thousands of audio and videocassettes, televisions, computers and CDs. A similar episode took place simultaneously in Brikot village in Malakand. Furthermore, the aftershocks from the October 8 earthquake are still occurring and continue to frighten the region's inhabitants. On April 11, for instance, another powerful aftershock jolted the whole area. These aftershocks make the local populace in these districts more determined to set their music-related appliances on fire (*Mashraq*, April 19, 2006).

As a result of Sufi Mohammad's imprisonment, his son-in-law Maulana Fazalullah is now leading the TNSM movement. Although it is not operating at a high level and does not enjoy the influence it has had in the past, the earthquake has revived the organization to the extent that thousands of people tune into its FM radio transmission. This radio station was recently banned by the government which prompted thousands of people to stage demonstrations. Fazalullah established this FM radio station at Imamdairi, a small town in Swat district. The station is used to deliver teachings of the Quran and persuade people to destroy their musical appliances by arguing that listening to music and performing other sinful acts caused the recent earthquake. According to the broadcast, if believers do not give up their musical and electronics equipment, it may invite the anger of God. As a result of these teachings, thousands of inhabitants voluntarily destroyed their electronic goods in just a few days and this chain of events has continued. Additionally, as a result of TNSM's religious speeches, 50 families announced the end of their long-standing rivalries, hundreds gave up the use of drugs and unaccountable numbers disconnected their cable television connections.

Religious parties called the government's decision to ban the radio station a conspiracy to prevent religious teachings, and accused the Musharraf government of acting on the orders of the United States (*Mashraq*, April 13, 2006). On April 20, the English-language daily *The Post* reported that so far 10,000 people have set their electronic goods on fire due to the motivation given by Fazalullah's radio station, who declared that watching television is un-Islamic.

The October 8 earthquake hit a vast area of northern NWFP and Azad Kashmir (the part of Kashmir controlled by Pakistan). Devastation in the rest of the areas, which were just as damaged as Malakand and Swat, did not lead to the same developments. The reason is that outside of Malakand and Swat, no leader is persuading people to destroy their electronic appliances on a powerful tool of communication like FM radio run by a cleric pushing extreme religious views does not exist.

The provincial government that banned this FM radio station must be concerned about the increasing influence of TNSM, an organization that once caused a major threat to the writ of the government in these areas during the mid-1990s when the government had to use force to control the volunteers of this movement who were demanding the enforcement of Sharia. The provincial government, due to political reasons, cannot afford the revival of TNSM. The ruling religious alliance, the Muttahida Majlis-e-Amal, and particularly JI consider Malakand and Swat their strongholds and will not allow TNSM to damage their positions in the region. It is worth mentioning that Sufi Muhammad is a JI dissident

TNSM is now increasing its activities. *Nawa-i-Waqt* reported on May 1, 2006 that TNSM has decided to launch a movement—consisting of protests after Friday prayers and additional rallies—against the government. Five leaders of TNSM held a press conference on April 30, 2006 at Chakdara in Dir district and alleged that their workers are being harassed. They said that the government has failed to enforce Sharia in Malakand district against which TNSM will launch a movement; however, they did not specify when the movement would begin. While the leaders attempted to make clear that they are against terrorism and do not have any link with al-Qaeda terrorists, the revitalization of the TNSM movement could create further instability in Pakistan's NWFP, adding to Islamabad's existing difficulties of maintaining stability over the entire country.

[From Terrorism Focus, Volume III, Issue 19]

Al-Suri's Treatise on Musharraf's Pakistan

Stephen Ulph

Originally published on May 9, 2006

Ayman al-Zawahiri's new video release, titled "Message to the People of Pakistan," closely meshes with the work of Abu Musab al-Suri (also known as Mustafa Setmariam Nasar), one of the chief political thinkers of al-Qaeda, who was arrested last November in Pakistan (*Terrorism Focus*, March 28, 2006). Al-Suri's own treatise on the subject, titled "Pakistan Musharraf: Al-Mushkila wal-Hall, wal-Farida al-Muta'ayyana" (Musharraf's Pakistan: The Problem and the Solution... and the Incumbent Ordinance), was completed in November 2004 and is 161 pages long. Methodically ordered and meticulously researched, the treatise sets out to demonstrate how Musharraf's government, in its structure, policy and actions, is an infidel government, and therefore in itself illegitimate, in much the same way as al-Zawahiri presents his case. In many respects, the treatise by al-Suri forms the ideological framework for al-Zawahiri's homily.

Al-Suri's word for al-Zawahiri's "dark fate" of Pakistan is karitha, the "disaster," and avoiding this "disaster" forms the theme of his work. The "disaster" is the progressive secularization of Pakistan. "It pains us," al-Suri laments, "to see Pakistan, the redoubtable citadel of Islam—due to a gang traitorous to God, His Prophet and the Believers—become day-by-day an American citadel for the war on God and His Prophet." Al-Suri gives much space to Musharraf's alleged "war against Islam," singling out his subordination to the U.S. war on terrorism. For al-Suri, Musharraf has "openly declared war on Islam, its ulema, madrassas and students." Just as al-Zawahiri laments how Musharraf "provided all the backing needed to expel the Islamic Emirate from Kabul," al-Suri discusses at length how "Muslims in Pakistan must support the Emir of the Faithful Mullah Omar and the Taliban." Like al-Zawahiri, al-Suri is also at pains to counter the negative perceptions on the presence of the Arab mujahideen in Pakistan as causing the present crisis. In his opening note, al-Suri argues that the conflict they are waging is all one, against a common global enemy: "all we need do is change the name Pakistan for Saudi Arabia, or Yemen, or Syria, Egypt, Turkey, Indonesia or any other Islamic country...and the enemy name, whether America,

Crusader Europe, Israel, or enemies of Islam such as India, they are all one and the same." The disaster befalling Pakistan, al-Suri argues, is simply a local manifestation of the disaster that has befallen all of Islam. Pakistanis should, therefore, think more globally, less parochially, and lend their support to the mujahideen unstintingly: "Muslims in Pakistan are obligated to shelter migrant mujahideen fleeing for their faith, whether Arab or Afghan or others, from whatsoever nationality, and they must conceal them and aid them with all that they have."

Al-Zawahiri's case against Musharraf promoting a "jihadless Islam" forms the subject of an entire section of al-Suri's treatise. Under the rubric "The Essence and Demands of the Sharia," al-Suri lists obligations of government policy that conforms to the mujahid interpretation of Islam: the universality of Islamic law in religious and mundane affairs, the legitimacy of the ruler judged by this standard and conduct of foreign relations according to the doctrine of al-Wala wal-Bara (Friendship and Enmity), which regulates relations on the basis of religious propriety alone.

Al-Zawahiri's claim that Musharraf is compromising national security is fleshed out in full in this treatise. A significant portion of the fifth section is taken up with the war with India and its influence on the progress of jihadist currents within Pakistan. Al-Suri turns on its head Musharraf's argument (deplored by al-Zawahiri) of the need to "take care of their interests without paying attention to any moral or religious considerations." The nation, he argues, is everyone but the government. The combined threats of "India, America behind her, and Europe," he states, "require Pakistan to maintain internal unity, in particular between the army and the Pakistani people, and especially its militant forces, which are the Islamic organizations and the ulema and the students, and especially the armed jihadi groups which have gained fighting experience in Kashmir and Afghanistan."

Al-Zawahiri's emotional call upon the army's sense of honor and fear of the afterlife to foster non-cooperation with Musharraf is given chapter-and-verse treatment by al-Suri. Under "The Essence and Demands of the Sharia" section, the author expounds at length on the implications of "soldiers and collaborators with tyrant rulers who befriend the enemies of Islam and who fight against Muslims." The argument is subtly presented, with jurisprudential examinations made into the case of a soldier being ignorant, collaborating unintentionally or "being forced into working for the infidel powers." From there, categorizations follow of "legitimate and illegitimate obedience to orders from commanders, scholars and elders," but the treatise concludes that they may be killed "if they attempt to protect the infidel imams or act as bodyguards for Americans or Disbelievers."

Al-Suri sums up the present state of the country. With the myriad agents of the FBI and the CIA operating out of annexes to Pakistani security institutions, or even independent bases, "it appears that Pakistan under Musharraf has become an American colony dependent on the American administration and its orders on the political, economic, military and security fronts, and all that follows this in cultural and social terms." General Musharraf labors "under the American threat of their support for India" and is dependent on Washington for his position in power. "Events are going from bad to worse every day," al-Suri warns. "What can be avoided or resisted today will be difficult to avoid tomorrow as the tentacles of the American octopus and its collaborators spread…and the seeds of secularism and treason take root and grow." To avert this "disaster" in Pakistan, al-Suri formulates the strategy of resistance:

- Maintain the coherence of the Pakistani forces;
- Prevent the apostate government from filtering out the Islamic forces in the army (which is what they claim the United States is attempting to do);
- Do not allow Musharraf's government to weaken the broad Islamic base of the ulema, students and Islamic and jihadi groups in Pakistan;
- Maintain the jihadi alliance of mujahid Islamic forces in the territories (Afghan mujahideen led by Mullah Omar and the Taliban; Arab mujahideen led by Sheikh Osama, al-Qaeda and the Afghan Arabs; the mujahideen in Kashmir; the Central Asian mujahideen led by the mujahideen of Uzbekistan);
- Remove the Musharraf and Karzai regimes and eliminate them;
- Expel U.S. forces from Pakistan, Afghanistan and the entire region and eradicate their presence.

Given al-Suri's argument that "jihad against the Pakistani government and its U.S. backers is an individual obligation," he states bluntly: "Muslims in Pakistan are to target all manifestations in Pakistan of the Western Crusader presence, American, British or other infidel allies, [all actions hostile to] their blood and wealth is therefore authorized."

The treatise is uncompromising, unemotionally argued and consequently commands all the more weight as an authority, as one would expect from the composer of the encyclopedic 1600-page "Call to Global Islamic Resistance." The recent confirmation of al-Suri's arrest (after early reticence, Pakistani officials stated that al-Suri had been flown out of the country to an undisclosed destination) may mean that his writing days are over, but his ideological influence and legacy remain considerable and will continue to influence the coming generation of mujahideen. As Pakistan climbs up the scale of weakening or failing states, the need to understand the intellectual and ideological structures of Pakistan's growing jihadist current becomes all the more urgent. For political observers, analysts and strategists, Abu Musab al-Suri's "Musharraf's Pakistan: The Problem and the Solution" should be required reading.

[From Terrorism Focus, Volume III, Issue 18]

Inside Pakistan's Madrassas

Farhana Ali

Originally published on January 9, 2006

In the northern hills of Quetta, girls from the ages of eight to their early twenties study the holy Qur'an in Madrassa Tul Banat (literally, an all-girls seminary), the oldest religious school for girls with nearly 900 students. Established in 1989 by a graduate from Cairo's infamous Al-Azhar University, Qari Abdul Rashid opened the seminary to provide predominantly Afghan girls more than just a free Islamic education. "When I looked around me, I realized that there was nothing for these girls," he said. "They were not permitted to go outside their homes, even if the school was in front of their house. When the madrassa opened, I convinced the men—mostly of Afghan origin from the Pathan tribe—to allow their girls to study behind closed doors."

An encounter with these girls is like revisiting a period in ancient history. Some girls from distant villages never leave the seminary, except for the two Islamic holidays, Eid al-Adha and Eid al-Fitr. They also receive room and board, in addition to an education in Islam, which includes memorization of the Qur'an for younger girls, and lessons in history and the Arabic language for older students. Not every girl lives in the compound, nor is from a poor family, a Western misperception. Many students come in vans provided by the madrassa and some belong to affluent families, including the daughters of Quetta's high-ranking officials and army officers. The Dean of Islamic Studies at Karachi University, Dr. Qari Abdul Rasheed, dispelled the myth that madrassas are factories for the poor. He insisted that the hostel for Karachi's Dar ul-Uloom seminary is "not below a four star hotel." Rasheed indicated that at least 25 percent of all madrassa students are from well-to-do families, which contradicts the picture of madrassas as educational institutes for boys and girls living below or at the poverty line.

Most of the money that supports madrassa activities comes from the "public." The public could include several sources, from the richest families of Pakistan to local organizations. As one Deobandi madrassa leader explained to me, "we offer free education to the public, and in return receive monthly gifts from the parents. We accept whatever the public wants to give." The public gives freely to the madrassas in the form of charity, which means that madrassas seldom have to write it down. Accordingly, madrassas are not held accountable by the government for gifts they receive. This holds true even for madrassas who have registered with the Pakistani government in support of President Pervez Musharraf's new madrassa reform law.

What these students do with their religious education is a personal or family decision. Girls in Quetta and Rawalpindi, a congested town outside of Islamabad, reveal that after graduation they intend to open madrassas in their villages to teach others what they have learned. Whether the more conservative men will allow female graduates to continue their education is a separate issue, but most girls (and boys) seek to establish their own Islamic networks and schools. Others have high hopes. For example, boys in the Dar ul-Uloom Naeemia seminary, one of Karachi's largest, aspire to be Islamic scholars ('alim), while others understand the need for secular education. A senior student and manager of the computer lab at the Naeemia School is pursuing an advanced degree in computer science at Karachi University.

When asked about the madrassas' links to al-Qaeda—a common Western fallacy and accepted truth—every imam or hafiz (one who has completely memorized the Qur'an) boldly told me, "there is no link, and if there is, where is the proof?" A teacher at Karachi's Dar ul-Uloom Amjaddia madrassa, a boys school with nearly 1,000 students, insists that "international propaganda wrongly accuse Pakistan's madrassas of supporting terrorist networks, and we have no resources to defend ourselves against these accusations." Without evidence from the U.S. government, teachers and students alike refuse to accept that violent jihad is propagated behind closed doors of the madrassas. That is not to say that jihad is absent from the curriculum. "It is in our religion," said one madrassa leader, "but it is defensive jihad—the same type of jihad that we fought against the Soviets with the support of the Americans."

Conspiracy theories abound; it is not difficult to understand why many seminaries respect bin Laden, though reject his call for arbitrary violence. Al-Qaeda expert and Islamabad talk show host, Hamid Mir, says that "bin Laden is the hero by default," or according to a madrassa manager from an Ahl al-Sunna School, "he is the lesser of two evils." Many madrassas in Pakistan, particularly those in the Northwest

Frontier Province, blame the U.S. for failing to secure Afghanistan after the Soviet withdrawal and argue that U.S. foreign policies, such as the war in Iraq, continue to fuel the fire for jihad.

The other problem lies with definition. Several religious leaders contend that terrorism has different meanings for different individuals and states. The chairman of the national madrassa society declared, "reactionaries are terrorists, but freedom fighters are not terrorists." He, like others, also says with a wry smile that Al-Qaeda and the jihadi organizations in Pakistan are the creation of "agencies," and dismiss the U.S. Department of State's list of terrorist organizations, of which Al Rashid Trust and Jama'at al-Dawa, formerly Lashkar-e-Taiba, are included. The general argument offered is that "there is no proof."

The danger in Pakistan is that everyone acknowledges that the various jihadi outfits, most of which the government banned after 9/11, continue to exist. With only a name change, their central leadership and organizational structure remains. Why they exist and how they garner support is a subject of debate among researchers and concerned citizens, but it is a problem no one can resolve. According to the leader of the Naeemia School, the only solution to eradicating terrorism is "to negotiate with the Muslim world," but what that involves is an open question.

[From Terrorism Focus, Volume III, Issue 1]

The Re-Orientation of Kashmiri Extremism: A Threat to Regional and International Security

Peter Chalk and Christine Fair

Originally published on November 17, 2005

Since the onset of Operation Enduring Freedom (OEF), the activities of foreign jihadists in Pakistan have been a major source of concern for both Washington and Islamabad. However, an equally if not more serious problem that has emerged over the last four years has been the progressive reorientation of Kashmiri Islamist tanzeems (organizations) toward an increasingly explicit anti-Musharraf agenda. These developments not only directly threaten the stability of a key U.S. ally in South Asia, but also appear to raise serious concerns about wider regional and even global security.

Catalysts for Kashmiri Reorientation

Historically, jihadist tanzeems operating in Indian-administered Jammu and Kashmir (J&K) have fallen into two categories: (a) those that are comprised of primarily Kashmiri cadres, for example Al Badr and Hizbol Mujahideen (HM); and (b) those that are predominantly non-Kashmiri in composition, including, the Ahle-e-Hadith tanzeem Lashkar-e-Taiba (LeT), and the prominent Deobandi groups such as Jaish-e-Mohammad (JeM), Harkat-ul-Mujahadeen (HuM), and Harakat-ul-Jihad-e-Islami (HUJI). While most of the indigenous groups have retained their focus on Indian-administered Kashmir, many of the Deobandi outfits are now targeting Musharraf and other elements of the Pakistani state. This recent reorientation of prominent jihadist tanzeems constitutes a serious threat to Islamabad and is a phenomenon that stems from two main factors.

First, was the Government of Pakistan (GOP)'s decision to ally itself with the United States in the Global War on Terror (GWOT). JeM was one of the earliest Kashmiri outfits to bridle at this relationship and, in fact, specific elements within the group wanted to immediately attack American interests in Pakistan after the launch of OEF in Afghanistan.

This internal demand was initially denied by Jaish's then-chief Masood Azhar, who favored compliance with the GOP's new policy direction as politically expedient. Other group leaders such as Maulana Abdul Jabbar (alias Umar Farooq) vociferously disagreed, however, and have since managed to seize the reins of power within the organization. These militants are currently at the forefront of many of the anti-government attacks [1].

Second, is what Pakistan-based analysts describe as the GOP's adoption of a "moderated jihad" strategy, which has involved the imposition of tighter limits upon Islamists seeking to operate in J&K and the Indian hinterland. In large part, pursuit of this calibrated approach stems from external compulsions that became increasingly prominent in the wake of the JeM- (and possibly LeT-) backed assault on the Indian National Parliament (Lok Sabba) in December 2001. Prompting a yearlong standoff with Delhi, this attack brought Pakistan's policy of proxy warfare under renewed scrutiny, not least because it raised the potential to spark a full nuclear exchange in South Asia. Reflecting western concerns, then-Deputy Secretary of State Richard Armitage went to Islamabad in June 2002, during which he managed to extract a promise from the GOP to both abandon its reliance on Kashmiri militants and cease their infiltration across the Line of Control (LoC).

According to commentators in Islamabad, the strategy of a moderated jihad approach has acted as a double-edged sword for Pakistan. On the positive side, it has significantly reduced international pressure on the GOP as well as allowed Musharraf to continue the peace process with Delhi while simultaneously giving him the option of resuming militant activities should negotiations collapse or fail to produce tangible results. On the negative side, however, moves to limit jihadist attacks have clearly been interpreted by groups such as JeM and HuJI as a sell-out of the Kashmiri cause and confirmation that Islamabad, under the present government, is no more than a puppet of Washington. Certain analysts also believe that the strategy has prompted renegade factions within the armed forces and intelligence services—whose raison d'etre for most of their existence has been wresting control of J&K from India—to side with and actively support organizations seeking to redirect their ideological fervor against the Pakistani state.

Target Musharraf

The reorientation of Kashmiri groups toward an internal agenda has been particularly apparent with JeM and HuJI. As noted, Jaish was one of the first tanzeems to advocate the targeting of American interests in Pakistan and over the last four years has systematically moved to expand this focus to an explicit anti-GOP footing. This evolutionary tract has been mirrored by HuJI, which now routinely defines its operational priorities in terms of overthrowing the incumbent Musharraf regime. Both organizations have been directly implicated in high-level attacks on institutional pillars of the Pakistani establishment, including assassination attempts against the President (December 14 and December 25, 2003), Prime Minister Shaukat Aziz and the Karachi Corps Commander General Ahsan Hayat [2].

Somewhat more worrying are indications that JeM and HuJI are acting in concert with enlisted cadres as well as junior and non-commissioned officers in the armed forces. The December 2003 attack on Musharraf, for instance, is widely thought to have involved lower ranking members of the military in addition to at least one commando drawn from the Special Services Group (SSG). Moreover, one of the key persons who infiltrated the army and trained the hit-men for the earlier attempt on the President's life was Amjad Hussain Farooqui, a former member of JeM who is known to have sheltered Khalid Sheikh Mohammad until his capture in March 2003 [3].

A Globalized LeT?

Besides JeM and HuJI, U.S. officials have further suggested the possibility that "globalized" elements within LeT have taken on explicit non-Kashmiri designs and are moving to extend their operations beyond this theater and India proper. If confirmed, this would represent an especially dangerous development given that Lashkar has traditionally been one of the strongest and disciplined groups operating in J&K.

American concerns are predicated upon, inter alia, recent Pakistani reports of the group's annual three-day ijtimah (convention), during which speakers were described as making virulently anti-Western proclamations as well as the "internationalist" content of LeT web-based materials. U.S. commentators fear these rhetorical signposts may be indicative of Lashkar leaning toward a more explicit global jihadist outlook, which, at least certain analysts assert, has been reflected in the establishment of residual logistical contacts with al-Qaeda, facilitation with Islamic recruitment drives for the Iraqi insurgency and readiness to provide military training for foreigners wishing to carry out attacks well beyond the Kashmiri theater (for example, Jack Roche, who has been linked to alleged terror strikes in Australia, and Shehzad Tanweer, one of the British Muslims involved in the July 7, 2005 bombings in London).

Long-time observers of the LeT, however, believe U.S. concerns are misplaced, arguing that Washington's current perception of the group is based on a fallacious understanding of its historical lineage and reflects more post-9/11 biases than any genuine reorientation of the organization's intentions. Analysts within Pakistan similarly reject the notion of a globalized LeT, noting that Lashkar is one of the more ideologically unified groups that has fought in J&K, and is therefore not as prone to the type of wider, non-Kashmiri metastasization that JeM and HuJI have undergone. They also point out that there is currently no evidence to substantiate claims about LeT's supposed internationalist activities, further arguing that anti-Western rhetoric is nothing new and certainly not something that has translated into assaults outside J&K and India [4].

Yet it is important to stress that LeT does not have to be global to be of great significance for South Asia and beyond. The group is known to have been behind the attack on India's Red Fort in December 2000 and it may have been deeply involved in the strike against India's parliament in December 2001—an event that nearly precipitated all-out war between India and Pakistan. The potential to initiate such conflict, with the attendant specter of nuclear escalation, readily underscores the latent threat LeT poses to regional and international security that is irrespective of the actual bounds of its physical presence. Most recently, Indian officials believe that LeT may have been involved with the October 2005 serial blasts in New Delhi. The Islamic Inquilabi Mahaz (Islamic Revolutionary Movement) claimed responsibility for the blast, but some Indian analysts speculate that the Mahaz is tied to LeT.

Conclusion

The reorientation of Kashmiri Islamist terrorism has had a decisive impact on Pakistan's internal stability. As noted, President Musharraf has already been the target of two concerted assassination attempts. Moreover, many Pakistanis believe entities such as JeM and HuJI are directly contributing to a noticeable expansion of radical Islamist sentiment across the country and that, unless constrained, will result in a highly polarized state that lacks any effective middle ground of political compromise. The 2002 elections that brought the Muttahida Majlis-e-Amal (MMA) to prominence in the North-West Frontier Province (NWFP) and Balochistan are often singled out as a salient case in point. This multi-party religious alliance, which is vigorously opposed to the GWOT and the modernist leanings of the Musharraf regime, has caused Islamabad a number of problems, not least by undermining efforts aimed at reforming madrassas and curtailing the activities of militants on the ground.

Beyond these national considerations, the various machinations of JeM, HuJI and LeT have significantly complicated Islamabad's external relations. This is particularly the case in relation to India, which has repeatedly portrayed Pakistan as a bastion of Islamist extremism that poses a fundamental threat to the stability of South Asia and even the world. More seriously, attacks such as Lok Sabba in December 2001 clearly underscore the potential of these groups to trigger a wider inter-state conflict on the sub-continent. That a situation of this sort should arise is especially unnerving given that both countries possess nuclear weapons and that India has pursued an explicit war doctrine since 1999 and a "cold start" doctrine since 2002.

Peter Chalk is a Policy Analyst with the RAND Corporation in Santa Monica, California. Christine Fair is the coordinator for South Asia research programs at the United States Institute for Peace (USIP). This article draws from their ongoing work for USIP Research and Studies Program.

Notes
1. Fair interviews with analysts of Pakistani militant organizations in Lahore, January 2005 and June 2005.

2. Massoud Ansari, "Divine Mission," *Newsline* (Pakistan), June 2004; Zahid Hussain, "Al-Qaeda's New Face," *Newsline* (Pakitan), August 2004, Abbas, Zaffar . "The Pakistani Al-Qaeda," *The Herald*, August 2004.
3. Zaffar Abbas. "What Happened," The Herald, June 2005, p. 71; "Pearl Murder Plotter Orchestrated Bid to Assassinate Musharraf," *The Daily Times*, May 24, 2004; Amir Mir, "Uniform Subversion," *South Asia Intelligence Review*, October 19, 2005; Zahid Hussain, "Al-Qaeda's New Face," *Newsline*, August 2004.
4. This judgment of LeT's anti-western rhetorical orientation is based upon Fair's collection of LeT materials since the mid-1990s. For more information about connections to the London bombings and Pakistan, see Massoud Ansari, "The Pakistan Connection," *Newsline* (Pakistan), August 2005.

[From Terrorism Monitor, Volume III, Issue 22]

India

Students Islamic Movement of India: A Profile

Animesh Roul

Originally published on April 6, 2006

Following the October 2005 deadly bombings in New Delhi, the Union Home Department claimed that Islami Inquilabi Mahaz, or the Islamic Revolutionary Front (a hitherto unknown outfit), which accepted responsibility for the Delhi blasts, is associated with the outlawed Students Islamic Movement of India (SIMI), a radical Islamist organization. Intelligence sources revealed that the masterminds behind the October blasts had several meetings with SIMI cadres in the southern cities of Gulbarga and Hubli. SIMI is also suspected of involvement in the blast at the Ahmedabad railway station in Gujarat on February 19, 2006 and the twin blasts in Varanasi on March 7 that killed 18 people and injured over a hundred others (*Daily News and Analysis*, February 22, 2006; *Hindustan Times*, March 30, 2006).

Although SIMI was outlawed immediately after 9/11, the Indian government claims its subversive activities have continued relentlessly. In 2005, SIMI allegedly struck twice in a single month; for instance, on July 5, 2005 suspected SIMI operatives staged an attack on the disputed temple complex in Ayodhya, and, on July 28, 2005 SIMI operatives allegedly played a role in the bombing of the Shramjeevi train that killed 12 passengers and injured at least 52 others (*The Hindu*, August 1, 2005).

Background

SIMI was founded on April 25, 1977 at the Aligarh Muslim University in Uttar Pradesh, as a radical student outfit with a mission to revive Islam in India and transform the entire country into an Islamic state. SIMI's founding president was Mohammad Ahmadullah Siddiqi, currently a professor of journalism and public relations at the University of Western Illinois. The group's three core ideological concepts were: Ummah, Caliphate and Jihad. SIMI's ideological inspirations were Muslim thinkers who had launched major Islamic movements in the subcontinent, in particular Shah Waliullah, Sayyid Ahmad, Haji Shariat

Allah and the legendary Maulana Maududi, the founder of Jamaat-e-Islami (JI).

Specifically, SIMI was deeply inspired by Maududi's goal to make Islam the supreme organizing principle for the social and political life of the Muslim community. In its annual report, SIMI reiterated these tenets, urging Muslim youths to struggle for the revival of Islam in the light of the Quran and Sunnah (*South Asia Analysis Group*, October 30, 2003). In fact, the Maududi influence was so deep-rooted that in the early years of SIMI's existence the organization was dominated by the Indian wing of JI, called Jamaat-e-Islami Hind (JIH). In due course, SIMI emerged as a coalition of student and youth Islamic bodies, namely the Muslim Students Association, Students Islamic Union, Students Islamic Organization and Muslim Youth Association.

SIMI's pro-Taliban stance in the wake of the 9/11 terrorist attacks, anti-U.S. demonstrations in the Indian states of Madhya Pradesh, Uttar Pradesh, Maharashtra, Gujarat and Rajasthan and the glorification of Osama bin Laden as the "ultimate jihadi" prompted the Indian government to impose a ban. Since the ban, some reports suggest that SIMI has been operating under the banner of Tahreek Ihya-e-Ummat or Movement for the Revival of the Ummah (*The Milli Gazette*, January 2002).

SIMI is believed to have 400 full time cadres called "Ansars" and some 20,000 ordinary members known as "Ikhwans." The leadership is in complete disarray following the ban in September 2001. The last known leaders of the outfit were Shahid Badar Falah and Safdar Nagori as the national president and secretary-general, respectively. While Falah was arrested and charged with sedition and communal tension in north India in September 2001, Nagori has so far evaded arrest. It has been reported that Nagori is trying to revive SIMI and has established links with Pakistani intelligence operatives, the Palestinian group HAMAS and other like-minded organizations beyond India's borders (*The Pioneer*, July 21, 2003).

The ideological affinity with HAMAS was revealed by SIMI's financial secretary Salim Sajid following his arrest in June 2002. According to Sajid, HAMAS' former spiritual leader Sheikh Ahmad Yasin had endorsed the "freedom struggle" in India's Jammu and Kashmir state and the reconstruction of the demolished Babri Masjid in Uttar Pradesh (*Times of India*, June 29, 2002). Sajid's interrogation also exposed SIMI's covert connections with Saudi Arabia's Jamayyatul

Ansar (JA) and Bangladesh's Islamic Chhatra Shivir, the student wing of Jamaat-e-Islami Bangladesh (*Times of India*, June 29, 2002). JA is primarily comprised of expatriate Indian Muslims working in Saudi Arabia and is suspected of channeling funds to SIMI. Other sources of funding have included the World Assembly of Muslim Youth in Riyadh, the International Islamic Federation of Students Organizations based in Kuwait and the U.S.-based Consultative Committee of Indian Muslims (*The Hindu*, September 28, 2001).

While SIMI's strong ties with Jamaat-e-Islami units in Pakistan, Bangladesh and Nepal are well documented, not much is known about its ties with Pakistan's notorious Inter-Services Intelligence Directorate (ISI). According to some reports, SIMI cadres were being trained by the ISI to launch terrorist attacks in India (rediff.com, April 27, 2004). One arrested Sikh militant revealed in 1993 that SIMI cadres, along with Kashmiri and Sikh militants, had been brought together by the ISI through the Jamaat-e-Islami in Pakistan to carry out training and subversive activities in India (*The Hindu*, September 28, 2001). Moreover, it has been reported that the ISI has maintained contact with key SIMI operatives during their trips to Saudi Arabia and other Middle Eastern countries, either for the Hajj or fund-raising activities (*Daily Excelsior*, October 9, 2001). In early 2003, a senior police official in Lucknow (tasked with investigating SIMI in Uttar Pradesh state), warned that the group was trying to re-organize with the help of the ISI. His claim was based on the confessions of two detained SIMI operatives, Obaid Ullah and Mohammed Arif (Press Trust of India, January 27, 2003).

Intelligence sources have stated that after proscription, large numbers of SIMI cadres fled to the northeastern parts of India and neighboring Bangladesh for sanctuary, training and bonding with other Islamic groups. In previous years, SIMI had formed local branches in West Bengal, especially in the border districts of Malda, Murshidabad, North and South Dinajpur and even Kolkata. They organized regional meetings in West Bengal and in Chittagong (Bangladesh) under a different banner in 2003, where they were reportedly planning to infiltrate Islamic education centers, libraries, and other cultural bodies (*Daily Excelsior*, December 12, 2003). SIMI is also believed to be active outside the Indian subcontinent, mainly in Saudi Arabia and other Persian Gulf states. In 2003, as many as 350 Indian Muslims working in Jordan, Libya, Saudi Arabia, Kuwait, Oman, Qatar and other Middle-Eastern states were allegedly recruited by SIMI to fight U.S. forces in

Iraq at the behest of the International Islamic Front (*Intelligence Online*, August 28, 2003).

Additionally, Pakistani terrorist outfits like Hizbul Mujahideen (HM), Lashkar-e-Taiba (LeT) and Jaish-e-Muhammad (JeM) have had strong logistical and operational ties to SIMI. In late 2002, Maharashtra police seized as many as 30 compact discs containing speeches of Maulana Masood Azhar, chief of Jaish-e-Muhammad, along with clippings of communal riots in Gujarat from SIMI offices in Aurangabad. Furthermore, there is clear evidence of operational ties between HM militants and SIMI. The arrest of Sayeed Shah Hasseb Raza and Amil Pervez with explosives in the Kolkata railway station in 2002 substantiated earlier claims of terror ties. Both Raza and Pervez were senior members of SIMI and earlier worked for HM. Investigation officers believed that the duo were in Kolkata to carry out subversive activities and recruit youth for jihadi activities (*Times of India*, March 2, 2002).

Conclusion

The major concern for the Indian government and the United States revolves around al-Qaeda's possible penetration of SIMI. While there is no evidence linking SIMI to al-Qaeda, SIMI leaders are known to have made declarations of support for Osama bin Laden and his organization. In October 2001, Safdar Nagori stated in Lucknow that declaring bin Laden as an international terrorist was part of "an evil design of the U.S." He later admitted to distributing audio cassettes of bin Laden's speeches in and around Kanpur city (*The Milli Gazette*, October 2001). This was not an isolated instance of SIMI's brazen anti-Americanism. Earlier, in July 1998, SIMI cadres held demonstrations in the major cities of India against the presence of U.S. troops in Saudi Arabia, which they called "a sinister plot on the part of the enemies of Islam to desecrate and capture its holiest site" (*South Asia Analysis Group*, October 30, 2003). Furthermore, during a special operation, security forces recovered CDs, tapes, books, journals, posters of bin Laden and documents urging all Muslims "to take revenge for the Babri Masjid demolition, to support the secession of Kashmir as well as the jihad of bin Laden in West Bengal" (*The Statesman*, October 5, 2001).

[From Terrorism Monitor, Volume IV, Issue 7]

Bangladesh

Islamists Pose a Growing Threat to Stability in Bangladesh

Andrew Holt

Originally published on January 18, 2006

Between August and December 2005, a series of attacks hit Bangladesh, collectively killing 12, wounding hundreds of others and involving the country's first suicide strikes. In the most audacious assault on August 17, 2005, 434 homemade bombs were set off in 63 districts over the course of just one hour. This unprecedented bout of violence has thrust the country to the forefront of regional and global terrorist attention, generating fears that a new jihadist beachhead is emerging in this predominantly Muslim nation of roughly 144 million people.

The Islamic Threat

Two main militant organizations currently exist in Bangladesh: Jama'at ul-Mujahedeen Bangladesh (JMB, or the Bangladesh Assembly of Holy Warriors) [1] and Harakat-ul Mujahideen Bangladesh (HuJI-B, or Movement of Islamic Holy war–Bangladesh).

The JMB, which first came to prominence in 2002, is alleged to operate in 57 districts across Bangladesh. According to regional sources, the group is able to call on roughly 10,000 full-time and 100,000 part-time cadres and has recently formed a 2,000-strong suicide squad. The organization is thought to be led by a triumvirate consisting of a spiritual emir, Maulana Abdur Rahman, and two operational commanders, Siddiqur Islam and Muhammad Asadullah al-Ghalib. Together, these three individuals have worked to forge a movement to replace Dhaka's secular legal system with one based on Islamic law, and to ensure the eradication of all non-Muslim influences in the country.

The JMB took responsibility for the August 17, 2005 bombings, as well as three subsequent suicide strikes during November and December that killed 18 people. Leaflets written in Arabic and left at the sites of several of the earlier mid-year attack locations appear to confirm that the group's immediate goal is to terrorize the Bangladeshi judiciary in preparation for the full institution of Sharia rule: "It is time to implement Islamic law in Bangladesh. There is no future with man-made law."

Similar to the JMB, HuJI-B aims to establish a fully-fledged Muslim theocracy in Bangladesh. Intelligence sources in Delhi, however, assert that the organization's real intent is to foster an Islamic revolution in India's northeast by working in conjunction with radicals based in Jammu and Kashmir, as well as Assam.

HuJI-B's roots date back to 1992, although it is only since 2000 that it has emerged as a prominent militant entity. Shauqat Osman leads the group, overseeing an operational cadre that is believed to number 15,000, of which 2,000 are described as hardcore. Most of these radicals are based in cells scattered along a stretch of coastline that runs from the port city of Chittagong to the Burmese border.

Most of HuJI-B's past actions have been directed against Bangladesh's Hindu minority as well as the country's moderate Muslim population. Western officials have expressed concern, however, that this focus has steadily expanded in recent years to include aggression against international aid agencies. There is widespread speculation that the group was responsible for a slate of firebomb attacks on Christian-oriented non-governmental organizations (NGOs) in early 2005.

Government Response

The Bangladesh National Party (BNP), the dominant party in the coalition government that was formed in 2001, has moved to stymie the activities of domestic Islamic militants. JMB and HuJI-B were both been outlawed in 2005, following the August, November and December attacks, and the government authorized widespread detentions. The BNP's actions reflect a growing awareness of the internal threat posed by these two outfits, as well as pressure for more concerted counter-terrorist action by international financial and donor institutions (upon which Bangladesh is heavily dependent).

Despite these efforts, JMB and HuJI-B continue to enjoy broad latitude, largely because they retain the backing of the Jamaat-e-Islami Bangladesh (JIB) and Islami Oikya Jote (IOJ). Both parties, which are part of the ruling administration and forceful advocates of a Sharia system, have studiously worked to limit the scope of measures aimed at disrupting the activities of fundamentalist Islamists. This allows the JMB and HuJI-B to steadily expand their national presence. Indian commentators additionally allege that the two outlawed organizations directly benefit from support provided by elements within Dhaka's Directorate of Field Intelligence (DFGI) and that it is this that accounts for the scale and sophistication of recent attacks.

International Support

Just as importantly, JMB and HuJI-B are thought to have established at least tenuous ties with foreign Islamist entities to buttress their current militant activities. Financially, funds have reportedly been sent from individual donors in the Middle East, allegedly channeled through prominent Arab NGOs such as the Revival of Islamic Heritage and the al-Haramaine Islamic Institute. Operationally, there is speculation about the external provision of training and expertise. The advent of suicide attacks has been taken as evidence of outside influence, as well as the make-up of the improvised explosive devices (IEDs) used in many of last year's assaults

Outlook

The BNP-dominated administration now faces an overt challenge to its authority, which, worryingly, manifest the operational hallmarks common in the wider international jihadist movement. At the same time, the coalition government continues to be constrained by the actions of its JIB and IOJ partners and arguably lacks the complete loyalty of the country's security and intelligence apparatus. Under such circumstances, the future prospect for stability in Bangladesh is bleak.

Notes
1. Another group, the Jagrata Muslim Janata Bangladesh (JMJB), is thought to be a front name for the JMB.

[From Terrorism Focus, Volume III, Issue 2]

Part IV

The Caucasus and Central Asia

Islam, Jamaats and Implications for the North Caucasus - Part 1

Andrew McGregor

Originally published on June 2, 2006

In the last few years, Russian security forces have inflicted considerable damage on Chechen resistance forces, most notably with the elimination of Chechnya's president, the late Aslan Maskhadov. Like hitting a pool of burning oil with a hammer, however, their military blows have sent the fires of insurgency across the North Caucasus. These flames are now nurtured by the evolution of a new resistance structure, the military jamaat.

The traditional jamaat is not a new social structure in the Caucasus. Its roots can be found in the early jamaats of Dagestan at the time of Islamization. The jamaats were tribal-based communal organizations with political and economic roles. In time, the jamaats also assumed a defensive military role and commonly merged into more powerful confederations when the external threat was severe.

Today, in its simplest terms, a jamaat is a local community of Muslims, organized at an often basic level to share spiritual pursuits. Jamaats may be found from Wisconsin to Wessex, and in general have little to do with radical Islam. There are others, however, like Egypt's notorious Gama'a al-Islamiyya that have been responsible for acts of terrorism carried out in pursuit of an Islamic state. In the North Caucasus, the modern jamaat movement has been growing for nearly 20 years, producing both peaceful and militant varieties of the organization. In the last few years, however, there has been a tendency for North Caucasian jamaats to form the basis for military resistance to the administrative and security structures of the Russian Federation. Not all militants are members of a jamaat, but these organizations have taken the lead in the fighting against Russian federal forces outside of Chechnya.

Origins of the Caucasian Jamaats

In South Russia's present cauldron of religious, political and ethnic conflict, many jamaats have developed an Islamist political agenda. Their concerns, like their origins, tend to be local in nature. Land claims, mosque closings, moral laxity, political corruption, police brutality and other local problems dominate their public statements. Rarely is there mention of other theaters of the war on terrorism, or references to the so-called "global jihad."

The involvement of the jamaats in the fight against Moscow appears to have been part of a plan conceived by Aslan Maskhadov not long after the expulsion of his forces from Grozny in 2000. As a veteran Soviet officer, Maskhadov understood the strategic need to broaden military resistance beyond the confines of Chechnya. Shortly before his death in 2005, Maskhadov declared that, by his orders, "additional sectors were established [early in the conflict]: Ingushetia, Kabardino-Balkaria, Dagestan, etc. Amirs of these fronts were appointed, and they are all subordinate to the military leadership of the Chechen resistance" (RFE/RL, March 7, 2005). Despite their many differences, the agent of Maskhadov's efforts to expand the conflict was warlord Shamil Basayev.

Are the Jamaats Wahhabist?

Russian Interior Minister Rashid Nurgaliyev, who is himself a Muslim, has described the entire North Caucasus as a "breeding ground for Wahhabism," a very loaded term in Russian political discourse (*Interfax*, September 21, 2004). Can the jamaats actually be described as Wahhabist? Their adopted brand of Islam is Salafist in nature, drawing on the example of the model community established by the Prophet Muhammad and his companions. In this way, they earn themselves the deprecating name of "Wahhabists" from Russian authorities (the term is borrowed from Saudi Arabia's Wahhabist movement, the most severe example of Salafi beliefs).

The Wahhabis were, and are, a puritan-style Islamic revivalist movement started in 18th century Arabia to eliminate the religious innovations that had attached themselves to Islamic worship since the days of Muhammad. The Wahhabist movement has used their alliance with Saudi Arabia's ruling family to spread their version of Islam internationally. Roaming Arab preachers made some inroads in the Caucasus in the early 1990s, but members of the generation that now provides the young membership of the jamaats are to a large degree discovering Salafi Islam on their own initiative.

The Salafists of the jamaats, like the Wahhabis of Arabia, reject the veneration of saints, requests for their intercession or pilgrimages to their tombs. These are all cornerstones of Sufi worship, which has until recently dominated Caucasian Islam. In some places, a war of words has erupted between the leaders of official state-sponsored Islam and the independent jamaats. Fairly typical is a recent condemnation of the official imams of Dagestan by the local Sharia Jamaat. The jamaat denounced official Islam as nothing more than "ancestor worship," closer to Buddhism than Islam as it involves the veneration of "tombs, amulets and sacred monks." These conflicts have impeded the growth of Salafism in Sufi religious communities, and the jamaats' insistence on the rule of Sharia law alienates the still overwhelmingly secular population of the North Caucasus republics.

Of course, in Russia "Wahhabi" now refers to nearly all Muslims acting outside of official Islam, with the added association since 2001 of somehow being linked to al-Qaeda. It appears that none of the active jamaats have expressed any solidarity with Osama bin Laden's group, though they do cooperate with the diminishing number of Arab mujahideen still active in the Caucasus. Since the September 11 attacks, when all "Chechen bandits" became "international terrorists," Russian security services have maintained that the Chechen resistance is directed and funded by bin Laden's al-Qaeda. The Chechen conflict, far from being directed by al-Qaeda, seems to have barely registered with bin Laden and his associates. Russian security forces have spent so long dealing with the elusive threat of al-Qaeda and the pursuit of terrorist non-entities like Achimez Gochiyayev that they have failed to notice the growth of a more concrete threat to the Federation's stability. The jamaats enjoy a flexibility and insularity that have allowed their proliferation without much interference from the police.

Strategic Advantage of the Jamaat Organization

Islam in the Caucasus survived the long period of Soviet rule by decentralizing. Kremlin-directed official Islam sought to create rigid hierarchies and careful documentation of observant Muslims and their activities. Unofficial Islam went in the opposite direction. The Caucasus region's leading order of Sufis, the Naqshbandi Brotherhood, continued to thrive by rejecting a traditional Sufi hierarchy of hereditary leadership. Naqshbandi spiritual leaders were chosen largely by consensus (with some exceptions), so that their arrest or demise did not threaten the continued existence of the lodge. Generally small in numbers (40 or less), their strong local base, reinforced by ethnic, clan and family ties, usually defied all Soviet attempts at infiltration. The other leading Sufi brotherhood, the Qadiris, maintained a hierarchal system that exposed their leaders to targeting by Soviet police.

It is important to recognize that the Soviet-era Naqshbandi Sufi lodges were not intended to wage any kind of military resistance. They do, however, provide a proven method of organizing locally while avoiding the attention of authorities. The jamaats are similar to the Sufi lodges in many ways, even if they represent conservative rather than popular forms of Islam. They rely almost exclusively on local membership and leaders. In most cases the jamaats are created spontaneously, fulfilling the spiritual needs of those returning to the Islamic fold. Official Islam, stained by corruption and pro-Kremlin subservience, has failed in its attempts to rein in the Islamic revival. It is the energy of the underground jamaats that Chechen warlord Shamil Basayev has devoted the last few years to harnessing.

Both Dagestan's Sharia Jamaat and Kabardino-Balkaria's Yarmuk Jamaat have made attempts to broaden their ethnic membership from the original core group. The Salafist interpretation of Islam practiced by the jamaats is open to a broader membership than the old Sufi lodges. The Yarmuk Jamaat made a statement explicitly rejecting any attempts to represent the jamaat as a "monoethnic organization" (Utro. ru, February 4, 2003). Russian converts to Islam have also joined the jamaats, and a few of these converts have been involved in combat actions. According to pro-Russian Chechen militia leader Sulim Yamadayev, these individuals have found their way to the jamaats from Krasnodar, Volgograd, Stavropol and the Astrakhan Oblast.

[From Terrorism Monitor, Volume IV, Issue 11]

Islam, Jamaats and Implications for the North Caucasus - Part 2

Andrew McGregor

Originally published on June 15, 2006

Many of the military leaders of the North Caucasian jamaats were trained by warlord Ruslan Gelayev in the Pankisi Gorge before he led his guerrilla forces back into Ingushetia and Chechnya in the fall of 2002. Gelayev, like Shamil Basayev, was a graduate of the pan-Caucasian movement and commanded fighters from the Kabardino-Balkarian Republic (KBR) and the Karachai–Cherkessian Republic (KCR) in the 1999 raids on Dagestan. A young fighter named Muslim Atayev emerged as the leader of approximately 30 Kabardino-Balkarians in Gelayev's command. Shortly after participating in the battle of Galashki in Ingushetia, Atayev was detailed to lead his men back into the KBR to set up a resistance group. Based in the mountains, this group evolved into the Yarmuk Jamaat. The name of the jamaat reflects its military intent, referring to the Yarmuk River near the Golan Heights where an outnumbered army of Muslims inflicted a decisive defeat on the forces of the Byzantine Empire in 636 AD.

The Yarmuk Jamaat armed itself through an attack on the Federal Drug Control Service (FSKN) headquarters in December 2004. Atayev justified the attack (in which four Kabardin policemen were killed) by accusing the Drug Control Service of being the main distributor for narcotics in the region (Kavkaz Center, December 15, 2004). Basayev visited Atayev in Baksan where future operations were planned. Atayev was eventually killed in a Nalchik gun battle in January 2005.

Shamil Basayev also has deep roots in the pan-Caucasian movement, particularly with his involvement in the military activities of the Confederation of the Peoples of the Caucasus in the early 1990s. His raids on Dagestan in 1999 also had a strong pan-Caucasian element, with many of the fighters under his command originating from North Caucasus republics other than Chechnya. It is these contacts that Basayev has exploited successfully in building a centralized command for the region's disparate resistance groups. Aslan Maskhadov's successor as president, Sheikh Abdul-Khalim Sadulayev, appears to share Basayev's sentiments, calling for the liberation and unification of the entire Caucasus. Recently, he went so far as to offer Chechnya's complete support to Georgia's struggle with what Sadulayev termed "Russia's terrorist activity and imperial ambitions" (*Chechenpress*, May 15, 2005).

The Caucasian Jamaats in Action

Russian authorities still claim that the 1999 bombings of Moscow apartment blocks were carried out by a KCR jamaat under the direction of the late Arab mujahideen commander Ibn al-Khattab. In recent years, urban shootouts with members of the KCR's Jamaat No. 3 have become common. The organization has been accused by security services of directing suicide bombers in Moscow.

In the last two years, the jamaats have engaged in urban warfare in cities across the Caucasus. This fighting is usually of two types, the first being planned actions by insurgents designed to eliminate selected targets and seize arms for further operations. The second arises when federal intelligence or police discover the presence of jamaat members in urban safe houses. In these cases, a crisis typically develops when the insurgents refuse to surrender. Long gun battles have followed in most cases that have exposed a tendency by state security forces to use maximum force, often with mixed results. The inevitable security sweeps and abductions that follow do little to reassure residents of the North Caucasus that Moscow can be called upon to protect the local population.

Jamaats are active elsewhere besides the KBR. In Ingushetia, the local Sharia Jamaat has been active in bombings and attacks on security forces as well as participating in the Basayev-led raid on the Ingushetian city of Nazran in June 2002. In Dagestan, another Sharia Jamaat is engaged in a violent struggle with the republic's Interior Ministry forces that threatens to rival the conflict in Chechnya. According to Sadulayev, these jamaats, as well as others in the Adygea, Stavropol and Krasnodar regions, pledged their allegiance to him after the death of Aslan Maskhadov (*Gazeta Wyborcza*, September 9, 2005). Sadulayev himself was amir of the Argun military jamaat before the current Chechen war erupted.

The Raid on Nalchik

The Nalchik raid of October 2005 differed from the previous year's raid in Nazran in that it was directed and carried out almost exclusively by local militants, rather than by Chechen fighters who needed to be transported to Nazran and back to safe bases in Chechnya. Even Russian Defense Minister Sergei Ivanov announced that there were no "outside gunmen" present at Nalchik (Pravda.ru, October 16, 2005). The KBR's minister of culture noted that the militants did not belong to any one ethnic group, suggesting that the attacks were not just an eruption of Balkar dissatisfaction. The raid demonstrated how independent jamaats could mobilize in the "Caucasus Front" envisioned by Aslan Maskhadov, and now pursued by his successor, Sadulayev. KBR President Arsen Kanokov noted that low income and unemployment had "created the soil for religious extremists and other destructive forces to conduct an ideological war against us" (AP, October 14, 2005).

Yet, while the militants were mostly local, their commanders were not. A look at the operational command demonstrates how the Chechen-style command structure works in action. Basayev carried out what he describes as "general operative management." By accepted rules, the amir responsible for the sector in which the action is to take place assumes operational command (Kavkaz Center, October 15, 2005). In this case, it was Anzor Astemirov (also known as Amir Seifulla). The amirs of other sectors were each given responsibilities under Astemirov's command. One of those killed in the assault on Nalchik's FSB headquarters was Ilyas Gorchkhanov, the leader of the Ingush Jamaat. The amirs of Ossetia and Krasnodar regions were also wounded.

After the raid, Astemirov correctly pointed out that despite months of preparation, no one in the local population betrayed the militants. For his part, Russian Presidential Representative Dimitri Kozak was vocal in his criticism of the lack of intelligence available on the Yarmuk Jamaat. In fact, Russia's advance knowledge of the raid came from the interrogation of a captured militant, Anzor Zhagurazov, who revealed plans for a large-scale attack on Nalchik five days before it happened. A cache of a half ton of explosives was discovered based on his information, and several hundred members of the Russian special forces were sent to Nalchik. Despite this, the militants carried out an assault on government and military targets that lasted several hours and reaped large quantities of captured weapons; at least 40 militants were killed. The attack on Nalchik appears to have been planned to coincide with a similar attack in Dagestan that was prevented by the death of several of its main planners in a Russian operation.

Astemirov compared the raid to the Battle of Uhud, fought in 625 AD by the Muslims of Medina against the Meccans (Kavkaz Center, January 10, 2006). The Muslim army of Muhammad suffered a setback that day due to their overconfidence, but eventually regrouped to emerge triumphant. Astemirov also suggested that the anti-Russian jihad must be fought on the home ground of all the Muslims of the North Caucasus.

The militarization of the jamaat movement may yet provide Sadulayev with the power base he needs to assume the role of Imam of the Caucasus. The job of centralizing control will be difficult, and will ultimately expose members of the network. The Chechen leadership, however, realizes that the Kremlin has succeeded in closing Chechnya to the outside world. The conflict with Russia has settled into a war of attrition, which the Chechens cannot possibly win. Without spreading the conflict, their best hope is for a withdrawal of Russian forces, allowing for a civil war with the pro-Moscow forces of Ramzan Kadyrov. A full blown fratricidal struggle would reduce the fighting strength of Chechnya to insignificance, a solution to the "Chechen Problem" that might prove satisfactory in Moscow.

Recent political developments in the Caucasus have reminded many residents of the troubled history of the region's relations with Russia. As memories surface of the Circassian exodus and Stalin's deportations, the limited benefits of Russian rule threaten to be overwhelmed by history. Imam Shamil's 19th century rebellion is undergoing a revival in popularity. In current conditions, the attraction of a revived Imamate under the direction of Abdul-Khalim Sadulayev may be great enough to make young militants forget that Shamil's three decades of rebellion ended in the utter devastation of his followers in Dagestan and Chechnya (as Vladimir Putin has lately taken to reminding citizens of the North Caucasus).

Conclusion

While it is difficult to envision the jamaats as a military threat to the Russian Federation, it may prove impossible for the Kremlin to deal effectively with five insurgencies at once, or to address international questions as to why Russian rule in the region has spun out of control. Bombings and other attacks have spread right into the Stavropol and Krasnodar regions of the Russian Republic, indicating an ever-widening scope of operations for anti-Russian militants.

The Islamic combat jamaat in the North Caucasus is more than a religious phenomenon. Economic and territorial issues are also important factors in the recruitment of young fighters, who otherwise find themselves unemployed and disenfranchised. Last November, President Putin's envoy, Dimitri Kozak, warned that the proliferation of what he describes as "Islamic Sharia enclaves" in remote areas of the Caucasus would soon immerse the entire region in conflict. This result was inevitable if military measures were taken without addressing state corruption and other social and economic problems. In these conditions, the revival of the dormant pan-Caucasus movement has found a rallying point in Salafist Islam, but one rooted in local tradition with local leaders. Russia's pre-emptive counter-terrorism policy and repression of Islamic activities outside the realm of state-approved Islamic structures continues to feed the insurgency. The emergence of the "military jamaat" threatens to stretch Russian resources to the limit and turn the North Caucasus into a minefield of anti-Russian resistance.

[From Terrorism Monitor, Volume IV, Issue 12]

The Rise and Fall of Foreign Fighters in Chechnya

Paul Tumelty

Originally published on January 26, 2006

The recent killing of Saudi Sheikh Abu Omar Muhammad al-Sayf, a religious adviser to the Chechen resistance since 1995, heralded the demise of the first generation of Arab mujahideen in Chechnya. Their presence has had a profound effect upon the ongoing war in the Russian North Caucasus, with Chechnya widely viewed as another jihadi front controlled by al-Qaeda. This article aims to contextualize Chechnya's "Arab" fighters.

Background

Chechen and North Caucasian links with the Middle East stretch back to the Russian Imperial Period when these peoples migrated by the thousands to modern day Jordan, Turkey, Syria and Iraq. While the Chechens were assimilated in the latter three countries over time, in Jordan today there still exists a unique community of around 8,000 Chechens who have preserved their language and cultural traditions.

After 1990, dozens of Jordanian-Chechens traveled to see their newly independent homeland. Among them was Sheikh Ali Fathi al-Shishani, an elderly veteran of the war against the Soviets in Afghanistan and an ethnic Jordanian-Chechen. In 1993, Fathi formed a Salafi Islamic Jamaat consisting of scores of young indigenous Chechens and some Jordanian-Chechens. Following the onset of the Russo-Chechen war in December 1994, he was instrumental in facilitating the recruitment of Arab fighters from Afghanistan. Among those he personally invited was Samir Salih Abdallah al-Suwaylim, better known as "Khattab."

The Emir

Emir Khattab was a young, but experienced Saudi Arab-Afghan mujahid, who commanded one of the three Arab units that fought in the Tajik civil war from 1992. Apparently, he made the decision to fight alongside the Chechens after seeing television images of the latter wearing Islamic headbands. From Afghanistan, he traveled to Baku's airport and met with a fellow mujahid. While investigating travel routes to Chechnya, he received a letter from Sheikh Fathi via the already extant network of Arab financiers and facilitators in Baku, inviting him to join the jihad.

Khattab formed a unit of eight experienced Afghan-Arabs who together traveled to Chechnya in February 1995. Once there, he met Fathi and arranged the transfer of two-thirds of Fathi's approximately 90 followers into his personal military command, thus furnishing himself with immediate military clout. This company-sized unit was then subdivided into sections headed by his deputies (*al-Sharq al-Awsat*, May 2, 2002).

Khattab was also able to enhance his status by befriending the Chechen warlord Shamil Basayev, who later declared him his brother. This symbolic gesture was important given that the fiercely independent Chechens are wary of outside influence in their internal affairs. Khattab fully cooperated and coordinated with the Chechen rebel command, and he and his commanders—including his first deputy Abu Bakr Aqeedah, Aqeedah's successor Hakim al-Medani, Abu Jafar al-Yemeni, Yaqub al-Ghamidi and his then deputy and the future emir of the foreign fighters, Abu Walid al-Ghamidi—were able to impart some of their tactical experience from the anti-Soviet jihad.

Over time, the logistical networks from the Middle East and Afghanistan via Georgia, Azerbaijan and Turkey solidified, with Fathi continuing to play a role in recruitment, largely through the dissemination of rebel videos and CDs, at that time a novel tool that was conceived of by Khattab.

In total, approximately 80 Middle Eastern Arabs fought against the Russians during the 1994-96 war [1]. Alongside them were some North Africans and Turks, or in other words, the three main constituent groups of the foreign contingent that continue to fight today. They were regarded by the rebel leadership as an anomaly, although useful nonetheless and welcomed as a result, particularly for their ability to attract finances. While their military influence was negligible within the larger war effort, their militant ideas and religious influence began to percolate through war-torn Chechen society after August 1996.

An Islamic State

Khattab's vision for an Islamic State in the North Caucasus was only partially complete with the Chechens' 1996 victory. He believed that jihad must establish God's law in one country, which can then be used as a base for expanding the Islamic state. To that end, he established a number of training camps after 1996, paying young North Caucasians to attend two week courses in which they acquired religious training and weapons instruction. A trickle of Arabs continued to arrive in the region via established networks, adding to his original core that survived the war almost intact.

President Aslan Maskhadov's secular rule after 1996 was opposed by an array of Islamists who formed a pseudo-military-religious alliance that eventually forced him to implement Sharia law. Around 30 "courts" were established throughout the republic, with religious guidance from Sheikh Abu Omar al-Sayf, operating from the template of the Sudanese model. It received additional religious sanction by Abdurakhman, a young Jordanian-Chechen who succeeded Sheikh Fathi as head of the Islamic Jamaat following the latter's death in 1997.

This botched attempt to impose alien concepts on this devastated and highly Sovietized society failed, at the very least, to restore order. Maskhadov soon decreed that Abdurakhman, two of his Arab deputies and the Dagestani Islamist Bagautdin Magomedov needed to leave the republic. Yet, he did not single out Khattab, who by then had acquired too much power.

Al-Qaeda

Khattab has often been described as an associate of Osama bin Laden, given that the two Saudis both fought in the anti-Soviet jihad. Yet although they were in Afghanistan at the same time, Khattab was only a 17-year-old mujahid when he arrived in 1987 and he persistently refuted any connection with bin Laden, stating that there is "no relationship because of the long distance and difficult communications" (al-Jazeera, January 21, 2000). He constantly reiterated this sentiment in interviews, simply referring to bin Laden as a "good Muslim."

There is now evidence, however, that both sides were in contact via representatives during the 1990s and early 2000s. That correspondence amounted to a rigorous debate over strategy, as both men had an entirely different worldview and each attempted to convince the other of the superiority of their respective approaches to jihad. This was also characterized by a personal rivalry between them, particularly as Khattab's stature grew within the Islamist community (al-Sharq al-Awsat, December 9, 2004).

Although he occasionally highlighted the oppression of Chechnya's Muslims, bin Laden was obsessed by the Judeo-Christian alliance and focused his strategy upon attacking the "far enemy." Khattab on the other hand sought to establish an Islamic system in Chechnya and then use it as a base from which to forcefully expand into neighboring territories. In August 1999, he and Shamil Basayev led hundreds of fighters in an invasion of Dagestan to implement this vision, which ultimately failed. Right up until his death in 2002, Khattab never threatened to attack the United States.

Bin Laden's deputy, Ayman al-Zawahiri, had a deeper interest in events in the North Caucasus: "if the Chechens and other Caucasus mujahideen reach the shores of the oil-rich Caspian, the only thing that will separate them from Afghanistan will be the neutral state of Turkmenistan. This will form a mujahid Islamic belt to the south of Russia..." [2]. Before al-Zawahiri's Islamic Jihad merged into bin Laden's umbrella group in 1998, he embarked upon a fact-finding mission to Chechnya to investigate the establishment of a camp for his followers.

In January 2000, links with Afghanistan deepened when a delegation led by Chechen ideologue Zelimkhan Yandarbiyev traveled to Kandahar and the Taliban formally recognized Chechnya as an independent state (Kavkaz Center, January 19, 2000). At the time, Yandarbiyev, who by this stage had moved to the Middle East together with other Dagestani ideologues, denied that Chechens were being trained in Afghanistan, although a training facility was established in Kandahar (The News, Pakistan, February 22, 2000).

Chechnya is well-known as one of the more difficult jihadi fronts, where the climate is extremely harsh and, due to linguistic and physical differences, Arab fighters have been prone to death or capture. For these reasons, the Chechen rebels sought to regulate the number of foreign fighters, and where possible only accept those with adequate military experience. Khattab employed a representative in Kandahar, known as Dahak, a Moroccan, who vetted recruits for their suitability.

By default, the number of foreign fighters was also regulated by logistics and the difficulties of traversing the terrain. Indeed, the biographies of dozens of jihadis reveal their desire to fight in Chechnya, but show their failure to do so. Moreover, the post-9/11 American invasions of Afghanistan and Iraq diverted would-be recruits to these fronts. Hence, external events caused a significant change in the Arab leadership's approach towards Chechnya.

New Approaches

The strictly controlled method of operating within the Arab leadership in Chechnya allows only the emir to air his views; the sole exception was Abu Omar al-Sayf. After Khattab's death in June 2002 and the smooth ascension of Abu Walid, he began to alter the tone of his interviews, which strongly contrasted with those of his predecessor. Both Abu Walid and his successor, Abu Hafs al-Urdani, began to advocate attacks against the U.S. Despite the Arab presence being partially influential in Chechnya on religious terms, for example when Abu Omar al-Sayf issued a fatwa to justify the first Chechen suicide bombing, the rationale for the change in emphasis was driven by the necessity for the Arab fighters to continue their primary role as fundraisers. Their utility otherwise, in the eyes of the rebels, is defunct.

After 9/11, U.S. pressure on Persian Gulf-based organizations suspected of terrorist financing drastically slowed funding to the Chechens, as openly confirmed by both Abu Walid and Abu Hafs (*al-Watan*, December 12, 2003). In an attempt to attract new potential contributors amid the diversification of funds to clearer cut causes, both leaders broadened their rhetoric, aligning it roughly with the aims of al-Qaeda.

Abu Hafs has been thrust into an information campaign by the post-Maskhadov leadership under Sheikh Abdul-Khalim Sadulayev. Both men appear to have a close relationship, assisted by Sadulayev's ability to speak Arabic. A new video shows Abu Hafs, whose real name was recently revealed as Yusuf Amerat, sitting to the left of Sadulayev, together with his Sudanese deputy, giving the impression of real Arab influence in decision making [3].

Amerat has also exploited the links the U.S. claims he has with Abu Musab al-Zarqawi, who strongly supports the Chechen cause. Both men have sent one another moral support via jihadist websites. Al-Zarqawi's home city of Zarqa hosts some of the Jordanian-Chechen/Circassian population and he previously expressed a desire to fight in Chechnya. Interestingly, a source has claimed that at one stage Khattab lived in Zarqa (*al-Sharq al-Awsat*, October 13, 2005).

While Arab military influence was negligible during the 1994 to 1996 war, Khattab was instrumental in organizing the invasion of Dagestan in 1999, which led to the resurgence of the ongoing war. The Arab financial and religious input has sustained and changed the dynamic of the Russo-Chechen wars, as well as allowed the Putin administration to paint the Chechen resistance as al-Qaeda. Since 1994, the number of foreign fighters has rarely, if at all, risen above 50 at any one time and is not likely to have exceeded 500 combatants.

Notes
1. Aslan Maskhadov's and his deputy's estimate, RFE/RL Russian Service.
2. *Knights Under the Prophet's Banner*, A. Zawahiri.
3. See Kavkaz Center, video section (Russian version).

[From Terrorism Monitor, Volume IV, Issue 2]

Al-Qaeda in Azerbaijan: Myths and Realities

Anar Valiyev

Originally published on May 18, 2006

After the events of September 11 and the subsequent war on terrorism, Azerbaijan became one of the active members of the anti-terrorism coalition. Besides providing a small contingent of troops for peace operations in Afghanistan and Iraq, the Azerbaijani government actively cooperates with the United States and other members of the coalition to fight against al-Qaeda. For a short period of time following the September 11 attacks, Azerbaijani special services arrested 23 international terrorists and extradited them to Middle Eastern countries (Arif Yunusov, *Islam in Azerbaijan*, 2004). Late President Heydar Aliyev claimed that state security agents had arrested "big figures" from the al-Qaeda network. Supposedly, Aliyev was speaking about two members of Egyptian Islamic Jihad who were apprehended in Azerbaijan in 2002 with the assistance of the CIA. They were handed over to Egypt. Later in 2004, both local and foreign newspapers reported that al-Qaeda might implement large-scale attacks against some countries, including Azerbaijan, that have handed al-Qaeda members to the Egyptian government.

In most of the cases, the majority of arrested terrorists and radicals were foreign citizens, usually from Arab countries, in addition to Turkey, Pakistan and Afghanistan. For the last couple of years, however, ethnic Azerbaijanis have become involved in the activities of radical terrorist organizations. In March 2005, for example, an Azerbaijani court imprisoned a group of six people. The gang, headed by Amiraslan Iskenderov, who allegedly fought in Afghanistan from 1999-2003, was planning terrorist attacks against public and governmental buildings, strategic facilities and residences of foreign citizens. The terrorist group also planned to implement mass-scale chemical attacks in some regions of Azerbaijan. The group prepared a statement on behalf of al-Qaeda in the Caucasus, threatening the Azerbaijani government with carrying out bombings in Baku. According to the Ministry of National Security, the terrorists' main aim was to force the Azerbaijani government to change its secular and democratic regime, as well as to quit the anti-terrorism coalition (Day.az, March 17, 2005). In June 2005, another group consisting of foreign and local citizens was indicted. The group received special instructions from the Abu Hafs, the coordinator of al-Qaeda in the Caucasus, and was planning to commit terrorist acts, bombings and arson to cause political instability (Today.az, July 6, 2005).

Later in March 2006, Eldar Mahmudov, the Azerbaijani Minister of National Security, warned the public on activities of religious-extremist groups in the country. Mahmudov claimed that before September 11, Azerbaijan was only a transit country for terrorists. After becoming a member of the anti-terrorism coalition, however, terrorists began to target Azerbaijan as well (*Echo Newspaper*, March 18, 2006).

Independent analysis would doubt the existence or even the interest of al-Qaeda in Azerbaijan. After September 11, it became fashionable among some autocratic regimes in Central Asia to "neutralize" al-Qaeda cells in their respective countries and to show their importance to the anti-terrorism coalition. Azerbaijan was no exception. Officials, special services and the media actively circulate a variety of myths, stressing the importance of Azerbaijan as well as the potential danger from al-Qaeda. Some of these myths are below.

Myth I: Al-Qaeda is planning attacks on Azerbaijan for its participation in the international anti-terrorism coalition.

One of the most circulated myths that can be found in the local Azerbaijani media implies al-Qaeda's plans to launch attacks in Azerbaijan as punishment for participating in the anti-terrorism coalition and to force the Azerbaijani government to withdraw its troops from Afghanistan and Iraq. Despite the fact that Azerbaijan was one of the first countries that answered the call of U.S. President George W. Bush to wage a war against terrorism, it is unlikely that al-Qaeda would target Azerbaijan. As previous actions of al-Qaeda and its affiliated organizations have shown, the leaders of these groups are rational actors who do not generally attack merely for the sake of terrorism. Al-Qaeda prefers to attack cities where a terrorism strike would lead to both high casualties as well as a huge resonance. Baku, the capital of Azerbaijan, is not of great global importance. Attacking Baku would offer little benefit to al-Qaeda.

Secondly, Azerbaijan does not offer many attractive targets. The only possible targets might be the U.S., British or the Israeli embassies, or the Baku-Ceyhan pipeline. After September 11, there were several reports claiming al-Qaeda was planning to attack the U.S. Embassy in Baku. Those reports, however, were not independently confirmed.

Myth II: Al-Qaeda might attack the Baku-Ceyhan pipeline and disrupt oil supplies to the West.

In 2004, the Azerbaijani government stated that the country's special services had obtained information that members of al-Qaeda were planning acts of sabotage designed to derail the construction of the Baku-Ceyhan pipeline—a $3 billion project intended to transport oil from the Caspian Sea region to the world markets. The news caught the eye of many security experts and government officials. In the wake of the Limburg bombing—the French-flagged oil tanker—and al-Qaeda's adoption of the new tactic to disrupt oil supplies from the Middle East to the West, government officials called for tighter security measures for the pipeline. Thorough analysis, however, can explain that al-Qaeda is not very interested in the destruction of the Baku-Ceyhan pipeline.

First of all, the pipeline transports approximately one million barrels per day, supplying only 1.2 percent of all the world's oil consumption. A disruption of the pipeline will hardly be a massive hit global oil supplies. Second, the pipeline and its infrastructure can be easily reconstructed within weeks or even days. Third, an attack on oil installations in the Middle East region, especially in the Gulf countries, which give al-Qaeda more attention than the Baku-Ceyhan pipeline, has more regional and less global significance. It is worth mentioning, however, that disruption of the pipeline would lead to anxiety or even panic in the world market and affect prices. The attack on the pipeline would show that al-Qaeda is targeting, and capable of attacking, oil facilities outside the Middle East. Meanwhile, a terrorist attack on a pipeline could become a mini-catastrophe for the country. Azerbaijan could lose its attractiveness to investors due to elevated financial risks.

Myth III: Al-Qaeda recruits Azerbaijanis for terrorist attacks.

In March 2006, Minister of National Security Mahmudov shocked the public with the information that an al-Qaeda Caucasus terrorist cell was planning to recruit Azerbaijani women for suicide missions. The minister maintained that although the country has extensive experience with fighting extremism, the information "was the worst discovery for us over the past years" (*Echo Newspaper*, March 18, 2006).

The real situation in Azerbaijan, however, is different. Despite the fact that Azerbaijan is a Muslim country, a majority of the population consider themselves secular. It should be mentioned that while most

Azerbaijanis consider Islam part of their national identity, any mixing of religion with the political sphere is discouraged by a vast majority. Critical to understanding this issue is the fact that the Azerbaijani view of Islam is one of a common national characteristic, inseparable from its Azerbaijani ethnic identity, which no single group can monopolize. Compared to other Muslim countries such as Jordan, Saudi Arabia, Turkey and Pakistan, al-Qaeda will have a hard time influencing and recruiting local Azerbaijanis for suicide terrorist missions. Furthermore, up to 75-80 percent of the population is Shiite, to which the ideology of al-Qaeda is hostile. Finally, a majority of the mosques, where al-Qaeda usually recruits its followers, are under tight surveillance by the Azerbaijani government.

The Reality

It cannot be denied, however, that members of other radical organizations are active in Azerbaijan. During the last couple of years, members of terrorist organizations such as the Caucasian Islamic Army, the Islamic Movement of Uzbekistan, Jeyshullah, Hizb ut-Tahrir and Jamaat al-Muvahidun have been neutralized.

On April 18, 2006, a group of Azerbaijani citizens calling itself Jamaat al-Muvahidun were sentenced to terms in prison. According to the Ministry of National Security, the group planned to bomb the U.S., Israeli and Russian embassies. In addition, they were planning the assassination of members of government and law-enforcement bodies in retaliation for their cooperation in the anti-terrorism coalition. The group was also planning to blow up buildings of The State Oil Company, National Bank and other strategic facilities. It was revealed that the young people were ready to get military training in the camps of Afghanistan, Pakistan, Iran and Turkey in order to fight "infidel countries" (*Turan News Agency*, April 18, 2006). On April 19, the Azerbaijani court sentenced an international group consisting of 16 people to terms in prison. The group, mostly comprised Azerbaijani citizens—although there were citizens of Russia, Turkey and Yemen among them—were supposedly members of al-Qaeda, trained in the Pankisi Gorge in Georgia (*Terrorism Focus*, April 25, 2006). The gang members were accused of terrorism, illegally obtaining arms and murdering a police officer in Baku in July 2005. Group members, meanwhile, were recruiting young Azerbaijanis to fight in Chechnya against Russian troops. For the last year, over 100 people were sentenced to various jail terms for the participation in the war in Chechnya—or for preparing to do so (*Turan News Agency*, April 19, 2006).

Recent trends show that local radical organizations pose more of a danger to Azerbaijan than does al-Qaeda. Yet, the Azerbaijani government is trying to connect the surge of local radicalism with the influence of al-Qaeda. There are several reasons for this. First, the country's regime is trying to show the United States its loyalty concerning the war on terrorism. Thus, the sentencing of al-Qaeda "members" was done in order to demonstrate the activity of Azerbaijan's special services. Secondly, by exaggerating the danger from al-Qaeda, the Azerbaijani government is trying to portray itself as the one and only pro-democratic force in a region dominated by anti-Western religious extremists. For many years, the current regime in Azerbaijan successfully sold this propaganda, often depicting outbreaks of social unrest as the work of Islamic extremists.

The most important aspect, however, is that the government of Azerbaijan, as well as in many countries in the Middle East, falsely interpret the issue of religious extremism. They believe that terrorist attacks occurring in their countries as well as the establishment of cells of radical Islamic organizations are attributable to some "nerve" center headed by bin Laden's al-Qaeda. It is easier for the Azerbaijani government to connect jihadi phenomena in the country with al-Qaeda rather than to look at the real factors leading to the emergence of such organizations. The core of these radical extremist organizations usually consists of a group of religious young men who are mostly unemployed and dissatisfied with the autocratic regime of their country. They tend to see a theocratic state as the only alternative for a highly corrupt and debauched government. One might conclude that the government's preoccupation with al-Qaeda targeting Azerbaijan is a deliberate attempt to divert attention from daily problems by creating a straw man.

Historical experience shows that cracking down radical cells in the country will hardly bring long-term benefits. Instead, it could further alienate religious minority groups and lead them into the trap of jihadi organizations. For the Azerbaijani government, it is time to address important issues such as corruption, poverty and democratic development. Otherwise the country will be bogged down in eternal conflict with the growing influence of radical organizations.

[From Terrorism Monitor, Volume IV, Issue 10]

Resurgence of Islamic Radicalism in Tajikistan's Ferghana Valley

Igor Rotar

Originally published on April 18, 2006

The Ferghana Valley is one of the most unstable regions in Central Asia. In early 1989, pogroms of Jews and clashes with Meskhetian Turks broke out and resulted in the deaths of 150 people. Subsequently, 15,000 Meskhetian Turks fled from the Ferghana Valley. In 1990, clashes between Uzbeks and Kyrgyz resulted in the deaths of more than 200 people and in the destruction of more than 1,000 houses. An uprising in the Uzbek city of Andijan in May 2005 seriously aggravated the situation in the Ferghana Valley.

Social instability in the Ferghana Valley is a result of the high population density (the highest in Central Asia) and a shortage of arable land. The fact that a great majority of the population of the valley lives in rural areas is the main destabilizing factor. Additionally, the population of the valley is more religious than the population of any other region in Central Asia. It was here that the Islamic Movement of Uzbekistan (IMU) emerged. Currently, the radical Islamic organization Hizb ut-Tahrir is the most active in the valley.

Although the Uzbek authorities managed to suppress the Andijan uprising, there is little confidence that the peace will last. The central problem is that in the 1920s, the single ethnocultural region of the Ferghana Valley was divided between three states: Uzbekistan, Tajikistan and Kyrgyzstan. Even today, the Tajik, Uzbek and Kyrgyz parts of the Ferghana Valley remain closely linked. Therefore, even if Uzbekistan manages to maintain control over its part of the valley (which seems unlikely), there is no guarantee that the metastasis of the Andijan crisis will not spread to the neighboring countries of Tajikistan and Kyrgyzstan.

The Andijan Link

In mid-January, in the Tajik city of Kayrakkum, the events in Andijan were replicated on a smaller scale. Armed people stormed and seized a detention center and in the process killed a policeman and also freed an associate who belonged to an Islamic terrorist organization. According to Tajik authorities, after the attack the militants managed to hide in neighboring Kyrgyzstan. Two days later, Abdugafor Kalandarov, the chief prosecutor of the Sogd district of Tajikistan, stated that the IMU has become noticeably active in the Ferghana Valley. According to the prosecutor, authorities managed to find whole arsenals of weapons concealed by militants (*Eurasia Daily Monitor*, February 15, 2006). "Today, the IMU has become an international organization," Kalandarov told Jamestown. "It includes Tajiks as well. [The IMU is] united in its wish to build an Islamic state in Central Asia by military means. It is possible that after the suppression of the Andijan uprising, some militants moved to Tajikistan along with their weapons."

In addition to Kayrakkum, the Tajik town of Isfara has also been affected by Islamic militants. The town of Isfara is located in the Isfara region of the Sogd district and is regarded as the unofficial capital of the Tajik part of the Ferghana Valley. The population is much more religious than in other cities of Tajikistan. About a year ago, the special services in Isfara detained 20 members of the extremist organization Bayat. According to local authorities, members of the organization killed protestant pastor Serghey Bessaraba, who had been actively involved in spreading Christianity among Tajiks. They also torched a few mosques whose imams cooperated with the authorities. While being apprehended, the members of Bayat put up resistance. It is noteworthy that members of Bayat had not resorted to such radical measures before. Initially, they planned to order the district in line with the norms of Sharia and create some semblance of the Iranian revolutionary guards.

In 1990, the current leader of the IMU, Tahir Yuldashev, created a similar Islamic militia in the Uzbek part of the Ferghana Valley. It can be assumed that Bayat maintained close links with the IMU. According to Muzasharif Islamuddinov, the former mayor of Isfara and a current deputy of the Tajik Parliament, who spoke to Jamestown, "It was in 1997 that people in our district heard for the first time about Bayat when law enforcement agencies arrested a citizen of Uzbekistan for committing a murder who was a close relative of one of the leaders of the IMU. At that time, the investigation discovered that the murderer was linked with the underground organization Bayat."

According to the imam of the Hazhan mosque, Huri Ibadulo Kalozade, Bayat probably emerged in northern Tajikistan in the early

1990s. "At that time a flood of foreign Islamic priests rushed to Tajikistan," Kolozade explained to Jamestown. "There were members of the organization called Bayat among them." According to authorities in Dushanbe, Tajik citizens belonging to Bayat fought on the side of the Taliban in Afghanistan and some of them are now in captivity at the U.S. base in Guantanamo (*Eurasia Daily Monitor*, May 3, 2004).

Speaking with Jamestown, the mayor of Isfara, Mukhiba Yakubova, said, "I believe that Bayat is a purely terrorist organization which aims to destabilize the situation in northern Tajikistan." Yakubova also said that policemen have been finding buried caches of shotguns on the outskirts of Isfara. "We can only guess whom these weapons belong to. Maybe they simply belong to hunters, or to terrorists," Yakubova said.

The activity of Islamic radicals in the Isfara district is a very alarming signal since Isfara is located at the crossroads of the Kyrgyz and Uzbek sections of the Ferghana Valley. Isfara is only 10 kilometers from the Batken district of Kyrgyzstan through which mujahideen of the IMU were fighting their way to Uzbekistan in 1999 and 2000. Additionally, Isfara is located about 50 kilometers from the Uzbek city Kokand, where in November 2004 an uprising against Uzbek authorities broke out. Indeed, according to Ahmadzhon Madmarov, a human rights activist from the Ferghana Valley, many residents of Kokand participated in the Andijan uprising.

Chain Reaction

Uzbeks make up about 30 percent of the population of southern Kyrgyzstan. The majority of Uzbeks in southern Kyrgyzstan have relatives in Uzbekistan. Today, no one in Kyrgyzstan denies that there were Kyrgyz citizens among the participants of the Andijan uprising. "It is not a secret that there are members of the Akramiya movement in the south of Kyrgyzstan," said Sadikdzhak Mahmudov, the head of the Osh human rights organization Rays of Solomon. "Almost all of them are local Uzbeks," Mahmudov continued. "It is interesting that they all had known in advance about the planned uprising and a few days prior to the events went to that city."

It appears that Akramiya—founded in 1996 after an ideological split within Hizb ut-Tahrir—has been active in Kyrgyzstan for many years (RFE/RL Uzbek Service, May 11, 2005). According to Samsibek Zakirov, a representative of the Committee for Religious Affairs of the Osh district, "In 1998 some people tried to convince people not to visit mosques saying that it is a sin and urged people to pray at home instead. As far as I understand, a refusal to visit mosques is one of the conditions of Akramiya's teachings."

Despite the fact that the last 439 Uzbek refugees were sent from Kyrgyzstan to Romania, a great number of refugees from Uzbekistan still remain in the Republic. Their number, according to the estimates of some Kyrgyz human rights activists, may be as high as several thousand (fergana.ru, December 8, 2005).

Last fall, one of the leaders of the uprising in Andijan, Kabul Parpiev, granted several interviews to the Western media. According to the Central Asian website fergana.ru, both Uzbek and Kyrgyz special services are still looking for Kabul Parpiev on the territory of Kyrgyzstan. The Uzbek special services fear that "Kabul Parpiev is assembling people in Kyrgyzstan to invade into Uzbekistan" (fergana. ru, December 8, 2005).

In the opinion of Aselbek Eghembediev, an employee of the Fund for Social Tolerance, based in Batken, the situation in southern Kyrgyzstan has become increasingly tense since the May Andijan events. For example, as Eghemberdiev says, leaflets calling for revenge against the Uzbek authorities for the carnage in Andijan were circulated in the Kyrgyz city Kizil Kiya which borders Uzbekistan (located 40 kilometers southeast of the Ferghana Valley).

Policemen Found Weapons in the Same City

The ideology of Hizb ut-Tahrir is in fact quite exotic from the Western point of view. The party believes that democracy is unacceptable to Muslims. At the same time, the members of Hizb ut-Tahrir always stress that they condemn violence. The softer policy of the Kyrgyz authorities toward extremist organizations accounts for the fact that the main centers of Islamic radicals are located in this country. Here, they control their followers both in Uzbekistan and in Kyrgyzstan. For example, the unofficial "capital" of Hizb ut-Tahrir in Central Asia is located in the Kyrgyz city Karasu.

The imam of the central mosque in Karasu, Rafik Kamaluddin, told Jamestown that "the Uzbeks live on both sides of the Ferghana Valley both in the Andijan district of Uzbekistan and in Osh district of Kyrgyzstan." He continued, stating, "During the Soviet Union, the city Karasu, which was one single city, has now been divided by the border into two parts: Kyrgyz and Uzbek. Nowadays, Islamic radicals of Uzbekistan flee to Kyrgyzstan in fear of repression. The majority of these people settle down in Kyrgyz Karasu. A narrow channel separates us from the Uzbek part of the city. Perhaps that is exactly why our city is called the capital of Hizb ut-Tahrir." For instance, as witnessed by this author, every five minutes a homemade boat with people unwilling to pass the customs check crosses the border channel. In the opinion of Kammaluddin, the people cross the border illegally to avoid paying bribes to the Uzbek customs officials. One factor is obvious: the border remains transparent and one can transport not only leaflets, but also weapons.

Destabilization of the situation in southern Kyrgyzstan is also promoted by the lack of firm authority in post-revolutionary Kyrgyzstan. As Jamestown has stated in the past, the current vacuum of power in Kyrgyzstan provokes inter-ethnic clashes. For example, the relationships between Uzbeks and Kyrgyz have become heated in the Kyrgyz part of the Ferghana Valley. The fact that the population of neighboring Uzbekistan may become involved in the clash if it erupts makes possible consequences hard to predict. An example of this spillover effect took place in 1990 in Osh district. Osh is situated just a few kilometers from the Uzbek border and is about 60 kilometers from Andijan. During the Kyrgyz-Uzbek carnage in the Osh district in 1990, crowds of residents of the Andijan district who were coming to help their compatriots were stopped at the Uzbek–Kyrgyz border with great difficulty (*Eurasia Daily Monitor*, February 10, 2006).

One can assume that the Andijan turmoil was simply the first symptom of the destabilization of the situation in the Ferghana Valley. In fact, a chain reaction effect has taken place here. A crisis in any part of the valley inevitably leads to cataclysms in adjacent territories, and that, in turn, provokes new shocks in neighboring countries.

[From Terrorism Focus, Volume III, Issue 15]

Part V
Southeast and East Asia

Thailand

A Breakdown of Southern Thailand's Insurgent Groups

Zachary Abuza

Originally published on September 8, 2006

Thailand has faced an Islamist secessionist movement since 2001-2002 that has led to the deaths of more than 1,500 people. There have been nearly 400 successful bombings, many more attempted bombings and more than 400 arson attacks. Militants have assassinated more than 600 people. Ten of the 33 districts in the deep south are "plagued by violence" according to the Thai Ministry of the Interior, and the number is increasing. Yet, little is actually known about the insurgents' structure and capacity. To date, there has not been a single credible claim of responsibility, nor have the insurgents publicly stated their goals or political platform. Their unwillingness to disclose any details has worked to their advantage and left Thai intelligence in a quandary. There are a number of insurgent groups working together, and unlike the insurgency in the 1960s to the early-1990s, when groups were sharply divided over their goals and ideology and proved absolutely incapable of working together, today's organizations share a common Islamist agenda and are demonstrating unprecedented coordination and cooperation. No organization is trying to discredit another to build up its own power base.

The Pattani United Liberation Organization (PULO)

PULO was founded in India in 1968 by Kabir Abdul Rahman, a Pattani aristocrat and Islamic scholar educated in the Middle East. The founding ideology was "religion, race, homeland, humanitarianism." His goal was to establish an independent Muslim state through armed struggle. PULO splintered, and by the mid-1990s it was all but defunct, with much of its aging leadership living in exile in Europe. PULO held a watershed "reunification congress that brought together some 40 leading PULO figures from Thailand, Europe and the Middle East between April 29 and May 1, 2005 in Damascus" in an attempt to bring itself back from irrelevancy [1].

PULO has taken a degree of responsibility through website postings warning foreigners to stay away from southern Thailand, but they have no control over the insurgents [2]. PULO has held secret talks with the government, but this seems to be an attempt by them to leverage their limited degree of influence. A PULO spokesman recently caused controversy in an August 9 report aired by the BBC when he suggested that PULO could carry-out terrorist attacks in Bangkok: "Maybe we will target other areas, like Bangkok or Phuket—I can't guarantee it won't happen" (BBC, August 9, 2006). Yet, this goes against most of what the PULO leadership has stated and against the reality that PULO has no operational control over the insurgents.

PULO has always been a very secular organization, emphasizing Pattani secessionism, not religion. Yet this fact ignores the extreme religious undertones and forced implementation of Salafi values on the society. Former PULO members are very clearly involved in the insurgency, but it is not clear whether they are fighting in PULO's name or whether they have joined forces with newer and more radical organizations. Clearly, their experience in cross-border operations and their control or ownership of land that can be used for training has been important for the younger insurgents. Yet, even PULO leaders admit that the Barisan Revolusi Nasional-Koordinasi (BRN-C) is spearheading the insurgency.

Barisan Revolusi Nasional-Koordinasi

The BRN-C was one of three splinters of the Barisan Revolusi Nasional (National Revolution Front, BRN), which was opposed to the nationalist agenda of PULO. The BRN was founded in March 1963 by Ustadz Haji Abdul Karim Hassan and developed close ties to the Communist Party of Malaya and was influenced by the ideology of pan-Arab socialism. By 1984, the BRN had three discernible factions: BRN-Congress, BRN-Coordinate and BRN-Uran. The BRN-Congress, under the leadership of Jehku Peng (Rosa Bursao), pursued a military struggle. The BRN-Coordinate, or BRN-C, under Haji M, pursued a more political struggle in the mosques and emerged as the largest and best organized of the three groups.

BRN-C is distinctly Islamist and developed through a large network of mosques and Islamic schools. Thai intelligence now speaks of the insurgency as being a "pondok-based" movement. General Pisarn Wattanawongkeeree, the former commander of Thai armed forces in the south, said, "There is no doubt that the basis for this new insurgency are the ustadz (religious teachers). This is something that has been in the making for a long time" (*Time Magazine Asian Edition*, October 11, 2004). A police official stated, "We suspect some [Islamic] schools might have played a significant role in these shootouts. We think that they might have been used as training grounds for militants, or teachers might have indoctrinated their pupils with fundamentalist ideologies" (Reuters, May 7, 2004). There is now a critical mass: some 2,500 graduates of Middle Eastern institutions who have returned to the south.

The BRN-C is attempting to become a mass organization. In a BRN document that was found in Narathiwat's Joh I Rong district, the authors outlined a plan to increase popular support to between 200,000 and 300,000 people, 10 percent of whom were to be recruited into the paramilitary wing (author interview, Bangkok, April 20, 2005). Its main recruitment vehicle is a student organization, Pemuda (Youth), established in 1992. The Thai government has "blacklisted some 4,000 youths for suspected involvement in Pemuda" (Thai News Agency, January 13, 2005).

The number of members in the BRN-C is not known, but Thai officials estimate that there are approximately 1,000 members. Its current leaders are, for the most part, schoolteachers and ustadz from roughly 18 schools, including the Thamawittiya Foundation School in Yala, the Samphan Wittaya School, Jihad Wittaya School and Pattana Islam. Teachers at these schools have been arrested with weapons, bomb-making materials and bomb-making instructional videos. The current known BRN-C leadership includes Afghan-trained Masae Useng, Sapaeng Basoe, Abdullah Munir, Dulloh Waeman (Ustadz Loh), Abroseh Parehruepoh, Abdulkanin Kalupang, Isma-ae Toyalong, Arduenan Mama, Bororting Binbuerheng and Yusuf Rayalong (Ustadz Ismae-ae). The BRN-C is structured along strict cellular lines. It is estimated that 70 percent of the villages have a cell of between five and ten people. Many villages have two or more cells.

Gerakan Mujahideen Islami Pattani (GMIP)

The GMIP was founded in 1986 by Wae-Hama Wae-Yuso, but broke up by 1993 as a result of internal squabbling. In 1995, Nasori Saesaeng (Awae Kaelae), Jehku Mae Kuteh (Doromae Kuteh), Nasae Saning and a handful of other Afghan veterans consolidated power. For most of the 1990s, the GMIP was more of a criminal gang than a group of freedom fighters. It was thought to have run guns for other Muslim insurgent groups, in particular the Moro Islamic Liberation Front (MILF) and the Free Aceh Movement (GAM). The GMIP was engaged in kidnapping, extortion, contract killings and "enforcement." As one senior Thai Intelligence official said, "The Gerakan mujahideen had a poor record in the past. It was really a criminal gang. But they purged their leadership" (author interview, Bangkok, March 16, 2005).

Thai authorities seemed to take the GMIP more seriously beginning in August 2003, when security forces gunned down two senior members in Pattani—its Afghan-trained operations chief Nasae Saning and Mahma Maeroh.

In January 2004, the government announced that it was searching for Doromae Kuteh, the head of the GMIP and "the mastermind of many evil attacks on the south." On January 26, 2004, Thai authorities announced that the Malaysian government had detained him under the Internal Security Act (ISA). Unconfirmed reports suggest that Malaysia deported Kuteh to Syria. Other Afghanistan-trained members of the GMIP include Nasori Saesaeng (Awae Keleh) and Wae Ali Copter Waeji. Karim Karubang (Doromae Lohmae) is another top leader.

Jemaah Islamiyah (JI) approached the GMIP in 1999–2000 as part of the Rabitatul Mujahideen, but it is unknown how deep or strong a relationship was forged. Following the 9/11 attacks on the United States, the GMIP distributed leaflets in Yala calling for a jihad and support for Osama bin Laden. It has a stated goal of turning Pattani Raya into an Islamic state by 2008. The GMIP probably maintained a close relationship with the Kumpulan Mujahideen Malaysia (Malaysian Mujahideen Group, KMM), also founded by a veteran of the Afghan mujahideen, Zainon Ismail. Nik Adli Nik Aziz, another former leader of the KMM, trained with Nasori Saeseng in Afghanistan, and the two became close friends. The KMM was founded at approximately the same time as the "new" GMIP on October 12, 1995. Members of the KMM procured weapons and engaged in training in southern Thailand. In return, many of the Thai secessionists were able to seek sanctuary in parts of Malaysia where the KMM had influence or where government officials were sympathetic.

The GMIP tried to raise its profile in early 2002 by staging a number of raids on police and army outposts to steal weapons in the three southernmost provinces of Yala, Narathiwat and Pattani. Between 2002 and 2004, the group was responsible for the deaths of 40 police officers. Raids on armories have been the group's modus operandi for the past five years. Karim Karubang is believed to have been the leader of the January 4, 2004 raid that restarted the insurgency.

The GMIP is a rural-based organization and its operations reflect this. Thai officials have linked the GMIP to attacks on military convoys using roadside IEDs and on rural police and military outposts. Thai intelligence documents estimate that the GMIP has 40 well-trained cell leaders in the south.

The Runda Kumpulan Kecil (RKK)

In late 2005, the Thai government began to acknowledge that a number of BRN-C militants had been trained in Indonesia, although it was not known by whom. Both Thai officials and the media began to discuss the group known as the Runda Kumpulan Kecil (*Bangkok Post*, November 24, 2005). The RKK, however, is not a completely independent group per se, but simply a name for BRN-C militants who received some training in Indonesia; mostly, it seems, while studying there. Police believe that the head of this cell is Rorhing Ahsong, also known as Ustaz Rorhing, and that the cell has some 500 members (*Bangkok Post*, June 17, 2006).

The 17 suspects arrested in connection with the October 16, 2005, killing of a monk all claimed to be part of this group. Police asserted that they were trained in Bandung, Indonesia (*Bangkok Post*, November 28, 2005). The commander of Police Region 9 said that the group that decapitated an army commando in early January 2006 had also been trained by Islamic scholars in Indonesia. Likewise, three men suspected of participating in an ambush on a commando unit in Yala's Banang Sata district on January 2, 2006 said they had received training in guerrilla tactics from the RKK in Indonesia. In late July, police detained Udeeman Samoh, 21, and Sapee-aree Jehkor, 21, both of the RKK. Investigators said Udeeman is a very skilful bomb maker, while Sapee-aree was considered one of the cell's top members (*Bangkok Post*, July 29, 2006).

In December 2005, Thai army chief General Sonthi Boonyaratglin traveled to Indonesia where the two sides agreed to further cooperate in counter-terrorism. The Indonesians agreed to monitor links between the southern Thais and the Free Aceh Movement (GAM).

New PULO

Two members of PULO—Ar-rong Moo-reng and Hayi Abdul Rohman Bazo—founded New PULO in 1995. Bazo and his deputy, Hadji Mae Yala, were two of the four Thai Muslim leaders arrested by Malaysian authorities in 1998 and turned over to Thai authorities. After that, Saarli Taloh-Meyaw headed New PULO until his death in February 2000. The current leadership of New PULO is unclear; the organization may be under the control of Kamae Yusof. A handful of arrests in the past two years suggest that members have some involvement in the unrest. Many of New PULO's leaders and original members were trained in Libya and Syria and have considerable technical bomb-making skills. Two members of New PULO—Marudee Piya, who is the head of the group's Narathiwat operations, and Paosee Yi-ngor, a top demolitions expert—are on the Thai government's most wanted list.

Jemaah Salafi

Muhammad Haji Jaeming (Abdul Fatah) founded Jemaah Salafi in the late 1990s. He trained in the Sadda Camp in Afghanistan in 1989 and returned to southern Thailand, where he established the madrassa Hutae Tua in Narathiwat. Abdul Fatah represented Jemaah Salafi at JI's three Rabitatul Mujahideen meetings in Malaysia in 1999–2000. He served as a liaison and moneyman for Hambali and seems to be one of the few Thais who favors the pan-Southeast Asian agenda of JI. Yet,

Jemaah Salafi has played a very limited role in the violence as Abdul Fatah is under intense scrutiny by Thai security forces and is in no position to get involved in the current unrest.

Conclusion

The preceding groups are responsible for the continuing insurgency in southern Thailand. The past few months have seen repeated coordinated bombing campaigns by these insurgents, such as an operation in June that involved more than 70 bombs, an operation on August 1, 2006 and the most recent operation on August 31, 2006 that targeted at least 20 commercial banks in Yala province. Coordination between the groups will continue to evolve as they pursue their shared Islamist agenda.

Notes
1. The congress elected Tengku Bira Kotanila as titular president and the head of a 17-member executive council. Anthony Davis, "Interview: Kasturi Mahkota, Foreign affairs spokesman, Patani United Liberation Organization (PULO)," *Jane's Intelligence Review*, August 6, 2006.
2. PULO and Bersatu's joint "Statement of Protest," issued on October 31, 2004, can be found at http://www.pulo.org/statement.htm. Also see, Ed Cropley, "Exclusive: Malay Separatists Say Behind Southern Thailand Unrest," Reuters, August 28, 2005; Tony Cheng, "Behind the Bombs," BBC, August 30, 2005.

[From Terrorism Monitor, Volume IV, Issue 17]

The Indigenous Nature of the Thai Insurgency

Peter Chalk

Originally published on January 12, 2006

The recent upsurge of unrest in southern Thailand has increased concerns that the country's Malay Muslim provinces—Pattani, Yala and Narithiwat—may be emerging as a new front for cross-border terrorism in Southeast Asia. In particular, regional and western authorities fear that outside militants, including cadres with ties to Jemaah Islamiyah (JI) and the broader international jihadist movement could be establishing a logistical and operational foothold to further the objectives of international Islamists. Yet while the nature and tempo of violence in southern Thailand has certainly changed over the last 24 months, there is no firm indication that this transformation is the result of external influences.

The Nature of the Insurgency

The nature of the current conflict in southern Thailand differs in several key respects from the limited, sporadic and largely ad-hoc insurgency that was waged throughout the 1980s and 1990s. First and foremost, the intensity of violence today is of a far higher order than in the past. During 2004, 878 attacks were recorded in the region, which represents a 25 percent increase over the average annual incident rate for the 1990s. The total casualties reached 841, including 325 deaths and 516 injuries. Figures in 2005 have continued to exhibit a rapidly escalating trend. Between January and September some 1,084 assaults took place, killing 367 people and wounding another 282 (Interview, Chulalongkorn University, November 2005).

Besides intensity, there are indications that the militants have developed the means to both produce and deploy larger, more powerful bombs. One improvised explosive device (IED) that was detonated in a car trunk on the Thai-Malay border in February 2005, for instance, weighed 50 kilograms. This stands in stark contrast to earlier rudimentary IEDs, most of which were in the 5 and 10 kilogram range and usually packaged in simple everyday items such as shopping bags, Tupperware lunch boxes and PVC tubing (Interviews, *The Nation* and Australian Embassy [Bangkok], November 2005).

In line with a higher tempo of violence, the mechanics of individual operations have steadily improved. This has been most apparent with cell phones, which are now routinely used to trigger improvised IEDs. These mechanisms are far more effective than the older, Chinese-made analog clocks that extremists have traditionally relied on, not least because they allow for external detonations in clear line of sight of a specific target and at a particular time (*Jane's Intelligence Review*, May 2005). In addition, attacks are now routinely being integrated and executed along a full modality spectrum—often embracing coordinated bombings, arson, assassinations and random shootings—to maximize overall impact.

The audacity and range of attacks have also expanded. In January 2004, one of the most brazen robberies ever to have taken place in the south occurred when a group of roughly 100 unidentified Muslims raided a Thai army camp in Narithiwat and made off with over 300 weapons, including assault rifles, machine guns and rocket propelled grenades (*Far Eastern Economic Review*, January 27, 2004). Two equally bold operations followed quickly on the heels of this now infamous foray. The first occurred on March 30 and involved masked gunmen who descended on a quarry in the Muang district of Yala and successfully stole 1.6 tons of ammonium nitrate, 56 sticks of dynamite and 176 detonators (*Jane's Intelligence Review*, May 2005). The second, known as the Krue Se Siege, took place on April 28 when machete-wielding militants attempted to overrun a string of police positions and military armories in Pattani. Over 100 attackers were ultimately killed in the incident, 31 of whom were shot after seeking refuge in the central Krue Se mosque.

More recently were the April 2005 simultaneous bombings of the Hat Yai International Airport, the French-owned Carrefour supermarket and the Green Palace World Hotel in Songkla. The three attacks generated widespread concern throughout the country, not least because they represented the first time that Malay extremists had struck outside the three separatist provinces and focused on venues liable to have consequences for wider Western and/or international interests (*The Bangkok Post*, April 4, 2005).

Finally, the nature of the current bout of instability in the south has been marked by an explicit jihadist undertone not apparent in past years. Reflective of this have been frequent attacks against drinking houses, gambling halls, karaoke bars and other establishments associated with Western decadence and secularism; the distribution of leaflets (allegedly printed in Malaysia) specifically warning locals of reprisals if they do not adopt traditional Muslim dress and observe the Friday holiday; and the increased targeting of monks and other Buddhist civilians—often through highly brutal means such as burnings and beheadings (2005 witnessed six decapitations)—in an apparent Taliban-style effort to undermine society by fostering religious-communal fear, conflict and hatred (Interviews, *The Nation*, November 2005).

External Influences or Local Imperatives?

Commentators have expressed concern that the altered and more acute nature of unrest in the Malay Muslim provinces could be indicative of growing external extremist penetration involving radicals with links to both JI and (through this movement) the broader global jihadist network. In particular, these officials remain worried that a process of fanatical Arabization similar to that which has occurred in Indonesia and the outlying Moro areas of the Philippine archipelago may now be taking place in Thailand's deep-south, possibly heralding the emergence of a new strategic theater for anti-Western terrorist attacks in Southeast Asia (Interviews, November 2005).

Compounding these fears are reports that money from Saudi Arabia, the United Arab Emirates (UAE) and Pakistan is increasingly being channeled to fund the construction of local Muslim boarding schools (or "ponoh," known as pondoks in Malaysia and pesenteren in Indonesia), private colleges and mosques dedicated to the articulation of hardline Wahhabist and Salafist teachings. A number of prominent clerics alleged to be connected to international Islamist elements have been tied to these institutions, including Ismail Yaralong (a.k.a Ustadz Soh, who is widely suspected of acting as spiritual inspiration for the Krue Se Siege) and Ismail Luphi (who has been directly connected to convicted Bali 2002 bombers Ali Ghufron and Amrozi) (Interview, *The Nation*, November 2005). A 2004 assessment by Thai military intelligence suggests there are at least 50 educational establishments scattered throughout Pattani, Yala and Narithiwat that have been decisively penetrated by Islamist forces to recruit and/or train their students for holy war (*Jane's Intelligence Review*, November 2004).

To a certain extent, it is reasonable to speculate that at least some outside Islamist entity has attempted to exploit the ongoing unrest in southern Thailand for its own purposes. To be sure, gaining a logistical and operational presence in this type of opportunistic theater is a well-recognized and established practice of networked movements such as al-Qaeda and JI. That said, there is as yet no concrete evidence to suggest the region has been decisively transformed into a new beachhead for pan-regional jihadism. While it is true the scale and sophistication of violence have increased, there is nothing to link this change in tempo to outside militant forces. Indeed, in the opinion of informed local commentators, the heightened intensity of attacks reflects learning and development on the part of indigenous rebel groups, possibly combined with the infusion of an increasingly competitive criminal interplay involving gambling syndicates, drug lords and corrupt members of the security forces and political elite. Moreover, these same sources are quick to point out that unlike the situations in Mindanao and Indonesia, there is no established expanse of rebel-held territory in Pattani, Yala or Narithiwat that external extremists could use to institute a concerted regimen of international terrorist training (Interviews, November 2005).

Equally, although there is a definite religious element to many of the attacks that are currently taking place in the three Malay provinces, it is not apparent that this has altered the essential localized and nationalistic aspect of the conflict. At root, the objective is to protect the region's unique identity and traditional way of life—both from the (perceived) unjust incursions of the Thai Buddhist state and, just as importantly, the unprecedented influx of cross border movements of trade, commerce and people. As one Bangkok-based journalist puts it: "Muslims are now standing up for Muslim rights, which together with globalization, has catalyzed the insurgency [onto a more explicit] religious plane" (Interview, Chulalongkorn University, November 2005).

Perhaps the clearest reason to believe that the southern Thai conflict has not metastasized into a broader jihadist struggle, however, is the fact that there has been no migration of violence north, much less to other parts of Southeast Asia. Indeed, there appears to have been a deliberate strategic decision on the part of rebels on the ground—including those associated with the Barisan Revolusi Nasional Co-ordinate, an ad-hoc, loosely based alliance that has claimed responsibility for many of the attacks that have occurred over the last 24 months—to not explicitly tie the Malay cause to wider Islamic designs (Interview, *The Nation*, November 2005). Again, this stands in stark contrast to organizations such as the Abu Sayyaf Group and the Rajah Soliaman Revolutionary Movement, both of which claim to be fighting for Moro Muslim interests in the southern Philippines, but each of which has been directly connected to JI as well as bombings that have occurred well beyond their primary theater (such as the 2005 Valentine's Day bombings in Manila).

As noted above, one cannot dismiss the possibility that at least some external penetration may have taken place in southern Thailand. Accurately disaggregating the extent to which this has actually taken place, however, is of vital importance—both as an issue of substance and policy. To inappropriately conflate local grievances and objectives with outside imperatives will not only serve to greatly complicate the possibility of peace agreements on the ground, but also risk creating the very conditions for the type of cross-border radicalism that governments in this part of the world so fear.

[From Terrorism Monitor, Volume IV, Issue 1]

Alternate Futures for Thailand's Insurgency

Zachary Abuza

Originally published on January 25, 2006

The Thai insurgency has formally entered its third straight year. Between January 2004 and January 2006, more than 1,200 people were killed. In January 2004, violent incidents averaged 30 per month; by December 2004, violent incidents averaged 120 per month. By June 2005, bombings averaged more than one per day. More than 300 were killed and more than 300 wounded in the six months following the introduction of the Emergency Decree in July 2005 (*The Bangkok Post*, October 24, 2005). In 2006 alone, 19 people have been killed, seven in one day—five of whom were policemen. The presence of over 40,000 security forces has done little to stop the insurgency.

While the majority of victims are killed in drive-by shootings and assassinations, the technical capacity of the bombs has increased dramatically. Thai Muslim bomb-makers now assemble 10 kilogram bombs composed of a variety of components, including powergel, TNT, potassium chlorate and ammonium nitrate. The detonators have become sophisticated to the point that the government had to block all un-registered pre-paid cell phones in the three southernmost provinces. Authorities also have evidence that the militants are now experimenting with infrared devices as detonators, although they have not consistently deployed these bombs (*The Nation*, November 29, 2005). The Thai militants are also learning techniques from abroad. According to a senior intelligence official, "They have stolen cement kilometer road markers to make bombs, for which we have seen instructions posted on some web sites in the Middle East" (Reuters, October 6, 2005).

The insurgents have also become more sophisticated in a number of other ways. Not only are attacks becoming more clinically precise, but there was an increase in coordinated attacks in 2005. For example, October 26, 2005 saw 34 coordinated night-time attacks that left six people dead in raids (Associated Press, October 27, 2005). In another incident, 18 locations in six different districts were hit in one night. In another, militants hit two dozen outposts in one night, killing five and seizing 42 firearms (*The Nation*, October 27, 2005). More than 100 government weapons were stolen by militants between November and December 2005. On January 18, 2006, militants launched 101 coordinated arson attacks across three provinces.

What was also notable about attacks in 2005 was that they became more shocking and more brutal with the purpose of inciting revulsion and fear. There have now been 24 beheadings, one of which was done before a crowded tea house. In October 2005, 15 militants stormed a Buddhist temple and hacked to death a monk, killed a novice monk, torched their bodies and set the living quarters on fire. The incident gripped the country (*The Nation*, October 17, 2005).

While the government claims it has arrested 190 insurgents responsible for conducting or planning operations, there are still glaring shortages of information. Very few if any of the leaders of the insurgency have been arrested. There are still some 247 "red zones," villages controlled by insurgents. There is little reason to share the government's optimism. Indeed, on January 19, 2006, Deputy Prime Minister Chidchai Wannasathit, who claimed credit for the 190 arrests, recently lashed out at the state's intelligence services for their inability to stop the bloodletting.

The intelligence failure has been so great because Thai officials have rounded up the usual suspects: the old ethno-nationalist groups, such as the Pattani United Liberation Organization (PULO), that were active through the mid-1990s, but are now defunct. The current insurgency is being led by two Islamist organizations that the Thai government has always considered peripheral: the Gerakan Mujahideen Islami Pattan (GMIP) and the Barisan Revolusi Nasional-Coordinate (BRN-C). Their leaders are younger, Middle-Eastern-trained ustadz who have never appeared on the government's radar screen.

There is also a misunderstanding about the nature of the insurgency. This is not an insurgency about physical space, but an insurgency about mental space. Moreover, it is an intra-Muslim conflict. Since March 2005, militants have killed more of their co-religionists than they have Buddhists. Put simply, the militants are ideologically and religiously motivated; they are trying to impose a very austere and intolerant form of Islam on their society and they countenance no opposition to this. The militants are going after not just collaborators, or individuals who receive a government salary, but also Muslim clerics who perform funeral rites for murtad, or apostates, as well as teachers who work in schools that have mixed curriculums.

The militants have issued a number of threats to their own community. Such threats include forcing businesses to close on Fridays, with the failure to obey resulting in death or the amputation of ears; militants also warn imams not to conduct funeral rites for Muslim security forces, guards at state schools, government employees, or "anyone who receive salaries from the state," and warn people not to send their children to state-run schools. These threats are made from a perceived position of strength. The militants have introduced the Wahhabi culture of takfiri—condemning fellow Muslims for their lax interpretation of Islam. They seem undeterred that the threats are broadly unpopular among the Muslim population. The militants are not trying to create a mass-based movement, but rather to impose a strict interpretation of Islam on society. They believe that this outcome will strengthen the Muslim community. It appears that their strategy is working since the stream of intelligence from the villages has dried up.

Three Potential Possibilities for the Future of Thailand's Insurgency

The least likely possibility for the future of Thailand's insurgency is the development of a broader insurgency. This development is unlikely because the insurgents do not have enough personnel, guns or a steady supply of ammunition. The insurgents would also face a more hostile external environment from the Malaysians. Additionally, it is likely that the insurgents understand that a broadened insurgency is one that the Royal Thai Army is the best equipped to counter. An emboldened insurgency would require 1,000 to 2,000 men and significantly more material resources. Moreover, the training and quality of the insurgency to date have wavered. Some groups have improved their hit and run tactics and have begun using roadside IEDs with a small arms assault. Yet these improved tactics have not occurred on a regular basis. Indeed, attacks seem disjointed because the cell structure is so compartmentalized and autonomous from the leadership.

The second possibility is for the insurgency to move to the next level by launching attacks on Bangkok or Phuket. This is obviously a nightmare scenario for the government, although one that it vehemently denies is a possibility. To date, the militants have shown an unwillingness to engage in this type of operation. They clearly have the technical capability to undertake such attacks, but are obviously alarmed at the government's reaction to such an operation. There are insurgent leaders, however, who precisely want to provoke a harsh government response that will legitimize them in the eyes of their constituents. Moreover, if the current rate of arrests remains steady, they may engage in terrorism out of desperation. Indeed, there have been a number of arrests— including three individuals scouting targets in Bangkok in November 2005—suggesting that an attack on an out-of-area soft target is being considered as an option. Such an attack would also attract greater attention and international support for their cause, which, to date, has been negligible.

The third and most plausible possibility is that the conflict remains at the status quo: a low-level insurgency coupled with intensified dakwah (religious propagation activities). It appears that this is the path upon which the insurgents have settled. First, in their eyes it has been very successful. The insurgency is much further along than was expected a year ago. Second, it is within their current range of material and human resources and technical know-how. Third, they need this type of violence within their community to enforce their values.

Yet, this strategy also makes the insurgents vulnerable in a number of ways. First, if they cannot raise the violence to the next level, then it becomes a menace in the region, but one that can be contained and that people learn to live with. Second, it gives the government time to improve their intelligence operations. For instance, there is already more actionable intelligence that has led to more arrests. Moreover, it gives the government ways to come up with additional counter-insurgent plans, such as the mobile phone registration.

In the face of a government counter-insurgency, the militants can easily retreat back to the mosques and pondoks in which they can recruit and proselytize anew. In such a scenario, the government would declare victory while the insurgency would simply incubate as it did over the past decade.

[From Terrorism Focus, Volume III, Issue 3]

Maritime Terrorism

The Threat of Maritime Terrorism in the Malacca Straits

Catherine Zara Raymond

Originally published on February 9, 2006

The Joint War Committee (JWC) of Lloyd's Market Association announced last week that the Malacca Straits would remain on its list of areas at risk from terrorism and other related perils. The announcement came despite a collective campaign by the three littoral states of Indonesia, Malaysia and Singapore to have the Malacca Straits removed from the list (*Jakarta Post*, January 22, 2006). The decision of the Joint War Committee is based on risk assessments of the region, which concluded that the Straits are a terrorist target. This will mean increased shipping costs for ships transiting the Straits. When similar war insurance premiums were applied to ships calling at Yemeni Ports following the terrorist attack on the French supertanker the MV Limburg in 2002, the impact on the Yemeni economy was severe.

The initial decision in June 2005 to put the Malacca Straits on the JWC list caused an outcry from the three littoral states. According to the Singapore Shipping Association, the classification is "unjustified and an exaggeration of the actual situation" and "the committee's decision does not do justice to the efforts put in by the littoral states" (*Jakarta Post*, January 22, 2006). This view was supported by Malaysian Deputy Prime Minister Datuk Seri Najib Razak who declared that "there existed an unfair perception of the security situation in the Straits" (*New Straits Times*, December 5, 2005). Indeed, over the last three decades maritime terrorist attacks have constituted only two percent of all terrorist attacks worldwide and, apart from a small number of hostage-taking incidents, none of these have taken place in the Malacca Straits. In addition, despite predictions by academics and the media alike that it was only a matter of time before the Straits were blocked by an attack or that ships in the Straits would be used as "floating bombs," this has not been the case.

This article seeks to assess the extent of the threat of maritime terrorism in Southeast Asia and in particular in the Malacca Straits, a waterway of great strategic and economic importance.

The Threat of Maritime Terrorism

It is well known that Southeast Asia is home to a number of militant Islamic groups. These include the Abu Sayyaf Group (ASG), which is based in the Philippines, the Free Aceh Movement (GAM) in Aceh, Indonesia, Jemaah Islamiyah (JI), which primarily operates from Indonesia, and the Moro Islamic Liberation Front (MILF) based in the Philippines. The al-Qaeda network is also believed to have established a presence in the region following the destruction of its bases in Afghanistan. All of these groups are known to use the maritime environment for logistical purposes, have developed maritime capability or have made preliminary steps toward acquiring capability in this area. In addition, either through statements or past activities, all of these groups have displayed a desire to target economic or maritime targets.

In 2001, it was revealed that JI had planned to attack U.S. naval warships visiting the region. More recently, evidence suggests that JI has been conducting training in the southern Philippines in order to develop underwater destruction capability. ASG was responsible for what has been labeled the most lethal maritime terrorist incident since 2000 with its attack on the MV Superferry 14 in Manila in 2004, which killed over 100 people (*Philippine Daily Inquirer*, June 13, 2004). GAM admitted to carrying out an attack on a boat being chartered by Exxon Mobil in 2002 in Aceh and is suspected to have carried out a number of kidnap-for-ransom attacks on vessels in Indonesian waters during the last four years. MILF is responsible for attacks on Philippine shipping, mainly placing bombs on inter-island ferries being used to transport members of the armed forces and Christians to and from Mindanao.

Another issue that has caused alarm and has reinforced the perception that the region and its waterways are at risk from terrorism is the massive increase in incidents of piracy during the last decade. Not only has the high frequency of pirate attacks drawn attention to the vulnerability of shipping in the region, but there has also been a worry that pirates and terrorists could join forces. In particular, terrorists could employ the pirates' great wealth of maritime knowledge to carry out a devastating attack on a commercial port or a shipping operation (*The Business Times Singapore*, May 21, 2004).

The evidence certainly points to the fact that the threat from maritime terrorism in Southeast Asia is real. Given that the Malacca Straits has been described as one of the arteries of the regional if not global economy, and is transited on an annual basis by approximately 63,000 ships, an attack on shipping in this waterway would also seem to be a real possibility. Nevertheless, no such attack has yet materialized.

ASG and MILF traditionally operate within their locality of the Philippines and its surrounding archipelagic waters; it would be uncharacteristic of them to carry out an attack on shipping in the Malacca Straits. This is related to the fact that they are both separatist groups, with the aim of establishing an independent Islamic state in the Philippines. Therefore, their targets tend to be either located within the country, or closely associated with it. GAM is also a separatist group and while there may be some overlap in terms of its area of operations and the Malacca Straits, its targets have traditionally included the Indonesian military and security forces. In addition, GAM has just signed a peace agreement with the Indonesian government, which includes the disarmament and demobilization of its 3000 fighters (*PNG Post-Courier*, August 23, 2005).

Through this process of elimination, the group that would appear to be the only real threat to shipping in the Malacca Straits is JI. The group has shown an interest in attacking shipping in the Straits and vessels visiting Changi Naval Base in Singapore and is suspected of developing more expertise in this area. Its maritime capability, however, remains underdeveloped when compared to its land capability. Attacks against targets in the maritime domain would require specialized equipment and skills; depending on the target, they may also require knowledge of shipping patterns, boat operation and maintenance, and boarding techniques. This explains the predictions of a piracy-terrorism nexus, of which there is still no evidence. Various explanations have been proffered as to why there is still no sign of any cooperation between pirates and terrorists. One explanation is that the majority of those committing acts of piracy in the Malacca Straits are largely unorganized petty criminals who use piracy as a way of supplementing their inadequate income. These small groups and individuals may not be willing to cooperate with terrorists who, through their high-profile activities, may trigger a complete crackdown on all maritime crime.

Carrying out an attack in the maritime domain also presents a number of difficulties that are not encountered on land. First, if the aftermath of an attack is to be captured by the media, which is often the wish of a terrorist group, then the attack needs to be carried out close to land. This then considerably compresses the theater of operations, as only coastal areas and ports would be suitable. Second, surveillance at sea of potential targets offers less cover and concealment than on land and entails the same environmental challenges as any maritime activity.

Conclusion

The threat of maritime terrorism in Southeast Asia and specifically in the Malacca Straits is real and should not be ignored. Yet, an accurate and comprehensive understanding of the threat is paramount. This is vital for the development and implementation of targeted and effective counter-measures. Due to the complexities of operating within the maritime domain and the unpredictable nature of the marine environment, attacking targets on land has remained the preferred choice of many of the region's terrorist groups. Until there is a significant level of target hardening on land, this is likely to remain the case in the future.

In addition, following 9/11 much has been done to enhance maritime security in the region. Measures include the introduction of the "Eyes in the Sky" aerial patrols last year, the Trilateral Coordinated Patrols implemented in 2004 and the creation of the International Ship and Port Facility Security Code in the same year. The implementation of these initiatives has helped to reduce some of the vulnerabilities of the maritime industry. If this level of cooperative activity continues, the result should be an even further reduction of the threat from maritime terrorism.

[From Terrorism Monitor, Volume IV, Issue 3]

Maritime Terrorism in Southeast Asia: Potential Scenarios

Catherine Zara Raymond

Originally published on April 6, 2006

In Southeast Asia, home to one of the world's most strategic sea lanes—the Straits of Malacca, and the world's second largest port, Singapore—the vulnerability of the maritime sector is of great concern. As a result, over the last few years various scenarios of how terrorists might carry out an attack in the maritime domain have been put forward by the media and academics alike. Many of these potential scenarios are extremely unlikely due to their complicated nature and their sheer impracticability. Nevertheless, a great number of these scenarios have remained unchallenged due to a lack of knowledge of the geography of the region, local shipping patterns and the nature of the commercial shipping industry in general. This has led to a misunderstanding of the threat posed by maritime terrorism.

This article seeks to address this problem by examining the credibility of a number of these scenarios. In addition, several other scenarios will be discussed which have received little or no attention in the literature on maritime security, but which if carried out by terrorist groups could potentially have a serious impact on both Singapore and the efficient flow of global trade through the region's strategic sea lanes.

Scenario: Ship Sunk to Block the Straits of Malacca

In an article in Singapore's major broadsheet newspaper, *The Straits Times* on March 27, 2004, an "expert" on maritime security is quoted as saying that "If terrorists want to mount a maritime strike here [Southeast Asia], sinking a ship in the Malacca Straits is the likely attack of choice." He goes on to say that "It would enable them to wreak economic havoc worldwide by blocking the sea lane, and is also the easiest way to attack."

This scenario is clearly impossible for one key reason: the narrowest point of the marked channel in the Malacca Straits is at One Fathom Bank, where the width is 0.6 nautical miles. Even if a ship was sunk at this point, which itself is not necessarily an easy task to accomplish, it would not block the Straits. Ships could continue to use the waterway by simply navigating around the sunken vessel.

Scenario: Tanker as Floating Bomb to Strike Ports

The second possible scenario was summed up by Singapore's Foreign Minister George Yeo in a speech given to the ASEAN Regional Forum on July 29, 2005: "Terrorists could hijack an LNG [Liquefied Natural Gas] tanker and blow it up in Singapore harbor. Singapore, of course, would be devastated. But the impact on global trade would also be severe and incalculable" (Ministry of Foreign Affairs, Singapore). As this statement implies, the potential threat of terrorists hijacking one of the many vessels passing through the region, particularly those carrying high-risk cargos, such as LNG, crude oil or other such inflammable chemical products, is of great concern to the Singapore government.

In addition, the high number of pirate attacks in the region, a number of which have involved the hijacking of these more high-risk vessels, has led to the worry that terrorists could use copycat methods to take over a vessel for more sinister reasons. In a visit to Malaysia in 2005, Vice Admiral Terry Cross of the U.S. Coast Guard told the media that the ease with which pirate attacks were taking place in the Malacca Straits could "alert terrorists to the opportunities for seizing oil tankers" and that "these could be used as floating bombs" (*The Straits Times*, April 18, 2005). In a similar vein, when the 1,289-ton MT Tri Samudra was boarded by pirates in the Malacca Straits, the regional manager of the International Maritime Bureau was quoted as saying: "This is exactly the type of tanker that terrorists would likely use to attack a shore-based port or other facility" (*The Business Times Singapore*, March 15, 2005). The Tri Samudra is a chemical tanker that was carrying a full cargo of inflammable petrochemical products when it was hijacked.

There are a number of issues related to this scenario that need to be considered when assessing how likely it would be and what particular form it would take. The first issue is the differing capacity of each vessel and its cargo to cause damage and the means by which this could be made possible by determined terrorists. The second issue is the actual impact on the port or facility itself.

LNG tankers and their potential role in a scenario of this kind have probably received the most attention. In its liquid state, natural gas is not explosive, and it is in this form that it is shipped in large quantities via refrigerated tankers. Once in the open air, LNG quickly evaporates and forms a highly combustible visible cloud. It has been reported that if ignited the resulting fire could be hot enough to melt steel at a distance of 1,200 feet, and could result in second-degree burns on exposed skin a mile away (Council of Foreign Relations, February 11, 2006). A fire of this magnitude would be impossible to extinguish. It would burn until all its fuel was spent. The impact of such a fire on a port like Singapore would be devastating. There would be loss of life and severe structural damage in the immediate area. This would mean that the port would have to operate at a reduced capacity, causing delays in trade and a loss of business.

The most likely way that terrorists would carry out an attack using an LNG tanker would be to create an explosion onboard the vessel as it is rammed into the target. If powerful enough this could rupture the hull and cause the gas to escape. The force required to breach the hull and tank, however, would almost certainly cause a fire at the tank location which would ignite the gas as it escaped rather than causing a cloud of fire or plume. Thus, the potential damage would be limited somewhat to the tanker's location.

If the vessel chosen was an oil tanker carrying crude oil or petroleum products, its explosive capability would depend on the nature of the cargo and whether or not the vessel had a full load. Crude oil itself is difficult to ignite; its vapor, however, which may remain in the tanks after the vessel has unloaded its cargo, is more easily ignited. The most likely risk to the target port or facility is that of a localized fire, explosion (particularly in the case of volatile petroleum products), and the consequences of a potential oil spill.

The risk from a vessel carrying chemical products is also worrisome. Chemical products may pose a toxicity risk in addition to being highly volatile. Like LNG tankers, chemical tankers are designed with the maximum provisions for safety. The vessels are designed in such a way as to maintain space between tank walls to prevent incompatible cargos from coming into contact with each other. The safeguards in place, however, may not always be sufficient and may not be designed to guard against deliberate sabotage. In addition, general cargo vessels and container ships (which may not have such safeguards in place) are also sometimes used.

Scenario: Malacca Straits Blocked by Mines

One scenario that has not received much attention is the potential for the Malacca Straits to be blocked by mines. There are two variations of this scenario, both equally alarming. The first is that terrorists mine the Straits and the authorities are alerted to this fact either by a declaration from the perpetrators or because a ship hits a mine. The second is that terrorists merely claim to have mined the Straits and simulate a mine attack on a ship to add credibility to their claims. In each scenario, assuming that there is little or no information on the exact area of the Straits that has been mined, the impact would be the same—the Malacca Straits would be closed to shipping traffic, forcing the vessels, particularly those on international voyages, to reroute around the Lombok and Sunda Straits. This would cause severe delays to shipping as these alternate routes are longer. Additionally, shipping costs would increase and world trade would be affected. The impact on the region's economies could be severe if the closure lasted more than a few days.

Scenario: Missile Launched at Aircraft from Vessel

The final scenario, and again one which has not been widely discussed, is terrorists using a portable surface-to-air missile (SAM), launched from a ship, to bring down a commercial airliner. This would be of concern to Singapore where planes coming into land must make their descent over the busy shipping lane—the Singapore Straits. While arrangements may be in place to reduce the possibility of a SAM being fired from the shore in Singapore, the same cannot be said about ships passing off-shore.

SAMs can be purchased on the black market for a starting price of $10,000 and have a range which puts aircraft that are landing or in a holding pattern waiting to land well within their targeting capability. The missile could be launched from one of the many hundreds of small vessels transiting the Singapore Straits. The impact on Singapore would be massive; not only due to the loss of life, closure of the airport and the immediate effect on the Singaporean economy, but also because there would be no way of guaranteeing that a similar attack would not be carried out in the future. Short of inspecting the contents of every ship that passes though the Singapore Straits, the law enforcement agencies can do very little to reduce this particular threat.

Conclusion

The key to gauging the extent of the threat posed by maritime terrorism lies not only in an assessment of the capabilities and motivations of the terrorist groups themselves, but also in an understanding of the maritime environment, shipping practices, the vulnerabilities of the commercial shipping industry and the response capabilities of those agencies tasked with safeguarding the region's shipping lanes. Uninformed claims regarding potential maritime terrorist scenarios, which are based on a misunderstanding or a complete lack of knowledge of these key factors, has led to a misinterpretation of the threat from maritime terrorism. This must be rectified if there is to be any hope of reducing the threat.

[From Terrorism Monitor, Volume IV, Issue 7]

Indonesia and Jemaah Islamiyah

The Emir: An Interview with Abu Bakar Ba'asyir, Alleged Leader of the Southeast Asian Jemaah Islamiyah Organization

Scott Atran

Originally published on March 9, 2006

This interview was conducted on August 13 and 15, 2005 from Cipinang Prison in Jakarta. Questions were formulated by Dr. Scott Atran and posed for him in Bahasa Indonesian by Taufiq Andrie. The interview took place in a special visitor's room, where Ba'asyir had seven acolytes acting as his bodyguards, including Taufiq Halim, the perpetrator of the Atrium mall bombing in Jakarta, and Abdul Jabbar, who blew up the Philippines ambassador's house. The transcript follows the short introduction below.

Background

In this interview, the alleged terrorist leader Abu Bakar Ba'asyir provides his justification for waging jihad against the West. He also explains the calculus of suicide bombers and discusses his interpretation of Islam concerning war and infidels. Despite accusations that he is head of the al-Qaeda-linked Jemaah Islamiyah (JI) terrorist organization and has planned the most lethal terrorist attacks in Southeast Asia, Ba'asyir has only been convicted on conspiracy charges in the 2002 attack on a Bali nightclub that killed 202 people. His 30-month sentence for his role in that bombing, which included scores of Australian tourists among the casualties, was recently reduced by four months and 15 days.

Just outside the visitor's cell is Hasyim, who runs Ba'asyir's daily errands. Hasyim is a member of Majlis Mujahideen Indonesian (MMI), the country's umbrella organization for militant Islamist groups headed by Ba'asyir. Like many Jemaah Islamiyah (JI) members, including Ba'asyir and JI founder Abdullah Sungkar, Hasyim originally came from

Darul Islam, a post-independence group banned by the Suharto regime that has operated semi-clandestinely in Indonesian society much as the Muslim Brotherhood has in the Middle East.

In 1993, Sungkar split from DI, bringing with him most of the Indonesian Afghan Alumni that he and Ba'asyir had sent to fight the Soviets. Until Suharto's downfall in 1998, Sungkar and Ba'asyir expanded their network of Islamist schools from exile in Malaysia, funneling students to training camps in Afghanistan and the Philippines, and expanding JI's influence across Southeast Asia. After Sungkar's death in 1999, Ba'asyir became "Emir" of JI – a position and organization whose existence he publicly denies but for which there is overwhelming evidence, including from current and former JI members Dr. Atran has interviewed. Although Sungkar himself established direct ties with bin Laden, it is under Ba'asyir's stewardship that JI has adopted key aspects of al-Qaeda's ideology and methods, targeting the interests of the 'far enemy' (the U.S. and its allies) with suicide bombings (Bali, Marriot Jakarta, Australian Embassy) in support of global jihad.

Referred to as Ustadz ("teacher"), Ba'asyir is surrounded by visiting family and students who offer him a daily assortment of news magazines and food, especially dates, his favorite. His disciples tend to be well-educated, often university graduates, and they wash his clothes. Ba'asyir's wife visits him once a month, and Ustadz offers to share the food she prepared with his prison mates, including Christians. He is a lanky, bespectacled Hadrami (a descendent from the Hadramawt region of Yemen, like bin Laden and Sungkar) who fasts twice a week, on Mondays and Thursdays. He is 66 and seemingly in good health. Dressed in a white robe, red sarong and white cap, he is sitting on a wooden chair, one foot up perched on the edge. He exudes politeness and is all smiles, with a strong voice and easy laugh he answers questions as if teaching.

Q. You say that it is fardh 'ain [an individual obligation] for Muslims to wage jihad against infidels.

A. There are two types of infidels. The infidel who is against Islam and declares war on Islam is called kafir harbi [enemy infidel]. The second type is kafir dhimmi [protected infidel]. These are people who don't fight against Islam, but don't embrace it either and basically remain neutral.

Q. When in Cipinang, did Ustadz meet Father Damanik? [1] Is he kafir dhimmi?

A. Yes, I was visited and was respected by him. I plan, if Allah allows me, to pay a visit to his house. That's what I call "muamalah dunia," daily relations in the secular life. Because al-Qur'an sura 60 verse 8 says that "Allah encourages us to be kind and just to the people who don't fight us in religion and don't help people who fight us" so we are encouraged by Allah to be good and just to them. It means that we can help those who aren't against us. On these matters we can cooperate, but we also have to follow the norms of Sharia. If Sharia says not to doing something, then we shouldn't do it. Sharia never prohibited business in the secular world except in very minor things. So it is generally allowed to conduct business with non-Muslims. We can help each other. For example, if we are sick and they help us, then if they become sick, we should help them. When they die we should accompany their dead bodies to the grave even though we can't pray for them.

Q. What is the principle of Hudaybiyah [the covenant between Prophet Muhammad and the People of the Book]?

A. Hudaybiyah means different things according to the legal situation. When Islam is strong, we come to the infidel's country, not to colonize but to watch over it so that the infidel cannot plan to ruin Islam. Everywhere, infidels conspire to ruin Islam. There is no infidel who wouldn't destroy Islam if they were given even a small chance. Therefore, we have to be vigilant.

Q. What are the conditions for Islam to be strong?

A. If there is a state, the infidel country must be visited and spied upon. My argument is that if we don't come to them, they will persecute Islam. They will prevent non-Muslims converting to Islam.

Q. Does being a martyr mean being a suicide bomber?

A. As I explained [the day before] yesterday, there are two types of infidel terms for suicide: first, those who commit suicide out of hopelessness, second, those who commit suicide in order to be remembered as a hero. Both are types of suicide and there is no value in it.

In Islam there are also people who commit suicide out of hopelessness and we call this killing oneself. But if a person defends Islam, and according to his calculations must die in doing so, although he works hard in life, he will still go and die for Islam.

The consideration is: "if I do this, will Islam benefit or lose? If I must die and without my dying Islam will not win, then my dying is allowed." If one can avoid dying that is better. But to die is also permitted. That we called istimata or istijhad. Istimata [to seek death, also istishhad to become a shaheed] means looking to become a shaheed [martyr] and istijhad [becoming a jihadi] means the same. Because to die in jihad is noble.

According to Islam, to die is a necessity because everyone dies. But to seek the best death is what we call "Husn ul-Khatimah," and the best way to die is to die as a shaheed.

Q. Would it be possible for an act of martyrdom to be aborted if the same results can be assured by other actions? For example, a roadside bomb.

A. For sure, if there are better ways to carry out an action and we don't have to sacrifice our lives, those ways must be chosen. Because our strength can be used for other purposes.

Q. Is it acceptable to postpone a martyrdom action in order to make the hajj [pilgrimage to Mecca]?

A. A martyrdom action cannot be postponed in this case because jihad is more important than making the hajj. For example one of most revered ulema, Ibn Taymiyya, was asked by a rich person, "O Sheikh, I have so much money but I'm confused about donating my money because there are two needy causes. There are poor people who, if I don't help, will die of starvation. But if I use the money for this purpose, then the Jihad will lack funding. Therefore, I need your fatwah [religious decision] O Sheikh." Ibn Taymiyya replied: "Give all your money for jihad. If the poor people die, it is because Allah fated it, because if we lose the Jihad, many more people will die."

There is no better deed than jihad. None. The highest deed in Islam is jihad. If we commit to jihad, we can neglect other deeds. America wants to wipe out the teaching of jihad through Ahmadiyah [an Islamic school of thought that believes that Pakistan's Mirza Ghulam Ahmad is the Prophet Muhammad's successor]. America works through this organization. Why? Because Ahmadiyah prohibits its followers to undertake jihad because [they argue] jihad is the teaching of Christians. This organization originates from India. Its headquarters are in London, and it is funded by America. Ahmadiyah is America's tool to destroy Islam, including JIL [Jaringan Islam Liberal, Islamic Liberal Network], an NGO in Jakarta that advocates a liberal form of Islam. It is funded by USAID.

Q. So postponement is not allowed in any circumstances, even in order to visit sick parents?

A. No, no. If we are in jihad, the jihad must come first. Unless jihad is in [the state of] fardh kifayah [a collective duty, for the nation]. If jihad is in [the state of] fardh 'ain [an individual duty], jihad must be number one. There is no obligation to ask permission from one's parents. But even if jihad is still in the fardh kifayah state, such as jihad to spy on infidel countries, Muslims don't require their parent's permission.

Q. Can a martyrdom action be permanently abandoned if there is a good chance that the martyr's family would be killed in a retaliation action? Similarly if the community where the martyr is from will also experience retaliation and casualties?

A. That is the risk and the consequence of jihad. If the martyr's family understands Islam deeply, they will obtain many rewards. Their reward will come, if they understand. A martyr must have ikhlas [sincerity]. The parent who understands this concept must be thankful to Allah. This is the spirit of jihad that most scares the infidels. This is a moral force. According to General De Gaulle, moral force is 80% and actual action only 20% [of successful combat]. For infidels the motivation is to be a hero or [to die for] the nation. Some are even encouraged to drink [alcohol] so that they can become brave. Russia was badly defeated in Afghanistan. [Afghanistan] is different than Eastern Europe which could be conquered in only a month or two. Russians thought [that they could conquer] Afghanistan in two weeks maximum because its people were backward, isn't that right? That was Russia's calculation based on their experience in Eastern Europe. But Afghanistan fought Russia back with their aqidah [by following Islamic doctrine] in the way of jihad.

I'll tell you a story so that you'll understand. There was an Afghan mother who made cakes. She asked her children to distribute the cakes to the mujahideen. One by one her children were hit by shells on their way to deliver the cakes. When the mujahideen informed her they said: "Dear mother, please be strong because your children are martyred." [The mother replied]: "I'm not crying for my children but I'm crying because I don't know who'll bring my cakes to the mujahideen." Then one of the mujahideen agreed to replace her children. So, this is the spirit of jihad. You find ikhlas and willingness. Prophet Muhammad said: "I want to make jihad then die, then live again, then do jihad again, then live again, then jihad - for ten times." This is because of the noble status for Muslims who became shaheed.

Q. Do you think the community which believes in martyrdom cares if the martyr only manages to blow up himself/herself and fails to kill any of the enemy?

A. No, [provided that] the ni'at [intention] to be a shaheed must be for Allah. During battle it is different. Istimata is also different. Still, the whole notion revolves around martyrdom. But in places like London and in America there must be other calculations. In battle it is best to cause as many casualties as possible.

Q. Do you think God favors or cares more for the martyr who manages to kill 100 enemies or one enemy?

A. The value [nilai] and reward [pahala] is the same.

Q. In regard to the global condition, what kind of things can the West, especially America, do to make this world more peaceful. What kind of attitudes must be changed?

A. They have to stop fighting Islam, but that's impossible because it is "sunnatullah" [destiny, a law of nature], as Allah has said in the Qur'an. They will constantly be enemies. But they'll lose. I say this not because I am able to predict the future but they will lose and Islam will win. That was what the Prophet Muhammad has said. Islam must win and Westerners will be destroyed. But we don't have to make them enemies if they allow Islam to continue to grow so that in the end they will probably agree to be under Islam. If they refuse to be under Islam, it will be chaos. Full stop. If they want to have peace, they have to accept to be governed by Islam.

Q. What if they persist?

A. We'll keep fighting them and they'll lose. The batil [falsehood] will lose sooner or later. I sent a letter to Bush. I said that you'll lose and there is no point for you [to fight us]. This [concept] is found in the Qur'an. The other day, I asked my lawyer to send that letter to the [U.S.] embassy. I don't know whether the embassy passed on my letter to Bush [telling him], "You are useless, you'll lose." There are verses in the Qur'an that say, "You spend so much money yet you'll be disappointed." The verse is clear so I'm not some one who can predict the future but I get the information from Allah, so I'll never be sad because I believe the time will come. Still, I feel that the Ummah [Muslim community] has a problem now. If the Ummah loses the [current] battle it isn't because of Islam. A Muslim, as long as he is not "broken" [and remains committed to Allah's rule] will get help from Allah.

Q. How about using nuclear weapons by Muslims, is it justified?

A. Yes, if necessary. But the Islamic Ummah should seek to minimalize [the intensity of the fighting]. Allah has said in verse 8 chapter 60 that we should equip ourself with weapon power—that is an order—but preferably to scare and not to kill our enemy. The main goal is to scare them. If they are scared they won't bother us, and then we won't bother them as well. But if they persist, we have to kill them. In this way, Prophet Muhammad sought to minimalize the fighting.

Q. In your personal view, what do you think of bombings in our homeland, namely the Bali, Marriott and Kuningan bombings?

A. I call those who carried out these actions all mujahid. They all had a good intention, that is, Jihad in Allah's way, the aim of the jihad is to look for blessing from Allah. They are right that America is the proper target because America fights Islam. So in terms of their objectives, they are right, and the target of their attacks was right also. But their calculations are debatable. My view is that we should do bombings in conflict areas not in peaceful areas. We have to target the place of the enemy, not countries where many Muslims live.

Q. What do you mean by "wrong calculation," that the victims included Muslims?

A. That was one of them. In my calculation, if there are bombings in peaceful areas, this will cause fitnah [discord] and other parties will be involved. This is my opinion and I could be wrong. Yet I still consider them mujahid. If they made mistakes, they are only human beings who can be wrong. Moreover, their attacks could be considered as self-defense.

Q. Does that mean you think they didn't attack?

A. No, they didn't attack because they defended themselves. They shouldn't be punished. In Bali where 200 people died, it was America's bomb. That was a major attack and Amrozi [the Bali plotter who bought the explosives] doesn't have the capability to do that. [2]

Q. Did Amrozi tell you this himself?

A. He was surprised to see the explosion. When he said that it was Allah's help he was right but he didn't make that bomb. America did. There is much evidence to this effect and so the police dare not continue their investigations. According to England's expert, that bomb was not Amrozi's bomb. You should ask Fauzan. He knows this subject. That bomb was a CIA Jewish bomb. The Mossad cooperates with the CIA. [3] I had an exchange of views with the police and they didn't say anything. I said to them, "You are stupid to punish Amrozi if he really knows how to make such a bomb. You should hire him to be a military consultant, because there is no military or police person [in Indonesia] who can make such a bomb." However, when I asked Ali Imron [4] in the court he said: "Yes, I did it" I believe him [that he made one of the smaller bombs that went off]. A bomb expert from Australia said that anyone who believes that Amrozi and friends made that [bigger] bomb is an idiot; [this is also the opinion of] a bomb expert from England whose comments I read in a magazine. If Amrozi really did make that bomb, he deserves the Nobel Prize. So, the death penalty is not fair.

Q. I want to ask your opinion of Nasir Abbas's book where he said that you are the Emir of JI? [5]

A. This is a traitor, a betrayer. I was in Malaysia and I had a jama'ah [congregation] named Jama'ah Sunnah. We just studied Islam.

Q. Were you aware that Nasir Abbas was your student?

A. Yes, I was. But he was not the only one there; he also studied with Ustadz Hasyim Gani. I joined his group. He died. I think Nasir Abbas's book is [written] on orders from the police and for money.

Q. According to you, the book is incorrect, especially on Jemaah Islamiyah and you being its Emir?

A. This is not a court and the real court has failed to prove it. [6]

Q. What was Nasir Abbas's motivation in writing that book?

A. I don't know. But basically he got orders from the police and received some money. I think that was his motivation. He doesn't have the courage to meet me. If I meet him, I'll send him to do jihad in Chechnya or to the Southern Philippines so that Allah will accept his remorse [taubah]. He invented his own story.

Q. I heard that Nasir Abbas came here. Did he meet you?

A. No, he came here to meet others.

Q. If I may know, when was the first time you heard the name al-Qaeda?

A. After the police questioned me; during the time I was filing a lawsuit against *Time* magazine. Do you remember when I did that? They wanted me to take 100 million rupiah to stop the case but I didn't. But I don't know anymore about the case. During that time, I was under suspicion but I wasn't arrested. That was the first time I heard the name al-Qaeda. [7] A policeman from the intelligence section whose name I forget interrogated me from morning until afternoon. He asked about that name [al-Qaeda]. That was the first time I heard of it. Before, I never heard of it. I went to Pakistan but I didn't hear that name. I went there to accompany my son [8] and meet some Arabs but I never heard that name.

Q. How about Sheikh Osama bin Laden?

A. I heard his name a long time ago. I read his writings, saw his tapes and met Arabs in Pakistan who talked about him when I accompanied my son, Abdur Rahim. Who didn't know Osama? He was a mujahid against the Soviets and he had his own military that he funded by himself. He was a hero who America also praised. He was then also supported by America. America was piggybacking on him because America didn't have the courage to fight against the Soviets. They were afraid of the Soviets and they relied on the Afghans.

Q. Have you ever met him?

A. No, no. I want to though. After my release, I hope I can meet him. [9]

Q. Where will you find him?

A. If he still exists—but how could I? On Osama, my stand in court was clear. I have sympathy for his struggle. Osama is Allah's soldier. When I heard his story, I came to the conclusion that he's mujahid, a soldier of Allah.

Q. So you will always be on his side?

A. Many say this and Osama is right. His tactics and calculations may sometimes be wrong, he's an ordinary human being after all. I don't agree with all of his actions. He encouraged people to do bombings. I don't agree with that. He said that JI followed his fatwah. His fatwah said that all Americans must be killed wherever they can be found, because America deserves it. Therefore [according to bin Laden] if Muslims come across Americans, they have to attack them. Osama believes in total war. I don't agree with this concept. If this occurs in an Islamic country, the fitnah [discord] will be felt by Muslims. But to attack them in their country [America] is fine.

Q. So it means that the fight against America will never end?

A. Never, and this fight is compulsory. Muslims who don't hate America sin. What I mean by America is George Bush's regime. There is no iman [belief] if one doesn't hate America. There are three ways of attacking: with your hand, your mouth and your heart.

Q. Does this mean America's government? Its policies?

A. If its citizens are good that's fine, especially the Muslim citizens. They are our brothers. Non-Muslims are also fine as long as they don't bother us. A witness at my trial, Frederick Burks, wrote that he's against Bush. [10]

Q. How can the American regime and its policies change?

A. We'll see. As long as there is no intention to fight us and Islam continues to grow there can be peace. This is the doctrine of Islam. Islam can't be ruled by others. Allah's law can't be under human law. Allah's law must stand above human law. All laws must be under Islamic law. This is what the infidels fail to recognize, that's what America doesn't like to see. You should read a book, *The Face of Western Civilization* by Adian Husaini. It's a good book, a thick one. The conclusion of the book is that Western scholars hold an anti-Islamic doctrine. It is true there will be a clash of civilizations. The argumentation is correct that there will be a clash between Islam and the infidels. There is no [example] of Islam and infidels, the right and the wrong, living together in peace.

Notes
1. Father Rinaldy Damanik is the leader of the Christian community in Poso District, Sulawesi where violence between Muslims and Christians led to hundreds of deaths on both sides between late 1998 and 2002 (and where intermittent violence continues to this day). I interviewed Father Damanik in his home in Tentena on August 10, 2005. It turns out that Father Damanik shared the same jail cell block successively for some months (September 2002 – January 2003) with Reda Seyam (legendary al-Qaeda film-maker), Imam Samudra (the JI computer expert condemned to death for planning the meetings and choosing the targets for the Bali bombings) and Ba'asyir. Damanik befriended all three. There are smiling photos of Reda and Damanik together, and Samudra and Ba'asyir have both confirmed their warm feelings toward Father Damanik. Damanik used to call Ba'asyir "Opa" (grandfather) and Ba'asyir's wife would bring gifts of food to Damanik. They discussed injustice, Sharia, faith in God, suicide attacks and opposing America. According to Damanik, they found much agreement on the sources of injustice but disagreed strongly over the means to overcome it.
2. Amrozi bin Nurahasyim was sentenced to death by an Indonesian court for having plotted the bombing of the Sari Club in Kuta, Bali along with Imam Samudra and Amrozi's older brother, Mukhlas.
3. The story about the CIA-Mossad conspiracy is widespread among JI leaders and foot soldiers and (usually with a laugh) used to illustrate that JI is itself a concoction of "Jewish Intelligence."
4. Ali Imron, the younger brother of Mukhlas and Amrozi, was sentenced to life in prison for the Bali bombings after having expressed remorse for his role in the attacks.

5. Muhammad Nasir bin Abbas, who trained Bali bombers Imam Samudra and Ali Imron, received his religious instruction from Sungkar and Ba'asyir in Malaysia before they sent him in 1991 for three years to Towrkhan military camp in Afghanistan. He became a top JI military trainer but also gave religious instruction. In April 2001 Ba'asyir appointed Abbas head of Mantiqi 3, one of JI's strategic area divisions, which covered the geographical region of the Philippines and Sulawesi and was responsible for military training and arms supply. Abbas turned state's evidence in Ba'asyir's trial, outlining the structure of JI and Ba'asyir's position as Emir. But Abbas refused to openly condemn Ba'asyir or accuse him of ordering any terrorist operations, always respectfully referring to Ba'asyir as Ustadz. In July 2005 Abbas published *Membongkar Jamaah Islamiyah* (Unveiling Jamaah Islamiyah). The first part of the book details JI's organization, ideology and strategy. The second part is a rebuttal to Samudra's own book, *Aku Melawan Terroris*, and what Abbas believes to be a tendentious use of the Quran and Hadith to justify suicide bombing and violence against fellow Muslims and civilians.

In between my interviews with Ba'asyir, I interviewed Abbas, who says that he quit JI over Ba'asyir's refusal to condemn or contain the operations and influence of Riduan Isamuddin (aka Hambali). In January 2000, Hambali hosted a meeting in an apartment owned by JI member Yazid Sufaat in Kuala Lumpur that included 9/11 mastermind Khalid Sheikh Mohammad and 9/11 highjackers Khalid al-Mihdhar and Nawaf al-Hamzi. As Abbas tells it, Hambali, who was JI's main liaison with Al-Qaeda and a close friend and disciple of Khalid Sheikh Mohammad, was given control of Mantiqi 1, which covered the geographical region of Malaysia and environs and was strategically responsible for JI finances and economic development. But Hambali was dissatisfied being saddled with the "economic wing" (iqtisod) and wanted to play a more active role in the conflict zones. The then-leader of Mantiqi 3, Mustafa (now in custody) blocked Hambali from muscling in on his area, but Hambali was able to send fighters to fight Christians in Ambon (Maluku) in 1999, which was under Mantiqi 2 (covering most of Indonesia and strategically responsible for JI recruitment and organizational development). Encouraged by his success in heating up the Maluku crisis, Hambali decided first to extend his (and al-Qaeda's) conception of jihad to all of Indonesia (including the 1999 bombing of the Atrium Mall in Jakarta, the August 2000 bombing of the Philippines Ambassador's house, and

17 coordinated church bombings on Christmas Eve 2000) and then to "globalize" the jihad by enlisting suicide bombers to hit Western targets and interests (including a failed plot to blow up Singapore's American, Australian and Israeli embassies in December 2001, and the successful 2002 Bali bombings and 2003 suicide attack on Jakarta's Marriott hotel). Although Abbas argues that JI shouldn't be outlawed because many in JI reject al-Qaeda's vision of global jihad, in fact JI's infrastructure and leadership continue to protect (with safe houses) and condone (as "self-defense") efforts by the likes of master bomber Dr. Azhari bin Hussain and his constant sidekick, JI's top recruiter Nurdin Nur Top, who some tell me recently established a suicide squad, called Thoifah Muqatilah, for large actions against Western interests.

6. According to Abbas, JI's essential organization and ideology is outlined in a set of general guidelines for the *Jemaah Islamiyah Struggle* (Pedoman Umum Perjuangan al-Jamaah al-Islamiyah, PUPJI), a 44-page manual that contains a constitution, outlines the roles of office bearers and gives details of how meetings must be organized (e.g., about what to do if a quorum cannot be obtained in the leadership council). The guidelines declare that anyone who adheres to fundamental Islamic principles that are devoid of corruption, deviation (e.g. Sufism) or innovation, can take the bayat (oath of allegiance) to the Emir of JI and become a JI member. Although JI would be, in principle, open to anyone who meets these conditions, in fact only carefully selected individuals, including the Mantiqi leaders, were allowed to take the bayat and obtain copies of the PUPJI. Such individuals generally (but not always) would have undergone previous training in Afghanistan or graduated at the top of their class in courses that Sungkar and Ba'asyir designed for JI recruitment (though designation of courses as JI-sponsored courses was unknown to potential recruitees). Abbas fulfilled both conditions. Although many people (including some Afghan Alumni I have interviewed) think of themselves as JI, or are not certain of whether or not they belong to JI, Abbas insists that if they did not formally take the bayat they are considered sympathizers or supporters of JI but not members (just as some prisoners at Guantanamo are sincerely uncertain as to whether or not they belong to al-Qaeda if they did not formally take the bayat to bin Laden).

Abbas says the PUPJI was drafted by a committee, including Ba'asyir, and then formally approved by Sungkar as the basis for

JI. When asked about the PUPJI in an earlier (untaped) part of the interview, Ba'asyir claimed, on the one hand, that the PUPJI manual was planted by police and intelligence services but, on the other hand, that it contains sound principles modeled on the doctrine of the Egyptian Islamic Group (Gama'at Islamiyah). Abbas says that the manual also contains elements of Indonesia's military organization, particularly in regard to the ranking of personnel (binpur) and responsibility for territory (bintur). He adds that although the PUPJI allows the JI to conduct itself as a "secret organization" (tanzim sir) - and conceal its doctrine, membership and operations from public view – it does not allow the practice of taqiyyah (dissimulation) to extend to lying to the (Muslim) public (another reason Abbas gives for his leaving JI).

7. Other members of JI who openly acknowledge sympathy with bin Laden and al-Qaeda say much the same thing. For example, I interviewed the JI member who founded the first mujahidin training camp in 2000 for the conflict in Poso, Sulawesi. He had earlier been sent by JI founder Abdullah Sungkar during the Soviet-Afghan War to train in Abu Sayyafs's Ihtihad camp in Sada, Pakistan and to study with Abdullah Azzam, bin Laden's mentor and the person who first formulated the notion of "al-Qaeda sulbah" ("the strong base") as a vanguard for jihad. This JI member also acknowledges hosting Khalid Sheikh Mohammad at his home in Jakarta for a month in 1996. Yet, he claims never to have heard of "al-Qaeda" applied to a specific organization or group headed by bin Laden until 9/11.

8. Ba'asyir sent his younger son, Abdul Rahim, to the Afghanistan border during the Soviet-Afghan war to spend time under the wing of Aris Sumarsono (aka Zulkarnaen, who became JI's operations chief) later enrolling Rahim in an Islamic high school in Faisalabad, Pakistan. Seeking a stricter salafist education for his son, Ba'asyir directed Rahim in the mid-nineties to Sana'a, Yemen, to study under Abdul Majid al-Zindani (like Abdullah Azzam, Zindani was a legend among self-proclaimed "Afghan Alumni" who fought the Soviets). By 1999, Rahim was in Malaysia and soon under Hambali's stewardship. Abdul Rahim now operates freely in Indonesia (reports in August 2005 place him in Aceh, heading a new charity, Camp Taochi Foundation [NB these reports now appear to be invalid - ed. 11/01/05]) but he is suspected of having taken over JI's contacts with al-Qaeda remnants after Hambali's capture.

9. Ba'asyir's statement that he never met bin Laden is contradicted by testimony from other JI members, both free and in custody. In the following letter (authenticated by Indonesian intelligence) dated August 3, 1998 and addressed to regional jihadi leaders, Ba'asyir and Sungkar state they are acting on bin Laden's behalf to advance "the Muslim world's global jihad" (jabhah Jihadiyah Alam Islamy) against "the Jews and Christians:"

Malaysia, 10 Rabiul Akhir 1419 [August 3, 1998]

From: Abdullah Sungkar and Abu Bakar Ba'asyir

To: Al Mukarrom, respected clerics, teachers (ustadz), sheikhs

All praises upon God who has said, "The Jews and Christians will never be satisfied until you follow their way of worship" al-Baqarah: 120

Praise and peace upon Prophet Muhammad who has said, "If I'm still alive, I'll surely expel the Jews and Christians out of the Arabian peninsula"

And may God bless us and any of his followers who want to follow his orders.

Respected clerics, teachers and sheikhs, this letter is to convey a message from Sheikh Osama bin Laden to all of you. We send you this letter because we can't visit and see you directly. However, we send our envoy, Mr. Ghaus Taufiq [a Darul Islam commander in Sumatra], to bring this letter personally to all of you.

We also attach bin Laden's written message in this letter and bin Laden also sends these messages to all of you:

1. Bin Laden conveys his regards (Assalamu'alaikum Warahmatullahi Wabarakatuh)

2. Bin Laden says that right now, after "Iman" (to believe in God), the most important obligation for all Muslims in the world is to work hard to free the Arabian Peninsula from the occupation of Allah's enemy America (Jews and Christians).

This obligation is mathalabusy syar'i (a consequence of the sharia) that every Muslim must not consider this obligation to be a simple matter. Prophet Muhammad, although he was sick, ordered the Muslim Ummah to prioritize their obligation to expel the infidels from the Arabian Peninsula. Therefore, as the Prophet has said, the Muslim Ummah must take this obligation seriously. It is very important for the Muslim world to work very hard to free the Arabian Peninsula from colonization by the infidel Americans.

If we can free the Arabian peninsula as masdarul diinul Islam (the source of Islam) and makorrul haromain (Holy Mecca) from occupation by the infidel Americans, Inshallah (God willing) our struggle to uphold Islam everywhere on God's land will be successful. Stagnation and the difficulty in upholding Islam at present stems from the occupation of the Arabian Peninsula by the infidel America.

This great struggle must be put into action by the Ummah (Muslim community) all over the world under the leadership and guidance of clerics in their respective countries. Under such leadership, we will prevail.

The first step of this struggle is issuing fatwah (Islamic edict) from clerics all over the world addressed to the kingdom of Saudi Arabia. The edict must remind the King what Prophet Muhammad said about the obligation for the Muslim Ummah to expel the infidels from the Arabian Peninsula. Otherwise, this world will suffer a catastrophe. These edicts will give strong encouragement and influence to the King of Arabia. This is the message from Osama bin Laden conveyed to all of you.

Sheikh Osama bin Laden really wants to visit all clerics and Islamic preachers everywhere in the world to share his views so that there will be a common understanding about this momentous struggle. In the end, we will have similar movements simultaneously across the world. However, bin Laden realizes that the situation outside his sanctuary is not presently safe. He also awaits your visit with his deep respect so that this great struggle may proceed. These are bin Laden's messages that we convey to all of you.

We take this opportunity to explain certain facts about bin Laden:

- At present, Sheikh Osama stays in Afghanistan, in the Kandahar area, under the protection of Taliban.
- He doesn't oppose either the Taliban or Mujahideen. He's trying to unify both groups.

From his camp in Kandahar, bin Laden organizes plans to expel infidel America from the Arabian Peninsula by inviting ulemas and preachers from all over the world. In this camp, bin Laden is accompanied by a number of Arab mujahideen, especially those who previously fought in Afghanistan. Bin Laden and these mujahideen prepare to form "jabhah Jihadiyah Alam Islamy" (The global jihadi coalition in the Moslem world) to fight against America.

The above information is about Sheikh Osama bin Laden that you should know. If you have the time and commitment to visit Sheikh Osama, Inshallah, we can help you meet him safely.

We praise God to all of you for your attention and cooperation.

Jazakumullah khoirul jaza (Thanks to God the best thanks)

Wassalamu'alaukim, Your brother in Allah

Abdullah Sungkar Abu Bakar Ba'asyir

10. Frederick Burks appeared at Ba'asyir's trial testifying that he had interpreted at a 2002 meeting about Ba'asyir between an envoy of President George W. Bush and Indonesia's then-president Megawati Sukarnoputri. Burks said the unidentified envoy accused Ba'asyir of involvement in a series of church bombings in Indonesia in 2000 and asked for the cleric to be secretly arrested and handed over to U.S. authorities. Megawati declined, he said.

[From Spotlight on Terror, Volume III, Issue 9]

Abu Dujana: Jemaah Islamiyah's New al-Qaeda Linked Leader

Zachary Abuza

Originally published on April 4, 2006

With the death of Jemaah Islamiyah's (JI) master bomb maker, Azahari bin Husin, there has been intense speculation over JI's current leadership, in particular the position of Amir, or "spiritual leader", which has been vacant since 2003. In recent weeks, Indonesian authorities have focused their sights on a little-known militant, Abu Dujana. Indonesian police have now made his arrest their "priority."

Dujana was born in Cianjur, West Java, around 1968. West Java was the traditional stronghold of the underground Darul Islam movement, and Dujana, like many JI members, appears to have close family connections to the Darul Islam movement. He was educated by Dadang Hafidz, a militant Islamist with deep ties to the Darul Islam organization.

After years of Quranic tutorial, Hafidz selected Abu Dujana for advanced training in Pakistan. He studied there for a few years before joining the mujahideen and leaving to fight in Afghanistan. Abu Rusdan, who would go on to lead JI in 2002, reported that he first met his compatriot in a mujahideen training camp in Pakistan in 1986 (indictment of Abu Rusdan). Dujana was trained in small arms, tactics and bomb-making. In Afghanistan he came into close contact and developed a deep friendship with Zulkarnaen, who would become head of JI's military operations. His other classmates in Pakistan were Riduan Isamuddin, better known as Hambali, who was the operations chief of JI until his arrest in August 2003, and Nasir bin Abbas (BBC, March 22, 2006).

In the early 1990s, Dujana returned to Southeast Asia, although there is little information about what he did in this period. JI was founded in 1992-1993 by Abdullah Sungkar and Abu Bakar Ba'asyir, and many of the Afghan veterans who were frustrated with Darul Islam's passivity became the core of JI's leadership, committed to waging an armed jihad against the Indonesian state. Cells were patiently established and recruiters began working as JI-controlled madrassas were established throughout the Indonesian archipelago and into Malaysia. Dujana spent a period of time as a teacher at one of those schools, the Luqmanul Hakiem School, outside of Johor, Malaysia, which was run by the leader of the Bali attacks, Mukhlas (*Tempo*, September 21, 2004; interrogation of Nasir bin Abbas).

It is not known if, after 1996, Dujana spent any time in Moro Islamic Liberation Front (MILF) camps in the southern Philippines, conducting training for JI and MILF members along with al-Qaeda instructors.

Following the fall of Indonesia's strongman Suharto in May 1998, sectarian conflict erupted in parts of the archipelago. Although not started by JI, the organization was quick to take advantage of the situation. Senior JI members Abu Jibril and Agus Dwikarna established paramilitaries in the Malukus and Central Sulawesi, respectively. Owing to his Afghan experience, Dujana spent some time in these conflict zones and helped to coordinate JI's efforts from 1998-2001. His former mentor Hafidz was himself a key supporter and procurer of weapons for JI's sectarian strife.

In this period of time, Abu Dujana's rise through JI's Mantiqi 2 division was swift. By 2000, he was the secretary of Mantiqi 2. One year later, he was attending almost every key meeting of JI's leadership that was held in Indonesia. Top JI members who have been arrested all cite his presence at key strategy sessions and leadership appointments. For example, Nasir bin Abbas states that Dujana was among the top 10 leaders present when he was elected to head Mantiqi 3 in April 2001 (interrogation of Nasir bin Abbas). In October 2002, following Abu Bakar Ba'asyir's arrest, Dujana and Zulkarnaen, Mukhlas and Sulaiman met to elect Abu Rusdan as JI's new Amir. At that meeting, Dujana was elected to be Rusdan's secretary (indictment of Abu Rusdan). Rusdan, however, was arrested soon thereafter and Indonesian officials believe that Dujana became the acting Amir, though he is not a religious leader.

Dujana assisted a number of JI suspects who had fled the dragnet in Singapore in late 2001. In 2002, he turned his sights on executing Hambali's line of attacking Western targets. Dujana was among the plotters of the October 2002 Bali bombings, and met with Zulkarnaen, JI's military chief, and Mukhlas in Bali days before the attack (interrogation of Nasir bin Abbas). The ICG reports that Azahari bin Husin and Noordin Mohammad Top consulted with him before the August 2003 bombing of the JW Marriott in Jakarta (*Tempo*, September 21, 2004). Following that attack, Dujana was placed on the government's 10 most wanted list.

Dujana is thought to be a key leader of the organization, and not simply a default candidate from group attrition. He is one of the remaining leaders who spent time in Afghanistan and Pakistan and is personally known by the al-Qaeda leadership. As a senior police official recently said, "He has good relations with al-Qaeda...[He is] trusted" (BBC, March 22, 2006).

Authorities thought they had arrested him in November 2004 (*Jakarta Post*, November 28, 2004). In January 2005, they tracked him to Subang, West Java, in conjunction with the investigations into the September 2004 bombing of the Australian Embassy, although he and others escaped arrest. In November 2005, police raided the home of Abu Dujana's father, Achmad Tamami (*Jakarta Post*, November 13, 2005). He now uses the alias Sorim.

Among the other top JI leaders at large are Dulmatin and Umar Patek, both believed to be in Mindanao; the Malaysian, Noordin Mohammad Top, JI's top recruiter and money man; Zulkarnaen, JI's chief of military operations; Qotada; Nu'im; and Zulkifli bin Hir.

[From Terrorism Focus, Volume III, Issue 13]

JI's Moneyman and Top Recruiter: A Profile of Noordin Mohammad Top

Zachary Abuza

Originally published on July 25, 2006

Of all the known leaders of Jemaah Islamiyah (JI) at large, no one strikes more fear than Noordin Mohammad Top. A Malaysian national, he along with his compatriot, the late Dr. Azahari bin Husin, were the masterminds behind seven past suicide attacks to hit Indonesia. While Azahari was the group's leading bomb-maker, Noordin is believed to be the top recruiter and strategist. Nicknamed "The Moneyman," he is also thought to be an important fundraiser for JI.

Noordin was born in Johor, Malaysia on August 11, 1968 and attended the Sekolah Islam Luqmanul Hakiem, a madrassa in rural Johor state, that was established by JI's founders Abdullah Sungkar and Abu Bakar Ba'asyir, and where the mastermind of the 2002 Bali bombing Mukhlas was the headmaster. He went on to study at the Universiti Teknologi Malaysia (UTM), where he befriended his professor, Dr. Azahari. He received a bachelor's degree (B.Sci.) from UTM around 1991, but his whereabouts in the following years are not well known. He was briefly an accountant before returning to teach at the Luqmanul Hakiem School. He became increasingly involved as JI developed its network and organization in the 1990s, although unlike other operatives he did not receive training in al-Qaeda camps. Like many JI members, he married within the JI family; he wed Rahmah Rusdi, a sister of another JI member.

Noordin was active in JI's Mantiqi 1 (one of JI's regional divisions), but fled with Azahari to Indonesia, probably in late 2001 or early 2002. Azahari was deeply involved in the planning of the 2002 Bali bombing that killed 202 people and was the first suicide attack by a Southeast Asian national. Noordin and Azahari made suicide attacks the weapon of choice for JI. While Azahari built the bombs, Noordin was the primary recruiter and has been described as a very charismatic individual. Noordin's magnetism has also been seen in his ability to co-opt other organizations. He recruited a member of Darul Islam to become a shaheed (martyr) in the August 2003 bombing of the JW Marriott in Jakarta.

Noordin and Azahari sought to institutionalize suicide attacks. While Azahari's cookbooks were widely disseminated, the two also made a video lecture on bomb construction. Azahari seemed to study other jihadist organizations for inspiration. The bomb-making video also taught recruits how to perform their final ritual acts, such as prayers and debt repayments, and how to narrate a video-will; several of these wills have now been recovered in Indonesia.

Perhaps the most glaring foreign innovation was Noordin's Abu Musab al-Zarqawi-like video threat that aired on Indonesian television in November 2005, following the death of Azahari who was killed in a police shootout. Like videos from Iraq, the footage of a masked man—believed to be Noordin—explicitly threatened the West: "As long as you keep your troops in Iraq and Afghanistan and intimidate Muslim people, you will feel our intimidation and our terror...America, Australia, England and Italy. You will be the target of our next attack. Especially for Australia, as long as its troops are in Afghanistan and Iraq and engage in intimidation there, you will also feel our intimidation" (BBC, November 18, 2005). While this type of video statement is commonplace in the Middle East, it had never been used in Southeast Asia. The video also included a "martyr's statements" recording by one of the Bali II bombers of October 2005, further evidence that JI is trying to develop a cult of martyrdom.

Noordin has been one of the top targets of regional security forces, but his repeated escapes have raised questions about corruption within Indonesia's police. In 2003, he and Azahari fled a cordon, as police feared they would detonate their suicide vests (Associated Press, November 12, 2003). In another case, Indonesian police announced that they had come within two hours of capturing him in the middle of the night on September 26, 2005 in a central Javanese village. He then traveled to Bali to plan the October attacks, but left before they were executed. In November 2005, Indonesian police raided a safe house in a small town in central Java. Although Noordin was not there, his two aides were apprehended and a cache of weapons was uncovered, including a backpack filled with explosives, a similar design of the bombs that were used in the October 2005 triple Bali bombings that killed 20 people. Noordin married a second woman, Munfiatun al-Fitri, also a sister of a JI member, who was sentenced to jail in June 2005 for giving him material assistance.

Noordin has been the leading proponent of targeting Western interests in Indonesia. In addition to the two Bali and two Jakarta attacks, Noordin has ordered his operatives to conduct reconnaissance on a large foreign-owned power plant southeast of Surabaya that provides much of the electricity for the province of East Java (*Yomiuri Shimbun*, April 17, 2006). Detained JI members have also revealed that Noordin ordered the targeting of Japanese targets, perhaps mirroring al-Qaeda statements that identified Japan as an enemy. In January, he announced the formation of a new organization, Tanzim Qaedat al-Jihad, although it is still unclear whether this is a distinctly independent organization from JI.

Noordin has been designated by the U.S. Treasury Department and the UN Security Council as a terrorist financier. He remains one of the most important JI figures at large. He is a charismatic leader and a recruiter, who has proven to be innovative and single-minded in his desire to implement the al-Qaeda line and target Western interests.

[From Terrorism Focus, Volume III, Issue 29]

The Role of Kinship in Indonesia's Jemaah Islamiyah

Noor Huda Ismail

Originally published on June 2, 2006

On April 29, 2006, the Indonesian police raided the safe house of Jemaah Islamiyah (JI) senior member Noordin Mohammed Top in Wonosobo, Central Java. Noordin, Southeast Asia's most wanted terrorist, eluded capture by escaping only hours before police arrived at his hideout. Two of his trusted men, however, were killed and another two were arrested (Detik.com, April 29, 2006).

JI has been weakened by arrests and other counter-terrorism measures since the 2002 Bali bombings that killed more than 202 people, mostly foreigners, with several hundred more injured. Terrorists have struck with murderous effects twice in Jakarta and once more in Bali since the first major bombings. These events demonstrate that all parts of the terrorist network have not ceased jihadi operations.

JI has survived partly because it is held together by an intricate pattern of kinship. Generally, people do not gravitate to JI due to some individual pathology. Indeed, most recruits look, dress and behave like normal individuals, at least until they are given a deadly mission or are deeply engaged with the JI ideology and group. The choice to become a terrorist or engage in terrorist activities is a gradual process with many routes toward this type of political violence.

Once inside the group, JI members tend to cement ideological and other bonds by marrying the sisters and daughters of their comrades-in-arms. This is a unique tool utilized for recruitment and for further engagement in the JI cause, thus limiting disengagement options for JI members and blocking effective counter-terrorism tactics.

Therefore, it becomes difficult for a member to defect from JI without seeming to betray his family in the process of disengagement. Kinship ties help to keep the network secure from infiltration. JI as a case study offers several examples highlighting the complexity of kinship links in terrorism, such as relationships between two or more male siblings, between in-laws, between fathers and sons, as well as more distant kinship relations.

Sibling Relationships

The use of sibling relationships in jihadi recruitment is to provide further ideological support for the recruits beyond the group itself. Sometimes two or more brothers are recruited for jihad, helping each other during an operation and providing each other inspiration and reassurance. This particular type of recruitment is an effective use of kinship to ensure deeper engagement with the cause and group.

One example of such sibling kinship and terrorism is the family of Achmad Kandai. In the 1950s, he belonged to the hard-core movement Darul Islam, which tried to assassinate the first Indonesian President Sukarno in 1957. Darul Islam is an Islamic Indonesian rebellion movement whose aim has been to turn the country into a state ruled by Islamic law. For more than five decades, Darul spawned many offshoots and splinters that committed violent acts in the name of jihad [1].

Nasir, a brother of Kandai's, worked with Abdullah Sungkar and Abubakar Ba'asyir, two successive spiritual heads of JI in Malaysia in the 1980s and 1990s. Kandai's sons Farihin bin Ahmad, Abdul Jabar, Mohammed Islam and Solahudin all became jihadists. In August 2000, Ahmad and Jabar participated in the attack on the Philippine ambassador's Jakarta residence that killed two people and injured 22 others, including Ambassador Leonides Caday (*Washington Diplomat*, August 1, 2000).

Mohammed Islam, the third brother, became involved in several bombings during the religious conflict in Poso in Central Sulawesi where violence between Muslims and Christians led to hundreds of deaths on both sides between late 1998 and 2002 (and where intermittent violence continues to this day) [2].

The fourth brother, Solahudin, was among those arrested in the April 29 raid in Wonosobo, Central Java. He is now under police interrogation for his involvement in a series of terrorist attacks including the bombing of the Atrium shopping mall in August 2001 where the designated bomber lost his leg and was arrested after the bomb he was carrying blew up prematurely [3].

The complex kinship relations found in terrorism, illustrated by the Kandai family, is not an anomaly in the JI terrorist faction. The al-Ghozi family is another jihadi family. Faturrahman al-Ghozi, who was shot and killed by the Philippine police in 2003, was one of JI's main bomb-makers. Among other actions, he was the perpetrator of the devastating Rizal Day bombing in Manila in 2000 that killed 12 people and wounded 19 others (Inquirer News Service, July 8, 2003).

Al-Ghozi's father was a Darul Islam member who was jailed during the Suharto era. A younger brother, Ahmad Rofiq Ridho, is now standing trial on several charges including sheltering the Malaysian JI member Noordin Mohammed Top. Last year, Ridho set a precedent for JI by marrying his brother's widow in a ceremony in a Jakarta police detention facility [4].

Gempur Angkoro, whose alias is Jabir, is al-Ghozi's cousin and was one of Top's most trusted men; he, too, was killed in the April 29 raid. Jabir assembled the bombs used in the deadly attacks in Jakarta at the Australian Embassy in 2004 and the JW Marriott hotel in 2003 (*Jakarta Post*, May 2, 2006).

The first Bali bombing introduced three brothers to the outside world: Ali Ghufron (Mukhlas), Amrozi and Ali Imron. The first two are now on death row. Ali Ghufron was in charge of overall supervision of the bombing. Amrozi procured the chemicals and vehicles needed for the attack, while the third brother coordinated transport of the bomb [5]. Another set of brothers, Herlambang and Hernianto, were also involved. Hernianto later died in jail, allegedly of a kidney complaint.

Hambali and Rusman Gunawan, whose alias is Gun Gun, are another set of JI brothers. Hambali, now in U.S. detention, was JI's liaison with al-Qaeda. Gun Gun was involved in the Marriott hotel bombing in 2003. He attended university in Pakistan and from late 2002 took over as the intermediary for e-mail messages between al-Qaeda and Hambali, who was then hiding in Cambodia [6].

There was also a set of JI brothers in Singapore, Faiz and Fatihi bin Abu Bakar Bafana. Faiz was treasurer of the first JI region, or Mantiqi 1 (JI's regional division that provides the economic wherewithal for JI operations), and has admitted to receiving funds from Osama bin Laden via Hambali. Fatihi carried out reconnaissance against Western targets in Singapore [7]. Mantiqi 1 was initially led by Hambali and subsequently replaced by Ali Ghufron (Mukhlas) in 2001 [8].

The cell in Singapore was started by Afghanistan alumni Ibrahim Maidin in 1988-1989. He was arrested in 2001 and another Afghanistan alumnus, Mas Selamat Kastari, assumed leadership until he was arrested in early 2003. Before it was broken up by the Singaporean intelligence agencies, JI had 60 to 80 members. No more than 25 members were operatives. As of May, there are 36 people detained in Singapore under the Internal Security Act (ISA) for terrorism activities in support of JI leaders and/or the Moro Islamic Liberation Movement (MILF) [9].

In-Law Relationships

Kinship ties also include in-laws. Ali Ghufron married Farida, younger sister of Nasir bin Abbas, a Malaysian who once served as Mantiqi 3 chairman. Nasir, who abandoned the JI cause and wrote a book entitled Exposing Jemaah Islamiyah, was sufficiently loyal to his brother-in-law to write that he had been the best possible husband for his sister. Another JI member, Syamsul Bahri, is another of Nasir's brothers-in-laws [10].

Taufiq Abdul Halim, the Malaysian who lost part of his leg in the Atrium bombing, is the brother-in-law of Zulkifli Hir, a leader of a Malaysian jihadi group, which was responsible for a series of crimes including the assassination of a state assemblyman [11].

Another example is Datuk Rajo Ameh, who participated in the Christmas Eve bombing in 2000 among other attacks. He is the father-in-law of JI member Joni Hendrawan, who was involved in the first Bali bombing and the 2003 Marriott attack [12]. Muhammad Rais, another Marriott figure, is the brother-in-law of Top. Rais recruited a suicide bomber for the Marriott bombing [13].

Fathers and Sons

Anxious for their offspring's safety and with an eye to regenerating JI, senior members sent their children to study in Karachi, where they formed the so-called al-Ghuraba (the foreigners) cell.

During university break, some members of the group went to Afghanistan for a course in urban warfare. Six of them traveled to Pakistan-controlled parts of Kashmir where Lashkar-e-Taiba, a guerrilla movement affiliated with al-Qaeda, gave them a month of physical and military training. Pakistan's Inter-Services Intelligence (ISI) agency discovered the group in September 2003 [14]. Abdul Rohim, Abubakar Ba'asyir's son, was the cell leader [15]. One of its members was Abu Dzar, whose father is a long-time associate of Hambali's and two of whose uncles are JI members. Abu Dzar's uncle, Muhamad Ismail Anwarul, who drove a taxi in Singapore, would later attend an al-Qaeda training camp in Kandahar during 2001. His sister had recently married Masran bin Arshad, the leader of Khalid Sheikh Mohammad's alleged suicide cell [16].

Another cell member was the Malaysian Muhammad Ikhwan, whose father, Abdullah Daud, attended an al-Qaeda surveillance course in Kabul in 2000. Ikhwan's older sister married another JI member. Likewise, the father of Singaporean student Mohammad Riza was sent by JI's Mantiqi 1 for military training in Mindanao [17].

Arranged Marriages

Arranging marriages between members of JI families was the ideal way of forging permanent alliances. JI spiritual leaders could play the roles of both matchmaker and marriage celebrant.

Abdullah Sungkar married two of his stepdaughters to senior jihadis—Ferial Muchlis bin Abdul Halim, a head of the Selangor JI cell, and Syawal Yassin, a prominent South Sulawesi figure and former military trainer in Afghanistan. Sungkar had been the celebrant at the 1984 marriage of future Mantiqi 4 leader Abdul Rahim Ayub and the Australian Rabiyah [18].

Haris Fadillah is a hard-core Darul Islam militia leader who fought and died in communal religious conflict in Ambon, Maluku, where thousands of Muslims and Christians lost their lives; many villages and places of worship were destroyed. He arranged the marriage of his daughter, Mira Augustina, to Indonesia-based al-Qaeda operative Omar al-Faruq. Following her husband's arrest in June 2002, Mira acknowledged that she had married al-Faruq the first day she met him [19].

In the same vein, Jack Thomas, an Australian jihadi, married the Indonesian Maryati in South Africa on the recommendation of his JI friends. Thomas, who even adopted the name "Jihad," likewise married his wife the day he met her. A Singapore jihadi called Jauhari testified in court that the Indonesian preacher Abu Jibril had helped choose his wife for him and that Abdullah Sungkar had married them at Abu Jibril's house [20].

As for Hambali, he married a part-Chinese woman, Noralwizah Lee, who converted to Islam. Like male JI members, Lee used several aliases and was active in recruiting women to the cause. The couple first met at a function held by one of the women's groups under Abdullah Sungkar's auspices. The author established in interviews with one of the participating lecturers that one topic offered was "Women and Jihad" [21]. Lee shared Hambali's fate by being arrested in Thailand with him in August 2003.

Noordin Mohammed Top found time to take a second wife, Munfiatun al-Fitri, in a marriage arranged by Surabaya JI members in 2004. Like Ali Ghufron's wife, Munfiatun is well-educated and graduated in agriculture at East Java's Brawijaya University (*Jakarta Post*, March 8, 2006).

Conclusion

Understanding kinship ties in the jihadi network in Indonesia and beyond is critical. Without such ties, many alienated young Muslim men would not have become or remained jihadis. Kinship is particularly important in a clandestine organization like JI where maintaining relations of trust and confidence is crucial for survival. Additionally, jihadi organizations have the unusual advantage of having their own religiously qualified members available to officiate at the creation of new marital bonds.

Relatives of identified terrorists need to be closely monitored and investigated wherever they reside. Especially important are those who went to the same mosque and school, or who participated in the same military training either in local areas or abroad such as in Afghanistan or in Moro Islamic Liberation Front camps.

It is essential not to underestimate previous informal membership in action-oriented groups such as soccer or cricket that may facilitate the passage from radicalization into jihad and onto joining suicide attack teams. Lastly, profiling of jihadi families by looking at their social backgrounds is useful. It is also crucial to look at the ways in which a person gets drawn into terrorism and from that to develop counter-terrorism strategies.

Notes

1. An interview with one of Darul Islam's leaders, Ghaus Taufiq, in 2005 in Medan, North Sumatra. Taufiq said that Darul Islam sent 360 members to participate in military training in Afghanistan. Some of these people would later emerge as the fighters of today's Jemaah Islamiyah.

2. In interviews in 2005, Nasir Abbas, head of Mantiqi 3, one of JI's strategic area divisions, which covered the geographical region of the Philippines and Sulawesi and was responsible for military training and arms supplies, said that Poso had the potential to develop into a qoidah aminah, a secure area where residents can live by Islamic principles and law. In their view, such a base could then serve as the building block of an Islamic state; Maluku and Poso, therefore, remain a focus for religious outreach and recruitment efforts.

3. An interview with Farihin bin Ahmad in Jakarta in 2005.

4. An interview with Ahmad Rofiq Ridho in Jakarta prison in 2005.

5. An interview with Ali Imron in Jakarta Prison in 2005.

6. An interview with Rusman Gunawan in Jakarta Prison in 2005.

7. Ken Conboy, *The Second Front Inside Asia's Most Dangerous Terrorist Network*, Equinox Publishing (Asia) Pte. Ltd. Indonesia, 2005.

8. ICG Asia Report No 63, August 26, 2003.

9. White Paper, "The Jemaah Islamiyah Arrests and the Threat of Terrorism," The Singapore Minister of Home Affairs, January 7, 2003.

10. An interview with Nasir bin Abbas in Jakarta in 2005.

11. An interview with Taufiq Abdul Halim in Jakarta Prison in 2004.

12. An interview with Joni Hendrawan in Jakarta Prison in 2005.

13. An interview with Muhammad Rais in Jakarta Prison in 2005.

14. Conboy.

15. An interview with Abdur Rahim in Solo, Central Java in 2004.

16. Conboy.

17. Conboy.

18. *ICG Asia Report No 63*.

19. An interview with Mira Agustina in Bogor, West Java in 2004.

20. *ICG Asia Report No 63*.

21. An interview with Muyazin in Solo in 2004.

[From Terrorism Monitor, Volume IV, Issue 11]

Philippines

MILF's Stalled Peace Process and its Impact on Terrorism in Southeast Asia

Zachary Abuza

Originally published on July 13, 2006

Early July saw a spate of fighting that has seriously challenged the peace process in the southern Philippines. The fighting began with attacks by pro-government paramilitaries on Moro Islamic Liberation Front (MILF) villages in Maguindanao. The MILF's counter-attacks provoked intervention by the Armed Forces of the Philippines (AFP). On July 3, 2006, after three days of fighting that produced 5,000 refugees, the MILF ordered its forces to stand down at the request of the small contingent of Malaysian truce monitors (*Philippine Daily Inquirer*, July 3, 2006; Reuters, July 3, 2006). The following day it declared a unilateral ceasefire for the sake of the peace process. The breakdown of the ceasefire that has held fairly well for more than a year-and-a-half is not surprising and is testimony to the increasing frustration within the ranks of the MILF; sadly, it has repercussions for the war on terrorism in Southeast Asia.

In April 2005, the Government of the Republic of the Philippines (GRP) and the MILF announced a breakthrough in their peace talks. Although only some of the details were made public, it is clear that the MILF renounced their bid for an independent Islamic state and accepted a degree of autonomy. In return, the government gave in on two key concessions: it expanded the size of the autonomous region (the 1996 accord with the Moro National Liberation Front (MNLF) created the Autonomous Region of Muslim Mindanao (ARMM), which is comprised of five provinces and one city), expanded the political and fiscal autonomy of the ARMM and gave the MILF control over subterranean resources. The agreement proposed the establishment of the Bangsamoro Juridical Entity, in which the MILF would have full fiscal, political and religious authority.

Since then, the talks have stalled on the issue of "ancestral domain"—the actual size and scope of the Bangsamoro Juridical Entity. Moreover, the agreement was conditioned on a constitutional amendment. Several MILF officials told this author a year ago that they would give the government up to two years to push through the charter changes so that an agreement could be finalized [1]. It has already been more than a year, with no charter change in site, and a president who is so politically weakened that it is unlikely that she will be able to push through the necessary amendments in the Philippine Congress, especially after the brief imposition of emergency powers to fight off a "leftist-rightist coup" in February.

There are additional stumbling blocks to the peace process. First, there has been little public explanation as to how this agreement will impact the GRP-MNLF agreement of 1996 that established the ARMM. Will the Bangsamoro Juridical Entity supersede the ARMM? Will the MILF share power with the MNLF? Will the MILF protect the MNLF's economic interests? Will the MNLF accept the establishment of Islamic institutions? Indeed, one of the causes for the recent outbreak of fighting was a June 23, 2006 car bombing-cum-assassination attempt on the anti-MILF governor of Maguindanao Andal Ampatuan that killed six people, including two of his relatives, which some say was perpetrated by MILF commanders Ombra and Pakiladatu. These two commanders were also suspects in the 2002 bombing that killed Ampatuan's son (*Manila Star*, July 4, 2006; ABS-CBN, July 4, 2006). Intra-Muslim rivalry is a major stumbling block to the peace process.

Second, there are many potential spoilers, not least of all the politicized Philippine military, many of whose leaders are against making significant concessions to the rebels. The military is politically strong because President Arroyo has become increasingly dependent on them. Third, the Philippine government is so fraught with corruption and institutional frailties that even if it were fully committed to the peace process it would have trouble implementing it.

The stalled peace process has implications to the war on terrorism in Southeast Asia. Frustration within the MILF is palpable. In early March, coup rumors circulated in Mindanao. Although the MILF quickly denied that there had been any move to unseat the moderate Chairman Ebrahim el Haj Murad, who has been behind the peace process, it is clear that a growing cadre of MILF members are questioning the wisdom of the ongoing peace process. Already, many in the MILF were skeptical of the agreement and many hardliners—such as Wahid Tondok, Salamat Samir and Ustadz Ameril Umbra Kato—saw it as a betrayal of the original goal to establish an independent Islamic state. It took

Murad two years to effectively consolidate power following the death of the group's founder Salamat Hashim in 2003, to the point where he could make these concessions (in early 2005, he also re-organized the MILF's military commands and installed loyal lieutenants in positions of command in an attempt to isolate the hardliners). MILF leaders are very concerned about the growing radicalism of their youth who are frustrated with the older leader's inability to win the revolution. Should the peace process completely break down, their ability to resort to war will be greatly diminished. If Murad cannot deliver a viable peace, he will be replaced by Islamist hard-liners, such as Kato and Tondok, or more likely by the vice chairman, Aleem Abdulaziz Mimbintas. While Murad is a popular leader, he is not a religious leader, a fact that has angered many, and his hold on power is not guaranteed.

Moreover, many in the MILF's armed wing contend that as each day passes, the MILF's ability to wage war (because of military dissipation and the short shelf life of ammunition and weapons in the tropics) diminishes. One of the ways that the MILF has augmented its military capacity is by forging tactical alliances with groups such as the Southeast Asian affiliate Jemaah Islamiyah (JI).

The MILF began to invite members of JI to train in its camps beginning in 1996. At the time, a number of al-Qaeda trainers were dispatched to Mindanao to train MILF and JI operatives. The MILF denies that these ties are formal (they admit that some individual commanders may maintain such relations) and that they have been severed [2]. Indeed, they cite the fact that they have established the Joint Ad Hoc Action Group with the government specifically to go after criminal elements and JI and Abu Sayyaf Group (ASG) terrorists; they have not, however, arrested or turned over a single individual. A steady stream of both high and mid-level JI operatives arrested in Malaysia (Zulkifli and the Darul Islam 12), Indonesia (Mustaqim and Abdullah Sonata) and the Philippines (Taufiq Riefqi and Rohmat) in the past two years has confirmed that training is still continuing, although at a much lower rate than in the late-1990s.

In addition, the MILF continues to provide sanctuary to a core cadre of high-level JI operatives—including Dulmatin, Umar Patek, Zulkifli bin Hir and possibly Abdul Rahim Ayub—who have continued to train members of JI and the ASG in MILF camps. Hardline members of the MILF continue to protect these operatives and contend that keeping channels open to the international jihadist community is in the

MILF's interest in the absence of a durable peace; indeed, continuing this relationship makes perfect sense.

For one, the MILF has not been punished for these actions. Since 2001, the Philippine government has pleaded with the U.S. government not to put the MILF on the Foreign Terrorist Organization list for fear of undermining the peace process, although last year the U.S. government came very close to designating them. Second, most fighters in the MILF see the JI members as their brothers, fellow mujahideen whom they have known since Afghanistan. There is a commitment to a global agenda, which speaks of the fard ayn (the religious obligation) to help other jihadis. Third, the MILF has low expectations for the outcome of the peace process and the government's seriousness and intentions to actually implement it. If history is any guide, their skepticism is well placed. They cannot afford to cut ties to JI and al-Qaeda. The MILF does not regularly or like to employ terrorism, but they use it like clockwork when they suffer battlefield losses—usually to good effect in that it ends the offensives.

The festering conflict in the southern Philippines has regional security implications beyond simple human security concerns in the Philippines. Weak states can easily become failed states and serve to legitimize the Islamic vigilantism of transnational jihadist organizations.

Notes

1. Readers should note that there have been two concurrent moves to amend the constitution. The first would abolish the U.S.-style presidential system and replace it with a Westminster style parliament. The second proposal would break down the strong centralized state and devolve significant political and economic power to the provinces. It is the latter constitutional reform that is the crux of the peace process. Both amendments are languishing because of fighting between the weakened President and a hostile Congress.

2. See, for example, the June 9, 2006 posting on the MILF's website at http://www.luwaran.com/modules.php?name=News&file=article&sid=195.

[From Terrorism Monitor, Volume IV, Issue 14]

Christian Converts and Islamic Terrorism in the Philippines

Peter Chalk

Originally published on April 20, 2006

For several years now, the Republic of the Philippines has attracted the attention of regional and Western authorities as an emergent hub—both logistically and operationally—for cross-border jihadist extremism in Southeast Asia. Most of this focus has been directed toward the Abu Sayyaf Group (ASG), largely on account of the group's historical ties to Osama bin Laden, persistent rejection of any form of religious compromise and/or cohabitation and recent attempts to re-establish itself as a credible and integrated Islamist force (between 1998 and 2001, the group appeared to be motivated more by financial greed than religious fervor). While the ASG is certainly a cause for concern, the activities of extremist Christian converts organized under the auspices of the Rajah Solaiman Revolutionary Movement (RSRM) may represent an even greater threat, not least because of their increasing interaction with militants from the Indonesian-based Jemaah Islamiyya (JI) movement.

The RSRM

The RSRM represents a highly fanatical fringe element of Balik Islam (BI)—a legal movement of Christian converts (or reverts as they like to be known) to the Muslim faith. Official records estimate BI's membership at around 200,000 (out of a total Islamic population of some 6.5 million)—20,000 of whom live in traditionally Catholic Luzon (which makes the movement the seventh largest of the Philippines' local Muslim tribes) (*The Manila Times*, November 17, 2003; *Christian Science Monitor*, November 28, 2005).

It is thought that the RSRM was established around 2002 with the ostensible aim of creating a theocratic Islamic state across the Philippines—supposedly to rectify what it views as the artificial influx of Catholic and Christian influences that had been first introduced by the Spanish and then consolidated under the United States. The group is believed to have a special commando unit that is responsible for carrying out acts of urban sabotage and terrorism and is allegedly financed by Saudi money that is channeled through charitable fronts located in Mindanao (*The Manila Times*, April 12, 2004).

The reputed commander of the RSRM is Ahmed Santos, who was born Hilarion del Rosario Santos III into a landed and squarely Catholic family in 1971 and who took the Islamic testimony of faith 20 years later while working in Riyadh (*The Manila Times*, November 17, 2003). Also acting as the ostensible and self-defined leader of BI, Santos was arrested in October 2005 and charged with inciting rebellion against the Philippine state (which is a non-bailable offense in the Philippines). He is currently being held in a maximum security facility located at the military's sprawling Camp Aguinaldo complex in Manila. Local sources maintain that while Santos almost certainly remains the undisputed leader of the RSRM, responsibility for the day-to-day running of the group now falls to Sheikh Omar Lavilla (formerly known as Reuben Lavilla)—a shadowy figure with a degree in chemical engineering who is thought to have participated in the Chechen jihad (author interviews with security and intelligence officials, Manila, March and November 2005).

The RSRM is small, probably constituting no more than 50-100 hard-core activists. Despite its size, the group has demonstrated both a willingness and ability to "strike well above its weight," and is now known to have played an important role in some of the more high-profile assaults and plots that have taken place in the Philippines since 2004. The most notable include:

- The 2004 partial sinking of Superferry 14, which with 116 fatalities remains the most destructive act of maritime terrorism in the modern age.

- Synchronized bombings in February 2005 that targeted civilian-centric venues in Manila, General Santos City and Davao City.

- A multi-dimensional plan discovered the following month that was allegedly to have involved truck bomb attacks against either the U.S. or Saudi embassies in Manila; mass and light rail transit tracks and stations across the capital region; and nightclubs, restaurants and other venues popular with Western businessmen and tourists in the central commercial district of Makati (author interviews with security and intelligence officials, Manila, March 2006).

For a number of reasons, these incidents generated considerable concern throughout the Philippines as well as among Western government officials and intelligence analysts: they were deliberately calibrated to maximize civilian casualties; they demonstrated that decisive acts of terrorism could be carried out well beyond the Mindanao theater; and at least with regards to the March 2005 plot, they underscored an operational focus on large-scale vehicular-borne devices—a first in the Philippine context—to destroy targets that would have direct implications for wider international interests.

What appears to have especially worried counter-terrorism officials, however, is the fact that the attacks also involved militants associated with JI. More specifically, there is a growing fear that the Indonesian-based movement is now moving to expedite bombings across the Philippines archipelago via the RSRM, which, for its part, appears to be actively prepared to facilitate such endeavors (author interviews with security and intelligence officials, Manila, March and November 2005).

The Rationale Behind the Presumed RSRM-JI Nexus

There are at least four factors that would seem to have salience in terms of explaining the emergent nexus noted above. First, many BI members (the movement from which the RSRM is drawn) are either based in or have intimate knowledge of Manila. This facet makes Christian converts uniquely suited for carrying out attacks that are able to impact directly on the seat of national political, economic and cultural power. JI would presumably have a strong interest in availing itself of such a conduit given the Philippines' overwhelming Catholic character, its universal endorsement of capitalism and liberal democracy and strong defense and security relationship with the United States (all of which symbolize much of what the group is violently opposed to).

Second, and very much related to the above, because RSRM cadres do not originate from ethnic Moro Muslim backgrounds, they are less likely to be identified as Islamist terrorists. Again, this characteristic trait is useful insofar as it provides greater functional and operational latitude for conducting indiscriminate, civilian-oriented attacks in non-Islamic areas. There is good reason to speculate that this has been an equally strong motivating driver behind JI's interest in instituting ties with the RSRM, not least because of the negative backlash it has suffered in Indonesia as a result of bombings that have left large numbers of Muslims killed or maimed (notable cases in point being the attacks on the U.S.-owned Marriott Hotel in 2003 and the Australian Embassy in 2004).

Third, and directly related to the above two points, it would be extremely difficult for JI to act independently in the Philippines given the enormous ethnic and linguistic diversity that exists across the Republic. According to one defense official, because people look, speak and even smell differently from one province to the next, outsiders attempting to infiltrate and operate in local communities under their own auspices would almost certainly stand out and be quickly exposed. Government sources in Manila contend that JI readily appreciates this reality and accepts the necessity of extending its operational and logistical presence in the country primarily by working through homegrown militants that are both known and trusted in their respective regions.

Finally, since the RSRM is made up of converts to Islam, the group arguably has more to prove in validating the credibility of its jihadist credentials. Working in conjunction with an organization that is broadly accepted as presently posing the greatest Islamist threat in Southeast Asia satisfies this requirement and, in so doing, provides a visible ideological fulcrum that can be used to further radicalize existing cadres, mobilize additional recruits and "positively" sway undecided "fence-sitters" (author interviews with security and intelligence officials, Manila and Singapore, November 2005).

The RSRM and the Question of Future Suicide Terrorism in the Philippines

One additional major question that is occupying the minds of security officials in the Philippines—local, regional and international— is whether the RSRM will emerge as an operational conduit for the execution of JI suicide strikes in the Philippines. As noted, the group is composed of converts to the Muslim religion who are keen to actively and visibly demonstrate their commitment to the militant Islamist cause. One of the defining hallmarks of this ideological movement—and one that is heavily imbued in JI—is a commitment to martyrdom, both as a highly effective force equalizer and, more intrinsically, as the most visible way of establishing a true pioneering vanguard to champion the Islamic faith. Speculation is now mounting that the RSRM, in an effort to burnish its jihadist credentials, will take it on itself to further JI's wider Southeast Asian struggle by either assisting Indonesians in carrying out suicide strikes in the Philippines or conducting such attacks independently. While the culture of militant martyrdom has yet to take hold in the Philippines, it is a potential contingency that cannot be dismissed and, should it occur, is one that many commentators believe will manifest through the RSRM.

Indeed, such a process may already have begun to take place. According to intelligence sources in Manila, during interrogation at Camp Aguinaldo, Santos declared that a small cell of RSRM members have not only affirmed the utility and legitimacy of martyrdom, but have also pledged to carry out suicide strikes should it ever be requested of them. If this is in fact the case, there is every possibility that the Philippines will decisively transplant Indonesia as the main operational center for JI jihadist terrorism in Southeast Asia (author interviews with security and intelligence officials, Manila, November 2005 and January 2006).

[From Terrorism Monitor, Volume IV, Issue 8]

Abu Sayyaf Group's Notorious Chieftain: A Profile of Khadaffy Janjalani

Zachary Abuza

Originally published on August 15, 2006

In the first week of August, intense fighting broke out against a faction of Abu Sayyaf Group (ASG) militants on the southern Philippine Island of Jolo (*Sun Star*, August 15, 2006). While the Armed Forces of the Philippines claimed to have killed five militants, their real target, ASG chieftain Khadaffy Janjalani, has continued to elude them. With a $5 million bounty on his head, Janjalani is one of the most wanted men in Southeast Asia (*Manila Times*, August 15, 2006).

Khadaffy Janjalani is the younger brother of ASG founder Abdurajak Janjalani, a fiery cleric, Afghan veteran and friend of Osama bin Laden, who was gunned down on December 18, 1998. His other elder brother, Hector, was captured by the Philippine government and arrested for masterminding a string of bombings in Manila in December 2000.

Abubakar Khadaffy Janjalani (known as Abu Muktar) was born on March 3, 1975 in Isabella City, Basilan, and later briefly studied computers at Mindanao State University before joining his brothers in the early-1990s. He was allegedly trained at an al-Qaeda camp near Mazar e-Sharif in the early-1990s, where he led a group of 20 Moros. He was arrested in 1995, but escaped from police headquarters in Manila under suspicious circumstances.

Khadaffy was involved in some of the ASG's most notorious kidnappings, including the Palawan Island incident of May 27, 2000 that led to the capture of 20 people, and the subsequent beheading of an American hostage (*Sun Star*, May 15, 2006). For this, he was indicted in U.S. federal courts. Yet Philippine National Police debriefs of six ASG members who were captured in October 2002 present a very clear picture that Khadaffy Janjalani was focused primarily on waging jihad through an urban bombing campaign. He became the ASG's top bomb-instructor by 2001-2002. He directed his underlings to reconnoiter targets and acquire bomb-making skills and ingredients, organized training by Middle Eastern operatives and ordered bombings in Zamboanga, General Santos and elsewhere. He organized the

December 2002 bombing in Zamboanga that killed a member of the U.S. Special Forces.

With the killing of ASG leaders Abu Sabaya in 2002 and the capture of Ghalib Andang in 2003, Khadaffy Janjalani became the titular head of the ASG, although he has no formal religious training (*Terrorism Focus*, May 17, 2006). The ASG, moreover, is a loose affiliation of groups, with each commander having significant autonomy. Yet under his leadership, as it is, the ASG has moved away from high-profile kidnappings and back into the realm of terrorism. Janjalani is "working very hard to get the ASG back to its roots," one Philippine intelligence official told this analyst. Yet this was more for personal reasons: he was "trying to assert his legitimacy based on the religious authority of his brother."

In 2001, Khadaffy approached Zulkifli, a top JI operative and the liaison to the Moro Islamic Liberation Front (MILF) in the southern Philippines. Khadaffy wanted to send his men to train in MILF camps, something that the MILF had always resisted. In 2002, however, JI's acting amir, Abu Rusdan, ordered JI operatives to forge an alliance with the ASG. At the same time, the MILF realized that a relationship with the ASG could be useful in terms of building their own network in the Sulu archipelago. (The Sulu archipelago is dominated by ethnic Tausigs, who comprise a very small number of the MILF cadre, but represent the vast majority of their rival, the Moro National Liberation Front.) Zulkifli also arranged for the training of JI operatives in ASG camps in Tawi Tawi and Basilan in return. Rohmat (also known as Zaki), an Indonesian JI member, was the primary liaison to the ASG.

Afterwards, the ASG's area of operations expanded to central Mindanao. According to captured JI leader Nasir bin Abbas, Janjalani provided RP100,000 (roughly $2,000) to Zulkifli to fund the February 2003 bombing of the Cotabato airport and later played a role in the Sasa Wharf and Davao airport bombings. Janjalani recruited and trained the 2005 Valentine's Day bombers, Abu Khalil Trinidad and Gamal Baharan, and has encouraged the recruitment of other Christian converts to extend the ASG's reach beyond Mindanao and the Sulu archipelago (*Sun Star*, October 29, 2005).

Khadaffy has been the focus of an intense manhunt, and following the 2002 U.S.-Philippine operations in Basilan, he is believed to have fled to Tawi Tawi. He was then reported in Palimbang, Mindanao, a MILF stronghold. He moved into the Liguasan Marsh area in Maguindanao, where he was given sanctuary by two MILF hardliners, Wahid Tondok and Salamat Samir, who were also protecting two senior JI operatives, Dulmatin and Umar Patek (*Terrorism Focus*, July 5, 2006). The three were reportedly the target of an air attack in 2004, although they all escaped unharmed. One Philippine intelligence official explained to this analyst, "Khadaffy Janjalani is consolidating the [MILF] radicals. He has the money to support the religious hardliners who will challenge [MILF Chairman Ebrahim el Haj] Murad." Murad, however, was able to isolate some of the hardliners and in late 2005 Khadaffy was purportedly back in Jolo. He travels with a small contingent of around 12-20 men.

There are contentions that the real power in the ASG is not Janjalani, but Radullan Sahiron (known as Commander Putol) and his son, Ismin Sahiron (known as IS). Nonetheless, Janjalani remains one of the most hunted men in Southeast Asia.

[From Terrorism Focus, Volume III, Issue 32]

Australia

Al-Qaeda in Australia

Trevor Stanley

Originally published on October 7, 2005

Al-Qaeda and its allies pose a credible threat to Australian security. While al-Qaeda affiliates have repeatedly bombed Australian interests in Indonesia, the organization has consistently singled out Australia itself as a high priority target. The terror network is determined to make good on these threats, and several plots to attack Australia at home have been thwarted in their early stages. Therefore, an effective Australian counter-terrorism policy must address the threat locally, regionally and globally.

The Region

Because of Australia's unique history, geography and demographics, Australians have a tendency to expect security threats to originate overseas, particularly from Asia. Australia is the world's largest island, and has a population density 1% that of the United Kingdom, producing enormous border security challenges. Radical Islamic insurgencies, cells and training camps are present in several countries in the immediate region.

Australia's nearest neighbor, Indonesia—the world's most populous Muslim-majority country—is the birthplace of the regional terrorist umbrella group, Jemaah Islamiyah (JI). JI's Operational Commander, Riduan Isamuddin, commonly known as "Hambali," was also a member of al-Qaeda's leadership council until his arrest in Thailand in August 2003.

However, Australia should not view the Southeast Asian region in isolation. On closer examination, the boundaries between al-Qaeda's activities in Australia, Southeast Asia and the Middle East are quite amorphous. Funding, ideology, training, logistical support and personnel flow back and forth between al-Qaeda networks in Australia, the immediate region and areas such as Afghanistan and even Europe.

An exclusive emphasis on the region obscures the potential for terrorist threats to infiltrate—or even originate in—Australia.

Within Australia

While neither al-Qaeda nor its regional franchises have yet succeeded in launching an attack on Australian soil, this is not for lack of trying. From the 1980s until 2004, Jemaah Islamiyah delegated Australian operations to the leadership of Abdul Rahim Ayub, an Australian citizen of Indonesian origin. He and his twin brother, Abdul Rahman, organized training for JI members and acted as the intermediaries between Australian JI members and the JI regional leadership. The brothers also taught Islamic studies at al-Hidayah Islamic School in Perth until they fled the country after the Australian Security Intelligence Organization (ASIO) raided their home [1].

It seems the Ayub brothers focused on guarding their nominal positions of authority at the expense of producing operational results. Over time, al-Qaeda sought to intervene more directly to mount a terrorist attack on Australian soil.

One such attempt involved French Lashkar-e-Taiba (LeT)—a Pakistani al-Qaeda affiliate banned by the Australian Government in 2003—operative Willie Virgile Brigitte, who was arrested in Australia in October 2003 after France's Direction de la Surveillance du Territoire (DST) discovered he was in Australia and informed ASIO [2].

While in Australia, Brigitte repeatedly met with Australian terror suspect Faheem Lodhi, whom police allege was planning to bomb either an army base or the electricity grid in New South Wales. Lodhi is alleged to have obtained maps and aerial photographs, contacted a chemical supplier and obtained a mobile telephone using false personal and company names. He is also alleged to have been the leader of foreign students at a LeT terrorist training camp during October 2001.

Brigitte was deported and is currently under indefinite detention without charge in France. Lodhi is in custody in Australia awaiting trial on nine terrorism-related charges.

The Brigitte case demonstrates that foreign terrorists are willing to travel to Australia in order to mount terrorist attacks. That terrorist traffic can also travel in the opposite direction was demonstrated by the case of Jack Roche [3].

Roche, a middle aged, British born-Australian family man and convert to Islam is currently serving a prison sentence over his plans to bomb the Israeli embassy in Canberra. He has contributed to the dissolution of the perceived barrier between the shady foreign terrorist and the ordinary member of society. Even before the London tube train bombings, Roche's case demonstrated that apparently trustworthy citizens can self-recruit and plan attacks within their own country.

Roche's case is also important because it demonstrates the level of hands-on collaboration and interaction between al-Qaeda's core organization, regional affiliates and local recruits.

During February 2000, Roche was sent by Abdul Rahim Ayub to meet with Hambali in Malaysia. Hambali gave Roche funds and instructed him to go to Afghanistan for basic training with al-Qaeda.

In a subsequent trip to Pakistan and Afghanistan, Roche reports that he met with al-Qaeda leaders Osama bin Laden, Khalid Sheikh Mohammad, Muhammad Atef and "Saif" (presumably Saif al-Adel). In the Afghan training camp, Roche was given explosives training and assigned a mission, along with further funds.

Roche was to be the founding member of an all-Caucasian cell that would launch sporadic guerrilla attacks against Jewish and American interests in Australia. In addition to plans to conduct bombings and assassinations against Israeli and American diplomatic missions, the al-Qaeda leadership discussed assassinating prominent Australian Jewish businessman "Diamond" Joe Gutnick.

Roche's first two tasks were to conduct surveillance and to recruit two more white Australian Muslims who would be sent to Afghanistan and trained in sniping and explosives respectively, completing a cell capable of blending easily into the Australian community.

Returning to Australia, Roche began implementing the first phase of the plan. In June and December, he conducted photographic and video surveillance of the Israeli consulate in Sydney and the Israeli embassy in Canberra, along with his (adult) son and a sympathetic taxi driver.

The plan, however, began to fall apart when Roche attempted to recruit his fellow Muslims. Already an impressionable person, Roche's credulity had been exacerbated when he converted to Islam, making him an easy mark for al-Qaeda. The disapproval of his fellow Muslims gave him pause for thought.

The plan received another blow when the Ayub brothers got wind of it, and reacted defensively to al-Qaeda's attempt to sideline them. By August 2000, JI's spiritual leader Abu Bakar Ba'asyir had ordered Roche to halt the operation, and by 2001 Roche had abandoned the mission.

The plan's initial success and eventual failure hinge on two factors. Firstly, the decentralized, somewhat ad hoc network of al-Qaeda, regional and Australian-based agents succeeded in formulating and carrying out the early stages of a plausible plan. However, the unclear lines of authority inherent in such a loose network ultimately led to failure.

Secondly, al-Qaeda's recruiting strategy made sense in an Australian context. In Britain, large and longstanding Pakistani and North African immigrant communities generate youths who are alienated both from the general community and from their own cultural traditions, and are therefore susceptible to radicalism. In Australia, no such enclaves really exist. The aggressive proselytism of radical Muslim fringe groups, however, has attracted converts who are already alienated from wider Australian society. These individuals, such as Roche, are susceptible to the overtures of terrorist recruiters. Yet, it was the negative response of converts that Roche himself attempted to recruit that led him to question his mission.

Incitement to Terrorism

In the wake of the July 2005 bombings in London, Australian public attention has focused on the role of Islamic fundamentalist fringe groups in the country. In particular, Sheikh Muhammad Omran, who has claimed that the London bombings were not carried out by Muslims, and that the September 11 attacks were an "inside job," has developed a media profile that threatened to overshadow the August 23 summit between the Prime Minister, Immigration Minister, security officials and mainstream Muslim leaders. Omran also calls himself a friend of Abu Qatada and Osama bin Laden, although he denies that either is a terrorist, and is reportedly critical of their anti-Saudi position.

Omran is the spiritual leader of Islamic Information and Services Network of Australasia (IISNA), a group that propagates a pro-Saudi Salafi position in Australia. There have been calls for foreign-printed books being sold at IISNA's Sydney bookshop to be banned because of their incitement to political violence and racial and religious hatred. Similar calls were directed at the bookshop of a smaller outfit, the Islamic Youth Movement (IYM).

While the sale of foreign-printed radical publications in two Sydney bookshops is obviously of concern to the community, banning these books would not close off the most important medium for terrorist propaganda, which is the Internet. Alongside its bookshop, IYM has been publishing a Qutbist, pro-al-Qaeda web publication, Nida'ul Islam (Call of Islam) for a decade [4]. Published in English and Arabic, Nida'ul Islam printed interviews with Osama bin Laden, Omar Abd al-Rahman, Ansar al-Islam leader Fateh Krekar and JI leaders Abu Bakar Ba'asyir and Abdullah Sungkar. The publication also featured regular updates on guerrilla battles and terror strikes around the Middle East. Articles on parenting and society described non-Muslims as filthy, corrupt and disgusting and encouraged home schooling. Democracy was condemned.

Nida'ul Islam is published by Bilal Khazal, a Lebanese immigrant who was convicted on terrorism charges by a Lebanese military tribunal in absentia in December 2003. A CIA report places Khazal at an Afghan training camp in 1998, as a confidant of bin Laden and Dr. Ayman al-Zawahiri. ASIO has kept tabs on Khazal since November 1994, and in 2004 he was arrested for compiling a terrorist instruction manual and posting it on the Internet. His trial will begin in April next year [5]. Although the law seems to be finally catching up with Khazal, it should be noted that until 2000 he was working as a baggage handler for Qantas airlines. And Nida'ul Islam continues to publish its militant message from the Sydney suburb of Lakemba.

Conclusion

An eventual terrorist attack in Australia could involve operatives from al-Qaeda proper infiltrated from abroad, JI terrorists, or even domestic operatives. Most likely, these elements will work together in any successful attack. The greatest terrorist threat may come from Australia's own citizens, and they may not look like "Islamic fundamentalists" or even like Muslims.

The examples given in this article are illustrative, not exhaustive. A worrying number of Australian citizens have trained with al-Qaeda or LeT in Afghanistan, and several are currently facing terrorism charges in separate cases in Australia and the United States.

Australia is not only the target of al-Qaeda's global terrorist message, but also in some cases its point of origin. Australian security depends on successfully constraining al-Qaeda and its allies in the Middle East, Europe, Southeast Asia and Australia itself, and ultimately ensuring that alternatives to violence and social alienation are available both in Australia and abroad.

Notes:
1. "Behind Closed Doors" *The Australian*, August 5, 2005, p. 15.
2. ASIO Report to Australian Parliament 2003-2004, part 2. http://www.asio.gov.au/Publications/Content/AnnualReport03_04/arhtml/Report_to_Parliament_20003.html.
3. Sentence in the case of The Queen and Jack Roche, District Court of Western Australia, June 1, 2004. http://www.districtcourt.wa.gov.au/ content/files/binaryFiles/Roche_sentence.pdf.
4. http://www.islam.org.au/articles/.
5. "The Baggage of Bilal Khazal" *Sydney Morning Herald*, June 4, 2004.

[From Terrorism Monitor, Volume III, Issue 19]

Japan

Japan: A Target for al-Qaeda?

Guido Olimpio

Originally published on March 9, 2006

While surprising, Japan is a secondary target for al-Qaeda. Tokyo backed the intervention in Afghanistan and deployed a small detachment of troops to Iraq; these two moves were interpreted by Osama bin Laden as a declaration of war. On October 18, 2003, in a message broadcast by al-Jazeera, al-Qaeda's leader said: "We reserve the right to respond at the appropriate time and place against all the countries participating in this unjust war, particularly Britain, Spain, Australia, Poland, Japan and Italy" (for an earlier assessment on al-Qaeda's threat to Japan, see Joseph Ferguson's *Terrorism Monitor* article from January 30, 2004). Threats against targets in the center of Tokyo have also been made by the elusive Abu Hafs al-Masri Brigades. Last summer, Jean-Louis Bruguiere, a French judge with considerable expertise and vast knowledge of the world of intelligence, said a devastating terrorist attack on Japanese soil was indeed a possibility (*Financial Times*, August 26, 2005).

In the spring of 2005, intelligence services were following the trail of a mysterious al-Qaeda operative. According to intelligence sources, the operative had left Pakistan to travel to Southeast Asia, where he was planning to recruit a cell for a terrorist attack in Japan. It is possible this cell was made up of Arabs supported by local Islamist extremists who may have been Jemaah Islamiyah activists. Intelligence sources believe al-Qaeda was contemplating an attack just before the September 2005 Japanese elections in an obvious attempt to reproduce the "Spanish" effect of 3/11. What is referred to as the "Spanish route" in some intelligence circles works like this: it starts with threats from al-Qaeda leaders on the Arab satellite TV networks; it continues with warnings on the internet; a debate starts to rage in online jihadi forums; actions are tested on a small scale, and eventually front-line terrorists strike against major targets. While no concrete proof exists, French intelligence has added an important piece to the puzzle: it is possible that a mission may be entrusted to a mixed group, with Lebanese and Iraqi extremists sent to assist fellow militants who are long-time residents of Japan. In any case, signals intelligence reports an increase in electronic communications between key figures living in Waziristan in Pakistan and others now permanently based in East Asia.

Possible Targets

Japan is an attractive target for terrorists for the following reasons. First of all, Japan's security services are unfamiliar with threats of this type and magnitude. In the past, they have been up against Japan's Red Army, minor radical groups and the Aum Shinrikyo sect (*Japan Times*, June 27, 2002). Second, Japanese society is open, and there is intensive movement of people and goods. Third, an attack would have an immediate adverse impact on Tokyo's global economic weight. According to the Japanese National Police, the country's ports are the most attractive targets for Islamist extremists. A major explosion in a Japanese port would lead to serious political and economic repercussions. More broadly, the country's transport infrastructure (in particular bullet trains), symbols of economic power, large corporations and multinationals constitute other primary targets. These targets are a constant in al-Qaeda's terrorist offensives against the West for three reasons: first, they replicate the effects in Madrid and London, with transportation systems left in chaos; second, they spread panic among cities' inhabitants by magnifying the sense of the terrorists' power; third, they further al-Qaeda's strategy of sabotaging the economies of key U.S. allies (*Terrorism Monitor*, March 25, 2004).

Moreover, terrorists might opt to target Japanese interests abroad. The oil tankers that ply the waters between the Persian Gulf and Japan are an enticing prey for Islamist extremists. In this case, the attackers' hunting ground is a geographical area they are familiar with. Simulations carried out in several intelligence centers have considered the hijack of a supertanker, followed by the threat to either sink or block it in one of the area's strategic passageways, such as the straits of Hormuz or Malacca (Institute for Counter-Terrorism, Herzylia, Israel, September 2004). Initially, there would be two protagonists involved in this attempted blackmail: the terrorists and Japan. Subsequently— especially if demands are made for the release of prisoners held in a third country—the crisis would acquire a wider impact, and lead to diverging opinions on how to respond. Furthermore, terrorists may attempt to strike either a U.S. military base or a warship in Japanese maritime territory. The likelihood of this, however, is very low, not least because U.S. military assets in Japan are highly secured.

Pakistani Presence

The Japanese authorities are always very cautious about disseminating information on the presence of terrorist cells and radical groups. It is an open secret, however, that the security services are closely monitoring the country's Muslim community. It is made up of between 70,000 and 90,000 immigrants, mostly from Indonesia, Pakistan, India, Iran and Turkey. The Sunni Pakistanis attract most of the suspicion and are monitored especially closely. In December 2005, local newspaper Sankei Shimbum published a police report alleging that members of Sipah-e-Sahaba Pakistan (SSP) are trying to establish a base in Japan. SSP (now ostensibly called the Milat-e-Islamia Pakistan) is widely regarded as the most ferocious Sunni supremacist organization in the world and is believed to have loose links to al-Qaeda (*Terrorism Monitor*, January 27, 2005). The group was outlawed in Pakistan—not primarily for massacring Pakistani Shiites—but because of its alleged al-Qaeda links.

SSP first caught the eye of Japanese security agents two years earlier when checks were being made on lists of foreigners who had entered Japan. The security agents spotted a 30 year-old Pakistani who was conducting political and religious propaganda. After careful investigations, it was determined that the man intended to establish a Sipah outpost between Tokyo and Yokohama. Police later arrested him together with an accomplice who was working as a trader. The authorities then investigated further to establish whether the detained men were in contact with possible accomplices abroad. The presence of Sipah is a cause of serious concern. On the one hand, the organization could provide support for al-Qaeda's activities since it operates in over 17 countries. On the other hand, the group has long waged a violent onslaught against Shiites and it could be looking for new battlefields in Asia. Obvious targets would include the tiny number of Pakistani Shiites in Japan in addition to Iranians. Japanese security services are also worried by increasing money-laundering activities in Asia and the proliferation of the hawala (informal network for money transfer) system.

The Dumont Case

In late May 2004, Japanese police units made a series of raids in and around Tokyo, netting five suspects. On checking documents, bank accounts, money movements and phone calls, the investigators established that the suspects were in contact with Lionel Dumont, a convert to Islam and one of the first Euro-jihadists. A Frenchman of Algerian origin and a former paratrooper, Dumont was a member of the notorious Roubaix gang which mixed organized crime with radical forms of Islam (*The Standard*, January 9, 2005). Forced to stay out of the limelight for a long period of time, Dumont eventually made his way to Japan and lived in the quiet town of Nishi-Kawaguchi from 2002-2003 where he developed a cover as a car salesman (*Japan Times*, June 2, 2004).

Police discovered a post office account on which the terrorist had conducted transactions involving thousands of dollars. It appears that Dumont was continuously receiving and withdrawing money, and only part of this intensive activity was connected with his job: in no way could certain deposits have been compatible with the sale of used cars to Russia and North Korea. Numerous international phone calls made by Dumont were of particular interest to the police. His direct and indirect acquaintances in extremist circles lead to the suspicion that his presence in Japan was connected with the preparation of some kind of terrorist action (*Japan Times*, May 20, 2004). The police found contacts with more than a dozen suspects: among them a Russian sailor tied to the Russian mafia (a possible channel for weapons), an immigrant from Guinea and a man from Bangladesh working in a mobile phone shop. The last suspect had access to a U.S. military base in Japan.

Dumont left Japan in 2003 and was later arrested in Germany where he was finally extradited to France. At his recent trial (after which Dumont was sentenced to 30 years imprisonment), magistrates reconstructed the journeys the accused had made and provided some important details. During his stay in Asia, Dumont visited Thailand, Indonesia, Malaysia as well as Japan. It was in Malaysia that he met up with Andrew Rowe, a Briton of Jamaican descent who had fought with

Dumont in Bosnia and, like him, was a globetrotter of Islamist terrorism (*The Standard*, January 9, 2005). According to unofficial reports, their assigned mission was to establish themselves in Asia (by using the cover of tourists and businessmen) in order to prepare the way for future operations. It was actually on Rowe's trail that German intelligence discovered Dumont in Munich. The long period spent in Japan by the French-Algerian terrorist brings to mind two other relatively distant episodes that relate to al-Qaeda and Japan. In 1987, Khalid Sheikh Mohammed, one of the masterminds of the 9/11 attacks, bought some tunnel digging machines in Japan which were later used to build hideouts for mujahideen in Afghanistan. In 1995, Mohammed Khaled Salim (aka Rashed Daoud al 'Owhali), who played a part in the African bomb attacks of August 1998, purchased electronic materials in Tokyo. These were later found in Ethiopia after the failed assassination attempt of Egyptian President Hosni Mubarak in Addis Ababa in June 1995.

Considered as a whole, the factual information and the more nebulous reports provide a disquieting picture. Japan, like Italy and Denmark, is seriously at risk of a terrorist attack (*Terrorism Monitor*, January 30, 2004). Al-Qaeda's propaganda machine has included it in its list of enemies and claims it has legitimate motives for doing so (al-Jazeera, October 18, 2003). It should, therefore, come as no surprise if Japanese politicians increasingly maintain—in much the same way as in Britain before July 7—that the question is not "whether," but "when" the terrorists will attack.

[From Terrorism Monitor, Volume IV, Issue 5]

Part VI
Europe and the Americas

New Reports Allege Foreign Fighters in Iraq Returning to Europe

Kathryn Haahr

Originally published on May 25, 2006

Recent pronouncements by a Spanish judge who has led high-level inquiries into al-Qaeda in Spain, Baltazar Garzon, and the head of France's domestic security service, Pierre de Bousquet, imply that Iraqi foreign fighters are already returning to Europe to re-establish or establish new networks to support terrorist operations in Europe (AFP, May 9, 2006). While Garzon's and Bousquet's official comments provide no concrete details about the number of European Islamists returning from Iraq nor their nationalities, it is apparent that there is terrorist activity. With Iraq being the new center of gravity for jihad, Europe has become the de facto center of gravity for recruitment, weapons and financial activities, all critical to ensuring the continuation of jihad in Iraq and, increasingly, in Europe.

The return of jihadists from Iraq and Afghanistan would transform European states from logistical platforms (support infrastructure) to "battle front stations" (operational structures). After their experiences in Iraq, jihadists are probably returning infused with the intention to engage in jihad in their respective European countries and to make Europe the new front in the international jihad. These jihadists will bring back ideological concepts and recruitment and fighting techniques that can assist their efforts in radicalizing and mobilizing segments of the Muslim populations in Spain, Italy and France. Of particular concern is training they may have received in fighting techniques (such as IEDs and suicide bombings) and the use of chemicals for unconventional attacks. Several jihadi personalities, including Abu Musab al-Suri, have legitimized the use of chemical, biological, nuclear and radiological weapons as a tool in jihad.

The debut of "mobile jihad satellite platforms" in Europe demonstrates how critical Europe is to sustaining al-Qaeda related terrorist operations on a global basis. European counter-terrorism officials have been concerned about the terrorist threat of returning foreign jihadists from fighting in Iraq since the discovery of extensive Iraqi jihadist support networks following the U.S. invasion of Iraq.

During the past two years, arrests of Islamists and Salafi-Jihadists have been made in Spain, France and Italy. Those arrested had close links to the GSPC, GICM and al-Qaeda, revealing a structured, and, at times, interconnected network of cells, each responsible for support such as recruitment of volunteers to fight in Iraq, falsification of paperwork for travel throughout Europe and to Iraq, and procurement of explosives materials. Counter-terrorism officials from these three countries now know that the heads of the cells in Spain, France and Italy—which were dispersed regionally throughout each country—and the members of each cell were predominantly foreign Muslims from Morocco and Algeria (*Terrorism Monitor*, May 4, 2006). It is probable that there remain sleeper cells and a loose underground network of terrorists, collaborators and sympathizers all capable of providing non-tactical and tactical assistance to the returning foreign fighters.

There are a few documented cases of Spanish and French Muslim citizens who traveled to Iraq. At least 50 French Arabs have traveled to Iraq for suicide operations over the last two years (Grupo de Estudios Estratégicos, http://www.gees.org). In Spain, there is some data about the increasing number of Spaniards who are members of terrorist cells responsible for sending suicide bombers to Iraq. The continuing arrests, especially in Spain, of new al-Qaeda sympathizers and Muslims indoctrinated to engage in jihad in Iraq indicates that the terrorist mission for radicalizing and recruiting fighters for Iraq is active.

Based upon Garzon's and other senior European counter-terrorism officials' comments about foreign fighters returning from Iraq, it would appear that the intelligence services of France and Spain have a way of monitoring the travel of some of these individuals. Those foreign fighters that do enter France, Spain or Italy without detection could do so by first traveling to a staging country—such as Syria or other countries in the region—where the jihadist could try to "hide" his travel from Iraq. From the staging country, the jihadist would pick up a falsified passport, if needed, and enter Europe by boat, train or car. The individual, once integrated into one of these countries, would easily disappear into one of the multiple Muslim pockets where he would be hidden and protected.

[From Terrorism Focus, Volume III, Issue 20]

Balkans

Al-Qaeda's Recruitment Operations in the Balkans

Anes Alic

Originally published on June 15, 2006

The recent arrest and pending trial in Bosnia of three young men believed to have been plotting terrorist attacks on Western targets in the capital of Sarajevo have sparked fears that al-Qaeda is recruiting "white Muslims" in the country. Bosnia's porous borders and weak law enforcement institutions, coupled with the presence of hundreds of Islamic fighters who arrived from Arab countries during the 1992-1995 war, make this small war-torn country an easy meeting point for al-Qaeda networks.

During the pre-trial hearing on May 3, 2006 of Bosnia's first-ever terrorism case, three men—Mirsad Bektasevic, Cesur Abulkadir and Bajro Ikanovic—pleaded not guilty to charges of plotting a terrorist attack either in Bosnia or elsewhere. Two others—Senad Husanovic and Amir Bajric—who were charged with possession of explosives and believed to be heading up the alleged network's logistics, also pleaded not guilty and were released on bail.

The five men, four of whom are teenagers, were arrested in October and December last year in the Sarajevo suburbs of Butmir and Hadzici. Bektasevic and Abdulkadir were arrested in late October in Butmir's apartment owned by Bektasevic's cousin. They also rented two apartments in downtown Sarajevo, an anonymous high-ranking Bosnian police source told The Jamestown Foundation. While Bektasevic is a Bosnian Muslim national with Swedish and Serbian citizenship, and Ikanovic is a Turkish national with Danish residency, the remaining suspects were all Bosnians.

On October 20, 2005, agents found some 30 kilograms of explosives and dozens of guns in raids on three apartments used by the suspects. They also said that they found a suicide vest. Yet, the most significant piece of evidence discovered was a videotape showing the two men asking God for forgiveness for the sacrifice they were about to make. Two of the suspects—Bektasevic and Abdulkadir—were wearing face masks and had videotaped themselves making bombs, the police source said.

Nevertheless, the first months of the investigation failed to turn up enough concrete evidence that the alleged network was plotting a terrorist attack in Bosnia, so the local authorities turned to Scotland Yard and the FBI for forensic assistance. FBI forensic tests on the face masks determined that they had been worn by Bektasevic and Abdulkadir, while Scotland Yard confirmed that the voice on the videotape belonged to Bektasevic.

Faced with the new evidence, the two main suspects changed their original statements in which they had denied plotting terrorist attacks, saying instead that they had intended to "warn" Bosnian and Western European authorities about Muslims suffering in Iraq and Afghanistan. They also said they were plotting to "warn" the Bosnian government to withdraw its soldiers from Iraq. Bosnia recently sent some 30 soldiers there as part of a de-mining unit, the source said. He also said the alleged network was most likely plotting an attack on the European Forces (EUFOR) base in Sarajevo, located just 100 meters from the house where the two main suspects were arrested.

The investigation, however, has extended well beyond Bosnia, indicating the possibility of a "white al-Qaeda" network operating from Western to Southeastern Europe. Bektasevic operated under the code name Maximus and kept in touch with a group of at least three men in Britain, all of whom were arrested by British police in early November. The British police have not revealed details on the arrests. Days after the Sarajevo arrests, police in Copenhagen detained seven men and one woman, most of them Danish converts to Islam, on suspicion that they were planning suicide bombings somewhere in Europe. Four of the suspects arrested in Denmark have been released due to lack of evidence against them, while three have been released on bail. Evidence linked those arrested in Denmark to those arrested in Sarajevo (*Slobodna Bosna*, April 22, 2006).

In the meantime, however, the trial in Bosnia has been postponed for at least three months while prosecutors and investigators attempt to collect more solid evidence against the five. Some experts say that the Bosnian authorities moved too quickly to arrest the five, preventing authorities from learning the intended target of the alleged terrorist plot and revealing the extent of a wider "white Muslim" network in Europe. Bosnian security agencies allegedly discussed the repercussions of making the arrests too soon, but chose to move to thwart a possible terrorist attack before it was too late (*Vecernji List*, April 26, 2006).

While there is largely agreement that al-Qaeda is attempting to recruit white Muslims in Bosnia, there is some disagreement on the extent of these efforts. EUFOR says that it has no evidence that Bosnia and Herzegovina or the Balkans represent a bigger terrorist threat than any other country in Europe (Fena.ba, April 26, 2006). "We cannot exclude the existence of the threat in any country and that goes for BiH as well," EUFOR Commander Gian Marco Chiarini said. "However, at this moment EUFOR has no data that would lead us to the conclusion that the threat of terrorism and terrorist attacks is larger in BiH than elsewhere" (*Dnevni Avaz*, April 25, 2006).

The U.S. State Department's 2005 report on terrorism, however, warned that while Bosnian authorities had been highly cooperative in the war on terrorism, Bosnia could be an attractive locale for terrorists because of its weak state comprised of semi-autonomous power centers. Additionally, while secular Bosnia is no friend to Islamic extremism, several hundred Arab mujahideen warriors who arrived in Bosnia to fight on the Bosnian Muslim side during the war are likely to be sympathetic to al-Qaeda. According to the Bosnian Foreign Ministry, it is believed that as many as 6,000 Arab volunteers arrived during the war. After the war, up to 400 of them acquired local citizenship, many of them marrying local women. They came from a variety of locations in the Middle East and North Africa, but largely from Saudi Arabia, Syria and Algeria.

Perhaps most significantly, the pending terrorism trial has ignited a fierce debate about these naturalized citizens, prompting fears of a backlash. Bosnia-Herzegovina security agencies are actively investigating individuals and groups, including al-Hussein Imad, also known as Abu Hamza, the informal leader of naturalized Bosnian citizens, who recently warned that revoking citizenship from these Arab fighters could result in protests, blockades and other forms of unrest (Radio B92, May 26, 2006).

Anonymous EUFOR sources told The Jamestown Foundation that Abu Hamza was believed to have recently formed an organization called "Ansarija" to provide legal assistance to former mujahideen threatened with deportation to their home countries. Abu Hamza told Bosnian FTV's "60 Minutes" political talk show on April 18, 2006 that those being targeted for deportation could not be legally expelled as they faced charges in their countries of origin. The Syrian-born Abu Hamza is among those who are facing deportation. He arrived in Bosnia in the early 1990s as a student. Investigators say he lied on his citizenship application.

Bosnian authorities have stepped up their investigation into how hundreds of Arabs obtained Bosnian citizenship. According to a high-ranking police source speaking to The Jamestown Foundation, 104 naturalized citizens are in the process of having their citizenship revoked. Yet, the whereabouts of 64 of those being targeted remain unknown. The Bosnian government believes that these people present a potential security threat, and Western intelligence agencies agree. Western agencies are cooperating with Bosnian authorities in the terrorism investigation and pressuring local officials to locate and conduct checks on the 64 naturalized citizens who remain unaccounted for—some of whom authorities believe may have been in touch with Bektasevic and the other suspects (*Nezavisne Novine*, May 25, 2006).

Most of these naturalized citizens are believed to live in Sarajevo and the central Bosnian towns of Zenica, Tuzla and Travnik. Since late last year, police have conducted several raids in the mountains surrounding those towns, suspecting that militants have training camps there and caches of weapons and explosives. Thus far, however, nothing has turned up.

Without a significant amount of technical and other assistance from Western intelligence and security forces, Bosnia is ill-equipped to prevent terrorist infiltration. Recent police reforms—including one significant reform that created a state-level police agency replacing the two separate Bosnian-Croat Federation and Republika Srpska agencies—are only embryonic and untested, as is cooperation between the present three agencies.

Although Islamic extremism is not nearly as prevalent in Bosnia as it is in many Western European countries, the threat must also be measured against its security forces' counter-terrorism capabilities, which in this case are starting from ground zero. Furthermore, while secular Bosnia is far from being a sympathetic haven for Islamic extremist activities, its institutional weaknesses and its wartime history of having been "saved" in part by Arab mujahideen could make it an easy and symbolic meeting and recruitment point for a new, white al-Qaeda network.

[From Terrorism Monitor, Volume IV, Issue 12]

Italy

Italy and Islamic Militancy: From Logistics Base to Potential Target

Guido Olimpio

Originally published on September 21, 2005

      Islamic radicals have been present in Italy in large numbers since 1992, shortly after the defeat of the Red Army in Afghanistan. Like in other European countries, the influx of former mujahideen volunteers from the Arab world had a great impact. Geographically and politically, the center of gravity for the Islamists was North Italy, where thousands of Muslim immigrants live and work. In Milan, the most active are from Egypt and Algeria, whereas Turin, Varese and Cremona are the territory of Moroccans and Tunisians. Further south, apart from a few small groupings in Rome, the most significant presence is in Naples, where Algerians have established a bridgehead. The Palestinians are of less importance, being fewer and generally more wary of extremist doctrines.

      In the mid-nineties, during the wars in the former Yugoslavia, Milan became the "hotbed" of Islamic extremism for five main reasons: 1) the activism of the Egyptian Imam Anwar Shaban, linked to al-Gamaa al-Islamiya and close to the positions of the blind Sheikh Omar Abdel Rahman; 2) the importance of its Viale Jenner mosque, a proselytizing and recruitment center with international connections; 3) its geographical position, which allows easy access to Northern Europe, the Balkans, the U.S. and the Middle East; 4) the presence of numerous Afghan war veterans and North African extremists linked to terrorist movements; and 5) the ease of collecting funds, documents and arms in North Italy for the jihad fronts, especially in Morocco and Chechnya.

      Shaban, with his many contacts in the Persian Gulf, was instrumental in keeping the rank and file of the Islamic networks in Italy together. While clearly inspired by the principles of international jihad, his main objective was to bring down the Egyptian regime. His sermons drew in new recruits, many of whom were sent to Bosnia to fight the Serbs, with a smaller number going to Chechnya [1]. Viale Jenner formed part of a network that linked up Islamist groups in Austria, Germany, Turkey and the U.S.. Milan was often visited by a then little-known character who was to gain notoriety in 2003: Mullah Krekar, head of Ansar al-Islam [2].

In the course of investigations into the February 1993 attack on the Twin Towers, telephone contacts between Milanese Islamic militants and the cell involved in the attack were uncovered. There were also close links with other prominent international exponents of jihad, including Ayman al-Zawahiri, who faxed over his orders and advice. Shaban gradually increased his involvement in Bosnia and became the emir of the Mujahideen Battalion. When the war ended, many of the volunteers went back to their countries (including Italy) and started forming the first al-Qaeda groups in Europe. The Imam's career ended in 1996 when he was killed at a Croatian road block. But his death didn't signal the end of radicalism in Italy as many of his followers went on to develop networks of their own.

Investigations by the Italian authorities (the Milan counter-terror unit in particular) since 1995 show the growth of this phenomenon. Operation Sfinge (targeted the followers of Shaban) brought 35 suspected Islamic militants to trial; Operation Ritorno led to the investigation and sentencing of 11 Islamists; Operation Fattar led to the sentencing of 10 individuals and three acquittals and the Essid Operation led to the successful sentencing of 13 individuals.

Various radical groups have a presence in either northern or southern Italy. The Armed Islamic Group, the Moroccan Islamic Combatant Group (the draft of a document about the formation of the group was found in Cremona in 1998), the Algerian Islamic Salvation Front, the Egyptian Gamaa, the Egyptian Jihad and the pan-Islamic (albeit non-violent) Hizb ut-Tahrir all have some presence in Italy. The extent of the phenomenon is demonstrated by the fact that, despite the police raids, the cells continue to reform—stronger than before— thanks to the activities of "veterans" such as Abdelkader Es-Sayed [3] and Nasr Mustafa, alias Abu Omar [4]. Investigations have proved that Es-Sayed knew about the September 11 attacks before they happened [5].

From 1995 to the present, northern Italy—with its mosques in Viale Jenner and Via Quaranta in Milan—has been an important base for Islamic militants, which have used it for: recruiting mujahideen for Afghanistan, Iraq and Chechnya; recruiting suicide bombers for the Zarqawi network in Iraq; supplying forged documents for international operations; illicit financial activities; illegal immigrant trafficking and providing a base of support for fugitives.

Since the anti-terrorism offensives prompted by 9/11, the extremists have changed their modus operandi. They visit mosques less frequently because of increased surveillance and they also establish small communities in provincial towns that do not have a strong police presence. Moreover, they have developed special and largely secure channels of encrypted communication with their reference contacts and task masters in Saudi Arabia, Pakistan and Iran. The networks are no longer led by charismatic figures like Shaban, but by local leaders who, although considered minor and unimportant, are capable of planning and ordering attacks [6]. These local leaders have the military expertise and connections with mid- to high-level operatives in al-Qaeda to successfully plan and execute attacks. For example, in an area north of Milan there is a small but very active group of Pakistani militants with links to London and Lahore. Some of them are veterans of the Afghan war. According to informed sources, the Italian military intelligence service (SISMI) is keeping a very close eye on this network, suspecting that they are controlled by a rogue agent in Pakistan's notorious Inter-Services Intelligence Directorate (ISID—better known as the "ISI").

As with the rest of Europe, the Italian intelligence services are concerned about the militants connected to the Islamic Moroccan Combatant Group, which has roots not only in rural areas but also in larger cities such as Milan and Turin. The arrest of Mohammed Rabei in Milan, alias Mohammed the Egyptian, one of the masterminds behind the Madrid bombings, has probably prevented an attack in Italy or in other European countries. After the attacks in Spain, Rabei traveled to Italy to find a safe place and recruit potential terrorists. Furthermore, recent developments have confirmed links between extremists in Italy and the Zarqawi network in Iraq.

Also noteworthy are changes in the funding methods and communication channels. Before 9/11 the money came from zakat (alms) and donations from the Persian Gulf States, which were usually routed through Middle Eastern banks. Since 9/11 the funds have been coming in cash, usually brought over by couriers with suitcases full of dollars, or from criminal enterprises such as forged documents, drug trafficking and forged residence permits. Moreover, Pakistanis and Somalis run call centers, which give excellent cover for fundraising and "clean" phones. According to investigative sources, one militant, involved in clandestine activities, would use 30-40 SIM cards for a single mobile phone. His method was very simple: he would make a first call and pronounce a few words, before changing the SIM card and ringing the number again to communicate a few words in code.

The Islamic extremists in Italy have proven themselves to be particularly adept at producing forged documents. Some of the forged passports ended up in the possession of the network involved in the killing of Afghan Northern Alliance leader Ahmad Shah Masood in September 2001. Others found their way to an organization active in Morocco. And yet others were found to have been sent to al-Qaeda leaders arrested in Malaysia in 2002. The militants have developed the expertise to produce not just Italian passports but also documents of North African countries (Morocco in particular).

The lives of cell members in Italy have always been governed by Spartan principles, putting security before all else. In some districts where they have safe houses, they have created "fortress" zones with a trusted network of look-outs. One of these was in the Porta Venezia district of Milan where a member of the cell spends hours in a little Arabic restaurant posing as a customer, the Tunisian barber keeps an eye on a junction, the Algerian merchant watches over a possible escape route; they are like sentries with eyes and ears everywhere. They note the faces of all "suspect" persons including Italian law enforcement agents, but above all spies from Arabic intelligence agencies. The militants display regimented behavior and have regulated and standardized conduct through the production of manuals, one of which was found by the Carabinieri (paramilitary police) in Milan in July 2002, in an apartment used by Islamic militants.

Given this impressive presence in Italy, if the order comes for an attack, there are various teams that are ready to act; all of which have people capable of preparing explosive devices, the hideouts, the documents needed for escape and the would-be martyrs. Moreover, it is very easy to procure explosives in Italy, the traditional sources of supply being either local (Calabrian mafia) or East European (particularly Albanian) organized crime networks. The going price for a kilo of plastic explosives is about $1,500, whereas civil-use explosives costs $1,000 per kilo and a machine gun can be bought for just a few hundred dollars [7]. A Tunisian detainee who agreed to cooperate with the authorities spoke of a cell, active from 2001 to 2002, that had looked into ways of fabricating bombs from substances freely available on the market: the ingredients and the formula were the same as those used in the London bombs [8]. In the attacks, they were to be packed in trucks specially reinforced to carry large quantities of explosives, rucksacks left in station luggage deposits and a police car that was to be stolen, filled with explosives and launched against the Cathedral in Milan. The possible targets considered were the U.S. Embassy in Rome, American Consulates, an international school in Milan and the Police Headquarters [9].

There are essentially two reasons why there have been no attacks in Italy thus far; several plots have been thwarted by police and intelligence action and in certain cases the Islamic extremists have elected to protect their logistics networks. But, as in London, this can change in the space of a few hours.

Notes
1. Islamic source in Milan.
2. From investigation papers, Operation Sfinge.
3. Possibly died in 2001 in Afghanistan.
4. Seized by the CIA in 2003 in Milan.
5. Police report.
6. Intelligence source.
7. *Corriere della Sera*, December 7, 2005.
8. Police report, 2003.
9. Intelligence source.

[From Terrorism Monitor, Volume III, Issue 18]

GSPC in Italy: The Forward Base of Jihad in Europe

Kathryn Haahr

Originally published on February 9, 2006

Italy has evolved from a logistics base for Islamic militants to a de facto base of operations for Algeria's Salafist Group for Preaching and Combat (GSPC) targeting Italy, other European countries and the United States. While the GSPC continues to engage in and support terrorist operations in Algeria, the group's emphasis on "out-of-Algeria" terrorist operations has made it the largest, most cohesive and dangerous terrorist organization in the al-Qaeda orbit.

GSPC cells in Italy employ a dual-track approach to planning terrorist attacks and provide support infrastructure—safe houses, communications, weapons procurement and documentation—to GSPC networks in other European countries.

Historical Timeline and Profile of the GSPC Network in Italy

Italian security services' detention of and investigations into the activities of Salafist Islamists recently culminated in the exposure of a deep and wide network of GSPC cells throughout Italy. In November and December 2005, Italian counter-terrorist operatives arrested five Algerian nationals on suspicion of planning terrorist operations in Italy and the United States, and of providing financial/weapons/logistical assistance to other jihadi cells in Europe (*La Repubblica*, November 17, 2005). The November arrests involved Yamine Bouhrama, Achour Rabah and Tartaq Sami. Italian security services believed Bouhrama was the head of the Salerno cell, and had contact with other GSPC cells in Milan, Brescia and Naples (*La Repubblica*, December 23, 2005).

Bouhrama's contact with other GSPC cell members in Italy enabled SISMI (the Italian military intelligence service) to identify two other GSPC members residing in Naples and Brescia: Khaled Serai and Mohamed Larbi. According to an intercepted conversation prior to his November arrest, Bouhrama discussed with Serai and Larbi an "attack against the infidel," and specifically discussed attacking a company somewhere in Italy (*Corriere della Sera*, November 17, 2005). According to Interior Minister Giuseppe Pisanu, Bouhrama, Serai and Larbi were

planning a new series of attacks in the United States and considered
targeting ships, stadiums or railway stations in an attempt to surpass
the September 11, 2001 strikes by al-Qaeda. Similarly, the Italian police
noted that these individuals were "primed" to strike targets in Italy (*El
Mundo*, November 17, 2005).

Based on the communication patterns of GSPC cell members,
Italian security services now believe that Bouhrama, Serai and Larbi
were members of GSPC cells in Naples, Brescia, and possibly Venice
that were headed by Lounici Dhamel, whom the Italian security services
suspected as a senior GSPC member (*Corriere della Sera*, November 11,
2005). In 2004, the Italian police arrested Dhamel and at least two other
Algerians after they were convicted of providing logistical support to
the GSPC: Dhamel was one of approximately 12 Algerians convicted of
supplying arms and false documents to the extremist group in 2002.

Connections between Italian GSPC and European Jihadi Cells

An interesting discovery arising out of the November
and December 2005 Italian arrests is the connections between the
Algerian jihadis in Italy and other Salafist Islamists in Europe. The
relationship is based on logistical support, weapons procurement,
communications venues, and propaganda mechanisms that enable
GSPC and Salafist Islamists cells in Europe to plan terrorist activities
in the countries in which they reside. Although the cells in Italy
appear to be composed exclusively of Algerian Salafi-Jihadists, their
interaction with mixed Moroccan and Algerian cells in Spain, Norway
and other countries demonstrates that the desire for global jihad has
overcome the historical animosity between these two national groups.

An additional finding of the Italian counter-terrorism
investigations is the extent of communications between the GSPC
cells in Italy and the Maghrebi-dominated networks in Spain and
other European countries. Italian police have been investigating
contacts between GSPC members in Italy and Algerian jihadis in
Belgium, France, Germany, the United Kingdom, the Netherlands and
Switzerland (*Corriere della Sera*, November 17, 2005). Bouhrama, Serai,
and Larbi, for instance, used false documentation to travel together
through France, Norway and other northern European countries. They
are alleged to have procured false papers and funds to finance GSPC

terrorist activities. For example, the computer of one of the Algerians, code named 007, registers contact with mujahideen in Bosnia and with Islamic militants in Norway, France, and the United Kingdom, as well as communication with elements of the Takfir wal Hijra organization (*Corriere della Sera*, November 11, 2005).

GSPC Cells in Italy

Special intelligence investigations into the activities of Algerian Salafi-Jihadists reveal that GSPC members established inter-connected cells throughout Italy. The Viale Jenner mosque in Milan and its cultural center stand out as the epicenter of jihadi-related activities.

Milan Cells:

2002: 13 Algerians and a Moroccan believed to be members of GSPC were arrested for illegally acquiring explosives and weapons. They operated out of the Milan mosque.

2003: Italian police arrested five Tunisians and a Moroccan imam, Mohamed El Mahfoudi, in raids at the mosque and at 40 sites associated with the GSPC. The six suspects were associated with the GSPC.

2004: Hassine Ben Moahmed Snoussi—forced to leave Italy for Tunisia—was associated with Arman Ahmed El Hissiny Helmy, an Egyptian imam of the Milan mosque.

Rabei Osman el Sayed Ahmed (a.k.a., Mohamed the Egyptian)— suspected head of al-Qaeda's networks in Europe—had many contacts in Milan, including the influential Yahia Payumi, who frequented the mosque.

September 2005: Italian police detained five of 11 Algerians suspected of membership in the GSPC, and investigated their involvement in planning a failed terrorist attack against the Spanish National Court in Madrid. Jamel Launici, alleged head of the Italian cell in charge of recruiting terrorists and obtaining explosives for the Madrid attack, was one of the detained.

Salerno GSPC Cell: Yamine Bouhrama, Achour Rabah, Tartaq Sami and Lounici Dhamel.

Possible Venice GSPC Cell: Lounici Dhamel

Naples and Brescia GSPC Cells: Khaled Serai and Mohamed Larbi, who were in contact with Yamine Bouhrama of the Salerno cell, and Lounici Dhamel. There are likely other members that have not yet been identified.

Ben Khemais GSPC network: suspected by Italian and Spanish security services as leading al-Qaeda's regional network and one of the senior leaders of the jihadi networks in Italy. Khemais was arrested in 2001 in Italy and was involved in planning an attack on the U.S. Embassy in Rome.

Profile of Algerian Jihadis in Italy

According to available information, the GSPC network operating throughout Italy is almost exclusively composed of Algerian nationals who immigrated to the country during the past decade. Italian GSPC members have the following characteristics:

- They are first generation immigrants born in Algeria who immigrated to Italy probably for the purpose of setting up cells in support of the ongoing Islamist insurgency in Algeria and the GSPC in particular.
- They are young, male and usually poorly educated. It is unclear if these individuals were employed in Italy and, if so, where they worked and with whom.
- It is unclear if any of the men have family members in Italy.
- The level and intensity of association with Italian Muslims remains unknown.

Al-Qaeda's Second Front in Italy: Observations and Gaps

While Iraq is the new center of gravity for jihad, Europe has become an important logistical center critical to ensuring the constancy of jihad in Iraq and, increasingly, in Europe. Some of the more significant observations include:

- The return of jihadis from Iraq is transforming Europe from a logistical base to a forward terrorist planning center.
- The recruitment of Muslims for jihadist activities likely remains in the cultural centers and mosques and through the internet, as well as the prisons (*La Repubblica*, June 19, 2002). Yet, given the surveillance of these sites by Italian intelligence services, it is possible that Islamists are being driven away from the central mosques to smaller, makeshift mosques and possibly schools, stores and homes.
- The inter-personal relationships of GSPC members in Italy are crucial to the viability of these cells. Understanding these relationships would help counter-terrorism officials in devising effective programs to target their recruitment and logistical activities.

Conversely, insofar as the gaps in knowledge are concerned, security officials should investigate the degree and depth of contact between cell members prior and subsequent to arrival in Italy in order to identify points of leverage and influence in the jihadi movement.

[From Terrorism Monitor, Volume IV, Issue 3]

France

Evaluating the Effectiveness of French Counter-Terrorism

Ludo Block

Originally published on September 8, 2005

Over the last decade, French counter-terrorism strategy has been recognized as one of the most effective in Europe. The French system emerged from painful experience—unlike other European countries France has faced the deadly threat of Islamic terrorism on its soil since the 1980s. A number of attacks in Paris by the Iranian-linked Hezbollah network of Fouad Ali Saleh in 1985 and 1986 triggered profound changes in the organization and legislative base of French counter-terrorism. These were reinforced after the Algerian Armed Islamic Group's (GIA) attacks in 1995 and 1996.

The key elements in the French counter-terrorism strategy are the privileged relationship between intelligence services and dedicated magistrates, as well as the qualification of acts of terrorism as autonomous offences punishable by increased penalties. The specific offence designated 'association' or 'conspiring to terrorism,' makes a preemptive judicial approach possible. Meanwhile a sophisticated system named Vigipirate (security alert plan) of nation-wide, pre-planned security measures was developed. After the July 2005 attacks in London, Vigipirate was put in stade *rouge* (level red) swiftly invoking a large number of extra security measures in public places and public transport throughout France and along its borders.

French authorities understood very early on that Islamist terrorism represented a new, complex threat and developed a system containing decisive advantages. This prevented acts of Islamic terrorism on French territory from December 1996 until October 2004, although various plots were disrupted during this period. These included a plan to bomb the Paris metro in December 2002 and a plot to attack tourist facilities on the French island of Reunion in the Indian Ocean in June 2003. Clearly France remains high on the list of targets for al-Qaeda and associated groups, while recent trends challenge the long term effectiveness of the French approach.

Trends and Future Concerns

The explosion near the Indonesian Embassy in Paris on October 8, 2004 was the first act of terrorism in France in eight years. It was claimed by the unknown Front Islamique Français Armé (FIFA) which threatened France and demanded—amongst other things—the liberation of two terrorists convicted for their participation in the 1995 attacks. The explosive device used was rudimentary, consisting of a gas tank in a bag pack, resembling the devices used in the 1995 attacks and showing once again that terror can be brought upon society cheaply. One person believed to be responsible for communicating the claims of responsibility for the attack was arrested soon after the incident.[1]

It is not this incident alone that has alarmed the French intelligence community. In the first six months of 2005, the French Secret Service (DST) made over sixty Islamic-related terrorism arrests, compared to seventy-six in 2004. This reflects the changes among international jihadists where, according to French counter-terrorism experts, new threats come in addition to existing ones, rather than replacing them. Several trends are regarded as especially worrisome by the French intelligence community.

First, there is the growing importance of what is called the filière Irakienne (Iraqi network), the recruiting network for the insurgency in Iraq. Recruitment seems to take place everywhere. As usual, it takes place in and near mosques, but recruiting also takes place in prisons and private gatherings. Moreover, the internet, where professional multimedia techniques are applied for this purpose, is actively used for recruitment.[2]

Secondly, the recruitment networks operate throughout Europe with recruiters traveling back and forth between various European cities. The Paris based Imam Ben Halim Abderraouf, a foreman of the extremist Jama'at al-Da'wa wal-Tabligh (Society for Propagation & Preaching) movement, apparently played a key role in the recruitment of young Dutch Muslims. Four of them recently traveled on fake Algerian passports via Paris and Damascus to the Syrian-Iraq border area to receive jihad training. A DVD containing footage of their training with explosives in the desert surfaced in the notorious 19th arrondissement of Paris. It demonstrates the making of suicide bombs hidden in jackets as well as the devastating effects of these bombs on an autobus and on a constructed scenery of a supermarket and a busy street. The DVD is used for recruiting and indoctrinating other young Muslims.[3]

Thirdly, French experts expect to find Iraq veterans back in France in due course to continue the jihad, just as happened after earlier conflicts. This time however, the insurgents avoid long stays in the combat zone, and instead use the conflict to gain sufficient training and motivation to return battle-hardened to Europe.[4] A dozen young Frenchmen are believed to be in Iraq as combatants. Several were arrested along the Iraq/Syria border and an unknown number have probably already returned to France.

Fourth, there is a new category of Islamic extremists, almost all offspring of immigrants, who seem to be younger, more frustrated, and more radicalized than the French jihadists of the 1990s. Over the last year, five young Frenchmen were killed in Iraq, one while executing a suicide attack near Fallujah. Although no plots for suicide attacks in France have been discovered yet, the DST fears that cells are planning such a strike and is working hard to discover and foil them. Fears of suicide attacks by young French Muslims were reinforced after the events in London.[5]

Finally, another dangerous trend is the apparent change in focus of the Algerian-based Salafist Group for Preaching and Combat (GSPC), an offshoot of the GIA, beyond the borders of Algeria. Intelligence shows that the purported leader of the GSPC, the explosives specialist Abdelmalek Droukdal, has active contacts with Abu Musab al-Zarqawi and is planning to combine efforts in the international jihad arena, focusing in particular on France. Since the GSPC is regarded as the most organized extremist organization in Algeria, with its tentacles already reaching far into Spain and presumably into France as well, French security experts take this development seriously.[6]

Developments in Counter-Terrorism

French law enforcement is highly hierarchical in nature, resulting in several agencies and departments within the same agency involved in counter-terrorism. In the National Police these are the aforementioned

DST, the General Intelligence Service (RG) and the National Anti-Terrorism Division (DNAT). Also the External Intelligence Service (DGSE) of the Defense Ministry has a role in countering terrorism and in addition both the Gendarmerie and the Judicial Police in Paris maintain counter-terrorist judicial and intelligence capabilities.

Frequently these bodies act as little kingdoms, invoking inevitable problems of coordination. Therefore several coordinating structures were created of which the anti-terrorist Operational Coordination Unit (UCLAT) is the most important. However, without having direct access to the information of the participating bodies and largely dependant on face-to-face meetings, UCLAT's coordinating role remains suboptimal.

A new—and against the French background, almost revolutionary—initiative aimed at streamlining this organizational jungle and boosting efficiency, is the sharing of one location and resources by the DST, RG and DNAT in 2006. Although ideas for sharing resources and even a fusion between them from time to time emerged since the 1995 GIA attacks, new threats are prompting a greater convergence of resources and capabilities.

Another initiative is last year's creation of a joint French-Spanish anti-terrorism investigation team in which officers will have equal operative powers on each other's territory. This is remarkable in contemporary European police cooperation. Another initiative of unprecedented caliber is the reinforced French-U.S. counter-terrorism cooperation under the name "Alliance Base" that has been in place since 2002, though only became public last July.

Although the London attacks predictably prompted several new repressive initiatives, like proposals to upgrade the 1995 legislation on video surveillance, tougher penalties for terrorism-related crimes and data retention on all communication, the French have already been searching for original alternatives to supplement conventional counter-terrorism strategies.

A first initiative in this regard was the decision in 2004 to elevate the fight against terrorism to the status of a Chantier National (Major Project); meaning a prioritized cause requiring nation wide efforts. [7] Among other things, this entailed an appeal to all government institutions to actively search for indications and information pointing to processes of radicalism in society. A following initiative is the recent announcement of the compilation of a white book on "the internal security and the threat of terrorism." [8]

The white book should receive input from various government departments and provide answers to strategic, operational and pedagogical questions involving:

- evaluating the actual threat level;
- mapping the types of threats and targets relevant for France;
- exploring new technological counter-terrorism possibilities;
- finding an equilibrium between liberties and security;
- enhancing the international counter-terrorism cooperation;
- informing society adequately without creating unnecessary fear.

When completed, the white book should serve as a basis for public action against the threat of terrorism in the coming decennia. [9]

The broad appeals to various government institutions and society in both the "Chantier National" and the white book are relatively new approaches in this field in Europe. These are necessary and important attempts to take countering terrorism out of the exclusive domain of law enforcement. After all, the recent attacks in London clearly indicate that Islamist terrorism will continue to threaten Western European societies for the foreseeable future. As far as the French are concerned, even a very efficient law enforcement and intelligence community will only be a part of the answer. To enhance its counter-terrorism approach, France has taken initial steps that ensure a wider participation of society to counter this growing menace.

Notes

1. "Attentat contre l'ambassade d'Indonésie à Paris : un homme en garde à vue," *Le Monde*, October 12, 2004.
2. Bunt, G. "Cyber-Terrorism: Using Internet as a Recruitment Tool," paper delivered at the IRIS conference "L'Europe face au Terrorisme," *Paris*, March 8, 2005.
3. "De Spin in het zelfmoord-net," *Dutch Daily De Telegraaf*, July 2, 2005.
4. "Alerte sur les nouvelles filières islamistes," *Le Figaro*, May 25, 2005.

5. "Le djihadiste français est plus fruste, plus jeune, plus radicalisé," *Le Monde*, May 24, 2005.

6. "Le GSPC algérien menacerait la France dans le cadre du 'djihad' international," *Le Monde*, June 26, 2005.

7. Speech by the Minister, D. de Villepin, at the June 24, 2004 French Ministry of Interior press-conference.

8. "Préparation d'un Livre blanc sur la sécurité intérieure face au terrorisme," statement at www.premier-ministre.gouv.fr , issued May 3, 2005.

9. "La lutte contre le terrorisme va faire l'objet d'un Livre blanc," *Le Monde* May 5, 2005.

[From Terrorism Monitor, Volume III, Issue 17]

Radical Islam and the French Muslim Prison Population

Pascale Combelles Siegel

Originally published on July 27, 2006

In the mid-1990s, after an unprecedented campaign of terrorist attacks in Paris, the French government dismantled several Algerian GIA-backed terrorist cells and sentenced both operatives and financiers of the attacks to lengthy prison terms. A new wave of convicts followed suit after the dismantling of another terrorist cell before the 1998 World Cup. Yet these anti-terrorism successes created a different set of problems as radical Islamists began proselytizing their views to fellow inmates and recruiting new followers in prisons. Pascal Maihlos, the director of France's domestic intelligence agency, Renseignements Généraux (RG), put it plainly in an interview with *Le Monde* earlier this year: "It is there, in prison, that a minority of radical Islamist terrorists (about 100) hook up with petty criminals who find their way back to religion under its most radical form" (*Top Chrétien*, November 25, 2005).

Maihlos is referring to the new dangers posed by the proselytism of some radical Islamist activists inside French prisons. In its seminal 2005 study of proselytism in prisons, the RG counted 175 acts of proselytism in 68 prisons (out of 188 prisons across the country). The 68 prisons in question are generally larger prisons located in urban areas. According to Maihlos and the RG, the most severe acts of proselytism include spontaneous calls for collective prayers (30% of all incidents) and pressures on fellow prisoners to follow certain religious-oriented rules (20% of all recorded incidents) (*Top Chrétien*, January 14, 2006). Other acts of proselytism include special requests, such as requests for prayer carpets, halal meat (meat killed and processed according to religious principles) and suitable places for worship; there are also calls for allowing the traditional Islamic dress code (instead of prison garments) and a few incidents of degrading Christian symbols such as Bibles and Christmas trees. The progression of proselytism appears to be linked to the rise of Salafism, a brand of Islam that preaches a strict observance of 7th century rules and a strong rejection of Western values. Even though the Tablighi movement—which is hostile to violence—remains the dominant Islamic movement in French prisons, an unnamed RG official told *Le Figaro* on January 13, 2006 that "we observe a steady increase of Salafism, with two particularities: a strong rejection of Western values and the legitimacy of violence" to achieve their goals. As a result, the Salafism brand of Islam is now found in jails all across France except for four regions (out of 22), and its influence continues to grow. The four regions that are not experiencing this trend are located in rural areas (*Top Chrétien*, November 25, 2005).

In the short term, the threat is considered serious because a number of those imprisoned for acts of terrorism in the mid-1990s have been (or will soon be) released from prison [1]. The fear is that once out of prison, they will reconstitute new networks with the assistance of former inmates. According to Maihlos, "Of course, the release of such individuals is a top priority for all intelligence services [involved in counter-terrorism]" (*Top Chrétien*, November 25, 2005). Such fears are not just theoretical. In September 2005, the French counter-terrorism agency, Direction de la Surveillance du Territoire (DST), dismantled Safé Bourada's terrorist cell in Trappes (near Paris). Safé Bourada, an Algerian, had been incarcerated for almost 10 years for his participation in the 1995 attacks on the Paris metro system. He stands accused of having reconstituted a terrorist network with delinquents he had met in prison. Bourada is now back behind bars.

Additionally, according to the RG, another network headed by a man named Cherifi was also created in prison and dismantled in 2005. A month later, in October 2005, the conservative daily *Le Figaro* announced that a prison guard in Bourges, in central France, was under investigation for radical proselytism. In 2003, both the RG and local prison officials realized that he "was involved in [radical Islamist] proselytism inside and outside the prison. Police sources indicated that he had encouraged youth to join the jihad in Iraq and elsewhere" (*Le Figaro*, November 30, 2005). Six other people were subsequently arrested and placed under investigation.

While the risk is certainly real, as attested by last year's incidents, it also appears to be quantitatively limited for the time being. Out of the nearly 60,000 inmates in French prisons, only 99 are being held on terrorism-related charges [2]. Of these, the RG estimates that 30 of the 90 are heavily engaged in radical Islamist proselytism. The RG considers them particularly dangerous because their previous "terrorist" experiences make them capable of leadership. The RG is also concerned with 20 isolated cases of new converts who are now actively engaged in proselytism; these 20 have been identified as being at risk of becoming overzealous in their actions in order to "prove" their sincerity to their newfound religion. Of these 175 acts of proselytism, the RG considers "that half-a-dozen, based on their past behaviors, could cross the red line into terrorism" (*Le Figaro*, January 13, 2006). This calculation validates prison officials who consider that "proselytism does not necessarily lead to terrorism" (*Le Monde*, February 4, 2006). A prison guard at Osny (a Paris suburb) declared to *Le Monde* on February 4, 2006: "These guys [proselytizing radicals] can exert great influence and have a courtship of 50 around them. Some arrive in prison with nothing, and within a week their cells are replete with gifts from fellow inmates. When the ring leaders are transferred to another prison, however, it all quickly disappears. Their influence is not that deep."

In the long run, two factors may decisively impact the threat that seasoned terrorists recruit common criminals into new terrorist networks.

First, if Islam is the religion of a large majority of French inmates, the prison system has only very recently decided to accommodate the practice of a moderate brand of Islam. In the first ever sociological study of Islam in French prisons, Farhad Khosrokhavar (Ecole des Hautes Etudes en Sciences Sociales), estimated that between 50% and 80% of French inmates are Muslims [3]. That number must be contrasted with France's overall Muslim population, which is 7-8%. Despite these numbers, the author found the almost "complete absence of institutional response" on the part of the authorities to accommodate Muslims (casafree.com, May 7, 2006). For example, Khosrokhavar notes that there are only 69 imams in French prisons (compared to 500 Christian ministers and 84 rabbis) to tend to the religious needs of tens of thousands of Muslim inmates. By comparison, at the time of the study, there were two imams tending to only 20 Shiite prisoners in the British prison system. Khosrokhavar also criticizes the strict security rules and a strict application of the principles of secularism that overly constrict the practice of Islam. For example, in many prisons, according to Khosrokhavar, collective prayers are forbidden; women cannot come to the prisoner visiting rooms veiled; halal meat may only be available for an additional fee and prisoners encounter difficulties in observing Ramadan [4]. According to Khosrokhavar, "inmates view these rules as manifestations of disdain toward them" and therefore turn toward a practice of "wild Islam" (un islam ensauvagé). "Prison administration leaves inmates to their own devices and to the hands of self-proclaimed, semi-clandestine radical leaders," he said. "As a result, the door is open for dangerous interpretations of Islam where rejections of others [non-Muslims], hatred of the West and jihad are the dominant elements" (casafree.com, May 7, 2006).

After the RG report of 2005 on the extent and dangers of radical proselytism in prisons, the French Ministry of Justice initiated a number of reforms to allow for a better practice of a moderate Islam. The cornerstone of the project is the recruitment of more imams to serve the Muslim prison population in conjunction with the Conseil Français du Culte Musulman (a representative organization of French Muslims headed by Dalil Boubakeur). The project is only in its initial stages and only time will tell how successful it is.

The second dimension of the problem lies in the socioeconomic profile of Muslim prisoners. Some of these prisoners—young, male, poor and brutally cut off from all familial support (after they land in jail)—may become easy prey for the radicals' recruitment machine. The statistics gathered by Khosrokhavar are quite telling. In his book, he estimates that the overwhelming majority of Muslim convicts are males between 20 and 30 years-old and who belong to the underclass. At the time of their arrest, two-thirds of the prisoners were unemployed. Those who were employed were mostly laborers. Only 10% were professionals, making this group more capable of tapping into the large pool of disenfranchised and poor youth to proselytize a radical and violent version of Islam and recruit them for terrorist networks. The risk is that a violent, confrontational version of Islam finds resonance in a population alienated from mainstream values and progress. If the French government fails to take effective measures to promote the practice of a moderate form of Islam in prisons, it runs the risk of breeding a new generation of terrorists.

Notes

1. This was the case of some of the terrorists who had provided financial and logistical support to the 1995-1996 attacks in the Paris metro as well as some of those indicted in the terrorist (failed) plot against the World Cup organization in 1998.

2. This number accounts for both convicts and suspects awaiting trial.

3. The numbers are imprecise because the French government does not ask for the religious affiliation of convicts. This is part of the French concept of "neutrality" toward people's origins. The figures are based on the author's educated estimates.

4. Farhad Khosrokhavar, *L'Islam dans les prisons*, Paris, Balland, 2004.

[From Terrorism Monitor, Volume IV, Issue 15]

Netherlands

"Mujahideen of the Lowlands" on Trial in the Netherlands

Judit Neurink

Originally published on December 20, 2005

The trial of 14 young radical Muslims is attracting widespread attention in Holland and elsewhere. This article examines the network and explains how young second-generation immigrants are radicalized to pose an unprecedented security threat to the Dutch state.

Mohammed Bouyeri, who is already serving a life sentence for the murder of controversial Dutch filmmaker Theo van Gogh in November 2004, is among the 14 young Muslims whose trial started in December 2005. All 14 have been charged with membership in a criminal terrorist organization, the so-called Hofstadgroup (Hofstadt being another name for The Hague), of which Bouyeri was one of the leading figures.

The Hofstadgroup is mainly comprised of second-generation Dutch youth of Moroccan descent. Members of the Hofstadgroup were under surveillance by the Dutch intelligence agency AIVD since 2002. Group members are thought to have been planning attacks on Dutch politicians and institutions. Houses where the boys lived were wired, and excerpts of the taped conversations form part of the evidence against them. Moreover, the contents of their computers and their postings on radical websites and in internet chat rooms will also be used as evidence.

This small organization has been called the Hofstadgroup because it was in The Hague where members used to meet. For some time they would gather for Qur'an meetings at a phone shop in the city. It was here that a number of them became radicalized after listening to their Qur'an teacher, the Syrian Abu Khaled, who disappeared just before Bouyeri murdered van Gogh. Abu Khaled would show them jihadi videos and convinced them that jihad was an obligation for

UNMASKING TERROR

"pure" Muslims. Some members traveled to Pakistan, presumably to attend training camps. They called themselves the Polder Mujahideen, or Mujahideen of the lowlands.

Apart from Bouyeri, who killed van Gogh, only two other members of the group were actually caught in a criminal act. Jason Walker is charged with throwing hand grenades at the police team that came to arrest him last year, badly wounding some policemen. Moreover, Nouredine el Fathni was arrested last June in Amsterdam with a loaded machine gun in his sports bag. Dutch intelligence had reason to believe he was on his way to assassinate a politician in Amsterdam. Both he and another of Bouyeri's friends, Samir Azzouz, provoked a state of high alert among the Dutch security services. Consequently, special security was put in place for all members of the Dutch cabinet, the parliament, the buildings of ministries and Amsterdam's Schiphol airport.

Their success in discovering and dismantling this network notwithstanding, the Dutch authorities have made clear there are likely many more similar networks in operation. Home Minister Johan Remkes has claimed that there are ten to twenty networks of radical Muslims in the Netherlands that have the propensity to resort to terrorism [1]. Hundreds of people are believed to be involved and the networks are described as "fluid," as members enter and leave the organization. Some of the groups are exclusively local, while some have strong and wide-ranging international contacts.

In order to deter members of these networks from engaging in violence, the Dutch police have been using what they call "interference," which is basically overt surveillance. Jason Walker's younger brother Jermaine has told the press he has been followed by the police ever since he was set free after the arrest of Jason and other members of the group in November.

Jermaine Walker is a good example of the problems associated with very young Muslim radicals who are under the strong influence of older people. He is 18 years old, the son of a Dutch woman and an alcoholic American man who converted to Islam. Subsequently both his sons became Muslims as well. After his release, Jermaine became more radical, telling Dutch journalists he understood Mohammed Bouyeri's murderous assault on van Gogh: "it was good...who dares to talk dirty about Islam now? No one!" [2].

Samir Azzouz was set free in April after being acquitted by the court (the appeals court later followed the ruling) of planning attacks on Amsterdam's Schiphol airport, the parliament and the AIVD building. In his house, police found maps and fertilizers and chemicals that could be used for bomb-making. Yet the court decided that evidence of planning alone was not enough to convict him.

While Azzouz was free, he established a new network which included drug addicts, and tried to turn them into takfiris [3]. Samir Azzouz is the only known member of the group who has made a video testament, in which he declares his admiration for Bouyeri, and advises other Muslims that armed jihad is their duty. When he was arrested again in October, the AIVD discovered that Azzouz was looking for weapons and explosives.

Nouredine el Fathni was also building a new network, while he was on the run from the police after most of the group's members were arrested in November 2004. It appears that Fathni had been giving Qur'an lessons at the house of a Dutch friend in The Hague. Three girls and a boy were present at three sessions or more [4]. One of them was a young Muslim girl with whom he had got married under Islamic law; another was a former girlfriend of Mohammed Bouyeri. As his knowledge of the Qur'an was negligible, Fathni used his laptop to read aloud Qur'anic verses and other details about what he called "pure Islam." The girls were also shown videos of decapitations.

These sessions became known to the police after the girls decided to report them. They were confused, because Fathni's sermons were radically different from the ones they had heard at the as-Sunna Mosque in The Hague, which is known as one of the most radical mosques in the Netherlands. Most members of the Hofstadgroep frequented this mosque, until they become even more radical than the Salafist Sheikh Jneid Fawaz who preached at as-Sunna. The girls initially reported their concerns to Fawaz, who called the takfiri group a bunch of madmen and advised the girls that they were on the wrong path [5]. Moreover, he urged them to report the matter to the police. The girls took this as a fatwa, religious guidance that they could not ignore. They consulted another Salafist imam in Tilburg, who gave them the same advice.

At the opening of the trial this week, one of the women refused to repeat her allegations in court, allegedly after receiving threats. The woman's testimony shows the spread of radical thinking between friends, as described by the American forensic psychiatrist Marc Sageman [6].

Sageman's study of Islamic terrorists showed that many of them had no religious background, and became radicalized among a group of people in the same position: in a foreign country, lonely, homesick and feeling in some way humiliated. The Hofstadgroup is interesting because it clearly shows the dynamics of the group as Sageman describes it and the attraction of it for other young people. For even after most of the members had been detained, the group remained attractive to other young Muslims. While in prison, Bouyeri and Samir Azzouz found new followers, prompting the authorities to incarcerate the two young men in solitary confinement.

Politicians in the Netherlands have called for stronger laws to prevent people like Samir Azzouz from being acquitted. Dutch law makes it difficult to try people for their intentions. This problem might arise in the trial of the Hofstadgroep, which is expected to last at least two months. The Dutch parliament is still waiting for the bill Justice Minister Piet Hein Donner promised last summer, which would make glorification of violence a crime, thus enabling judicial action against potential jihadis.

Political opinions are split between left and right over such a bill, with opposition parliamentary member Femke Halsema strongly against. This law would really be all about Muslims, she said. "The law seems mainly aimed at changing the minds of a rebellious group of young people...it will work the wrong way for this specific group as young people will be affirmed in their conviction that they are persecuted because of their opinions," she said [7].

Even Justice Minister Piet Hein Donner lately made clear he is not sure that strengthening the law would be the right step. "Prevention is important in the case of terror, but the law is made to punish actions... If a judge can also punish someone for what he is saying or thinking, then you also undermine the freedom of expression," he said [8]. Freedom of expression remains a contentious issue in the Netherlands, over a year after the murder of Theo van Gogh.

Van Gogh's distasteful verbal attacks on Islam and Muslims and his placement of Qur'anic texts on a naked woman's body in the film "Submission" led to his murder. Many Dutch people feel that the assault on van Gogh also murdered freedom of expression in the Netherlands. Yet, some people are also voicing criticism of van Gogh's extreme insults against the Islam and Muslims. Moreover, people feel that the anti-Islamic sentiments that have grown since van Gogh's murder are undermining multicultural Dutch society. The trial of the Hofstadgroep is not only seen as the trying of the Polder Mujahideen, but a trial for Dutch society as a whole at a time when it is nearly universally agreed that the terrorist threat is indeed real.

Notes

1. Ikon TV, interview with Home Minister Johan Remkes, July 17, 2005.
2. "Jermaine Walker Gets Star Treatment," *NRC Handelsblad*, October 15, 2005.
3. "Samir Azzouz Recruits Criminals," *Trouw*, November 5, 2005.
4. "How Nourddine El Fathni wanted to form a new group," *NRC Handelsblad*, August 6, 2005.
5. "Maneuvering between the Law and Allah," *NRC Handelsblad*, September 19, 2005.
6. Marc Sageman: *Understanding Terror Networks*, 2004.
7. "Donner's Law Goes Too Far," *Trouw*, September 20, 2005.
8. Buitenhof TV, interview with Justice Minister Piet Hein Donner, November 20, 2005.

[From Terrorism Monitor, Volume III, Issue 24]

Spain

After 3/11: The Evolution of Jihadist Networks in Spain

Javier Jordán and Robert Wesley

Originally published on January 12, 2006

Nearly two years after the March 11, 2004 terrorist attacks in Madrid, new militant Islamist cells continue to be disrupted in Spain on a regular basis. In 2004, Spanish police detained almost 100 jihadists. The trend continued in 2005 with more than 80 Islamic militants apprehended. In the latest arrests, on January 10, 2006, Spanish police detained 20 suspected Islamic militants alleged to have recruited sympathizers to join the Iraqi insurgency. The alleged militants were detained during pre-dawn raids in and around Madrid, Barcelona and the Basque town of Tolosa. These staggering figures do not even include the significant roles played by common delinquents and ideological sympathizers. This period has illuminated several emerging characteristics of jihadi groups that will affect the long-term evolution of Islamic terrorism in Spain.

The first two distinguishing characteristics are the increasingly mixed nationalities in these networks and the proliferation of individuals of Maghrebi origin, especially Moroccans and Algerians. When the first Armed Islamic Group (GIA) and then Salafist Group for Call and Combat (GSPC) cells were detected in Spain in the 1990s, the cells were characterized by their national homogeneity: all members were Algerian. The few jihadi Moroccans in Spain were integrated into the Syrian-dominated Abu Dahdah network. According to a senior Spanish police official, until that point, cooperation between Algerians and Moroccans had not developed because many Algerians considered the Moroccans weak, cowardly and untrustworthy. Conversely, the Moroccans viewed the Algerians as extremely violent (Personal Interview, January 2004). These prevailing attitudes seem to have been pushed aside in favor of a more multi-national approach. The reasons for this change are not presently clear, but it is likely that counter-terrorism efforts and the globalization of jihad have been the main driving factors.

The dissolution of the Abu Dahdah network at the end of 2001 had the inevitable consequence of elevating those who, at that time, had maintained a low militant profile into positions of greater prominence [1]. They were people of varying backgrounds, including Syrians, Tunisians, Moroccans and Algerians. In addition, some of them, like the Algerian Allekema Lamari or the Syrian Almallah brothers, played very important roles in the formation of the Madrid attacks group.

After the attacks of 2004, similar configurations have occurred in subsequent disruptions of jihadi cells. This was the case in a network that formed in various Spanish prisons, and which was disrupted in November 2004. The prison network was apparently preparing a new campaign of attacks in Madrid and included both incarcerated members and those who had already been released. There were also the disruptions of two large recruiting and support networks for the jihad in Iraq in June and December 2005. Besides these networks, there were further detentions of other smaller more homogeneous cells composed of Moroccans, Algerians and Pakistanis.

Detentions are not only revealing the diversity of cells, but also showing that Moroccans are increasingly assuming leadership roles. For example, the last network to be unraveled by police in 2005, allegedly included 11 Moroccans, an Iraqi, a Saudi, an Egyptian, a Belarussian, a Ghanaian, an Algerian and a Spaniard (Office of Information and Social Relations, Home Office, Spain, December 19/21, 2005). Moreover, in the arrests conducted on January 10, 2006, 15 out of the 20 alleged militants are thought to be Moroccans.

The increasingly diffuse boundaries of these groups are not solely explained by the dismantlement and disintegration of older networks marked by more homogeneous national character (e.g., the Algerian GIA and GSPC; the Syrian Fighting Vanguard; or the Moroccan Islamic Combatant Group [GICM]) and their subsequent reconstruction from dispersed elements. What has also contributed to this interconnection between radicals of distinct nationalities is the more global political agenda of the jihad, which is overshadowing the previous national priorities. The disruption of Maghrebi networks involved in support activities for foreign jihads exemplify the threat posed by these networks to Iraq, North Africa and other European countries—as well as the threat of globalized jihad to Spain itself.

It is probable that the complexities of these Spanish networks will be compounded as groups previously focused on national jihads, such as the Algerian GSPC, attempt to extend their operational networks by partnering with other jihadi groups. The overtures of mutual assistance and affiliation from al-Qaeda to national groups have resulted in the call for the establishment of an "al-Qaeda Organization in the Arab Maghreb," which, while attempting to act as an umbrella organization, might also serve to support the continued interrelations between expatriate communities in Spain (*al-Hayat*, December 8, 2005).

Another new characteristic is the increasing prevalence in the number of individuals whose initiation into jihad occurred after settling in Spain. In the 1990s, militant jihad was an imported phenomenon, as cells that found refuge in Spain were principally involved in the support of jihad in other countries, primarily Algeria. Nevertheless, over the past years, the conversion to jihad has become an increasingly indigenous phenomenon.

A possible contribution to this problem has been the high immigration levels from the countries of the Maghreb, especially Morocco. The official figures place the total number of Muslim immigrants at close to a half-million, but the actual number is likely to be over one million [2]. The overwhelming majority of these immigrants are honest workers who came to Spain to improve their livelihoods. Nevertheless, a small minority are sympathetic to Islamic militants, thus enabling the recruitment drives of clandestine jihadi networks.

The radicalization of Muslims living in Spain constitutes an enormous challenge for the future. One of the areas of significant concern is the numerous Islamic centers espousing radical and militant interpretations of Islam. Recently the contents of an intelligence report concerning the state of radical preaching at Islamic centers was leaked to the press. The report notes that of the approximately 600 mosques and other Islamic centers, roughly 10 percent propagate radical ideas. In addition, six of them are thought to be in the orbit of Takfir wa al-Hijra (*El Pais*, December 19, 2005).

Takfir wa al-Hijra (excommunication and exile) is not so much an organization but an ideological current of Salafist jihadism, to which many of the members of the aforementioned Spanish networks adhere. With origins in the Middle East and the Maghreb, Takfir ideology justifies indiscriminate killing and is characterized by its clandestine nature and willingness to engage in prohibited activities (e.g. drinking alcohol in public and eating pork) as a means to deflect attention from its members' subversive activities. As in other European countries, Takfiri recruitment in Spain has fed on individuals previously engaged in delinquent activities and has had significant success. Spanish police have estimated that around 50 incarcerated Salafi jihadists are Takfiri [3].

The final characteristic of jihadi groups in Spain is the continued planning of Spain-based jihadi groups against targets within Spain. The hurried withdrawal of Spanish troops from Iraq by the new government of President Jose Luis Rodriguez Zapatero, which assumed power following the Madrid attacks, has not diminished the terrorism threat. In fact, there have been at least four foiled terrorist attacks since the withdrawal. One of these groups was composed of Pakistanis who had relationships with important members of original al-Qaeda cadres (*El Pais*, December 19, 2005). The other three networks were primarily composed of members with familial origins in the Maghreb. In addition to these groups, Spanish police arrested two Moroccans related to the Madrid attacks network in December 2004, who were in possession of a camera with photographs of a nuclear power plant (*El Pais*, December 15, 2004).

The continued hostility is perplexing on the surface, considering the distance that has developed between the Bush administration and the Zapatero government. There are several grievances that explain this hostility. They are, inter alia: the presence of Spanish troops in the NATO mission in Afghanistan; the repeated detention of scores of influential jihadists since 1995 and the continuing "occupation" (as jihadists see it) of the cities of Melilla and Ceuta on the North African coast.

Notes
1. Javier Jordán & Nicola Horsburgh, "Mapping Jihadist Terrorism in Spain," *Studies in Conflict and Terrorism*, 28, (2005), pp 169-191.
2. Gustavo de Arístegui, *La yihad en España*, (Madrid: La Esfera de los Libros, 2005), p. 243.
3. Ibid; Tamara Makarenko, "Takfiri presence grows in Europe," *Jane's Intelligence Review*, February 2005, 16-19; Petter Nesser, *Jihad In Europe: A Survey of the Motivations for Sunni Islamist Terrorism in Post-Millennium Europe* (Forsvarets Forskningsinstitutt Norwegian Defence Research Establishment, 2004).

[From Terrorism Monitor, Volume IV, Issue 1]

Emerging Terrorist Trends in Spain's Moroccan Communities

Kathryn Haahr

Originally published on May 4, 2006

Recent counter-terrorism operations in Spain have spotlighted an increasing presence of Salafi-Islamists and al-Qaeda "loyalists" in Andalucia and, more alarmingly, in the Spanish autonomous communities of Ceuta and Melilla (located on the northern coast of Morocco). Since the 2004 terrorist attacks in Madrid, Spanish security services have arrested dozens of GSPC-/GICM-affiliated members and al-Qaeda sympathizers in Ceuta, Melilla and Andalucia. There are no proven links between Islamist activities in the enclaves to the known terrorists associated with al-Qaeda and Salafi-Islamists in Andalucia and the enclaves. The proximity of Ceuta and Melilla to Andalucia, however, coupled with the "Maghreb-Andalucia" clandestine immigration pipeline, increases the risk of terrorist infiltration.

Cultural and Historic Setting

Historically, Ceuta and Melilla are multicultural cities in which Christians, Muslims, Jews and other ethnic groups live together. The majority of Muslims in the two enclaves consider themselves to be Spanish citizens. There are, however, segments of the population that have vocalized their allegiance to the King of Morocco. In 2002, the Counsel of the Moroccan government called for a "mobilization" to free the "occupied territories of Ceuta and Melilla" (http://www.gees. org, January 24, 2006), and the Moroccan Islamist Party of Justice and Development (PJD) called for a public march to "free Ceuta and Melilla" (*El Mundo*, July 18, 2002; February 8, 2002). The issue of Ceuta and Melilla—in terms of its political, religious and socioeconomic relationship to Morocco—will remain a challenge in Spain's domestic policy and in its bilateral relations with Morocco.

Melilla's Muslim population is 40 percent of the total population and is mainly of Moroccan origin. The city has 14 mosques. The most important religious organization is the Islamic Commission of

Melilla (CIM), which is very active in promoting the religious, social and political rights of its imams and Muslim members. The Badr Islamic Association, which engages in religious instruction of Muslim children in Melilla, was formed in the early 1990s by Mustafa Aberchan, leader of the Coalition for Melilla (CpM). Of note, the Badr Islamic Association disassociated itself from the CIM (*El Mundo*, October 24, 2001). Another organization, the CpM, a cross-section of Muslims, attempted to separate women from men in the municipal pools in 2003, prompting the Melillan government to warn the group against "sectarian" activities.

In Ceuta, there are approximately 25,000 Muslims and 12 mosques. Reportedly, the most radical is the Barella in the Radou quarter. In terms of organizations, there is the Islamic Community of al Bujari de Ceuta.

To date, there is a relative absence of radical Islamic groups in Ceuta and Melilla. The few "fundamentalists" who exist are more inclined to incite the youth to adopt a political rather than religious agenda (http://www.bladi.net). The burning of a tomb of a Muslim spiritual leader in Melilla in 2005, however, combined with other recent developments— including the appearance of pro-Osama bin Laden slogans in a Jewish cemetery, a Christian church and a synagogue—are worrisome. Some sources believe that the Badr Islamic Association was responsible for these actions and elements of the Muslim population are increasingly supporting this group. Abdelkader Mohamed Ali, the spokesman for Badr, denied the allegations, calling the attacks "repugnant" and "a barbarian act inappropriate for a Muslim" (*El Mundo*, October 24, 2005).

Counter-Terrorism Activities in Melilla, Ceuta and Andalucia

The profile of Melilla, Ceuta and Andalucia, as "hosts" to Islamist terrorist activities, demonstrates the degree to which various terrorist groups have penetrated mainstream Spanish cities and populations. Several significant counter-terrorism operations in 2005 (resulting in the arrest of approximately 85 individuals) netted an al-Qaeda cell with a nucleus in Andalucia, as well as GSPC members dispersed throughout southern Spain (*El Mundo*, December 20, 2005). Of significance, Spanish police arrested a Moroccan national, Bahbah El H. (last name not available) in Nerja, Malaga, who had formerly been the imam of a mosque in Ceuta (http://www.canalsur.es, December 12, 2005; *El Pueblo de Ceuta*, December 20, 2005). It is also important to note that the "first Spanish Taliban," Hamed Abderrahaman Ahmed, was from Ceuta. He spent two years at Guantanamo Bay on suspicions of being an "enemy combatant" allied to al-Qaeda (*El Mundo*, February 17, 2002).

According to Spanish Minister of the Interior Jose Antonio Alonso, the al-Qaeda network was broken into three command cells: a "command and control" decision-making cell, a cell that recruited mujahideen for Iraq and one devoted to falsifying documents. Alonso also noted that the network maintained "contacts with the nucleus of al-Qaeda in Iraq" (http://www.canalsur.es, December 12, 2005). The most important al-Qaeda leader to travel through Andalucia is Mustafa Setmariam Nasar (also known as Abu Musab al-Suri, who lived in Granada for two years (*El Mundo*, November 23, 2005). During that time, Nasar maintained contact with various al-Qaeda linked personalities, including Mohamed Bahaiah, the presumed courier of the terror network in Europe.

The Spanish Guardia Civil (a Spanish police force with both military and civilian functions) noted in an internal memo that "support cells for Islamist terrorists" exist in Ceuta and Melilla, in addition to other Spanish cities. Moreover, the report notes ties between these cities and some of the Islamists detained after the terrorist attacks in Casablanca in May 2003, and that the imams of several mosques (not identified) are radicalizing the Muslim community. The same report reflects a conviction by Spanish security officials that both autonomous cities are being utilized by individuals associated with "violent Islamism" (*La Razon Digital*, May 15, 2004).

As a result of the increasing presence of Islamists in the enclaves and Andalucia, Spanish security authorities have deployed counter-terrorism agents to Ceuta, Melilla and other cities in southern Spain. As part of their activities, they have stepped up efforts to identify Islamic extremists among the thousands of Spanish Muslims who attend mosques in the two enclaves and Andalucia. According to press reports, the Spanish security services have monitored all of the mosques in Ceuta and Melilla and "analyzed the number of Muslims who attended them, as well as the profile of each of the adherents" (*El Mundo*, November 24, 2001; *El Pueblo de Ceuta*, December 20, 2005).

In Ceuta, the Ministry of Interior specifically investigated those mosques that are "sponsored" by Morocco and reported its findings in a special intelligence report (*El Mundo*, November 24, 2001). Security officers noted that 200 and 500 Muslims attend the Benzu and Pasaje Recreo mosques respectively. The ideological orientation of the mosques' imams was recorded as well. The report notes that the Moroccan Ministry of Islamic Affairs office in Tetuan, Ceuta pays the salaries of the imams and that these community leaders owe their loyalty to the Moroccan king, whom they recognize as the most senior religious authority. The report notes that the same situation exists with most imams in Melilla.

In Andalucia, there are approximately 100 known mosques and around 250,000 Muslims. Major cities such as Granada and other towns have unwittingly hosted terrorists tied to 9/11 and Salafi-Islamists linked to terrorist activities in Spain. Due to the increase of Muslim immigrants flowing into Andalucia, unregistered prayer sites have multiplied (http://www.abc.es, February 26, 2006). According to the Ministry of Justice, there are only 36 registered Islamic entities, while the Islamic Council estimates that there are 74 groups with (mostly makeshift) prayer sites (*El Pais*, January 15, 2006).

Spanish security officials continue to worry that members of al-Qaeda will take advantage of the clandestine immigration pipeline route by inserting terrorists to make their way either to the enclaves or to the Spanish mainland. To this regard, the Directorate General of National police recently advertised 357 posts for anti-terrorist officers to monitor potential Islamists in areas where the presence of Muslim immigrants is well known, such as Melilla, Ceuta, Granada, Malaga and Alicante.

Trends in Ceuta and Melilla

According to a document from the Centro Nacional de Inteligencia (CNI, Spain's intelligence agency), intelligence officials are worried about the increase in the Muslim populations in the autonomous cities. The fear is that the burgeoning Muslim population (which in 15 years could become the majority), coupled with the suspected presence of militant Islamists, will, in due course, morph into a very serious threat to national security (*El Pais*, September 12, 2005; *El Telegrama Melill*, September 13, 2005; http://www.lejournal-hebdo.com, April 7, 2006).

Moreover, census information from the CNI and the Spanish Army predicts that Ceuta's and Melilla's Muslim populations will become the majority in about 13 years (http://www.madridhabitable.org, December 9, 2005). In addition to the demographic trend, another one to closely watch is the appeal of Muslim political parties in both autonomous cities: in Ceuta, for example, there are only 25 Muslim representatives in the Assembly. But they are organizing to win more seats in the autonomous elections of 2007. It remains to be seen whether the rise of Muslim political consciousness will interface with radical Islamism to create yet more potential terrorist threats.

[From Terrorism Monitor, Volume IV, Issue 9]

The Caribbean and Latin America

Al-Qaeda's Inroads into the Caribbean

Chris Zambelis

Originally published on October 21, 2005

Security threats emanating from the Caribbean Basin typically revolve around its position as a key trans-shipment point for South American narcotics to the United States and Europe, as well as illegal immigration, money laundering and other forms of banking and document fraud. Indeed, organized criminal networks from as far away as Western and Eastern Europe, Russia and Asia, in addition to U.S. and South American organizations, have a formidable presence in the region.

In the wake of the September 11 attacks, however, many observers began to look at the region's potential as a base of operations for radical Islamist terrorist organizations such as al-Qaeda to stage attacks against the U.S. and its interests in the Western Hemisphere. Upon cursory examination, the region's geographic proximity to the U.S., porous borders, widespread poverty, endemic corruption, and energy reserves, not to mention the tens of thousands of Americans and Europeans who vacation there at any given time of the year, make it an attractive target.

The potential threat of al-Qaeda using the Caribbean Basin as a base of operations came to the fore when allegations circulated that Adnan G. El-Shukrijumah, a known al-Qaeda operative, was reportedly spotted in Honduras in June 2004. Despite a lack of hard evidence, U.S. and regional security officials believe that Shukrijumah's alleged presence in the region stemmed from an al-Qaeda plot to link up with Central American gangs such as Mara Salvatrucha (MS) and Mara 18th Street (M18). U.S. Panamanian officials reported that Shukrijumah was in Panama as early as April 2001, possibly surveying high-value targets such as the Panama Canal, after which it is alleged he visited several neighboring countries [1]. Trinidadian sources go a step further and tie Shukrijumah to the Darul Uloom, an Islamic institute in Trinidad, and claim he may have infiltrated Central America via Trinidad and Tobago with a Trinidadian, Guyanese or Canadian passport [2].

The July 2004 arrest of Ashraf Ahmad Abdullah, an Egyptian man, at Miami International Airport for running a prolific smuggling ring from his home base in Guatemala for Egyptians and other Arabs seeking entry into the United States, did raise alarm bells for good reason. Although Abdullah has not been tied to al-Qaeda or terrorism, but is instead believed to have been interested solely in profit, the relative ease with which he was able to smuggle illegal immigrants originating from countries of "special interest" into the U.S. via Latin America and the Caribbean Basin highlights the vulnerability of the U.S. underbelly [3]. It is difficult to gauge whether terrorist networks deployed operatives to the U.S. through Abdullah's network without his knowledge.

Islam in the Caribbean Basin

The region's small Muslim population is comprised mostly of South and Southeast Asians with deep roots stemming back to the Colonial period, as well as Arabs. The region has also experienced an increase of migrants from the Middle East in recent decades. Some of the largest Muslim communities are found in Guyana, Suriname and Trinidad and Tobago. Adherence to Islam varies dramatically from country to country. In general, it reflects the diverse ethnic and cultural traditions that comprise the region and is often infused with distinctly "Caribbean" features. This is best evidenced by the Shi'a Muharram rituals known locally as Hosay, (derived from the regional transliteration of Husayn) performed by East Indian Shi'a Muslims in Trinidad and Tobago, Guyana, Suriname and Jamaica, that commemorate the martyrdom of Imam Husayn.

Recent Arab migrants from the Middle East tend to be more pious and traditional relative to their second and third generation Arab and Muslim counterparts. Moreover, there are a growing number of locals converting to Islam, especially among impoverished minorities such as the indigenous peoples of the Mexican state of Chiapas and marginalized populations of African descent in the Caribbean islands.

Most Muslim converts embrace Islam for purely spiritual reasons and do not harbor any inclination towards political or religious extremism. Many see Islam as a rite of empowerment in societies where they are underserved and experience discrimination. Nevertheless, there is a concern that al-Qaeda is targeting these groups for recruitment due to their perceived ability to travel and blend into Western cities more effectively.

Spotlight on Trinidad and Tobago

U.S. and regional security sources point to the activities of a number of obscure organizations based in oil- and natural gas-rich Trinidad and Tobago as evidence of the Caribbean Basin's potential to spawn homegrown radical Islamist organizations [4].

The Jammat al-Muslimeen (Muslim Group) is Trinidad and Tobago's most notorious Muslim organization. Although Trinidad's ethnically and religiously diverse population, split roughly between descendants of African slaves and indentured servants from India and a sizable "mixed" community, includes Sunni and Shi'a Muslim immigrants from South Asia and the Middle East, the Jammat is known almost exclusively as a Black Sunni Muslim organization comprised mainly of Afro-Trinidadian converts to Islam. The group is led by Imam Yasin Abu Bakr, a former police officer who was born Lenox Philip. The Jammat is best known for its violent 1990 attempt to overthrow the Trinidadian government over grievances related to land ownership, social and economic inequality and government corruption [5].

On July 27, 1990, Abu Bakr, along with leading Jammat figures Bilaal Abdullah and Maulana Hasan Anyabwile, led over 100 members of the group in storming Trinidad's Red House (National Parliament), taking Prime Minister A.N.R. Robinson and most of his cabinet captive. The group also took over Trinidad and Tobago Television, then the country's only television network, and the Trinidad Broadcasting Company, one of two radio stations. The ensuing standoff lasted for five days while rioting and looting gripped the capital, Port of Spain, leading to scores of deaths and the destruction of millions of dollars worth of property. Abu Bakr surrendered to the authorities after a period of negotiations that allowed the group to escape prosecution [6]. Significantly, many of the weapons used in the failed coup were imported from Florida through Louis Haneef, an Afro-Trinidadian Muslim convert based in the U.S.. Haneef spent four years in a U.S. federal prison after being convicted for his role in smuggling the weapons to Trinidad [7].

Many observers attribute the origins of the coup attempt to Trinidad's history of racially inspired riots and revolutionary social protest movements. Between six and eight percent of Trinidad and Tobago's population is Muslim, with the Jammat representing a tiny fringe of the community.

U.S. and Trinidadian authorities have kept a close eye on the Jammat's activities since the 9/11 attacks, but there is no hard evidence tying the group to international terrorism, let alone al-Qaeda. However, Abu Bakr did maintain links with Libya's Muammar Qadhafi in the 1980s and 90s and considers him a close friend to this day. The Jammat reportedly received funds through Libya's World Islamic Call Society (WICS) to finance the construction of its main mosque, schools and a medical center, but there is no evidence linking Tripoli with the failed 1990 coup attempt. Abu Bakr's most recent publicized links with controversial international figures include Venezuelan President Hugo Chavez.

In many respects, the Jammat al-Muslimeen's ideology and rhetoric mirror that of militant Black ethno-nationalist movements, including the most radical fringes of the Nation of Islam. Abu Bakr's supporters see him as a hero fighting for social justice. Interestingly, although most Trinidadians did not support his 1990 coup attempt, many at the time agreed with the issues raised by the Jammat during the crisis, especially impoverished Afro-Trinidadians. At the same time, the Jammat is seen by many locally as a well organized criminal empire involved in everything from drug smuggling, money laundering, kidnapping for ransom and extortion, with Abu Bakr running the show [8]. Abu Bakr has since been the target of a series of criminal investigations and indictments for his alleged role in ordering the murders of former Jammat members.

The Waajihatul Islaamiyyah (Islamic Front), headed by Omar Abdullah, himself a Black Muslim convert, has also been identified as a potential threat by U.S. intelligence and Trinidadian authorities. Like the Jammat al-Muslimeen, the Waajihatul Islaamiyyah is comprised mostly of Afro-Trinidadian converts to Islam. Local sources allege that Abdullah harbors extremist leanings. The Waajihatul has been accused of publishing material expressing support for al-Qaeda, but Trinidadian authorities have not provided conclusive evidence of any direct links with the group. He is often outspoken in his criticism of U.S. foreign policy in the Middle East and the Trinidadian government's policy towards Muslims. Trinidadian authorities also tie Abdullah to local crime and other illicit dealings [9].

The Jamaat al-Murabiteen (Almoravids, after the African Muslim dynasty that ruled Morocco and Spain in the 11th and 12th Century) and the related Jammat al-Islami al-Karibi (Caribbean Islamic Group) are associated with one time Jamaat al-Muslimeen chief of security Maulana Hasan Anyabwile, formerly Beville Marshall. He split with Abu Bakr in 2001 over what Trinidadian sources allege was a personal rift with the group's leader. Anyabwile hosted a radio show where he was known to criticize Trinidadian Hindus, Indian Muslims and his former Jamaat al-Muslimeen associates for their purported failure in improving the lot of Muslims in Trinidad and Tobago. Local sources also allege that he is an extremist [10].

Anyabwile was shot and critically wounded in 2002 by an unknown attacker in what many believe was part of a larger turf war between rival Muslim activists, most likely the Jammat al-Muslimeen. Now a paraplegic, Anyabwile continues to fear for his life, but remains an outspoken critic of Abu Bakr [11].

Conclusion

The Caribbean Basin will remain a region of concern in the war on terrorism. Despite a lack of hard evidence to date, international terrorist organizations such as al-Qaeda in theory can potentially feed off of the institutional weakness, political and economic instability, poverty, and lawlessness that characterize the Caribbean Basin to further their aims. But as the case of Trinidad and Tobago demonstrates, the mere presence of Islamist activist groups (or Muslims in general) does not necessarily equate to links to al-Qaeda. Therefore, in addressing the threat (or perceived threat) of radical Islam in the region effectively, it is imperative that policymakers consider the nexus between deep-seated social, political and economic grievances and international terrorism, and not simply settle for shortsighted solutions.

Notes

1. Mario D. Courteous Camarillo, "Al-Qaeda busca reclutas entre polleros de México y Maras entroamericanos," *La Cronica de Hoy* (Mexico), September 9, 2004 and "Sospechoso de terrorismo estuvo de paso en Panamá, *La Prensa* (Nicaragua), May 27, 2004.
2. Curtis Williams, "Special Branch in Terrorist Hunt," *Trinidad & Tobago Express*, May 28, 2004.
3. See "ICE Gets Special Interest Smuggler," *Inside ICE, US Immigration and Customs Enforcement*, Volume 1, Issue 7, July 19, 2004.
4. Ucill Cambridge, "Muslim Watch," *Trinidad & Tobago Express*, March 9, 2004.
5. Walter C. Soderlund, "The Jamaat al-Muslimeen Coup in Trinidad and Tobago, 1990," in *Mass Media and Foreign Policy : Post-Cold War Crises in the Caribbean* (Connecticut: Praeger, 2003).
6. Ibid. For a recent interview with Bilal Abdullah, see B.C. Pires, "The Saudis are Islam's Amish," *Trinidad & Tobago Express*, November 14, 2004.
7. Camini Marajh, "U.S. on Jammat Trail," *Trinidad & Tobago Express*, August 15, 2004.
8. Camini Marajh, "Bakr's Empire: Muslimeen Leader's Million-Dollar Properties," *Trinidad & Tobago Express*, August 8, 2004.
9. Darryl Hertaal, "Abdullah Unmasked," *Trinidad & Tobago Express*, December 2, 2002.
10. S. Edwards, "Ex-Muslimeen Hasan Anyabwile shot four times," *TriniView*, July 22, 2002.
11. Gail Alexander, "Ex-Jamaat Seeks Asylum in U.K.," *The Trinidad Guardian*, July 27, 2004.

[From Terrorism Monitor, Volume III, Issue 20]

Radical Islam in Latin America

Chris Zambelis

Originally published on December 2, 2005

In the wake of the September 11 attacks, the possibility of al-Qaeda infiltrating Latin America became a priority for U.S. intelligence and law enforcement officials. However, the most publicized incidents of radical Islamist activity in Latin America have not been linked to al-Qaeda, but instead to the Lebanese Shi'ite Hezbollah, which is ideologically and politically close to Iran. These include the March 1992 bombing of the Israeli Embassy in Buenos Aires, Argentina and the July 1994 attack against the Argentine-Israeli Mutual Association (AIMA), also in the Argentine capital, allegedly in retaliation for Israel's assassination of former Hezbollah leader Sheikh Abbas al-Musawi and his family in February 1992.

Hezbollah officially denies responsibility for these attacks and remains emphatic that it only operates in the Israel-Lebanon theatre, in what it declares to be the defense of Lebanese soil and sovereignty against Israeli threats and occupation. Many questions still surround the attacks in Argentina. Some observers suggest that the attacks were in fact out of character for Hezbollah, and instead point to al-Qaeda's possible involvement. This controversial theory throws into question the date of al-Qaeda's earliest attack, which is generally believed to be the failed December 1992 attack against U.S. servicemen en route to Somalia in a hotel in Aden, Yemen that killed two Austrian tourists instead. It also raises the possibility of a link between the attacks in Latin America and the first World Trade Center bombing in February 1993.

Many observers believe the evidence implicating Iran and Hezbollah in these incidents is scant and, at best, circumstantial. Yet this did not prevent opponents of Argentine President Carlos Menem from exploiting the attacks in an effort to discredit him. Menem's tenure in office was mired by corruption charges, which included allegations that he accepted a $10 million bribe from Iranian intelligence to cover up Tehran's alleged role in directing the attacks through Hezbollah. Some even pointed to Menem's Syrian Christian origins as evidence of his alleged pro-Hezbollah leanings. These reports stem from the testimony of a former Iranian intelligence agent known by his alias, Abolghasem Mesbahi, who defected in 1996 and whose credibility has been the subject of intense speculation [1].

Subsequent legal action against Iran for its alleged role in the attacks led to the brief detainment of Iranian officials, including former Iranian Ambassador to Argentina, Hadi Soleimanpour, who was apprehended in the United Kingdom in 2003. However, a London court rejected the evidence provided by Argentine officials against the Ambassador and his colleagues.

The Nexus between Terrorism and Organized Crime

In June 2005, Ecuadorian security officials uncovered a drug smuggling ring led by a Quito-based restaurateur of Lebanese descent identified as Rady Zaiter. Under the auspices of "Operacion Damasco," local security forces disrupted his syndicate, which stretched to the U.S., Europe and the Middle East. Although little evidence has emerged confirming that Zaiter was anything other than a prolific drug dealer, Ecuadorian sources are emphatic that Zaiter had ties to Hezbollah and was in fact laundering money for the group [2]. This seems to fit a pattern in Latin America, as more countries attempt to curry favor with Washington by claiming solidarity in the war on terrorism by linking narcotics traffickers to terrorism.

Zaiter was also known by his aliases David Assi Alvarez and Almawla Fares. He is accused of cocaine trafficking and money laundering through a network of local drug smugglers and contacts in the sizable Arab and Muslim immigrant communities of Maicao, a free-trade zone in northeastern Colombia, as well as the capital Bogota. Like Zaiter, the majority of Maicao's Arab Muslim population is of Lebanese descent. Others trace their origins to Syria and, to a lesser extent, Palestine [3].

Margarita Island, Venezuela, another free-trade zone that is home to a sizeable Arab Muslim (and Arab Christian) community, is also cited as a potential terrorist base. The alleged threat emanating from Margarita Island is receiving far more attention in Washington, but is as much a product of the simmering tensions between the Bush Administration and Venezuelan President Hugo Chavez.

Both Maicao and Margarita Island, along with the banking centers on the island of Curacao and elsewhere in the Netherlands Antilles, Colon, Panama, the Cayman Islands and the rest of the Caribbean Basin, are part of a multifaceted network that facilitates the transfer of illicit funds from drug and weapons sales, as well as counterfeiting, piracy and human smuggling. The warring factions in Colombia's civil war also have a lucrative stake in this system.

The Tri-Border Area (TBA) that binds Puerto Iguazu, Argentina; Ciudad del Este, Paraguay and Foz do Iguacu, Brazil, is another center of lawlessness and lucrative criminal activity in South America that includes Russian and Asian gangs, in addition to South American criminal syndicates. Hezbollah is reported to operate extensive operations involving fundraising and money laundering amidst the region's sizeable Arab community in the TBA.

The Black Market Peso Exchange (BMPE), the largest and most sophisticated system of laundering money in the Western Hemisphere, along with other Alternative Remittance Systems (ARS), including hawala, an Islamic form of money transfer traditionally used by Muslims that facilitates the movement of funds through informal and anonymous channels, is endemic to Latin America and a central feature of organized crime and the drug trade in the region [4].

Despite a lack of hard evidence demonstrating collaboration between Hezbollah and al-Qaeda in Latin America and elsewhere for that matter, many observers worry that al-Qaeda may be using the same networks exploited by Hezbollah and other organizations to generate funds. Members of the Egyptian Gamma al-Islamiyya, including Al-Sayid Hassan Mukhlis, who is tied to the 1997 attack against tourists in Luxor, Egypt, have been linked to the TBA, allegedly as local fundraisers for the group. Mukhlis was arrested in El Chui, Uruguay in January 1999 and eventually extradited to Egypt in 2003 [5]. Gammat al-Islamiyya is known to have links to al-Qaeda.

Islam in Latin America

Latin America is home to a sizeable and diverse Muslim population with deep roots throughout the region. Most Muslims are of Arab descent, typically of Lebanese, Syrian and Palestinian origin, although Christian Arabs from the Levant far outnumber their

Muslim kin. There are also sizeable South and Southeast Asian Muslim communities with roots in India, Pakistan, Afghanistan and Indonesia in Suriname, Guyana, Trinidad and Tobago and elsewhere in the Caribbean Basin. The region is also experiencing a steady stream of migration from the Middle East and South Asia in recent years, especially in vibrant free-trade zones such as Iquique, Chile and Colon Panama.

As a result of intermarriage and conversion, Islam is becoming one of the fastest growing religions in Latin America. There is evidence to suggest that Muslim missionaries based in Spain and their regional affiliates are making inroads into disenfranchised and underserved indigenous communities that were once the target of evangelical Christian sects for conversion [6]. The competition between Muslim and Christian missionaries for prospective converts has even led to confrontation and violent clashes in the Mexican state of Chiapas.

Spain's al-Murabitun (The Almoravids, after the African Muslim dynasty that ruled North Africa and Spain in 11th and 12th centuries) is believed to be the most prolific missionary movement operating in Latin America [7]. The group is an international Sufi order founded in the 1970s by Sheikh Abdel Qader as-Sufi al-Murabit, a controversial Scottish Muslim convert born Ian Dallas. Although no hard evidence has surfaced tying the group to international terrorism, let alone al-Qaeda, Dallas has been accused of harboring extremist leanings. Aurelino Perez heads the Murabitun's campaign in Chiapas, where he competes with Omar Weston, a British-born Muslim convert who resides in Mexico City and heads the Centro Cultural Islamico de Mexico (CCIM), for adherents in Chiapas and the rest of Mexico. Known locally as Muhammed Nafia, Perez is a Spanish convert to Islam who hails from the southern Spanish city of Granada in Andalucia.

The Murabitun's ambitious efforts to gain adherents in Mexico include an unsuccessful attempt to forge an alliance with Subcommandante Marcos and his Zapatista Army of National Liberation (EZLN), following the group's armed rebellion in Chiapas in 1994 [8]. The Murabitun are comprised predominantly of Spanish and European converts to Islam. There are also reports that Muslim missionaries are finding adherents among indigenous peoples in Bolivia and elsewhere in Latin America [9].

In an effort to win over converts in Latin America, the Murabitun emphasize the cultural links between the Arab world and Latin America through Spain's Moorish heritage. In doing so, the Murabitun and like-minded movements advocate a collective reversion to Islam, which in their view signifies a return to the region's true heritage, as opposed to what many see as conversion to the Muslim faith. In this sense, Islam not only represents an alternative to the colonial traditions imposed on the indigenous and mestizo peoples of Latin America, namely the Roman Catholic Church, but also is a nativist tradition that has been suppressed. The Murabitun also claim that Islam is not tainted by European and Western colonialism and imperialism, but instead serves as a remedy for the oppression and destruction brought about by the Spanish conquest.

Given al-Qaeda's documented successes in recruiting Muslim converts in Europe and the U.S. to its cause, many observers worry that Muslim converts in Latin America provide fertile ground for new recruits due to their perceived ability to circumvent travel restrictions and blend into Western cities more effectively.

There is no evidence to suggest that the recent trend toward conversion to Islam in Latin America stems from a turn to political and religious radicalism. On the contrary, most Muslim converts see Islam as a vehicle for reasserting their identity. They also see conversion as a form of social and political protest in societies where they are marginalized and experience discrimination [10]. In this context, it is no surprise that groups such as the Murabitun, with their message of social, political and cultural empowerment, are making inroads into disenfranchised and impoverished indigenous communities. The group also supports local education, social welfare and other projects that include Arabic language instruction and the publication of the Qur'an in Spanish and other local languages.

Conclusion

Although the evidence pointing to an alleged al-Qaeda presence in the region is often overshadowed and/or confused with the reported activities of Hezbollah and other groups, it is important for policymakers to consider each of these organizations separately and not fall into the trap of linking them as part of a unified network with a common agenda. At the same time, the diverse array of criminal organizations active in the region—from local drug gangs to radical Islamists—demonstrates that weak institutions, political instability, corruption and poverty provide ample opportunities for groups such as al-Qaeda and others to share the spoils.

Notes

1. Miguel Bonasso, "Un silencio de diez millones: Las estremecedoras declaraciones del testigo secreto Irani," *Pagina 12* (Argentina), September 30, 2001.

2. Sandra Moran Castillo, "Desmantelan a presunta banda de narcotraficantes vinculada con Hizbuláh," *CRE Satelital* (Ecuador), June 21, 2005.

3. Sakia Hassan Rada, "Los Musulmanes de Colombia," *WebIslam: Islam en Latinoamerica* (No. 277) January 4, 2005. http://www.webislam.com/numeros/2005/277/noticias/musulmanes_colombia.htm.

4. Britanico Julio Quesada, "Mercado Negro del Peso: Como se lavo dinero en la zona libre de Colon," *El Siglo* (Panama), June 25, 2003.

5. Julian Halawi, *Al-Ahram Weekly* (Cairo) 17-23, July 2003, Issue No. 647.

6. Thelma Gomez Duran, "Muslalmanes en Chiapas," *WebIslam: Islam en Latinoamerica* (No. 132) July 20, 2001. http://www.webislam.com/elementos_wi/WI_Latino/Musulmanes_Chiapas.htm.

7. For more information on Spain's Murabitun Movement, see the Comunidad Islamica en Espana website at www.cislamica.org

8. Natascha Garvin, "Conversion and Conflict: Muslims in Mexico," *International Institute for the Study of Islam in the Modern World Review* (Netherlands), Spring 2005.

9. Aliefudien Al-Almany, "Da'wa in Latin America," *Tehran Times* (Iran), October 2, 2005.

10. See transcript of presentation by Yahya Juan Suquillo, Imam of the Islamic Center of Quito Ecuador, "Islamic Principles in Latin America" at the Fourth Annual Conference of Latin American Muslim Leaders in Curacao [Curacao], 16-18 September 2003 in the *Latino Muslim Voice* (November 2003), official newsletter of the Latino American Da'wa Organization.

[From Terrorism Monitor, Volume III, Issue 23]

The Threat of Religious Radicalism in Guyana

Chris Zambelis

Originally published on July 27, 2006

The potential threat of radical Islamist infiltration in Latin America and the Caribbean is attracting increasing attention following the September 11 attacks. The region is already plagued by criminality. Local and international organized crime syndicates with a hand in the drug trade, money laundering, human and weapons trafficking, counterfeit goods and document fraud, as well as legitimate business interests, exert tremendous influence on regional affairs. Widespread corruption and poverty, institutional weakness and fluctuating levels of political instability also make the region ripe for infiltration by international terrorist organizations. Although largely underreported due to a lack concrete proof and widely varying assessments as to the true scope and nature of the threat, there is evidence that radical Islamist organizations have a presence in the region.

As a result, the region's small but diverse and dynamic ethnic Arab and Muslim communities have come under increasing scrutiny by local and international security officials. Al-Qaeda's documented international success in winning ideological sympathizers to its cause is one point of concern. Osama bin Laden's ability to inspire sympathizers with no direct links to al-Qaeda to act independently and take action in furthering their own radical agendas through the use of violence in their home countries and elsewhere also raises alarm bells. Given al-Qaeda's ability to lure certain Islamic converts to its cause, growing Muslim conversion trends in the region are also raising fears among some observers about the nature and intentions of Muslim converts.

Given this context, it is worth examining the nature of Islam and the outlook of Muslims in Guyana, one of the most ethnically and culturally diverse countries in the Western hemisphere. Little scholarly research or journalistic coverage exists on the subject. Despite its modest population, Guyana boasts one of the largest percentages of Muslims out of its total population in the Western hemisphere. It is also a member of the Organization of the Islamic Conference (OIC).

It is important to note that there is no substantive evidence to date pointing to a nascent radical threat in Guyana. Guyana did make headlines, however, when local sources reported sightings of Adnan

G. El Shukrijumah in the region in 2003, a known al-Qaeda operative whose whereabouts remain unknown. Many believe that Shukrijumah was born in Saudi Arabia to a Guyanese father and a Saudi mother, although some sources report that he was born in Guyana (*Guyana Chronicle*, March 26, 2003). U.S. and regional security and intelligence officials believe that Shukrijumah may have used a Guyanese passport to pass through one or both countries and elsewhere in the region as well (*Guyana Chronicle*, August 2003).

David "Buffy" Millard, also known as Mustapha Abdullah Muhammad, an Afro-Trinidadian Muslim convert and member of Trinidad and Tobago's Jammat al-Muslimeen wanted on charges of conspiracy to commit the murder of two former Jamaat members on the orders of Imam Yasin Abu Bakr, is believed to have been hiding in Guyana since 2003. He was recently arrested by Guyanese authorities and extradited to Trinidad to face charges (*Stabroek News*, May 7, 2006).

Islam in Guyana

Guyana's sizeable Muslim community, estimated to number between 10 and 12 percent of the country's population of nearly 800,000, boasts a long and rich history that stems back to the slave trade. West African Muslim slaves are believed to have been the first Muslims in Guyana. There is even evidence of popular slave rebellions led by Muslims. East Indians, who represent the vast majority of Guyana's Muslim community, were brought to Guyana as indentured servants by British colonial authorities in the 1800s to satisfy local demands for labor following the abolition of slavery. Guyanese Muslims trace their origins to South Asia, in particular India, Pakistan and Afghanistan, and are known locally as East Indians or Hindustanis. The majority of Guyana's East Indian community, however, is Hindu and, to a lesser extent, Christian. Most Muslims are Sunni, while a minority belongs to the Shiite branch of the faith [1].

Guyana is also home to followers of the Ahmadiyya movement, a sect claiming to be Muslim that originated in India in the late 1800s and continues to count a small following in contemporary Pakistan and other parts of South Asia (http://www.aaiil.org). Many Sunni Muslims consider Ahmadis as heretics. Ahmadis have been the target of violent attacks by Sunni extremists in Pakistan and Bangladesh (http://www.thepersecution.org).

East Indian Guyanese Muslims are well organized. They also look to a host of religious associations, many of which maintain close links with their counterparts in India, Pakistan and parts of the Middle East, including influential centers of Muslim learning such as Cairo's al-Azhar Mosque and university (http://www.alazhar.org). These include the Guyana Islamic Trust (GIT, http://www.gitgy.com) and the Central Islamic Organization of Guyana (CIOG, http://www.ciog.org.gy). GIT and CIOG and other groups organize religious schools, social services and charity, language training in Urdu and Arabic, publications and other programs.

Activism and Identity

Guyanese Muslims pay close attention to the issues affecting Muslims abroad, especially the plight of the Palestinians and the conflicts in Kashmir, Iraq, Afghanistan, Philippines and Chechnya, among others. Local organizations often host prominent Muslim scholars from South Asia and the Arab world as a means of encouraging solidarity and identification with the global ummah (the Muslim community). Guyanese Muslims also maintain close ties with the sizeable Guyanese community in the United States. Some groups such as GIT have raised funds for Muslim charities operating in the Balkans during the period of conflict and other regions.

Guyanese Muslim organizations feel empowered when it comes to influencing Guyanese foreign and domestic policy. CIOG has gone so far as to call on the Guyanese government to cut ties to Israel and has undertaken projects in Guyana on behalf of a number of influential Arab and Muslim charities based in the Middle East [2]. It is also a vocal critic of corruption and racism in Guyanese society (*Stabroek News*, April 11, 2006).

CIOG and other organizations organized protests against the controversial publication of cartoons depicting the Prophet Muhammad in European newspapers and called on all Muslims to do whatever they could to defend the honor of the Prophet. CIOG lent its support to small Muslim organizations in the Caribbean in their efforts to stage protests, including Grenada's Islamic Foundation (*Caribbean Net News*, February 13, 2006). Guyanese Muslims in general also maintain close ties to Muslims elsewhere in the Americas and are active in regional events such as the annual Caribbean Muslim Forum (http://www.centralzakah.org).

Despite theological and ideological disputes and rivalries, Muslim organizations in Guyana in general have a history of tolerance and unity. For instance, Guyanese Muslims were in consensus in their protest of the findings of the 2002 census that omitted the percentage of Muslims out of the total population. Some saw this as an intentional move on the part of the government to downplay or ignore the growing Guyanese Muslim community. Guyana is home to a small but reportedly growing community of recent converts to Islam from among East Indian Hindus, Christians and Afro-Guyanese (*Stabroek News*, October 19, 2005).

Muslims united in 2005 to protest the opening of a bar and restaurant serving alcohol opposite a mosque. The owner's decision to include halal (permissible) meals was seen as an irresponsible provocation against the Muslim community and a break from what one local source calls Guyana's unwritten tradition of respecting the sanctity of places of worship (*Guyana Chronicle*, October 20, 2005). A number of leading local Muslim organizations, including the Muslim Youth League of Guyana (MYL), Guyana United Sadr Islamic Anjuman (GUSIA), Guyana Islamic Forum (GIF), among others, have also set aside their ideological differences in issuing joint statements condemning the use of violence and terrorism following major terrorist attacks such as the bombings in Madrid (http://www.indocaribbeanworld.com, March 24, 2004).

Guyana's complex ethnic composition and often tense race-based political landscape pitting East Indians versus Guyanese of African origin have also influenced the outlook and identity of Guyanese Muslims. East Indians comprise approximately half of Guyana's population while Afro-Guyanese represent a little over one-third. Indigenous Amerindians and others of mixed ethnicity make up the rest of the population. As a result of their common origins and plight as indentured laborers, most Guyanese Muslims tend to identify closely with their East Indian Hindu and Christian kin (*Stabroek News*, October 19, 2005). In many respects, East Indian ethnic identity trumps sectarian affiliation. Significantly, the same trend can be found in other parts of the region that are home to sizeable East Indian Hindu, Christian and Muslim communities, namely Trinidad and Tobago and Suriname.

In April 2004 Muhammed Hassan Abrahemi, an Iranian Shiite cleric affiliated with Guyana's International Islamic College of Advanced Studies (IICAS) in the capital Georgetown, was abducted by armed assailants. Abrahemi's decomposed body turned up buried in a shallow grave approximately a month later just outside of Georgetown. Guyanese police and Iranian investigators who assisted in the search have not uncovered the motive for the crime. Targeted kidnappings for ransom by violent street gangs are a serious and growing problem in crime-ridden Guyana, but local authorities report that no demands for ransom were ever made. Some sources suggest rivalries between Sunni and Shiite Muslims may have played a role in prompting the attack, however, no conclusive evidence has surfaced supporting these claims. Nevertheless, the incident did raise concerns among Guyana's minority Shiite community and Tehran. Some Shiite Guyanese accused the government of being indifferent to the interests and concerns of Guyanese Shiites in order to placate the much larger and more influential Sunni Muslim community (*Caribbean Net News*, May 4, 2004).

Conclusion

Despite a lack of hard evidence implicating extremist elements operating in Guyana, many observers worry that radical ideologies will find resonance among Guyanese Muslims and others in the region. In many respects, these concerns mirror growing fears of al-Qaeda's ability to inspire Muslims and potentially others across the globe to its cause. By all accounts, the potential threat of radicalism in Guyana should be seen in this context and not as a unique case. Nevertheless, Guyana's porous borders and growing problem with violent crime remain a concern, especially as its security and intelligence capabilities are overwhelmed, thus presenting a potential opening for radical Islamists to gain a foothold.

Notes
1. Raymond Chickrie, "Muslims in Guyana: History, Traditions, Conflict and Change," *Journal of Muslim Minority Affairs* (Vol. 19, No. 2 October 1999).
2. See Raymond Chickrie, "History of Politicking of Islamic Organizations in Guyana," http://www.guyana.org/features/Guyana_Islam_org.May2006.pdf.

[From Terrorism Monitor, Volume IV, Issue 15]

Al-Qaeda in the Andes: Spotlight on Colombia

Chris Zambelis

Originally published on April 6, 2006

Colombian authorities claim to have dismantled an extensive counterfeit passport ring in January 2006 that allegedly supplied an unknown number of Pakistanis, Egyptians, Jordanians, Iraqis and others purported to be working with al-Qaeda with Colombian, Portuguese, German, and Spanish citizenship, enabling them to travel freely in the United States and Europe. Bogota also mentioned that the network had ties to HAMAS militants (*al-Hayat*, January 28, 2006; Caracol Radio, January 26, 2006).

In contrast, U.S. Justice Department and Department of Homeland Security officials expressed surprise at Bogota's announcement while emphatically disputing its claim, alleging that they had no knowledge of known links between the document forgery operation and any brand of Islamist terrorism, let alone al-Qaeda. Instead, they acknowledged that the sting operation involved Colombians posing as members of the Fuerzas Armadas Revolucionarias de Colombia (FARC) or Revolutionary Armed Forces of Colombia, the country's largest and most powerful rebel group, interested in purchasing forged documents and possibly even weapons (*U.S. Immigration and Customs Enforcement Report*, January 27, 2006). Washington classifies FARC as an international terrorist organization.

Since the September 11 attacks, Washington fears that radical Islamist terrorist organizations such as al-Qaeda may exploit Latin America's porous borders, endemic corruption and weak institutions to gain a foothold in the region in order to infiltrate U.S. territory or to stage attacks against vital U.S. interests in the region. Many observers believe that Colombia, a strong ally of Washington, with its vibrant narcotics trade, ongoing insurgencies, robust energy reserves, and proximity to the Panama Canal and other vital shipping lanes, represents an ideal target.

FARC's extensive involvement in the drug business and its documented ties to regional and international drug cartels and organized crime, coupled with the control it wields over large swathes of Colombian territory out of Bogota's reach, is of particular concern. In a worst case scenario, Washington worries that al-Qaeda may cultivate alliances of convenience with organizations such as FARC or others involved in the drug trade in order to raise finances or procure armaments. At the same time, it is important to note that there is no credible evidence pointing to this kind of formal cooperation. At the very least, however, terrorist organizations can exploit established money laundering and finance networks used by narcotics traffickers and organized crime syndicates in the region, especially the Black Market Peso Exchange (BMPE), to fund future operations (*El Siglo*, June 25, 2003).

It is against this background that Colombian and regional governments have played on U.S. concerns by moving to curry favor with the U.S. to further their own domestic agendas and international standing in the context of the Bush Administration's war on terrorism. In doing so, they often highlight the alleged threat of al-Qaeda or other brands of radical Islamist terrorism within their own borders.

Based on the evidence, this latest attempt by Bogota is a case in point in that it likely represents an effort to enhance its position in the eyes of Washington and the international community in its longstanding war with FARC guerillas. Since one of the alleged members of the smuggling ring, Jalal Saadat Moheisen, happened to be of Palestinian descent, it is likely that Colombia seized the opportunity to win political points in Washington by pointing to a possible link to Middle East terrorist networks.

What makes Colombia's bold claims especially interesting is that the sting operation was in fact led by U.S. Immigration and Customs Enforcement (ICE) officials and other investigators, who worked in concert with their Colombian counterparts in the Department of Administrative Security (DAS).

Normally, references to alleged al-Qaeda infiltration are enough to gain the attention and headlines governments in Latin America seek. For example, El Salvador, Nicaragua and Honduras have pointed to alleged al-Qaeda links with the Maras street gangs that terrorize their cities. Mexican officials have hinted at al-Qaeda involvement with rebel indigenous groups in Chiapas. Trinidadian authorities have employed similar tactics when it comes to discrediting their own homegrown Islamist opposition centered in the Afro-Trinidadian Muslim community.

U.S. concern over the strong showing by HAMAS in the recent Palestinian elections is likely responsible for Bogota's decision to include HAMAS alongside al-Qaeda in its recent claims of radical Islamist involvement in the document forgery ring.

Islam in Colombia

Colombia is home to a small, albeit diverse, Muslim population. Most Colombian Muslims are of Lebanese, Syrian and Palestinian origin, but Arab Christians from the Levant with a long history in the country dating back to the Ottoman era far outnumber their Muslim counterparts. In contrast, unlike elsewhere in the region, Arab Muslims made their presence felt in Colombia beginning in the late 1960s and 70s after a wave of migration from the Middle East that was prompted by the Lebanese Civil War and other regional tensions (*Los Cromos*, April 1, 2005).

Recent Muslim migrants from the Middle East tend to be more pious and traditional compared to their second and third generation kin who have become assimilated into Colombian society. For example, many still speak Arabic and live in tight-knit communities, not unlike immigrant communities elsewhere. Demographic assessments on Colombia's Muslim population vary. According to some local reports, Colombia's Muslim population numbers approximately 15,000 adherents (webislam.com, January 4, 2005).

As a result of intermarriage and religious conversion, Islam has become one of the fastest growing faiths in Colombia and Latin America. Growing disenchantment with the Roman Catholic Church establishment in Colombia and elsewhere in the region has also led many to seek spiritual guidance elsewhere. Many former Roman Catholics that have strayed from the Church have come to see Catholicism as a European colonial tradition that was imposed on the peoples of the Americas. Therefore, conversion to Islam represents an assertion of ethno-national, as well as spiritual, identity. Protestant missionaries have been making inroads into Latin America for many of the same reasons for decades, especially among underserved communities and indigenous populations.

Colombian Christians who become Muslims find solace in Islam's reverence of Jesus Christ and Mary. Other Muslim converts see

Islam as a native tradition untainted by the region's colonial experience. Many Muslims in Colombia also emphasize what they believe are their natural cultural and even ethnic links with Arabs and Muslims, stemming from Spain's Moorish heritage. In this regard, conversion to Islam symbolizes a reversion to their original state, which they see as having been suppressed by colonialism. There is also evidence suggesting that Colombian Muslims are becoming more open about asserting their identity, especially since Bogota abolished Catholicism as the official state religion in an effort to promote a broader definition of Colombian identity.

Many analysts are alarmed by increasing Muslim conversion trends, which they interpret as a sign of radicalization, especially in light of al-Qaeda's proven successes in luring Muslim converts to their cause. Despite these concerns, there is no evidence that Muslim conversion in Colombia or elsewhere in Latin America stems from a turn to political radicalization.

Maicao

Although accurate demographic measures are hard to come by, the municipality of Maicao, in northeastern Colombia in the department of La Guajira, an indigenous reserve located along the border with Venezuela and the Caribbean, is home to Colombia's largest Muslim community. Maicao's Muslim population is believed to number anywhere between 4,000 to 8,000 adherents. Maicao is also home of the Omar Ibn al-Khattab Mosque, which was completed in 1987. It is Colombia's largest mosque and is counted as one of the largest in South America (*Latino Muslim Voice*, December 2003).

Most of Maicao's Muslims are Sunni Arabs from the Levant, especially Lebanon, while a minority originates from Syria and Palestine. Maicao is also home to a small Shiite Arab population. The region's Arab community lives alongside the Way'uu, an indigenous group. As a result of its position on the coast, La Guajira has always lured immigrants seeking potentially lucrative trade opportunities and jobs, especially migrants from the Middle East.

Maicao is a free trade zone (FTZ) and a known center of smuggling of counterfeit goods such as cigarettes and electric appliances, arms, and narcotics, money laundering, and other illicit forms of commerce to Venezuela, Central America, and the Caribbean. According to some reports, recent efforts by Bogota to enforce tax codes and root out corruption and smuggling hit Maicao's merchants particularly hard, especially Arab Muslims who figure prominently in the local economy. This includes merchants engaged in both legal and illegal business. As a result, Maicao's Arab Muslim population is said to be dwindling, as local merchants seek out opportunities elsewhere in Colombia and in the region (*Los Cromos*, April 1, 2005).

Many observers worry that al-Qaeda and other terrorist organizations can exploit Maicao and the Colombian island of San Andres, another FTZ located off the coast of Panama, to raise funds to finance operations. San Andres is also home to a sizeable Arab Muslim and Christian community. FTZs in Colon, Panama, Iquique, Chile, Margarita Island, Venezuela, and elsewhere in the region are frequently cited as potential terrorist finance centers.

Conclusion

Despite a lack of concrete evidence to date, Colombia appears susceptible to al-Qaeda infiltration, but it is highly unlikely to come in the form of an alliance with FARC or the radicalization of Colombia's Muslims. In contrast, Colombia's weak institutions and ongoing conflict may present an opening for radical Islamists to gain a foothold. Given this background, it is important to consider the politics behind allegations of al-Qaeda infiltration, as they may divert attention away from the far more pressing themes shaping the threat at hand.

[From Terrorism Monitor, Volume IV, Issue 7]

Terrorism and Human Smuggling Rings in South and Central America

Thomas Davidson

Originally published on November 17, 2005

The road to the "American Dream" for many illegal immigrants usually leads from home countries through Mexico and then into the U.S.. Although almost all of these illegal immigrants are merely looking for a better life for themselves and their families, world-wide human trafficking routes provide ample opportunity for those wishing harm to the U.S. easy access into America. In spite of international efforts in the Americas to break up these human smuggling routes, there are still a number of avenues available whereby the potential terrorist can enter the United States.

Muslim and Middle Eastern Illegal Immigrants and Activities in Central and South America

During 2004 and 2005, a number of Muslim and Middle Eastern illegal immigrants were captured in Central and South America. Some of the more unusual cases include:

- A Turkish citizen with a false Dutch passport is arrested in Managua, Nicaragua on September 22, 2004. He had lived in Costa Rica for ten months and entered via Russia and Cuba. While attempting to board a flight to Canada, he was arrested by Nicaraguan authorities. [1]
- Two Jordanians with false European passports were arrested at the San José International Airport in Costa Rica. Their route of travel included Cuba and Guatemala. The two attempted to bribe the Costa Rican authorities with a "large sum of money" [2]. Almost all newspaper reports place the illegal immigrants as having passed through Moscow and/or Cuba.
- In early 2005, Spanish and Italian intelligence and police agencies informed Argentine authorities that members of the fundamentalist Jamaat Tabligh Movement were in Argentina after having attended a meeting in Chile. Spanish authorities

believe that members of the European wing of the Movement
had been recruited by al-Qaeda to participate in the Madrid
bombings. The arrival of 26 members of the movement was
confirmed by Argentine Muslim authorities. Members who had
entered Argentina included citizens of Malaysia, Syria, Egypt,
Qatar, Pakistan and South Africa. Argentine authorities believe
that the Islamic fundamentalists are in Argentina in order to
recruit members with Argentine passports. When traveling, such
individuals will receive considerably less scrutiny by security
personnel than those from obviously Muslim countries.

Defunct Smuggling Rings in Mexico and the Americas

Mexican, Honduran and Peruvian authorities were able to break
up three major human smuggling rings. The Mexican and Peruvian rings
specialized in transporting Middle Easterners and the Honduran Ring
specialized in transporting Chinese into the U.S.. All of these individuals
were brought into Central or South America and then through Mexico
into the U.S..

In mid-2003, one of the Mexican smuggling rings was run
by an individual named Salim Boughader Mucharrafille. Boughader is
identified only as an Arab. The ring worked primarily out of Tijuana,
Mexico. Mexican authorities believed that the ring consisted of 14
individuals, seven of whom have been captured. The Mexican Foreign
Ministry employee Imelda Ortiz allegedly worked with this gang while
stationed with the Mexican Consulate in Lebanon. She is alleged to have
provided a visa to Mexico for al Afani Sghir, an alleged Shi'ite extremist
[3].

In late 2003, the second Mexican ring was run by a Pakistani
national Ali Ganzafar Houssein. Ganzafar's ring operated from the
Mexican Southern states of Chiapas and Tabasco through Veracruz
up to Matamoros, Tamaulipas on the border with Brownsville, Texas.
Ganzafar is alleged to have had numerous connections to Central and
South American human trafficking rings. In November 2003, he was
arrested at the Mexico City International Airport attempting to board
an aircraft for Amsterdam, the Netherlands.

In April 2005, the Honduran Director for Immigration Affairs was arrested for involvement in human trafficking. He worked with Chinese "mafias" to smuggle Chinese, Afghan and Pakistani citizens into Honduras and then into the U.S.. One of the most common routes for the illegal aliens was through Havana, Cuba where they would be provided with false documents such as Honduran or European passports [4].

In September 2005, Peruvian and U.S. authorities were able to smash a human smuggling ring which ran from Peru to the U.S.. A Jordanian citizen was apprehended in Peru and three Iraqi-born U.S. citizens were arrested in Chicago. The Jordanian arrived in Peru from Amsterdam in June 2004. This ring allegedly specialized in smuggling Arab and Middle Easterners into the U.S..

Illegal Immigrants in Mexico

The chart below compares the number of illegal immigrants detained in Mexico by the Instituto Nacional de Migración (INM - Mexican National Immigration Institute) in 2004 and 2005.

In 2004, the number of Ethiopians was not significant enough to be on the official statistical chart; yet in 2005, there were a total of 128. In addition, Eritreans are known to use Ethiopian passports. The number of Chinese detained in 2005 nearly doubled from 2004. The number of "all others" increased by more than 100. Statistics for the capture of illegal immigrants in other Central and South American countries are not available.

Illegal Immigrants Detained by INM [5]		
Nationality	**2004**	**2005**
South American	5,087	5,803
Central American/Caribbean	163,911	160,948
Ethiopian	Not Provided	128
Chinese	861	513
All Others	854	968
TOTAL	172,117	170,365

Islamist Activities in Mexico and Central America

One of the active Salafi organizations in Mexico is run by Omar Weston. Born Mark Weston, he is a British subject who converted to Islam in Orlando, Florida, and established the Centro Cultural Islámico de México (Islamic Cultural Center of Mexico) in Mexico City. Weston has a master's degree in Shari'ah law from Medina University and is currently running an Islamic retreat on Lake Tequesquitengo near Cuernavaca, Morelos, Mexico. The original center in Mexico City has been renamed Centro Salafi de México (Salafi Center of Mexico) and is now being run by Muhammad Abdullah Ruiz, a Mexican convert and former deputy to Weston. Although the actual size of the retreat is not known, from photos it appears to encompass at least four acres. The retreat is directly on the lakeshore and is accessible by road, boat, and two airports. These two organizations maintain contact and are affiliated with Salafi groups and/or individuals in the Mexican states of Coahuila, Chiapas, Chihuahua, Jalisco, Nuevo León, Sinaloa, and Veracruz.

The Mexican Secretary of Governance (Interior) stated that there are a number of international terrorist cells active in Mexico, including ETA, FARC and Islamic groups. In a report issued by Centro de Investigación y Seguridad Nacional (CISEN - National Center for Investigation and Security), these three groups are allegedly operating primarily in the Federal District and the states of Distrito Federal, Querétaro, México State, Oaxaca, Nuevo León, and Coahuila. Although there are Muslim communities in the states of Coahuila, Veracruz, Morelos, Mexico City, Jalisco, Chiapas, Nuevo León, Quintana Roo, and Yucatán, Mexican authorities believe that there are radical support cells only in Torreón, Coahuila and Mexico City. The federal authorities believe that these support groups are involved in human trafficking, telephone fraud, and automobile theft [6].

In May 2004, Said Ould Bah, representative of the Islamic Organization for Culture, Science, and Education in Honduras sponsored a meeting of Muslims from 24 Latin American nations. The original meeting was to have taken place in San Pedro Sula, Honduras. However, for reasons of "pressure in Honduras" from unidentified sources, the meeting was moved to Guatemala City and scheduled for late June 2004 [7].

In late June 2004, Omar Weston scheduled an international meeting with Islamic speakers from all over the world to include the UK, Pakistan, Panama, and the U.S. at the retreat on Lake Tequesquitengo. The meeting was originally scheduled for late June or early July 2004. The meeting was postponed until July 24 through August 8, 2004 [8].

Possible Involvement of Transnational Gangs

According to Central American authorities, the transnational gang Mara Salvatrucha may have become involved with Islamic militants [9]. The Mexican train routes (both east and west) are the primary means for illegal immigrants to transit Mexico on their way to the U.S.. Up to 99% of these are freight and not passenger trains. The Mara Salvatrucha is controlling the eastern Mexican train route Transportación Ferroviaria Mexicana (TFM - Mexican Rail Line Transportation) which runs from Chiapas to Tabasco through Veracruz to northern Mexico. Rumors are that they are also beginning to control the west coast train route Transportación Marítima Mexicana (TMM - Mexican Maritime Transport) [10]. Salvatrucha members extort sexual favors or money from the illegal immigrants in order to allow them to board the empty freight cars. If the "taxes" are not paid, the immigrant could be beaten, thrown off the train, or even killed [11]. In addition to their control of the train routes, Salvatrucha members are known to be working as protection for drug cartels as they smuggle their contraband into the U.S. [12].

Conclusion

A number of Arabs, Middle Easterners and other Muslims are still using Central America and parts of South America as jumping off points. With the break-up of a number of human trafficking organizations specializing in Middle Easterners and Arabs, illegal immigrants (to include potential terrorists) have had to look for other avenues for entering the U.S. Two conceivable avenues of entry are: 1) the current Salafi network in Mexico which currently runs from the southernmost state of Chiapas to the northern Mexican border (many of the elements of this Islamic network are located at or near the train lines of the TMM and the TFM. These elements could provide any needed support to potential terrorists traveling via rail); and 2) The Mara Salvatrucha which is a violent gang with no allegiance to any country or cause except the gang. As they control the rail lines through Mexico, terrorists wishing to use the trains as a way of entering the U.S. would have to do via the Mara Salvatrucha.

Of further interest was the postponement of the two international Islamic conferences. Both conferences took place in rather isolated areas and occurred approximately one month before the al-Qaeda operative Adnan El Shukrijumah was alleged to have been seen in the northern Mexican state of Sonora. Part of the Salafi network includes several Muslims in Hermosillo, Sonora, not far from the U.S. border [13].

The number of illegal immigrants detained by Mexican authorities in 2005 decreased as compared to 2004. However, the number of South Americans, Ethiopians, Chinese, and "all others" increased significantly. This increase, in all probability, included a significant number of Arabs. South America, especially in the Tri-Border area, has a very large Arab/Muslim population. This combined with the recruitment efforts of the Jamaat Tabligh Movement in Argentina and the significant increase of Ethiopians and "all others" increases exponentially the possibility that terrorists are making their way from South and Central America through Mexico and into the U.S..

Notes

1. http://www-ni.laprensa.com.ni/archivo /2004/septiembre/22/nacionales /nacionales-20040922-17.html.
2. http://www.elsalvador.com/noticias/2004/09/21/nacional/nac6.asp.
3. http://www.lacronica.com/EdicionImpresa/Hoy/General/13.asp.
4. http://terra.com.hn/noticias/nacionales/articulo/html/nac37585.htm.
5. www.inami.gob.mx.
6. https://secure.milenio.com/nota.asp?id=148425.
7.http://www.laprensahn.com/nacionales.php?id=1091&tabla =August_2004&fecha=20040823.
8. http://www.islam.com.mx/index.php?art_id=29&categ=25&expand =25&file=view_article.tp#.
9. https://secure.milenio.com/nota.asp?id=148425.

10. http://www.am.com.mx/notap.asp?ANIOX=2005&ID=62373.
11. http://www.univision.com/content/content.jhtml?chid=3&schid=181&secid=182&cid=666912.
12. http://www.cronica.com.mx/nota.php?idc=195064.
13. https://secure.milenio.com/nota.asp?id=148425.

[From Terrorism Monitor, Volume III, Issue 22]

Islamic Radicalism in Mexico: The Threat from South of the Border

Chris Zambelis

Originally published on June 2, 2006

The ongoing controversy surrounding the debate over illegal immigration and border security issues in the United States, specifically as it applies to the porous U.S.-Mexico frontier and the status of millions of undocumented workers and other migrants that enter the country each year from Mexico, continues to dominate headlines. Although the overwhelming majority of those entering the United States from Mexico each day are in search of opportunity, many observers worry that it is only a matter of time before al-Qaeda exploits this vulnerability for its own ends.

In assessing this threat, Muslim communities in Mexico have come under increasing scrutiny by U.S., Mexican and international security officials both as potential enablers for terrorist infiltration and as ideological sympathizers for the brand of radicalism characteristic of al-Qaeda. Muslim conversion trends in Mexico and Latin America have also raised concerns, especially given al-Qaeda's successes in luring some Muslim converts to its cause. To date, however, these assessments have been way off the mark and in many respects divert attention away from the far more pressing threats at hand. A closer look at the nature of Islam and the outlook of Mexican Muslims may explain why.

Islam in Mexico

Compared to other countries in Latin America that are home to sizeable Muslim communities with longstanding ties to the region, Mexico's Muslim minority is tiny. At the same time, it is one of the most diverse and dynamic in the region. Despite varying figures and scant data, only a couple thousand Muslims are believed to live in the overwhelmingly Roman Catholic country. Nearly all are Sunni Muslims. Of this group, approximately half trace their origins to what is modern-day Lebanon, Syria and Palestine, mostly the descendants of traders and peasants who emigrated from the Middle East in the latter part of Ottoman rule. Mexico's Arab Muslim community is assimilated in major urban centers such as Mexico City. Significantly, Mexico is also home to a much larger Arab Christian community, also originating from the Levant, which numbers in the tens of thousands. Both communities share close ties and feel a mutual sense of pride for their common Arab heritage [1].

Mexican Converts

The other segment of Mexico's small Muslim community is made up of Mexicans who converted to Islam in recent years. Islam is one of the fastest growing religions in the world, partially as a result of intermarriage and religious conversion. This trend is also evident elsewhere in Latin America, despite the longstanding influence of the Roman Catholic Church. In fact, widespread and growing disenchantment with the Catholic Church is leading many Mexicans and others in the region to find spiritual solace elsewhere, including Islam.

One of Mexico's longest running and most influential Muslim organizations is the Centro Cultural Islamico de Mexico (CCIM). Founded in 1995, the CCIM is a Sunni Muslim organization based in Mexico City. It is led by Omar Weston, a British Muslim convert who was born Mark Weston. It runs two mosques and an array of social welfare and education programs that include Arabic language training and a dawa (call) for conversion. It also has links with Muslim communities elsewhere in Latin America and the Caribbean (http://www.islam.com.mx). Despite some vague and unsubstantiated reports, there is no evidence implicating Weston and the CCIM to radicalism or terrorism.

Mexico is also home to a number of small Sufi orders led by two women, Sheikha Fariha and Sheikha Amina, the most prominent being the Nur Ashki Jerrahi order, a branch of the Halveti-Jerrahi Tariqat community of dervishes based in the Masjid al-Farah in New York City and other major U.S. cities. The group has branches in Mexico City, Curernavaca and Oaxaca (http://www.nurashkijerrahi.org). The group has been described as adhering to an unconventional blend of traditional Sufi mysticism and New Age ideologies [2]. There is no evidence linking these groups to radicalism or terrorism.

The Murabitun (the Almoravids, after the African Muslim dynasty that ruled North Africa and Spain in the 11th and 12th centuries) also has a presence in Mexico (http://www.cislamica.org). The group is a well-funded international Sufi order based in Granada, Spain that claims thousands of followers across the globe, including many European converts. It is also regarded as one of the most aggressive missionary movements in Latin America and a major rival of Omar Weston's CCIM. It was founded in the 1970s by Sheikh Abdel Qader as-Sufi al-Murabit, a Scottish Muslim convert born Ian Dallas who was formerly a playwright and actor. Dallas is a controversial figure who, among other things, is a vocal critic of international capitalism and modern forms of finance. Although there is no evidence linking him or his organization to violence or terrorism, he has been accused of harboring pro-Nazi leanings and other radical ideologies. Othman Abu-Sahnun, an Italian Muslim convert and former ranking member of the Murabitun who had a falling out with the group, dedicates an entire website accusing his former leader of extremism, corruption and being party to alleged sinister conspiracies involving Freemasonry (http://www.murabitun.cyberummah.org).

Chiapas

In recent years, Mexico's volatile and impoverished southern state of Chiapas, which is home to a predominately indigenous population that traces its ethnic and cultural lineage to the Mayans, has been the target of Muslim missionaries. The indigenous peoples of Chiapas are underserved and face severe discrimination in Mexican society. In fact, these circumstances are one of the main reasons why Evangelical and other Protestant Christian sects target them in search of new adherents, an ongoing trend in Chiapas and elsewhere in Latin America. In an effort to win over converts, Christian missionary organizations have been running social welfare and humanitarian programs for decades targeting Mexico's indigenous communities. In doing so, they emphasize what they describe as the failure of the Roman Catholic establishment to cater to the spiritual and material needs of the people in the region, often with great success [3].

Muslim missionary groups, especially the Murabitun, which is led by Aurelino Perez in the region, and Omar Weston's CCIM, use similar tactics in an effort to win over adherents in Chiapas. In addition to providing much needed social welfare and humanitarian aid, the Murabitun argue that Catholicism represents a vestige of European imperialism that is directly responsible for the destruction of Mayan culture. Likewise, Catholicism is seen as a tool of the state that is to blame for the poverty and plight of the indigenous peoples. The anti-capitalist message of the Murabitun in particular also resonates with some of the impoverished locals. Murabitun discourse even emphasizes what it describes as the close cultural and ethnic links between the indigenous peoples of the region and the Muslim Moors who once ruled Spain. Therefore, conversion to Islam represents a reversion to their original identity, essentially an assertion of cultural and ethnic identity long suppressed by European colonialism. The Murabitun went as far as to engage Subcommandante Marcos and his Zapatista Army of National Liberation (EZLN), following the group's armed rebellion in Chiapas in 1994, in an effort to gain support (http://www.ezln.org. mx).

The number of indigenous peoples who have converted to Islam is believed to number in the hundreds. Significantly, the majority of indigenous peoples converting to Islam are among those who previously converted to Protestantism and other sects. Although religious affiliation in Chiapas tends to be more pluralistic relative to the rest of Mexico due to the influence of indigenous beliefs and customs, Mayans who turn away from the Catholic Church often face discrimination and violence. Many have even been expelled from their homes by violent gangs and are now known locally as the expulsados (the expelled). For example, many of the Muslims of Chiapas trace their lineage to the Tzotzil Mayan village of San Juan Chamula. A large segment of this community was expelled decades ago for adopting Evangelical Christianity. They now reside in Nueva Esperanza, an impoverished section of San Cristobal [4].

In addition to the Murabitun, Muslim missionary activity in San Cristobal has been attributed to the efforts of a group known as the Mission for Dawa in Mexico, represented locally by Esteban Lopez Moreno, a Muslim convert from Spain who is also linked to the Murabitun [5]. Organizations such as the Murabitun and other Muslim groups line up alongside Pentecostals, Jehova's Witnesses, Mormons and other proselytizers in the hunt for new adherents. Under these circumstances, impoverished locals will often convert to a new faith based on which congregation can provide the most benefits. Many, however, take their newfound faith seriously. With the financial support of local and international groups, Mayan Muslims made the pilgrimage to Mecca in 2005, the first group from Chiapas to do so [6].

Reports pointing to possible terrorist links with Muslim missionaries in Chiapas have surfaced in the Mexican and Spanish media. Spanish authorities have raised suspicions about possible links between Spanish members of the Murabitun living in Chiapas and radical Islamists in Spain. Other reports have even linked the group with Basque separatist movements such as ETA. Othman Abu-Sahnun is a proponent of this theory (http://www.murabitun.cyberummah. org). Mexican authorities have also investigated the activities of the Murabitun due to reports of alleged immigration and visa abuses involving the group's European members and possible radical links, including to al-Qaeda [7]. Despite these allegations and extensive media hype in Mexico and other Spanish-language press, no concrete evidence has surfaced substantiating such claims.

Conclusion

U.S. policymakers and security officials should continue to worry about border security and the potential for al-Qaeda infiltration into Mexico. Given the evidence to date, however, any potential inroads by al-Qaeda into Mexico is not likely to come through ties with Mexico's Muslim community—and this includes local converts or otherwise. Washington would be better served by concentrating its resources to confront Mexico's weak institutions, corruption, the influence of drug and other criminal gangs and poverty that may be exploited by al-Qaeda as a means to a greater end, as they have all too often in other parts of the world.

Notes
1. Luz Maria Martinez Montiel, "The Lebanese Community in Mexico: its Meaning, Importance and the History of its Communities," *The Lebanese in the World: A Century of Emigration* (New York: I.B. Tauris, 1993).
2. Natascha Garvin, "Conversion and Conflict: Muslims in Mexico," *International Institute for the Study of Islam in the Modern World Review* [Netherlands], Spring 2005.
3. Thelma Gomez Duran, "Muslalmanes en Chiapas," *WebIslam: Islam en Latinoamerica*, No. 132, July 20, 2001.

4. Bill Weinberg, "Islamic Sect Targets Chiapas Indians," *Native Americas Journal*, August 28, 2003.
5. "Los musulmanes del sureste mexicano," Univison, October 4, 2004.
6. *Dawn*, January 28, 2005.
7. Natascha Garvin, "Conversion and Conflict: Muslims in Mexico."

[From Terrorism Monitor, Volume IV, Issue 11]

The United States

Jihadi Doctrine on Killing Americans

Stephen Ulph

Originally published on January 31, 2006

On January 30, al-Qaeda's second-in-command, Egyptian national Ayman al-Zawahiri, reiterated Osama bin Laden's threat to carry out an attack in the United States. Given the controversy that bin Laden's threat stirred on the jihadi forums, it is worth taking a brief look at the ideological angle of the possible forthcoming attacks (*Terrorism Focus*, February 10, 2005).

Comments on the jihadi forums focused on bin Laden's offer of a truce, and his assurance of the bona fides of such a treaty in that "we are a Nation whom God has forbidden to use treachery or deceit." A critic on the forum pointed out that the attackers in the 9/11 events used deceit by employing subterfuge in using their Saudi passports to gain entry visas, thus claiming and receiving legal protection from the host state, which they then proceeded to betray. This issue has long been controversial and can be gauged from the publication in August 2004 of the "Epistle on the Basic Verdict on the Blood, Wealth and Honor of the Infidel." The article was produced by the online al-Tibyan Publications, a group posting on http://www.at-tawheed.com and aimed at providing jihadist-related materials for a general audience.

The anonymous authors of the Epistle concede that the rights of one entering the country may indeed be guaranteed by the host state—even if he should enter with false papers—but argue that if the Muslim in some way has his rights curtailed, then the mutual conditions for aman ("security guarantee") are nullified. Then, with recourse to the classical jurists concerning conflict, they claim that without explicit agreements made demanding their security from the Muslim, "it is allowed for him to assassinate them and to take whatever he can from their property."

The issue of "covenant" is a vexed one. In response to concerns on this matter, the radical Sheikh Nassir al-Fahd (famous for his treatise authorizing the use of weapons of mass destruction on the United

States) issued a Hukm mujahadat al-Amrikan kharij al-Iraq ("Verdict on Waging Jihad Against Americans Outside of Iraq") where he dealt with the issue of the restriction of jihad conditions to an established arena of war. For al-Fahd, there is no such restriction due to the United States' anti-Muslim activities in all places in the world. According to his argument, the Americans are harbis, understood in the jihadi conception to mean "enemy combatants as such, irrespective of a state of war." Added to that is the conviction that any agreements made by "Muslim" governments with them are illegal, built as they are on "the tyrannical treaties of the United Nations."

The authors of the Epistle on the Basic Verdict then go on to overturn what they term "misconceptions" regarding the fundamental concept of the permissibility of killing, and stealing from, the infidel. They dismiss the idea that the killing of infidels is to be considered an act that requires exceptional circumstances since that would imply an equivalence of worth. Secondly, the reference in the Quran that "Allah does not forbid you to deal justly and kindly with those who fought not against you" (LX, 8), used by Muslim critics of the mujahideen, is taken by the jihadist authors to mean that Allah does not obligate the Muslim to behave in this way either.

They also leave open the possibility that this constitutes one of the class of Quranic verses abrogated by subsequent verses, such as "kill the mushrikeen ("polytheists") wherever you find them" (IX, 5). Similarly, the authors dismiss the argument that the permissibility of killing and looting refers only to the battlefield, and instead contend that "the characteristic of Disbelief itself is what permits it."

Finally, the argument that killing and looting can only be done as an act of self-defense is refuted on the grounds that the self-defense stipulation only applies between two Muslim groups, not between Muslims and infidels. Besides, they argue, such a restriction would cancel out the possibility of Jihad al-Talab (offensive, preemptive jihad), which they hold as a fundamental duty.

The authors explicitly spell out the aim of the Epistle: to counter the "allied elements of infidels, apologists and defeatist Muslims, who have accepted such slogans as: 'Islam Means Peace,' and 'Jihad is for Self-Defense Only,' and to prevent the Sharia from being stripped of its 'principles of enmity toward the Disbelievers and its clearness concerning the inequality between them and the Believers.'"

The authors argue triumphantly that "whether they call this 'extremism' or 'radicalism,' the fact remains that the rulings of Islam are found in its texts and not in the slogans of the people who weakly adhere to its principles."

The value of examining internal debates provides important information on the robustness of the jihadi doctrine against criticism from moderate Muslims, and its ability to maintain morale and to retain necessary ideological support. Beyond theology, such documents have strategic significance.

[From Terrorism Focus, Volume III, Issue 4]

Radical Trends in African-American Islam

Chris Zambelis

Originally published on August 10, 2006

Since the arrest of members of the Seas of David, due to allegations that they sought al-Qaeda support in facilitating a plot to attack targets in Chicago and Miami, law enforcement and intelligence officials have been paying closer attention to radical trends in the African-American Muslim community. Despite its rhetoric and embrace of Islamic discourse, Seas of David is not a Muslim organization. Instead, its ideology appears to reflect an array of influences that includes a heavy dose of Judaism, Christianity and an affinity for pan-African nationalist ideals. Nevertheless, the group's predominantly African-American and Afro-Caribbean immigrant membership and its reported intent to seek out al-Qaeda raised alarm bells about the potential radicalization of Black Muslims in the United States, especially Muslim converts (*Terrorism Focus*, July 11, 2006).

Inner City Islam and Identity

Fears of the threat of al-Qaeda's influence spreading among African-American Muslim converts and underprivileged minorities in impoverished inner cities are in part based on alarming trends in Europe. Evidence of the presence of Black and Latino American-born Muslims in terrorism training camps in the Middle East and South Asia is one point of concern [1]. Richard C. Reid, the infamous "shoe bomber," also known as Abdul Raheem or Abu Ibrahim, was the British-born son of an English mother and a Jamaican father. He converted to Islam while serving a prison sentence and is alleged to have had close links with al-Qaeda [2]. Germain Lindsay, also known as Abdullah Shaheed Jamal since his conversion to Islam in his early teens and one of the four participants in the 2005 suicide bombings in London, was born in Jamaica and raised in Great Britain (*Telegraph*, July 17, 2005). Trinidad and Tobago's Jamaat al-Muslimeen, a radical Islamist organization comprised mostly of Afro-Trinidadian Muslim converts that has a history of violence and crime, also counts on support from impoverished Blacks in Trinidad's urban centers (*Terrorism Monitor*, March 9, 2006).

Despite these concerns, it is important to emphasize that Muslim conversion in the African-American community has a long history as a positive force for empowerment. In many respects, conversion to Islam has traditionally represented an assertion of social, political, ethnic and racial identity in a society where Blacks and other minorities face discrimination and obstacles. As the descendants of slaves who had adopted the Christianity practiced by their former slave owners, but who were at the same time subject to severe discrimination and relegated to churches and societies segregated along racial lines, many African-Americans see in Islam an opportunity to formally break with the injustices of the past. Others believe that they are reverting to the faith of their enslaved ancestors and hence are adopting a proud native tradition that they can call their own.

Many Muslim converts identify with the greater ummah (Muslim community). Some may learn Arabic in order to read and study the Quran in its original form. The plight of the Palestinians and U.S. foreign policy in the Middle East, issues typically important to Muslims, often becomes of interest. At the same time, many African-American Muslims identify with the issues affecting the Black community as a whole, regardless of sectarian affiliation.

Black Power and Nationalism

In order to assess the potential threat of radicalism in the African-American Muslim community, it is important to distinguish between the myriad of ideologies that influence the outlook of Black Muslims today from the groups and individuals on the extreme fringe implicated in terrorism. This holds especially true when one considers social protest movements that fought for racial equality during the U.S. civil rights struggle that continue to wield influence today, such as the Nation of Islam (NOI). Founded in 1933, in its early years NOI encompassed a mix of Islamic discourse and a worldview that held that Blacks were God's chosen people. Whites were seen as inferior, oppressors and regularly referred to as "devils," in what many observers contend was a reaction to the ideals of white supremacy that prevailed in society [3].

NOI borrowed heavily from the beliefs held by the Moorish Science Temple. Founded in 1913 by Timothy Drew, later known as Noble Drew Ali, the Moorish Science Temple of America (MSTA), as it is referred to today, is regarded as the first major Black identity movement. MSTA's worldview was shaped by Islam, Judaism, Christianity and other belief systems. MSTA declared that African-Americans are the descendants of the ancient Moorish Muslim civilization whose culture had been suppressed by the legacy of slavery.

NOI helped inspire the radical Black Power movement of the 1960s that broke with the non-violent approach of activists such as Martin Luther King, Jr., including the Black Panther Party for Self Defense, later known as the Black Panther Party (BPP). BPP did not rely on religious discourse and instead emphasized popular revolutionary struggle in the name of social justice and Black liberation. NOI also influenced Black identity movements across the English-speaking Caribbean, Canada and Great Britain. In many respects, the agendas of NOI and BPP converged in a number of areas.

The Nation of Gods and Earths, also known as the Five Percent Nation of Islam or simply as the Five Percenters (FP), represents another side of the Black identity movement that mixes aspects of Islam, Judaism, Christianity and other beliefs (http://www.allahsnation. net). FP, which split from NOI in 1964, is adamant that it is not a religion, but maintains that Islam represents a way of life. Its worldview declares Blacks as the original people of the earth and the founders of civilization. FP sees Black men as Gods, which they refer to as ALLAH (Arm, Leg, Leg, Arm and Head), not to be mistaken with the Arabic word for God. FP ideology also espouses the theory of "Supreme Mathematics," which among other things maintains that followers represent the chosen five percent of mankind who lead a virtuous life. FP enjoys a large following among popular Hip Hop artists and African-American activists [4]. It also has a following in the U.S. prison system, where some members have been linked with gang activity and violence [5]. FP made headlines when false allegations surfaced linking convicted Washington DC-area snipers John Allen Muhammed and John Malvo to the group. Muhammed was actually a former member of NOI, but had left the group years before the attacks.

Orthodox Sunni Muslim organizations regard MSTA, NOI and FP as heretical cults. India's Ansar us-Sunnah Library and Research Center refers to NOI as the Nation of Kufr (unbelievers) for its emphasis on Black nationalism and identity and what it describes as a blend of false Muslim and Christian beliefs. The group's website places NOI alongside Shiites, which they describe as rafidah (rejectors), and other groups they consider heretics such as Sufis, Druze and Amhadis in a section warning Muslims to guard their faith (http://www.allaahuakbar. net).

The NOI continues to grapple with the dilemma of reconciling its origins as a Black identity group with orthodox Islam. This has led to major rifts and splits within the movement over the years. Despite the influence of NOI under the charismatic leadership of Louis Farrakhan, the vast majority of Black Muslims today subscribe to orthodox Islam, a trend that has been growing over the years. Most African-American Muslims look to mainstream orthodox Muslim organizations such as the Muslim Society of America (*Christian Science Monitor*, February 14, 2002). This includes believers once affiliated with NOI who eventually parted ways with the group due to its emphasis on Black identity.

Homegrown Terrorism

The highly publicized Seas of David case was not the first of its kind. The case of the obscure Jamaat al-Fuqra (Community of the Impoverished, JF), a Muslim association with branches in South Asia and North America, once raised concerns about radical trends in the African-American Muslim community. According to some reports, JF was founded in the early 1980s by Sheikh Mubarak Ali Shah Gilani. Gilani is a Sufi cleric from Pakistan. In the United States, JF is reportedly comprised mostly of African-American Muslim converts. Gilani also heads the International Quranic Open University (IQOU), which is affiliated with the Muslims of the Americas (MOA).

U.S. and Pakistani intelligence officials have accused JF of militant and criminal activities in the United States and abroad, including the murder of religious and ideological rivals on U.S. soil [6]. Prior to his abduction and eventual murder, American journalist Daniel Pearl was on his way to interview Gilani to investigate reports that Richard C. Reid studied under him in Lahore, Pakistan. Gilani denies any links to Reid and Pearl's kidnapping and death (*Dawn*, February 1, 2002). In a statement on the IQUO-MOA website, Gilani also denies any connection to or knowledge of Jamaat al-Fuqra or radical activities and attributes such allegations to sinister political agendas meant to tarnish his image (http://www.iqou-moa.org).

JF made headlines when news spread that followers of Gilani established a series of isolated rural communities across the United States, including Baladullah (God's Village) outside of Fresno, California. According to MOA representatives, these communities were intended for believers to live and worship in peace. Given Gilani's background, however, U.S. security officials worried about their potential use as radical training grounds (*The San Jose Mercury News*, February 3, 2003). The group established other settlements in Colorado, Virginia, South Carolina and upstate New York (http://www.iqou-moa.org).

The recent case involving Jam'iyyat Ul-Islam As-Saheeh (Assembly of Authentic Islam, JIS), an extremist Islamist group based in the California prison system, was the first major publicized incident of its kind involving a homegrown terrorist plot hatched by radical African-American Muslim converts. Led by Kevin James, an African-American Muslim convert currently serving a lengthy sentence for a robbery conviction, JIS is alleged to have planned attacks against a number of targets in California in the fall of 2005, including U.S. military installations, Israeli government facilities and Jewish synagogues (*Terrorism Monitor*, January 26, 2006). JIS is comprised of African-American Muslim converts, as well as a legal U.S. resident of Pakistani descent. Members of the group allegedly swore a bayat (an oath of allegiance) to James [7]. The JIS case also highlights the threat posed by the spread of radical Islamist ideologies in U.S. prisons.

Conclusion

Given the current trajectory of the threat posed by radical Islamist terrorism in the form of homegrown cells or possibly individuals plotting and acting independently of organizations such as al-Qaeda, security officials need to be alert to emerging radical trends within U.S. borders. This includes extremist tendencies in the African-American Muslim community. Based on al-Qaeda's success in inspiring others to act on behalf of its radical agenda, however, this threat does not differ from the larger issue at hand and should instead be considered in the larger context of homegrown terrorist threats.

Notes

1. Hisham Aidi, "Jihadis in the Hood: Race, Urban Islam, and the War on Terror," *Middle East Report* (Fall 2002).
2. See United States District Court, District of Massachusetts Indictment of Richard Reid at http://www.fas.org/irp/news/2002/01/reidindictment.pdf.
3. Ogbar, Jeffrey, O.G., *Black Power: Radical Politics and African American Identity*, (Baltimore: Johns Hopkins, 2004).
4. Ted Swedenburg, "Snipers and Panic over Five Percent Islamic Hip-Hop," *Middle East Report Online* (November 10, 2002), http://www.merip.org/mero/mero111002.html.
5. Brian Levin, *Radical Religion in Prison*, Southern Poverty Law Center Intelligence Report (Fall 2003), http://www.splcenter.org/intel/intelreport/article.jsp?aid=120.
6. Narayanan Komerath, "Pakistani Role in Terrorism Against the U.S.A.," *Bharat Rakshak Monitor* (Vol. 5, September-October 2002).
7. U.S. Department of Justice Press Release, August 31, 2005, http://www.usdoj.gov/opa/pr/2005/August/05_crm_453.htm.

[From Terrorism Monitor, Volume IV, Issue 16]

Index

About the Authors

Dr. Zachary Abuza is one of the leading scholars on terrorism in Southeast Asia. He is currently Associate Professor for Political Science and International Relations at Simmons College.

Farhana Ali is an Associate International Policy Analyst at the RAND Corporation. She has done extensive research on jihadi networks and religious extremism.

Anes Alic is ISN Security Watch's senior analyst in Southeastern Europe. He is a former reporter for Bosnia's Federal Television (FTV) and the Open Broadcast Network (OBN), and the former host of FTV's "Echoes" political talk show. He is based in Sarajevo.

Dr. Scott Atran is a director of research at the National Center for Scientific Research in Paris and professor of anthropology and psychology at the University of Michigan. He is the author of *In Gods We Trust: The Evolutionary Landscape of Religion* and the organizer of a NATO working group on suicide terrorism.

Abdul Hameed Bakier is an intelligence expert on counter-terrorism, crisis management and terrorist-hostage negotiations. He also is an English-Arabic-Chechen translator. He is based in Jordan.

Ludo Block is a former Dutch senior police officer and served as the Dutch police liaison officer for Russia and surrounding countries between 1999 and 2004. He is currently writing a Ph.D. dissertation on police cooperation in the European Union.

Anneli Botha is a senior researcher on terrorism at the Institute for Security Studies (ISS) in Cape Town.

Christopher Boucek is the editor of the *RUSI/Jane's Homeland Security & Resilience Monitor* at the Royal United Services Institute in London.

Dr. Anouar Boukhars is a specialist on politics of the Muslim world. Dr. Boukhars is currently a visiting assistant professor and Director of the Center for Defense and Security Policy at Wilberforce University in Ohio. He is also editor of *Wilberforce Quarterly Journal*.

James Brandon is a freelance journalist based in the Middle East. He holds an M.A. in Middle Eastern Studies from the School of Oriental and African Studies (SOAS) and has reported on Islamic political movements from around the Middle East, Europe and Africa for a wide range of newspapers and broadcast media.

Dr. Peter Chalk is an analyst at RAND specializing in South East Asia, international terrorism and emerging threats.

Dr. John C.K. Daly is a UPI international correspondent. He received his Ph.D. in Russian and Middle Eastern Studies from the University of London and was an Adjunct Scholar at the Middle East Institute in Washington, DC.

Thomas Davidson was formerly a Senior Military Intelligence Analyst at the Foreign Military Studies Office (FMSO) of the U.S. Army Training and Doctrine Command at Ft. Leavenworth, Kansas. He has extensive experience working on border and security issues.

Christine Fair is the coordinator for South Asia research programs at the United States Institute for Peace (USIP).

Audra Grant is a political scientist at RAND. Her research focuses on the Middle East, and issues related to the development of political Islam, terrorism, as well as the attitudinal orientations of Middle East publics. Prior to joining RAND, she was an analyst at the U.S. Department of State, Bureau of Intelligence for five years.

Kathryn Haahr is a foreign affairs and counterterrorism consultant in Washington, D.C.

Andrew Holt is a Southeast Asia analyst based in Los Angeles.

Noor Huda Ismail is a consultant on the impact of religion on political violence in Southeast Asia. Mr. Ismail has been doing extensive research on jihadi networks and religious extremism. His works have been published in numerous publications, including the *Washington Post*, YaleGlobal online, *The Australian*, *The Straits Times* and *The Jakarta Post*.

Dr. N. Janardhan is the editor of Gulf in the Media at the Gulf Research Center, Dubai, United Arab Emirates.

Gregory Johnsen is a former Fulbright fellow in Yemen and is currently a Ph.D. candidate in History and Middle Eastern and Islamic studies at New York University.

Dr. Javier Jordán is a lecturer in the Department of Political Science, University of Granada (Spain). He was a Research Fellow at the Training and Doctrine Command of the Spanish Army and a NATO Research Fellow. He is currently a participant in a research project on terrorism sponsored by the European Commission Program AGIS. He is author of *Profetas del Miedo. Aproximación al terrorismo islamista* [*Prophets of Fear: A Study of Islamist Terrorism*] (Pamplona: EUNSA, 2004).

Lydia Khalil recently returned from Iraq where she worked as governance policy advisor for the Coalition Provisional Authority in Baghdad. Prior to that, Lydia was appointed to the White House Office of Homeland Security. She has worked at home and abroad for the U.S. government, international organizations, private companies and think-tanks on a variety of Middle East political and terrorism issues.

Erich Marquardt is the Program Manager of The Jamestown Foundation's Global Terrorism Analysis.

Omid Marzban has worked for Good Morning Afghanistan Radio Station and Radio Free Europe. He is based in Afghanistan.

Dr. Andrew McGregor is the director of Aberfoyle International Security Analysis in Toronto, Canada.

Hayder Mili is an independent researcher specializing in terrorism and security issues in Central Asia and the Caucasus.

Dr. Sami Moubayed is a Syrian writer and political analyst. He is the author of many books on Syria including *Steel & Silk: Men and Women Who Shaped Syria 1900-2000* (Cune Press 2005).

Sohail Abdul Nasir is an Islamabad-based journalist. He writes on foreign policy matters, regional security issues and the war on terrorism.

Judit Neurink is editor of the Middle East section at a Dutch daily. Neurink recently published a book on the Iranian terrorist group, the Mojahedin-e-Khalq, entitled *Misled Martyrs*.

Dr. Tarique Niazi teaches Environmental Sociology at the University of Wisconsin, Eau Claire. He specializes in Resource-based Conflicts.

Guido Olimpio is security correspondent for *Corriere della Sera* and has been a researcher on international terrorism for the past 20 years.

Jeffrey Pool is a freelance consultant, specializing in security and terrorism issues in the Middle East. He is a former U.S. Army linguist, having received his diploma in Arabic from the Defense Language Institute in 1996. He completed a Masters in International Relations at the Institut d'Etudes Politiques de Paris in July 2005. He is fluent in Arabic and French.

Waliullah Rahmani is a freelance journalist in Afghanistan.

Catherine Zara Raymond is an Associate Research Fellow at the Institute of Defense and Strategic Studies (IDSS), Nanyang Technological University, Singapore.

Igor Rotar is a Central Asia correspondent for Forum 18 News Service.

Animesh Roul is the Executive Director of Research at the New Delhi-based Society for the Study of Peace and Conflict (SSPC).

Dr. Michael Scheuer served in the CIA for 22 years before resigning in 2004. He served as the Chief of the bin Laden Unit at the Counterterrorism Center from 1996 to 1999. He is the once anonymous author of *Imperial Hubris: Why the West is Losing the War on Terror* and *Through Our Enemies' Eyes: Osama bin Laden, Radical Islam, and the Future of America.* Dr. Scheuer is a Senior Fellow with The Jamestown Foundation.

Stephen Schwartz is a frequent commentator on terrorism and related issues in national periodicals and websites. He is also the author of nine books on political history, the most recent being *The Two Faces of Islam: The House of Sa'ud from Tradition to Terror* (Doubleday Anchor paperback).

Pascale Combelles Siegel is a France-based independent defense consultant specializing in perception management. She is currently working on how to counter Islamist terrorist propaganda.

John Solomon is Head of Terrorism Research for World-Check, a provider of structured risk-related intelligence. He was formerly with the Centre for the Study of Terrorism and Political Violence at the University of St. Andrews in Scotland.

Trevor Stanley researches Islamic terrorism. He is the editor of *Perspectives on World History and Current Events.*

Donald Temple is a research assistant at the RAND Corporation specializing in national security.

Paul Tumelty is a researcher specializing in the Russian North Caucasus, the Caucasus and Central Asia. He holds an M.Phil. in Russian and East European Studies from the University of Glasgow and a B.A. in War Studies, King's College, London.

Stephen Ulph is a Senior Fellow with The Jamestown Foundation. One of the preeminent analysts of the Islamic world, Mr. Ulph specializes in the economic and political developments of the Middle East and North Africa. He is the founder and editor of the *Terrorism Security Monitor* and editor and analyst of *Islamic Affairs* for Jane's Information Group.

Anar Valiyev is a Ph.D. candidate in Public Affairs at University of Louisville in Kentucky. His area of interests includes urban terrorism, public policy of post-Soviet countries, governance and democracy.

Sunguta West is an independent journalist based in Nairobi.

Chris Zambelis is an independent analyst and consultant based in Washington DC, specializing in Middle East politics and international terrorism issues.

About the Editor

Jonathan D. Hutzley is the Program Officer for The Jamestown Foundation. He has received two M.A.'s from George Washington University; one in Russian and East European Studies and the other in Political Science. He previously received a B.A. in Political Science from Davidson College.

I